CW01463873

Buddha Shākyamuni

Ārya Nāgārjuna (first–second centuries c.e.)

Ārya Asaṅga (fourth century c.e.)

Guru Padmasambhava

༄༅། །རྡོ་རྗེ་ཐེག་པའི་ཐུན་མོང་གི་སྔོན་འགྲོ་སྤྱི་ལ་སྦྱོར་ཆོག་པའི་
ཁྲིད་ཀྱི་རྒྱབ་ཡིག་ཀུན་མཁྱེན་ཞལ་ལུང་རྣམ་གྲོལ་
ཞིང་རྟ་ཞེས་བྱ་བ་བཞུགས། །

པདྨ་ཀ་རའི་སྒྲ་བསྒྱུར་མཐུན་ཚོགས་ནས་
སྒྲ་བསྒྱུར་ཞུས།།

The Padmakara Translation Group gratefully acknowledges the generous support of the Tsadra Foundation in sponsoring the translation and preparation of this book.

A Chariot to Freedom

Guidance from the Great Masters on the Vajrayāna Preliminary Practices

Shechen Gyaltsap Gyurmé Pema Namgyal

TRANSLATED BY

the Padmakara Translation Group

SHAMBHALA

Shambhala Publications, Inc.
2129 13th Street
Boulder, Colorado 80302
www.shambhala.com

© 2021 by Association Padmakara
All line drawings by Olivier Philippot.

Cover art: Thangka of Shechen Gyaltsap Rinpoche from Dilgo Khyentse's collection.
Painted by Gen Tragyal and kept at Shechen Monastery, photo Shechen Archives/
Matthieu Ricard
Cover design: Gopa & Ted 2, Inc.

All rights reserved. No part of this book may be reproduced
in any form or by any means, electronic or mechanical, including
photocopying, recording, or by any information storage and retrieval
system, without permission in writing from the publisher.

9 8 7 6 5 4 3 2 1

First Edition
Printed in the United States of America

♾ This edition is printed on acid-free paper that meets
the American National Standards Institute Z39.48 Standard.
♻ Shambhala Publications makes every effort to print on recycled paper.
For more information please visit www.shambhala.com.

Shambhala Publications is distributed worldwide by Penguin Random House, Inc.,
and its subsidiaries.

LIBRARY OF CONGRESS CATALOGING-IN-PUBLICATION DATA
Names: Zhe-chen Rgyal-tshab Padma-'gyur-med-rnam-rgyal, 1871–1926, author.
Comité de traduction Padmakara, translator.
Title: A chariot to freedom: guidance from the great masters on the Vajrayāna
preliminary practices / Shechen Gyaltsap Gyurmé Pema Namgyal;
translated by the Padmakara Translation Group.
Other titles: Rdo rje theg pa'i thun mong gi sngon 'gro spyi la sbyor chog pa'i khrid kyi rgyab yig
Kun mkhyen zhal lung rnam grol shing rta. English
Description: Boulder: Shambhala, 2021. | Added title page in Tibetan. |
Includes bibliographical references and index.
Identifiers: LCCN 2021008415 | ISBN 9781611804584 (hardback)
Subjects: LCSH: Tantric Buddhism—Rituals. | Tantric Buddhism—Customs and practices. |
Meditation—Tantric Buddhism. | Spiritual life—Rnying-ma-pa (Sect)
Classification: LCC BQ8920 .Z44 2021 | DDC 294.3/925—dc23
LC record available at https://lccn.loc.gov/2021008415

Contents

Foreword

Jigme Khyentse Rinpoche

Among the many well-known Tibetan Buddhist teachers of the twentieth century, two in particular—Dzongsar Khyentse Chökyi Lodrö Rinpoche and Dilgo Khyentse Rinpoche—stand out for the vast influence that they exerted on the entire tradition. From the many great lamas who were their disciples down to the most humble practitioners, no one was impervious to the wisdom, compassion, and ability of these two great beings. All who met them were soothed by their kindness, comforted by their wisdom, and disarmed by their power. Even to this day, decades after these teachers passed away, we can still see and feel the effects of their blessing. Now both Dzongsar Khyentse Chökyi Lodrö Rinpoche and Dilgo Khyentse Rinpoche were disciples of Shechen Gyaltsap Rinpoche, a master of immense learning and compassionate power, the heart son of the great Jamgön Mipham. They both looked up to him as the Buddha in person, and Dilgo Khyentse Rinpoche in particular regarded him as his most precious root teacher.

I remember when I was once in the room of my most precious root guru Dilgo Khyentse Rinpoche in Bhutan. I noticed a newly printed text and asked him what it was. Rinpoche told me to take it down from the shelf and said that I could keep it. It was an offset print of Gyaltsap Rinpoche's commentary on the preliminary practices that, at that time, had only recently been brought out of Tibet. As Rinpoche gave it to me, he said that the book was more precious to him than all the riches of the world. It was the text that has been translated here, the text that you are holding in your hands.

In this time of turmoil, it is such an amazing good fortune even to hear the name of this book, let alone to be able to read, study, and put it into practice. So I am deeply grateful not only to Shechen Gyaltsap Rinpoche, the inestimable author, but also to our teachers, the translators, the publisher, and the sponsor who have made this translation possible. I pray that they live long and continue their excellent work. And on behalf of all the readers who will study and benefit from this book, I thank them from my heart.

Foreword

Pema Wangyal

It is truly beyond words that such a precious and wonderful book as this has been made accessible in our time, and it is an incredibly great honor and fortune for the Padmakara Translation Group to have translated it. This book is a distillation of the teachings and practices that have come down to us from Buddha Shākyamuni, Guru Rinpoche, Longchenpa, and the masters of the lineage.

The text is taken from the writings of Shechen Gyaltsap Rinpoche, which in total amount to over twenty volumes. Among all of them, it was this particular volume, containing the text of the *Namdrol Shingta* (*A Chariot to Freedom*), that was Kyabje Dilgo Khyentse Rinpoche's favorite. Whenever he taught, there would always be some trace of this book in what he said. This is why, when we read or study this book, we can be reminded of the atmosphere of Dilgo Khyentse Rinpoche's teachings.

With the Cultural Revolution, this book became exceedingly rare, and then, like many other texts, was thought to have been lost. Nobody knew that one copy had in fact been preserved in a cave. This copy was finally brought to Dilgo Khyentse Rinpoche, who became so happy—just having the book brought into his presence moved him so much that tears of joy came to his eyes. From then on, until further copies of the book were printed, he would always keep it close to him; he cherished it so much. He used to say that if one has the fortune to study this book, it is really like studying the Buddha's teachings in their entirety.

The author, Shechen Gyaltsap Rinpoche, was born in the Tsolung region of Derge, the "Land of Lakes," in the year of the iron sheep (1871), on the nineteenth day of the twelfth lunar month. While he was still young, many important teachers recognized him as Shechen Gyaltsap Rinpoche. These teachers included the First Khyentse the Great, Jamgön Kongtrul the Great, the great Kathok Situ Rinpoche, the Fourth Dzogchen Rinpoche, and Minling Trichen Rinpoche. Even though they were all unanimous about the recognition, Jamyang Khyentse Wangpo checked thoroughly, again and again, to ensure they were right. When he was satisfied, he enthroned the young Shechen Gyaltsap, giving him the name Gyurmé Pema Tenzin Khedrup Gyamtso Wangpoi De, and wrote a prayer for his long life. Shechen Gyaltsap Rinpoche went on to become one of the most learned and accomplished teachers of the nineteenth and twentieth centuries. He was one of the main root teachers of our own most precious and beloved teacher, Dilgo Khyentse Rinpoche, as well as that of Jamyang Khyentse Chokyi Lodrö, Shechen Kongtrul, and Khenpo Kunpel.

Shechen Gyaltsap Rinpoche's predecessor was Ugyen Rangjung Dorje, who was a very great teacher. Not only was he learned and accomplished, he was also incredibly kind. As a great practitioner of love and compassion, he would always extend these to everyone with total equality, regardless of whether they were human or animal. For this reason, he had great difficulty living in the nomadic region where he was from and made strong prayers and aspirations to always be able to help others and never bring harm to anyone, including animals. In keeping with this, he was strictly vegetarian.

Lochen Vijaya, Shechen Gyaltsap's father, was very learned and accomplished. In a vision, Shelkar Dorje Tso, the closest disciple of Yeshe Tsogyal, appeared to him singing and dancing, telling him that she had manifested from the space of unborn and unceasing activity in order to protect the awareness child of the great Namkhai Nyingpo, who would arrive riding on the rays of the sun. This meant that she would come to take care of Namkhai Nyingpo's manifestation and protect him from all kinds of obstacles. The emanation of Shelkar Dorje Tso prophesied in this vision was Namkha Drolma, who became Shechen Gyaltsap Rinpoche's mother. She was a great practitioner in her own right, and also very learned. Even though she was always busy taking care of the family and a number of duties, she still managed to bring her body, speech, and mind into harmony with her practice. She hardly let any time be wasted in an ordinary way. Whatever actions she did with her body she would use to benefit others with love and compassion. With her speech she would ceaselessly recite sublime mantras, and, maintaining the proper view, she would never allow her mind to be stained by ordinary perception. She was so diligent that, during the course of her life, she recited the mantra of Amitabha one hundred million times, the Mani mantra of the Lord of Great Compassion two hundred million times, the precious mantra of Padmasambhava one hundred million times, and the mantra of Vajrasattva one hundred million times. She also read the *Prayer in Seven Chapters* daily, as well as *The Life of Guru Rinpoche*. She had incredible devotion and pure vision and was always very kind to those in difficulties. She was completely free of all defects and negative qualities and was also very wise. Throughout the pregnancy, she experienced many auspicious signs and dreams and would always wake up filled with great peace. She never felt even the slightest discomfort or fatigue.

Right after Shechen Gyaltsap Rinpoche was born, he adopted a meditative gaze, and his parents saw that the lower part of his body bore birthmarks resembling a tiger-skin skirt. His father then undertook all the necessities, giving him long-life pills and pills to increase his knowledge and intelligence, marking his tongue with the syllable DHĪḤ, endowing him with protective substances, and bathing him in consecrated water. He also gave him his first name, Tsering Drukgyel (Victorious Long-Life Dragon). Even from a young age he had a very compassionate and kind nature and was clearly not an ordinary child. He was very concerned about protecting animals from being killed and abused and would burst into tears if he saw such things happening, provoked by his immense love. With such a disposition, it is hardly surprising that he was strictly vegetarian, just like his predecessor. Even as a child he refused to eat meat. In fact, there was never even a question of his eating it—he could not bear seeing the flesh and blood of slaughtered animals, and the smell alone would make him sick. He was also persistent in his requests for his family and all those around him to give up eating meat.

After a few years of being with his parents, the young Shechen Gyaltsap was recognized and enthroned at Shechen Monastery and entrusted to the care of Pema Wangchen. Under his tutelage, he learned such things as reading, writing, grammar, poetry, Sanskrit, astrology, and astronomy. As a student he was extremely diligent, always learning things very quickly and without any difficulty. On many occasions, just like Kyabje Dudjom Rinpoche, he would make it obvious to his tutors that he had already studied in his previous lives the subjects he was being taught. When the time came, he was ordained by Pema Damcho, one of the greatest khenpos of Dzogchen Monastery, and given the name Gyurmé Pema Namgyal. He later received full ordination in the Shantarakshita lineage from Khenpo Yonten Gyamtso of Gemang monastery. He was very disciplined and kept his vows very strictly.

Over the years, he met many of the great teachers of his time. In his biography, we can find an enumeration of all the teachings that he received from the vast number of teachers he studied with. To include such a list here would likely fill many pages! Nevertheless, it is important at least to know this and to understand that it was with the intention of ensuring that all the teachings that still existed would be upheld and transmitted for the benefit of future generations that great teachers such as Shechen Gyaltsap Rinpoche studied with so many teachers and received so many teachings. Among all these teachers, his two root teachers were Jamgön Kongtrul and Jamyang Khyentse Wangpo. Upon meeting them, he felt as though he was once again encountering the root teachers with whom he had been connected for many lives. Another of his main teachers was Jamgön Mipham Rinpoche, who was one of the root teachers of both Kyabje Dilgo Khyentse Rinpoche and Kyabje Kangyur Rinpoche.

It was at Dzongsar Monastery that Shechen Gyaltsap first met Jamgön Kongtrul Rinpoche, receiving from him many empowerments and transmissions. His first meeting with Jamyang Khyentse Wangpo was extremely auspicious, and the First Khyentse offered him all the teachings and transmissions that he held. He particularly bestowed upon him the empowerment of Vajrakīlaya according to the lineage of Rongzom Mahapandita, in order to remove all obstacles to his life and practice, and requested that he focus on this practice until he had attained the sign of perfect realization. As advised, Shechen Gyaltsap went into retreat, sealing his door with mud and resolving not to set foot outside until he had attained perfect accomplishment. Since he had in fact already perfected the practice of Vajrakīlaya in his previous lives as Prabahasti, Namkhai Nyingpo, and Lang Lab Jangchub Dorje—the most accomplished mahasiddha of Vajrakīlaya in the Land of Snows—when, after only a short time in retreat, he opened his door and stepped outside, his foot sunk into the solid entrance stone as if it were mud. This footprint that he left in stone was the sign of his accomplishment, and it can still be seen at Shechen Monastery in Tibet.

After marking his footprint in stone, Shechen Gyaltsap Rinpoche remained in retreat, studying, practicing, and teaching for the rest of his life. Having absorbed within himself all the teachings that he had received, he then composed many texts, like the *Namdrol Shingta*, containing their quintessence. In this way, he kindly left over twenty volumes for us to study and make use of as references for our practice. The collection of his writings is so complete that there is hardly a subject it doesn't cover.

Early in the morning, on the eighteenth day of the fifth lunar month of the fire tiger year (1926), Shechen Gyaltsap Rinpoche entered into parinirvāṇa accompanied by many auspicious signs. His last piece of writing was a detailed commentary on Jamgön Mipham Rinpoche's *Aspiration Prayer for the Teaching of the Ancient Tradition to Flourish*. Before passing away, he placed this text upon the head of Kenchen Kunzang Pelden and made many prayers of aspiration. He also blessed Shechen Kongtrul, the incarnation of Jamgön Kongtrul Rinpoche, with a long-life arrow and ingredients for longevity. His teachings have been continued by Dilgo Khyentse Rinpoche and his many other hundreds of students.

For such a book to still exist in a time like ours is truly something to rejoice in. I was so happy when the translation was completed, and over the past two years I have been trying to read through and check it. I think it has been very well translated, although this opinion is, of course, according to my limited understanding. Quite a lot of effort goes into translating a text, and so I would like to offer my sincere thanks to Lodrö Zangpo (Stephen Gethin), who took the trouble of making this translation accessible, trying his best to find the right words and so on. I would also like to take this opportunity to express my gratitude to every one of the translators within the Padmakara Translation Group for all the many unique texts that they make available in modern languages.

Translators' Introduction

Among the different series of Buddhist teachings that were propagated in India and subsequently in Tibet, those of the Diamond Vehicle, or Vajrayāna, provide a means by which a person can progress rapidly on the spiritual path and attain buddhahood in a relatively short time. In contrast to the bodhisattvas' path described in the sūtras, in which buddhahood is a goal to be achieved after many aeons of dedicated effort, the Diamond Vehicle, based on the tantras, provides a whole panoply of potent methods by which full enlightenment can be reached in a few lifetimes, or even, for certain practitioners, within a single life. Central to Vajrayāna practice is a special relationship with a qualified master, from whom the disciple receives the necessary empowerments and instructions. None of this, however, can be undertaken without specific preparation, and it is this preparation, comprising the so-called preliminary practices, that is the subject of this book.

In most traditions, these preliminary practices consist of five stages, beginning with taking refuge, which are each performed one hundred thousand times. For these to be effective, however, most people need first to acquire the appropriate mental orientation by going through the so-called four practices for turning the mind. And since all meditation depends on receiving the relevant teachings and reflecting on them, Shechen Gyaltsap begins this book with instructions on the attitudes and behavior, based above all on respect for the teachings, that both the teacher and the students must adopt during a teaching session. It should be noted here that, in a traditional context, a book like this would rarely be picked out of a bookcase and read by the student in private. In order for the students to receive the oral transmission of these teachings, which have been passed down through an unbroken lineage of realized masters to their disciples since the time of the Buddha, the teacher usually reads the text out loud, often giving detailed explanations of particular topics in the process. Shechen Gyaltsap's advice on how to approach these teachings should be applied not only to those attending formal sessions of teaching but also to all situations in which this book is read, whether on one's own or in a study group.

Progress in spiritual practice is impossible unless the mind is properly directed toward the spiritual goal. To this end, the four practices for turning the mind begin with meditation on the difficulty of finding a human life with access to the Buddhist teachings. Unless one fully appreciates this unique opportunity for taking the path toward enlightenment, one may never begin that path. Second, it is essential to understand, by reflecting on death and impermanence, that one's progress may be interrupted at any moment by changes in one's circumstances and that it is urgent to practice while one has the opportunity. As well as acting as a spur against laziness and procrastination, meditation on impermanence, especially on its subtle aspects, serves as an important introduction to the Buddhist teachings on emptiness. Third, reflection on karma and the law of cause and effect enables one not only to direct one's activities away from the negative deeds that will hinder one's progress but also to gain a more open-minded appreciation of the factors that produce one's own and others' situations. Finally, it is only by reflecting carefully on the defects of the cyclic existence in which we are all trapped that one will really want to free oneself and attain enlightenment.

It is this desire for protection from the suffering of cyclic existence that leads one into the first of the five preliminary practices: taking refuge in the Buddha, Dharma, and Saṅgha. These represent the guide, the path, and the companions on the way, respectively. The faith and commitment developed in this practice is deepened in the second phase, arousing the mind set on enlightenment. Here, the wish to attain buddhahood is extended to wishing enlightenment not only for oneself but for all beings as well. This practice is based on first training the mind in boundless love, compassion, joy, and impartiality, and from this point onward one enters the path of the bodhisattvas and engages mainly in the practice of the six transcendent perfections, beginning with generosity.

The essence of the bodhisattva path consists of purifying the negative factors that obscure one's ability to see the enlightened state and accumulating the positive factors that will enable one to reach one's goal and benefit other beings. These two aspects of the path—purification and accumulation—are comprised in the third and fourth preliminary practices—namely, the meditation and recitation of Vajrasattva (a manifestation of buddhahood whose special activity is the purification of negative deeds and obscurations) and the offering of the maṇḍala (a symbolic representation of the universe). Finally, there is the fifth preliminary, the Guru Yoga, in which the disciple's relationship with the teacher, based on trust and commitment, is nurtured, preparing the way for the practice of sādhana and mantra recitation and the advanced practices of the Great Perfection.

These preliminary practices are so important that in a traditional three-year retreat they occupy the whole of the first year. Even during the subsequent stages of the "main" practice, not a day passes without the practitioner going through the preliminary practices again, however briefly. Many teachers consider them to be as profound as the main practice, if not more so. Without having thoroughly mastered the preliminary practices, and in particular the Guru Yoga, the practices of the generation and perfection phases, and especially of the Great Perfection, will, in all likelihood, prove fruitless. This book, therefore, is not only an introduction for anyone setting out on the Vajrayāna path but also an indispensable manual for those already on the path.

Shechen Gyaltsap Gyurmé Pema Namgyal (1871–1926)

The fourth Shechen Gyaltsap[1] (also known by his bodhisattva name, Jamyang Lodrö Gyamtso Drayang) was the heart son of Ju Mipham Namgyal Rinpoche (1846–1912) and was largely responsible, with Khenchen Kunzang Pelden (c. 1870–c. 1940), for continuing Mipham Rinpoche's teaching tradition. He studied with the greatest teachers of his day, including Jamyang Khyentse Wangpo (1820–1892) and Jamgön Kongtrul Lodrö Thaye (1813–1899). He was undoubtedly one of the most learned lamas of his time: his collected writings fill thirteen volumes, one of which comprises the detailed explanation of the preliminary practices translated in this book. His other works include an extensive commentary on Atisha's *Seven-Point Mind Training*,[2] a treatise on the nine vehicles, and a commentary on Zurchung Sherab Trakpa's *Eighty Chapters of Personal Advice*.[3] He was also a highly accomplished practitioner, as Pema Wangyal Rinpoche points out in his foreword. He once completed what was intended to be a three-year retreat in only three months and left the imprint of his foot in a rock at the entrance to his hermitage. It is said that when Shechen Gyaltsap's body was cremated, it vanished without a trace, and that where the smoke settled on the leaves in the surrounding countryside, crystal relics were found. His many disciples included Dzongsar Khyentse, Chökyi Lodrö (1896–

1959), the sixth Shechen Rabjam, Nangdze Drubpai Dorje (1910–1959), and Dilgo Khyentse Rinpoche, Tashi Paljor (1910–1991), whom Shechen Gyaltsap recognized and enthroned as the incarnation of Jamyang Khyentse Wangpo's mind.

A Chariot to Freedom

For many years, it seemed that *A Chariot to Freedom* had been lost, for with the dramatic exodus of hundreds of thousands of Tibetans from their homeland at the end of the 1950s, only a handful of Shechen Gyaltsap Rinpoche's writings found their way across the Himalayas. Some thirty years later, however, as access to Tibet was opened up, a lama brought Dilgo Khyentse Rinpoche a book—this very same commentary on the preliminary practices. Khyentse Rinpoche considered the rediscovery of this important text so precious that he subsequently carried a copy of it with him wherever he went.

This book is the third large-scale commentary on the preliminary practices that the Padmakara Translation Group has translated into English. While its subject is broadly similar to that of the other two, it differs from them both in its intended readership and in its style. While it is true that students of almost all lineages can easily relate the principles set out in all these works to their own particular practice, some of the practice details in each of these commentaries, especially the visualizations, are specific to certain lineages. In writing *The Words of My Perfect Teacher*, for example, Patrul Rinpoche had in mind particularly people practicing the preliminary practice related to Jigme Lingpa's sadhana cycle Heart Essence of the Vast Expanse (Longchen Nyingtik); Dudjom Rinpoche's *A Torch Lighting the Way to Freedom* is specifically intended for practitioners of the cycle called Heart Essence of the Ḍākinī (Khandro Nyingtik). Shechen Gyaltsap, on the other hand, describes his commentary as "a universally applicable guide to the common preliminaries," though he illustrates his descriptions of the practice by referring to sections from the preliminary practice for the Vajrasattva sadhana cycle known as Minling Dorsem, a treasure discovered by the seventeenth-century master Terdak Lingpa, who founded Mindrölling Monastery in Tibet.

These minor differences in detail should not deter students of a specific lineage from reading all these commentaries, for each of them complements the other two. Repeated familiarity with their general content is a vital aid to whichever practice one may be doing, and the differences between these works can serve only to deepen one's understanding, as will their stylistic differences. Patrul Rinpoche was writing for the largely nomadic inhabitants of East Tibet, setting down for the first time oral instructions that had been passed down through the masters of his lineage. His practical, down-to-earth style, combining anecdotes with direct personal advice, gives few hints of the erudition he exhibits in some of his other works. Dudjom Rinpoche's approach is altogether different: presenting his topics systematically and with scholarly clarity, he backs up each point with a quotation from the scriptures. Shechen Gyaltsap takes yet another approach. Relatively sparing in what he has to say, he makes use of lengthy quotations from the Buddhist canon to communicate his intended message, drawing from the original words of the Buddha in the sūtras and from the later treatises of Indian masters such as Nāgārjuna, Asaṅga, and Shāntideva; and he bases much of his presentation on the works of the great lineage masters, in particular Guru Padmasambhava and the Omniscient Longchen Rabjam. His commentary reads more like a commonplace book—a carefully selected anthology of Buddhist wisdom—and a literary feast for his readers.

Technical Note

The task of translating the numerous quotations in Shechen Gyaltsap's text has necessitated frequent recourse to the original canonical sources. In many cases, consulting these has helped us make sense of passages that appeared to contain misprints, scribal errors, or omissions. In a few cases, this has revealed discrepancies in the attribution of certain quotations to named works or authors. Some of these attributions appear to have been copied from commentaries written many hundreds of years ago, when it would seem likely that certain canonical works existed in versions different from those now available to us, while some sources available then are no longer extant. At the present time, when it is an easy matter, thanks to the tools and resources now accessible via the internet, to identify the sources of many quotations, it seems to us that any such apparent inaccuracies could lead some people unnecessarily to criticize the writings of the lineage teachers. It is solely with the intention of avoiding such criticism that we have taken the liberty to update some of the attributions in line with information currently available to us.

To facilitate reading for those who are not familiar with the diacritics used in romanized Sanskrit spelling, we have adopted the following modifications in the text: *ś* is rendered as *sh*, *ṣ* as *ṣh*, *c* as *ch*, and *ṛ* as *ṛi*. For the Sanskrit titles of cited works, bibliographic entries, and Sanskrit words used in definitions, we have retained full diacritics.

Footnotes have been supplied mainly to explain difficult terms and points. Further information is also to be found in the glossary. The endnotes, on the whole, provide bibliographic references for some quotations and other less essential information.

Acknowledgments

The translation of this work was made at the request of our teacher Pema Wangyal Rinpoche. The recordings of teachings he gave on the text enormously facilitated our work, as did his answers to individual queries. He took the trouble, moreover, to go over the completed translation as he taught *A Chariot to Freedom* to Western practitioners undertaking the traditional three-year retreat in France. Our gratitude to him cannot be measured. We are also indebted to Jigme Khyentse Rinpoche, Khenchen Pema Sherab, and Khenpo Tenzin Norgay for their time and patience in resolving many of our questions, and similarly to Gelong Konchok Tenzin (Matthieu Ricard), who kindly gave us a copy of Shechen Monastery's new edition of the work, answered our questions, and further checked numerous points with Dagpo Rinpoche. Stephen Gethin carried out the bulk of the translation work and is alone responsible for its many imperfections. He would like to thank all his colleagues in the Padmakara Translation Group for their translations, published and unpublished, of some of the works cited by the author and Artemus B. Engle for sharing his research on Ārya Asaṅga's *Bodhisattvabhumi*. Thanks are also due to 84000 for permission to use a passage from the *Play in Full*. Larrie Gethin and Hannah Sadwith kindly read through the whole text and suggested many improvements. And Sarah Noble went over it meticulously while practicing in retreat and helped to polish the manuscript. Once again, we are indebted to Tsadra Foundation for their ever-generous funding of this project, and to Nikko Odiseos, Michael Wakoff, and the whole team at Shambhala Publications for their dedication and expertise in producing this book.

A Chariot to Freedom

Oral Instructions of the Omniscient Ones, a Universally Applicable Guide to the Common Preliminaries of the Diamond Vehicle

Kunkhyen Longchenpa (1308–1364)

Preamble

Namo Padmākaraye

Truly perfect from the beginning, you dwell eternally as the body of truth,
Yet with great compassion you manifest as the net of illusory display,
Benefiting according to need until the end of existence.
All-pervading teacher endowed with the wisdom body, care for me!
The quintessence of the sublime teachings, profound and extensive,
Has been transmitted in its entirety and without error by the lineage of *vidyādharas*.
This I shall now write down as an introduction for fortunate beginners,
A guide to the preliminaries—a chariot to freedom.

Our Teacher,* who was skilled in means and endowed with great compassion, gave teachings in accord with the different intellects of beings to be trained, and the sections of the Dharma therefore number some eighty-four thousand. Yet all of them are simply different means for guiding beings in stages, in ways that match their various temperaments. As it is said in the *Sūtra of the Treasury of Jewels*,[4]

> Just as newborn babes are reared
> On breast milk and the like, in stages,
> And later on eat quantities of rice and other solid food,
> From which they grow and gain in strength,
> So too, my children, being taught
> These pith instructions and following in stages

*"Our Teacher" refers to Buddha Shākyamuni.

The Vinaya, Sūtras, and Abhidharma,
Will accomplish unsurpassable enlightenment.

And in the *Extensive Magical Manifestation Tantra*,

Those who have great compassion
Must be learned in all the paths to liberation;
Those who have supreme wisdom
Should teach sentient beings, according to their level,
The meanings of the higher and lower vehicles,
In ways appropriate to each individual.

In particular, we read in the *Tantra on Seizing the Essential Meaning*,

After completing the preliminaries, the means for training one's mind stream,
By reflecting on the difficulty of finding this present support,
On impermanence, and on the defects of cyclic existence,
By purifying negative actions, taking the refuge vow, and so on,
And then being properly introduced, in stages, to the philosophical tenets—
Those of the listeners and others—
Beings with compassion and wisdom
Should be introduced to this true definitive meaning.
It is thus that they will accomplish the great goal.

This is why the Omniscient Dharma King Longchenpa says in his *Precious Treasury That Fulfills All Wishes*,

If that sublime teacher is to thoroughly explain
The sacred Dharma to fortunate disciples,
It is important, first, to examine the disciples' faculties.
For just as children and grown-ups need separate food,
The teachings, too, should differ in their nature.
Then he should teach by guiding them in stages:
By this means, they will understand the order of the vehicles,
Their qualities will grow, they'll have no fear or dread,
Make no mistakes, and bring together view and conduct.[5]

In general, when we speak of matching the teachings to the disciples' mental aptitudes, the best individuals are those with karmic fortune from having trained in their past lives: they have very sharp faculties and are of the "instantaneous" kind.* In such cases, there is an enduring karmic connection with the teachings, and these can be introduced to them directly. In this degenerate age, however, individuals of that sort are rare, and without clairvoyance it is impossible to know what kind of disciples one is dealing with. Those with a weak or uncertain karmic connection will gain no benefit from the instantaneous path, and their potential will be wasted. Initially, therefore, they should be guided in accordance with the stages of the path. In this way, the qualities of the path will grow in them. They will not be intimidated by the profound teachings and will be able to unite the view, meditation, and conduct without any deviations or conflicts on the path. The reasons and benefits of proceeding like this are limitless.

On the other hand, it is said that there are enormous negative consequences and numerous faults occur when disciples with ignorant minds are given the definitive teachings on the instantaneous path right from the start, without their first training gradually from the lower levels upward. As the Omniscient Teacher says,

> Failure to teach in such a way brings boundless faults:
> By dispensing with the proper sequence,
> The traditional order of the teachings will be lost,
> Small minds will take fright and abandon the Dharma out of false views,
> And ignorant of the order, they will not understand the profound teachings;
> Scorning relative virtue,
> They will be subject to criticism, and mixing up cause and result,
> They will not know what to adopt and reject, be ignorant of the points they need to know,
> And reject compassion and the Mahāyāna spiritual intent.
> Because of their nihilistic views, the faithful will be enticed into the lower realms;

*Tib. *cig car ba*. Such disciples attain a high degree of realization as soon as they receive the profound teachings of the Great Perfection and gain full accomplishment at a single stroke.

> For all their talk about nonaction, they will remain completely
> ordinary
> Yet proclaim the secrets to beings who are not ripe.
> Because such negative consequences are many, teach the vehicles
> in stages.[6]

These negative consequences, then, are as follows. The traditional way in which the teachings are given will be corrupted. Small-minded beings will be intimidated and reject the Dharma and the teacher. They will not understand the definitive teachings; and even if they do understand them, they will not gain profound realization. They will scorn the conceptualized practice of virtue. They will be subject to criticism by people with little intelligence. They will be ignorant with regard to the things they need to know and confuse the adoption of virtue and avoidance of nonvirtue. And they will abandon the ways of the bodhisattvas. In particular, they will have the fault of clinging to the extreme of emptiness and therefore denigrating the karmic law of cause and effect, with the result that they will go to the lower realms. In the *Heap of Jewels*, we read,

> Kāshyapa, an egotistic view as big as Mount Meru can be dealt with, but not so arrogant people's view of "emptiness," for that is incurable.

Furthermore, there is the fault of saying, "All phenomena are, from the very beginning, like the sky in nature, so there is no need for any activity: activity is ruinous." And as a result of one's attachment to taking things easy physically, verbally, and mentally, one remains quite ordinary, as is explained in the same sūtra:

> In the future, there will be proud monks, as stupid as sheep, who will say, "The Bhagavan has said that all phenomena are like the sky, so there is no need to exert oneself in any practice." They will render the sharing of merit on their alms rounds fruitless.* They

*As the Tibetan expression *bsod snyoms* (meaning literally "equalizing or sharing merit" but often translated as "begging alms") suggests, monks gain merit by providing laypeople with an opportunity to gain merit when they give the monks food.

> will not even attain the happiness of the higher realms, let alone unsurpassable enlightenment.

Proclaiming the secret teachings to people who are not ready will result in one's being obscured by the deed of giving up the Dharma, as is mentioned in the *Middle Sūtra of the Perfection of Wisdom*:

> Subhūti, do not speak about the emptiness of all phenomena, the absence of attributes, and the absence of expectancy in the presence of beginners who have only just engaged in this vehicle. Should you ask why, it is because they will take fright and give up.

And in the *Fourteen Root Downfalls*, we read,

> Proclaiming the secret teachings
> To beings who are not fully ripe is the seventh.

It is for these reasons that the great vajra holders of India and Tibet have guided fortunate beings to the level of buddhahood in line with the graded teachings. In this book, I have taken as my main sources the actual, adamantine* words of the Great Master Padmasambhava, of the Omniscient Dharma King Drimé Öser,† and of other vidyādharas of the Ancient Translation tradition who attained the supreme accomplishment, for the power of their blessings is much more potent than that of others. These I have embellished with a few relevant words as appropriate, to provide a complete instruction on the common preliminary practice.

The text is divided into three parts:

*The terms *adamantine* and *diamond* translate the Tibetan word *rdo rje* (lord of stones), which is used to represent the unchanging, indestructible nature of reality and to thus qualify an enlightened being's body, speech, mind, wisdom, concentration, posture, and so forth. In this context, the diamond is described as having seven characteristics: it cannot be cut, it is indestructible, true, hard, enduring, unimpeded, and invincible. The symbolic implement of the same name, originally a weapon used by Indra, is denoted in this book by its Indian name, *vajra*.

†One of the names by which the Omniscient Longchen Rabjam is referred to. See glossary, s.v. "Longchenpa."

- a virtuous beginning, explaining how the teachings should be presented and received
- a virtuous middle part, on training one's being through the four common practices for turning the mind
- a virtuous conclusion, the main preliminaries for the path of the Diamond Vehicle

PART ONE

The Virtuous Beginning, Comprising an Explanation of How the Teachings Should Be Presented and Received

This first part has three sections: attitude, conduct, and a supplementary, inspirational section describing the benefits of teaching the Dharma and listening to it.

1. Attitude

Attitude is divided into (1) the attitude related to the vast intention of bodhichitta and (2) the attitude related to the vast skill in means of the Secret Mantra Vehicle.

I. The attitude related to the vast intention of bodhichitta

Just as space has no end or limit, the realm of sentient beings is without end or limit. Throughout their series of lives since time without beginning, they have all been circling repeatedly in cyclic existence, and during this time there is not a single one with whom we have not been connected as a parent or relative. The Glorious Protector, Noble Nāgārjuna, has said,

> Not a single being is there
> In whose womb I have not dwelt—and not just once—
> Nor one who has not dwelt in mine.
> And so we're all related in this way.

Indeed, this has been the case, not just once but again and again, an infinite number of times. In *Letter to a Friend*, we read,

> To count one's mother's lineage by making pills
> The size of pips of juniper, the earth would not suffice.

At those times, we were linked by the same feelings of affection as we now have with our actual parents and children. In caring for us by doing whatever they could to help us and doing whatever they could to protect us from harm, they have been nothing but kind to us. All of these beings want to be happy, yet because they are quite ignorant of the means, they are unable to carry out the positive actions that are the causes of happiness. They do not want to suffer, and yet, in their ignorance, they are unable to avoid the negative actions that lead to suffering. The consequence of all this is that they are divested of happiness and subject to much suffering. Their very actions go against what they most deeply wish for. It is as if they were completely crazed and had eaten some deadly poison. How pitiful all these sentient beings are!

What good, though, will it do to just say, "How pitiful!" and leave it at that? At present we have obtained a human body with the freedoms and advantages, we have met a qualified teacher, and we have received instructions on the profound and extensive teachings. We know a little bit about how to put the teachings into practice, and we also have the freedom to do so. All the conditions favorable to the practice of the Dharma have come together, so with such an opportunity, we should do whatever we can to deliver all sentient beings, our mothers, from the ocean of suffering that is cyclic existence and set them in the everlasting happiness of perfect liberation. The wondrous great master Chandragomin has said,

> Our relatives, caught in the ocean of cyclic existence,
> Are born and die and transmigrate as if swept along upon its waves.
> Nothing could be more shameful than to fail to recognize this,
> And to abandon them and seek liberation alone.

Who, you might wonder, has the means and compassionate ability to bring them all to liberation? No one, apart from a perfect buddha. So we should think, "First, I must attain the precious state of buddhahood, and having done so, I must then do whatever I can, alone, to liberate the infinite sentient beings without leaving a single one out. And in order to do so, I must be diligent in hearing, explaining, and practicing the nectar-like teachings of the profound and extensive Dharma." Such an attitude, with its two aspects or points—focusing on sentient beings with compassion and focusing on perfect enlightenment with wisdom—is bodhichitta, the mind intent on enlightenment, as has been stated by the Protector Maitreya:

> Bodhichitta is the wish to attain
> Perfect enlightenment for the benefit of others.[7]

It is extremely important to have this attitude of bodhichitta in all situations, whether we are listening to the Dharma, teaching it, or practicing it. However great or small are the sources of good we create, it is essential to imbue them with the three supreme methods:

- the preparation, giving rise to bodhichitta, which imbues the source of good with skillful means
- the main practice of nonconceptuality, which prevents it from being destroyed by circumstances
- the conclusion, sealing the good deed by dedication, which makes it grow greater and greater

In the *Tantra of Vairocana's Enlightenment*, we read,

> Lord of Secrets, the wisdom of omniscience
> Springs from the root of compassion.
> What causes it to arise is bodhichitta.
> It is consummated by skillful means.

And Orgyen, knower of the three times, says,

> The essence of the path of the Great Vehicle is bodhichitta, based on love and compassion. Without these, nothing is possible. By relying on these, one's own and others' goals will all be fulfilled. They determine the direction that the path takes, just as a horse's bit determines the way the horse goes.

And again, in the *Introduction to the Middle Way*,

> The shrāvakas and those halfway to buddhahood are born from the Mighty Sage,
> And buddhas take their birth from bodhisattva heroes.
> Compassion, nonduality, the wish for buddhahood for others' sake
> Are causes of the children of the Conqueror.*

*Chandrakīrti, *Introduction to the Middle Way*, chap. 1, v. 1. "Those halfway to buddhahood" refers to solitary realizers (pratyekabuddhas). "The Mighty Sage" translates the Tibetan *thub dbang* (Munindra), an epithet of the Buddha.

So in all situations, whether we are listening to the teachings, explaining them, meditating, or practicing, this attitude is of the greatest importance. In *Treasury of Precious Qualities*, it is said,

> Intention, good or ill, dictates the act's effects
> And not the size of the apparent right or wrong.[8]

However much we teach or listen to the Dharma, if it is with an attitude that consists of pursuing our own desire for greatness, our desire for fame, and other such mundane goals in this life, we will not be following the authentic Dharma. It is absolutely crucial, therefore, that both teacher and disciple begin by looking inside themselves and correcting their attitude. If we know how to correct our attitude like this, every positive deed we perform will be imbued with skillful means. It will be transformed into the path of the great beings and enable us to access boundless merit.

II. The attitude related to the vast skill in means of the Secret Mantra Vehicle

Generally speaking, both the sūtra and mantra traditions have the same goal, which is to attain perfect enlightenment. However, the Diamond Vehicle, that of the secret mantras, is said to be superior to the Sūtra Vehicle in the following respects: Its methods (the entrance through empowerment, and so on) are unobscured by ignorance.* It comprises numerous methods for effortlessly accomplishing both one's own and others' goals. Its methods are easy, for one can realize the result without needing to go through great difficulties. And it is meant for those with sharp faculties. This is stated in the *Torch of the Three Methods*:

> It has the same goal but is free from all confusion,
> Has numerous methods, is without difficulties,
> And is for those with sharp faculties:
> The Mantra Vehicle is superior.

*Tib. *thabs la rmongs pa*. According to Khenpo Ngawang Pelzang, this refers to the fact that the view in the Diamond Vehicle is unobscured. See Khenpo Ngawang Pelzang, *Guide*, 31–32.

The root of this vehicle depends on the transformation of one's outlook. In this context, the Omniscient Teacher states in his *Precious Treasury That Fulfills All Wishes*,

> For the teachings of the manifestation body, think of the King of the Shākyas;
> For the secret mantras of the enjoyment body, think of Vajradhara of the five families;
> For the space-like teachings of the body of truth, think of Samantabhadra and his consort Prajñāpāramitā.
> Alternatively, think of the teacher of the respective teaching.

Accordingly, one should meditate specifically on one's teacher as being in the form of each of these teachers with their retinue. Here, however, as a general rule, rather than considering the present teaching hall, teacher, circle of disciples, and so forth to be in their ordinary form, we should think of them as

- the perfect place, the Unexcelled,* the palace of the expanse of reality, a measureless palace made of the five wisdom lights, utterly transcendent and boundless in its layout;
- the perfect teacher, in whom all faults have come to exhaustion and all qualities perfected, the central deity in the particular maṇḍala—for example, the glorious Vajrasattva, sovereign of all the buddha families;
- the perfect retinue, having the nature of male and female bodhisattvas appearing as the deities and female deities of the vajra family, or whichever family is appropriate; or otherwise, all the male disciples visualized as Ārya Mañjushrī and all the female disciples as Ārya Tārā;
- the perfect time, the ever-revolving wheel of eternity;
- the perfect teaching, the unsurpassable supreme vehicle, the melody of the indestructible primordial sound that transcends deliberate articulation, resounding as unborn sound-emptiness, present as clear sounds dispelling all imperfection in existence and peace.

*Tib. *'og min*, the Akaniṣhṭha buddha-field.

It is not as if we are imagining all this as being present when it is not. It is simply a question of keeping in mind the recognition that something which is there *is* actually there, as is mentioned in the *Secret Essence of the Magical Display*:

> Something other than the nature of buddha
> The buddhas themselves cannot discover.

In particular, the teachers are the embodiments of all the buddhas. They are the manifestations of the buddhas of the past, the sources of the buddhas of the future, and the regents of the buddhas of the present. Because they care for us unruly beings of the degenerate age, whom even the thousand buddhas of this fortunate kalpa cannot tame, they are the equals of the buddhas in terms of qualities yet superior to the buddhas in their kindness. As it is said,

> The teacher is the Buddha, the teacher is the Dharma,
> So too, the teacher is the Saṅgha.
> The teacher is the one who manifests all.
> The teacher is glorious Vajradhara.

And in the *Sūtra of the Supreme Concentration*, we read,

> Child of good family, in future ages, I will manifest as spiritual friends and teach this concentration. Therefore, since the spiritual friends will be your teachers, until you reach the heart of enlightenment, follow them and serve them with respect.

In the *Sūtra of Untainted Space*,

> Ānanda, the Tathāgata cannot appear to all sentient beings, but since spiritual friends will appear and teach the Dharma, planting the seed of liberation, you should consider the spiritual friends as superior to the tathāgatas.

In particular, those who teach the Diamond Vehicle of the secret mantras are said to be blessed by the Buddha in person, as we see in the *Guhyagarbha Tantra*:

> Whoever has realized and speaks of
> This great secret seal,
> The essence of all the tathāgatas,
> Is myself, empowered and complete.

We should also consider the circle of disciples listening to the teaching. Their ground is the sugata essence, their support is the precious human body, their condition is the spiritual friend, and their means is being guided by the latter's instructions. They are thus the buddhas of the future, as is stated in the *Two Segments*:

> Sentient beings are buddhas,
> Yet they are obscured by adventitious stains.
> Rid of those stains, they are truly buddhas.

2. Conduct

The chapter on conduct is divided into two parts: (1) conduct to be avoided and (2) conduct to be adopted.

I. Conduct to be avoided

Conduct to be avoided is divided into three sections, concerning conduct to be avoided respectively by (1) the disciples listening to the teachings, (2) the master giving the teachings, and (3) both in common.

A. Conduct to be avoided by the disciples listening to the teachings

The *Precious Treasury That Fulfills All Wishes* states,

> Regarding the conduct of the disciples who are listening,
> They should listen respectfully, avoiding all faults.[9]

When one is listening to the teachings, one must be free of the three defects of the pot, the six stains, and the thirty-six faults.

The three defects of the pot

The three defects of the pot are analogous to an upside-down pot, a leaky pot, and a pot containing poison.

The first of these refers to not paying attention to the teachings, or, even if one is paying attention, to feeling dull and sleepy, or playing around, or busying one's mind with other things. It is as if one were an *upside-down pot* into which not a drop of the nectarous rain of the teachings pouring down on it will go inside. If each time you listen to teachings, you do not familiarize yourself with them once the teaching is over, repeatedly reminding yourself of them, you will forget them. You will be like a *leaky pot*: the rainwater that collects in it while it is on the ground will all leak out when it is picked up.

If you are influenced by defilements, and feel proud when you hear the teachings again, you will be like a *pot containing poison*: it might stay filled to the brim with rainwater, but anyone who drinks it will become ill.

Avoid these three and, as instructed in the *Middle Sūtra of the Perfection of Wisdom*,

> Listen properly, listen well, and remember. Then I will teach you.

Or, in other words,

> Listen properly, without defilements;
> Listen well, without the mouth turned upside down;
> Remember, without the bottom leaking.

The six stains

In the *Well-Explained Reasoning*, it is said,

> It is a stain to listen with pride,
> With lack of faith, or without interest,
> While distracted outwardly,
> Introverted, or discouraged.

Accordingly, these six stains are as follows:

- pride, thinking that one is better than the master who is giving the teaching
- lack of faith in the teacher and the teaching
- lack of real interest in the teaching
- mental distraction by the objects of the six consciousnesses outside
- excessive withdrawal of the five senses
- feeling fed up—on account of the teaching being too long, and so on

It is important to rid yourself of these six.

The thirty-six faults

The *Precious Treasury That Fulfills All Wishes* lists these as follows:

> The six works of the devil, lack of respect and so on,
> The six obscuring deeds—pride and the rest,
> The six deeds that lead to rejecting the Dharma—hypocrisy and others,
> The six faults of distraction—pursuit of material gains and the like,
> The six faults of perversion—attachment to offerings and veneration, and so forth,
> And the six errant ways—acting otherwise and the rest—
> Avoid these six and thirty faults, and listen![10]

Of these, the six works of the devil are as described in the *Sūtra of the Full Array of Qualities*:

> Laziness, indifference,* lack of faith in the teachings and teacher, failure to bow down respectfully to the spiritual friend, failure to take the teachings to heart, and, with this life in mind, contempt for the karmic law of actions and their ripened effects.

The six obscuring deeds† are mentioned in the *Sūtra of the Questions of Sāgaramati*:

> Excessive pride, from one's mind having been penetrated by demons; giving up the Dharma on account of karmic obscurations; being confused by the secret words of the Chārvākas and

*Tib. *snyoms las*. This refers to a tendency to interest oneself in something other than what one is supposed to be doing.

†Throughout this book, the term *deed* translates the Tibetan *las* (Skt. *karma*), also translated as "action" or "past deed." Implied in the use of this term is the force created by a positive or negative action (physical, verbal, or mental), which is then stored in an individual's stream of being and persists until it is experienced as pleasure or pain (usually in another life), after which the deed is said to be exhausted.

> listening to their instructions;* not listening to the bodhisattva-piṭaka; wrong view with regard to spiritual friends; and wrong view with regard to the teachings.

The six deeds that lead to rejecting the Dharma are detailed in the same sūtra:

> Acting hypocritically, physically and mentally, out of a liking for evil; disrespect for the teacher because of pride; disrespect for the Dharma because of doubt; hypocritically using the teachings for profit; disrespect for one's parents, preceptors, and instructors; and constant conflicts as a result of coarse behavior and attitudes.

The six faults that distract one from the Dharma are described in the same sūtra as follows:

> A multitude of worldly activities, much hankering after material acquisitions, much engaging in worthless chatter, a lot of friends inclined to evil, numerous wrong thoughts, and a lot of illness and negative forces due to past evil deeds.

For the six faults involving perversity, we read in the *Sūtra of the Questions of Rāṣṭrapāla*,

> Being deceitful and ungrateful for kindness rendered, practicing the Dharma out of attachment to gain and respect, being jealous with regard to others' gains and acting stingily, looking for faults instead of thinking of the teacher's qualities, having faith in and following an evil master, and seeking intellectual qualities and failing to seek the qualities of merit.

And for the six errant ways that stray from the Great Vehicle, the *Chapter on Mañjuśrī's Magical Display* states,

> Seeking to achieve the *tīrthikas'* magical powers rather than seek-

*This refers to being led astray by false views that repudiate the law of karma, past and future lives, and so on.

> ing the bodhisattva-piṭaka, seeking worldly advice and not seeking to receive many teachings, seeking to receive teachings while not seeking liberation through them, seeking the *piṭakas* of the listeners and solitary realizers but not the bodhisattva-piṭaka, seeking to bring the defilements to an end without mastering skill in means, and wanting to be learned in the sciences but not seeking a spiritual friend.

Rid yourself of faults like these and listen to the teachings in the proper manner.

B. Conduct to be avoided by the master giving the teachings

The masters giving the teachings should also avoid any faults. As far as their attitude is concerned, they should be free from the defilement of pride, from distraction, lack of respect for the teachings and individuals, carelessness, and any kind of wrong motivation such as the eight ordinary preoccupations. As for their conduct when they are teaching, they should avoid mistaking the context, failing to convey the meaning, mistaking the words and their meanings, and indulging in thoughts and words that are motivated by defilements such as jealousy. They should not use unclear words, add or omit anything, or say things that undermine their own arguments. While teaching, they should not make use of hints to praise themselves and disparage others. They should not adulterate their words with vulgar colloquialisms, or waste the disciples' potential by giving teachings that do not match their intellects.

While avoiding the above faults, they should explain the teachings with the most appropriate words, communicating clearly and audibly to everyone in the hall, using pleasant expressions that are universally inspiring. The words and meanings should be precise, so that all doubts are resolved. Through the skillful use of analogies, the teachings should be made accessible and easy to understand for the disciples. And they should be matched to the disciples' mentalities, so that they truly benefit them. From time to time, the teacher should tell inspiring stories to prevent those listening from becoming dull and sleepy or getting fed up. They should draw from the treasure trove of scriptural authority and reasoning so as to eliminate any errors or confusion. They should be skilled in countering objections by eliminating opponents' assertions and criticisms. They should use explanations that are common to all the vehicles so that they are acceptable to everyone. Everything they say should be seemly—easy to understand and free of vulgar expressions and colloquialisms. They should use their ability to elaborate and condense to make their explanations complete in themselves. They should teach in a way that is relaxed and spacious, without any sense of fatigue or being forced. Teaching in this manner is what we call "a teaching rich in qualities."

C. Conduct to be avoided by both the teacher and the disciples

While they are engaged in teaching the Dharma and listening to it, master and disciples should all avoid anything that acts as an obstacle to giving and receiving the teaching. Thus they should avoid such things as diversions and material concerns that lead to their minds being distracted; delays from inviting people to pay their respects and so forth; and intoxicants and dullness or sleepiness, which reduce mental clarity. The Omniscient Teacher expresses this as follows:

> Avoid all obstacles to hearing the Dharma—
> External and internal diversions, veneration, and material concerns,
> And alcohol and dull, sleepy states, which diminish attention.[11]

II. Conduct to be adopted

This section on conduct to be adopted is divided into the same three parts as the one that has just been explained.

A. Conduct to be adopted by the disciples listening to the teachings

This part is divided into four: (1) thirty-six qualities that one should possess, (2) four correct notions that one should cultivate, (3) the six transcendent perfections that one should have, and (4) additional instructions on conduct.

1. Thirty-six qualities that one should possess

These are listed in the *Precious Treasury That Fulfills All Wishes* as follows:

At that time, you should listen in the correct manner, with
Six metaphorical considerations in valuing the teachings, such as the thought of the jewel,
Six kinds of tolerance in the face of difficulties, such as putting up with afflictions,
Six shields against being swayed by circumstances, such as an appetite for learning,
Six qualities that should be emphasized, such as cultivating compassion,
Six necessities, such as knowing the different teachings,
And six ways of seeking, such as seeking the teachings—
Take hold of these thirty-six qualities and listen.[12]

Of these, six metaphorical considerations in valuing the teachings are described in the *Sūtra of the Questions of Subāhu*:

Consider the master teaching the Dharma as a treasure of precious things,
Likewise, consider that the teaching is a wish-fulfilling jewel,
That to listen to the teachings is extremely rare,
That to remember and reflect on the teachings is something meaningful, to be cherished,
That to be able to investigate the teachings is something not to be found in a hundred lifetimes,
And that to give up seeking the teachings is to throw away nectar and consume poison.
Rely on such enthusiasm to make your listening and reflection meaningful.

The six kinds of tolerance in the face of difficulties are to be found in the same sūtra:

In connection with the spiritual friend and the teachings, it is important to put up with being afflicted by heat and cold; and likewise, to put up with being afflicted by hunger and thirst, by criticism and abuse, and by the ordeal of traveling; to put up with the difficulty of giving away one's worldly possessions or of trying

> to obtain things that one needs; and to put up with even risking the life that one holds so dear.

Of the six shields against being swayed by circumstances, the same sūtra declares,

> When teaching the Dharma and assiduously practicing it, exert yourself so that not even darts can stop you. Receive the teachings numerous times, retain the many teachings you have received, gain a knowledge of the meaning of the teachings, practice in accordance with them, rely, moreover, on those who do so, and venerate such beings.

For the six qualities that should be emphasized, the sūtra states,

> Know all the roots of virtue; knowing them, practice them accordingly; cultivate great compassion for sentient beings; hold the sacred Dharma; do not interrupt the lineage of the Three Jewels; and bring sentient beings to full maturation—these are the particular qualities you should possess.

As for accomplishing the six necessities, these are described in the *Sūtra of the Discourse for Kāśyapa*:

> The need to hear and then know the teachings in detail; likewise, the need to know and then avoid wrong action; the need to teach this to others too; the need for oneself and others to attain perfect liberation by means of such teaching; the need for oneself and others to train in wisdom; and the need to resolve the doubts of those who approach one from all directions. Be diligent in listening with these six.

The six ways of seeking the teachings are listed in that great body of extremely extensive teachings, the *Sūtra of the Ornament of the Buddhas*:

> Seek the teachings with deep-felt interest, without deceit or pretense. Likewise, seek them not for your own sake but for the ben-

efit of all. Seek them with a wish to eliminate beings' defilements rather than a desire for gain and respect. Seek them with wisdom and not with pretense. Seek them unhesitatingly, in order to resolve everyone's doubts. Seek them in order to complete the qualities of buddhahood, and not with arrogance and desire. It is in this manner that you should seek the teachings.

2. The four correct notions that one should cultivate

In the *Sūtra of the Arborescent Array*, we find extensive explanations using numerous analogies such as the following:

> Fortunate child, think of yourself as someone who is sick. Think of the teaching as a medicine. Think of the spiritual friend as an experienced physician. Think of your diligent practice as the treatment for your sickness.

3. The six transcendent perfections that one should have

The Omniscient Teacher has said,

> Generosity—offering flowers, a seat, and so forth,
> Transcendent discipline—full restraint of one's three doors,
> Patient acceptance of difficulties, joyful diligence,
> Concentration—maintaining one's listening without distraction,
> And supreme wisdom, which cuts through doubts and
> misinterpretations.[13]

When one receives teachings, acts such as setting up a teaching throne for the teacher, adorning it with offerings such as flowers, offering the maṇḍala, and so forth constitute generosity. Restraining one's body, speech, and mind and avoiding harming any beings in the area, even the minutest insects, fleas, and lice, is discipline. Putting up with heat, cold, and other difficulties is patience. Joyful enthusiasm in praying to the teacher and listening to the teachings constitutes diligence. Listening one-pointedly without the mind getting distracted is concentration. Resolving doubts and misinterpretations with regard to the meaning of what one hears constitutes wisdom.

All these appear, yet they are devoid of intrinsic nature, and it is in this way that you should listen, with the concepts of the three spheres completely purified.

4. Additional instructions on conduct

In the *Precious Treasury That Fulfills All Wishes*, we read,

> Abandon all distractions and diversions,
> And having made offerings, real and imaginary, for the teachings,
> Make prostrations, sit straight with your palms joined,
> And listen respectfully, without distraction.[14]

Distractions refer to mundane activities like commerce that distract the three doors. Diversions, on the other hand, refer to one's being tied up with amassing wealth and entourage, so that one's body, speech, and mind are engaged and caught up in such things.* In a venue free of any disadvantages that could constitute an obstacle to the teachings, set up a lion throne for the teacher, draped with brocade and so forth, and invite him or her to be seated on it. Then make prostrations to them and offer incense, flowers, lamps, and other material offerings that you have prepared. As you do so, imagine that you are offering dense clouds of offerings filling space—both things that are owned and those that have no owner. Avoid dressing ostentatiously and carrying parasols, walking sticks, weapons, headwear, or shoes. Without turning your back on the teacher or sitting sideways, sit cross-legged or in an upright posture, with your eyes lowered and your palms joined together. Listen to the teaching without letting your mind wander elsewhere. As you listen, you should be full of respect, joy, and enthusiasm with regard to the teachings and the teacher. It is said in the *Verses That Summarize the Perfection of Wisdom*,

> Applying the highest joy, respect, and faith,
> Rid of obscurations and defilements, quite beyond all stains,

*Shechen Gyaltsap here gives a definition of the Tibetan word *'du 'dzi* (translated in this case as "diversion") in terms of its two component syllables: *'du ba* means "gathering" and *'dzi* signifies "being busy."

> And determined to engage in beings' good, with transcendent wisdom,
> Conduct yourself as do the brave, and listen.

Besides that, never let yourself think, even for an instant, that the teacher does not know the Dharma, is of lowly birth, is not very rich, has gross defilements, is short-tempered, irritable, does not speak very pleasantly, is badly dressed, is poor and destitute, is surrounded by low sorts of people, and so on. If such thoughts should occur, confess them and vow never to have them again. Think of his or her kindness and give rise to the thought that he or she is a buddha.

What should we concentrate on when listening to the teaching? The instructions are to consider that from the teacher's mouth the light rays of the Dharma issue forth and strike the heart of each one, clearing away the darkness of ignorance and causing the lotus of intelligence and understanding to blossom.[15]

B. Conduct to be adopted by the master giving the teachings

It is said in the *Sūtra of the White Lotus of the Sacred Dharma*,

> In a pure and lovely place,
> Well set up a beautiful throne,
> And don fine clothes, clean and pleasing.
> With cloths spread out and cushions for the feet,
> Be seated on the throne.
> Amid an assembly of disciples listening one-pointedly,
> Teach without any thought of material gain or fame,
> With a loving mind, and without laziness.

First of all, teachers should wash themselves and dress properly in Dharma robes and so on. Conducting themselves purely, they should sit cross-legged on the teaching throne. Then, they should begin by melodiously offering the seven branches, reciting mantras to subjugate negative forces, requesting the disciples to listen, and so forth. Without any thought of gain, honor, or other personal advantage, they should arouse the mind intent on enlightenment, both in aspiration and in action. And thinking, "I shall acquire the eye of Dharma for all sentient beings; I shall light the lamp of gnosis; I shall do everything to ensure that the Buddha's teaching remains for a long time," they should bring to mind the points of the generation and perfection phases.* In this way, they should proceed to give the teaching.

As for the manner in which the teaching should be given, the Omniscient Teacher has this to say:

> Teach the words and meanings of the Dharma without mistake or misinterpretation,
> With clear meanings, pleasant tones, and in accordance with the listeners' aspirations.
> Consider that the sound fills the whole universe:
> It is heard by all beings and clears away their ignorance.[16]

Consider that the sound of the teaching, with its sixty expressive qualities, fills the whole universe and that by hearing it, all sentient beings are cleared of the gloom of ignorance. They all acquire the power of memory as an entrance to the Dharma, along with confident eloquence and concentration. With this in mind, use clear, pleasant words to give explanations that are suitably detailed or condensed, so that they are easy for the disciples to understand, they resolve their doubts, and they accord with each one's mind and karmic inclinations. As we read in *The Way of the Bodhisattva*,

> Do not teach the highest way to those on lower paths.
> Those suited to the teachings of great scope
> Should not be introduced to lesser paths.[17]

For this reason, we find in the *Great Array of the Sublime*,

> The teachings for the three of lowest capacity
> Are the Vinaya, Sūtras, and Abhidharma.
> The true teachings for the three of middling capacity
> Are Kriya, Yoga, and Upa.
> For the three who are at the stages of great capacity,
> Teach the generation, perfection, and Great Perfection.

*In other words, the teacher should perform the visualization appropriate to the subject being taught while also maintaining the view of emptiness.

Accordingly, teach in accord with the disciple's level and capacity. In particular, to disciples who are truly determined to be free of cyclic existence and for whom the practice is the most important thing, one should teach the profound essential instructions, in which everything is condensed into a few words and that make for rapid progress toward liberation. For life is so short, there are so many conventional teachings, and nothing else is of much importance, as Atisha Dīpaṃkara-shrī-jñāna has said:

> This life is short and there is much to learn.
> Since we do not know how long we have to live,
> Like swans extracting milk from water,
> We must eagerly undertake what we most desire.

And,

> Look outside, at the world and its activities:
> All we do is meaningless and leads to suffering.
> Nothing we can think of can bring us benefit,
> So train yourself in looking at your mind.

When we teach the sacred Dharma properly in this way, the six transcendent perfections will be complete. The Omniscient Teacher has said,

> At that time, teach with the six transcendent perfections:
> The gift of Dharma, in properly explaining the words and meanings;
> Transcendent discipline, in teaching without defilements;
> Forbearance, in putting up with weariness; diligence, in teaching enthusiastically;
> Concentration, in being undistracted; and wisdom, in exercising discernment.[18]

Properly explaining the words and meanings of the Dharma is generosity. Giving explanations unadulterated by defilements such as attachment and aversion and refraining from saying anything unwholesome constitute discipline. Putting up with such difficulties as physical and mental fatigue, hunger and thirst, and heat and cold while one is teaching constitutes patience. Untiring enthusiasm in teaching constitutes diligence. Teaching without the mind being distracted elsewhere is concentration. Distinguishing the points that are being explained and realizing that they are devoid of intrinsic nature, while knowing, when one is teaching the Dharma, that everything is like a dream or magical illusion, constitute wisdom. Thus, by teaching the Dharma properly, one will complete the two accumulations of merit and wisdom.

C. Conduct to be adopted by both the teacher and the disciples

When teacher and disciples have both finished teaching and listening in the correct way, we should recognize that we ourselves, those listening, and the teachings all appear from the illusion-like state but are devoid of intrinsic existence. As we do so, we should dedicate the merit with such prayers as the following:

> With this vast act of generosity,
> May we spontaneously rise from among beings and attain buddhahood.
> May the host of beings who have not been liberated by the buddhas of the past
> Be brought to complete liberation.

And,

> By this precious accumulation of merit, may all beings
> Never be parted from the sacred Dharma.
> May our own and others' goals be completely fulfilled,
> And may the world be graced by the beat of the Dharma drum.

We should also reflect as follows. The fact that we can hear the sacred teachings has come about because of the teacher, the spiritual friend, so be grateful to the root and lineage teachers. Since the Dharma comprises the words that the Buddha spoke, be grateful to the Buddha. Since we have listened with our sublime companions, be grateful to the Saṅgha—our Dharma friends who aspire so keenly to virtue.* The fact that there have

*Tib. *dge ba la 'dun pa'i grogs*. "Aspiring to virtue" is a literal translation of the Tibetan term for Saṅgha (*dge 'dun*).

been no interruptions to the teachings is due to the kindness of the ocean-like *ḍākinīs* and loyal protectors, so be grateful to the infinite guardians and loyal protectors. Thanks to our parents giving birth to our physical body and bringing us up, we are able to practice the Dharma, so be grateful to them too. And since all these have come about through the kindness of the Buddha's sublime doctrine, be grateful for the Buddha's teaching, the source of benefit and happiness, and think, "Long may it endure!"

3. A Supplementary, Inspirational Section Describing the Benefits of Teaching the Dharma and Listening to It

The benefits are described in two parts.

I. The benefits obtained by the master giving the teaching

The Omniscient Teacher says,

> The benefits of this are memory and concentration,
> Freedom from defiling thoughts, inexhaustible confidence and eloquence.
> They will hold the treasury of the Dharma, hear the teachings from the sugatas,
> Be praised and honored by gods and humankind, and accomplish everything they wish.
> Never parted from the Dharma in all their lives,
> They will swiftly achieve buddhahood and cause the rain of Dharma to fall.[19]

If one teaches the Dharma properly without any thought of material gain, one will acquire the power of memory, concentration, and confidence and eloquence, and be completely freed from defilements. One will hold the treasury of the teachings, hear the Dharma from the buddhas, and receive the praises and devotion of hosts of gods and humans. All one's positive wishes will be fulfilled, and in all one's lives one will never be separated from the sacred Dharma. Having swiftly attained buddhahood, one will bring beings to maturity with the great rain of the teachings, and one will fulfill all one's own and others' goals. The benefits will thus be boundless, as we find in the *Sūtra on the Concentration of the Magical Display That Ascertains What Is Peace*:

> One will acquire sharp intelligence, inexhaustible confidence and eloquence, and the magical powers of universal monarchs, Indra, and Brahmā; and one will attain unsurpassable buddhahood.

And in the *Sūtra of the Questions of Gaganagañja*,

> One will delight many beings, be protected by the Dharma protectors, and be praised by the gods. One will be immune to harm from nonhumans. One will preserve the sacred Dharma, become renowned throughout the ten directions, and be praised by all the sugatas. One will acquire the Dharma robes and so forth and live off alms in accordance with the activities laid down in the Vinaya.* One will possess intelligence and realization, reduce the three poisons, eliminate one's own and others' defilements, and hold the Buddha's teachings. One will have no fear of the lower realms and will, without difficulty, be reborn as a god or human. One will remember one's past lives and be reborn in pure buddha-fields. One will have one's faculties complete and will never be parted from the Three Jewels. One will be able to gain inexhaustible confidence and eloquence, acquire a brilliant memory, and be attended by learned beings. One will hold the stream of great wisdom, swiftly acquire the vision of reality, and have no improper thoughts. One's teaching the Dharma will eclipse all material generosity, and one will obtain the thirty-two major marks and hold the inexhaustible treasure of the Dharma.

There are innumerable such descriptions, beginning with the *Sūtra That Inspires a Superior Intention*, which speaks of twenty benefits from teaching the Dharma, and the *Sūtra of the King of Concentrations*, which mentions ten benefits. Even reciting in someone else's ear just a few of the different names, incantations, and mantras of the secret mantra deities results in the

*In other words, one will be able to lead a simple life conducive to Dharma practice.

purification of obscurations accumulated over many kalpas, in the completion of the accumulations, and so on. The benefits are inconceivable.

The *Verses That Summarize the Perfection of Wisdom* concludes,

> When a bodhisattva meditating on the supreme wisdom
> Arises from that state and teaches the immaculate Dharma,
> Dedicating it as the cause for enlightenment for the benefit of beings,
> The merit of that has no equal in the three worlds.

And the *Extensive Sūtra of the Great Realization*,

> After I have gone beyond,
> There will be some among humans
> Who will be able to inspire beings, saying,
> "All forms of sentient beings
> Have the essence of the sugatas."
> Thus will they repay the Buddha's kindness.

And in another sūtra, too, we read,

> Excellent, excellent it is to teach the tathāgata essence.
> Wherever it is excellently taught, those who hear the tathāgata essence
> Will always be reborn as humans in the world
> And will in the future become buddhas, the Tathāgata has said.

And,

> Those who teach the tathāgata essence,
> Whether they have defilements
> Or are without defilements,
> Are known as perfect buddhas.

And in the *Heruka Galpo*,

> Henceforth, those who read aloud
> Or even think of this practice

Of the vajra body, speech, and mind,
Will be like Vajradhara.

More detailed accounts may be found in other texts.

II. The benefits obtained by the disciples listening to the teaching

The Omniscient Teacher says,

The benefits of that are utterly boundless:
If beings who hear just the beat of the Dharma drum*
Will be liberated from the lower realms,
Need one speak of the benefits for those who actually receive the teachings?
They will acquire wisdom, concentration, and the power of memory;
They will distinguish what to avoid and adopt, increase in virtue, and lessen all wrongdoing.
Gods and humans will praise them; the darkness of ignorance will be cleared away.
Adorning a lotus seat, they will hear the vast Dharma
And swiftly attain the state of Dharma King, beyond all misery.[20]

They will acquire perfect liberation, wisdom, concentration, and powers of memory such as that associated with the concentration of the stream of Dharma.† Distinguishing between what they should abandon and what they should adopt, they will increase in virtuous activities and attenuate nonvirtue. They will receive the praises and devotion of the gods and the rest of the world. The darkness of their ignorance will be cleared away. When they die and transmigrate, they will take a miraculous lotus birth in a pure buddha-field, receive teachings from the supreme manifestation body of a buddha, and having swiftly attained buddhahood, turn the Wheel

*The drum used to summon beings to the teaching.

†The concentration of the stream of Dharma is so called because by remaining in equanimity in that concentration, bodhisattvas receive countless instructions on the sacred Dharma from innumerable buddhas and are able to continuously retain the words and meanings.

of Dharma. These and others are the boundless benefits they will gain. As it is said in the *Sūtra of the Questions of Nārāyaṇa*,

> If one has heard the teachings, one will gain in wisdom.
> If one has wisdom, one's defilements will be stilled:
> If one has no defilements, demons will be unable to harm one.

The *Sūtra of the Prophecy for the Magician Bhadra* speaks of four benefits: training oneself and others in wisdom, resolving the doubts of all those to be trained, being praised by the buddhas and bodhisattvas, and holding the sacred Dharma. And in the *Chapters of Utterances on Specific Topics* and in other scriptures too, listening to the Dharma is extensively praised. In the *Perfection of Wisdom in One Hundred Thousand Lines*, we read,

> Lord Buddha answered Shāriputra's question thus: "Having heard this transcendent wisdom, sentient beings with faith will definitely attain enlightenment. They will come closer and closer to enlightenment. They will be regarded as the Buddha himself."

And in the *Sūtra of the Questions of the Devaputra Susthitamati*,

> If all those with the belief in a self were to venerate buddhas as numerous as the sands of the Ganges River and their retinues with all kinds of material offerings for as long as they live, that would bring great benefit. But greater still is the benefit of hearing and having faith in the profound teachings on the doors of emptiness, absence of attributes, and absence of expectancy, which counter all worldly views. Why is that? Because, as a result of doing so, even though one may reject the profound teachings and fall into the hells, one will very swiftly rise out of them and be liberated. Hearing those teachings is as if the buddha bhagavans were appearing in the world.

And in the *Succession of Ṛṣi Teachers*, a section of the *Sūtra of the Ornament of the Buddhas*,

> To respectful bodhisattvas who wish for the teachings and have perfect motivation, the buddhas dwelling in other worlds will

> manifest and teach them the Dharma. Bodhisattvas resplendent with an untainted wish for the teachings will hold in the palms of their hands infinite entrances to the Dharma in the form of books that have been placed as Dharma treasures in mountains and trees. Likewise, the gods who have seen the buddhas of the past will help them achieve confidence and eloquence. Even when their lives are at an end, the buddha bhagavans and gods will give them strength, and because of that, they will live even a thousand years if they so wish and remain for a kalpa or as long as they wish. The sugatas will increase their joys, dispel their illnesses, and enable them to practice mindfulness and to accomplish understanding, intelligence, and confident eloquence. Wrong views will be dispelled, and they will achieve the correct view. They will not fear harm from others. Thus, those bodhisattvas should be truly diligent in listening to a great number of teachings.

And in the *Sūtra of the King of Concentrations*, it is said,

> Once one has heard this sacred sūtra,
> For seventy-three measureless kalpas
> In the future, it will be impossible
> To fall into the lower realms.
> At a time when the teachings are about to disappear,
> Those who retain this sūtra
> Will swiftly acquire confidence and eloquence.
> If retaining just a single verse
> Results in an immeasurable mass of merit,
> Need one mention the benefit for those who,
> With a wish to listen, retain all the sūtra sections:
> They will bring all sentient beings to enlightenment.

And in the *Sūtra That Teaches the Tathāgata Essence*,

> In the past, when I was following the practice,
> I heard the name of this sūtra
> From the sugata Leonine Victory Banner.
> Filled with respect, on hearing it, I joined my palms.

As a result of that excellent deed,
I swiftly attained supreme enlightenment.
Therefore, wise bodhisattvas
Should always hold this sublime sūtra.

And in the *Guhyagarbha Tantra*,

Anyone with faith in this
Will be considered as their dearest son
By all the maṇḍalas of buddhas
Throughout all space, throughout all time.

These and similar benefits are mentioned in detail in all the sūtras and tantras.

The prize the supreme protector sought for countless aeons
And gave his life ten million times to find
Is this treasure house of jewels, the sacred teachings of the Dharma,
So teach and listen with respect, O fortunate ones!

This completes the virtuous beginning comprising an explanation of how the teachings should be presented and received.

CHOKGYUR DECHEN LINGPA (1829–1870)

PART TWO

The Virtuous Middle, Comprising an Explanation on Training One's Being through the Four Common Practices for Turning the Mind

The four common practices for turning the mind are treated in two sections: the preliminaries to beginning a session and the specific, individual practices. The first section comprises a single chapter, devoted to the manner in which one should begin each session of practice.

As for the specific, individual practices,[21] in his commentary on the *Precious Treasury That Fulfills All Wishes*, the *White Lotus*, the Omniscient Teacher speaks of five topics on which we need to reflect:

> Begin by reflecting on these five topics: the difficulty of finding the freedoms and advantages, impermanence, the benefits of faith, the karmic law of cause and effect, and the defects of cyclic existence.
>
> Out of all the supports for accomplishing enlightenment, the best is a human body with the freedoms and advantages, so you should feel delighted at having obtained one. If you do not reflect on this, you will have the negative consequence of wasting your freedom.
>
> Even if you have obtained it, there is nothing one can be certain of, so you will need to reflect on the impermanence of life, which acts as the whip of diligence, encouraging one to accumulate virtue. If you do not reflect on this, you will have the negative

consequence of never beginning the path to liberation, due to laziness and indifference.

Then, you will need to back this up by cultivating single-minded faith. If you fail to do so, you will have the negative consequence of losing the very root of the Dharma.

Next, you must reflect on even the minutest positive and negative actions and their effects. If you do not, you will have the negative consequence of never ever being liberated from the suffering of cyclic existence.

After that, you should reflect on the defects of the higher and lower realms of cyclic existence. Unless you do so, you will have the negative consequence of not knowing what to reject and adopt with regard to saṃsāra (cyclic existence) and nirvāṇa (the transcendence of suffering), and therefore of never really embarking on the path to liberation and enlightenment.

By reflecting on these five topics, a person will not mistake the way for undertaking the journey to liberation.

Of these five, faith will be explained below in the chapter on taking refuge. In the section on the specific, individual practices, therefore, there are four chapters, presented in the usual order:

- instructions for reflecting on the difficulty of finding the freedoms and advantages, as a result of which one turns the mind away from pointless worldly activities and pursues the path to liberation
- instructions for reflecting on death and impermanence, as a result of which one turns the mind away from laziness and indifference and develops diligence in the practice of Dharma
- instructions for reflecting on the karmic law of cause and result, as a result of which one turns the mind away from all forms of nonvirtue and makes a one-pointed effort to engage in positive, virtuous activities
- instructions for reflecting on the sufferings of cyclic existence, as a result of which one turns the mind away from worldly comforts and pursues the path to everlasting liberation

4. Preliminaries to Beginning a Session

In an isolated place where nothing will happen to adversely affect your concentration, such as visitors and people moving about during the day or disturbances from noise at night, sit on a comfortable seat and adopt the essential point for the body, the seven-point posture of Vairocana, as follows: Assume the vajra posture, with both legs crossed, the right leg on top of the left. Stretch your fisted hands down, with the thumbs pressing on the base of the ring fingers, and place them on the crook of your right and left thighs. Straighten your arms, with the shoulders drawn upward. Let the belly relax forward. Keep the spine straight, with the vertebrae stacked on top of each other like gold coins and the chin pressing in on the Adam's apple. Without moving the eyes or blinking, look straight into space in line with the tip of your nose. Holding your head up straight, keep your whole body erect.

The purpose of all this has been explained by former learned and accomplished masters as follows: The body is like a city, the subtle channels in it are like the streets, the wind-energy like a horse, and the consciousness like a crippled person. If your movements are restricted, the street junctions are blocked and it is impossible for the rider and horse trapped inside to move. And just as the scales a snake uses for locomotion* do not stand out unless one twists the snake, we need to adopt the essential point for the body and use skillful means to control it more so that the wisdom perceptions will increase. By bringing about the right conditions in the body, realization will take birth in the mind.

*Tib. *yan lag*, lit. "limbs," refers here to the scales on the underside of a snake adapted to locomotion. Unless one forcefully twists the snake, they do not stand out. Similarly, one has to use forceful means in adopting the posture in order to create the right conditions for meditation.

Once you have adopted the essential point for the body like this, begin the session with the essential point for the speech, which is to expel the stale air nine times. First, expel three times through the left nostril—gently, more forcefully, and very forcefully. Do the same three times through the right nostril, and then three times through both nostrils together, making nine times in all. At the beginning of subsequent sessions, expel the stale air through the left, right, and both nostrils once each, making three times in all. As you do so, visualize as follows: Consider that all the negative actions, obscurations, illnesses, negative forces, obstacles, and adverse factors that you yourself and all other sentient beings have accumulated in your series of lives since time without beginning are gathered together and flushed out with the air through the nostrils. Alternatively, imagine that all the deeds, defilements, and stains accumulated with attachment are flushed out through your left nostril, those accumulated with aversion through the right nostril, and those accumulated with ignorance through both together. Consider that in this way, the inside of the body is completely rinsed. This is like washing out a container before pouring some valuable substance into it.

After that, there is the essential point for the mind, which, as has been explained above, is to correct your attitude—that is, to arouse the mind intent on enlightenment.

Next, considering yourself in your ordinary form, visualize above the crown of your head an eight-petaled multicolored lotus (symbolizing the pure nature of the eight conceptual extremes)* with its pistil-cup and anthers. On top of this are the maṇḍalas of the sun and moon, symbolizing skillful means and wisdom, the moon above the sun, touching but not stuck together.

When these have become clear, visualize on top of them your own root teacher, in whichever form you wish—Vajrasattva or the Great Orgyen, for example; or alternatively, in the everyday form he or she usually takes, with the two hands in the gesture of teaching the Dharma or of meditation, whichever you prefer. Visualize them vividly present, physically in the full bloom of youth, with all the major and minor marks, utterly resplendent. If there is a difference in the way it arouses your faith and devotion, you should visualize the teacher in the form that inspires you most; but if it makes no difference, then visualize the teacher as he or she actually is. Whichever the case,

*The eight conceptual extremes (Tib. *rtog pa'i mtha' brgyad*) are birth, cessation, eternalism, nihilism, going, coming, unicity or sameness, and multiplicity or difference.

beginners should not be in a hurry to visualize a multitude of details precisely right from the start. The important thing is to train in concentrating one-pointedly, vividly imagining the teacher's presence.

When this becomes clear, seeing the teacher as the Buddha, pray with intense longing and devotion, thinking, "Whatever you do, you know best!" and recite whichever prayers you can, for example:

> Precious, glorious root teacher,
> Dwell on a lotus seat on the crown of my head.
> Guide me with your great kindness,
> And grant me the accomplishments of your body, speech, and mind.

And,

> Precious Teacher, essence of all buddhas past, present, and future, in you I place my trust.
> Grant your blessings to mature and liberate my mind stream.
> Grant your blessings that the extraordinary realization of the profound path take birth in my mind stream.
> May I attain the sublime accomplishment of Mahāmudrā in this very life!

If you like, you can also say the *Prayer for Calling the Teacher from Afar** and other prayers. In short, until the realization of true devotion develops, pray ardently from the bottom of your heart to achieve your desired goal. At the end, the teacher, his heart greatly gladdened, melts into a ball of five-colored light and dissolves through your crown into the middle of your heart. Rest in equipoise, for as long as it lasts, in a state of great bliss free from elaboration, without any concept of your three doors and the teacher's three vajras being distinct, like water poured into water, indivisible in nature.

After that, conclude by dedicating the merit with prayers such as the following:

> By the merit of this
> May I swiftly accomplish the glorious teacher,

*Tib. *bla ma rgyang 'bod,* any one of a genre of prayers used to invoke one's teacher.

> And, not leaving out a single being,
> May I establish them all in his level.

This is a practice that the Dharma King Terdak Lingpa,* the unique sun of the doctrine of the true secret, the ancient tradition of the Diamond Vehicle, gave as a way to begin and precede each session or practice. It leads swiftly to the entrance of blessings and is a particularly sublime gateway for the swift birth of experiences and realization in the main practice, whichever it may be.

*Gyurme Dorje, Terdak Lingpa (1646–1714), the founder of Mindrölling Monastery in Tibet.

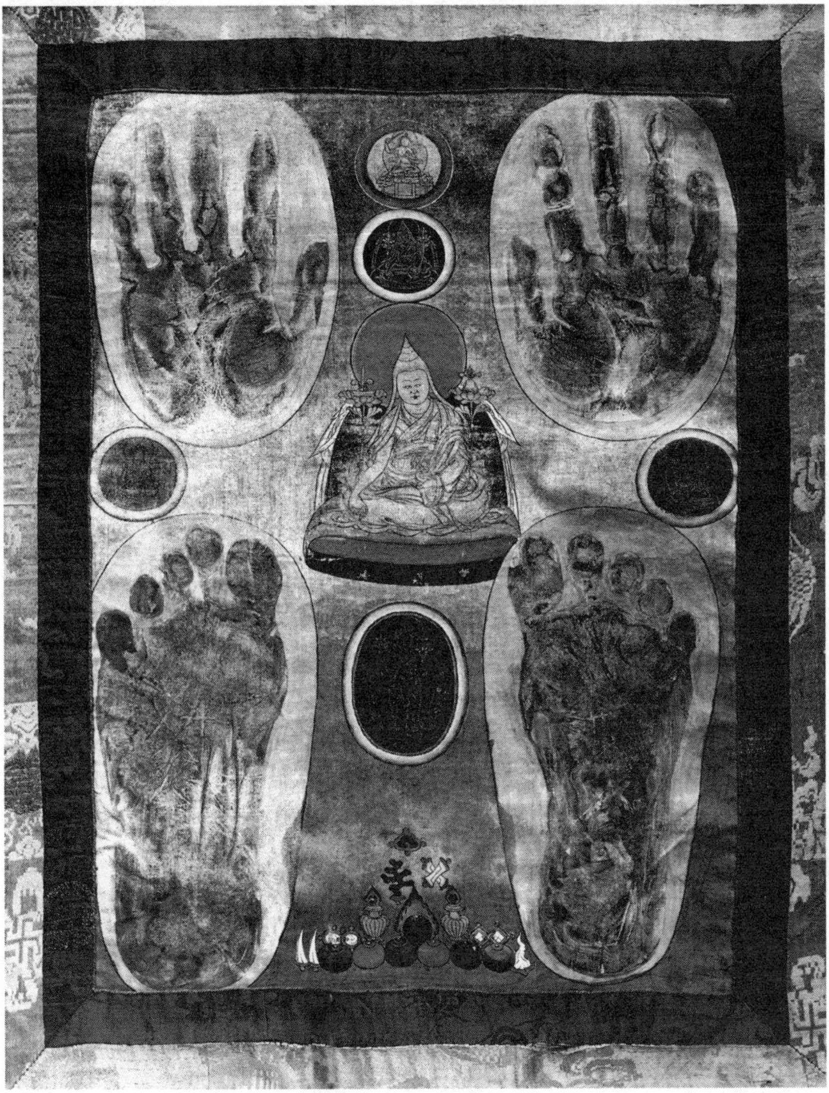

Jamyang Khyentse Wangpo (1820–1892)

5. Reflecting on the Difficulty of Finding the Freedoms and Advantages

The instructions for reflecting on the difficulty of finding the freedoms and advantages enable one to turn one's mind away from pointless worldly activities and to pursue the path to liberation. They have generally been taught using the ten outline headings or instruction sections in the Omniscient Teacher's *Essential Instructions for Finding Rest in the Nature of the Mind*, but here, for ease of explanation, I will present them under four headings: (1) identifying the freedoms and advantages, (2) the difficulty of finding them, (3) the importance of finding them, and (4) the benefits and signs of having meditated on them.

I. Identifying the freedoms and advantages

Identifying the freedoms and advantages is divided into two: (1) identifying the essence, freedom, and (2) identifying the particular qualities, the advantages.

A. Identifying the essence, freedom

The basis of the precious human body is freedom, which is the opposite of states without opportunity. These states without opportunity can be categorized under three headings: (1) the eight states without opportunity that depend on one's own stream of being, (2) the eight intrusive circumstances that leave no freedom to practice the Dharma, and (3) the eight incompatible propensities that leave no freedom to practice the Dharma.

1. The eight states without opportunity that depend on one's own stream of being

In the *Jewel Garland*, Padmasambhava's autocommentary on his *Great Treatise on the Graded Path*, we read,

> The only support that can be used to accomplish enlightenment is one that has the freedoms and advantages. The term *freedoms* is used to refer to the absence of the eight states without opportunity, these being described as follows:
>
> The hells, preta realm, and animal realm,
> The long-lived gods and barbarians,
> The Buddha's not coming, false view,
> And dumbness—these are the eight states that lack opportunity.
>
> The three lower realms and the long-lived gods are four nonhuman states. Then there are the following four states that concern human beings: the absence of the Buddha's doctrine; birth as a barbarian, with no access to the Buddha's teaching even if it is present; having the false view that actions do not have results; and having incomplete faculties (deafness, blindness, stammering, dumbness, and so on). Someone in whom these two sets of four disadvantages are absent has freedom and is thus an appropriate support for the extraordinary Dharma.

And in his *Essential Instructions*, the Omniscient Teacher writes,

> Feel joyful that rather than falling into those states, you have acquired the freedoms, and be diligent in practicing the Dharma. Reflect as follows: "If one is born in the hells, one experiences the sufferings of heat and cold and there is no opportunity to practice the Dharma. If one is born as a hungry spirit, one is tormented by the fires of hunger and thirst, so there is no opportunity to practice the Dharma. If one is born in the animal realm, one is in danger of being eaten by other animals and so on, so there is no opportunity to practice the Dharma. If one is reborn as a long-lived god, one continues for kalpas in a state of insensi-

> bility and then, at the moment of death, develops false views, so there is no opportunity to practice the Dharma. If one is born in a border land, where the light of the teachings is absent, there is no opportunity to practice the Dharma. If one is born as a non-Buddhist or a similar type of person, because of one's false views there is no opportunity to practice the Dharma. If one is born in a dark kalpa, in which the names of the Three Jewels are never uttered, there is no opportunity to practice the Dharma. If one is born dumb, one's mental faculties do not constitute a suitable vessel for the teachings, so there is no opportunity to practice the Dharma. Right now, as I have not been born in those eight states, I have that opportunity. I must make every effort to practice the Dharma!" Take refuge, arouse bodhichitta, and then reflect on the freedoms that you have obtained, which are the opposite of the eight states without opportunity. Thinking, "I must do nothing but practice the Dharma," reflect again and again. Conclude by dedicating the merit, and combine this reflection with all your everyday activities too.

You should understand that this way of training applies to all the instruction sections below, so practice them all complete with the preparation and conclusion.*

2. The eight intrusive circumstances that leave no freedom to practice the Dharma

In the *Precious Treasury That Fulfills All Wishes*, the Omniscient Teacher writes,

> Those who are buffeted by the five poisons, who are stupid, possessed by demons,
> Lazy, overwhelmed by the effects of past evil actions,

*Each of the instruction sections (Tib. *khrid rkang*) in Longchenpa's *Essential Instructions for Finding Rest in the Nature of the Mind* includes the admonition to reflect with the three supreme methods (see above, p. 11), beginning with refuge and bodhichitta and concluding with the dedication of merit.

> Dominated by others, in search of protection from danger, and
> whose practice is a pretense
> Have the eight intrusive circumstances that leave no freedom:
> They are unsuitable vessels for the Dharma, turned away from the
> path to liberation.[22]

Even if they are born as humans in a place where one can practice the Dharma, there are some whose minds are constantly troubled by the sheer power of the five poisons. There are some who are stupid and find themselves being guided by companions who indulge in negative activities. Or they may be possessed by evil forces and mistake the path on account of their erroneous views and conduct. Some, even though they want to train in the Dharma, are lazy and lack diligence. Others, however diligent they may be, are overwhelmed by a flood of bad karma and have so many negative deeds and obscurations that they fail to develop any good qualities. Then there are those, servants and the like, who are put to work for others and who have no control over their own destiny. Some people take up the Dharma with this present life in mind—to have food and clothes, or because they are afraid of some difficulties—but as a result of their old habits from the past, they lead lives that conflict with the Dharma. Some are impostors, pretending to practice the Dharma while actually working to win possessions, honors, and fame. These eight kinds of people, too, lack the opportunity to practice the Dharma.

3. The eight incompatible propensities that leave no freedom to practice the Dharma

These are described in the *Precious Treasury That Fulfills All Wishes* as follows:

> Those who are bound by ties, lead wicked lives,
> Are not afraid of cyclic existence, have not a scrap of faith,
> Indulge in evil deeds, give no thought to Dharma,
> And break their vows and sacred commitments
> Have the eight incompatible propensities that leave no freedom:
> They are remote from the Dharma; the lamp of liberation has
> gone out.[23]

Some people are tightly bound by the ties to the things in this life—possessions, riches, children, relatives, and the like. Others have such a bad character, without the slightest scrap of humanity, that there is no improving their behavior. There are some people who feel not the slightest apprehension when they hear of the lower realms and the defects of cyclic existence or when they are faced with suffering and difficulties in this present life. Others might hear laudatory descriptions of liberation and the Three Jewels, or they might see sublime beings, but they still feel not the slightest degree of faith. Certain people take pleasure in harmful, negative activities, with no control over their thoughts, words, and deeds. Others are as uninterested in good qualities, virtue, and the sacred Dharma as a dog that is offered some grass. Those who enter the Common Vehicle and then break their spiritual commitments and vows have nowhere to go but the lower realms. Others, who have entered the vehicle of the secret mantras, damage their sacred samaya commitments with their teachers and spiritual brothers and sisters. These eight kinds of people are a long way from the sacred Dharma. For them, the lamp of liberation is said to have gone out.

When Longchenpa speaks here of incompatible propensities (lit. "interrupted potential"),* this negative notion is used in the sense of a deficiency, meaning that one will circle in cyclic existence for a long time; but it is not that one will lack the potential forever, for in the realm of sentient beings, there is not a single being that does not have the naturally existing potential.†

It is often held that the Great Omniscient One created these last two groups‡ and added them to the pith instruction tradition. However, they also appear in an old manuscript from the Zur tradition, before his time, so it is probable that they were taught in a tantra of the Ancient Translations.

Perfect freedom, then, is being master of one's own destiny so that one can practice the sacred Dharma, instead of being born with any of these sets of eight states without opportunity. The *Verses That Summarize the Perfection of Wisdom* explains,

*Tib. *rigs chad*, deprived of the potential for enlightenment, or cut off from the family of enlightenment.

†Tib. *rang bzhin gnas rigs*, that is, the Buddha nature, tathāgatagarbha.

‡That is, the eight intrusive circumstances and eight incompatible propensities.

> Those who are rid of the eight states without opportunity will always find freedom.

B. Identifying the particular qualities, the advantages

There are two sections: (1) individual advantages, and (2) circumstantial advantages.

1. The five individual advantages

The individual advantages are detailed in the *Great Treatise on the Graded Path* as follows:

> To be reborn as a human, in a central land,
> With one's faculties complete, faith in the teachings,
> And likewise, a correct lifestyle.

If one has not obtained a human body, there is no practicing the Dharma. At present, however, you have been born as a human being, so you have one individual advantage. If one is born in a place where there are no teachings, it is impossible to practice the Dharma. But at the moment, you have been born in a place in which the teachings are propagated, which is what is meant by "a central land," so you have another individual advantage. People whose faculties are incomplete cannot practice the Dharma, whereas you have all your sense faculties, which is also an individual advantage. If, through wrong livelihood, one is constantly indulging in negative deeds, then again, there is no practicing the Dharma. You, on the other hand, have a correct lifestyle and are inclined to virtue, so you have yet another individual advantage. Without faith in the teachings, there is no practicing the Dharma; but you have faith in the Buddha's teaching, so that is another individual advantage. Since it is in relation to one's own situation that these five have to be complete, they are called "individual advantages." In a sūtra that teaches twelve perfect freedoms,[24] we read,

> Obtaining the human state, being born in a sublime land, with all one's faculties complete, a correct lifestyle, and faith in the Dharma—these five constitute a perfect individual.

And in the *Direct Instructions of the Teacher* from the *Treasure of Nyang*,

> Born in a central land, having obtained a human body, with all the faculties complete, faith in the Dharma, and a correct lifestyle.

2. The five circumstantial advantages

The five circumstantial advantages are listed in the *Great Treatise on the Graded Path* as follows:

> The buddhas have come, they taught the Dharma,
> Their teachings have endured, they are accessible,
> And there are beings who have compassion for others, making five.

When there are no buddhas appearing in the world, the word *Dharma* does not even exist. In this present age, there has been a buddha who has come, so one sublime circumstantial advantage is complete. Even if a buddha appears, it does not benefit anyone unless he teaches the Dharma. Our Buddha, on the other hand, turned the Wheel of Dharma three times, so another sublime circumstantial advantage is complete. If, despite his having taught the Dharma, his teachings had not endured, they would not have helped us. But we are still in an age when the doctrine has not disappeared, so another sublime circumstantial advantage is complete. Although the teachings have endured, they would be of no use if we did not have access to them. Yet we do have access to the teachings, so another sublime circumstantial advantage is complete. Even with access to the teachings, if there were not the favorable condition of spiritual friends, we would never know what to adopt and what to avoid. Nonetheless, there are authentic, loving spiritual friends who, moreover, are skilled in compassionately caring for beings, so another sublime circumstantial advantage is complete. There are thus five circumstantial advantages.

While most of these are easy enough to understand in this context, what we call "having access to the teachings" should be understood according to the explanation in the *White Lotus*, the commentary on the *Precious Treasury That Fulfills All Wishes*:

> Even though the teachings are present, they would be of no

> use to us if there were no friends to instruct and inspire us and thus bring us benefit and happiness. But there are extraordinary Dharma friends who follow the Buddha's teachings and enable us to listen, reflect, and meditate, so this advantage is complete. The *Sūtra of the Questions of Candragarbha* states, "It is hard to find someone in the world who enables us to apply ourselves in accord with the Dharma."

Since it is in relation to extraneous factors that these five have to be complete, they are referred to as "circumstantial advantages." As the aforementioned sūtra says,

> A Buddha has come, he taught the Dharma, the sacred Dharma endures, others, too, practice it, and there are beings with love for others who help them to practice the Dharma. These five constitute perfect circumstances.

And the *Direct Instructions of the Teacher* states,

> The five circumstantial advantages are a Buddha has appeared in the world, he taught the Dharma, his doctrine has lasted a long time, moreover there are friends who follow the teaching, and they practice compassion for others' sake.

Any factors, even of minor significance, that differ from these two sets of five individual and five circumstantial advantages lead to misfortune, so we need always to be careful about avoiding them. They include unfavorable places and conditions, mixing with negative companions and so forth, conflicting lifestyles, losing faith, and being parted from one's spiritual teachers and virtuous companions. As the Omniscient Jigme Lingpa says,

> Many are those who are free but lose their freedom through false views.
> In each of the two sets of five advantages, individual and circumstantial,
> Besides the first three, reflect thoroughly on the last two,
> For it is these that connect or separate us from the Dharma.

In particular, lack of faith and wrong view spoil perfect freedom, and there is nothing more destructive than that. Yet most people nowadays, bereft of good fortune, have their eyes veiled by the distorted vision of their own perceptions, their wrong views, like someone with jaundice who perceives a conch shell as yellow. Thinking, "I am learned in the Dharma, I have heard so many teachings, I have so many good qualities," they bellow falsehoods and find fault in the teachings and the teacher like a heron on the lookout for a fish. Even if the Buddha were to come to them in person, they would not be able to see him purely. Because of this, the initial link between teacher and disciple goes wrong, the gateway for blessings is closed, the eye of pure vision becomes dim, and they pile up punishments from the gods and protectors. The more they listen to the Dharma, the wilder their minds become, the grosser their defilements become, the more their desires increase, and the coarser their conduct becomes. Finally, without even having passed through the gateway to the Dharma, they end their lives, as anyone can see, even worse than ordinary laypeople.

To make matters worse, even though the ultimate goal of the teachings, the very intention of the profound sūtras and tantras of the definitive meaning, is the same, these people take into account only the differences in the provisional teachings, with their various ways of commenting on the Buddha's words in terms of the philosophical tenet systems and their various definitions of the two truths. Subsequently, they maliciously criticize the true Dharma and authentic individuals and adopt biased, sectarian attitudes. Thus, they abandon the Dharma, accumulating in the process an immense amount of negative karma. This is extremely dangerous, and we should take every care to prevent such a fault occurring. As we read in the *Jewel Garland of the Middle Way*,

> The intentions and words of the Tathāgata
> Are not easy to understand.
> That is why, though there is but one vehicle, he taught three.
> So guard yourself by being impartial.
> Impartiality does not have negative results.
> Criticism is negative and never virtuous.

Now regarding the human body, *Finding Rest in the Nature of the Mind: A Teaching of the Great Perfection* mentions three kinds:

Three kinds of human life may be attained:
Mere, superior, or that which is most precious.[25]

The first of these refers to ordinary, or ill-fated, persons, who are described in the same text as follows:

Those who have the first, not knowing right from wrong,
Do evil deeds. And though their faculties are whole,
They're only human in the commonly accepted sense.
They may be born within a central land,
And yet they act like savage borderers.[26]

Such people are of the kind that do not know the meaning of good and evil and who constantly indulge in negative actions. Since this will anchor them in the lower realms and the hells, they are referred to as "ill-fated," as is stated in the *Sūtra of Precious Space*:

> As a result of their previous virtuous deeds, they are born in the world of humans, with their faculties complete. Even though they have been born in a region in which the Dharma is constantly practiced, they do not know about the ripening of deeds. They follow and engage in numerous unvirtuous ways, and even though they are called human, they are of the lowest sort, for after they die, they fall into the endless lower realms.

Second, with regard to superior human beings, *Finding Rest in the Nature of the Mind* continues,

Then there are those, not entering the Doctrine,
Whose actions are a mixture of both good and ill.
Thinking of this life alone,
They're utterly distracted by their busy occupations.
Rough, untamed, they cast away all thought of lives to come;
They do not strive for freedom.
Though the Dharma they may hear,
Their state is not supreme but mediocre.
To some slight good they may at times incline;
More often is their minds' sight veiled by negativity.

They have the semblance of practitioners,
And yet what good do they achieve
For others or themselves?
Whether they assume the guise of monks or laity,
They are a little higher
Than the beings in the lower realms.
And so the Conqueror described them as "superior."[27]

Whether they have taken monastic ordination or are laypeople, they are for the most part overpowered by carelessness and are completely distracted. From time to time, they give rise to a few virtuous thoughts, and their activities are a mixture of positive and negative deeds. They thus plant the seed for liberation at some time in the distant future, so they are described as having a "superior human body" compared to the previous kind. The abovementioned sūtra gives the following description:

> There are some in the realm of sentient beings who, whether or not they have entered Dharma, perform a mixture of positive and negative actions and devote themselves to diversions and distractions. Physically, verbally, and mentally coarse and undisciplined, they fall into the three lower realms. Despite their evil destiny, the Buddha, with his sunray-like compassion, sees that they possess the seed for liberation at some time in the distant future, and it is for this reason that he speaks of a "superior human body."

As for the third kind, the precious human body, *Finding Rest in the Nature of the Mind* says,

Beings who are utterly sublime are vessels for the stainless Dharma.
Through learning and reflection they attain its essence.
They discipline themselves, and others they establish in the
  virtuous life.
Their practice, like the king of mountains, is unshakable.
They are the ensigns of the Sage's victory.
Householders or, better,
Those who have gone forth to homelessness,
The Teacher has declared them both to have a precious human form.[28]

Passing through the excellent doors of the sacred Dharma—listening, reflection, and practice—they tame their minds and encourage others, too, to practice virtue. They have donned the great armor of liberation and are thus the Sage's great victory banners—a term that does not refer merely to their style of dress.* Someone like this who is diligent and incites others to practice virtue is said to have a precious human body, whether he or she lives the life of a householder or takes the appearance of a monastic, as is mentioned in the *Śrīgupta Sūtra*:

> Shrīgupta, someone who studies by listening to many teachings, reflects on their meaning, practices by meditating without defilements, and moreover encourages others to do so is the most beautiful being in all the world and its celestial realms. That is what we call making full use of the freedoms and advantages. That is what we call "the precious human body."

And in the *Middle Sūtra of the Perfection of Wisdom*, we read,

> Subhūti, bodhisattvas who practice virtue themselves and incite others, too, to do so, make full use of the freedoms and advantages and are praised, lauded, and revered by all the buddhas.

Now that we have obtained the freedoms and advantages, therefore, if we fail to use them as a support for accomplishing the sacred Dharma, after we die our karma may lead us to be reborn in the three lower realms, and during that time we will neither hear the sound of the Dharma, nor meet a spiritual friend, nor understand what is good and what is evil. Everything we do will be evil, with no virtue at all, as a result of which we will circle constantly in cyclic existence. What a disaster that would be! Instead of that, we must practice, thinking, "I will make the best of my freedoms and advantages!"

*In other words, they are shining examples of true practitioners of the Buddha's teachings, not just in their outer appearance ("victory banner of the teachings" is an expression also used to denote monastic robes) but particularly in their inner ability to train their minds. The "great armor of liberation" here refers especially to patience and diligence.

II. The difficulty of finding the freedoms and advantages

The reasons for which the precious human body, with its perfect freedoms and advantages, is so difficult to find can be considered under four headings: (1) the very nature of the precious human body that makes it so difficult to find, (2) the causes and conditions that make a precious human body so difficult to find, (3) analogies of how difficult it is to find a precious human body, and (4) reflecting on numerical comparisons of how difficult it is to find a precious human body.

A. The very nature of the precious human body that makes it so difficult to find

In the *Precious Treasury That Fulfills All Wishes*, we read,

> Considering how many sentient beings there are,
> Gaining a human body seems as rare
> As becoming a universal monarch.
> And out of all the human beings there are,
> The kind that have faith and practice the Dharma
> Are rarer still, as rare as the advent of a buddha.
> I beg you, therefore, constantly reflect upon the freedoms and
> advantages.
> Consider likewise how extremely numerous are those
> Who are born with faculties incomplete, in border lands,
> With no karmic propensity for the Dharma, with wrong lifestyles,
> With no faith in the teaching, and with evil, irreligious friends.
> Then be sure to spend your days and nights reflecting
> On this body that you have found, which has the Dharma and is
> not like them.[29]

If we reflect generally on the different levels of sentient beings and their numbers, they are boundless. Even if we consider just the number of worms and other minute creatures in our world, obtaining a human body would seem to be as difficult as becoming a universal monarch. And if we think of all the human beings there are in the villages, cities, and marketplaces of countries like India and China, most of whom have no spiritual path and indulge exclusively in negative actions, it seems barely possible that anyone might have an interest in the Dharma and listen to the teachings. And of those who do, people with faith, who have wholeheartedly entered the gateway of the true Dharma and are following and practicing it properly, are even rarer than the advent of a buddha in this world. Then if we think of all the human beings whose faculties are incomplete—who are crippled, blind, deaf, dumb, and so on—it is extremely hard to find anyone with all his or her faculties in working order, who is a suitable support for listening and reflecting. Look at border lands like the northeastern frontiers and Mongolia, where no one has even heard of the Three Jewels. How incredibly lucky we are not to have been born there. Then there are people who have no karmic connection with the Dharma: whatever they are doing—eating, lying down, moving around, or sitting still—they never think of the Three Jewels even for an instant. They have never once recited the refuge prayer. And there are those who have previously led conflicting lifestyles, so that even if they have entered the door of the Dharma, they revert to committing all sorts of negative actions. There are communities who have no faith in the Buddha's teachings and people who perform only negative deeds. Think of them all—you can be sure that there are other countries as well that are full of people like them. How amazing it is that instead of being born as people like them, we have, as a result of our enduring good deeds from the past, gained a body with all the freedoms and advantages.

Yet there are a great many people who have obtained a human existence in this life but will never gain a human body in the future, as we read in the *Sūtra of the Ten Wheels of Kṣitigarbha*:

> There are ten kinds of people for whom it is hard to find the human state in cyclic existence. What are they? Those who have not produced sources of good, those who do not accumulate a store of merit, those who follow evil companions, those who are continually carried away by defilements, those who are not afraid of suffering in subsequent lives, those whose minds are disturbed by defilements, those who constantly neglect the Dharma on account of laziness and distraction, those who, despite having taken up the Buddha's teachings, do not practice them accordingly, those who pursue wrong views, and those who champion wrong views.

Thus *The Way of the Bodhisattva* says,

And yet the way I act is such
That I shall not regain a human life!
And losing this, my precious human form,
My evils will be many, virtues none.
Here is now my chance for wholesome deeds,
But I have failed to practice virtue.[30]

It is for this reason that the *Sūtra of the Meeting of the Father with the Son* states,

Once rid of all eight states without opportunity,
With perfect freedom, so hard to find, obtained,
The wise gain faith in the doctrine of the Sugata
And proceed to train in the correct practice.

The circumstantial advantages, too, are difficult to find. In general, there are two kinds of kalpas: light kalpas in which buddhas appear in the world and dark kalpas in which they do not appear. Of these, it is said in the *Compendium of the Buddhas' Wisdom*,

> With regard to light kalpas, long ago there was a great kalpa called Manifest Joy, in which there appeared thirty-three thousand buddhas. After that there were one hundred dark kalpas. Then in the kalpa called Perfect, there appeared eight hundred million buddhas. This was followed by one hundred kalpas without Dharma. After that, in the kalpa called Excellent, there appeared 840 million buddhas. This was followed by five hundred dark kalpas. Then, in the kalpa Delightful to Behold, eight hundred million buddhas appeared, after which there were seven hundred dark kalpas. Then, in the Joyous Kalpa, there appeared sixty thousand buddhas. After that came the present Good Kalpa, in which one thousand buddhas will manifest. This will be followed by sixty bad kalpas without Dharma. After that, in the Kalpa of Vast Numbers, ten thousand buddhas will appear. That will be followed by ten thousand bad kalpas. In this endless succession of myriad light and dark kalpas, when a dark kalpa is encountered, not even the word *Buddha* is ever heard.

Thus, the advent of a buddha in the world is a rarity. Even when a buddha does appear, it is generally rare for them to teach the Dharma. And in particular, the teachings of the Diamond Vehicle appear on only three occasions,* as rarely as the *udumbara* flower, for the *Tantra of Vairocana's Enlightenment* explains,

> In this world, the omniscient ones
> Are yet as rare as the udumbara flower.
> Sometimes they appear,
> Sometimes they do not.
> Rarer still is this practice of the secret mantras,
> For no beings are equal to it—
> They are unable to reach the unsurpassable goal.

Even though the Buddha taught the Dharma, as his teachings disappear, they are losing their benefit. We have now reached the final five-hundred-year period,† and people's attitudes and conduct are all the worse. The sun of the Buddha's doctrine is about to set behind the western mountains, and most of the supreme spiritual teachers are thinking of beings to be trained in other realms and are not staying. Even ordained monks and nuns are concerned only with their dualistic monastic affiliations and material preoccupations. Those who have a proper attitude to the Buddha's teachings and are upholding and preserving them are as rare as stars in the daytime. Foreign armies and barbaric dark forces are sweeping through the world like clouds of hail. Wherever one looks, all the signs have appeared that the teachings will not last for long, and in the future it will be even more difficult to encounter them.

Now the teachings may still be present, but they are of no use to anyone if there are no Dharma companions following the Buddha's words and no qualified spiritual teachers giving proper instructions on what to abandon and what to adopt. Such beings are extremely hard to find. And other favor-

*The Secret Mantrayāna teachings have been taught on a wide scale once in the past, during the first kalpa, once in the present kalpa, during the era of Buddha Shākyamuni, and they will be taught once in the future. See Patrul Rinpoche, *Words of My Perfect Teacher*, 26.

†This is the age of the five degenerations, when beings' life spans are shorter, their defilements are stronger, they are much more difficult to help, war and famine are on the increase, and false views proliferate.

able conditions for practicing the Dharma, like food and clothes, are also difficult to get hold of. All these necessarily depend on causes and conditions that have been accumulated in the past, so they are very difficult to come by, as we learn from the *Sūtra of the Arborescent Array*:

> Difficult it is to manage to avoid the eight states without
>   opportunity,
> Difficult to gain the human state,
> Difficult to find freedom, perfect and complete,
> And difficult to meet with the advent of a buddha.
> Difficult it is to have all one's faculties complete,
> Difficult to have the chance to hear the Buddha's Dharma,
> Difficult to find supreme beings and companions,
> And difficult to find a genuine spiritual friend.
> Difficult it is to have access to genuine instructions,
> Difficult to find the correct means of subsistence,
> And difficult in the human world to follow the teachings and
>   apply oneself to Dharma.

And in the *Sūtra of the Questions of Ratnacūḍa*, we read,

> To see a guide* is very hard indeed,
> To hear them speak the peaceful Dharma is also very hard,
> To be reborn a human, free and well endowed, is very difficult,
> To keep on finding discipline and faith is very hard as well.

It is thanks to the precious human body that one can meet an authentic teacher, listen to the profound teachings, and train on the path to liberation. Now that you have obtained it, it is as if you had reached an island of jewels. If you return empty-handed, there will have been no point in journeying across the ocean. You will have reached the jewel island—your precious human body—and failed to take your share of the jewels—the sacred Dharma. If instead of setting out on the path to liberation you are distracted by the activities of this life, you will have let the precious human body that you obtained go to waste.

*Guide (Tib. *'dren pa*), that is, a buddha.

The practice of the sacred Dharma depends on the mind, and the mind is dependent on the body, with its freedoms and advantages. So, reflecting on how hard it is for all the right conditions to coincide, think, "I am not afflicted by illness and difficulties; I am not dominated by others; I am free to do as I wish. I must at all costs use this support to exert myself in the sacred Dharma!"

B. The causes and conditions that make a precious human body so difficult to find

This perfect state of freedom and advantage does not happen without causes or conditions. It is the result of merit accumulated in the past. And even if one has an immense amount of merit from having practiced generosity and so forth, without discipline, one will not obtain the perfect body of a celestial being or human, as is explained in the *Introduction to the Middle Way*:

> The fruits of generosity enjoyed in lower realms
> Occur through fracturing the limbs of discipline.*

Not only that, but even if one has other excellent qualities, such as great learning from having heard many teachings, they will not help much, as the same text points out:

> And high rebirth derives from discipline alone.[31]

In the *Sūtra of the King of Concentrations*, we read,

> Because of lax discipline, one will go to the lower realms,
> And no amount of learning can protect from that.

And the *Mahāparinirvāṇa Sūtra*,

*Chandrakīrti, *Introduction to the Middle Way*, chap. 2, v. 4. Certain beings in the lower realms, such as *nāgas* and hungry spirits with miraculous powers, are wealthy as a result of generosity practiced in previous lives, but they have been reborn in the lower realms because they lacked the discipline that brings about rebirth in the higher realms. Generosity on its own is not a protection against lower rebirth.

> Look at the monk Devadatta. Because of his negative actions, he fell into the lower realms even though he had heard and memorized as many sūtras as a Nepalese elephant could carry.*

Even if we have observed discipline and been diligent in accumulating an immense amount of virtue—for example, by making offerings and gifts—these will be of no use if we have dedicated† them to gaining positions of power and wealth in realms such as the worlds of demons and the Lord of Death. A precious human birth depends, above all, on our former aspirations and our state of mind at the moment of death. Since it is rare for all these causes and conditions to coincide properly, it is exceedingly rare to obtain their result, the perfect state of freedom and advantage. The fact that we have now obtained this perfect support for practicing the Dharma is an infallible sign that we accumulated a vast amount of merit in the past. As we find in *Letter to a Friend*,

> To dwell in places that befit the task,
> To follow and rely on holy beings,
> Aspiring high, with merit from the past—
> These four great wheels are yours for you to use.[32]

If we do not put our efforts into practicing the Dharma by speedily applying diligence at the very moment that we have obtained this precious human body and have the four great wheels, the favorable conditions for the path, it will be extremely difficult to find them again in future, as is mentioned in *The Way of the Bodhisattva*:

> So hard to find the ease and wealth
> Whereby the aims of beings may be gained.
> If now I fail to turn it to my profit,
> How could such a chance be mine again?[33]

*The Nepalese elephant (Tib. *bal glang*) is defined in the Tibetan dictionary (*Tshigs mdzod chen mo*) as a type of immensely strong elephant with a quick pace.

†Dedication is the condition or contributory factor that determines whether the primary causes (accumulated merit and discipline) will result in a precious human life.

C. Analogies of how difficult it is to find a precious human body

Imagine that on the vast ocean, buffeted by the wind, there is a yoke with a single opening, tossed about by the waves and never staying still, and under the water, a blind turtle that comes to the surface once every hundred years. It would be difficult enough for the turtle to come upon the yoke and put its neck through the opening in the yoke. But it is even harder to leave the lower realms and obtain a human body.

Or imagine, if one were to throw a handful of peas at the smooth surface of a wall, how difficult it would be for even one of them to stick to it. Obtaining a human body is even more difficult than that.

These and other analogies are given in the sūtras. *Letter to a Friend* reiterates,

> Harder, harder still than that a turtle chance upon
> The opening in a yoke that's tossed upon the ocean
> Is rebirth as a human after rebirth as a beast,
> So heed the sacred Dharma, King, and make your life bear fruit.[34]

The Great Orgyen said,

> As difficult to find repeatedly as the udumbara flower,
> When found, it is of greater value than a wish-fulfilling gem.
> Now, when you have gathered all the right conditions,
> With the greatest diligence, free yourself from existence.

And in the *Precious Treasury That Fulfills All Wishes*, we read,

> It might be possible for a turtle to put its neck
> Through the hole in a yoke tossed around in the middle of the sea,
> But it is harder, from the lower realms, to find the human state.
> Likewise, a pea might stick to the plaster on a wall,
> But rarer is it, even if reborn a human, to be born in a central land.
> Difficult it is to see an udumbara appear in the world,
> But rarer still to enter the Dharma and chance upon the authentic path.
> Difficult it is to insert a cotton cloth through the eye of a needle,

But even rarer are those who find the path and practice it properly.
Hard it is to find a wishing jewel from islands in the ocean,
But even harder to find an authentic teacher.
So reflect on all these and practice diligently, I beg you.[35]

D. Reflecting on numerical comparisons of how difficult it is to find a precious human body

In *Detailed Explanations of Discipline*, we read,

> Monks, consider the beings in the lower realms: it is extremely difficult for them eventually to obtain the human state. Think of all the teachers there are who teach mistaken paths: it is exceedingly difficult to encounter an authentic spiritual friend. Look at all the people there are whose degenerate ways deteriorate their discipline and liberation. Practice virtuous ways combined with ascetic virtues,* and spend the rest of your life delighting in your abodes, under trees or in secluded places.

And in another sūtra,

> Shāriputra asked, "Lord, how many beings are there in the hells? How many hungry spirits are there? How many animals? How many demigods? And how many gods and humans are there?"
>
> The Buddha replied, "The number of hell beings is comparable to the number of particles of dust on the earth. The hungry spirits are as numerous as grains of sand.† The animals are as numerous as the fermenting grains in a beer barrel. The demigods are as numerous as snowflakes in a blizzard, and the gods and humans are as many as specks of dust on a fingernail."

*There are said to be twelve ascetic virtues (Tib. *sbyangs pa'i yon tan bcu gnyis*): living off alms, eating at a single sitting, not eating afterward; wearing the three Dharma robes, coarse woolen clothes, and discarded rags; staying in isolated places, under trees, in the open without shelter, and in charnel grounds; sleeping sitting up and sleeping wherever one finds oneself.
†This is often explained as the grains of sand in the Ganges River.

The *Book of Analogies* gives similar comparisons. And according to the *Bodhisattva's Scriptural Collection*, it is said that there are not even as many gods and humans in the billionfold universe as there are beings—invisible to all but the Omniscient One—on the surface of a chariot wheel. This and other such quotations show how inconceivable in number beings' karmic experiences are.

The Great Orgyen sums this up,

> This precious human body, with its freedoms and advantages, is so hard to find,
> So truly rare when examined in terms of its causes and conditions, analogies and numerical comparisons.
> In dependence on it, all the buddhas have been produced.
> Reflect, therefore, on how hard it is to find the freedoms and advantages,
> And rejoicing, like a poor man discovering a treasure,
> Practice the sacred Dharma day and night, without respite.

And in the *Sūtra of the Questions of Rāṣṭrapāla*, we find,

> The Buddha, the Great Ṛiṣhi who benefits the world,
> Will manifest but once in a billion kalpas.
> Now that you have found supreme freedom,
> If you wish for liberation, avoid all carelessness.

And in the *Sūtra on Correct Moral Discipline*,

> Monks, it is so hard to obtain a human birth and thence to take ordination in the Buddha's doctrine. So why do you not practice with diligence and strong determination? When old age, sickness, and death arrive, and the Capable One's teachings, too, disappear, later you will surely have regrets.

Meditate in this way again and again.

III. The importance of finding the freedoms and advantages

The precious human body is an exceptional support for attaining buddhahood, so to find it is enormously meaningful, as we read in *Finding Rest in the Nature of the Mind: A Teaching of the Great Perfection*:

> To see the Buddha in this life is meaningful,
> To hear the Dharma and to practice it is also meaningful.
> This meaningful existence and the fruitful one to follow
> Arise from the attainment of a form endowed with freedoms and advantages.
> Reflect on this with great joy constantly.[36]

Whether we are following the lesser beings' path for attaining the higher realms or the middling and superior beings' paths for attaining the ultimate excellence of the three kinds of enlightenment, we need the proper provisions for this life and the next that will enable us to follow those paths—namely, meeting the Buddha, hearing the Dharma, practicing assiduously, and so forth. All these come about thanks to the perfect support of the freedoms and advantages, as is mentioned in the *Great Close Mindfulness Sūtra*:

> Nandaka, whatever you see that is good, whatever you hear that is good, it comes from reflecting on the freedoms. Look, likewise, at how it is from this that all human happiness and excellence also come about.

Moreover, in the previous text, we read,

> The ground of primal wisdom
> Where the truth beyond all concepts is beheld
> Is reached more easily by humans than by gods.
> The essence also of the deep path of the Vajrayāna
> Is more easily attained by those who find a human form.
> The basis of the Dharma of both great and lesser vehicles
> Is said to be supremely noble—
> This human state endowed with freedoms and advantages.[37]

Thus, the human form is also the support for giving rise to the untainted gnosis of the noble beings, which is the essence of the paths of all the vehicles. This is mentioned in the *Treasury of Abhidharma*:

In the three; above there is no way to see,

referring to having the support of a human body in the three continents.*
And in the *Letter to a Disciple*, we read,

The path of those who set out to guide beings, following the
sugatas' way,
Who have found a human body and have great strength of mind,
Is not for gods and *nāgas*, or for demigods,
Garuḍas, vidyādharas, *kinnaras*, or *mahoragas*.
The human state is very hard to find, and having found it,
Whichever goal you have in mind, be diligent and practice.

In particular, only this vajra body with its six elements† is recommended as a suitable support for the path of the secret mantras, the Diamond Vehicle, as we find in the *Tantra of the Exhaustion of the Four Elements*:

If human beings diligently practice
This marvelous, kingly secret mantra way,
In this very life they will attain buddhahood.
No need is there to speak of other yogas and accomplishments.

Moreover, in *Finding Rest in the Nature of the Mind*, it is said,

In the midst of śrāvakas, pratyekabuddhas, bodhisattva heirs,
Our Lord, the first of beings in this world endowed with godly
realms,
Declared that the immortal nectar of enlightenment
Derives from the supremely precious human form.
Extolling thus its freedoms and advantages,
He praised this form more highly than the body of a god.
Rejoice therefore in your humanity![38]

*Humans in the northern continent and celestial beings in the higher worlds cannot realize untainted gnosis.

†Tib. *khams drug ldan pa'i rdo rje'i lus*—the vajra body endowed with the six elements—the five elements and the element of mental objects.

Since the results of the paths of the three vehicles—arhathood for the listeners and solitary realizers, and buddhahood for the bodhisattvas—are obtained from the support of the freedoms and advantages, the Buddha praised it as "a body better than that of the gods," as we find in the *Sūtra of Manifest Enlightenment*:

> Having seen that manifest enlightenment is not possible in the abodes of the gods, for the pride in those realms prevents one from realizing the truth, and that it is only possible in the human state, with its freedoms and advantages perfect and complete, the Bodhisattva departed for Kapilavastu.

And in *The Way of the Bodhisattva*,

> With bodies greater than the gods, . . .[39]

So look at your own freedoms and advantages and rejoice in the same way as a pauper discovering a jewel, thinking, "Am I dreaming, is this really true?" Turning your mind away from worldly activities, which will result in your freedoms and advantages being rendered worthless, you must apply yourself diligently to the Dharma, as the *Precious Treasury That Fulfills All Wishes* advises:

> This life's occupations, company, counsels and guidance,
> Enjoyments, partialities, and wrong philosophies
> Waste the freedoms and advantages and lead to ruin, so give them up.[40]

Whatever worldly activities we get involved in will not help us much in the future. They will only cause us to sink into the mire of cyclic existence. We need to be quite definite about this and apply ourselves diligently to the Dharma. There is no lasting benefit from living off the land through agriculture. Neither is there any lasting benefit from the company of partners and relatives. Nor from the pursuit of pleasure, of food and riches, nor from advice and guidance on how to achieve greatness in this life. Partiality concerning enemies and those close to us merely leads to conflicts, and the rejection and acceptance of extreme philosophical beliefs is of no lasting benefit either. We need to give up all these and other activities that will be of no use to us in the long run. And rather than waste our freedoms and advantages, we must be diligent in sincerely practicing the sacred Dharma.

Ordinary laypeople find themselves having to take sides against their enemies and for their own kin. They have to provide for children and family. With their minds crushed by obligations and worries, they toil from dawn to dusk, enslaved by their efforts to acquire food and clothes. Whatever they do, they are never finished. Whatever the result, it is not what they want. However hard they try, no one is ever content. With no leisure during the day and no sleep at night, however much they work, there never comes a time when they can stop being busy. Rarely do they give a thought to the Dharma. Everything they do worsens their lot, for it is mixed with negative actions. With their neighbors, the flames of attachment and hatred flare up. They are crippled by the weight of the karmic debt they owe their children. Whatever they do, they are loaded down with suffering. They cannot bear the suffering that befalls them and the fortune that comes to others. With so many difficulties, they are completely distanced from the Dharma. As we read in a sūtra,

> A household life beset with defilements
> Destroys all wholesome qualities.

In this degenerate age, even those who have taken monastic ordination give up their little households for bigger ones.* They get involved in commerce and agriculture and in attending to horses, donkeys, yaks, and cattle. They are embroiled in creating and increasing wealth and possessions and become occupied with making provisions for when they get old and with taking responsibility for their relatives. They are completely distracted by their attachment and craving for the pleasures of the senses, by their desire for the gratifications of food and drink and wealth, and by being neverendingly busy with work on their property and buildings. Day and night, they surround themselves with attachment and aversion. They load themselves with responsibilities for their superiors and subordinates. With their

*It is said that those who take ordination renounce their large families and households and take up residence in the "small households" of their monastic cells. But, says the author here, it is only to find themselves once again involved in the worldly activities of life in a monastery. This passage can also be interpreted as referring to monks who have left a simple home life to end up holding positions of responsibility in the running of large monasteries.

yearning for esteem and their mundane outlook, they make a hypocritical show of receiving the teachings and reflecting on them. Their minds are ablaze with attachment, hatred, and rivalry. Constantly pricked by dissatisfaction, everything they do is for this life. They are forever occupied with trying to fulfill their expectations. In the ties they have with their teachers or students, there is a complete absence of faith. They jealously compete with their spiritual fellows, and their sense of superiority turns them into mountains of ambition, obsessed with the eight ordinary preoccupations. They behave as if they have no time for those who are weaker than them. Their minds are completely at odds with the Dharma. Such reprehensible practitioners are extremely numerous. Compared to them, those who practice the sublime Dharma are exceedingly rare. It is said in the Vinaya scriptures,

> Though they take ordination, they are not vessels for good qualities;
> Though they cut their hair and beards, they have not engaged in the training in virtue.
> These ordained persons are neither monastics nor laypeople:
> They are like wells without water, like lamps in a painting.

If you are to practice the Dharma properly, it is most important to turn your mind away from worldly perspectives. If now you do not set out on the path to liberation, it will be as if you had returned from a golden island empty-handed. Nothing could be worse. So do your best to practice the profound Dharma and set out on the path. In all your activities, in the six periods of the day, you should be guided and supervised by mindfulness and vigilance, and without getting distracted by the objects of the six senses, remind yourself of the following analogies. When you have a boat, use it to cross the river. When you have a thoroughbred horse, that is the time to proceed on the long journey. When you have warm weather, moisture, water, and manure all together, sow as much seed as you can. When you have an army of brave men, use them to put down the enemy. When a treasure cache of gold and silver is broken open, take as much as you can. When the autumn crops ripen, harvest all you can. When you have an escort in a dangerous place, that is the time to get to safety. When you have managed to borrow what you need, that is the time to make the most effort.[41] When you have servants to do the work, get the job done. Similarly, now that you have found a precious human body with the freedoms and advantages, rather than taking it easy, you need to make every effort to practice the Dharma, for impermanence strikes swiftly. If you think about this, you ought to be putting all your efforts into practicing the Dharma without even taking the time to sleep or breathe. As *The Way of the Bodhisattva* urges us,

> So take advantage of this human boat.
> Free yourself from sorrow's mighty stream!
> This vessel will be later hard to find.
> The time that you have now, you fool, is not for sleep![42]

Thus, in all situations, whatever you are doing, whether eating, lying down, moving around, or staying still, you should avoid laziness, indifference, apathy, distraction, diversions, and indeterminate, restless states of body, speech, and mind. Thinking, "I am someone who has entered the door of the sacred Dharma, so I should be different from other, ordinary people," examine your mind with mindfulness and vigilance. Should you happen to commit any negative actions, confess them and vow not to repeat them. And if you have not committed any, rejoice! Like a starving person finding some food, do not be choosy, but throw yourself into whatever virtuous activity presents itself at the time, whether conceptual or nonconceptual. Never scorn relative virtuous deeds. Maintaining the state in which everything is like a magical illusion, train in combining the two accumulations, the path that delights the victorious ones, and encourage others to do so too, passing your time day and night in the practice. By really setting out on the path that focuses on future lives, you will make your freedoms and advantages truly meaningful. As the Omniscient Teacher says,

> Even when moving, lying, sitting, eating, and so forth,
> Avoid the six faults—laziness and the rest,*
> And if you are to accomplish the goals of higher rebirth and
> ultimate excellence,
> Apply the analogies of a hungry person seeing food and so on,
> Diligently practicing virtue day and night.[43]

And Padampa Sangye,

*The six faults listed at the beginning of the previous paragraph.

With its freedoms and advantages, human life is like a treasure island;
People of Tingri, do not come back an empty-handed failure.[44]

Familiarize yourself with the meanings of these quotations, reflecting on them again and again, and verbally remind yourself of them by reciting these lines from the preliminary practice text *Illuminating the Path to Freedom*, by our Lord Teacher, the Omniscient Jampel Gyepa:*

The freedoms and advantages are difficult to find, like the udumbara,
To find them is more beneficial than finding a wish-fulfilling jewel.
Now, for once, we have found them,
Yet we are failing to achieve the most worthwhile, lasting goal
And are pointlessly wasting them.
Teacher, embodiment of the Three Jewels, look on us with compassion:
Bless us that we may make full use of the freedoms and advantages.

Say this prayer again and again, from the depth of your heart.

IV. The benefits of meditating on the freedoms and advantages and the signs of having done so

The *Precious Treasury That Fulfills All Wishes* describes the benefits as follows:

The benefits of this are that one gives up thoughts of this life;
Diligence in pursuing the goals of future lives blazes like fire.
Spending one's time practicing virtue, without a moment's leisure,
One swiftly proceeds to the other side of the ocean of the three worlds.[45]

*Shechen Gyaltsap's teacher, Jamgön Mipham Rinpoche (1846–1912).

Although the benefits of reflecting day and night on the difficulty of finding the freedoms and advantages are boundless, they can be summed up as follows: Having realized that all activities related to this present life are futile, we no longer engage in them. Applying ourselves wholeheartedly to fulfillment for future lives, we practice without doing anything that conflicts with the karmic law of cause and effect. Not pausing to rest, we put all our efforts into listening, reflecting, and meditating, as our diligence blazes like fire. We avoid evil companions and constantly practice virtue, so that our conduct remains wholesome. Having rejected samsaric preoccupations, we do not waste the opportunity to practice, and thus, at the time of death, we are full of joy. With the knot of stinginess untied, we are generous, accumulating provisions for the journey so that wherever we are reborn, we will never be poor or destitute. Because we are always content with what we have, we are unattached to wealth and possessions, and our thoughts, words, and deeds are in tune with the Dharma. We realize that since nothing has any essence, activities are pointless, and we cut the ties of attachment and clinging. Since we know that everything moves on, we are not afflicted by conflicts and our natural disposition is deeply virtuous. As we come to see that everything we might do is unnecessary, the wall of worldly conventions collapses and the mountain of the eight ordinary preoccupations is destroyed. We set out on the path to liberation: thus it is that we properly practice the sacred Dharma and swiftly accomplish buddhahood.

As for the signs of having properly trained, we should be like Geshe Chen-ngawa, who spent all his time practicing and never even slept. Geshe Tönpa said to him, "You'd better rest, my son. You'll make yourself ill."

"Yes, I should rest," Chen-ngawa replied. "But when I think how difficult it is to find the freedoms and advantages that we have, I have no time to rest." He recited the mantra of Miyowa nine hundred million times and went without sleep for the whole of his life.

To sum up, the signs of having properly trained in this are that we have reflected on the fact that if we do not do some genuine Dharma practice in this present body, we can despair of ever finding such an excellent support in the future. As a result, we have given up all activities undertaken for this life and have integrated everything into the sole practice of the sacred Dharma. Train, therefore, until such signs have definitely appeared in your stream of being.

Now, for once, your merit from the past
Has given you a wishing gem—this precious form so hard to find.
So do not leave it uselessly, distracted by life's busy works,
But make the very best of it, O fortunate ones!

This completes the instruction on reflecting on the difficulty of finding the freedoms and advantages.

6. Reflecting on Death and Impermanence

The instructions for reflecting on death and impermanence enable one to turn one's mind away from procrastination and idleness and to develop diligence in the practice of Dharma. There are four sections: (1) a general teaching on the impermanent nature of the vessel and contents, (2) a detailed classification using twelve instructions, (3) essentializing the practice with nine reflections on death, and (4) the benefits of meditating in this way and the signs of having done so.

I. A general teaching on the impermanent nature of the vessel and contents

In his *Graded Path of the Practice of Dharma*, the Great Orgyen says,

> The universe that contains us is impermanent, for it is destroyed
> by fire and water.
> The sentient beings it contains are impermanent, for body and
> mind must part.
> The seasons—summer and winter, autumn and spring—are
> impermanent.
> Bless us that disenchantment may arise from the depth of our
> hearts.
> Last year, this year, the seasons, and the phases of the moon,
> Day and night—each instant is impermanent.
> If we reflect well, we are constantly brushing with death.
> Bless us that we may be able to practice tenaciously.

And in *Finding Rest in the Nature of the Mind: A Teaching of the Great Perfection*,

So now you have your freedom, hard to find,
And yet its time is passing; it is subject to decay.
Look closely; see its hollowness like bubbling foam.
It is not worthy of your trust!
Think night and day upon the utter certainty of death.[46]

The outer universe that contains us—the Sahā realm of a billion world systems with Mount Meru and the four continents—appears to be so rugged, so hard and solid. And yet there will finally come a time when even it is destroyed by fire, water, and wind and it becomes empty space. In the *Sūtra of the King of Concentrations*, we read,

One day this world appears,
And once appeared, this world is then no more.
As in the past, so it will be in the future.
Know that thus it is with all phenomena.

As for its inner contents, sentient beings, none of them are exempt from the cycle of birth and death. The long-lived gods, who can live for kalpas, die. Beings with short lives that last no more than an instant die. And those in between, who might live for a matter of years, months, or days, are also, all of them, subject to death. As we read in the *Mahāparinirvāṇa Sūtra*,

Know that, for this whole world and all that it contains,
Where there is birth, there is death;
Where there is gathering, there is parting.
Even lives that last for countless years
At last come to an end.

Even this present age, when we live for so short a time, has been subject to change as the past age of complete endowment has progressed through the age of threefold endowment and that of twofold endowment to the final age of strife, making four ages in all.* Within a human life span there

*Numerous explanations exist concerning the four ages from complete endowment through threefold endowment and twofold endowment to the present age of strife, but they all involve a gradual decline from an age when beings have a complete set of qualities, which are progressively lost in the subsequent ages. One explanation is to be found in Jigme Lingpa and Longchen Yeshe Dorje, Kangyur Rinpoche, *Treasury*, bk. 1, 484n256.

is also change, through its four periods: infancy, childhood and youth, the prime of life, and old age and infirmity. A single year, too, changes over its four seasons: spring, the season of plowing and sowing seed; summer, the season of new leaf growth and increased moisture; autumn, when the fruit is perfectly ripe; and winter, when the soil is dry and the stones are frozen. Similarly, there is change from day to night, as the minutes and seconds tick by. In all this, impermanence is obviously present. And although the subtle impermanence that is the true nature of things is not directly visible to ordinary beings, it is unfailingly established by the fact that the noble beings see it. In truth, there are no phenomena, either material or mental, that are not subject to the sequence of momentary instants, as is stated in the *Chapters of Utterances on Specific Topics*:

> Ah! All compounded things are impermanent.
> Arising and perishing, they change.
> Since they arise and then will be destroyed,
> Those who swiftly wish for peace
> Should view all things that are compounded
> As like the stars, like visual aberrations, lamps,
> Illusions, dew, and water bubbles,
> Like dreams and lightning, and like clouds.

Moreover, everything that is accumulated is impermanent: it will be used up. Everything that appears to be high is impermanent: it will be brought down. Everything that flourishes is impermanent: it will decline. All that comes together is impermanent: it will be dispersed. Everything that is good is impermanent: it will change. All that is built is impermanent: it will collapse. All those who are born are impermanent: they will die. There is absolutely nothing, therefore, that can be relied upon, as is stated in the Vinaya scriptures:

> The end of all that is accumulated is its being used up.
> The end of all that is high is its falling.
> The end of all that is born is its dying.
> The end of gathering is dispersion.

In the *Mahāparinirvāṇa Sūtra*, we find,

Where things flourish, they will decline.
Where there is gathering, there will be parting.
Even youth is not eternal:
Lovely complexions are robbed by disease.
There is nothing at all that lasts forever.

And in the *Chapters of Utterances on Specific Topics*,

The end of all hoarding is consuming,
The end of rising is falling,
The end of meeting is parting,
The end of living is dying.

The Great Orgyen says,

In short, those who are born will finally die.
Those who keep company will, likewise, finally part.
All that is hoarded is spent, wealth leads only to decline.

And Padampa Sangye,

Families are as fleeting as a crowd on market day;
People of Tingri, don't bicker or fight.[47]

II. A detailed classification using twelve instructions

In his *Essential Instructions*, the Omniscient Teacher writes,

There are twelve ways of reflecting on the impermanence of life.
Reflect on the aggregates, the support: everything is impermanent.
Reflect on the lords of beings: everything is impermanent.
Reflect on the formation and destruction of the universe and beings: everything is impermanent.
Reflect on the sublime beings: everything is impermanent.
Reflect on how uncertain it is when we will die: everything is impermanent.
Reflect on the nature of compounded phenomena: everything is impermanent.

Reflect on how powerful are the causes of death: everything is impermanent.
Reflect on how one has to depart alone: everything is impermanent.
Reflect on beings in time: everything is impermanent.
Reflect on how there is nothing one can rely upon: everything is impermanent.
Reflect on the unpredictability of events: everything is impermanent.
Reflect with intense longing: everything is impermanent.

A. Reflecting on the aggregates that form the support

Look at your own and others' bodies, which are collections of limbs and minor appendages. However much at present we pamper them with suitable food and clothes and deck them with ornaments and clean them, there will eventually come a time when we die, when we will be carried, naked and stripped of our clothes, to a deserted site, to be eaten by foxes and vultures. Our limbs and appendages will separate, and even our bones will become fragmented. So, thinking, "I must practice the sacred Dharma right now!" put this into practice, making sure that the preparation, main practice, and conclusion are complete. As we read in *The Way of the Bodhisattva*,

> Your body that you've cared for with food and clothes,
> Acquired with so much difficulty,
> Will not go with you but will be eaten by birds and dogs,
> Or else burnt in a blazing fire,
> Or left to disintegrate in a river,
> Or hidden in the depths of the earth.[48]

And,

> My body is like something briefly lent.[49]

B. Reflecting on the lords of beings

Consider the lords of the gods Brahmā, Indra, Īshvara, and Viṣhṇu, and the great ṛiṣhis Vyāsa and Vālmīki, and the rest. They have beautiful bodies, their splendor is immense, and they live for kalpas on end. Yet for all their great qualities of knowledge and their boundless visionary abilities, clairvoyance, and miraculous powers, none of them is exempt from death, as we can read in the Vinaya scriptures:

> Look at those who have become Brahmā, the powerful, thousand-eyed Indra,
> And Viṣhṇu. Even they are impermanent and pass on.
> Look at the fleeting display of the sun and moon,
> At the world with its ground and four continents, which all becomes void.

And,

> Gods who have accomplished concentration, spirits who can take human form,*
> Demigods, sages, and ascetics, refulgent with splendor
> And living for kalpas on end—if even they are impermanent,
> Need one mention human beings,
> Whose frail bodies will perish and disintegrate like bursting bubbles?

And the *Mahāparinirvāṇa Sūtra* says,

> Even the five great ṛiṣhis, who have preternatural powers
> And travel great distances through space,
> Are unable to reach the level
> Where they experience deathlessness.

Moreover, of all the ordinary beings there are, like the universal monarch, ruler of the four continents, and kings, ministers, monks and nuns, brahmins, and laypeople, not one of them is exempt from death, as is mentioned in the *Chapters of Utterances on Specific Topics*:

*Tib. *mi'am ci*, one of the eight classes of gods and spirits (Tib. *lha srin sde brgyad*), who take on human form and listen to the Buddha's teachings on earth.

Emperors who possess the seven precious attributes,*
Kings and ministers,
Monastics, brahmins, householders, and the rest—
All these beings are impermanent:
They are like beings in a dream.

So reflect on this, thinking, "Why should someone like me not die? From now on, I will practice the sacred Dharma!"

C. Reflecting on the formation and destruction of the universe and beings

Starting with the mountains, valleys, and so on, the whole universe that contains us—the arrangement of Mount Meru, the four continents, and the abodes of the gods—seems to be quite hard and solid. Yet in the beginning it is formed in stages from the separation and gathering of the elements and the manifestation of sentient beings' karmic perceptions. And in the end, after it has been destroyed by seven conflagrations and one deluge, there is a period of emptiness.

As for the beings contained in the universe, they all, starting with the men and women in it, begin by being formed in their mothers' womb, driven there by the wind of ignorance, conceptual thoughts, and deeds. And in the end, after the outer and inner elements have dissolved and ceased in stages, they have a period when everything is space-like emptiness. Thinking, "Why should I not die?" reflect on this quotation from *Letter to a Friend*:

The ground, Mount Meru, and the oceans too
Will be consumed by seven blazing suns;
Of things with form not even ashes will be left,
No need to speak of puny, frail man.[50]

And the Omniscient Teacher says,

*Seven precious attributes of a universal monarch (Tib. *rin chen sna bdun*) are the precious wheel, jewel, queen, minister, elephant, horse, and general. These are described in detail in the Maṇḍala chapter on pp. 441–42.

The world and its inhabitants will pass.
The universe is formed and then destroyed
By seven fires, a flood, and then the scattering wind.
The all-encircling sea, the continents,
And even mighty Sumeru compounded of four jewels,
All girded by the rings of lesser peaks—all this will pass.
And time will come when all will have dissolved
Into a single space.
Remember this and practice Dharma from your heart.[51]

D. Reflecting on sublime beings

In this present kalpa, seven buddhas have come—Vipashyin, Shikhin, Vishvabhū, Krakucchanda, Kanakamuni, Kāshyapa, and Shākyamuni—along with their retinues of hosts of listeners and bodhisattvas. And in between them, there have appeared countless solitary realizers with their retinues. Yet one by one, they have all departed. Even their teachings, the sacred Dharma, have gradually disappeared. At present, we are nearing the end of the era of Buddha Shākyamuni's teachings. So how could beings like us, who are the product of negative actions, along with our relatives, last forever? For this reason, thinking, "I will practice the sacred Dharma from this very moment onward," we should reflect on the *Sayings on Impermanence*:

If even the body of the Sugata, blazing with a thousand marks,
The product of hundreds of meritorious acts, is impermanent,
How will one's own body, as undependable
As a bursting bubble, not surely perish?
Look at how the sun will set—the Buddha who came for beings' sake;
And the moon as well—the treasury of the sublime Dharma.
And know that in all one's prosperity, one's retinue and wealth,
There is nothing that is eternal.

And,

If even the buddhas, solitary realizers,
And the buddhas' listener disciples
Abandon their bodies,
Why need mention ordinary beings?

E. Reflecting on how uncertain it is when we will die

One's span of life is not something that can be prolonged; it can only diminish. Day and night, with every minute and second that passes, death comes closer, like a mouse gnawing its way through a hemp rope. There is no certainty where we will die, or whether we will not die now, for the causes of death are so numerous. So we should meditate, thinking, "Oh, when will I die?" As we find in *The Way of the Bodhisattva*,

> Never halting night or day,
> My life drains constantly away,
> And from no other source does increase come.
> How can there not be death for such as me?[52]

And in the *Sūtra of the Questions of Subāhu*,

> In mountains or ravines, gorges or abysses,
> At home or in the street, or on a riverbank—
> Where on earth will be my final resting place?
> Please know that no one can be sure,
> And turn away from pleasure in the world.

And the *Jewel Garland* states,

> Many are the things that can cause death,
> While few are those that help one stay alive—
> And even they may serve to cause one's death.
> Therefore, practice Dharma constantly.[53]

F. Reflecting on the nature of compounded phenomena

In general, compounded phenomena are impermanent. In particular, people's lives are impermanent. And especially, the support that is an assemblage of body and mind is impermanent. As with the cities and monasteries that grew and flourished in the past and are now ruined and empty, there will come a time when the cities of our bodies will be emptied of their inhabitants, our minds. Reflecting in this way, we should meditate on this quotation from *Finding Rest in the Nature of the Mind*:

This shelter built of the four elements,
Endowed with mind adorned with its inhabitants—
The thoughts that move—
Arises through conditions.
Thus it is compounded.
Being so, it is destructible.
Like a village crumbling down, it will not last.
Be swift to practice holy Dharma![54]

And Lord Buddha has said,

All that is compounded is impermanent.

G. Reflecting on the power of the causes of death

Take the example of a burning butter lamp, which quickly burns out. It is impermanent. With a sudden gust of wind, it goes out instantly. Like it, from the moment we are born, we are heading for death. And if illness, negative forces, serious injury, or some other cause of untimely death should suddenly occur, we are powerless to stay alive—even for an instant. It is therefore important to reflect, thinking, "There is no knowing when something like that could happen to me as well." As we read in the *Letter to a Disciple*,

As with the flame of a lamp flickering in a gale-force wind,
There is no assurance that this life will last a single second.

H. Reflecting on how one will depart alone

There will come a time when the perceptions of this world will abandon us and we will set out on the road to the next life. We will lie on our bed for the last time, eat our last meal, wear our last set of clothes, and utter our final words. We will have to leave everything behind—our entourage, possessions, relatives, and all—and proceed alone. This is something that will be extremely hard to bear. So think, "There is no knowing when that will happen to me too," and reflect on the words in the *Sūtra of Advice to the King*:

When the time comes and you, O King, depart,
Your riches, friends, and relatives will not follow.

Wherever people stay, wherever they go,
Their deeds, like shadows, follow them.

And in the *Sūtra of the Questions of Vīradatta*,

Those who, with mixed deeds, seek wealth,
Providing for their wives and children,
Will suffer greatly, and when they die
Their wives and children will be no help.
They'll take with them the various deeds they've done,
But leave behind their families,
While they themselves will suffer, all alone.
At that time, their kindred cannot share their fate.
Parents, siblings, wives,
Servants, wealth, and relatives—
None of them can follow those who have died.
Only their own deeds follow as the childish* depart.

I. Reflecting on beings in time

Reflect on how, of all the beings—people, animals, and so on—who were alive more than a hundred years ago, not one is alive today. And most of the beings on earth today will not be around in a hundred years' time. We are no different, and for beings in the future, it will be the same. Things change with the seasons and become old. All those who were there when we were born—our family, their neighbors, their friends and relatives, the dogs, goats, and cattle, the enemies they hated, our contemporaries, brothers, sisters, and the rest—one by one, they have died or will die. As we find in the *Practice of the Great Vehicle* by Aro Yeshe Jungne,

Of all those in this world, the great or small, the rich or poor,
Not one is there who is not preyed on by the Lord of Death.
All those people who in the past have died
Spent all their time collecting families and wealth,
Yet these they had to leave behind—they were no use to them
As they departed with their deeds, both good and bad, for company.

*Tib. *byis pa*. Ordinary, spiritually immature people.

> Now, too, have I not seen or heard that
> During all the time that I've been here
> My friends and family, beloved ones and enemies—
> Younger, older, those my age—have died?
> Of all those beings, too, on earth today,
> A hundred years from now, not one will still be left:
> It's natural, therefore, that I, too, will die.
> Who can know if I will die tomorrow or today?
> No one can foretell my death or take away my fear:
> How, then, can I tell if I will die next year or else this very day?
> The day I cease to live, my parents, children,
> Siblings, relatives and friends, servants and riches
> Will, none of them, come with me as I die,
> And none will share with me my pain:
> My good and evil deeds will go with me.
> Thus was I born, and born alone,
> And when I finally die, I'll die alone.
> For this one life, my relatives and friends, whose karmic lot is shared,
> Are but visitors to a common venue who'll then go separate ways.
> What good, then, are my relatives to me?
> My wife and children, relatives and friends,
> Land and servants, money, herds, possessions,
> From which I cannot for an instant bear to part—
> I'll leave them all behind and, this day or the next, depart alone.
> I've done much wrong and taken risks to gather wealth,
> But now the fool I've been will bear the burden of the fruits of sin.
> The riches I have gathered my children will take away,
> So what's the good of having hoarded wealth?

And the Omniscient Teacher says,

> Of former generations countless beings have already passed,
> And most of those who now are on this earth
> Within a century's time will surely be no more.
> For those who follow after, it will be the same.
> Look how they pass! The old and young have all an equal destiny.
> From them you are no different in your nature.
> Remember that your death is certain; practice Dharma![55]

J. Reflecting on how there is nothing that one can rely upon

Wherever one is—deep in the mountains, in the middle of the ocean, or in the air—there is nowhere that death will not strike. And because one will die without any control over the cause of death, whether timely or untimely, one cannot be confident of anything. Therefore, thinking, "There is no knowing when I will die," reflect on this passage in the Vinaya scriptures:

> Wherever one may be, no place is there
> Not struck by death:
> Not in the air, or in the ocean,
> Or even in the mountains, hidden away.

K. Reflecting on the unpredictability of events

Even if one excludes sudden causes of death, death is approaching us like the lengthening shadows before sunset. Death comes in many, many forms, caused by poison, weapons, fire, drowning, enemies, disease, negative forces, and even the wrong food, clothes, or lifestyle. So thinking, "When will I too die?" reflect from the depth of your heart, as is written in *The Way of the Bodhisattva*:

> Today, indeed, I'm hale and well,
> I have enough to eat and I am not in danger.
> But this life is fleeting, unreliable,
> My body is like something briefly lent.[56]

And in the *Verses That Summarize the Perfection of Wisdom*,

> As rare as are the precious teachings, as numerous too are the constant dangers.

And in a scripture,

> Some die choking on their food,
> Others die from taking medicine,
> Not to speak of lethal causes:
> There is no way one can be sure.

L. Reflecting with intense longing

When you go somewhere, ask yourself, "Might I die soon? Is there any knowing whether I will ever come back here?" When you set out on the road and stop to rest, think, "Will I die here?" Wherever you are staying, think, "Will I die now?" And whatever everyday activities you are engaged in, whether eating, moving around, or lying down, think, "This might be the last thing I do in this world." In such ways, meditate intensely on nothing but death. As we read in *The Way of the Bodhisattva*,

> "Today, at least, I shall not die."
> So rash to lull myself with words like these!
> My dissolution and my hour of death
> Will come to me, of this there is no doubt.[57]

And in the *Advice on Abandoning the Four Errors*,

> No pity for the little kids, and for the old he has not the least respect,
> No kindly look for lovely maids, no mercy for the destitute—
> The Lord of Death ignores all social mores, so do not think,
> While you're still young, your body fully fleshed and strong,
> "For me he'll bide his time."

III. Essentializing the practice with nine reflections on death

In Padmasambhava's *Great Treatise on the Graded Path*, we read,

> Meditation on impermanence is threefold.
> From the moment one is born, one is certain to die:
> That is the nature of impermanence,
> Like someone struck by a weapon in the heart.
> The time of death is uncertain:
> That is the characteristic of impermanence,
> Like dewdrops on the tips of grass.
> At death, whatever one does, nothing will help:
> That is the particular quality of impermanence,
> Like the lengthening shadows from the setting sun.

And for each of these, he gave three reasons.

A. Three reasons why death is inevitable

1. There is no one in the past whose life has been spared, who has been born and has stayed without dying, so we, too, are sure to die

As we read in the *Letter of Consolation*,

> Of all those born upon this earth
> Or in the upper realms,
> Did you ever see, or hear, or even pause to doubt
> That some were born and have not died?

And in the *Discourse on Impermanence*,

> "Like me, you too will die."
> Should I even entertain a doubt
> Regarding counsels on impermanence such as this
> I'd be, alas, just like an animal.

2. There is no adding to one's life span, it is constantly decreasing, so again, one is certain to die

As we read in the *Discourse on Impermanence*,

> As with a pond whose affluent stream is blocked,
> One cannot top it up, its level only falls:
> Everyone has set out on the road to death,
> So who can rely on this fleeting life?

And in the *Great Collection Sūtra of the Incantations of Ratnaketu*,

> Friends, this life swiftly passes by,
> Like a racing torrent down a mountainside;
> Immature beings are ignorant of this,
> Undiscerning and intoxicated by the arrogance of desire.

While the *Sūtra of the Magical Tree* states,

> Like a prisoner being led to the scaffold,
> With each step, we draw nearer to death.

3. One's body and mind are compounded, so again, one is certain to die

As we find in a sūtra,

> Nowhere will you find a state
> That is compounded and that lasts forever:
> All compounded things are impermanent,
> Therefore, Ānanda, do not grieve.

And in the *Sayings on Impermanence*,

> Oh, compounded things are impermanent:
> It is their nature to arise and perish.

The *Play in Full* states,

> Compounded things are unstable, impermanent:
> Their nature is to perish like unfired clay pots.
> They are like someone else's things, on loan.

B. Three reasons why there is no certainty when one will die

1. One's span of life has not been fixed in time, so there is no certainty when one will die

In general, with the exception of beings in Uttarakuru,* the length of time other beings live is not fixed, and this is especially true in our world, Jambudvīpa, where beings' life spans are quite unpredictable. This is even more the case in an age when the five degenerations are rampant: it is impossi-

*Uttarakuru is the northern continent in the cosmology of ancient India. Its inhabitants have fixed life spans.

ble to ascertain how long people will live. As the *Treasury of Abhidharma* expresses it,

> Here it is not fixed: at the end
> Ten years, in the beginning immeasurable.*

And the *Chapters of Utterances on Specific Topics* has this to say:

> From that very night
> When a person first enters the womb,
> His life is running out, it cannot be topped up;
> And there is no going back on what is past.
> In the morning, one sees many people;
> In the evening, some are no longer to be seen.
> In the evening, one sees many people;
> In the morning, some are no longer to be seen.
> Many men and women are there
> Who will die even in the prime of life,
> And one will say "They were so young!"
> But what guarantee is that for staying alive?
> Some will die inside the womb,
> Others while they are being born,
> Some just when they have begun to crawl,
> Some when they can fully run,
> Some when old, and some when young,
> Some are people in the prime of youth;
> One by one they will depart
> Like ripe fruit dropping from a tree.

2. The causes of death are numerous, so again, there is no certainty when one will die

The *Bodhisattva's Scriptural Collection* gives an indication of the countless causes as follows:

*At the beginning of a kalpa, human beings live for an immeasurably long time, but at the end their life expectancy falls to only ten years.

> There are nine causes of sudden death:
> Eating inappropriate food,
> Eating a lot of food when one is already full,
> Eating before the previous meal has been digested,
> Retaining excreta rather than eliminating it at the right time,
> Not obeying the doctor's and nurse's instructions when one is sick,
> Traveling at night and being attacked by negative forces and powerful spirits,
> Suppressing the urge to vomit and failing to vomit after taking an emetic,
> Unconsidered, dangerous behavior,
> And careless sexual intercourse.

The Omniscient Teacher states,

> Especially this human state is plagued by many perils.
> Disease and evil forces are the source of numerous ills.
> Fire and sword, vast chasms, poisons, savage beasts,
> And kings and robbers, enemies and thieves,
> And all the rest destroy prosperity and life.[58]

And in *Letter to a Friend*, we read,

> With all its many risks, this life endures
> No more than windblown bubbles in a stream.
> How marvelous to breathe in and out again,
> To fall asleep and then awake refreshed.[59]

3. The body is frail and essenceless, so again, there is no knowing when it will perish

As we read in *The Way of the Bodhisattva*,

> First, with mind's imagination,
> Shed the covering of skin,
> And with the blade of wisdom, strip
> The flesh from off the bony frame.

And when you have divided all the bones,
And searched right down amid the very marrow,
You yourself should ask the question:
Where is the essential core?[60]

And the Great Orgyen said,

Even the buddhas' adamantine bodies,
Refulgent with the major and minor marks,
Will not last eternally, so what is there to say
About the forms, like cesspools, made of filth,
That are impermanent and will perish soon?

The sublime scholar Mātṛicheṭa sums this up,

The Lord of Death is no one's friend,
Without warning he will fall on you.
So do not think, "I'll do it tomorrow,"
Hasten, instead, to practice the Dharma.
There is no good in people who say,
"I'll do this tomorrow; I won't do it today."
Never doubt that there will come
A tomorrow when you will be no more.

C. Three reasons why nothing can help one when one is dying

1. The wealth that one has accumulated cannot help one

Even if you have the greatest riches, such as the universal monarch's glory and wealth, complete with his seven precious divine attributes, or the whole treasury of Vaishravaṇa, you will have to leave it all behind and depart. We read in the Vinaya scriptures,

When a tree falls down,
What use are the branches and leaves?
Likewise, when a person dies,
What use are all their possessions?

2. Those to whom one is related cannot help one

We may have won the friendship of the universal monarch, be surrounded by five hundred young goddess consorts, and have a thousand godling children playing. Our nephew and uncle might be the lords of the gods, our clan might consist of demigod soldiers, and our subjects may be the four continents and the celestial realms. Our paternal uncles may be Brahmā and Indra, our friends the gods of the realm of the Four Great Kings. We might have a thousand celestial servants to serve us, and our palace might be the Mansion of Victory.* Our monastic estates might be like the city of the gods, our following of monks as numerous as the stars in the sky, and our patrons as many as the grains of sand on a riverbank. But none of these can keep us alive, provide help, prolong our life, escort or accompany us. There will be nowhere we can hide or lie low. We will have to depart alone, like a hair plucked out of butter,† proceeding along the narrow defile of the intermediate state with no one to accompany us. As it says in the *Sūtra of the Play of Mañjuśrī*,

> Your parents will not protect you,
> Neither will your friends and relatives.
> They will abandon you,
> And into the next life you will depart alone.

And the Lord of Yogins, Shrī Jagatamitrānanda said,

> Your majesty, however wealthy you may be,
> When you depart and leave for other worlds,
> Like one defeated in a plain of misery,
> You'll be alone, without prince or queen.
> You'll have no clothes, or food,
> No kingdom, or palatial court.
> Even the boundless might and armies you possess
> Will all be out of sight, beyond your hearing.
> Not a single one of these
> Will follow you to your future life.

*The Mansion of Victory is Indra's palace in the Heaven of the Thirty-Three,
†None of the butter sticks to the hair.

To summarize, at that time you'll have nothing,
Not even your own name, not to speak of other things.

And the Bodhisattva Shāntideva said,

There I'll be, prostrate upon my bed,
And all around, my family and friends.
But I alone shall be the one to feel
The cutting of the thread of life.[61]

3. The body with which one was born cannot help one

In the *Practice of the Great Vehicle*, we read,

This body too, which I have cherished so,
Will, this day or the next, be cast aside like broken pottery.
The flesh and bones with which I was born will separate,
And powerless, I'll wander all alone.
Where, by karma's force, will I then be reborn?
Therefore, I must do no evil for my body's sake.
This body, like the earth, is never satisfied;
Made from filth, it's just a heap of filth,
The source of all my woes—like aging, sickness, death.
Once dead, the body is abandoned, the earth around polluted;
It's food for all—birds, dogs, jackals, and the like.
I pampered it with so much effort,
Only to have the ogreish Lord of Death make off with it.
For the wise, the body is an object of disdain,
For fools, a source of lust,
So who with any sense would be attached to it?
For your body's sake, do not bring suffering upon yourself.
Reward it, if you like, with food and clothes,
But for your long-term good, put it to doing virtuous deeds.

And in *Letter to a Friend*,

This body ends as ash, dry dust, or slime,
And ultimately shit, no essence left.

Consumed, evaporated, rotted down—
Thus know its nature: to disintegrate.[62]

Moreover, influential talk cannot help: there is no chance of talking or arguing your way out. Courage and skill will not help: there is no way you can fight your way out. An athlete's speed will not help: there is no chance to escape. A beautiful face will not help: there is no seducing death. Intense activity will not help: this is not the moment for starting anything. Craft and cunning will not help: there is nowhere you can slip away to. Instead, you have to go alone. As we read in the Vinaya scriptures,

Here, even mighty long-lived gods
Living in their lofty abodes,
Their lives exhausted, will grow weak,
So who today can escape from death?
Even heroes and champions cannot protect one.
Kings, renunciates, and ascetics,
Activities, diligence, determination,
Vast retinues, and intelligence
Have no power to free one from death.

Powerful friends and allies cannot help us. Even such mighty beings as Brahmā, Indra, Īshvara, and Viṣhṇu, great sages, and Nārāyaṇa are not exempt from death. "Malignant" *yakṣhas* and *rākṣhasa* ogres, demons, serpentine nāgas, and the like cannot escape it. Medicine, science, divination, crystal gazing,* and other methods cannot help us escape. The power of such things as secret mantras, charms, magic, and clairvoyance will not help. Male gods, Dharma protectors, and ḍākinīs cannot provide a refuge. We will die without any help from the power of elixirs, special substances, or medicines. Again the Vinaya scriptures say,

Power and wealth they have,
Their fame spreads far and wide—
Brahmā, Indra, and Viṣhṇu,

*Tib. *pra*. The Tibetan equivalent of crystal gazing was to tell the future from signs seen in a mirror, on the surface of a lake, on a fingernail, or in a cup of tea.

Rāhu, the Kauravas and Pandavas*—
But even they are powerless to stop death.
From He Who Puts an End To All† neither medicines
Nor the activities of mantras, neither soldiers
Nor gods, neither guardians nor magical rituals,
Neither wealth nor relations can protect one.

The Great Orgyen said,

When the time arrives to leave behind your loved ones and depart,
Death will not delay, it will come to take your life:
The king of doctors might come to you in person,
But even he can't add some vital force to your spent life,
And like a hair pulled out of butter, you will depart.

Food, clothes, and the other things we enjoy will not help. The gods' sweet nectar, their finest clothes of five-colored silk, the most delicious human foods "with a hundred tastes," the finest satin and cotton—in short, the whole variety of beautiful forms, pleasant sounds, sweet scents, delicious tastes, and stuff that is soft to touch—none of these will help us when we die. As we find in the *Play in Full*,

Constantly these beings are caught and snared
By lovely forms and beautiful sounds, sweet smells,
The most delicious tastes, blissful sensations, and death.
Like a monkey caught in a hunter's net,
The pleasures of the senses bring much pain and harm,
With fear, with constant enmity and affliction,
Like a sword's sharp edge and the leaves of a poisonous plant.

And in the *Sūtra of Advice to the King*, we read,

*Brahmā and Viṣhṇu are the creators of the world according to the Hindu tradition; Indra is an all-powerful god in Indian mythology. Rāhu, the maker of darkness, is a demon who swallows the sun and moon, thereby causing eclipses. The Kauravas and Pandavas are warring clans that figure in the famous Indian myth Mahābhārata.
†Tib. *mthar byed pa*—that is, the Lord of Death.

> Great King, let us take an example. Imagine that from the four directions, the lofty masses of four great mountains—solid to the core, unfissured, indestructible, and extremely hard—were to come crashing down. All the plants and trees and animals and other living creatures would be completely pulverized. There would be no chance of using speed to run away, money to pay them off, strength to push them back, skillful means to get free, or the power of medicines, mantras, and special substances to avert them.
>
> Great King, in the same way, the four great dangers that are birth, aging, sickness, and death will occur. There will be no chance of using speed to run away from them, or wealth, strength, and so on to push them back. Aging will destroy your youth. Sickness will destroy your good health. Decline will destroy your prosperity. Death will destroy your longevity and life force. There is nothing you can do to stop them.

In addition to the above, we should also reflect on a variety of examples and analogies, as we find in the *Answers to the Questions of Yeshe Tsogyal* in the *Direct Instructions of the Teacher* from the *Treasure of Nyang*:

> The Lotus of Orgyen spoke, "Listen, Tsogyal, people who are not mindful of death will never come to the Dharma. It is necessary to train in remembering death. Those who are not mindful of death will remain strongly attached to this world.
>
> "First, there is outer impermanence. Take as your object someone dear to you, and look at how they died. How were they before they became sick, and how were they subsequently during their illness? Before they fell ill, they had a bright complexion, but as they sickened, their teeth and lips became stained, their complexion faded, and they fell into a coma. Imagine this for yourself: it will surely be the same for you.
>
> "Then consider how, when they were alive, everyone cherished them, they were surrounded by all their relatives, and given things to eat. But once they died, no one needed them anymore. People were only too glad to get rid of the body as fast as they could. Look at their death like that, and reflect that you too are not exempt from that.

"After that, look at when the corpse was taken out and carried to the cemetery. There were corpses that had disintegrated and decomposed, some that were still fresh, and so on. Reflect on the fact that you too will not be exempt from that. Furthermore, when you see your contemporaries die, whether relatives, friends, or neighbors, you should imagine yourself in their place: for you too, it will be no different.

"You should make use of the changes in the seasons—autumn, spring, and so on—to realize that your life is running out. Those who are unaware of this never give a thought to death. Nor do people perceive the moment-to-moment nature of impermanence. From the moment we were born until now, with every instant, our lives have been running out. With each instant that has passed, our lives have become that much shorter, and thus we have reached the age we are now. Even if we were to live for a predetermined length of time, or could live even longer, with every instant that passes, our lives are running out. Every second that ticks by brings us closer to death, and death will swiftly be upon us. Just as animals being led to the slaughterhouse come closer to death with every step they take, we, too, are drawing nearer to death. With every moment, life passes by as quickly as the lengthening shadows at sunset; it does not wait for an instant, yet we arrogantly carry on.

"Most people are unaware of the continuing stream of impermanence. From the moment our mother gave birth to us until now, by how many days has our life got shorter? By that many days, our life has slipped away. And even though we are still managing to continue living, each day that we do so, our life is running out. Today has gone, tonight has gone. In a flash, a whole twenty-four hours has gone by. In two flashes, two days have gone by. As days and nights flash by, life runs out, and it will not be long before we are dead. We might think, as our lives get shorter by the day, that the day is longer or shorter, the night longer or shorter. But however long they are, that will not help the length of time we have to live.

"People are also unaware of their own impermanence. This life of ours is like a boat in the ocean without oars; the demon of death is like the water in the ocean. Our own life is like a tree on a cliff; the demon of death is like a mountain torrent eroding it away. Our life is like a bird's feather stuck on top of a cairn; the demon of death is like a strong wind, which will blow it away. Our life is like a wounded deer; the demon of death is like a hound on the scent, giving chase. Yet we fail to see the way in which our own life is getting shorter, and we become deeply distressed when other people die. How can this be? People fail to perceive the fleeting nature of impermanence. Even if they were able to live for a predetermined length of time, they will never be exempt from death.

"Without any certainty as to whether we will die today or tonight, we have no power over death. Our own body can be the implement by which we die. The body is produced from the four elements, and when the combination of the four elements in the wind, bile, and phlegm humors becomes unbalanced, this acts as a cause of death. Food nourishes the body but can cause death by choking. Seasoned swimmers can die in the water. Smiths can kill themselves with the weapons they have made. We can die from poisoned meat and indigestible food. Expert horsemen can die falling from their steeds. Brave warriors can be killed by their weapons. Powerful people may be poisoned or stabbed to death. There is nothing, basically, that cannot cause death. In telling ourselves that we will live even a single day longer without dying, we are, it seems, simply lying to ourselves.

"What with all the different causes of death, there is no knowing when death will come. There is no knowing how we will die. There is nothing we can rely on as far as life is concerned. It is definite that we will die. The young cannot be certain of not dying. There are no old people who can escape. Before one sick person has died, a hundred healthy people might die. Even if we survive some terrible illness once, it does not mean we can escape sickness and death forever. Disliking death is not going to help. You are not the only one who disparages death. Saying that everyone else dies will not help either.

"If you were not going to be reborn after you had died, that would be fine. But you will have to take another birth. And you will have no freedom of choice as to where you will be reborn.

"When we die, only our positive and negative deeds will follow us. Yet even if they know they are going to die, people commit negative deeds without caring about the law of karma. What are they all thinking about? Tsogyal, after you die, you won't just disappear. Because of your deeds, you will have to be reborn. Of the three kinds of deeds (virtuous, nonvirtuous, and indeterminate), virtuous deeds result in happiness in the higher realms and so on. The result of nonvirtuous deeds is suffering in the three lower realms and so forth. Indeterminate deeds are like a rotten seed: they do not yield any fruit. In general, the causes of rebirth in the three lower realms are negative actions and attachment. Negative actions result in rebirth in the hells. Attachment results in rebirth as hungry spirits and animals."

Again, we read in the *Instructions to the King* by Orgyen, knower of the three times,

Unless you subjugate the defilements, your enemies and hatred will increase and you will be unhappy for no purpose: of this you should be firmly convinced.

Unless you have devoted yourself to virtuous activities and the practice of Dharma, the time you pass with your beloved relatives will not help you at the time of death: of this you should be firmly convinced.

If you do not follow in the Buddha's footsteps,[63] as a result of grasping at worldly gain you will again be thrown into the cycle of existence: of this you should be firmly convinced.

Unless you have taken up residence in the unchanging citadel,* you will have to abandon your well-built fortress of earth and stone and depart: of this you should be firmly convinced.

Unless you have accumulated merit and wisdom, even if you have gathered riches and possessions, once dead, you will not be able to enjoy them: of this you should be firmly convinced.

Unless you rely on the nectar of the true nature, all the tasty food you eat will turn into impurity: of this you should be firmly convinced.

Unless you attain the body of truth free from birth, however

*"The unchanging citadel" refers to enlightenment.

much your ego has cherished this heap of flesh and blood, its elements are on loan and will be carried away by their owner.* Of this you should be firmly convinced.

Unless you keep the company of skillful means and wisdom, even if you have a thousand like-minded friends for company, you will soon have to leave them and depart: of this you should be firmly convinced.

Unless you realize the truth beyond words, even if your fame fills all the billion worlds in the universe, it is only a deceptive trick by the demons: of this you should be firmly convinced.

Unless you gain mastery over your own mind, even if you have the immense power of a universal monarch, when the time comes for you to die, you will have no freedom to act as you please: of this you should be firmly convinced.

Unless you possess the skill of wisdom-awareness, even if you are as heroic as the strongest fighter, you will not ward off the attacks of cyclic existence: of this you should be firmly convinced.

Unless you have realized the meaning of primordial purity, sound-emptiness, even if you are the Lion of Speech,† you will not be able to argue your way out of the ripening of your karma: of this you should be firmly convinced.

Unless you discover the great bliss within yourself, even if you are mounted on the all-knowing horse,‡ you will not be able to escape the sufferings of cyclic existence: of this you should be firmly convinced.

Unless you are adorned with the immense qualities of buddhahood, even if your body is as beautiful as those of the gods in the heavens, you will not be able to seduce the demon of death: of this you should be firmly convinced.

Unless you place yourself under the protection of the teacher and the Three Jewels, no one will be able to protect you from your enemies, the defilements: of this you should be firmly convinced.

*That is, the Lord of Death.

†Tib. *smra ba'i seng ge*, an epithet of Mañjushrī, also, one of the forms of Guru Rinpoche, inseparable from Mañjushrī.

‡Tib. *cang shes kyi rta*, a magical horse in Indian mythology, renowned for its speed and intelligence.

Unless you realize your own mind to be the Buddha, you will be deceived by all other thoughts: of this you should be firmly convinced.

All mundane activities that do not lead to liberation and enlightenment are worthless; like the plantain tree, they are devoid of essence: of this you should be firmly convinced.

Again, Guru Padmasambhava said,

Cyclic existence is the result of your not giving up dualistic concepts of "I" and self. You and all sentient beings are the same in having the bodhichitta,* yet you distinguish between yourself and others. That shows that you have no real heart.

All the beings of the three worlds have been your father or mother in your previous lives, yet you consider some as friends and some as enemies. That shows you have no real heart.

At this moment when you can distinguish between saṃsāra and nirvāṇa, you find time to nurture the eight ordinary preoccupations. That shows you have no real heart.

This life lasts but an instant, yet you are busy building castles. That shows you have no real heart.

This body is full of unclean constituents, yet you cling to it as a self and cannot bear its being pricked by a tiny thorn. That shows you have no real heart.

All your friends and relatives are dying, subject to impermanence, yet you still expect to live forever. That shows you have no real heart.

When you die, you will leave empty-handed, yet you still seek food and riches by indulging in all sorts of negative deeds. That shows you have no real heart.

The things you perceive outside are constantly changing, yet you still hope your possessions will last forever. That shows you have no real heart.

Your life is diminishing as inexorably as the lengthening shad-

*"Bodhichitta" here refers to the buddha nature or tathāgatagarbha present in every single being.

ows at sunset, yet you still indulge in laziness and indifference. That shows you have no real heart.

Turning away from the Dharma, which brings happiness in this life and the next, you devote yourself to family life. That shows you have no real heart.

By doing negative actions, you are sure to go to the lower realms, but still you do not shy away from the ripening of karma. That shows you have no real heart.

At present, you cannot bear it when a spark of fire touches you, but you still expect to be able to bear the heat of the hot hells. That shows you have no real heart.

You cannot resist the cold of winter for a single night, yet you still expect to be able to bear being frozen in the cold hells. That shows you have no real heart.

You cannot stand going without food and drink even for three days, yet you still expect to be able to bear the sufferings of the hungry spirits. That shows you have no real heart.

You would not be able to bear things like being forced to labor, even for a short while, yet you still believe that you will be able to put up with the sufferings of the animal realm. That shows you have no real heart.

At this moment, when you need advice, you do not even listen to your teacher's instructions. That shows you have no real heart.

At this time, when you have gained the freedom to do as you wish, you are a slave to desire. That shows you have no real heart.

Without practicing the Dharma even for an instant, you still hope that things will be the same in the next life. That shows you have no real heart.

Once you are born, death is shadowing you, yet you still take your time, making plans for next year. That shows you have no real heart.

At present, when you have the freedom to choose between progressing or regressing, you fail to undertake the practice for liberation. That shows you have no real heart.

Whatever you do in cyclic existence will bring nothing but suffering, yet you do not give up your activities. That shows you have no real heart.

Now you will have to wander endlessly in cyclic existence, yet

> you still continue lying to yourself. That shows you have no real heart.
>
> O King, these people, with bodies that are human but minds like cattle, will end up filled with regret.

The only ones who can guide us as we are dying, who can dispel the terrors of the intermediate state and set us on the level of liberation, the state of great bliss, are our teachers, who embody the Three Jewels. So from this day on, follow sublime teachers without ever separating from them. Take refuge in the Three Jewels. Put all your efforts into practicing the Dharma and performing virtuous activities, without getting distracted. Gather the two accumulations as provisions for the journey. Build the mansion of concentration. Keep the company of mindfulness and vigilance. Seize the citadel of the three buddha bodies. This is most essential, as is affirmed in the *Sūtra of Advice to the King*:

> Great King, at that time the Dharma will be an island, a shelter, a protector, and a support. It will be like a fire for someone afflicted by cold, a cool pavilion for someone suffering from the heat, cool water for someone parched with thirst, shade for a weary traveler, a vehicle for someone embarking on a long journey, a comfortable bed for someone who is sleeping, good food for someone who is hungry, consolation for one tormented by grief, a guide for one who has lost their way, a doctor for someone who has fallen sick, a lifeline for someone sinking in a swamp, a boat for someone carried away by a river, a bridge over a difficult crossing, a resting place for one who is exhausted, a torch in a dark cave, a ship on the ocean, riches for a poor man, a helper for one who labors, a tool for a woodcarver, armor for one going into battle, a good escort on a perilous journey, reinforcements in battle, grain in a famine, space for someone in a tight squeeze, a place to stay for a vagrant, and a protector giving refuge to someone in danger.

Using these various analogies and reasonings, in all your daily activities—walking, moving around, lying down, sitting, eating, dressing, having a conversation, and so on—think only of death and impermanence, as the *Hundred Parables on Action* advises:

All the time, in everything you do,
Be mindful of the lord of death.

And *The Way of the Bodhisattva* says,

This should be my one concern,
My only thought both night and day.[64]

Reflecting in this manner, remind yourself again and again, using your speech as well to recite the following lines and underscoring your practice with the three supreme methods:

> Compounded things are all impermanent, flickering like lightning.
> All that we reflect upon, the world and its inhabitants, will naturally perish.
> We are sure to die, and there's no knowing when.
> Yet believing it is all eternal, we fool ourselves,
> Lulled into a state of carelessness.
> Teacher, embodiment of the Three Jewels, look on us with compassion:
> Bless us that we may be mindful of death and impermanence.[65]

IV. The benefits of meditating on impermanence and the signs of having done so

A. Benefits

The *Precious Treasury That Fulfills All Wishes* describes the benefits of reflecting on impermanence as follows:

The benefits of that are utterly infinite.
One rids oneself of the faults of cyclic existence,
Good qualities are naturally gathered.
One is freed from the belief that things are eternal,
Attachment to loved ones and hatred for enemies is pacified.
One is supremely diligent in virtuous practice

And realizes that the things of this life are delusory.
The two accumulations are perfectly completed,
And illustrious deities watch over one.
Dying peacefully, one proceeds to the higher realms,
And swiftly attains the nectarous state of immortality.[66]

We gain a deep feeling of disenchantment with the things of cyclic existence, as a result of which we turn our minds away from the affairs of this life. Numerous qualities that we did not have before take birth in our being. We turn away from the belief that everything will go on forever. We no longer feel attachment to loved ones or hatred for enemies, and we are constantly diligent in practicing virtue. We realize that the things of this life are illusions. We complete the two accumulations and are cared for by eminent beings sympathetic to the Dharma* and by the buddhas and bodhisattvas. We end our lives peacefully and are reborn in the higher realms. As soon as we are reborn, we will encounter the sacred Dharma and a spiritual friend. We will always be free to choose our destiny and will take ordination in the doctrine, bring discipline to perfection, pass our time day and night practicing the Dharma, and engage in the teachings of the Great Vehicle. Keeping the company of sublime beings, we will swiftly attain buddhahood. These are among the boundless benefits it is said that we will obtain.

When the Precious Lord of Dagpo† was about to begin a retreat, Lama Cha-Yulwa[67] said to him,

> Even if you tear my heart out, it is just a lump of flesh: more essential is meditation on death and impermanence. If you don't meditate on that, you won't get to the crucial point of the Dharma.

Taking faith in this, Gampopa made it the foundation of his practice. All his disciples, and their disciples in turn, cherished it above all.

And the Dharma Lord, Sangye Tönpa[68] said,

*Tib. *chos mthun gyi grags pa*, famous, powerful beings such as Brahmā and Indra, who approve of the Dharma.

†A name by which Gampopa, who came from Dagpo, is known. Gampopa was one of Milarepa's disciples and an important master in the Kagyu lineage.

Death and impermanence is the most precious thing for a teacher
to teach.
It is the most precious thing for disciples to receive.
It is the most precious thing for meditators to meditate upon.
Yet this profound teaching gets left aside in obscurity.

When Ga Lotsawa went to study with Chen-ngawa,[69] he asked him to kindly grant him a profound teaching. The latter answered, "Meditate on death and impermanence."

"I already know this teaching. Could you teach me something more profound?" requested Ga.

Chen-ngawa replied, "Geshe Drom Tönpa[70] has 1,500 bodhisattvas as disciples, and he says that this is the most profound teaching he gives them. I do not have a more profound teaching than this."

Sangye Öntön[71] declared,

Unless you keep the thought of death in mind,
There is nothing deep about the Guhyasamāja teachings.
Once you give birth to the thought of death,
You are taking refuge in the path. Nothing is more profound than
that.

And Mokchokpa[72] said,

The experiences of one who has not thought of death
Are like the autumn mists.
A monk who has not thought of death
Is like a queen.*
The determination of one who has not thought of death
Is like glacial ice in summer.

Padampa Sangye and all the other holders of the practice lineage recommended only this and made it the basis of their practice. Lord Buddha himself said, "Just as the elephant's footprint is the largest of all footprints, the greatest of all thoughts is the thought of impermanence." And in the Vinaya scriptures, we read,

*That is, a monk who does not meditate on death is just dressed up as a monk.

> Far better than giving the midday meal and other offerings to a hundred of my disciples like Shāriputra and Maudgalyāyana, who are perfect vessels,* is being mindful for an instant of the impermanence of compounded phenomena.

B. The signs of having trained

On the signs of having trained in meditating on impermanence, the Omniscient Teacher writes,

> From seeing that everything that appears perishes, there arises in the depths of one's mind a disgust for outer objects. Diligence in virtuous activities arises in one's mind like a blazing fire. One develops an extraordinary heartfelt dread of samsaric suffering.
>
> From recognizing that at the time of death nothing can help one, one abandons the activities of this life. Without, for a single instant, biding one's time in ordinary relaxation, one devotes one's body, speech, and mind to the practice of Dharma.
>
> From seeing the ripening of the results of one's deeds, one gives rise to disenchantment and determination to be free. Knowing that there is no certainty when one will die, one does not put one's trust in anything.
>
> These are the signs and measure of having truly meditated, from the depths of one's heart, on impermanence.

An example of someone in whom these signs have occurred is Kharak Gomchung. When he went to practice in the mountain solitudes of Jomo Kharak in Tsang, there was a thornbush at the entrance of his cave that caught on his clothes. At first he wondered whether he should cut it down, but then he thought, "I could die inside the cave. I don't know whether I might ever come out again. It is far more important for me to get on with my practice," and he left the bush uncut. The same thing happened when he came out again, but he said to himself, "I cannot be sure that I'll ever go back inside." And so it went on. He stayed in that place for twelve years, becoming an accomplished master, but he never cut down the thornbush. He himself said,

*That is, perfect vessels for receiving and holding the teachings.

> Whatever you do, you will have enough food and clothes for this life.
> Once you have died, it will be impossible to seek the fruit of enlightenment.
> Without being attached to anyone, friends or enemies,
> Make haste to gather a large amount of merit.
> There is no time to waste in life, conventional activities are endless.
> You should, rather, take up the teachings of the sublime beings:
> Give up diversions and make use of solitude;
> Stay alone like a rhinoceros.

Accordingly, it is important to do all you can to strictly curtail all unnecessary projects. Adopting the ways of the noble beings, with few desires and content with what you have, practice alone, in solitude.

The masters of the past used to say,

> If you have few desires, yours is the family of the noble beings.
> If you have put an end to desires, you are a noble being.
> Always train, therefore, in having few desires.

And the *Sūtra of Individual Liberation* gives this instruction:

> With certainty of mind, they've tamed their senses
> And grow old in peaceful solitudes.
> Much they've heard, and now, deep in the woods,
> Those whose youth is past lead happy lives.

Amid the clouds of those impermanent illusions, the world and beings,
Our lives flash by like lightning's playful dance.
With no confidence that tomorrow you will not die,
Accomplish enlightenment alone, O fortunate ones!

This completes the instruction on reflecting on the impermanence of life.

7. Reflecting on Actions: Cause and Result

The instructions for reflecting on actions, cause and result enable one to turn one's mind away from all unvirtuous activities and put one's efforts one-pointedly into positive, virtuous practice. They comprise four sections: (1) identifying the nature of deeds, (2) a specific explanation of the ten actions, (3) additional teachings on distinctions and categories, and (4) understanding that everything is determined by deeds.*

I. Identifying the nature of deeds

Padmasambhava's *Great Treatise on the Graded Path* outlines this as follows:

> Negative or unvirtuous deeds are unwholesome forms of conduct that give rise directly or indirectly to suffering. Of these, there are three kinds:
>
> - Naturally shameful deeds: the very fact of committing them has a negative effect. These include the five crimes with immediate retribution, the five crimes that are almost as grave, and the ten negative actions.
> - Shameful deeds that violate edicts: the very fact that such

*Throughout this book, the term *deed* translates the Tibetan *las* (Skt. *karma*), also translated as "action" or "past deed." Implied in the use of this term is the force created by a positive or negative action (physical, verbal, or mental), which is then stored in an individual's stream of being and persists until it is experienced as pleasure or pain (usually in another life), after which the deed is said to be exhausted.

deeds have been proscribed makes them downfalls. They are the faults that contravene the rules of the three vows.

- Mundane shameful deeds: these create the conditions for other negative deeds. They include ignorance, carelessness, disrespect, and an abundance of afflictive emotions.

Virtuous deeds are wholesome forms of conduct that give rise directly or indirectly to happiness. Of these, there are three kinds:

- virtuous deeds conducive to merit, which are those that are performed with the concepts of the three spheres
- virtuous deeds conducive to liberation, which are those motivated and performed with the thought of determination to be free
- virtuous deeds of unsurpassable liberation, which are those related to perfect knowledge without any concepts of the three spheres

Acts that are neither virtuous nor negative are indeterminate deeds.

There are therefore three categories: (1) nonvirtuous deeds to be avoided, (2) virtuous deeds to be adopted, and (3) indeterminate deeds.

A. Nonvirtuous deeds to be avoided

1. Definition

Nonvirtuous deeds are deeds that are motivated by the three poisonous defilements, as stated in the *Jewel Garland*:

> Deeds that are produced with attachment,
> Aversion, or bewilderment are nonvirtuous.[73]

2. Etymological definition

Unwholesome conduct, or shameful deeds, are so called because they give rise, directly or indirectly, to suffering as their result, or because merely speaking of them, not to mention actually perpetrating them, is inadmissible.

3. Categories

There are three categories. Naturally shameful deeds are any deeds that, simply by being committed, cut the path to liberation and have negative consequences. Shameful deeds that violate edicts are deeds that have negative consequences through their having been proscribed. Mundane shameful deeds are deeds that are disparaged by people in the world and have negative consequences. These will now be dealt with in turn.

a. Naturally shameful deeds

Naturally shameful deeds include the following:

The five crimes with immediate retribution

These are deeds that are particularly powerful because of the objects on which they are perpetrated:

- to kill one's father in this present life
- to kill one's mother in this present life
- to kill an arhat
- to create a split in the assembly of the Saṅgha
- with evil intent, to cause a tathāgata's body to bleed

Committing any of these five leads to one being reborn in the evil destiny that is the great Hell of Torment Unsurpassed without passing through any other intervening lives, which is why they are termed "crimes with immediate retribution."

The five crimes that are almost as grave

These are as follows:

- to destroy a stūpa*
- to kill a bodhisattva dwelling on the levels†

*The Tibetan term *mchod rten*, meaning "a support of veneration," refers to any sacred object, such as a statue, and does not necessarily refer only to stūpas.
†Tib. *byang sems nges gnas*. A bodhisattva who is on one of the ten bodhisattva levels.

- to engage in improper sexual relations with an arhat*
- to kill a stream enterer or other noble being training on the path
- to appropriate the property of the Saṅgha

These are similar to the above negative acts and so are termed "the five crimes that are almost as grave."

The ten nonvirtuous deeds

Physically taking life and the other nine nonvirtuous deeds will be listed and explained in detail below.

The sixteen serious faults

The four serious faults entailing reversal

These are as follows:

- to sit at the head of a row of scholars who have greater qualities than one's own
- to accept the homage of a realized being or of a monk who is senior to one in terms of the precepts
- to inconsiderately consume the food of someone doing intensive practice†
- to use the ritual materials of a mantra practitioner who has sacred commitments,‡ such as the ingredients necessary for the feast offering and *tormas*

Since these involve engaging in unworthy conduct that is the opposite of what one should do, they are termed the "four serious faults entailing rever-

*Tib. *dgra bcom ma la log par g.yem pa*, lit. "improper sexual relations with a female arhat," but it implies sexual relations with an arhat of either sex.

†This does not mean eating the food of any Dharma practitioner in general but rather eating the provisions of someone practicing intensively in retreat, with the result that the practitioner runs out of food prematurely and is thus prevented from completing the intended period of practice.

‡Performing the feast offering, offering tormas, and so on form part of a mantra practitioner's sacred commitment, or samaya.

sal." An exception is made for situations such as those in which one is oneself teaching the Dharma.

The four serious faults entailing impairment

These are as follows:

- to break a promise
- to impair the vows of the listeners*
- to impair the bodhisattva precepts
- to impair the commitments of the Secret Mantra Vehicle

Committing any of these four impairs one's character, so they are termed the "four serious faults entailing impairment."

The four serious faults entailing contempt

These are as follows:

- because of the defilement of ignorance, to show contempt for the authentic teachings of the Buddha
- out of pride, likewise, to show contempt for the good qualities of other wise and learned persons
- out of jealousy, to show contempt for the words of truth of others
- out of prejudice, to assert faults in others' teachings when there are none and to attempt to disprove them and prove one's own

Because these involve contempt for sacred objects, they are termed the "four serious faults entailing contempt."

The four serious faults entailing scorn

These are as follows:

- To think nothing of causing a tathāgata to bleed (one of the five crimes with immediate retribution). This is so serious because although the other four crimes with immediate retribution can

*That is, any of the vows of individual liberation. See glossary, s.v. "individual liberation."

be confessed by using a buddha as a support, in this case, by injuring a buddha, one has rejected the very object of confession.

- To think nothing of wrong view (one of the ten nonvirtuous deeds). This is so serious because, as long as one has the view of confidence in the karmic law of cause and effect, it is possible to counteract the other nine nonvirtuous deeds, but wrong view interrupts every source of good, and so any countermeasures are impossible.
- To favor the ultimate teachings and show contempt for the others, even though they are equivalent. This is so serious because it leads to the obscuration of giving up the Dharma.
- To criticize other bodhisattvas, falsely accusing them of faults without any grounds or causes for doing so.

It is because these involve scorning such exceptional objects that they are extremely serious faults, so they are termed the "four serious faults entailing scorn."

The eight perverse acts

These are so called because they involve engaging in the activities that are the opposite of what is right. They are as follows:

- maligning virtue
- praising evil
- disturbing the minds of the virtuous
- preventing the faithful from accumulating merit
- forsaking one's kind teacher
- forsaking the *yidam* deity, the root of accomplishment
- forsaking the spiritual brothers and sisters with whom one is connected by the sacred commitments
- violating the sacred maṇḍala

b. Shameful deeds that violate edicts

Although the simple fact of committing these does not have a negative effect for everyone, when they are committed by someone who has taken vows, they become faults. Some examples of these are as follows: for ordained monks, eating after midday and separating from their Dharma robes; for bodhisattvas, failing to dispel others' suffering, failing to nurse the sick, and so on; and for practitioners of the secret mantras, considering the universe and beings to be ordinary. In short, these refer to the different kinds of faults that constitute downfalls of the three classes of vows decreed by the Capable One, the Perfect Buddha.

c. Mundane shameful deeds

These are deeds that respectable people in the world would disparage if they were to see or hear of them. They include the following:

- not knowing what conduct to avoid and what conduct to adopt
- not respecting such conventions even if one knows them
- carelessly engaging in everything one does without checking what one is doing
- lacking faith and confidence in the Three Jewels, the karmic law of cause and effect, and so on
- having an unpleasant, uncontrolled character dictated by gross defilements

In short, these are negative actions that are universally condemned and shameful.

Of all these, some of the most serious deeds include inflicting harm on bodhisattvas who have aroused bodhichitta, on one's teachers and vajra masters, and on one's spiritual brothers and sisters, and giving up the sacred Dharma. There are innumerable mentions of these. The *Sūtra of the Marks That Inspire the Development of Faith*, for example, states,

> A greater evil than imprisoning all the beings in the ten directions is getting angry with, and turning one's back on, someone who has aroused bodhichitta. More serious than destroying as many stūpas as there are grains of sand in the Ganges River are the negative deeds of malice, anger, insults, and criticism directed toward a bodhisattva.

In the mantra tradition, it is said that as a result of deteriorating one's sacred commitment with the teacher, spiritual brothers and sisters, and so forth, one will be reborn in the great vajra hell, a place that will not be destroyed even in the kalpa of destruction.* And in numerous sūtras, it is stated that giving up the sacred Dharma is more serious a fault that accumulating the five crimes with immediate retribution and destroying all the stūpas in our world. The *Chapters of Utterances on Specific Topics* sums this up as follows:

> Even a small negative act
> Will cause, in other lives,
> Great fear and devastation,
> Like some insidious poison.

B. Virtuous deeds to be adopted

1. Definition

Virtuous deeds are all deeds whose motivation is characterized by an absence of the three poisons, as is stated in the *Jewel Garland*:

> Deeds that are produced without attachment,
> Aversion, or bewilderment are virtuous.
> Virtue leads to all the higher realms
> And happiness in all one's lives.[74]

2. Etymological definition

Virtuous or excellent conduct is so called because it gives rise exclusively, directly or indirectly, to happiness or excellence.

3. Categories

There are three categories: virtuous deeds conducive to merit, those conducive to liberation, and unsurpassable virtuous deeds.

*The kalpa during which the universe is destroyed. See Jigme Lingpa and Longchen Yeshe Dorje, *Treasury*, bk. 1, appendix 1, 364.

a. Virtuous deeds conducive to merit

These refer to deeds such as giving generously, observing discipline, and training in the concentration of meditative absorption, performed by ordinary beings who have little skillful means and wisdom. Such beings have not realized the meaning of no-self and have not given rise to the determination to be free from the whole of cyclic existence. Their goal is merely to achieve the happiness in the celestial and humans realms that will result from these deeds in future lives.

b. Virtuous deeds conducive to liberation

These refer to all sources of good imbued with partial skillful means and wisdom, performed by beings who possess the wisdom that has realized only the no-self of the individual and who are determined to become free from the whole of cyclic existence. Their goal is not so much to attain excellent states in existence but rather to achieve the limited result of their particular path—that is, liberation for themselves alone.

c. Unsurpassable virtuous deeds

These are sources of good imbued with extraordinary skillful means and wisdom. They unite compassion and love for sentient beings with wisdom, which through the knowledge of realization of both kinds of no-self, is perfectly free from the concepts of the three spheres.

In other texts, these last two are classed together as virtuous deeds conducive to liberation, while the virtuous deeds of someone on the path of joining are classified as "virtuous deeds conducive to definite differentiation,"* so again there are three categories.

Of all these, actions such as holding the sacred Dharma, ransoming the lives of sentient beings, and positive acts imbued with bodhichitta are especially noble, as is stated in the *Sūtra of the Questions of Sāgaramati*:

> The mind intent on perfect enlightenment, holding the Dharma,
> Practicing the Dharma, and loving compassion for beings—

*Tib. *nges 'byed cha mthun*. These are deeds that distinguish practitioners on the path of joining, who are approaching the path of seeing, from ordinary beings.

These four virtues have infinite qualities,
Which even the buddhas could never fully describe.

And the *Chapters of Utterances on Specific Topics* sums this up as follows:

Even a small positive act
Will lead, in other lives,
To great happiness and fulfillment,
Like fruits that ripen to perfection.

C. Indeterminate deeds

1. Definition

Indeterminate deeds are physical and verbal deeds whose motivation is neither virtuous nor nonvirtuous.

2. Etymological definition

They are indeterminate because they cannot be definitely determined as either virtuous or nonvirtuous.

3. Categories

Indeterminate deeds include walking, sitting, eating, lying down, having a conversation, making things, and so on. Since they do not give any other result, they are like rotten seeds. Nevertheless, they are very potent in wasting one's freedoms and advantages, so it is important to skillfully transform them into the path of virtue. Their root, too, depends on one's intention, as the Bodhisattva Shāntideva said:

Aspiration, so the Sage asserted,
Is the root of every kind of virtue.
Aspiration's root in turn
Is constant meditation on the fruits of action.[75]

And,

But if my acts are good, sincerely intended,
Then no matter where I turn my steps,
The merit gained will honor me
With its resulting benefits.[76]

II. A specific explanation of the ten actions

Finding Rest in the Nature of the Mind states,

> Actions that compound saṃsāra are of two kinds, white and black.
> They have the nature of the virtues and nonvirtues, ten by ten.[77]

It thus shows that deeds are of two kinds: the ten nonvirtuous deeds to be avoided and the ten virtuous deeds to be adopted.

A. The ten nonvirtuous deeds to be avoided

There are two parts: (1) a synopsis according to the Great Omniscient One's *Finding Rest in the Nature of the Mind* and (2) a presentation of the actual words of Orgyen, knower of the three times.

1. A synopsis according to the Great Omniscient One's *Finding Rest in the Nature of the Mind*

The root text condenses the ten nonvirtuous deeds into three groups:

> When differentiated [nonvirtue] is tenfold,
> Classified as three of body, four of speech, and three of mind.[78]

These will now be described in turn.

a. The three nonvirtuous deeds of the body

Finding Rest in the Nature of the Mind continues,

> The act of killing is to put to death
> A living being, intentionally, without mistaking the identity.

And similar to this are all aggressive actions,
Beating, striking, and so on, whereby beings are assaulted.
The act of taking what has not been given
Is to steal another's property, and similar to this
Is the acquisition through deceit of others' goods.
Sexual misconduct is to have relations
With one who is committed to another, and similar to this
Are all improper modes of intercourse.[79]

In this way, the actual deed of taking life involves recognizing the victim, be it as small as an insect, and killing it. Hitting, beating, and so on are the deeds related to taking life. The actual deed of stealing is stealing someone else's property, while related to it are deeds such as gently inducing someone to hand over their property. Actual sexual misconduct entails having sex with someone who is committed to another partner, with a relative, by another orifice, and in an inappropriate place or time. The related deeds are sexual acts involving desire for objects that one should not have intercourse with, such as one's hand.

The results of these deeds are generally taught as being four separate effects—the fully ripened effect, the effect similar to the cause, the conditioning or environmental effect, and the proliferating effect. Here, however, we shall summarize them by quoting directly from the *Essential Instructions for Finding Rest in the Nature of the Mind*:

> By taking life, wherever one is reborn, one will have a short life and many illnesses. One's environment will be disagreeable, with ravines, precipices, and other places where one's life is at risk. One will experience the sufferings of the three lower realms and so on.
>
> By taking what is not given, one will be poor and live in evil places stricken by frosts, hail, and famine. Of the three lower realms, one will be reborn especially in the land of the hungry spirits and so on.
>
> As a result of sexual misconduct, one will have an ugly, hostile partner. One will live in filthy places that are salty and utterly foul smelling. And one will experience the sufferings of the lower realms.

> So, thinking, "From now on, I must avoid the three nonvirtuous deeds of the body," practice with the preparation, main practice, and conclusion complete.

Here, where Longchenpa speaks of being reborn in the lower realms, he is referring to the *fully ripened effect*. Experiencing a short life and so on is the *effect similar to the cause*. Unpleasant places refer to the *conditioning* or *environmental effect*. "And so on" implies both the *effect similar to the cause*, whereby in future lives one delights in repeatedly engaging in those negative deeds, and the *proliferating effect*, which means that unless they are suppressed by antidotes, those deeds will grow more and more. It should be understood that these observations apply to all the corresponding passages cited below.

b. The four nonvirtuous deeds of speech

> Lying means to utter falsehood which,
> When understood, effects a change in someone else's mind.
> And similar to this is speaking truth in order to deceive.
> Divisive speech is saying things that bring estrangement,
> And like this is repeating others' words to create discord.
> Worthless chatter is to talk about unwholesome texts and fooleries,
> And this includes light, careless conversation
> Unrelated to the Dharma.
> Harsh speech is violent words that pierce the heart,
> And similar to this is sweet talk that brings misery to others.[80]

The actual act of lying is saying untrue words that alter other people's thinking, while the related deed is seeing that saying something true will deceive another person and then saying it. The actual act of divisive speech is repeating words that divide others, while the related deed is repeating things that one person has said to another person. The actual deed of worthless chatter is saying things that go against the Dharma—different kinds of worldly worship, poetry, and so on, and pointless conversations. The related deed is speaking in an untimely manner. The actual deed of harsh speech is saying words that others find unpleasant and that hit sensitive points, while related to it are words that, even if said pleasantly, make others unhappy.

Of these, the above mention of "poetry" refers to one of the four non-Buddhist Vedas, called Poetry or Sāmaveda. It does not refer to the poetical writings that exist nowadays in Tibet, for these were permitted by Lord Buddha, as is mentioned in a sūtra:

> In order to illuminate the Buddha's teachings, express them in the poetry of the victorious ones.

Speaking in an untimely manner is said to include such things as explaining the teachings to unsuitable recipients and to people who lack respect. The rest is easy to understand.

The results of these negative actions are as follows:

> By lying, one will be much criticized and constantly deceived. Divisive speech will result in one being surrounded by unfriendly people, and even though one helps them, they will treat one in a hostile, hateful manner. As a result of harsh speech, one will hear only unpleasant things and one will get into quarrels. Worthless chatter will lead to one's words not being respected and their being all mixed up. And it is certain that one will repeatedly fall upside down into the lower realms and experience the sufferings there. So thinking, "I must avoid those deeds," put that into practice.

c. The three nonvirtuous deeds of the mind

> Covetousness is not to tolerate the wealth of others
> And the wish to have it for oneself,
> And like this is to want another's glory: erudition and the like.
> Malice is to hate and wish harm to another;
> And similar to this is angrily refusing to give help.
> Wrong view is to believe in permanence or nihilism
> And to disbelieve the karmic law.
> Similar is every kind of false ascription and denial.[81]

Actually coveting is thinking how nice it would be if someone else's possessions were one's own; related to that is angrily thinking, "I wish it were mine," with regard to another person's learning and so on. Actual malice is the intention to harm others, while the related deed involves refusing to help and getting angry. Actual wrong view involves disparaging the karmic law of cause and effect and falling into the extremes of eternalism and nihilism; related to it are views that comprise false ascriptions and denials with regard to the true teachings, the spiritual friends who teach them, and anything else to do with the Dharma.

The results of these are as follows:

> Because of covetousness, one will not accomplish one's wishes, and things one does not wish for will befall one. As a result of malice, one will constantly be afraid, beset by numerous fears and misgivings. Because of wrong views, one will continue to have unwholesome views that deny cause and effect and follow wrong traditions like eternalism and nihilism. And one will be tormented by the sufferings of cyclic existence in the lower realms. So meditate on this, thinking, "I must avoid all these."

To sum up, the Vinaya scriptures say,

> Nonvirtue is like poison: even a little gives rise to great suffering.
> It is like a wild savage: it destroys one's accumulation of virtue.

Anyone who indulges in negative deeds will experience their harsh ripened effects, so it is important to avoid them completely, without hypocrisy. The *Sūtra of the Wise and the Foolish* declares,

> Do not take lightly small misdeeds,
> Thinking that they'll do no harm:
> Even tiny sparks of fire
> Can set alight a giant stack of hay.

And in the *Series of Lives*, we read,

> Unseeingly, they commit evil deeds:
> Like someone poisoned, how could they be happy?
> This the gods and yogins, with their pure sight,
> Can never fail to see.

2. A presentation of the actual words of Orgyen, knower of the three times

The following description of the ten nonvirtuous deeds has been taken from the *Direct Instructions of the Teacher* from the *Treasure of Nyang*, slightly abridged and rearranged.

Of the ten nonvirtuous deeds, there are, first, the three acts of the body: taking life, taking what is not given, and sexual misconduct.[82]

a. The three nonvirtuous deeds of the body

i. Taking life

Taking life is defined as discontinuing a living being's life. It can be divided into three categories, in terms of the three poisons:

- To take life out of attachment is to kill out of a desire for meat, leather, and so on.
- To take life out of hatred is to kill someone in a blood feud, for example, with one of the nine kinds of vindictive attitude.*
- To take life out of ignorance is to kill without any such intentions, as when children kill little birds or when one crushes ants underfoot as one walks.

Killing has four branches. The first is to precede the deed with the intention "I am going to do this evil deed." The second is to willingly prepare the deed and deliberately engage in it. The third, the actual act, involves the victim experiencing the deed—that is, being killed. And the fourth, the conclusion, is to feel glad about what one has done, without having any regret. These four make the act complete.

Its result occurs in three forms. The fully ripened effect of taking life with attachment is, in most cases, rebirth as a hungry spirit; that of killing with anger is rebirth in the hells; and that of taking life with ignorance is rebirth as an animal. The conditioning effect is that, on account of those previous

*The nine kinds of vindictive attitude (Tib. *mnar sems kyi gzhi dgu*) are the nine hostile feelings one may have toward someone who has harmed, is harming, or will harm oneself; or who has harmed, is harming, or will harm one's relatives and friends; or who has helped, is helping, or will help one's enemies.

wrong deeds, even if one is born as a human, one will have a short life. The effect similar to the cause is that because of one's previous propensities, one will enjoy killing.

These, therefore, are not actions that we should indulge in. On the other hand, it is said in the sūtras that if we make an effort to avoid them, the fully ripened effect, the effect similar to the cause, and the conditioning effect will be the opposite of those just mentioned, and we will enjoy the happiness and prosperity of gods and humans.

This last paragraph Guru Rinpoche also repeated in the sections below, so we should bear this in mind when reading those sections.

In the context of taking life, there are some important supplementary points that merit a little explanation. Although it is not stated in this text, other texts explain that the real "killing out of ignorance" mentioned above refers to ritual sacrifices. There are non-Buddhists who slaughter water buffalo and other animals as an offering to Mahādeva, Durgā, and other deities; and there are uncivilized people who consider the killing of animals to be a meritorious activity. Our views and philosophical tenets may be different from theirs, but nowadays, when we have animals killed even for virtuous activities such as holding Buddhist festivals and building stūpas, temples or other Dharma supports, we are engaging in exactly the same forms of conduct as they do. It is important to understand that this sort of thing is quite incompatible with the Buddhist way. As it is said,

> The Buddha strove to help the world;
> His teaching is to do no harm.
> Those who trust and follow it
> Express themselves nonviolently.
> For ages long they practice helpful deeds;
> Through this they reach enlightenment
> And, shunning violence, forever benefit others.
> They teach their followers, too, to strive to help.
> Even when his words are heard by other beings—
> Brahmins or ordained renunciates—
> They are not taken in a way that will bring harm.
> In all respects, this is the virtuous way.

And in the *Praise of the Most Noble*, we read,

Those who take the lives of beings
For shrines and sacrificial rites
Pursue the paths of worldly folk.
They show contempt for what you taught
And constantly bring harm to those that live.
Where is the true Dharma in such ways?

And,

The ṛiṣhis, it is said, are advocates
Of killing cattle as offerings and charity.
But you, who are entirely free of evil deeds,
Do not consent to doing any harm, not even to an ant.

Such practices will never be the way to please the buddhas, as the Bodhisattva Shāntideva says:

Buddhas are made happy by the joy of beings.
They sorrow, they lament when beings suffer.
By bringing joy to beings, then, I please the Buddhas also,
By wounding them, I wound the Buddhas too.
Just as there's no sensual delight
To please the mind of one whose body burns in fire,
There is no way to please the great compassionate ones
While we ourselves are causes of another's pain.[83]

Such actions could never result in benefit and happiness for either oneself or others, as is affirmed by *The Way of the Bodhisattva*:

But if, through seeking happiness, my deeds are wrong,
No matter where I turn my steps,
The knives of misery will cut me down,
The wage and retribution of a sinful life.[84]

And in the *Series of Lives*, we read,

Do no evil if you wish for happiness,
For yourself or for someone else.

> When childish beings, seeking joy, do evil deeds,
> They'll taste the fruit of each and every one.

And in the *Approach to the Ultimate*,

> In all the scriptures of the Omniscient One,
> He never spoke of freedom brought about by taking life.

Thus it is that the Protector Noble Nāgārjuna says in the advice he gave to King Surabhībhadra,

> Perform no evil, even for the sake
> Of brahmins, bhikṣhus, gods, or honored guests,
> Your father, mother, queen, or for your court.
> No share they'll take of suffering in hell.
> Although performing wrong and evil deeds
> Does not at once, like swords, create a gash,
> When death arrives, those evil acts will show,
> Their karmic fruit will clearly be revealed.[85]

In particular, if one is a teacher or monk, taking life is an even more serious fault. To begin with, it violates the precepts of the refuge, which is the foundation for all vows. This is explained in a sūtra:

> If you seek refuge in the sacred Dharma,
> Rid yourself of any wish to harm.

And there could be no more harmful deed than stopping someone from living. It is also contrary to the rules of individual liberation, for the avoidance of harming others, along with its basis, is the most important of the seven deeds to be avoided with one's body and speech. It was with this kind of fault in mind that the Buddha declared that monks should avoid eating meat other than that which is pure in three ways.* He did not even allow

*Meat that is pure in three ways is meat that is eaten without one's having any knowledge of the living animal, without one's having ordered its slaughter, and without one's specifically having had the dead animal's meat prepared for one as food. See also, Shabkar Tsogdruk Rangdrol, *Food of Bodhisattvas*, 20, 75, 128n6.

them to use grass or water in any manner that might injure sentient beings. It is for this reason that monks are required to have certain articles like water strainers.

For bodhisattvas, there are instances where it is permissible to commit the seven nonvirtuous deeds with body and speech if doing so is beneficial for others, but this does not apply to killing for meat: such conduct is not mentioned even once in any of the accounts (whether according to the Common Vehicle or the Great Vehicle) of the Buddha's life and series of past lives. The principal precept for bodhisattvas is that of cherishing others more than oneself so that one never mentally abandons sentient beings. Killing them, therefore, is a flagrant transgression of that precept.

In the mantra tradition, there is mention of such practices as union and liberation.* This concerns the conduct of accomplished beings like the masters Padmasambhava and Vimalamitra, the great Indian siddhas like Shavaripa, Tibetan masters of the secret teachings like Zurchenpa and Zurchungpa, and Bhutan's crazy yogin Kunga Lekpa, whose power was such that they could both liberate and compassionately revive beings. But we need to understand that this is not something that ordinary people can do, for it has been said that beginners should not adopt the conduct of experienced practitioners, experienced practitioners should not adopt the conduct of accomplished beings, and accomplished beings should not adopt the conduct of the omniscient ones. Indeed, the *Extensive Magical Manifestation Tantra* states,

> If those without realization attempt to act like this,
> They will be born as hungry ghosts and ogres.

We can also know this from the stories of Black Salvation and others.†

Taking life goes against the promise we make when we take the vows of the first empowerment, "Henceforth, I will never kill." And killing is

* *"Liberation"* refers to the practice by highly realized masters of liberating beings with very negative karma by killing them and transferring their consciousness to realms in which they can advance on the spiritual path.

† Black Salvation (Tib. *Thar pa nag po*) was a bodhisattva who received tantric empowerment but understood the teachings in the wrong way. After countless ages spent in the hells, he was eventually reborn as a terrible monster, the very incarnation of evil, called Rudra.

included in the transgression of the sugatas' word, which is a root downfall of the main practice.* This is why the *Vajra Pinnacle Tantra* declares,

> Until you attain stability,
> Without an atom's worth of shameful deeds,
> Abide by the three kinds of vow.

It was also with this in mind that, in the context of the feast offering, the samaya ingredients taught in India included the five fleshes (human flesh and the others)† of beings that had not been killed for consumption. Should we be unable to acquire such ingredients without committing negative actions, the *Guhyasamāja Tantra* tells us,

> Even if there is no meat and the like,
> Everything can be imagined as such.

And the *Tantra of the Union of All the Buddhas* confirms the meaning of this quotation, showing that the feast offering may be performed by imagining that dough effigies dyed with sandalwood and the like represent meat:

> Cows fashioned from dough
> And colored with red sandal,
> And meat made of wheat dough—
> These are said to be the food of kings.

Whether you do the killing yourself or you get someone to kill an animal out of sight, there will not be the slightest difference in the fully ripened effect that is produced, as the *Treasury of Abhidharma* says:

> General or troops—they're just the same:
> They all have the face of the perpetrator.

*Not to transgress the word of the sugatas is the second of the fourteen root samayas, the transgression of general and particular precepts related to the vows of individual liberation, bodhisattvas, and Mantrayāna.

†The five fleshes are the flesh of humans, and the meat of dogs, horses, cows, and elephants. In India, these animals were never killed for human consumption.

Moreover, even rejoicing at an act of killing is said to be the same as the deed itself, for it is said in the *Sūtra in Three Sections*:

> I have engaged fully in taking the path of the ten negative deeds, induced others to do so, and rejoiced at their doing so, and as a result of such karmic obscurations, I will become a being in the hells.

It is said in the *Close Mindfulness Sūtra* that if we make preparations to kill just one sentient being, the fully ripened effect that we will have to experience is one intermediate kalpa as a being in the ephemeral hells. Furthermore, beings with bad karma habitually make negative wishes, and so the dying prayers of the beings we kill may be extremely powerful. Long ago, some Shākya fishermen killed two big fish by tying them to a pole. The two fish thought to themselves, "We are both being killed now without having done anything wrong," and they made a wish: "In the future, may we likewise kill you all without your being at fault." As a result, the two big fish were subsequently reborn as King Virūḍhaka and his minister Mātropakāra, and in a single day they massacred eighty thousand members of the Shākya clan, even though those Shākyas had attained the noble path.

Then there were the thirty-two robbers who stole a cow and slaughtered it. By the power of its negative prayers, the cow, reborn as King Prasenajit, in a single day beheaded thirty-two little boys, the children of Anuradhā.

At the time when the stūpa of Jarung Khashor was being built and the Abbot, the Master, and the Dharma King* had been born as the three sons of a poultrywoman, there was an elephant being used to transport stones. As a result of its being left out of the dedication of merit, it became angry and made an evil wish. It was subsequently reborn as King Langdarma,† who disrupted all the results of the work the Abbot, Master, and Dharma King had done.

There are numerous stories like these. Since we can never be certain that

*Tib. *mkhan slob chos gsum*, referring to the Bodhisattva Abbot Shāntarakṣhita, the Master Guru Padmasambhava, and the Dharma King Trisong Detsen.

†In accordance with the elephant's wish, it was reborn as the great grandson of King Trisong Detsen, King Langdarma, who was instrumental in destroying the Dharma in Tibet. See Dowman, *Legend of the Great Stūpa*.

things will not turn out in the same sort of way, it is important to be very careful how we act.

Noble Kātyāyana was out on his alms round when he came to a village, where he saw a woman with a child on her lap. She was eating a fish and throwing stones at a bitch that was eating the bones. Using his clairvoyance to examine the situation, Kātyāyana realized that the fish had been the woman's father in this life, and the bitch had been her mother. As for the child, it had been an enemy that she had killed in a previous life. At this, Kātyāyana declared,

> She eats her father's flesh, she beats her mother off.
> She dandles on her lap the enemy that she killed;
> The wife is gnawing at her husband's bones.
> The things that happen in saṃsāra make me laugh!

We can never be sure, therefore, that the beings we are killing have not been our own deceased parents or other loved ones in this present life. What we can be certain of is that they have been our parents in previous lives, so whether we are laypeople or ordained monks and nuns, it seems we have to be extremely careful with regard to the act of taking life. These days, however, there are not many ordained persons, let alone laypeople, who count killing among even the most minor of the things that they should avoid doing. Yet this is what the Buddha said would destroy spiritual practice, as we read in the *Sūtra of Individual Liberation*:

> When those who have renounced the world and taken vows
> Do violence to others and injure them, where are their religious ways?

Related to this is the custom in some monasteries and other places of giving the monks the meat of slaughtered animals and eating meat offerings. This is a terrible state of affairs, as the *Sūtra on Entering Laṅka* points out at great length in passages such as these:

> Mahāmati, if I consider that all sentient beings are as my only child, how could I allow the listeners to eat the flesh of my children, let alone eat it myself? Mahāmati, it is wrong to say that I

have given the listeners permission to eat meat and that I myself have eaten it.

Also,

Those who slaughter animals for gain,
And those who give their money in exchange for meat—
Both of them will share the evil deed
And boil in hell, with fearful cries and calls for help.
Those who contravene the Buddha's word,
Whose mean intent leads to their eating meat,
Destroy their lives, both this and that to come.
Their practice is outside the Shākya faith.
To hells impossible to bear
Those beings who carry evil deeds will go.
In hells where beings scream with dreadful cries
Those carnivores will boil and cook.
There is no meat that is three-ways pure—
Meat that has not been earmarked,
Or been taken, or been ordered—
So please refrain from ever eating meat.

This is reaffirmed in the *Synopsis That Asserts the View of Mañjuśrī*, along with the reasons:

Those who kill to gain some wealth
And those who pay to eat the meat
Are both of them the murderers:
They'll roast in Screaming and the other hells.
If for laypeople there is no sin
In paying for the meat they buy,
Then where's the merit if they likewise pay
For building stūpas, temples, and the like?
Slaughterers who hanker after wealth
Will cook for a hundred thousand kalpas.
Those who crave the taste of meat
Will boil for ten million kalpas.
Any person who eats meat

> Will first become a hungry ghost
> And in the next life go to Screaming Hell.

First, they will be born as rākṣhasa ogres with the karma of a kind of hungry spirit and after that they will go to the Screaming Hell. Even worse, specifically ordering the butchering of animals is a hundred times more negative, with much more serious results:

> Worse than a hundred animals killed by someone else
> Is meat one has killed oneself or ordered to be killed—
> A fault one hundred times more grave.

In the same category as eating meat is the custom in some traditions of inviting members of the Saṅgha to partake of alcoholic beverages. It appears that some individuals in monastic attire even act as connoisseurs. Well they may, but by doing so, they are flaunting their real selves, proclaiming the fact that they are not followers of the Buddha, for as we read in the Vinaya texts:

> Upāsakas and those of higher orders who pretend that I am their teacher, and who do not refrain from brewing, serving, and drinking alcohol, are not my followers, and I am not their teacher.

And in other sūtras, we find,

> If one drinks alcohol in this life, one will be reborn in hell, drinking molten copper. Even if one is reborn as a human, one will be mentally disturbed for five hundred lives. If one serves alcohol to others, for five hundred lifetimes one's hands will be maimed.

Indeed, the faults are boundless, as is stated in the *Series of Lives*:

> Beings who partake of it will follow evil ways
> And fall into the hells, where fear and terror reign.
> They'll be reborn as animals or, destitute, among the hungry ghosts.
> What being is there who wishes to see that?
> The ripened fruit of just a little drink

Is, even if one gains a human birth,
Degeneration of one's discipline and view.
And one way or another, one will burn
In Torment Unsurpassed, within its blazing fires,
Or dwell in hungry spirits' lands, or lowly beasts' abodes.
One's discipline will fail and evil talk will abound,
One's sense of shame will disappear,
One's intelligence will be obscured.

Besides this, there is not the slightest difference between people like businesspeople, who make profits dishonestly, and most present-day practitioners, who call themselves monks and go around saying that they can see deities, that they can see ghosts, when in fact they are not above stealing, sexual misconduct, lying, and the rest, and are thus destroying the precepts and vows. It is extremely important to be aware of this and to guard ourselves with mindfulness, vigilance, and carefulness.

Having explained these few supplementary, but related, points, let us now return to the main text containing Guru Padmasambhava's adamantine words, with the second of the negative acts of the body—taking what is not given.

ii. Taking what is not given

The definition of taking what is not given is to appropriate someone else's property.

It is divided into the following categories:

- taking things by force—that is, direct robbery
- stealing things by stealth, unnoticed
- taking things by trickery, by such means as falsifying weights and measures

For these deeds to be complete, all four branches have to be present, as indicated in the previous section.

There are three kinds of result. The fully ripened effect depends on the gravity of the deed (great, middling, or small). It leads to one's falling into one of the three lower realms, and, in particular, to rebirth as a hungry spirit. The conditioning effect is that even if one should be reborn as a human, one will have few possessions and will be repeatedly robbed and deprived of what one has. The effect similar to the cause is that because of the evil habitual tendencies in one's ground consciousness, in all one's lives one will also take pleasure in taking what is not given.

iii. Sexual misconduct

Sexual misconduct is defined as having sexual relations with someone whom one desires but who is not free to do so.

Such persons fall into the following categories:

- those protected by the authorities—for example, the king's consort, with whom it is improper for a subject to have sexual relations, and those with whom sexual relations are forbidden by law
- those protected by parents—that is, those in traditional societies who are forbidden to have casual sexual relations because they are under the guardianship of their parents until they are married*
- those protected by conventional taboos—that is, those with whom it would be shameful to have sexual relations, such as one's mother or sister
- those protected by religious convention—for example, the master's consort or someone who holds the vows of monastic discipline

There are also instances when it is improper to have sexual relations even with one's own partner:

- at improper times—for example, on the eighth of the lunar month, full moon, and new moon
- in an improper place—for example, in the presence of representations of the Three Jewels
- in improper ways—for example, with unsuitable parts of the body or in the manner of animals

For sexual misconduct to be complete, all four branches must be present, similar to those described above.

The result is again of three kinds. The fully ripened effect is rebirth in

*Although the Tibetan text specifies that this applies to persons in India, it refers to those in any country or community in which there is a tradition of arranged marriages and a taboo on premarital sex.

the three lower realms. Even if one should attain the higher realms, one will be prone to marital conflicts and so on. The conditioning effect is that in all one's lives one's partner will be lacking in affection and do all sorts of things to upset one. The result similar to the cause is that on account of one's unwholesome desires, one will delight in sexual misconduct.

b. The four nonvirtuous deeds of speech

i. Telling lies

Telling lies is defined as verbally stating that something is not as it is in reality.

Lying is divided into the following categories:

- telling lies that are to no one's advantage or disadvantage—for example, the lies an old person might tell
- telling lies that are to one person's advantage and to another person's disadvantage
- telling lies about one's qualities—for example, a phony teacher who falsely claims to have clairvoyance

For lying to be complete, all four branches must be present, as described earlier.

Of the three kinds of result, the fully ripened effect is that one will fall into the three lower realms. The conditioning effect is that even if one is reborn as a human being, the things one says will carry no weight. The effect similar to the cause is that in all one's lives one will enjoy telling lies.

ii. Divisive speech

Divisive speech, or sowing discord, is defined as speech that divides others who are friendly with each other.

It comprises the following categories:

- sowing discord forcefully, by creating a conflict between the two parties in their presence
- sowing discord sneakily, by making hints
- sowing discord secretly—that is, saying things about the other person to each party privately

The branches are as previously mentioned.

Of the three kinds of result, the fully ripened effect is that one will fall into the three lower realms. The conditioning effect is that even if one is reborn as a human being, one will have few friends and many enemies, one will always have numerous disputes of different kinds, one will never be appreciated by people, and everything one says will be ineffectual. The effect similar to the cause is that in all one's lives one will take pleasure in sowing discord.

iii. Worthless chatter

Worthless chatter is defined as talk that wastes time.

It is divided into the following categories:

- making political speeches
- telling fanciful stories
- engaging in irrelevant chatter

It is completed by four branches, as mentioned earlier.

Of the three kinds of result, the fully ripened effect is rebirth in the three lower realms. The conditioning effect is that even if one is reborn as a human being, one's words will never be respected, one will be subject to criticism, and all one says will be irrelevant. The effect similar to the cause is that in all one's lives one will take pleasure in joking and gossiping.

iv. Harsh speech

Harsh speech is defined as speech that hurts someone else's feelings.

It is divided into the following categories:

- exposing someone's faults directly
- hurting someone's feelings indirectly
- hurting someone's feelings secretly

It is completed by four branches.

Of the three kinds of result, the fully ripened effect is rebirth in the three lower realms. The conditioning effect is that even if one is reborn as a human being, whatever one says, one will manage to hurt others' feelings and one will always have one's own feelings hurt. The effect similar to the cause is that in all one's lives one will delight in speaking harshly.

c. The three nonvirtuous deeds of the mind

i. Covetousness

Covetousness is defined as attachment to fortune.

It is divided into the following categories:

- an inability to give others what one has oneself
- a desire to make what others have one's own
- attachment to fortune that belongs to neither oneself nor others (NOTE: for example, treasure under the earth that has no owner)

It is completed by four branches. (NOTE: Although, for the three mental deeds, the last three of the basis, intention, application, and completion are essentially the same, I think they are probably categorized as four simply for the sake of distinguishing different aspects.)

The fully ripened effect is rebirth in the three lower realms. The conditioning effect is that even if one is reborn as a human being, one will always find oneself in unpleasant surroundings, afflicted by hunger and thirst. The effect similar to the cause is that in all one's lives one will tend to covet things.

ii. Malice

Malice is defined as having evil thoughts concerning others.

It is divided into the following categories:

- malice arising out of hatred
- malice arising out of resentment
- malice arising out of jealousy

It is completed by four branches.

The fully ripened effect is rebirth in the three lower realms. The conditioning effect is that even if one is reborn as a human being, one will be subject to other people's aggressive attitudes even though one is not at fault and one will always have many enemies and legal disputes. The effect similar to the cause is that one will have a propensity for malice.

iii. Wrong views

Wrong views are defined as those that are mistaken and err from the truth.

They are divided into the following categories:

- views that add to or subtract from reality
- the views of eternalism and nihilism, like those of the tīrthikas
- views of ethical superiority, such as those related to ascetic practices in which one acts like a dog or an ox
- the view of the transitory composite*

They are completed by four branches.

The fully ripened effect is rebirth in the three lower realms. The conditioning effect is that even if one is reborn as a human being, one will take birth in places such as the border regions and the lands of barbarians where not even the words *Three Jewels* are ever heard. The effect similar to the cause is that the habitual tendency to wrong views will become firmly imprinted in one's ground consciousness and one will be attracted to wrong views.

These ten nonvirtuous deeds are condemned by noble beings. They are rejected by the wise. For gods and humans who have obtained the extraordinary freedoms and advantages, they constitute unwholesome conduct. You must therefore avoid them.

The negative consequences of these ten nonvirtuous deeds differ in magnitude as follows: as a general rule, when they are classified in terms of the defilements, any of the ten nonvirtuous deeds perpetrated with anger lead to rebirth in the hells, those perpetrated with desire, or attachment, give rebirth among the hungry spirits, and those perpetrated with ignorance give rebirth as an animal.

The magnitude of the negative consequences is also determined by the object of the nonvirtuous deed. Any of the ten nonvirtuous deeds performed with regard to special objects† will lead to rebirth in the hells. Those performed with regard to ordinary objects will give rebirth as a hungry spirit. And those performed with regard to lowly objects result in rebirth as an animal.

The negative consequences are also determined by the frequency with which the nonvirtuous deed is performed. If one does it many times, one will be reborn in the hells; if one does it a few times, one will be reborn in the hungry spirit realm; and if one does it just once, one will be reborn in the animal realm. (NOTE: this has been quoted from another text.)

*The view of the transitory composite, see glossary, s.v. "transitory composite."

†Special objects refers to spiritual teachers, parents, and so on.

There are also specific differences. Of the different kinds of taking life, the greatest evil, with the worst fully ripened effect, is to kill a bodhisattva who has aroused bodhichitta. The worst form of taking what is not given is to steal the property of the Three Jewels. The most negative form of sexual misconduct is to have sexual relations with an arhat of the opposite sex.* The most negative form of lying is to deceive one's teacher and the Saṅgha—that is, those who are worthy of veneration. The worst kind of divisive speech is that which divides the Saṅgha. The harshest form of speech is to say unpleasant things to a member of the Saṅgha. The most negative kind of worthless chatter is that which disturbs the mind of a monk who is in concentration, meditating on nonduality. The worst kind of covetousness is coveting the property of the Three Jewels. The most evil form of malice is to prepare to commit one of the five crimes with immediate retribution. The most negative kind of wrong view is to negate the correct view. All these are to be avoided even if one's life is at stake.

Another difference between the ten nonvirtuous deeds is that, on the whole, taking life, divisive speech, harsh speech, and malice result in rebirth in the hells. Sexual misconduct, taking what is not given, and covetousness lead to rebirth as a hungry spirit. Lying, worthless chatter, and wrong view lead to rebirth as an animal.

B. The ten virtuous deeds to be adopted

The teaching on the nature of the ten virtuous deeds to be adopted again has two parts: (1) as described in *Finding Rest in the Nature of the Mind*, and (2) as presented in the adamantine words of Guru Rinpoche.

1. A synopsis according to the Great Omniscient One's *Finding Rest in the Nature of the Mind*

The root text lists them as follows:

> The ten good actions that propel one to the higher realms
> Consist in virtuously and consciously

*Although the Tibetan specifies a female arhat (*dgra bcom ma*), this holds true for an arhat of either sex.

Abandoning the ten nonvirtues.
Reject all killing, stealing, sexual misconduct;
Avoid all lying and divisive calumny;
Do not indulge in idle chatter, harsh words, covetousness;
And throw far away from you ill will and wrong views.[86]

It may happen that one is not committing any of the ten nonvirtuous deeds, but this on its own does not constitute performing any of the ten virtuous deeds unless mental restraint is involved. It is the conscious intent to avoid the ten nonvirtuous deeds that defines the ten virtuous deeds. The *Middle Sūtra of the Perfection of Wisdom* devotes a line each to these, beginning:

I, too, have abandoned the taking of life.

The simple fact of stopping nonvirtuous deeds such as taking life prevents one from being tainted by their fully ripened effects, but if one's mind is not restrained, there will be no increase in one's merit and one's actions will not genuinely be one of the ten virtuous deeds. It is extremely important, therefore, to restrain your mind stream by making a promise in the presence of a special person or support. In the *Analysis of Actions*, written by Jowo Atisha, we read,

That which makes one attain the higher realms,
The state of gods and humans,
Is the discipline of restraint.

In brief, the essence of the ten virtuous deeds is that they are rooted in the intention to avoid the above-mentioned ten nonvirtuous deeds and acts related to them, and this is, in fact, the essence of the discipline of avoiding evil. This is reiterated in *The Way of the Bodhisattva*:

Deciding to refrain from every harmful act
Is said to complete transcendent discipline.[87]

Of the four kinds of results of the ten virtuous deeds, *Finding Rest in the Nature of the Mind* describes the fully ripened effects as follows:

These actions, when of less intensity, result in human birth.
When of moderate strength, in birth among desire-realm gods.
Actions of a great intensity are linked with the samādhis
And the formless concentrations. They bring attainment
Of the bliss of the two higher worlds.
Virtuous actions have likewise their four effects,
And by examples contrary to those just now supplied,
You will realize that the fruits of the ten virtues
Are the higher realms.[88]

By performing small and middling virtuous deeds, one will be reborn as a human being or a god in the world of desire. Great deeds related to concentration result in rebirth in the two higher worlds. This accomplishment of the higher realms and the closing of the door to the lower realms is mentioned in the *Jewel Garland*:

Through these practices, one is liberated
From the hells and the hungry spirit and animal realms.
One will obtain abundant happiness, glory, and dominion
Among gods and human beings.
Concentrations, boundless attitudes, and formless meditations
Will lead one to experience the bliss of Brahmā and others.[89]

Virtuous deeds, if imbued with partial means and wisdom or the unsurpassable means and wisdom, will act as causal factors for any of the three kinds of enlightenment and yield their respective results.

The effect similar to the cause is described in the root text[90] as follows:

The consequence resembling the cause
Is, actively, a natural proclivity to virtue;
Passively, it is enjoyment of long life and vast possessions
And a loyal, harmonious spouse.
One is not scorned, and friends return one's love;
One's words are trusted, pleasant to the ears of everyone.
One is contented, loving, and has wholesome views.

The effect similar to the cause is thus twofold. As actions similar to the cause, wherever one is reborn throughout one's series of lives, one will naturally and enthusiastically engage in the ten virtuous deeds. The experiences similar to the cause are as follows: Because one has refrained from taking life, one will have a long life, free of illness. Refraining from taking what is not given will result in one's having abundant wealth. Refraining from sexual misconduct will result in one's having a spouse who is easy to get on with, good-looking, and loyal. As a result of one's having refrained from telling lies, everyone will praise one and make one happy. Because of refraining from divisive speech, one's companions and helpers will be cooperative and show one the greatest respect. Avoiding harsh speech will result in one's hearing pleasant things and being praised. As a result of avoiding worthless chatter, what one says will be worth retaining and recognized as valid. Refraining from covetousness will result in one's hopes being realized. Because of refraining from harmful intent, one will be free from danger. Abandoning wrong views will result in one's having the right views.

The conditioning effect is described in the same text as follows:

> The conditioning effect of virtue
> Is to be born in perfect circumstances,
> Prosperous and wonderful.
> Food and drink and medicine
> Are easy to digest and great in healing strength.
> One's habitat is unpolluted, and its herbs are sweetly fragrant.
> It is free from danger and from harm,
> And one is not deceived by others.
> It is a sweet environment, where pleasant people live,
> Where harvests ripen in due season with abundant fruit.
> It is a smooth terrain adorned by meres and cooling lakes,
> Where flowers and fruits are perfect and abundant.
> It is a region where great increase in prosperity is seen,
> Where things like grains and medicines
> Are supreme in their taste and quantity,
> Their sources excellent and plentiful,
> A place secure and safe on every side.[91]

Thus, by refraining from taking life, one will be reborn in a pleasant, delightful place. By refraining from taking what is not given, one will be born in a place where the food and drink is tasty and easy to digest, and the medicines efficacious. By refraining from sexual misconduct, one will be born in a clean place where the medicinal plants and trees are fragrant with the smell of incense. By refraining from telling lies, in whichever land one is reborn, there will be no harm or danger from enemies, robbers, and the like; no one will cheat one. By refraining from divisive speech, one will be born in a land where people everywhere get on well together and the earth is relatively free of stones, pebbles, and thorns. The result of refraining from harsh speech is that one will be reborn in a place where the seasons are not inverted and the flowers and fruits ripen on time. The result of refraining from worthless chatter is rebirth in a flat, level place adorned with lakes and ponds. Refraining from covetousness will result in birth in places where one sees good flowers, fruits, and crops growing. Refraining from harmful intent will result in birth in leafy places with many trees bearing delicious fruits. The result of abandoning wrong views is birth in a place that is a rich source of grains, precious stones, and so forth, and where protectors and helpers are abundant. All this is indicated in a sūtra that teaches the ten virtuous deeds.[92]

The proliferating effect is that unless one meets with conditions that destroy it, such virtue grows more and more, becoming infinite, as the same text shows:

> Through the proliferating consequence,
> Virtue is productive of yet further virtue.
> Every good desire comes to fulfillment.[93]

The *Sūtra of the Wise and the Foolish* sums up,

> Do not take lightly small good deeds,
> Believing they can hardly help:
> For drops of water gathered one by one
> In time will fill a giant pot.

We need to be diligent, therefore, in doing whatever we can to engage in even the smallest virtuous deeds. Moreover, it is very important to transform them into sources of good conducive to liberation. Whatever positive acts we perform, we should do so with the thought that they are for gaining liberation from cyclic existence and attaining the peace of nirvāṇa. Although there are three kinds of liberation, those of the listeners, solitary realizers, and perfect buddhas, in the present case, we should be aiming to attain perfect buddhahood. We must therefore be diligent in practicing the ten virtuous deeds, the four concentrations, the four formless absorptions, sustained calm and profound insight, the four boundless attitudes, the six transcendent perfections, and so on. All these should be backed by the three supreme methods—the preparation of arousing bodhichitta for the sake of others, the main practice free of the concepts of clinging to true existence, and the conclusion of dedicating the merit to enlightenment. We should accomplish these without relaxing for a single moment, for without completing the accumulations of merit and wisdom we will never attain buddhahood. With this in mind, we should practice with the preparation, main practice, and conclusion complete. In the above-mentioned text, we read,

> The full accumulation of merit and wisdom
> Is the gateway, true freedom is its result.
> It could never be otherwise, so practice virtuous deeds
> To make the cloud of purity appear with its refreshing rain.

2. A presentation in the adamantine words of Guru Rinpoche

The following description of the ten virtuous deeds is taken mainly from the section describing the discipline of gathering virtue* in the *Direct Instructions*. There they are presented in positive terms.†

For the ten virtuous deeds, there are four topics.

a. Definition

Virtuous deeds are physical, verbal, and mental acts that enable us to accomplish higher states.

*One of the three categories of the transcendent perfection of discipline, see p. 348 below. This section is in fact based on the part of the *Direct Instructions* that deals with the precepts of bodhichitta in application.

†In contrast to the above presentation in *Finding Rest in the Nature of the Mind*, in which the ten virtuous deeds are defined in terms of what they are not (not killing, not stealing, and so on), here they are established explicitly in terms of their being virtuous (saving lives, being charitable, and so forth).

b. Etymological definition

Virtuous deeds are so called because if someone who has obtained the freedoms and advantages engages in them properly, they yield desirable results.

c. Categories

As the opposites of the ten nonvirtuous deeds, the ten virtuous deeds consist of saving lives, giving generously on a vast scale, observing pure conduct,* telling the truth, settling disputes, saying things in a peaceful, restrained manner, speaking sincerely, acting lovingly toward sentient beings, acting without attachment, and being free of doubts with regard to the karmic law of cause and effect and to the true reality.

There are ten accessory factors that enable one to maintain these virtuous deeds in one's stream of being: faith in the true Dharma, keeping a sense of shame and a sense of decency, desisting from gambling and quarreling, avoiding public gatherings and spectacles, always conducting oneself carefully, not being lazy, avoiding the company of friends devoted to evil, thoroughly training one's body, speech, and mind, and meditation on the four perception spheres that focus on attentiveness to extraordinary qualities.

d. Results

The fully ripened effect is rebirth as a god or human being, possessed of a melodious voice like Brahmā's, a beautiful form like Indra's, and wealth like that of a universal monarch.

The conditioning effect is that one will have learning and wisdom, one will meet with the teachings of the buddhas, and one will finally attain the result of the three kinds of enlightenment.

The effect similar to the cause is that in all one's lives one will refrain from nonvirtuous deeds and be diligent in performing virtue.

III. Additional teachings on distinctions and categories

Although there are many expositions of these in the Abhidharma and other texts, here we shall explain their explicit presentation in the text of Pad-

*In practice, "pure conduct" (Tib. *tshangs par spyod pa*) implies chastity or celibacy.

masambhava's *Great Treatise on the Graded Path*, for which there are two sections: (1) distinctions, and (2) different kinds of deeds. The first of these he taught in seven sections.

A. Distinctions

1. The distinction between virtue and nonvirtue in terms of their object

> True virtue is the uncompounded actual mode of things,
> True nonvirtue is the compounded phenomena of cyclic existence.

The great uncompounded absolute space—nondual, profound and radiant, the ultimate mode of being of all phenomena—is, by nature, the highest bliss, for all suffering has been completely extinguished. It is the domain of the personally realized gnosis of noble beings. It is the source of the teachings of the buddhas, which are as numerous as the grains of sand in the Ganges River. All other sources of good are the substantial causes, or means, for realizing it. For these reasons, it is the ultimate virtue. The *Sūtra on Entering Laṅka* declares,

> The virtue that is the essence of the Tathāgata
> Is not the domain of intellectuals.

And,

> The radiant nature of the mind,
> The virtue that is the essence of the Tathāgata.

And the great master Noble Asaṅga says,

> What is ultimate virtue? It is suchness.

All the compounded phenomena of cyclic existence are, by nature, full of faults; they are the roots that give rise to the vessel and support of all suffering. For these reasons, they are nonvirtue.

2. Distinction in terms of the subject

> By nature, awareness-gnosis is virtue,
> By nature, the five poisonous defilements are nonvirtue.

The awareness-gnosis that is realized individually is the perfect gnosis of someone who is in meditation in a state of awareness of the unmistaken meaning of the true mode of being. Its essence is freedom from the three poisons, so it is virtue. Defilements are the supports for the tainted thoughts arising from improper use of the mind. They are the roots that give rise to all nonvirtue. They are, therefore, nonvirtue.

3. Distinction in terms of acting as the direct antidote to, and direct cause of, existence

> The empty, ultimate reality is innately virtuous,
> Ignorance is innately nonvirtuous.

Emptiness is the true nature, or true way of being, of all phenomena. Realizing that and getting used to that realization acts as the antidote to all the compounded phenomena that constitute cyclic existence and is, therefore, virtue. Ignorance is the root of existence, the ground of the whole origin of suffering, and so it is nonvirtue.

4. Distinction in terms of obscuration and nonobscuration of the way things are and of compatibility and incompatibility with the way things appear

> Genuine virtue is beyond the intellect,
> Genuine nonvirtue is that which is tainted by the mind.

The ultimate transcends objects of clinging that have attributes that can be expressed or conceived, so it is outside the domain of the dualistic mind.* By its very nature, it is devoid of nonvirtuous phenomena, and so it is virtue. The relative, related to the elaboration of dualistic appearance, is an adventi-

*Tib. *gzung 'dzin gyi blo*, the mind that perceives an apprehending subject and an apprehended object.

tious contamination that obscures the truth, and it is, therefore, nonvirtue. This is stated in *The Way of the Bodhisattva*:

> The ultimate is not within the reach of intellect,
> For intellect is said to be the relative.[94]

5. Distinction in terms of the presence or absence of samsaric, conceptual elaboration

> The absence of conceptual thoughts is nirvāṇa—virtue,
> The presence of conceptual thoughts is saṃsāra—nonvirtue.

In *Distinguishing the Two Truths*, it is said,

> Mind and mental factors, the three worlds,
> Are thoughts taking the form of misconceptions.

Absence of thoughts, where all concepts—that is, the mind and mental factors related to the three worlds—are stilled, is virtue, for as Lord Buddha has said, "Not to use the mind at all is to remember the Buddha, to remember the Dharma, to remember the Saṅgha." The elaboration of concepts, of the mind and mental factors, is the compounding of cyclic existence itself, so it is nonvirtue. The Master Dignāga states,

> Apart from conceptual thoughts
> There is nothing at all one can call "saṃsāra."
> Having freed yourself of conceptual thoughts,
> You have attained perfect nirvāṇa.

6. Distinction in terms of the fully ripened effect

> Virtue slightly mixed with the three poisons gives rise to the three higher realms,
> Nonvirtuous deeds motivated by the three poisons give rise to the three lower realms.

Tainted virtuous deeds performed without any realization of the meaning of no-self and associated with the ignorance of belief in a self propel one to the higher realms. Nonvirtuous deeds produced with negative motivations, which are the manifestations of the three poisons, propel one to the lower realms.

Here, a direct distinction is made between tainted virtuous deeds conducive to merit and nonvirtuous deeds, from the point of view of how the fully ripened effect is produced, as described in detail above.

7. Distinction in terms of the degree of skillful means and wisdom

> Virtue with means and wisdom gives the nondwelling nirvāṇa,
> Virtue with some means or wisdom gives partial nirvāṇa.

As explained above, virtuous deeds imbued with unsurpassable skillful means and wisdom bring about perfect enlightenment. Virtuous deeds partially imbued with skillful means and wisdom enable one to attain a partial nirvāṇa, the result of the listeners and solitary realizers.

In this case, the distinction is made between two degrees of virtue conducive to liberation—that is, between sources of good that are imbued with skillful means and wisdom to a vast degree and those that are so imbued to a lesser degree.

B. Categories of deeds

There are five headings.

1. A general exposition of the different kinds of deeds

> There are three categories: wholly positive deeds, wholly negative deeds, and deeds that are mixed.

Virtuous deeds where the act and the fully ripened effect are both entirely positive create the experience of bliss in the higher worlds, depending on the level of concentration. Those that are wholly negative are nonvirtuous deeds that give rise exclusively to suffering in the world of desire. Mixed deeds are those that create alternating experiences of happiness and suffering for those who have a body in the world of desire. It is not that these different deeds are in themselves positive, negative, or mixed, but they are presented like this in terms of the manner, or process, by which, given the many sorts of deeds there are, their fully ripened effect is experienced.

In addition to these, the Abhidharma mentions a fourth category, untainted deeds, which bring an end to all these tainted positive and negative deeds.

2. Deeds that differ according to their intention and application

> There are deeds that are positive in their intention but negative in their application, deeds that are negative in their intention but positive in their application, deeds that are positive both in their intention and their application, and deeds that are negative both in their intention and their application.

Deeds that are positive in their intention but negative in their application are like that of the captain Compassionate Heart when he killed Black Spearman.* An example of a deed that is negative in its intention but positive in its application is throwing a party for someone in order to kill them. Deeds that are positive both in their intention and their application include protecting the lives of others in order to attain buddhahood. An example of a deed that is negative in both intention and application is hatefully stabbing someone to death.

This shows how deeds become virtuous or evil mainly on account of their principal, causal motivation or intention.

3. Differences from the point of view of the way in which the effects are experienced

> There are deeds that have results in this life, deeds whose results are experienced in the next life, and deeds whose results are experienced in subsequent lives.

Deeds whose results are experienced in this life refer to certain deeds of

*Compassionate Heart performed the negative deed of killing Black Spearman, but with the positive intention of preventing him from killing five hundred bodhisattvas and thus of saving their lives and sparing Black Spearman the fate of innumerable kalpas in the hells. See Patrul Rinpoche, *Words of My Perfect Teacher*, 125.

great karmic force, motivated by powerful intentions and aimed at particularly important objects such as the Three Jewels or one's parents. Their results are not to be expected in the next life or subsequent lives but ripen on the very body that one has in this present life.

Deeds whose results are experienced once one has been reborn are "next-life" deeds that ripen only on the body one will have in the next life, without any intervening rebirths after this life.

Deeds that are experienced in subsequent lives are those that are certain to ripen on the body that one will have three rebirths from now.

In addition to these, there is also said to be a fourth category, consisting of certain deeds whose seeds are suppressed and rendered impotent by powerful antidotes. These are not certain to be experienced.

These four are presented in terms of the relative power of the deeds.

4. Differences from the point of view of the way in which the effects are produced

> There are positive deeds with positive effects, negative deeds with negative effects, positive deeds with negative effects, and negative deeds with positive effects.

These are explained in a note in Padmasambhava's text. An example of a positive deed leading to a positive effect is the performance of virtue resulting in rebirth in the higher realms. An example of a negative deed with a negative effect is the performance of a negative action resulting in rebirth in the lower realms. An example of a positive deed with a negative effect is one that gives rebirth as a human being with much suffering. And an example of a negative deed resulting in a positive effect is shown in the case of the celestial elephant Rabten.

In this case, the different deeds are distinguished by the way in which they produce fully ripened effects and effects similar to the cause.*

*A human being with much suffering is experiencing the fully ripened effect of a positive deed and the effect similar to the cause of a negative deed. The celestial elephant is experiencing the fully ripened effect of a negative deed (resulting in birth as an animal) and the effect similar to the cause of a positive deed (resulting in the marvelous conditions in which it finds itself).

5. Differences from the point of view of the classification of deeds as propelling and completing

> There are positive propelling actions with positive completing actions; positive propelling actions with negative completing actions; negative propelling actions with negative completing actions; and negative propelling actions with positive completing actions.

Examples of both propelling and completing actions being positive are those that result in human rebirth as a universal monarch or in celestial rebirth as Indra.*

A positive propelling action propels one to the higher realms, but as a result of a negative completing action, one may be reborn as a human who is always sick or as a god who is afflicted by poverty.

When both the propelling action and the completing action are negative, the result is rebirth in the lower realms with very intense suffering—as is the case for beings in the Hell of Torment Unsurpassed or those born as gangrenous *kaṭapūtanas*.†

A negative propelling action propels one to the lower realms, but because of a positive completing action, one may be reborn, for example, as a wealthy nāga or as a hungry spirit with magical powers.

In this regard, it is said that there are deeds that act as both propelling and completing actions and deeds that can act as one or the other. Moreover, for both propelling and completing actions, there are four possibilities: one action giving rise to several existences, several actions giving rise to several existences, several actions giving rise to one existence, and one action propelling a single existence.

You can learn more about the different aspects of karma from accounts in a variety of sūtras (the *Sūtra of the Wise and the Foolish*, the *Hundred Parables on Action*, the *Sūtra on the Classification of Acts*, and others). Stories that inspire confidence in the karmic law of cause and effect can be found in such

*The propelling action results in birth as a human or a god, on top of which the completing action results in the highest possible form of rebirth in those states, as a universal monarch or Indra, respectively.

†Kaṭapūtanas are a kind of hungry spirit with a rotting body.

treatises as my own compilation *Stairway on the Path to Perfect Liberation*. You should also read or listen to the detailed accounts in the sūtras.

To sum up, Ashvaghoṣha says,

> Evil deeds result in suffering,
> Merit will ripen as happiness,
> Mixed deeds give mixed results.
> Such is the reasoning—examine it well.

And in the *Sūtra of the Questions of Suratā*, we read,

> Hot seeds will ripen as hot fruits,
> Sweet seeds will produce sweet fruits.
> From these analogies, the wise will know
> That evil ripens as heat, white deeds' fruit is sweet.
> Always refrain from evil deeds with body, speech, or mind,
> And if others do them, the wise should not rejoice.
> Always have good thoughts and words and deeds,
> And rejoice as well at those who practice good.

The Great Orgyen says,

> The deeds that you have done will not ripen on others. The deeds that others have done will not ripen on you. You will not meet with deeds you have not done. Your deeds will not go to waste. Without confusing black and white deeds, even the most trifling, abandon the former and adopt the latter.

If we wish to do the best for ourselves, it is very important to follow this advice and to apply ourselves to the practice of adoption and avoidance.

IV. Reflecting on how everything is determined by deeds

In the Omniscient Teacher's *Essential Instructions*, he writes,

> Thus, the whole of the happiness and suffering of cyclic existence and its higher and lower realms is created by one's own positive and negative deeds. The three kinds of enlightenment

> and all their happiness and excellence, too, are produced by the particular deeds conducive to each kind of liberation. Karma is like an artist: a single deed can be transformed into many different things. Our deeds follow us like the shadow cast by our body. Our own deeds cannot be transferred to someone else, and others' deeds cannot be transferred to us; this is why different individuals can be happy or miserable. Intensely powerful deeds propel us to the higher and lower realms, as if at the command of a great and mighty king. The reach of karma is as vast as space, and its many different forms are as varied as the different wares in a market. Yet they are perfectly distinct, like the patterns on a brocade. The essential nature of our deeds, whether white or black, never changes, like the colors of the *utpala* and the *kumuta*.* Whatever deeds we have accumulated will each yield the corresponding result. So think, "Knowing that everything is karma, I must be diligent in adoption and avoidance," and practice with the preparation, main practice, and conclusion complete.

In this regard, all these impure, dependent phenomena of cyclic existence, which comprise the aggregates, constituents, and senses-and-fields, are nothing but the appearance aspects of interdependence, arising from their causes—tainted deeds and the defilements. This is stated in the *Hundred Parables on Action*:

> The joys and sorrows of beings
> All come from their deeds, the Buddha said.
> The diversity of deeds
> Creates the diversity of beings
> And impels their diverse wanderings.
> Vast indeed is this net of deeds!

The pure, dependent phenomena of nirvāṇa too, the whole of the buddha bodies and wisdoms, are simply illusion-like dependent arising. They are the natural expression of the consummation of the two accumulations, as is stated in the *Jewel Garland*:

*The utpala lotus is blue, and the kumuta (a sort of water lily) is white.

Stated briefly, the form body
Arises from the accumulation of merit.
Stated briefly, the absolute body,
O King, is born from the accumulation of wisdom.[95]

And the *Sūtra of the Ornament of the Light of Gnosis* states,

The Tathāgata is the natural reflection
Of untainted virtue,
And in it there is neither thusness nor gone-to-thusness.
It appears everywhere, reflected in all the world.

Thus all the phenomena in appearance and existence, in saṃsāra and nirvāṇa, constitute the very nature of dependent arising. They do not stand up to analysis. Unexamined, they simply manifest as they are. This is explained in *Finding Rest in the Nature of the Mind*:

Actions, when examined, are without intrinsic being.
Yet they make, as in a dream, all kinds of joy and sorrow.
They are not real existing things, although the mind believes them so.
And yet the causal process is infallible.
Such is the deep nature of arising through dependence.
Not existent, yet not inexistent, neither is it both.
Howsoever is the deed so will its fruition be.
This is the domain of the two wisdoms,
Which behold the nature and the multiplicity of things.
It has been well expounded by the Omniscient.[96]

And in the *Root Stanzas on the Middle Way*,

Because there's nothing that is not comprised
In dependent arising,
There is nothing
That is not emptiness.[97]

Although karma does not exist on the level of the ultimate nature, here, in the dreamlike state that is the relative level, there are the delusions of the dualistic belief in a subject and an object. As long as these have not been purified in the absolute space, actions and the results of actions will never go to waste. It is impossible that the karmic process will ever fail. The *Hundred Parables on Action* makes this clear:

> Even after a hundred kalpas,
> Beings' deeds will never go to waste.
> When the time and conditions are right,
> Each will ripen with its own result.

And the *Close Mindfulness Sūtra* says,

> Fire might one day turn to icy cold,
> The wind might just be captured in a noose,
> The sun and moon might one day fall to earth,
> But never could our deeds once fail to yield their fruit.

And the *Heap of Jewels*,

> Whatever the way a deed is done,
> In that same way will it mature.
> Not even in a billion kalpas
> Will it ever show the slightest change.

Furthermore, even if the cause is small at the time it is accumulated, it will increase in size and ripen as great happiness or suffering at the time the result is experienced. It is very important, therefore, to avoid and adopt even the most trifling deeds, as is stated in the Vinaya texts:

> Do not take lightly small misdeeds,
> Thinking that they'll do no harm:
> Even tiny sparks of fire
> Can set alight a giant stack of hay.
> Do not take lightly small good deeds,
> Believing they can hardly help:
> For drops of water gathered one by one
> In time will fill a giant pot.

This manner of teaching is unique to the Omniscient One: it is an extraordinary and marvelous truth that is not present in other, non-Buddhist traditions, as Bhavya's *Precious Lamp of the Middle Way* affirms:

> No other treatises explain
> What you, the Bhagavan, have taught—
> That dreamlike deeds will never fail:
> Cause inevitably leads to fruit.

And in the *Commentary on Bodhichitta*, we read,

> To know the emptiness of things,
> And to rely on virtue, cause, and fruit—
> How much more wonderful this is than wonderful,
> How much more marvelous than marvelous![98]

If we truly realize the profound ways of dependent arising, we will attain the level of enlightenment—liberation in the nirvāṇa that does not dwell in either of the two extremes. The *Jewel Garland* says,

> Those who believe in nonexistence go to lower realms,
> Those who believe in existence go to higher realms.
> One who fully knows the truth just as it is
> Will thus rely on neither of the two and hence be freed.[99]

In short, we find in the *Sūtra of the Prophecy for the Magician Bhadra*,

> Illusory are the stores that one collects,
> Illusory the buddhahood attained,
> Illusory the beings that are helped,
> Illusory the deeds done for their good.

Accordingly, it is from the knowledge that all phenomena are like magical illusions or dreams—appearing, yet devoid of intrinsic nature—that one gathers the two accumulations in an illusory manner and thereby attains the result, the two illusion-like buddha bodies. Subsequently, one fulfills the benefit of illusion-like sentient beings on a vast scale. This is the profound natural process of the dependent arising of pure causes and effects, which constitute the unsurpassable tradition of the Great Vehicle.

Even if we have not realized this essential point, this subtle secret of dependent arising, if we can genuinely hold the correct mundane view—the understanding that there are other lives and that there is cause and effect—this will bolt the door to the lower realms and be the starting point for boundless merit. This is affirmed in the *Chapters of Utterances on Specific Topics*:

> Those who have the true great view,
> The view that's right in worldly terms,
> Will never in a thousand lives
> Depart to evil destinies.

The opposite case is that of people influenced by perverted, demonic views, who talk meaninglessly about virtue being empty and negative actions being empty. These people, who scorn the law of actions and their results, have been beguiled by demons. As a result, they will wander endlessly in the lower realms, and there will never come a time when they will be liberated. The *Tantra of the Questions of Subāhu* makes this clear:

> There are some who say, "There is no karma or ripening of karma; it's just an expedient teaching for guiding children." You should understand that they are accumulating a great many nonvirtuous deeds. Even though they claim to be Buddhists, they are following the tradition of the Chārvākas, who throw their next lives to the wind; they are being beguiled by Māra.

And in the *Jewel Garland*, we read,

> In brief, the view of nihilism,
> That karmic deeds have no results,
> Is nonvirtuous; it leads to lower realms.
> This is taught as being "wrong view."[100]

The Omniscient Teacher says,

Those who scorn the law of karmic cause and fruit
Are students of the nihilistic view outside the Dharma.
They rely upon the thought that all is void;
They fall in the extreme of nothingness
And go from low to lower states.
They have embarked upon an evil path
And from the evil destinies will have no freedom,
Casting happy states of being far away.

"The law of karmic cause and fruit,
Compassion and the gathering of merit—
All this is but provisional teaching fit for children:
Enlightenment will not be gained thereby.
Great yogins should remain without intentioned action.
They should meditate upon reality that is like space.
Such is the definitive instruction."
The view of those who speak like this
Is of all views the most nihilist:
They have embraced the lowest of all paths.
How strange this is!
They want a fruit but have annulled its cause.[101]

To sum up, the Great Orgyen says,

Someone who claims to be a practitioner of the secret mantras and then indulges in coarse, unrefined conduct is not a secret mantra practitioner. What we call the Great Vehicle involves cherishing all sentient beings and having impartial compassion. You cannot claim to be a secret mantra practitioner and not refrain from negative actions. It is essential for secret mantra practitioners to cultivate great compassion within. Unless compassion takes birth in one's mind, even if one claims to be a secret mantra practitioner, one is a non-Buddhist, going the wrong way. What we call the Secret Mantra Vehicle is the Great Vehicle. And what we call the Great Vehicle is working for others' benefit. To benefit others, one has to obtain the result of the Great Vehicle—that is, the three buddha bodies. To obtain the three buddha

> bodies, one has to gather the two accumulations. To gather the two accumulations, one must have bodhichitta. And as the path, one has to practice the union of the generation and perfection phases. Without bodhichitta, the secret mantrayāna is completely impossible; the Great Vehicle is impossible. Though we speak of two vehicles—the vehicle of the secret mantras and the vehicle of characteristics—they have a single goal. Without both the view and the conduct, you will err. So the view should be established from above, while the conduct should be engaged in from below. This is my instruction.

Accordingly, those who are skilled in distinguishing the two truths rely on the view during formal meditation and are very discerning in their conduct during the postmeditation period. This is the incomparable long tradition of the Ancient Translations, so you should definitely practice in this way. Verbally too, pray again and again as follows and train in truly mingling the meaning with your mind:

> The results of black and white deeds never go to waste;
> Cause and result are unfailing, and in this way
> Appear as the phenomena of saṃsāra and nirvāṇa.
> What we do is certain to ripen on us, and yet we fail
> To do what's right—to engage in good and turn away from wrong.
> Teacher, embodiment of the Three Jewels, look on us with
> compassion:
> Bless us that we may adopt virtue and refrain from evil.[102]

V. The signs of having trained

As a measure of how well one has trained in reflecting on the karmic law of cause and effect, one should be like the brahmin Ravi. It is said that he would carefully examine his mind, and if he had a virtuous thought, he would put aside a white pebble; if he had an evil thought, he would put aside a black pebble. At first, there were only black pebbles. Later on, as he trained in giving rise to antidotes, there was a mixture of black and white pebbles. In the end, he reached a stage where there were only white pebbles. This is the way in which we should train and practice.

Saṃsāra and nirvāṇa, happiness and suffering, are the manifestation of
our deeds:
Actions unfailingly give rise to results, said the Buddha.
Now, when you only partly understand the precious treasure of his
words and have the freedom to choose,
Practice adoption and restraint, O fortunate ones!

This completes the instruction on reflecting on actions, cause and effect.

8. Reflecting on the Sufferings of Cyclic Existence

The instructions for reflecting on the sufferings of cyclic existence enable one to turn one's mind away from the comforts and pleasures in existence and to strive for lasting liberation. There are four sections: (1) reflecting generally on the sufferings of cyclic existence, (2) reflecting specifically on the sufferings in each of the six realms, (3) an instruction on the importance of accomplishing the means to become free from suffering, and (4) a teaching on the benefits and signs of having trained in this way.

I. Reflecting generally on the sufferings of cyclic existence

Padmasambhava's *Great Treatise on the Graded Path* provides the following outline:

> Cyclic existence comprises the sentient beings of the three worlds. Their nature is suffering, their very essence is suffering, their whole variety is suffering. There are
>
> - four root sufferings, which are linked one after another, as in a chain;
> - six branch sufferings, which never come to an end or fade away, like the waves of the ocean; and
> - secondary branch sufferings, which, like the stars in the sky, are countless and limitless.
>
> Thus, wherever we are reborn, there is suffering, in all its multiplicity and variety. Whoever accompanies us, we have suffering for company. Wherever we go, our destination is suffering.

> Whatever we do, it adds to our suffering. Thus, all the good things in the world are the causes that lead to suffering, all the bad things are the suffering that results: sufferings like a chain, each one linked to the next; sufferings like ripples on water, that never die out or come to an end; sufferings like the stars in the sky, countless and limitless.
>
> In short, there is nothing that is not suffering: mental suffering from wanting things, physical suffering in our experiences, suffering in our perceptions, and suffering in the efforts we make physically, verbally, and mentally. It is when one reflects in this way that one turns one's mind away from this cyclic existence.

The Omniscient Teacher says,

> Everything occurring in the three worlds of saṃsāra is
> impermanent.
> Change is everywhere. Great suffering abounds:
> By sufferings of pain itself, of change, and suffering in the making,
> The beings in the six realms are completely overwhelmed.
>
> As though burned in a fire or caught by savage men,
> Or by wild beasts or else imprisoned in a tyrant's jail,
> Beings suffer torment in a seamless continuity.
> There's no escape for them, and sorrow grows to think of it.[103]

From time without beginning, while we have all been circling continuously in the three worlds of cyclic existence, there are no beings who have not been a father, mother, or relative to one another, or who have not been a friend, a hated enemy, or one to whom we felt indifferent. A pile of all the heads and legs from our rebirths as ants alone would be higher than Mount Meru. All the tears each one of us has wept would exceed the waters in the ocean. The heads and limbs we have had cut off in our pursuit of pleasure are beyond counting. Even those who have wealth and riches, a large entourage, and power and fortune in this life may die and be reborn in a state of poverty and destitution, as if all those comforts and happinesses had been a dream and they awake to find they have disappeared. The perceptions of this life to which we ourselves and others are attached and that seem so pleasant are no different from that. So, thinking, "What can I do about it? My future lives will go on much longer than this, so I must spend my time practicing the teachings for attaining liberation," practice with the preparation, main practice, and conclusion. The *Close Mindfulness Sūtra* states,

> O monks, you should be weary of the world of existence. Why is that? All the while that you have been circling in cyclic existence since time without beginning, the bodies that you have left behind from your births as ants, if piled together, would make a heap even higher than Meru, the king of mountains. The tears that you have wept exceed the waters in the four oceans. The volume of boiling molten copper, blood, lymph, pus, and snot that you have drunk in your countless lives in the hells and as hungry spirits is greater than that of the four great rivers that flow from the interior of the four continents into the surrounding ocean. The heads, eyes, limbs, and minor appendages that you have had cut off in your pursuit of pleasure exceed in number the molecules of earth, water, fire, and wind in worlds as numerous as the grains of sand in the Ganges River.

Furthermore, we suffer from the fact that we can never know for sure who are our enemies, who our friends, where we will be born, or the form we will take, as is stated in *Letter to a Friend*:

> Men who've fathered sons in turn are sons,
> And mothers likewise daughters. Bitter foes
> Turn into friends, the converse too is true.
> Because of this saṃsāra's never sure.[104]

And the *Letter of Consolation* tells us,

> All the friends and beloved ones
> You've cared for and rejected in saṃsāra—
> The grains of sand in all the Ganges
> Could never equal them in number.
> The ones who have your full concern,
> Considered as your dearest child,
> In other lives you beat
> And thought of as your enemies.

And those who drink your milk
And suck your very breasts—
In other lives you drank their blood,
And ate the flesh from off their backs.

Even in this life the changes that take place between friends, enemies, and those that are neither are quite uncertain. In the *Tantra of the Questions of Subāhu*, it is said,

> Those who were once our enemies become our friends. Those who were once our friends become our enemies. Likewise, some become neither friends nor enemies. And those same ones to whom we feel indifferent will become enemies, or likewise friends. Once they have understood this, the wise are never attached.

Again, there is the problem that however much happiness we have experienced in the higher realms in the past, we are never satisfied. However much suffering we have experienced in the lower realms, we are never fed up. In the *Letter to a Disciple*, we read,

There are no sufferings that we have not experienced many times
in the past,
There are no desires beings have that anything can ever satisfy,
There are no beings who have not lain in one's belly,
Yet how is it that there is no one in saṃsāra who is rid of
attachment?

Similarly, even in this life, because of our attachment, we are never content with what we have, and this brings numerous problems, as the *Play in Full* declares:

A person might get everything they want,
But not content with that, they look for even more.
The pleasures of the senses never satisfy,
Like salty water thirsty people drink.

The specific drawbacks of attachment to the pleasures of the senses—forms and so forth—are described by Noble Vasubandhu as follows:

Deer are killed by simple sounds,
Elephants by the touch of what they crave,
Moths are killed by forms, and fish by taste,
And bees by their desire for fragrant smells:
For each of them there is a cause.
Those born in the human realm
Have all these five together, constantly,
Destroying them by night and day,
So how will they attain to happy states?*

There is also the difficulty of repeatedly abandoning one's body and being reborn, as we read in *Letter to a Friend*:

A heap of all the bones each being has left
Would reach to Meru's top or even higher.
To count one's mother's lineage with pills
Like juniper pips in size, the earth would not suffice.[105]

And *Letter to a Friend* continues on the difficulty of repeatedly changing between the higher and lower realms:

Indra, universally revered,
Will fall again to earth through action's force.
And he who ruled the universe as king
Will be a slave within saṃsāra's wheel.[106]

In the *Letter of Consolation*, we read,

Those who formed your entourage
And honored you a hundred times
Then had you as their servant
And marked you with their kicks a hundred times.
Beings, due to causal forces,

*Deer are lured to their death by hunters playing flutes. Elephants get trapped in the mud they hoped would cool them. Moths burn in candle flames, attracted by the light. Fish are caught by the bait on the fisherman's hook. Bees get caught in carnivorous plants, attracted by their smell.

Appeared as others in the past
And will in future change again,[107]
As do the constellations and stars.

And in *The Way of the Bodhisattva*,

From time to time they surface in the states of bliss,
Abandoning themselves to many pleasures.
But dying, down they fall to suffer torment,
Long, unbearable, in realms of sorrow.[108]

We know from what we actually see and hear that even in this present life things variously prosper and decline, come together and fall apart. And in the end, we too encounter the difficulty of suffering as we depart alone, without anyone to accompany us, as we find in the same text:

And when this life is left behind,
And with it all my kith and kin,
I must set out on strange paths all alone:
Why make so much of all my friends and foes?
This body, now so whole and integral,
This flesh and bone that life has knit together,
Will drift apart, disintegrate,
And how much more will friend depart from friend?
Alone we're born, alone we come into the world,
And when we die, alone we pass away.
No one shares our fate, and none our suffering.
What need have I of "friends" who hinder me?[109]

In short, all the aggregates, constituents, and senses-and-fields contained in the impure, dependent world and its beings are the sample subjects* of the truth of suffering: they are, by nature, nothing other than the three kinds of suffering, as we read in the *Sūtra of Advice to the King*:

*Tib. *mtshan gzhi*, the particular instance of something (in this case, suffering) used to establish a defining characteristic (Tib. *mtshan nyid*). For example, the sample subject used to establish the defining characteristic of fire (which is that it is hot) could be the flame of a candle or a fire in a fireplace.

> Great King, this existence is change, this existence is impermanent, this existence is suffering.

And the sūtra the *White Lotus of Compassion* states,

> The dominion of the gods is a source of suffering. The dominion of human beings is a source of suffering as well.

Accordingly, in everything that appears to be happiness in cyclic existence, there is nothing that is eternal. In the end, it changes and ceases, and at that time it acts as the cause of suffering. Thus it constitutes the suffering of change. This is analogous to eating a rice dish mixed with poison.

Everything that is unpleasant—birth, aging, sickness, and death, heat and cold, hunger and thirst, encountering things we do not like, and so on—constitutes the suffering of suffering. From the simple fact of its arising, it appears as essentially painful. This is analogous to being caught by a terrible epidemic. The *Analysis of Actions* describes it thus:

> The suffering of existence is like a pit of fire, with no chance of ever being cool,
> Like dwelling in the midst of fearful carnivores and savages,
> Like a tyrant's prison, with little chance of escape,
> Like the waves of the ocean, coming again and again.
> Like the poison of the deadly aconite, extinguishing the very life of happy states.

All the tainted aggregates are causal factors that perpetuate existence, and in this respect they are actually the essence of the all-pervading suffering of everything composite. This is analogous to an abscess that has not ripened. Ordinary beings do not feel this all-pervading suffering of everything composite: they are like people who are stricken by some violent infectious disease and are no longer aware of any other minor bodily aches and pains. Noble beings see this all-pervading suffering of everything composite: they are like people who have almost recovered from that disease and can feel their minor bodily aches and pains.

Another analogy is to be found in the commentary on the *Precious Treasury That Fulfills All Wishes*:

A single hair upon the palm
Is not perceived by anyone,[110]
But when it enters in the eye,
It causes pain and suffering.
The immature are like the palm,
They do not feel the hair of universal pain.
Noble beings are like the eye,
They see suffering in all compounded things.

Thus, all enjoyable feelings are nothing other than the suffering of change. All painful feelings are nothing other than the suffering of suffering. Neutral feelings are nothing other than the all-pervading suffering of everything composite. So it is that all feelings are said to be of the nature of the truth of suffering. But that is not all, for if we check carefully, the things people do these days in order to have food and clothes—things like killing animals and stealing others' possessions—actually create the sufferings of the hells, hungry spirit realms, and so forth in the next life. There is nothing that is other than the nature of suffering.

It is also said that the beings in the three lower realms mainly experience the suffering of suffering, human beings and the gods of the world of desire mainly experience the suffering of change, and those in the two higher worlds mainly have the all-pervading suffering of everything composite. In a sūtra, we read,

> The world of desire is full of defects, the world of form is likewise full of defects, and the formless world full of defects too. I see that only nirvāṇa is without defect.

II. Reflecting specifically on the sufferings in each of the six realms

This section contains six parts, of which the first, reflecting on the sufferings in the hells, is divided into two: the hot hells and the cold hells.

A. The sufferings in the hells

1. The eight hot hells

Orgyen, the Second Buddha, lists these as follows:

First, in the world of the hells,
The suffering from heat and cold is inconceivable.
Reviving, Black Line, Crushing,
Screaming, Great Screaming,
Heat, Intense Heat,
And Torment Unsurpassed are the eight hot hells.

a. The Reviving Hell

The beings who inhabit this hell are all assembled in a land of fiercely blazing embers on a ground of burning iron. As if seeing each other as mortal enemies, they kill each other with weapons spontaneously produced by the power of their past deeds. As soon as they die, a voice resounds in the sky, "Revive!" whereupon they come to life again. Again they die, and again they come to life. They have to experience this until their karma is exhausted. *Finding Rest in the Nature of the Mind* gives the following account:

In the Reviving Hell, upon a ground of burning iron,
Beings meet and fight with weapons to the death.
And then there comes a voice that cries, "Come back to life!"
And they must suffer once again.
Know that this they undergo until their karma's spent.[111]

And in *Letter to a Friend*, we read,

For one whole day on earth three hundred darts
Might strike you hard and cause you grievous pain,
But that could never illustrate or match
A fraction of the smallest pain in hell.
The frightful pains and torments just described
Are lived and felt throughout a billion years.
Until those evil deeds are fully spent
One will not die and shed this life in hell.[112]

The duration of life in the hells is generally difficult to define consistently. It is said that, on the one hand, powerful antidotes and the like can lead to one's suddenly being transferred out of the hells; on the other hand, as a result of actions like treating one's vajra master contemptuously, one has to remain in the hells for many great kalpas. Nevertheless, one can consult the texts of the Common Vehicle tradition, such as the *Treasury of Abhidharma* and the *Close Mindfulness Sūtra*. For ease of understanding, the Omniscient Teacher has written,

> To calculate their life span, fifty human years
> Are as one day in the divine realm of the four Great Kings.
> One month is thirty of these days; twelve months make up one year.
> Five hundred of these years
> Is as one day in the Reviving Hell.
> And here the days are added one by one until
> Five hundred years have passed—
> The time of pain these beings must endure.
> The span of life is thus computed,
> So the sūtra stipulates,
> As ten million human years
> Multiplied by one hundred, two and sixty thousand[113]

b. The Black-Line Hell

In the Black-Line Hell, the executioners, who are the wardens of hell, mark beings' bodies from the crowns of their heads to the tips of their toes with numerous black lines—four, eight, and so on. Then they cleave their bodies along these lines with swords, saws, and axes blazing with fire. Each time, the bodies stick together again, and once again they are chopped up and suffer, as *Letter to a Friend* explains:

> Some are cut and carved as if with saws,
> Others hacked with axes, razor-honed.[114]

As for the duration of life there, it is said in *Finding Rest in the Nature of the Mind*,

> In the Heaven of the Thirty-Three,
> One day is equal to a hundred human years.
> And in that heaven, a thousand years

Is but a single day in Black-Line Hell,
Whose denizens must live a thousand years.
This corresponds, the Teacher said,
To one million, two hundred six and ninety thousand years and twelve—
All multiplied again by ten million human years.[115]

c. The Crushing Hell

The beings here are herded together and crushed between mountains that look like the heads of goats, sheep, and elephants. Like sesame grains being pounded in a mortar, their bodies are turned into a red pulp, at which point they recover as before. They have to undergo such suffering until their karma runs out. The *Letter to a Disciple* states,

Caught between the fearsome horns of two gigantic rams
Their bodies are completely smashed and pulverized.
A slightly cooling breeze then stirs, restoring them,
And then again, a hundred times, they are in that way crushed and ground.

And in *Letter to a Friend*,

Some are squeezed and pressed like sesame,
Others likewise ground like finest flour.[116]

The duration of life there is mentioned in *Finding Rest in the Nature of the Mind*:

Two hundred human years are as one day
In the heaven of the *yāma* gods called Free of Conflict,
Two thousand of whose years, so it is said,
Are counted as one day spent in the Crushing Hell,
Where beings endure two thousand of their years.
This comes to ten million times
Three hundred, eight and sixty thousand human years.[117]

d. The Screaming Hell

Their terror at the sight of all this gives rise to the appearance of somewhere to hide, and they find themselves pushed into a blazing iron house, from which there is no escaping for great lengths of time. There they suffer, crying and calling for help, as they are cooked in boiling molten copper and their bodies blaze with fire. *Finding Rest in the Nature of the Mind* gives the following description:

> In the hell called Screaming, the beings wail and cry
> As in the blazing fires they burn.
> They suffer, boiled in molten steel.[118]

And on the duration of life there, the same text continues,

> Four hundred human years are as one day
> In the heaven called Joyous, where
> Four thousand years are as one day in Screaming Hell,
> Where beings are tortured for four thousand years.
> One hundred and eighty trillion human years are thus computed,
> And to this are superadded nine hundred, four and forty billion years.[119]

e. The Great Screaming Hell

Here the beings are trapped inside double-walled iron buildings where the heat is twice as great as in the previous hell. Even if they manage to escape through the first door, they will not escape through the second door for great lengths of time, and they will suffer from being burned by the fiercely blazing fires and being beaten by the henchmen of the Lord of Death. As we read in *Finding Rest in the Nature of the Mind*,

> In Great Screaming, beings are roasted in a blazing fire,
> In houses made of incandescent iron,
> Where they are bludgeoned by the Lord of Death.[120]

With regard to the duration of life there, it says,

Eight hundred human years are as one day
In the celestial realm Delight in Magical Creations,
Eight thousand of whose years are as one day
In the Great Screaming Hell, where beings must suffer
For eight thousand of their years, which is, in human terms,
Three quadrillion, five hundred, two and fifty trillion,
Six hundred and sixty billion years.[121]

f. The Hell of Heat

After entering an iron building blazing with fire, the beings in the Hell of Heat are impaled on spears, and molten metal is poured into their mouths, burning their insides. Thrown onto their backs on the burning metal ground, they are beaten with fiery maces, as described in *Finding Rest in the Nature of the Mind*:

In the Hell of Heat, in houses made of burning iron,
Beings have brains and bodies torn out and smashed
By spikes and hammers. They burn inside and out
With tongues of blazing fire.[122]

It presents the duration of life there as follows:

One thousand and six hundred human years
Are equal to a day spent in the heaven called
Mastery of Others' Emanations, where sixteen thousand years
Are equal to a single day spent in the Hell of Heat,
Where beings must live for sixteen thousand of their years.
This means eighty-four million and one trillion and
Six thousand five hundred and thirty human years,
All multiplied again ten millionfold.[123]

g. The Hell of Intense Heat

The beings in this hell are burned in double-walled iron houses, blazing intensely with fire inside and out. They are impaled on burning iron tridents from the soles of their two feet and the anus up to the crown of the head and their two shoulders. Their bodies are entirely wrapped in sheets of flaming steel, and they are cooked in great iron cauldrons of boiling metal. *Finding Rest in the Nature of the Mind* describes their suffering as follows:

> In Great Heat, beings are trapped in buildings,
> Double-walled, all made of blazing iron.
> There they are impaled on tridents with prongs
> That pierce through their heads and shoulders.
> They're wrapped in blankets made of burning metal,
> Boiled in molten copper.
> And in this torment . . .[124]

With regard to the duration of life there, it says,

> . . . they must live
> For half an intermediate kalpa,
> Which in human terms exceeds all counting.
> One such kalpa is made up of four small kalpas:
> Formation, and duration, destruction, and the void.
> One great kalpa is made up of eighty intermediate kalpas.[125]

h. The Hell of Torment Unsurpassed

This is an iron building blazing with fire and surrounded by the sixteen neighboring hells. In it, all the sufferings of the above mentioned hells are experienced. Apart from the wails emitted by its inhabitants, it is impossible to distinguish the beings from the fires. *Finding Rest in the Nature of the Mind* says,

> In the Hell of Torment Unsurpassed,
> Beings are trapped in buildings made of blazing metal.
> Other than their cries and screams,
> There's no way to distinguish them
> From the all-engulfing blaze.
> Their vital strength is in the middle of the fire
> As if adhering to the heart of blazing flame.[126]

And of the duration of life, it says,

This they must endure for one intermediate kalpa.
And since there is no greater suffering than this,
It is described as Torment Unsurpassed without reprieve.[127]

The Great Orgyen says,

> Since there is nothing worse than the suffering in the Hell of Torment Unsurpassed, it is the ultimate torment. The beings in that hell would be so happy to die, but it is impossible for them to do so. They are constantly revived and the suffering they have experienced returns. The causes of rebirth in the Hell of Torment Unsurpassed are the five crimes with immediate retribution and using the teachings for commercial purposes. Otherwise, those who mainly commit the act of taking life are born in the other hells.

In the hells that have been described here, the fires and so forth in each hell are seven times greater than those in the one above it, making the heat and sensations seven times more gross, and thus the suffering seven times more intense, as is mentioned in *Finding Rest in the Nature of the Mind*:

The fiery heat and corresponding pains
In each of these hell realms, in order given,
Grow seven times more intense.
And beings have to suffer it until their karma's spent.[128]

And in the *Analysis of Actions*, we read,

An ordinary fire, a fire of sandalwood, the fire at the kalpa's end,
Together with the fires in the hells, are placed in order:
For each the heat is multiplied by seven,
And likewise sevenfold are the sufferings.

The lesser hells

The lesser hells are included in the hot hells. They have no definite locations: they can be in mountains, rocks, water, fire, the sky, and other places. The beings in these hells may perceive themselves as mortars, ropes, brooms, bits of charred wood, logs, and diverse living forms, alone or in groups.

Accordingly, they suffer from heat, cold, hunger, thirst, being hewn up, chopped into pieces, boiled, and so on. In each case, they are tormented unbearably, day or night in alternation, for a brief instant, or constantly, depending on the different kinds of retribution for their deeds. This is why they are called "lesser" hells.* The story is told in the Vinaya texts of Maudgalyāyana traveling to the ends of the oceans and seeing a very great many lesser-hell beings resembling mortars, brooms, and trees, tormented by suffering. And in *Finding Rest in the Nature of the Mind*, we read,

> The beings who endure the lesser hells
> Are isolated or else live in groups both great and small.
> They live in various places: mountains, trees, the sky, rocks, fire, or water,
> Where they are tormented by a corresponding pain,
> And thus these are described as lesser hells.[129]

The neighboring hells

The neighboring hells comprise sixteen additional hells surrounding the Hell of Torment Unsurpassed. In each of the four directions with respect to the latter, there are four hells: the pit of hot embers, the swamp of putrefying corpses, the plain of sharp weapons, and the unfordable river of hot ashes. This makes sixteen in all. There is also the hill of iron *shālmali* trees in each of the intermediate directions.

When the effect of the deeds that have made them suffer so intensely in the iron mansion of the Hell of Torment Unsurpassed lightens, the beings in that hell have the impression that the doors in the four directions have opened. As they emerge from each of these doors, they see what looks like a pleasant, shady trench and they go into it, only to find themselves in the midst of glowing embers, where they suffer from all their flesh and bones being burned:

> They sink up to their knees in fiery embers.
> They cross. Their flesh is burned; their white bones show.
> And then they're healed to suffer all again.[130]

*The Tibetan *nyi tshe ba* has several meanings, reflected in the numerous translations of these hells, including "ephemeral," "occasional," "local," and so on.

Next, thinking that they can escape, they see a cool, flowing river. Plunging into it, they find themselves in a foul-smelling, muddy swamp of rotting corpses and excrement, where they are bored into by worms with steel mouthparts:

> They hurry then to what appears a cooling marsh,
> But there they sink into a stinking swamp of rotting dead,
> Where worms with jaws of gold or steel or copper bite them.[131]

Fleeing this, they see a delightful meadow, but when they arrive there, the whole meadow turns into razors, slicing their legs and shredding them to bits. As they lift their feet, they are restored, and thus they suffer. They then see a pleasant grove of trees, but on arriving there, the leaves turn into swords, which, stirred by the wind, hack their bodies to pieces, whereupon they are restored and the suffering begins again:

> And then they see a pleasant plain,
> But as they run there, burning razors
> Slice their flesh in pieces.
> They hasten into pleasant-seeming woods
> But are destroyed in groves of sword blades
> That lash and flail in winds their deeds have wrought.[132]

Again, they see the hill of iron shālmali trees, where they catch sight of their relatives and friends and the men and women with whom they had sexual relations in the past, who call to them from the top of the hill. As they begin scaling it, downward-pointing steel stakes pierce their bodies. When they get to the top, ravens and vultures gouge their brains out. Again they see their loved ones calling them from the foot of the hill. As they descend, they are pierced by steel stakes pointing upward. When they embrace, their former lovers turn to iron—men or women blazing with fire, who hug them tightly, burning and devouring them. Such are their sufferings:

> And then, upon the summit of a pleasant hill,
> They see the former object of their passion calling them.
> And as they hasten there, sharp metal scalpels cut them;
> Flesh and blood drips down.
> And when they reach the summit, vultures mash their brains.

They then think that their lovers call them from below.
As they descend, the upward-turning scalpels wound them yet
again.
Then, when they have come down,
Those men or women take them in their fiery arms
And with their sharpened fangs cause dreadful pain.
They're then devoured by packs of dogs and wolves.[133]

Although there are three such hells—the plain of razors, the forest of swords, and the hill of iron shālmali trees—they are all described together as parts of the "plain of sharp weapons."

Proceeding from there, they see in the distance a gently flowing river, but when they try to cross it, they find themselves sinking up to their waists in hot ashes. With their flesh burnt down to the bone, they try to escape, but find both banks guarded by Yama's henchmen. Thus they suffer:

They see a cool and flowing stream and run there in delight.
In they leap but sink up to their waists
In fiery ash that burns their flesh and bones.
Upon the banks they see the sentries of the Lord of Death.
This pain they must endure for many a thousand years.[134]

It is said that there are two possibilities with regard to these neighboring hells. One is that beings are first reborn in the Hell of Torment Unsurpassed and then, as the effects of their deeds gradually lighten, they take birth in the neighboring hells. The other possibility is that, as a result of certain deeds, beings are reborn there from the start and then are freed.*

Although some authorities, like the listeners in the Vaibhāṣhika school, believe that the hosts of vicious guardians, executioners, and animals in these hells exist in their own right, in truth, they are nothing other than one's own mind's perceptions that arise on account of one's evil deeds. This is affirmed in *The Way of the Bodhisattva*:

Who has forged this burning iron ground;
Whence have all these demon-women sprung?

*This latter case occurs if one has regretted one's negative deeds, thereby attenuating their effects.

> All are but the offspring of the sinful mind,
> This the mighty Sage has said.[135]

And in a sūtra, we read,

> The three worlds are merely the mind.

This accords with the thinking of both the Middle Way and Mind-Only traditions of the Great Vehicle.

So, thinking, "I have surely already experienced sufferings like these innumerable times, and I will definitely experience them again, so I must attain certain deliverance from them," practice with the preparation, main practice, and conclusion complete, and meditate intensely on compassion for sentient beings who have been reborn in those realms.

2. The eight cold hells

The eight cold hells are described in *Finding Rest in the Nature of the Mind* as follows:

> There are eight cold hells where beings are tormented.
> In glaciers and dark places of great freezing cold,
> Beings are lashed by swirling snowstorms.
> They are covered with blisters, bursting blisters.
> Their teeth are chattering in the cold;
> They cry and they lament.
> Their flesh splits open like utpala flowers,
> Then like lotuses and then great lotuses,
> And in the wounds are worms with jaws of burning iron
> That burrow in the flesh, consuming it.
> And thus they live until their karma is exhausted.[136]

a. The Hell of Blisters

In snowy mountains and glacial regions swept by blizzards, beings in the Hell of Blisters are afflicted by cold twenty times greater than that in the middle of winter, and they suffer from hundreds of blisters that appear on their bodies.

b. The Hell of Bursting Blisters

Because the Hell of Bursting Blisters is twenty times colder than the previous hell, its inhabitants' blisters burst. The resulting sores ooze blood and lymph; worms with steel mouthparts bore into them and devour them. Thus they suffer.

c. The Hell of Lamentation

In the Hell of Lamentation, the cold is overwhelming, twenty times greater than in the previous hell, and the beings here weep unceasingly.

d. The Hell of Groans

The cold in the Hell of Groans is even more intense, so that the beings cannot even cry. Instead, they emit whispered groans of pain.

e. The Hell of Chattering Teeth

The cold in the Hell of Chattering Teeth is even greater than in the previous hell. As a result, the beings in it cannot utter a sound but remain frozen stiff, their teeth chattering.

f. The Hell of Utpala-Like Cracks

It is even colder in the Hell of Utpala-Like Cracks, so that its inhabitants' bodies split into four pieces.

g. The Hell of Lotus-Like Cracks

As the cold is even greater in the Hell of Lotus-Like Cracks, its inhabitants' bodies split into eight parts.

h. The Hell of Great Lotus-Like Cracks

Afflicted by the extreme cold in the Hell of Great Lotus-Like Cracks, the inhabitants' bodies split into sixteen, thirty-two, or even more parts. In this way, the inhabitants have to experience the most terrible pain as their bodies freeze and are devoured by tiny creatures that infest the sores exposed by the cracks.

The duration of life in these hells is mentioned in the *Close Mindfulness Sūtra*:

> Thus it is: imagine a vessel with a capacity of twenty *koshala* measures* filled to the brim with sesame seeds. Imagine how long it would take to empty that vessel by removing one sesame seed every hundred years. That is how long it takes before beings in the Hell of Blisters die. In the other hells, the beings have to bear enormous suffering for successively longer periods of time, multiplied in each hell by a factor of twenty.

Thus it is that *Letter to a Friend* declares,

> The very instant that they cease to breathe
> The wicked taste the boundless pains of hell.
> And he who hearing this is not afraid
> A thousandfold is truly diamond hard.
> If simply seeing pictures of the hells
> And hearing, thinking, reading of them scares,
> Or making sculpted figures, need we say
> How hard to bear the ripened fruit will be?[137]

Reflect accordingly on these boundless forms of suffering from heat and cold. Be glad that you have not at present been born in states like those, and with thoughts of boundless compassion for others who have been born there, do the practice, thinking, "I must put all my efforts into the Dharma for my own and others' benefit."

B. Reflecting on the sufferings of the hungry spirits

The hungry spirits are divided into two groups: (1) those that live in the underworld, and (2) those that move through space.

*An ancient measure named after the Indian city of Koshala (near modern Ayodhyā), said to be one pint.

1. Hungry spirits that live in the underworld

The Great Master divides these hungry spirits into four classes:

> In the world of hungry spirits,
> The miseries of thirst and hunger know no bounds.
> Spirits who are outwardly obscured do not see anything to eat or drink,
> And even if by chance they do, it is perceived as filth.
> Spirits who are inwardly obscured cannot take in their food and drink,
> But should they manage, they are burned by violent heat.
> Those who are specifically obscured cannot find anything to eat or drink,
> And even if they find some, others keep it under guard.
> The ones who are generally obscured
> Never find any form of food or drink.

a. Hungry spirits whose perception of the outer world is obscured

Hungry spirits whose perception of the outer world is obscured have emaciated bodies and minute limbs. They are tormented by constant hunger and thirst. They never even hear the words *food* and *drink*. Should they ever happen to see something to eat or drink, they perceive it as a mire of vomit and other filth and they are unable to eat or drink it.

b. Hungry spirits whose perception of their inner world is obscured

Hungry spirits whose perception of their inner world is obscured have enormous bodies with huge bellies, spindly arms and legs, and mouths no bigger than the eye of a needle. As a result, they never find anything to eat or drink. Even if they should happen to find some, they cannot put it into their mouths. Those that somehow manage to do so find that it will not go down their throats, which are as narrow as a horse hair. Even if they do swallow it, it can never fill their stomachs, which are as huge as a whole country. Should they ever eat their fill, their limbs, which are as thin as straws, cannot carry them. What they have eaten bursts into flames, burning their hearts and lungs and sending smoke pouring out from their mouths and noses. Thus they suffer.

c. Hungry spirits whose perceptions are specifically obscured

Hungry spirits whose perceptions are specifically obscured suffer from never finding any food or drink. Even if they do find some, they perceive it as being guarded by others. In each of these hungry spirits' bodies, there appear to be many other beings living there, eating their flesh.

d. Hungry spirits whose perceptions are generally obscured

Hungry spirits whose perceptions are generally obscured live in fear of destitution and having nothing at all to eat or drink. For them, the seasons are reversed, so that in summer, the moonlight burns them, while in winter, the sun feels unbearably cold. They have to live off all kinds of food that make them suffer—filth, burning embers, and the like. Their hostility toward each other leads to fights and quarrels. They are driven aimlessly by the wind of karma. Such are their infinite sufferings, as *Finding Rest in the Nature of the Mind* describes:

> There are pretas living in the depths
> And pretas that can move through space.
> Those that live below are vast in size.
> Their arms and legs are small and thin, their stomachs cavernous.
> Their throats are narrow, their mouths like needle-eyes.
> They find no food or drink: great thirst and hunger torment them.
> When they see wholesome flowers, plants, and trees,
> They dry before their eyes.
> Repulsive is their dwelling place, and vomit is their only food.
> And even when from far they have a glimpse of food and drink,
> It seems as though it's under guard, forbidden them.
> Pretas that have inner defects
> Have blazing conflagrations in their stomachs;
> Smoke and flames come from their mouths.
> Through defects that are shared by all their kind,
> Pretas are distressed and poor; they're fearful and assailed.
> Protectorless, they suffer in wild and frightful places.[138]

2. Hungry spirits that move through space

Hungry spirits that move through space include yakṣhas, rākṣhasa ogres, *tsen* spirits, and ghosts. As they are classified as hungry spirits, they suffer immeasurably from unpleasant perceptions, dangers, intimidation, and hunger and thirst. When these spirits go to the places where the people they loved are, they inflict on them the illness that previously proved fatal to them as they were dying. Since they themselves constantly suffer from that illness, they want to give it to others. They do only things that harm others, like robbing them of their lives and vitality. In this way, they repeatedly create the causes for rebirth in the hells and so forth. Moreover, they are forcibly restrained by exorcists. These and others constitute their infinite sufferings. *Finding Rest in the Nature of the Mind* says,

> Pretas that can move through space are spirits,
> Yakṣhas, rākṣhasas, the *tsen* and *gyalpo* spirits, and more.
> They have miraculous powers by virtue of their karma
> And can move from place to place without obstruction.
> They produce all kinds of harm.
> They cause disease and steal the radiance of beings,
> Shortening their lives.[139]

The duration of their lives is mentioned in the same text, which accords with what is said in the *Treasury of Abhidharma*, *Letter to a Friend*, and other texts:

> Regarding their own length of life,
> One human month is as a day for them
> And therefore in the worlds of Yama, Lord of Death,
> They are tormented for five hundred of their own,
> Or fifteen thousand human, years.[140]

The Great Orgyen says,

> The cause of being reborn as a hungry spirit is being stingy and uncharitable. Stinginess is the inability to give things away oneself. What we call "lack of charity" consists of stopping others from being generous.

So reflect on this, thinking, "I must do whatever I can not to be reborn in states like those."

C. Reflecting on the sufferings of the animals

The Great Master says,

> Then, in the world of beasts, the animals,
> Who are by nature dull, unable to communicate,
> Bewildered, and dumb, as if in dark obscurity,
> Must suffer, devoured by one another,
> Killed by butchers and others,
> Or, helpless, forced to work.

Animals are of two main kinds.

1. Animals that live in the depths

The great outer oceans and the dark regions between the continents, unlit by either sun or moon, teem with fish, shellfish, reptiles, and so forth, packed together without any space in between, like the dregs of fermented grain in a brewery. There they endure boundless sufferings. The smaller ones are devoured by the bigger ones, the bigger ones are fed on by the smaller ones, and some even eat their own flesh. These and other miseries are described in *Finding Rest in the Nature of the Mind*:

> Animals that live down in the depths
> Teem everywhere in all the four great oceans.
> They prey on one another, and their suffering is endless.
> They dwell in the dark oceans that divide the continents.
> They are tormented by the heat and cold,
> By hunger, thirst, and fear of predators.[141]

2. Animals that live scattered in different places

The animals that live scattered in different places are animals such as birds, deer, and aquatic creatures that live in the human world. Wild animals are preyed on by hunters, fishers, and bird hunters. They are killed for their meat, skins, bones, and so forth. They are eaten by other animals. These are just some of their infinite sufferings. Domestic animals are forced to work as pack animals, yoked to plows, castrated, and have their hair pulled out.* After being exploited in these ways, they end their lives being turned out or dispatched to the slaughterhouse, where they are killed, beaten, bled, eviscerated, and skinned. Along with these and other unimaginable torments, they suffer from being generally bewildered and dumb.

Nāgas experience happiness and suffering alternately. Some suffer only in the morning or during the day, others only in the afternoon or at night. At these times, their numerous afflictions include heat and cold, and hunger and thirst. For some, hot sand rains down on their bodies, causing the flesh to separate from the bones. Others are unable to join a group of nāgas and suffer from loneliness. Among their other infinite forms of suffering is their fear of eagle-like garuḍas and sorcery.

Animals' life spans are indeterminate. Some live for only a short instant or for a single day. Others, like the nāga king Takṣhaka, are said to live for as long as an intermediate kalpa.

In *Finding Rest in the Nature of the Mind*, we read,

> There are animals also that live scattered and dispersed,
> Like birds and beasts that live in lands where humans dwell.
> By hunters they are harmed and live in danger of each other.
> Horses, oxen, camels, donkeys, goats, and so forth
> Are reduced to slavery.
> They're beaten and must suffer endlessly,
> And for their meat and fur and bones they are condemned to death.
> Their very nature is unbounded suffering.
> For half the day and night, the nāgas may find happiness,
> But sorrow in the other half.
> Their morning's joy transforms into an afternoon of pain.
> Rains of hot sand fall upon the habitats of some.
> Some are lonely, friendless, tortured by their poverty.
> Mostly they have small intelligence and live in fear of the garuḍas.

*This refers to the practice of pulling out the soft wool of the yak's belly rather than shearing it.

> A great variety of suffering afflicts them, and their life span is not fixed.
> Some live but a day, while some like Takṣhaka, their king,
> Have lives that last for one entire kalpa.[142]

The Great Orgyen says,

> The cause for being reborn there is failure to avoid the smallest negative deeds.

So meditate again and again, thinking, "I must do whatever I can not to be reborn like that."

D. Reflecting on the sufferings of human beings

In general, the sufferings of human beings are the three kinds of suffering:

(1) The suffering of suffering, where one kind of unwanted event such as illness has not been cleared away before another occurs on top of it. An example of this is someone suffering from leprosy developing an abscess as well.

(2) The suffering of change, which afflicts people when the happiness they have at the moment immediately changes into suffering. An example of this is the disaster that befalls newlyweds when their dancing causes the house to collapse.

(3) The all-pervading suffering of everything composite, where suffering is produced later, bringing misery and unhappiness. An example of this is eating poisoned food or inflicting harm on others.

The specific sufferings of human beings are listed in *Finding Rest in the Nature of the Mind*:

> Birth and aging, illness, death;
> Meeting with adversities
> And losing what is pleasant,
> To be deprived of what one wants,
> To have continuous suffering in one's aggregates—
> From all these eight there comes unbounded pain.[143]

There are thus said to be eight categories: four root sufferings and four branch sufferings.

1. The four root sufferings

a. The suffering of birth

When a sentient being wandering in the intermediate state merges with the father's semen and the mother's blood, its body takes form over seven weeks through the different stages—oval jellification, oblong solidification, and so forth. From then on, as it grows in its mother's belly, it is pitilessly tormented by the foul smell, nausea, and cramped space, and by the unsuitable things the mother eats, wears, and does. Sometimes it is too hot, as if thrown into a fire pit; sometimes it is too cold, as if immersed in a glacial river. Sometimes it feels under a great weight, as if crushed by a mountain; sometimes it feels too light, as if suspended over an abyss. When the time comes for it to be born and it is turned upside down, it suffers terribly, as if it is being churned. The birth process itself is akin to the Crushing Hell. The baby is so exhausted that for a while it loses consciousness. The touch of hands is unbearable: it feels as if it were being cut to the quick with a razor. When it is bathed, the heat feels like being flayed alive. And so the suffering continues. The Great Orgyen gives the following description:

> First, when the ground consciousness is smothered in the parents' semen and blood, it thinks it is being pushed into a land of darkness, or it thinks that it is being crushed under a great mountain. Then, as an embryo, its mother's movements and her being full of food make it think it is being pressed between stones. When its mother is hungry, it thinks it has been attached to a dangling rope. When she is doing heavy work, it feels it is being crushed by rocks. Next, the birth process is like being squeezed between rocks and forced out. The baby suffers as if it is falling onto the open ground, being flayed, and being tossed into a pit of thorns, or otherwise it thinks that it is being trampled under hooves. Its sufferings are thus exceedingly great. These are followed by the intense miseries of hunger, thirst, pains in the arms and legs, and so on.

b. The suffering of aging

As one's physical strength declines, getting up, sitting, and moving around become increasingly difficult. One's faculties dull: one's eyesight dims, one's hearing is less clear, one's memory fades, and one loses one's intellectual powers. As a result, one has less interest in life and depression sets in. With the swings of energy in one's channels, one becomes childishly silly and one's feelings become more gross. The changes inside the body and mind result in numerous illnesses and injuries, and everything is unpleasant. Even though old people say they would like to die, the truth is that they dread dying. There are no end of sufferings like these, as is stated in the *Play in Full*:

> Aging turns your beauty into ugliness;
> Aging takes away your splendor, it diminishes your strength.
> Aging snatches happiness away and brings you misery;
> Aging brings on death, it robs you of your radiance.

c. The suffering of illness

Disturbances in the balanced combination of the four elements* lead to grossly painful sensations. The body's usual character changes; one is irritated and feels depressed. One's faculties weaken, and it becomes difficult to get up from one's bed or sit. Everything one is given to eat and drink is unpleasant; one's perceptions are constantly disturbed. As a result of negative forces, obstacle makers, and other hindrances arising, one is very sensitive and accident-prone. There is the fear that one's wealth is running out and that one is dying. The boundless range of these sufferings is indicated in the *Commentary on the First Part of the "Hundred Parables on Action"*:

> Those who ail, their bodies racked with pain,
> Feel much the same as beings in the hells,
> Repeatedly tormented, more and more.
> Such are the afflictions of existence for those who crave.

And the Great Orgyen says,

> The sufferings of illness are manifold and overwhelming. Whichever part of the body is affected, it is completely unbearable: if it is the eye, one thinks, "If only it could be somewhere other than the eye." Thus one suffers terribly as the body's vitality diminishes,

*The four elements: earth, fire, wind, and water.

one's organs and strength deteriorate, and all one's money, grain, and possessions come to an end.

d. The suffering of death

People who are dying lie on their final bed, eat their last meal, wear their last clothes, and utter their last words. Even though their numerous relatives and entourage gather round, they are not the slightest help. They are tormented by the sensations of dying. Escorted by hallucinations, they set out on the perilous path of the intermediate state. The elements of their body gradually dissolve, and they abandon the perceptions of this life and hasten toward the next life. Having left everything behind, they proceed alone, like a hair plucked out of butter.* At that time, however much food and riches they may have, they are powerless to take even a handful of food with them. However many relatives and servants they have, not a single person will be able to accompany them, and they will have to depart alone. There is no limit to the sufferings of dying, as the Great Master affirms:

> After that, the suffering of death,
> Like lightning striking, befalls us all.
> Lying on your final bed, you start to die.
> You wear your final clothes, a corpse's shroud.
> You're fed a final meal—of cemetery food.†
> You speak your final words—your testament.
> And though your family all gather round,
> You fail to recognize them; your words are all confused.
> All round the bed are things to eat and drink,
> Yet nothing save some water passes down your throat.
> There's nothing that can help you; all your strength has gone.
> All hope is lost, and at that time
> You see you've spent this human life in vain, distracted uselessly.
> You failed to practice Dharma; you passed your life in evil deeds.
> Alas! Remorsefully, your nails tear at your chest.

*None of the butter sticks to the hair.

†This refers to the offerings of food, particularly that of the burnt offering (Tib. *gsur*), left in the cemetery for the dead.

Well may you feel regret, but now it is too late for anything to
help,
And in despair and dread as you approach saṃsāra's precipice,
You stare with bulging eyes and hold on tightly in the face of
death.
Your mind and subtle energies cannot stay still;
The breath is forced, you breathe more out than in.
Your body's elements gradually dissolve
And as perceptions start to change,
You briefly fall unconscious in luminosity.
Arising from that state, you panic, terrified,
And though you turn away and flee this way and that,
There's no communication, no refuge, no guide to help.
Knowing that you're dead, you start to cry,
And as you tremble, overcome with fear,
The messengers of death now lead you, powerless, away.
Your own inherent gods and demons draw you on,
Counting up the good and evil deeds that you have done:
The Lord of Death, the King of Law,
Reveals your next existence in the mirror of your deeds.
The owner of the five paths that beings take
Connects you to the path you have attained.*
Your mental body takes the form you had before
And undergoes all sorts of sufferings in the intermediate state.

And in the *Answers to the Questions of Yeshe Tsogyal*, he states,

> The suffering of death is more terrifying that the sufferings in the hells.

So we need to accomplish the sublime path of deathless liberation, thinking, "Until now I have always been involved with the appearances of this life—getting the better of my enemies and protecting those close to me,

*The five paths of beings (Tib. *lam rgyud lnga*) are the five realms of the gods (and demigods), humans, animals, hungry spirits, and the hell beings. Depending on one's past deeds, one now takes rebirth in one of these realms.

making future plans for where to live and things to have, and taking care of my children and entourage. What is the point of it all?"

2. The four branch sufferings

a. Encountering those we do not like

When we meet hated enemies, we suffer. We feel unhappy because they put our bodies, lives, and possessions in danger or because we fear that they will do so.

b. Being separated from those we like

If we are parted from our relatives and friends when they die or when they go somewhere far away, as soon as we think of their good qualities, their physical appearance, and the way they spoke, our hearts ache and we feel sad.

c. Being deprived of what we want

When we do not find some desired object that we have been looking for, when the nice things that we already have are damaged, or when we are afflicted by some sort of deprivation like the decline of our fortune, we become distressed.

d. The natural suffering of being tainted

This refers to the suffering that occurs because of our five perpetuating aggregates—form, feeling, perception, conditioning factors, and consciousness. These are the location, support, and source of suffering. Form attracts the harm that is suffering, so it is its location. Feeling is what receives it, so it is the vessel of suffering. Perception is the initial channel through which the movement of thoughts is created, so it is the support of suffering. Conditioning factors and consciousness are the creator and the knower, so they are the source of suffering. For example, when one is pricked by a thorn, the pain happens to the body and that feeling is recognized by the mind. The immediate notion of pain is perception. And what makes it painful is conditioning factors. Awareness of the pain from the thorn is consciousness. Any ailment that affects the body or any distress that affects the mind occurs on these five aggregates and nowhere else. Therefore, thinking, "I must do whatever I can not to have that part of the truth of suffering, the tainted perpetuating aggregates, and to acquire the gnosis of the noble beings," practice with the three aspects—preparation, main practice, and conclusion—complete.

The Great Orgyen says,

> Then, when one grows up, there are also the various sufferings of exhausting oneself looking for and not finding what one does not have; the various sufferings and fears of losing what one has—when it is stolen by robbers and the like; the various sufferings and fears of meeting hated enemies; the various sufferings and fears of parting from beloved kin; and the all-pervading suffering of everything composite, the heavy burden of suffering that arises simply from grasping the aggregates—all kinds of different sufferings such as one's inability to bear heat, to stand the cold, to bear hunger, or to bear thirst.

E. Reflecting on the sufferings of the demigods

The demigods are propelled into their particular realm by the action of jealousy. In conformity with that cause, they fight among each other, and when they see the glory and riches of the gods in the Heaven of the Thirty-Three, they are tormented by the fire of resentment and jealousy. From time to time, they do battle with the gods. On those occasions, they suffer from having their heads and limbs chopped off and being injured by vajras, arrows, wheels, and other weapons. Some of them are afflicted by the fear and suffering of dying or coming close to death. According to the lower vehicles, demigods have obscurations associated with the full ripening of deeds,* resulting in a great many negative consequences and faults. In particular, they are not suitable supports for seeing the truth of the listeners' and solitary realizers' paths, as is stated in *Letter to a Friend*:

*Obscurations associated with the full ripening of deeds (Tib. *rnam smin gyi sgrib pa*) are especially strong obscurations that prevent one from changing, so that practice and realization become impossible.

The asuras begrudge the gods their splendor,
Their inbred loathing thus torments their minds.
Though clever, they're obscured as all their kind,
And so it is they cannot see the truth.[144]

This is why the Omniscient Teacher gives the following instruction:

And for asuras too, contentment has no chance.
They are caught up in enmity and pointless strife.
Their envy of the glory of the gods is unendurable;
They suffer countless pains, I tell you, in their wars.
Therefore practice Dharma that with all speed
Sets beings free in states of peace and happiness.[145]

F. Reflecting on the sufferings of celestial beings

For the gods of the world of desire—those in the realm of the Four Great Kings, the Heaven of the Thirty-Three, the Twin Gods, the Joyous Realm, Enjoying Magical Creations, and Mastery over Others' Creations—there appears to be happiness for a while, but when the time comes for them to die and transmigrate, they know through their clairvoyance that their previous positive karma has come to an end and that as a result of their negative deeds they will be reborn in the lower realms. For seven days—in terms of their respective celestial realms as mentioned above[146]—they have to experience intense suffering, writhing like fish on hot sand. The Great Orgyen gives the following account:

> For the gods, there is the suffering of falling and the suffering of being stricken by fever. The suffering of falling is particularly great. The signs that herald death occur as follows: the colors of their bodies change, their seats become uncomfortable, their garlands of flowers wither, their clothes smell foul, and, for the first time, they begin to perspire. Once they see, with their clairvoyance, that they are going to be reborn in places like the three lower realms, they suffer as much as a fish drawn out onto dry land, a snake carried off by an eagle, a camel that has lost its calf, or someone on a ship sinking in the ocean. You should reflect on this, thinking that their mental anguish is seven or sixteen

times greater than that of the beings in the Hell of Torment Unsurpassed.

When the gods are stricken by fever, their suffering is sixteen times greater than that of the beings in the Hell of Torment Unsurpassed. Even if they are reborn in the higher realms again, they have innumerable sufferings such as those.

Likewise, in the world of form and the formless world, although there is no manifest suffering and the beings there enjoy the tainted bliss of concentration for a while, in the end their good karma runs out, and the force of their negative deeds creates the suffering of falling into lower existences. Thus, they are not exempt from experiencing the suffering of change, by taking the aggregates of their next rebirth, and the suffering of everything composite, as Nāgārjuna explains:[147]

All those within the Pure and other realms spontaneously produced
By concentration have boundless color, radiance, and light,
And yet they fail to see their latent concept of a self,
And when they die, they might take birth in hell.

To sum up, the Great Orgyen states,

From the peak of existence in the higher realms down to the bottom of the Hell of Torment Unsurpassed, there is nothing that is beyond the nature of suffering.

So, thinking, "Now I must do whatever I can to attain liberation from these three worlds and six realms," practice with the preparation, main practice, and conclusion complete.

III. An instruction on the importance of accomplishing the means to become free from suffering

The Omniscient Dharma Lord* says,

The up-and-down nature of cyclic existence is like the rim of a

*See glossary, s.v. "Omniscient Dharma Lord."

> waterwheel. We transmigrate and cannot last forever: this is the great problem. The supreme way not to enter cyclic existence is the liberation of enlightenment. Apart from this there is nothing we can rely on; it is all deceptive, alas! If we set out on the path to liberation, like the bodhisattvas, the buddhas' children, we will gain temporary happiness in the higher realms and acquire good qualities. And like the buddhas, we will accomplish the lasting happiness of unsurpassable enlightenment. Reflect, therefore, thinking, "I must accomplish perfect happiness, temporary and ultimate."

And the Great Orgyen declares,

> The decision point from which you will go up or down is this present moment. It is now that you must distinguish between happiness and suffering, now that you must decide between saṃsāra and nirvāṇa. If you do not make the distinction at this time, in the future it will be extremely difficult to get out of saṃsāra. If you can reverse the present chain of existences in saṃsāra, you will not need to go on taking a body forever; and it is just that not taking a body that constitutes the distinction between saṃsāra and nirvāṇa. So, man or woman, this is the time for you to check whether you are being prudent or rash, clever or stupid. Do not throw away what is good for you and while away your human life for nothing. Do not come back from the island of jewels empty-handed.

Liberation is something you have to accomplish yourself: no one else can help you. This is stated in the Vinaya texts:

> I have shown you the path to liberation,
> But liberation depends on you, so exert yourselves.

That is why the Omniscient Teacher says,

> Your liberation thus depends on you.
> The Teacher of both gods and humankind
> Has shown to us the means.
> No one else can save you through their sudden intervention,

Just as no one can prevent your dreams
When you are dazed in sleep.
If this indeed were possible,
The blissful buddhas and their offspring
Would indeed have emptied all saṃsāra
With the rays of their compassion.
Therefore you must don the armor of your diligence:
The time has come—exert yourself ascending freedom's path.[148]

Although countless buddhas came in the past, because of our faults, we did not fall within the range of their compassion and we have been repeatedly circling in this state of existence. Now, if we are still influenced by the defilements, carelessness, and distraction, we will likewise wander endlessly in cyclic existence. It will be impossible for the noble beings' compassion to have any effect on us, and so it will be difficult to ever be liberated, as the Omniscient Teacher points out:

You must reflect that sinful beings like yourself,
Who have not been the object of the healing action
Of unnumbered buddhas of the past,
Must wander in the wilderlands:
The pathways of existence.
And if, as in the past, you fail to make an effort,
You will suffer in the six realms of saṃsāra
Time and time again.

The sorrows of saṃsāra are like space unbounded,
Like fire, they are unbearable,
As various as the objects that appear.
Simply to submit to them, O mind, is abject and unfitting.
How can the compassion of the buddhas
Enter those bereft of conscience, care, or sense of decency?
Enlightened action, working skillfully, is called forth, it is said,
By the good karmic state of those who might be trained.
Admit therefore your faults,
And from your heart reflect upon the sorrows of existence.
To free yourself and others from saṃsāra,
Set out and climb the perfect path that leads to peace.

> If now you cannot bear the least discomfort,
> How can you withstand the dreadful sorrows of existence?
> If when it's explained you are not moved to sadness,
> Your heart inert like iron or a piece of stone,
> It's clear you have no mind at all![149]

At present, we have obtained a human body with the freedoms and advantages, and we have the freedom to decide for ourselves. If while we have this human life, we cannot bear a tiny spark touching our body, going hungry for one night, or the slightest hardship and fatigue, how, when we die, are we going to be able to endure the intense, long-lasting sufferings of heat and cold in the hells, hunger and thirst in the hungry spirits' realm, and being exploited as animals? If at present we cannot stand being sick and in pain for one day, how can we put up with the endless pains of cyclic existence? How can we be sure that we will be reborn as humans? And how can we bear to think that all the beings in cyclic existence have been none other than our own parents in our previous lives? So think, "Now I would rather die than not practice the sacred Dharma properly in order to free myself and others from the enormous suffering that is cyclic existence." Make this an intense, sincere commitment as you repeat aloud the following lines, and be sure to back your practice with the three supreme methods—preparation, main practice, and conclusion.

> We have much suffering that is hard to bear,
> And even what appears to us as happiness is deceptive and
> changeable;
> The tainted aggregates are the cause of suffering,
> The three worlds of saṃsāra are like a pit of fire,
> And yet, ignorant of that, we remain attached.
> Teacher, embodiment of the Three Jewels, look on us with compassion:
> Bless us that determination to be free may be born in us.[150]

IV. The benefits and signs of having trained in this way

In his instructions to King Trisong Detsen, the Great Orgyen told him,

> If you know the real nature of cyclic existence, your mind will naturally turn away from the world.

This is extremely important. Without turning our minds away from cyclic existence, however much we listen to the teachings, however much we practice, our attitude will be influenced by concerns for this life. Whatever we do will never be genuine Dharma, and it will not be the slightest help in beginning the path to liberation. The Great Orgyen said,

> There are many who have entered the gateway of the Dharma but have not traveled the path, so it is important not to go the same way. If you have taken ordination, but your lifestyle and possessions are like any layperson's, you are not a Dharma practitioner. Even if you have left aside worldly affairs, if you have not given up ordinary, idle chatter, you are not a Dharma practitioner. You might live in a secluded place, but if your activities are still worldly, you are not a Dharma practitioner. You may well have abandoned your homeland, but if you have not given up associating with worldly people, you are not a Dharma practitioner. However much you practice, if you have not turned your mind away from desire, you are not a Dharma practitioner. You might do all sorts of ascetic practices, but if you cannot put up with being harmed by others, you are not a Dharma practitioner. You may be practicing the generation and perfection phases, but if you have not kept the sacred commitments, you are not a Dharma practitioner. You may be meditating on nonduality, but if you have hopes that the gods will help you and are afraid that demons might harm you, you are not a Dharma practitioner. Even if you have entered the Great Vehicle, if you are not practicing to benefit sentient beings, you are not a Dharma practitioner. If you are working for beings' welfare, but your deeds are not imbued with bodhichitta and free of self-interest, you are not a Dharma practitioner. You might have realization of the view, but if you are not wary about the ripening of deeds, you are not a Dharma practitioner. You might be knowledgeable about the nine vehicles and their order, but if you do not blend the teachings with your own mind, you are not a Dharma practitioner. You might be constantly in one-pointed meditation, but if you have not destroyed the belief that appearances are real, you are not a Dharma practitioner. Even if you hold the three trainings, if you indulge in conceit, you are not a Dharma practitioner. Whatever virtuous activities you are doing, if they are not

> backed by the preparation, main practice, and conclusion, you are not a Dharma practitioner. Even if you adopt physical and verbal behavior that is basically wholesome, if on the mental level you are carried away by defilements, you are not a Dharma practitioner. If you let drop things that you can do today and hopefully aspire to do them later, you are not a Dharma practitioner. If you have not recognized the nature of mind yourself and are hoping for a result sometime in the future, you are not a Dharma practitioner. Even if your actions are virtuous activities, if you are not free of the eight ordinary preoccupations, you are not a Dharma practitioner.
>
> The eight ordinary preoccupations are being pleased when you are praised and displeased when you are criticized; being pleased when you are famous and displeased when you are not famous; being pleased when people say nice things about you and displeased when they say unpleasant things; and being pleased when you acquire things and unhappy when you do not. With regard to all your physical, verbal, and mental sources of good, you should check whether or not your past deeds were performed with these eight ordinary preoccupations in mind, whether or not your present deeds are accompanied by them, and whether or not your future deeds will be done with them. It is very important that they should not be associated with these eight.
>
> Great King, if you wish to follow me, Padma, whichever practice you undertake, pursue the unmistaken path that will enable you to swiftly attain the great enlightenment of the buddhas. Practice according to the extensive and profound teachings. Practice according to the words of the truly perfect buddhas. Practice in such a way that the meanings of the nine graded vehicles are complete within a single individual's mind stream, with the higher vehicles incorporating the lower. Practice in such a way that there is no practice to be done and no practitioner doing it. Practice in the state of the sole essence, all the phenomena of saṃsāra and nirvāṇa being the body of truth. Practice solely in accordance with this, my instruction. Then, there is no doubt that you will achieve the result, enlightenment.

All the defects mentioned above come from our failure to turn our minds away from cyclic existence and renounce the things of this life. The remedy for that is this reflection on the sufferings of cyclic existence. There is no more profound instruction than this. Lord Buddha himself, who turned the Wheel of Dharma three times, began first of all by teaching the importance of recognizing suffering, saying, "O monks, this is suffering."

If we train our minds in this, all the right conditions for the path of the three vehicles will occur. Disenchantment and a determination to be free will take birth in us. We will get rid of pride and carelessness. We will gain faith in authentic teachers and their instructions. We will gain confidence in the karmic law of actions and their effects, enabling us to avoid negative actions and undertake positive ones. Love and compassion for all other sentient beings will arise, and so on. The benefits, therefore, are boundless.

This is shown in the story of Nanda.* One day, Lord Buddha manifested a hell realm and showed it to him. As a result, there arose in him a genuine determination to be free. By never transgressing even the most minor precepts, he realized the level of arhat and was commended by the Buddha as the disciple who had most successfully controlled his senses.

As for the sign of having trained in reflecting on the sufferings of cyclic existence, we should be like Geshe Langri Thangpa. One day, one of his attendants told him, "The others call you Langri Thangpa Gloomy-Face."

"How could my face be cheerful when I think about all the sufferings in the three worlds of cyclic existence?" the geshe replied.

The story goes that at one time there was a turquoise on his maṇḍala. A mouse was trying to move it, but it was unable to do so on its own. Summoning another mouse with its squeaks, it set about pushing the turquoise while the other pulled. When he saw this, Langri Thangpa's face broke into a smile. But that was the only time he ever smiled.

We should train in the same way as he did, constantly.

Here in this pit of fire, this island of ogres that is saṃsāra,
The suffering, fear, and violence are inconceivable.
Those who cling to it, alas, are more stupid than cattle.
Cultivate genuine renunciation, O fortunate ones!

This completes the instruction on reflecting on the sufferings of cyclic existence.

*The story of Nanda, the Buddha's cousin, is related in full by Patrul Rinpoche, *Words of My Perfect Teacher*, 95–96.

PART THREE

The Virtuous Ending, Comprising an Explanation of the Main Preliminaries for the Path of the Diamond Vehicle

It should be understood that the number and order of the different sections that appear in the practice guides on the main preliminaries generally vary according to each instruction text.* In this case, they will be explained, as commonly accepted, in five sections:

- instructions on taking refuge, which distinguishes the path from wrong paths
- instructions on arousing the mind set on enlightenment, which distinguishes the path from lower paths
- instructions on the meditation and recitation of Vajrasattva, which purifies the negative deeds and obscurations that act as unfavorable conditions
- instructions on the maṇḍala offering, which enables one to complete the two accumulations that act as favorable conditions
- instructions on the Guru Yoga, which enables the extraordinary blessings to enter one's mind stream

*In particular, when the instructions are given depending on the practitioner's experience and progress (Tib. *myong khrid*), they may differ from one individual to another.

Jamgön Kongtrul Lodrö Taye (1813–1900)

9. Taking Refuge, Which Distinguishes This Path from Wrong Paths

This chapter has three sections: (1) a teaching on the nature of faith, the principal causal factor in taking refuge, (2) an explanation of the actual practice, the way to take refuge, and (3) a concluding explanation of the different precepts and benefits of taking refuge.

I. A teaching on the nature of faith, the principal causal factor in taking refuge

The causal factor, or root, as it were, that gives rise in one's mind stream to all the qualities of virtuous practices such as going for refuge in the Three Jewels is perfect faith. Lord Buddha has stated in a sūtra,

> Prerequisite for all that's good
> Is faith, which one must cultivate.
> Those who wish to reach the end of suffering
> And proceed as well to ultimate peace
> Should firmly plant the root of faith,
> And then resolve to gain enlightenment.

The Glorious Protector, Ārya Nāgārjuna, said,

> Because one has faith, one follows Dharma;
> Because one has wisdom, one's knowledge is correct.
> Of these two, wisdom is the chief,
> But faith it is that must come first.[151]

And the sublime scholar Ashvaghoṣha spoke of faith as the first of the seven noble riches:

> Faith is like the precious wheel,
> It leads us day and night along the virtuous path.

If one's mind stream is devoid of faith, it is impossible for all the positive qualities to arise, as we read in a sūtra:

> No virtue will appear
> In those who have no faith.
> How can green shoots sprout
> From seeds that have been burned?

It is, therefore, very important to give rise to faith in one's mind. And for this, the essence of faith is a perfectly clear state of mind, aware of what should be adopted and what should be avoided. As for its categories, the Omniscient Dharma Lord speaks of six different kinds of faith:

> Eager faith enables one to adopt and avoid in accord with the law of cause and effect.
> Inspired faith settles the mind on sublime objects.
> Respectful faith helps one have the utmost carefulness.
> Vivid faith is the clarity that comes from thinking of good qualities.
> Confident faith puts an end to doubts concerning the teachings.
> Certain faith is extraordinary faith in the highest teachings
> From listening, reflection, and meditation.[152]

Eager faith is the desire to abandon cyclic existence (saṃsāra) and adopt the state beyond suffering (nirvāṇa). It has three aspects: eagerness to abandon saṃsāra, eagerness to attain nirvāṇa, and eagerness to engage in respectively abandoning and adopting their causes.

Inspired faith is delight that arises in the mind when one encounters a teacher or the Three Jewels. Its four subdivisions are the inspiration to follow the teacher, inspiration to accomplish buddhahood, inspiration to take the Dharma as the path, and inspiration to take the Saṅgha as companions.

Respectful faith is based on a clear state of mind and involves carefully adopting virtue and avoiding evil, so that one does not transgress the Buddha's words. Its three subdivisions are physical respect through obeisance and veneration, verbal respect by means of praises and courteous words, and mental respect in seeing the Three Jewels and one's teachers as worthy of veneration and paying homage to them.

Vivid faith is the clarity of mind one experiences when one thinks of the qualities of superior objects. It has three subdivisions: vivid faith in virtue related to the relative, apparent aspect; vivid faith in virtue related to the ultimate, wisdom aspect; and vivid faith in virtue related to the union, sameness aspect.*

Confident faith is freedom from doubt with regard to the teachings on the ground, path, and result. Its three subdivisions are confidence in the law of cause and effect in relation to saṃsāra and what is to be abandoned, confidence in the law of cause and effect in relation to nirvāṇa and what is to be adopted, and confidence that everything that is neither positive nor negative is worthless.

Certain faith is the wish to settle the mind in equipoise in the profound ultimate reality that is taught in the profound sūtras and tantras on the definitive meaning. It has three subdivisions: certainty that comes from listening to the teachings that indicate that meaning, certainty from reflecting on them, and certainty from meditating on them.

These six kinds of faith can be condensed into three: vivid faith, eager faith, and confident faith. In this case, inspired faith, respectful faith, and vivid faith constitute vivid faith. Eager faith and confident faith constitute confident faith. Certain faith is actually eager faith, because, says Longchenpa,[153] it is the eagerness to engage in the unmistaken path and in cessation, the ultimate nature of things, thus abandoning suffering and its origin and attaining liberation.

Thus, most texts give three kinds of faith: vivid faith, which is the intense mental clarity that arises with regard to the Three Jewels; eager faith, which is the wish to practice avoidance and adoption in accordance with the four truths; and confident faith, which is confidence in the law of actions and their results. Some texts also speak of a fourth kind, irreversible faith. When

*Tib. *zung 'jug cha mnyam gyi dge ba*, refers to the union of the relative and ultimate truth and the sameness of appearance and wisdom.

one has this, it is impossible to turn back from the other three kinds of faith. All these are merely different ways of classifying faith: the essential point is the same.

If such faith is present in one's mind stream, it is like a fertile field, in which the shoot of enlightenment will sprout. Faith is like a good boat: it carries one across the river of cyclic existence. It is like an intrepid escort: it protects one from the hostile forces of demons and defilements. It is like an excellent steed: it carries one to the land of freedom. It is like a wish-granting gem: it fulfills one's every wish. It is like a warrior: it is capable of subjugating all that is evil and nonvirtuous. Moreover, it has boundless qualities such as banishing lack of opportunity and enabling one to gather sources of good, as we find in this extract from the detailed praise in the *Sūtra of the Precious Lamp*:

> Faith comes before everything, like a mother giving birth,
> Protecting and increasing all good qualities.
> It dispels all doubts and enables us to cross all the rivers.*
> Faith ushers us to the city of happiness.
> Faith clears the mind of cloudiness,
> It gets rid of pride and is the root of respect.
> Faith is like a treasure, a gem, the best of feet,
> Like a hand, the root for gathering virtue.
> Faith inspires one to give everything away,
> Faith gives rise to delight in the Buddha's teachings,
> Faith produces extraordinary qualities and wisdom,
> It shows the way to buddhahood and enables us to attain it,
> It sharpens our faculties and makes them very clear.
> Nothing else can crush the strength of faith,
> It is the foundation for dispelling defilements.
> Faith seeks out the good qualities that are naturally there.
> With faith, there is no attachment to desirable things,
> Faith banishes lack of opportunity,† it is the best of all freedoms.
> Faith enables us to go beyond the paths of demons,
> It is what shows us the supreme path to freedom.
> In the field of good qualities, faith prevents the seed from rotting,

*That is, the four great rivers of suffering: birth, illness, aging, and death.
†"Lack of opportunity" (Tib. *mi dal*), in this context, implies "distraction."

So that it grows into the tree of enlightenment.
It causes extraordinary gnosis and qualities to increase.
Faith reveals to us all the buddhas.
How those with faith, with extraordinary joy and interest,
Pursue their faith is something that must be taught in stages.
Such a quality is very rare in the world,
As rare as the king of jewels in the ocean.

For people whose minds are devoid of faith, even if the Buddha were present in person, he would be unable to help them. Like a rock on the bottom of the ocean, they will never be able to reach the dry land of liberation. Like a ferry without a helmsman, they will never traverse the river of suffering. Like someone with no hands arriving on an island of gold, they will be unable to nurture good qualities in themselves. As if the seed had been burnt, the shoot of enlightenment will never grow. Like blind people going into a temple, they will never see the light of the Dharma. As it is for someone caught in a whirlpool in the sea, there will never come a time when they can escape from cyclic existence. This is why those who wish to attain liberation and enlightenment must cultivate faith in their mind streams.

The sources of faith are as follows: Eager faith arises from seeing the nature of cyclic existence. Inspired faith arises from becoming weary of the company of people who commit negative actions. Respectful faith arises from coming into contact with supports of the Three Jewels that inspire wonder. Vivid faith arises from hearing stories such as those that tell of sacred supports* or those in the *Lives of the Bodhisattva*.† Confident faith arises from seeing the process of cause and effect. Faith based on thinking of the teachings arises as a result of hearing the profound teachings. So, reflecting on these sources, give rise to faith.

Furthermore, there are the following factors that cause faith to grow: following a teacher, a spiritual friend, and giving rise to the devotion of seeing him or her as the Buddha in person; relying on and following extraordinary companions who have definitely blended their minds with the teachings; studying the profound sūtras and tantras and reflecting again and again on death and impermanence; reading or listening to parables, in the sūtras and

*An account of the building of a stūpa or the history of a statue.

†Tib. *Byang chub sems dpa'i skyes rab*, the Jātaka tales that recount the Buddha's former lives as a bodhisattva.

elsewhere, that illustrate the qualities of the Three Jewels and the karmic law of cause and effect; and cultivating ever greater diligence in the practice and accomplishment of the profound teachings.

On the other hand, the conditions that lead to one's faith diminishing, which are signs that demons have entered one's mind stream, are as follows: finding fault in the teacher and spiritual friend; generally seeing defects in those who practice the Dharma; keeping the company of ordinary people, the wrong kind of friends; a decrease in one's diligence in the practice; indulging in pleasure regardless, without any moral principles; and lack of respect and devotion to the Three Jewels. The way to counter these when they occur is to reflect on the excellent qualities of the teacher, the Three Jewels, and one's fellow practitioners; to cultivate pure perception and respect with regard to all who practice the Dharma; to tell oneself that seeing faults in other people is a sign of one's own impurity, as if one had liver disease and perceived conch shells as yellow; to avoid befriending ordinary people; and to remind oneself of the drawbacks of the pleasures of the senses. We should recognize that all the faults that lead to our faith diminishing are demons and so give rise to their antidotes.

Furthermore, when we see transitions and changes such as birth and death, these are opportunities for giving rise to faith: we should think about other beings who have died and cultivate faith. Similarly, when we encounter obstacles that make us sick or harm us, we should cultivate faith, recognizing them as teachers urging us to practice virtue. When we suffer some misfortune, we should cultivate faith by recognizing that it is leading us to enlightenment. When we are listening to the sacred teachings, we should cultivate faith by considering that they are inspiring us to take the correct path and preventing us from taking the wrong one. When we hear the life stories of previous masters, we should cultivate faith by putting up with difficulties on the path. When we hear, in the *Series of Lives* section of the sūtras, of the great waves of activities of the buddhas and bodhisattvas, we should cultivate faith by thinking of the enlightenment of the Great Vehicle. All in all, it is important to make an effort to use everything, or every situation, in our daily lives to cultivate faith: it is essential not to be carried away by our habits, remaining impervious to situations, like grease-hardened leather.[154]

What are the signs that we have cultivated faith? We reject the deceptive appearances of cyclic existence like someone with nausea seeing food. We ache with devotion and longing for the teacher and the Three Jewels, like a small child yearning for its mother. We throw ourselves enthusiastically into studying and reflecting, like a thirsty person longing for water. We treasure the training,[155] like a poor person who has found some gold or turquoise. We delight in practicing virtuous activities, like a merchant traveling to an island of gold. We take great care to avoid negative actions, like someone avoiding getting dust in their eyes. Our faith and interest in all the different vehicles is like that of a keen shopper arriving at a market. When these signs occur, they are indications that we have given rise to faith, so it is important not to let them diminish but to make them increase. At such a time, it is said that the Dharma has tamed our mind, and the teachings and the individual have not gone different ways.[156]

Should our faith decrease, we should employ the methods for developing it mentioned above. Reflect on death and impermanence; on actions, cause and effect; on other people's good qualities; on how rare it is to have a chance to hear the teachings; on the teacher's kindness; on pure vision with regard to one's spiritual companions; on the qualities of buddhahood, and so forth. By these means, you should train in faith without any fluctuation or partiality and subdue your mind stream so that you are able to maintain firm faith, avoiding the sort of short-lived, inconstant faith that is easily sidetracked. In this regard, some people who are beginning to practice the Dharma act as if they have immense faith when they are with their teachers, but as soon as they are no longer with them, they are worse than ordinary people. Some are quick to give rise to faith when they encounter difficult circumstances, but it does not last for long and all at once fades away. Some people appear to have great faith when it is a question of obtaining teachings and possessions that they want for their own selfish ends, or when they are the victims of illness and negative forces, but once things are better or they have got what they want, they abandon their devotion. Some have not finished one virtuous activity before they start another, and in the end they never manage to complete either. Some people, instead of having unshakable faith in one profound teaching and one root teacher follow different ones according to their whims, and they end up producing the causes for degenerating the sacred commitments. Some give rise to a little bit of faith, but it fades away as soon as they encounter the slightest adverse situation.

To avoid these different kinds of superficial faith, prone to obstacles, you should begin by properly checking that the teaching and teacher are authentic. Once you have adopted them, whatever happens to you, you should rely on them with unflagging, unfluctuating devotion. Such devotion should have the following ten characteristics: It should be unchanging, like Mount Meru. Like the sun, it should not wax or wane. It should be like the ocean, with no difference between the surface and the depths.* Like a mother, it should never complain or expect to be thanked. It should be like space, without boundary or center; like the string of a bow, neither too taut nor too slack; like the sky, never prey to circumstances such as being influenced by others or being chastised; like a boat or bridge, untiring and uncomplaining; like a great river, flowing unceasingly. And like the string of a prayer flag, it should be respectful, supple and adaptable, and embellished with reverence.

The benefits of relying in this way on sacred objects like the teacher and the Three Jewels and of developing faith in them are innumerable, but they can be summarized as follows: Cultivating faith is the foundation for all virtuous practice. It clears away all the sufferings of cyclic existence and is the first step on the path to liberation. Because of your faith, you will be a fit vessel for the profound teachings, and the buddhas and bodhisattvas will constantly keep you in mind. You will have a host of qualities such as a sense of shame, a sense of decency,† mindfulness, carefulness, and wisdom, as a result of which you will be reborn in a pure buddha-field. In all your lives, as soon as you are born, you will meet a sublime teacher, the sacred teachings, and spiritual companions; you will thus be able to practice the Dharma. You will be protected by those gods who delight in virtue. Falling asleep peacefully, in your dreams, too, you will have pleasant visions of your teacher and the Three Jewels and of practicing the Dharma, and you will wake in a happy frame of mind. You will accomplish all your wishes and die peacefully, happily guided by the buddhas and bodhisattvas. You will have none of the terrifying experiences of the intermediate state. You will be reborn wherever your aspirations lead you, and you will uphold the lineage of the Three Jewels. Swiftly, you will attain buddhahood. A detailed account of these benefits would take endless kalpas, and it would still not be finished. This is explained in the *Sūtra of the Precious Lamp*:

> Though for kalpas one might serve beings
> Numerous as the atoms of all the worlds in the ten directions,

*Tib. *kha gting med pa*—that is, the same throughout, in all circumstances.

†See glossary, s.vv. "sense of shame"; "sense of decency."

> Bringing them every kind of happiness,
> In comparison, nothing is more sublime
> Than the merit of faith in this Dharma.

And,

> Those with constant faith and respect for the Buddha
> Make vast offerings to the victorious ones:
> Those who make vast offerings to the victorious ones
> Have inconceivable faith in the Buddha.
> Those with constant faith and respect for the Dharma
> Will never tire of listening to the teachings of the victorious ones:
> Those who never tire of listening to the teachings of the victorious ones
> Have inconceivable interest in the Dharma.
> Those with constant faith and respect for the Saṅgha
> Have faith in the Saṅgha of nonreturners:
> Those with intense faith in the Saṅgha of nonreturners
> Will never, through the strength of their faith, fall back.

And in the *Sūtra of the Inconceivable Secrets*,

> If one has faith, one will never fail to see the Buddha, hear the Dharma, and serve the Saṅgha, and wherever one is reborn, one will never be separate from them.

And,

> Those who have faith are reborn in the presence of the buddhas and are diligent in seeking all kinds of virtue. They are not interested in a household, wife, children, and the rest. From their childhood they do not take delight in play, and because of their faith, they renounce worldly life and follow a spiritual friend. Because of their virtuous attitude, they get to the heart of listening to the Dharma and earnestly practicing the teachings, not confining their efforts to the words. Diligent in hearing many teachings, they also explain to others the teachings they have heard, with compassion and without any regard for material gain.

And in the *Prayer of Good Action*,

> If one has given rise to faith just once,
> This is of the highest, supreme merit.

And in his *Story of Losel Ribong*, the Omniscient Teacher gives the following instruction:

> Of all riches, faith is the most precious:
> In this life and the next, it brings a rain of every excellence,
> Surpassing, thus, the nāga king's sublime wish-fulfilling gem.
> Of all foods, faith is the food of bliss:
> It gives rise to every wished-for joy in concentration,
> Surpassing, thus, all the food and drink we could desire.
> Of all clothes, faith is the sublime attire:
> It clothes us with a sense of shame and decency, and carefulness
> And is thus unmatched by gods' and humans' finest dress.
> Of all ornaments, faith is the most beautiful:
> It signifies a sublime being, replete with good qualities,
> And is lauded, thus, by buddhas and praised by beings in the three worlds.
> Of all dwellings, faith is the best of all:
> It is the unequaled abode of the sublime, granting all wishes,
> Excelling all the finest palaces of gods and men.
> Of all companions, faith is the most loyal:
> It never parts from us even in numberless lives,
> Tirelessly and forever bringing benefit and happiness.
> Of all attendants, faith is the closest:
> It follows us even in our dreams,
> Accomplishing all we wish, performing virtuous deeds.
> Of all relatives, faith is the nearest:
> It shows us what is right and stops us from doing what is wrong,
> Accompanying us in all that's virtuous, fulfilling all our goals.
> Of all friends, faith is the truest friend:
> It remains ever close and turns our perceptions toward Dharma,
> Our ally at all times, through misery and joy.
> Of all protectors, faith is the supreme refuge:
> It blocks off the lower realms, bestows happiness in higher birth,

Eliminates the cycle of existence, and sets us in nirvāṇa.
Of all teachers, faith has the greatest influence:
It makes those who have it accomplish everything that's good
And ultimately adorns them with the riches of conquerors.
Of all the Dharma, faith is the very root:
It is the great chariot, the way the sublime beings take;
It is the ground of all excellence in this life and the next.
Give rise, therefore, to this excellent quality—faith!

II. An explanation of the actual practice, the way to take refuge

This section has three parts: (1) a general presentation of distinctions, (2) a condensed presentation from the oral teachings of Orgyen, knower of the three times, and (3) the main explanation of the instructions for taking refuge.

A. A general presentation of distinctions

There are two topics: (1) the refuge of the causal vehicle of characteristics, and (2) the refuge of the system of the resultant Diamond Vehicle.

1. The refuge of the causal vehicle of characteristics

What kind of persons go for refuge? *Finding Rest in the Nature of the Mind: A Teaching of the Great Perfection* describes them as follows:

Refuge is the sure foundation of all paths.
Beings of small scope dread the lower states;
The two of medium scope are frightened by existence in saṃsāra;
While those of great scope see saṃsāra's pain in all its aspects
And cannot bear that other beings suffer.
What they fear is their own peace and happiness.
They thus embark upon the Great Way of the Buddha's heirs.
And so there are three kinds of beings who take refuge;
There are three approaches: ordinary, supreme, and unsurpassed.[157]

Because it is indispensable as the foundation for all the vows that are formally taken on the individual liberation, bodhisattva, and mantra paths, the root of the path is going for refuge. There are three kinds of beings who go for refuge. Someone who takes refuge in the Three Jewels out of fear of the sufferings in the three lower realms and with an aspiration to gain the happiness of fortunate states in the higher realms is termed a "being of small scope." Because this amounts to no more than the simple pursuit of a temporary resultant happiness, such beings are ordinary or inferior.

Those, on the other hand, who take refuge in the Three Jewels out of fear of all the sufferings of cyclic existence and in order to seek the happiness of a peaceful nirvāṇa for themselves alone are termed "beings of medium scope." Because they have in mind the result of liberation from cyclic existence, albeit just for themselves, they are classified as superior to the previous kind of beings.

Those who have seen the endless sufferings of other sentient beings in cyclic existence and who take refuge in the Three Jewels in order to deliver those beings from cyclic existence are termed "beings of great scope." Because they have in mind the wish to attain buddhahood for the benefit of sentient beings, and there is nothing higher than that, they are indicated by the word *unsurpassed*. At present, therefore, we should turn away from the perspective of the beings of small and medium scope and try to emulate the beings of great scope for the sake of all sentient beings.

The different durations for which these beings go for refuge correspond to their different intentions. Thus, beings of small scope take refuge until they attain the resultant happiness in their next life: being reborn in the higher reams. Beings of medium scope take refuge temporarily for as long as they live and ultimately, as listeners or solitary realizers, until they attain their respective results. Beings of great scope take refuge until they reach the heart of enlightenment—that is, until they have realized the gnosis of buddhahood. In this context, we should do as they do.

What are the objects in which they take refuge? It is possible to take refuge in beings who are renowned for their greatness in the world—beings like Brahmā, Viṣhṇu, and Mahādeva, who are well known to non-Buddhists; or in the different classes of gods, nāgas, yakṣhas, and nonhumans who live in their respective abodes, such as mountains, rocks, and trees; or in one's parents, relatives, friends, and so forth. But none of these are really able to protect us. Since they themselves have not been freed from the fears of cyclic existence, they should never be relied on as a refuge, as is stated in the *Supreme Victory Banner Sūtra*:

Men afraid of danger
Mostly go for refuge
In mountains, forests, gardens,
Reliquaries, and trees.
For those who use them, such refuges
Cannot protect from every kind of fear.

And in the *Sūtra of the Play of Mañjuśrī*, we read,

Your parents are not your refuge,
Neither are your relatives and friends.
They will abandon you
And depart wherever they please.
Today, take refuge in those who clear away
The fears of beings who are afraid,
Who protect those who are protectorless—
The Buddha, Dharma, and Saṅgha, the supreme assembly.
One who goes for refuge in these,
Rather than in gods, *gandharvas*, or humans,
Will be delivered from all fears
And find happiness without difficulty.

Thus, the only source of refuge that can protect us from both temporary and ultimate fear and suffering is the Three Jewels. It is in them that one should take refuge. For this, there are numerous points of view according to the different tenet systems of the higher and lower vehicles. We shall confine our discussion here to the approaches for taking refuge according to the Basic Vehicle and the Great Vehicle.

According to the Basic Vehicle, the Buddha is a supreme manifestation body. The Dharma comprises the twelve branches of his excellent speech, embodying transmission (the piṭakas of the Lesser Vehicle) and realization (the path, concentration, and so forth present in the individuals' mind streams). The Saṅgha is divided into the Saṅgha of ordinary beings and the Saṅgha of noble beings. The Saṅgha of ordinary beings comprises the lesser Saṅgha, which is a Saṅgha by virtue of the fact that it is a field of merit for beings, consisting of the male and female intermediate ordinees and lay practitioners, and the greater Saṅgha, consisting of fully ordained individuals, the "great Saṅgha of monks."* A group of four such monks is known as a "gathering of the Saṅgha." The Saṅgha of noble beings consists of stream enterers, once-returners, nonreturners, and candidates for arhatship. Arhats abiding by the result are held to be grouped with the buddhas.

The accepted viewpoint in the Great Vehicle is as follows: The Buddha is the embodiment of the three buddha bodies, possessed of the twofold purity,† the ultimate state in which the two fulfillments are fully present and perfect. This is stated in the *Sublime Continuum*,

> It is uncompounded, spontaneous,
> Not realized through anything extraneous,
> And has knowledge, compassion, and power—
> Buddhahood has the two fulfillments.[158]

Since it is not created anew by causes and conditions, it is uncompounded. It is not actuated by any effort, so it is spontaneous. It is seen with the self-arisen gnosis of buddhahood, so it is not realized through extraneous conditions. These are three qualities related to one's own fulfillment as the body of truth. Then there are three qualities related to others' fulfillment in the form body—namely, knowledge, which is the unmistaken comprehension of the meaning of the first three qualities; compassion, which is the wish to set other beings to be trained in that state of the body of truth; and the power to dispel the causes of suffering and resultant sufferings from others' minds. Together with the first three qualities, this makes six qualities in all, or eight qualities if the two categories are counted as qualities on their own.‡

The Dharma is in essence inexpressible. By nature, it is the path, or remedy, that leads to buddhahood. Its aspects are the Dharma as meaning, which is defined as both path and cessation, and the Dharma as word, comprising the twelve branches of excellent speech. The same text states,

> It is inconceivable, devoid of the two, and devoid of concepts;
> It is purity, clarity, and counteraction. Thus,

*Tib. *dge slong gi dge 'dun chen po*. This expression appears in numerous sūtras, such as the *Heart Sūtra*.

†Tib. *dag pa gnyis*. See glossary, s.v. "twofold purity."

‡The two categories here are fulfillment for oneself in the body of truth and fulfillment for others through the form body.

The Dharma is, and causes, freedom from attachment—
The two truths, which are its characteristics.
Freedom from attachment is summarized
As the truths of cessation and of the path.[159]

Because the Dharma is not an object to be evaluated by means of conventional knowledge using symbols, designations, analogies, reasoning, and so on, it is inconceivable. It is at peace from karmic deeds and defilements, so it is devoid of the two. It is free of the concepts associated with the incorrect ways of thinking that cause the latter, so it is devoid of concepts. These three qualities are associated with the truth of cessation, which is freedom from attachment. As it is unstained by the obscurations of the defilements, it is perfectly pure. Being free of cognitive obscurations, it shines with the light of gnosis. And in destroying the three poisons, it is counteractive. These three qualities are associated with the truth of the path, which causes freedom from attachment. The jewel of the Dharma thus has six qualities, or eight qualities if the two categories into which these are divided are counted separately.*

The twelve branches of excellent speech that comprise the Dharma of transmission are discourses, poetical declarations, prophesies, teachings in verse, teachings spoken intentionally, life stories, historical accounts, narratives, detailed expositions, accounts of the Buddha's previous lives, teachings establishing specific topics, and marvelous teachings.[160]

Cessation is twofold: analytical cessation, in which the stains that were previously present have been dispelled by counteragents and elaborations are absent, and nonanalytical cessation, which refers to settling in equipoise in the space-like natural absence of stains or elaborations. As for the path, it is the aspect of realization associated with the paths of accumulation, joining, seeing, and meditation.

In short, the Dharma refers to all the aspects of transmission and realization that show the characteristics of the two truths.

The Saṅgha comprises those who dwell on the ten levels of noble beings and who now see the luminosity that is the nature of the mind. Again, in the *Sublime Continuum*, we find,

Because, truly and to the full extent,
They see with inner gnosis,

*The two categories here correspond to the truth of cessation and the truth of the path.

> The assembly of the irreversibly wise
> Possesses unsurpassable qualities.[161]

They know truly, seeing unmistakenly the essence of the sugatas, the expanse of reality that is pure from the very beginning. They know to the full extent, seeing that that very state is intrinsically and equally present as the true nature of all the infinity of sentient beings. And they see these two with their own inner individual self-cognizing gnosis, which is not common to others. These are their three qualities of knowledge. They are also perfectly pure, being free from three obscurations—from attachment (the obscuration of the defilements), from obstruction (the cognitive obscurations), and the obscuration of the inferior views of the listeners and solitary realizers. These are their three qualities of freedom. Some authorities count these two categories separately and hold that they have eight qualities in all. The assembly of these wise, irreversible bodhisattvas thus possesses unsurpassable qualities, superior to those of the listeners and solitary realizers.

Besides these definitions of the Three Jewels, the sūtras speak of the "Buddha present in front of one," and the same expression is used with regard to the Dharma and Saṅgha. The Buddha present in front of one refers to images and stūpas. The Dharma present in front of one appears in the form of the books and letters of the sūtras and mantras. The Saṅgha present in front of one refers to the Saṅgha of ordinary beings who are keeping their vows. As far as beings to be trained are concerned, all these are the Buddha himself manifesting in those different forms, so they are to be considered as the objects of refuge. This is mentioned in the *Sūtra of the Ornament of the Buddhas*:

> Oh, the Tathāgata's manifestations are boundless,
> Benefiting the beings to be trained by different means
> With their appropriate colors and names.

And in the *Root Tantra of Mañjuśrī*, we read,

> Manifesting in those many different images,
> He benefits beings by introducing them to virtue.

And in the *Sūtra of the Ornament of the Buddhas*,

In the final period of five hundred years,
I will be present in the form of writings.
Consider them as identical to me
And show them due respect.

The *Mahāparinirvāṇa Sūtra* states,

During the age of degeneration,
I will manifest as spiritual friends
To benefit you and other beings.

Why are the Three Jewels called "rare and supreme"?* The *Sublime Continuum* gives the following explanation:

Because they exist rarely, are flawless,
Have power, are an ornament for the world,
Are supreme, and do not change,
They are indeed rare and supreme.[162]

The term "rare and supreme" was used to translate the Sanskrit word *ratna*, a precious jewel, which was taught as having six analogous qualities:

- Because beings who have not given rise to sources of good will not meet with them in many kalpas, the existence of the Three Jewels is rare.
- They are entirely free of stains and are therefore flawless.
- They possess inconceivably powerful qualities such as the six kinds of preternatural knowledge,† and so they have power.‡
- They are an ornament for the world because they are the source of all beings' positive aspirations.
- Because they transcend the world, they are supreme.
- Since they are uncompounded by nature, they do not change.

*This question introduces a discussion of the Tibetan term for the Three Jewels, *dkon mchog gsum* (literally "three rare and supreme ones").

†For the six kinds of preternatural knowledge (Tib. *mngon par shes pa drug*), see Jigme Lingpa and Longchen Yeshe Dorje, *Treasury*, bk. 1, appendix 5, 387.

‡A jewel's power lies in its hardness and its ability to cut through other stones.

As for why they are presented as *Three* Jewels, the same text states,

> With these points—the teacher, what he teaches, and the disciples—
> Were presented three refuges
> With regard to the three vehicles
> And those inclined to observances of three kinds.[163]

In order, on a temporary level, to introduce disciples progressively, the Buddha presented three sources of refuge from the point of view of six kinds of individuals. These six are related to the three vehicles and to three kinds of observances. Of the followers of the three vehicles, followers of the Great Vehicle strive to attain perfect enlightenment and, recognizing that the Buddha is the greatest of all human beings, they devote themselves to the observance (out of the three kinds of observance) of practices in which the Buddha is venerated and so on. For these beings, therefore, he presented the Buddha as the source of refuge.

Similarly, those following the vehicle of the solitary realizers wish to understand and attain by themselves the profound teachings on dependent arising. Recognizing that the Dharma is the supreme freedom from attachment, or the method for becoming free from attachment, they devote themselves to the observance of practices such as reading the scriptures. For them, therefore, the Dharma is the source of refuge.

Those in the listeners' vehicle, having followed the teachings given by others, wish to attain the eight resultant states of the four pairs of noble beings.* Recognizing that the Saṅgha is the greatest of all assemblies, they devote themselves to the observance of practices such as providing the prescribed articles. For them the Saṅgha is the source of refuge.

In short, the objects that are taken as the sources of refuge in the context of the causal vehicle are the Three Jewels, which are contained in others' streams of being. In the *Precious Treasury That Fulfills All Wishes*, we read,

> The objects of refuge are the Three Jewels,
> The causal objects that have already appeared in others' streams of
> being:

*Tib. *zung bzhi ya brgyad*, refers to the four kinds of noble being in the listeners' vehicle (stream enterer, once-returner, nonreturner, and arhat) for each of which there are two stages—candidates, and those who abide by the result.

> The Buddha who possesses the three bodies, elimination and realization, and activities;
> The Dharma, whose two aspects are the truths of cessation and the path;
> And the Saṅgha of noble bodhisattvas who have entered the levels.
> Temporarily, we take refuge in these three equally.[164]

How do we take refuge in these three? We consider the Buddha as our teacher, requesting him to teach us, for he knows what to avoid and what to adopt, while we do not. We take the Dharma as our actual refuge, for the Dharma is what the Buddha taught regarding avoidance and adoption. By putting the Dharma into practice as it appears in those teachings, we will attain the sublime happiness of freedom from all fear. We take the Saṅgha as our companions, guiding us as we travel an unknown road. Just as we have to go wherever the guide goes, we need to emulate whatever the Saṅgha does. Ideally, this would depend on meeting noble beings in person, but if there is a pure Saṅgha of ordinary beings who possess the essential instructions that have been transmitted in a lineage from one noble being to another and who maintain the continuity of the practice, it is also acceptable to put our trust in them. Nowadays, such beings are our main guides: all the sūtras and tantras state that a spiritual friend is the best guide for teaching the path.

Furthermore, the Buddha possesses infinite knowledge, love, and power. On account of his knowledge, he knows every one of the methods for protecting all beings who take refuge in him from fear and suffering and from all the defilements. With his love, he constantly protects beings without ever being indifferent with regard to their welfare. And with his power, he is able to protect his followers in accordance with their particular fortune. It is thus that the Buddha is capable of providing refuge. Apart from differing from the Buddha in the extent of their influence, the members of the noble Saṅgha, too, are worthy refuges, for they are similar to him in possessing extraordinary knowledge, love, and power, and they do protect us.

The main way in which the Three Jewels afford protection is through our practicing the sacred Dharma as taught by the Buddha and Saṅgha. This will enable us to eliminate the defilements and thus be delivered from all the fear and suffering that they cause. There are other, ordinary ways in which they will protect us. Regardless of our abandoning the deeds and defilements that cause our fear and suffering, simply remembering the names of the buddhas, performing prostrations, and praying to them will, on the temporary level, directly protect us from all kinds of harm such as the eight or sixteen dangers.[165] Even if we are to be reborn in the lower realms, the Three Jewels can permanently reverse or postpone such rebirth and thus protect us in all sorts of ways. Indeed, there are no limits to the miraculous display of the buddhas' and bodhisattvas' skillful means, prayers of aspiration, concentration, and gnosis, as we read in the *Sūtra Teaching on the Magical Display of Miracles*:

> O children of the buddhas, many are the Tathāgata's skillful means and many are the sentient beings to be brought to full maturation. Knowing what sentient beings are thinking, how they are to be trained, what are their sources of good, and the course their varied aspirations are taking, he reveals the Dharma. Some beings are trained by bodhisattvas, some by listeners, some by solitary realizers; some are trained by celestial beings, some by Indra, some by Brahmā, some by the nāgas. Some are trained by great miraculous displays, some by kings, some by concentration, some by hearing the Dharma, some by miracles. Some are trained by the Tathāgata's passing into nirvāṇa, some by his relics, and some by being inspired to meritorious activities such as constructing stūpas, building temples, and laying out pleasure gardens. Some are trained by being inspired to meritorious activities such as fashioning images, painting pictures, and making images out of gold, silver, and brass. Some are trained by being inspired to meritorious activities such as venerating and serving the Saṅgha of monks. Some are trained by being inspired to copy the sūtras, to cause others to copy them, and to study them. Some are trained by being inspired to offer adornments such as lamps, incense, flowers, scented water, garlands, and necklaces. The Tathāgata's skill in means is not limited to his knowledge of the ultimate truth and his attainment of nirvāṇa.

And the *Sūtra of the Ornament of the Buddhas* states,

> A spark no bigger than a mustard seed can burn
> A stack of hay as lofty as the highest peak.
> So too, a single offering to the sugatas
> Can burn up all defilements and lead beyond all pain.

The Himalayan herb called "Excellent to See"
Will clear up every ill when seen or touched.[166]
And those who, likewise, see the tenfold strengths or hear of them
Will gain the wisdom of the buddhas, possessed of all good qualities.

In the *Sūtra of the White Lotus of the Sacred Dharma*, we read,

Those who draw or else commission
An image on a wall of Buddha's form,
Perfect with the marks of a hundred merits,
Will all attain enlightenment.
When people or even children
Who are learning to draw,
Just for fun or to while away the time,
Use their fingernail or a stick
To draw the Buddha's image on a wall,
They will all attain enlightenment,
They will all come to have compassion,
They will all save ten million beings,
Setting on the path great numbers of bodhisattvas.

And in the *Verses for Prasenajit*,

Human beings who build stūpas of the bhagavans
And create images of them
Will, as many times as there are atoms in those things,
Win dominion over the celestial realms and on earth.
In the form and formless realms, they will experience
All the highest levels of perfect concentration
And finally attain buddhahood,
Free of the sufferings of birth, aging, and the rest.

And the *Incantation of the Pure Immaculate Rays of Light* states,

Again, if someone, in another's name, writes the letters of the secret mantras and places them inside a stūpa, to which they earnestly make offerings, the person who has died will be freed from the lower realms and be reborn in the higher realms; indeed, they

> will be reborn among the gods of the Joyous Realm. Through the blessings of the Buddha, they will not fall into the lower realms. A son or daughter of noble family who circumambulates that stūpa or makes offerings to it will, by the Tathāgata's blessings, never turn back from the path to unsurpassable enlightenment. The obscurations related to their past deeds will also all be purified, without exception. Even the birds and wild animals on whom that stūpa casts its shadow will never again be reborn as animals or in the other lower realms. Even the wrong deeds of those who have committed the great evil of the five crimes with immediate retribution and who touch that stūpa or come under its shadow will all be purified and brought to an end.

And,

> Even those who dream of that stūpa, or see it from afar, or hear the ringing of its bells, or hear the story of how it was built will have all their evil deeds and obscurations, the five crimes with immediate retribution and the like, purified: the tathāgatas will always protect them and think of them, and they will attain the perfectly pure path of unsurpassable, complete, and perfect enlightenment.

All this is further corroborated in the *Incantation of the Casket of Secret Relics*, the *Incantation of Sarvanīvaraṇaviṣkambhin*, the *Sūtra of Dependent Arising*, the *Incantation and Practice of Uṣṇīṣavijayā*, and other sūtras. And it is said in the *Sūtra Teaching on the Magical Display of Miracles* that greater than the benefit of filling a stūpa in Jambudvīpa made of the seven kinds of jewels and containing the Tathāgata's relics, of making all kinds of celestial offerings to it for one hundred thousand years, and of setting all the sentient beings in Jambudvīpa on the Noble Eightfold Path and continuously offering them everything they need for a thousand years is the benefit of writing, explaining, hearing, and reading a single verse of this discourse. The *Sūtra That Teaches the Tathāgata Essence* says that anyone who explains that sūtra, hears it, copies it, or causes it to be explained may immediately give rise to the thought, "I shall attain enlightenment," and is worthy of veneration by the gods and the whole world. And in the *Sūtra That Teaches the Conduct of a Bodhisattva*, it is said that the merit of listening to this discourse, even if one has doubts, is greater than that of a bodhisattva practicing the six transcendent perfections for one hundred thousand kalpas without skill in means. And there are infinitely many other statements of this sort. In the *Verses That Summarize the Perfection of Wisdom*, we find,

> Some, at the time the sugatas pass into nirvāṇa,
> Build stūpas made of the seven precious substances and venerate them.
> Now, imagine billions of worlds filled with stūpas containing the sugatas' relics and as numerous as the Ganges's sands,
> And in those infinite billions of worlds,
> As many sentient beings doing nothing but offering divine flowers, the finest incense,
> And perfumes for all the kalpas in the three times—could any offering be better than that?
> Yet that merit of erecting and worshipping those stūpas could never match
> The merit of copying in a book this Mother of the Sugatas,
> The source of the ten strengths of a buddha,
> And of preserving it and venerating it with flowers and scented offerings.

And,

> Some, in worlds as numerous as the Ganges River's sands,
> Might benefit as many beings and bring them to the arhat level,
> Yet far greater is the merit of copying this Transcendent Wisdom
> And giving the book to beings of supreme intelligence.
> The reason is that, having trained in it, those supreme exponents
> Then teach its message—that all phenomena are emptiness.
> Listeners who hear them will reach full freedom through this swift path,
> Solitary realizers will attain the level of bodhisattvas,
> And bodhisattvas, the enlightenment of the buddhas.

In the *Jewel Cloud Sūtra*, we read,

> If one were to ask what are the most perfect offerings and acts of respect that bodhisattvas can make, they are deeds that

> bodhisattvas perform in relation to the Buddha, Dharma, and Saṅgha. What deeds should they perform in relation to the Buddha? They should make offerings of perfume, flowers, incense, or scented unguents to stūpas containing the tathāgatas' relics and to images of the tathāgatas, or coat their stūpas with plaster, or repair stūpas of the tathāgatas that have disintegrated. These are the deeds they should perform in relation to the Buddha. What deeds should they perform in relation to the Dharma? They should listen to the teachings, study them, expound them, copy them, recite them, master them, reflect on them, and train in them by applying them correctly. These are the deeds they should perform in relation to the Dharma. What deeds should they perform in relation to the Saṅgha? They should offer to the Saṅgha robes, food, bedding, medicine for when they are sick, provisions, and, at the very least, a cupped handful of cold water. These are the deeds they should perform in relation to the Saṅgha. Such are the perfect offerings and acts of respect that bodhisattvas should make.

In the *Garret Sūtra*, we find,

> Ānanda, these three ways of cultivating sources of good in relation to the Buddha, Dharma, and Saṅgha will never be exhausted in cyclic existence; they will never come to an end but will lead to one's attaining the inexhaustible state of nirvāṇa.

These and other extensive explanations in the sūtras appear in detail elsewhere, though they will also be mentioned briefly below. Through knowing how the boundless miraculous display of the Three Jewels protects beings in these ways, we should develop even greater faith and respect.

After this short supplementary explanation, let us now continue with the main subject. Put briefly, the temporary refuge, as mentioned above, includes all three of the Three Jewels, but the ultimate, resultant refuge is the Buddha alone, as we find in the *Sublime Continuum*:

> Ultimately, the refuge for beings
> Is buddhahood alone.[167]

The reasons for this are as follows: The Buddha's excellent speech, the Dharma of transmission, is like a boat that has been used to cross a river: once one has realized the meaning, there is no longer any need for the words, so one abandons, or discards, it and continues on one's way. Those on the path of training who have attained realization through the Dharma of realization proceed higher and higher. As they do so, they discard the lower paths, so the Dharma of realization is inconstant and deceptive. The cessation of the lower vehicles is like a lamp being extinguished: it is a mere absence—the divestment of suffering and the origin of suffering—and that mere absence will neither protect nor not protect. Even the noble beings training in the Great Vehicle have not yet attained the level of eternal fearlessness, so they still need to make an effort to guard their minds and to go for refuge to the Buddha. For all these reasons, none of these are the true, unfailing refuge. The ultimate, absolute refuge is solely the body of truth of the Buddha, because it is the ultimate Dharma of realization, the truth of cessation, and because the ultimate quality that the assemblies* can achieve is the body of truth. From the ultimate point of view, there is not the slightest difference between the three refuges. The *Precious Treasury That Fulfills All Wishes* expresses this as follows:

> The ultimate is solely the truth-body buddha:
> It is the ultimate jewel, the supreme refuge,
> For the truth of the path is relative and bodhisattvas have
> obscurations.
> Other than buddhahood, what ultimate refuge is there?
> This is the resultant refuge,
> The Three Jewels which we aspire to achieve ourselves.[168]

We therefore distinguish between the causal refuge and resultant refuge. In the causal refuge, we go for refuge to the teacher, the path, and the companions in order to attain the ultimate state of buddhahood. The resultant refuge is the wish to accomplish in one's own mind stream the truth-body buddha, which is the inseparability of the ultimate, absolute Three Jewels. This is affirmed in the *Sūtra of the Questions of the Householder Ugra*:

*"Assemblies" here refers to the Saṅgha.

Taking refuge in the Buddha is wishing to obtain the qualities of Buddha.
Taking refuge in the Dharma is wishing to obtain the qualities described in the teachings.
Taking refuge in the Saṅgha is wishing to obtain the qualities of the Saṅgha.

What, then, is the difference between this and bodhichitta in aspiration? Among other things, the difference is said to be that bodhichitta in aspiration considers others' fulfillment, while this definition of refuge considers one's own fulfillment.

To sum up, the causal factors for taking refuge are fear, faith, and compassion. Its essence is a meaningful commitment, which is to be understood as follows: The causal refuge is the commitment to rely on the Buddha as one's teacher, the Dharma as the path, and the Saṅgha as companions helping one to accomplish the path. It therefore involves a promise not to rely on other teachers as one's teacher, on their traditions as the path, and on those who hold those traditions as companions. The resultant refuge is the promise and commitment to attain the ultimate state of buddhahood, which is the inseparability of the three refuges, and to turn the wheel of the Dharma and so on in order to preserve the lineage of the Three Jewels in the world without its being interrupted.

2. The refuge of the system of the resultant Diamond Vehicle

Considering the object of refuge in the Diamond Vehicle from the common point of view, one needs to go for refuge in the universal object of refuge described above—that is, the Three Jewels, and in the specific objects of refuge, which are the teacher, yidam, and ḍākinī. Their characteristics are as follows: Here, in the context of the Diamond Vehicle of secret mantras, one needs to receive blessings from an object who is full of kindness; and one needs to be mindful of his or her kindness. This object is the teacher. Then there is the extraordinary object from whom one receives the supreme and common accomplishments—the host of deities in the maṇḍala of the yidam. And because one needs to entrust the activities of dispelling obstacles and accomplishing one's temporary aims to someone, there are the ḍākinīs and protectors of the teachings. Although these are mentioned separately, the yidam is part of the jewel of the Buddha, the ḍākinīs and wisdom Dharma protectors are part of the jewel of the Saṅgha, and the teacher is the essence of all Three Jewels. This is affirmed in the *Tantra of the Arising of Saṃvara*:

> The Teacher is the Buddha, the Teacher is the Dharma,
> Likewise, the Teacher is the Saṅgha:
> The Teacher is the glorious Vajradhara.

And in the *Vajra Garland*, we read,

> His uncontaminated mind is the buddha state,
> The Dharma is fully included in his speech,
> His body is known as the Saṅgha.

And in the *Accomplishment of Gnosis* composed by Indrabhūti, it is said,

> The teacher is the Buddha, the Dharma,
> And the Saṅgha too.
> Through his kindness, one will know that this is so.
> Thus he is the embodiment of the Three Jewels.

Some scriptures also speak of a fourth jewel. In the *Tantra of the Union of All the Buddhas*, for example, we find,

> The Buddha, Dharma, and Saṅgha,
> And the teacher is the fourth.

And the *Vajra Mirror* has,

> Vajrasattva, the principal deity in the maṇḍala,
> Is the teacher, equal to the Buddha in person.

And the *Guhyasamāja Tantra*,

> Because their natures and activities
> Are essentially the same,
> The teachers are the equals of all the buddhas.
> But because they show beings the path,
> They are superior to the buddhas themselves.

In each case, these texts give extensive explanations of how the teachers are the lords of the maṇḍalas, how they are equal to the buddhas, and how they are superior to the buddhas.

Considering the object of refuge from the uncommon point of view, *Finding Rest in the Nature of the Mind: A Teaching of the Great Perfection* states,

> The final and resultant refuge is the dharmakāya.
> It is the essence of the Buddha, Dharma, and Assembly;
> It is the ultimate divinity, the luminosity of your own mind
> Free from all conceptual construction.[169]

In the vehicle of characteristics, the resultant refuge is simply the desire to attain the result, buddhahood, oneself. In this context, it is included in the causal refuge. Here, however, the ultimate, resultant object of refuge is the body of truth, for the ultimate Three Jewels are the body of truth. When the body of truth has already appeared in another's mind stream, it is the causal refuge, but the resultant refuge is one's own mind, the state free of all limitations due to conceptual elaboration, present as the nature of the Three Jewels. It is in this that we go for refuge, as is explained in the *Accomplishment of Gnosis*:

> The mind free of anything to be purified and anything to be attained is the Buddha,
> Its unchanging, uncontaminated nature is the Dharma,
> And its spontaneously perfected qualities are the Saṅgha;
> One's own mind, therefore, is supreme.

And in his *Great Treatise on the Graded Path*, Padmasambhava states,

> The natural state that is awakened from the very beginning is one's own awareness, bodhichitta. It is a state in which the delusion of duality has been purified and the nondual gnosis has been developed, which is why it is called "buddha."* It is not that a

*This is a definition of the term *buddha* (the awakened state) based on the two elements that make up the equivalent Tibetan term *sangs rgyas*: *sangs* means "purified" or "awakened," and *rgyas* means "developed" or "unfolded."

> delusion that was present has been purified and is no longer there, and that a nondual gnosis that was not there has been developed and is now present. In one's fundamental nature, there is no delusion; its essential nature unfolds as nondual gnosis, so it is awakened from the very beginning. Its empty nature is the body of truth. Its natural, clear radiance is the body of perfect enjoyment. The inseparability of clarity and emptiness is the body of manifestation. It is the primordial wisdom that knows the empty nature as it is, the natural radiance in its multiplicity, and the nondual nature, or the inseparability of clarity and emptiness. In the fundamental nature, there is no delusion: this is perfect elimination. Its essential nature is present as nonduality: this is perfect realization. If one were not, in this way, buddha from the very beginning, even if one were to meditate, buddhahood could never happen. It is as with fine gold: if it were not golden from the very beginning, however much one worked it, it could never become golden.

As for how one takes refuge, it is to rest in the state free of conceptual elaboration, for the Three Jewels (the objects to which one goes for refuge) and the persons taking refuge (oneself and all sentient beings) are, in truth, not in the slightest way distinct from the magical display of one's own mind. The nature of mind is in essence like space, utterly free of biased tendencies. This is explained in the *Middle Sūtra of the Perfection of Wisdom* as follows:

> Subhūti, to not think of the Buddha, or think of the Dharma, or think of the Saṅgha is the correct way to go for refuge.

And in the *Accomplishment of Gnosis*, we read,

> To realize the mind of radiant clarity
> As the lord of the three maṇḍalas
> And rest in equipoise one-pointedly
> Is perfectly explained as the supreme result.

B. A condensed presentation from the oral teachings of Orgyen, knower of the three times

The following account is a summarized extract from the *Answers to the Questions of Yeshe Tsogyal* in the *Direct Instructions of the Teacher* from the *Treasure of Nyang*.

The foundation of all Dharma practice is the refuge. The supports for all Dharma practice are the Three Jewels. The means for putting an end to birth and death is the refuge and its branches.

In this regard, the essence of taking refuge is the wish to attain unsurpassable enlightenment together with a commitment to do so, based on compassion.

Its etymological definition is that one goes for refuge because it affords protection from the fears of the three lower realms and from the inferior views of the transitory composite held by the tīrthikas and others.

There are three categories: the outer, inner, and secret refuges.

1. The outer refuge

There are three causal factors for giving rise to the outer refuge: fear of the sufferings of cyclic existence, confidence in the Three Jewels as a source of refuge, and taking them as one's refuge.

In what object does one take refuge? One takes refuge in the Three Jewels. By what means are they able to put an end to birth and death? The omniscient Buddha, who is free of all defects and in whom all qualities are complete, the teachings that he gave, and the Saṅgha who holds his teachings are together capable of putting an end to our own and others' birth and death. They therefore constitute the sole object of refuge, and it is to them that we go for refuge.

What sort of person takes refuge? Someone who has interest, respect, and faith and is mindful of the Three Jewels' qualities. He or she must also have three particular attitudes: first, the thought "Since cyclic existence is without beginning and end, I must turn away from it now"; second, the thought "The gods of the tīrthikas and others are not an object of refuge for me"; and third, the thought "The omniscient Buddha alone is my supreme object of refuge." These three apply to when one is giving rise to the common refuge.

How, or in what way, does one take refuge? One takes refuge out of fear of the lower realms and cyclic existence, with confidence in the blessings of the Three Jewels, and having firm faith and compassion.

With what particular attitude does one take refuge? One takes refuge with a deep concern for others' welfare. One does not attain buddhahood simply by rejecting cyclic existence and wanting to attain the result, nirvāṇa. So one takes refuge with the thought "In order to free all sentient beings from the sufferings of cyclic existence, I take refuge until I and all the beings in the three worlds attain the heart of enlightenment."

The precepts will be explained below.

2. The inner refuge

In what object does one take refuge? In the teacher, the yidam, and the ḍākinī.

What sort of persons take refuge? Those who have entered the gateway of the secret mantras.

How, or in what way, does one take refuge? With devotion, physically, verbally, and mentally.

With what particular attitude does one take refuge? One takes refuge with the attitude of seeing the teacher as a buddha, never abandoning the yidam even to save one's life, and continuously venerating the ḍākinī.

For how long? From the moment one first receives empowerment and arouses the bodhichitta until one attains the level of Vajradhara.

What are the conditions under which one takes refuge? One must have given rise to devotion and respect for the secret mantras.

The purpose, or benefit, of taking refuge is that it makes one a suitable vessel for the secret mantras and a recipient for the extraordinary blessings.

The precepts will be described below.

3. The secret refuge

In what object does one take refuge? In the view, meditation, and conduct.

What sort of person takes refuge? Someone of the very highest capacity who wishes to attain buddhahood in a single lifetime.

How, or in what way, does one take refuge? By means of the view, meditation, and conduct—that is, with confidence in the view, experiences in meditation, and one taste in conduct.

With what particular attitude does one take refuge? As regards the view, one takes refuge without dogmatic opinions—that is, without holding that buddhahood is something to be attained or that cyclic existence is something to be abandoned. In the meditation, there is nothing to be identified and no falling into extremes. And as regards one's conduct, there is nothing to adopt or avoid, and one is free of effortful activity.

For how long? Until one attains buddhahood.

Under what conditions? With the wish to never take a body.*

The purpose, or benefit, of taking refuge is that it enables one to attain perfect buddhahood in this very lifetime.

The precepts will be explained below.

As well as this, in Padmasambhava's autocommentary of the *Great Treatise on the Graded Path*, we read,

> The detailed explanation of taking refuge has three parts: the common refuge, the extraordinary refuge, and the unsurpassable refuge.
>
> The common refuge is again divided into three sections.
>
> First, the source of refuge is identified as follows: The Buddha is the manifestation body, Shākyamuni, who alone is held to be supreme. The Dharma is the four truths of the causal vehicle, with emphasis on the training in superior discipline. The Saṅgha is the assembly of those who, through their outer dress and conduct, bear the outward physical signs of the Vinaya.
>
> Second, the individuals who take refuge are the listeners and solitary realizers.
>
> Third, the way of taking refuge is to do so for one's own benefit.
>
> On the basis of the common refuge, one can then take the vows of individual liberation. The refuge is obtained at the time of the ritual. The path consists of training in the four truths. By this means, one attains the result, that of an arhat, in three existences.
>
> Second, the extraordinary refuge is divided into three sections.
>
> First, the source of refuge is identified as follows: The Buddha is one who has perfected elimination and realization. He comprises the three bodies—the body of truth, the body of perfect

*That is, to transcend the cycle of birth and death.

enjoyment, and the manifestation body. The body of truth is that which possesses the twofold purity. The body of perfect enjoyment is that which possesses the five certainties.* And the manifestation body is that which possesses the five uncertainties.† The Dharma is the wheel of the definitive, absolute teachings, or teachings without characteristics, of the causal vehicle, with emphasis on the training in superior wisdom. The Saṅgha is the assembly of those who think of others' welfare—that is, of those who practice the vast activities of the bodhisattvas.

Second, the individuals who take refuge are bodhisattvas. They are of two kinds: those with keen faculties, and those with dull faculties.

Third, the way of taking refuge is to work for one's own and others' fulfillment, using the four boundless attitudes.

On the basis of this extraordinary refuge, one takes the bodhisattva vows. This refuge is obtained at the time of arousing bodhichitta. The path consists of training in the six transcendent perfections. By this means, one attains the result, buddhahood, after three measureless kalpas.

Third, the unsurpassable refuge has two parts: the general refuge of the secret mantras, and the extraordinary refuge of Atiyoga.

The general refuge of the secret mantras has three sections.

First, the source of refuge is identified as follows: The Buddha is the inseparability, neither single nor multiple, of the five bodies. The Dharma is the resultant Diamond Vehicle, which has been prophesied and is to be marveled at. In it any of the three trainings may be taught, with emphasis on the teachings of the secret mantras. The Saṅgha is the true and ultimate assembly, which naturally never engages in nonvirtue.

Second, the individuals who take refuge are vidyādhara yogins of the secret mantras, those who hold the three kinds of vows.

*The five certainties (Tib. *nges pa lnga*), or five perfections, are the perfect place, perfect teacher, perfect retinue, perfect time, and perfect teaching. See p. 13.

†In contrast to the five certainties just mentioned, a manifestation body buddha appears in many kinds of different places, in unpredictable forms, to different kinds of beings, and at different times, and it gives different kinds of teachings to accord with beings' different needs.

Third, the way of taking refuge is to go for refuge free of any subject-object duality, one's own and others' body, speech, and mind being inseparable from the Three Jewels.

On the basis of this unsurpassable refuge, one gives rise to the vows of the Secret Mantra Vehicle. This refuge is received at the time of the empowerment. The path consists of training in the two phases, and by this means one attains buddhahood in one, two, three, or five lifetimes.

The second unsurpassable refuge, the extraordinary refuge of Atiyoga, also has three sections.

First, the Three Jewels are identified as follows: Awareness present as the four buddha bodies is the jewel of the Buddha. That state is inseparable from the empty expanse of reality. The wisdom that knows that is the jewel of the Dharma, the extraordinary, marvelous definitive teachings of Atiyoga. The true, ultimate Saṅgha comprises those who remain in the state of virtue, where fundamentally there is no evil and the essential nature is untainted.

Second, the individuals are identified as supreme beings of the very highest faculties, practitioners of Atiyoga.

Third, the way of taking refuge is threefold: (1) taking refuge with the active aim of understanding that the Three Jewels are present in one's own mind, (2) taking refuge in a way that excludes any possibility other than the realization that there are no separate Three Jewels that are not one's own mind, and (3) true, unsurpassable refuge, the realization that the nature of mind is inseparably one with that of the Three Jewels and is spontaneously free and nondual, dwelling in no extremes at all.

Thus, whoever says, "Practice in accordance with the Buddha's words," is a teacher. Whoever practices in accordance with what the teacher says is a disciple. Whoever provides the right conditions for the disciples is a benefactor. And wherever such beings exist, there is the Buddha's teaching.

C. The main explanation of the instructions for taking refuge

The instructions for taking refuge should be learned in accordance with the interpretations in the individual instruction manuals.[170] Here we will give an example of the visualization according to the Minling Dorsem tradition.*

Thinking that you are beseeching the Three Jewels, the rare and supreme ones, to be your unfailing source of refuge, your protectors and helpers in freeing all sentient beings from the sufferings in the fearsome firepit that is cyclic existence, settle your mind in a relaxed state. At the same time, keep in mind your own fear of cyclic existence, faith in the qualities of the Three Jewels, and compassion for other sentient beings.

The place in which you are is a delightful, inspiring buddha-field made of all kinds of precious substances. Alternatively, imagine that the ground is of beryl, checkered with gold, completely surrounded by a jeweled fence. The place abounds with rivers of nectar, wish-fulfilling trees, meadows of flowers, goddesses offering all the pleasures of the senses, and flocks of magically manifested birds with delightful calls. The ground is even and gives slightly when trodden underfoot, springing back when one lifts one's foot. In the center of this vast and spacious environment is a wish-fulfilling tree whose trunk is made of all kinds of precious substances. It is firmly rooted, with leafy branches bending under the weight of its flowers and fruits, spreading out to fill the whole sky. Its branches—one in the center and four spreading in the four directions—are bedecked with all kinds of beautiful ornaments: golden chains spread from one branch to another, garlands of flowers and many-colored silk hangings, jeweled filigree ornaments, and gold and silver chimes and tinkling bells. With the slightest breeze, there clearly resonates the sound of the Dharma—teachings such as those on impermanence, suffering, emptiness, and no-self. Visualize all this not as something solid and real but as light, having the nature of a rainbow.

Once this appears clearly, visualize on the central branch a lofty, broad, jeweled throne borne by eight great lions, and upon it a seat of lotus and moon, on which is your root teacher in the form of the Buddha, Glorious Vajrasattva. He is white in color, with one face and two hands. The right hand holds a vajra at the level of his heart, the left hand rests on his hip, holding a bell. He is in union with his consort Vajragarvā, who is white and holds a knife and skull. They are seated cross-legged in the vajra and lotus postures, respectively, and bedecked with all the silken garments and jewel

*The Minling Dorsem refers to a Vajrasattva sādhana cycle discovered as a treasure by Gyurme Dorje, the great Terdak Lingpa (1646–1714), the founder of Mindrölling Monastery in Tibet.

ornaments. His body radiates infinite rays of light and is adorned with the thirty-two major and eighty minor marks of excellence. His speech has the sixty expressive qualities, proclaiming the sound of the teachings. His mind rests in equipoise in many hundreds of different kinds of concentration.

Tiered upward above the crown of his head are the teachers of the lineage: the Vajradhara Lodrö Thaye; Jamyang Khyentse Wangpo; Jetsunma Trinle Chödrön; Trinle Namgyal, the reincarnation of Nubchen;[171] Pema Tenzin, an emanation of Hayagrīva; Rinchen Namgyal, an emanation of Vimalamitra; Rigdzin Gyurme Dorje, the revealer of profound treasures; the great translator Vairotsana; the mother of the buddhas, Yeshe Tsogyal; Padmasambhava of Uḍḍiyāna; the great *paṇḍita* Vimalamitra; the accomplished vidyādhara Hūṃkara; Shrī Siṃha, who perfected the union state; the manifestation body Garab Dorje; the body of perfect enjoyment Vajrasattva; and the body of truth Samantabhadra. Consider that they are present as the embodiments of the Three Jewels.

Next, on each of the branches in the four directions, visualize a high, wide throne. On the front one is the specific jewel of the Buddha, comprising the inconceivable display of the peaceful and wrathful yidam deities of the four and six tantra sections. On the right-hand branch is the universal Buddha, our teacher Munindra, surrounded by a retinue of the buddhas of the ten directions and four times in the form of supreme manifestation bodies attired as renunciates. On the branch to the rear is the *Sūtra of Transcendent Wisdom* in the form of a mountainous mass of sacred volumes stacked inside a lattice of five-colored light. On the left-hand branch is the universal Saṅgha, the assembly of noble bodhisattvas, listeners, and solitary realizers, including the Eight Great Close Sons,[172] the Eight Supreme Listeners,[173] and the Sixteen Sthaviras.[174] Around all these are the specific Saṅgha, comprising the *ḍākas* and ḍākinīs of the three places and the wisdom guardians who protect the teachings, massed together like clouds. Consider that they are all truly present.

All these are never anything other than the manifestations of your root teacher's mind, the state of bliss and emptiness; constant in their compassion and equal in their realization, they are visualized like the stars and planets shining in a clear sky.

The above concerns the objects of refuge. Now, with regard to the individuals taking refuge, imagine that on your right is your present father, on your left is your mother, in front of you are your enemies, and behind you are your friends and relatives. All around are the totality of beings with no particular feelings toward you, who are neither your adversaries nor your friends, disposed like dust on the surface of the earth. With yourself leading the chant, they join in as you show respect physically by kneeling and folding your hands. Verbally you all express your respect through the sonorous, heartfelt* recitation of the words of the refuge prayer. And mentally you express your respect by intense longing and devotion, thinking, "Whatever happens to me, favorable or unfavorable, pleasant or painful, good or bad, I have no one to rely on but you. Whatever happens, you know best. I beg you immediately to protect me and all sentient beings, my mothers, from all suffering and danger—the danger in general of the sufferings of cyclic existence, the danger in particular of the lower vehicles' concern for one's own welfare alone, and the danger especially of ordinary deluded grasping." In this manner, recite the refuge prayer, accumulating the numbers—a hundred, a thousand, ten thousand, one hundred thousand times, or more:

> NAMO In the sugatas of the ten directions and the three times,
> and their bodhisattva children,
> From now until we attain enlightenment,
> I and all beings as numerous as the sky is vast, without exception,
> Constantly take refuge with respect in body, speech and mind.[175]

You should take refuge in order that conditions adverse to accomplishing enlightenment may be dispelled, that favorable conditions like the two accumulations may be completed, and that enlightenment may be swiftly attained. Pray for the fulfillment of everything you wish for: pray that you may be protected from the fears of this life, from the confused experiences in the intermediate state, from the fears of your rebirth in the next life, from engaging in wrong paths, and so on; pray that you may develop the qualities of the path that you have not yet developed and stabilize and increase the qualities that you have developed.

At the end of the session, consider that the bodies of all the objects of refuge emanate rays of light, which strike you and all the sentient beings, purifying your negative deeds and obscurations. All the sentient beings fly up with a whirring sound like a flock of birds, ascending on a path of rainbow light into a pure buddha-field. Finally, consider that the root teacher's body

*Tib. *kha tsam tshig tsam ma yin pa*, reciting the prayer while thinking of its meaning and not simply mouthing the words.

emanates rays of light, striking the surrounding objects of refuge, which all melt into a ball of light and dissolve into the teacher, who shines more resplendently than ever. Your root teacher comes down onto your crown and with great joy melts into light and dissolves into you. Free of any dualistic concepts regarding your own mind and the teacher's mind, rest evenly as long as you can in the state of great bliss free of conceptual elaboration. This is the ultimate, absolute way of taking refuge.

Conclude by dedicating the merit. In the evening when you go to sleep, instead of dissolving the object of refuge into its support,* go to sleep with your head directed toward it, on your right side in the lion posture, in a state of constant devotion. At dawn, when you awake, think that the objects of refuge are waking you up with the sound of hand drums and bells. Consider that your upper garment symbolizes skillful means, your lower garment wisdom, your belt the union of means and wisdom, and your hat, if you are wearing one, symbolizes your teacher. Whatever you are doing, think, "I will never abandon the teacher and the Three Jewels." When you are eating and drinking, make an offering of the first part. When you are going up, climbing a mountain and suchlike, think, "I am going to draw all beings up into the buddha-field of Great Bliss." When you descend, think, "I am going down in order to draw all beings out of the lower realms." When you are traveling on the level, visualize the objects of refuge next to you at shoulder height, and recite the refuge prayer, considering that you, accompanied by all sentient beings, are circumambulating them. In this way, carry the practice on the path, never giving up your devotion and respect, whichever of the four forms of daily conduct† you are engaged in.

III. A concluding explanation of the different precepts and benefits of taking refuge

Mention was made above of the different precepts of taking refuge. These will now be explained. They are divided into (1) general precepts and (2) particular precepts. The general precepts are considered under two headings: (1) the actual precepts, and (2) the benefits of keeping them. The actual precepts are again divided into (1) precepts of the causal refuge and (2) precepts of the resultant refuge.

*The support of the object of refuge might be a statue or a painting of the refuge tree.
†Four forms of daily conduct: eating, sleeping, walking, and sitting.

A. General precepts

1. The actual precepts

a. Precepts of the causal refuge

There are three sets of precepts related to the causal refuge: (1) three precepts regarding things one must avoid, (2) three precepts regarding things one should do, and, as a follow-up to these, (3) three ancillary precepts.

i. Three precepts regarding things one must avoid

In his *Six Points of Refuge*, Vimalamitra says,

> The first precept of taking refuge
> Is not to rely on, or pay homage to, those who do harm.
> The second is to avoid harming any sentient beings
> And to treat them with love.
> The third is not to keep the company
> Of evildoers, whether "Buddhists" or non-Buddhists.

And in the *Mahāparinirvāṇa Sūtra*, we read,

> Those who take refuge in the Buddha
> Are perfect pursuers of virtue.[176]
> Never do they go for refuge
> In gods and others.
> Those who take refuge in the sacred Dharma
> Are devoid of harm and malice.
> Those, too, who take refuge in the Saṅgha
> Do not side with tīrthikas and others.

Furthermore, the Omniscient Dharma Lord adds, in *Finding Rest in the Nature of the Mind*,

> When you have taken refuge in a teacher,
> You must not deceive him, worthy as he is of reverence.
> Holy beings should be neither criticized nor denigrated.[177]

And he quotes from the *Sūtra of the Arborescent Array*:

> Those who follow a spiritual friend must not deceive anyone worthy of veneration; they should completely avoid saying unpleasant things about sublime beings and should follow the sacred teachings.

ii. Three precepts regarding things one should do

Vimalamitra lists these as follows:

> To images, verses, and stitched yellow patches
> You should be respectful and view them as the Buddha;
> Everything that he has said
> You should not disparage but take upon your crown;
> Individuals, pure and impure,
> You must regard as sacred.

iii. Three ancillary precepts

The *Compendium of Topics* explains that to follow a sublime being, to listen to the sacred teachings, and to practice them taking the example of the Saṅgha is what is called "taking refuge."

Moreover, whatever happens to you, never abandon the Three Jewels. Remember their great qualities. Offer them at least the first part of anything you eat or drink. And be diligent in taking refuge day and night, six times. As Vimalamitra says,

> Even for your life or body never give up the Three.
> Now, whatever happens to you,
> Do not seek any other protector or refuge.
> Always remember their immense qualities,
> And make offerings of food.
> Constantly recite the refuge prayer,
> And encourage this, six times a day.

b. Precepts of the resultant refuge

With the view that knows that all the phenomena of saṃsāra and nirvāṇa are, from the very beginning, the great sameness, the nature of the enlightened state, one should settle evenly on the point that has been ascertained, and recognize everything as the great maṇḍala of phenomenal appearance.* *Finding Rest in the Nature of the Mind* expresses this as follows:

> According to the precepts of resultant refuge,
> You should train at all times
> In the equality of all phenomena.
> You should not think in terms of good or bad,
> Taking or rejecting that which is of great or lesser worth.
> You should not trust your mind's elaborations,
> But cleanse them in the natural state of ultimate reality.
> All should be experienced as a maṇḍala spontaneous and perfect.[178]

And in the *Middle Sūtra of the Perfection of Wisdom*, we find,

> Those who wish to meditate on transcendent wisdom should train without conceptualizing or regarding any phenomenon whatsoever. How is that? Do not judge things with dualistic vision, saying, "This is best, this is worse, this is wrong, this is the Buddha's teaching, this a teaching by another wandering mendicant."†

This is a crucial point in the oral instructions that we and everyone else nowadays should take to heart. How different this is from the plethora of talk we hear that is based on attachment to different teachings and tenet systems: "This is our tradition," "Those are others' traditions," "This is the correct teaching," "That is not correct," and so on. You should understand that all these are signs of having been blessed by demons. Not only do they contravene the precepts of taking refuge, but we will experience terrible

*In other words, the precepts of the resultant refuge can be summarized in terms of view, meditation, and conduct.

†That is, a non-Buddhist teacher.

obscurations as the ripened effect of giving up the Dharma. The *Complete Compendium of Vaidalya*[179] declares,

> Thus are foolish people blessed by demons, leading them to the lower realms. So it is that they want to find fault with everything and seek to criticize even the teachings given by the Tathāgata.

And,

> Mañjushrī, there are some who think well of certain teachings given by the Tathāgata and think badly of other ones. They are rejecting the Dharma. By rejecting the Dharma, they are criticizing the Tathāgata. They are speaking ill of the Saṅgha.

And in the *Supplementary Tantra of Vairocana's Enlightenment*, we read,

> It will happen that confused people, without determining what is the condition of their minds, will say, "This is not the Buddha's teaching. It has been made up by charlatans." Vajrapāṇi, you should know that those fools will have two kinds of rebirth. What are those two? Rebirth as beings in the hells and as animals. Vajrapāṇi, I cannot say whether they will have anything at all that could be a source of good.

The *Sūtra of the King of Concentrations* states,

> Much worse than destroying
> All the stūpas here in Jambudvīpa
> Is the evil of rejecting the Buddha's teachings.

And in the *Perfection of Wisdom in One Hundred Thousand Lines*, we read,

> Do not indulge in rejecting the teachings, compared to which, in gravity, the five crimes with immediate retribution are a mere shadow. Shāriputra, those who have the attitude of rejecting the teachings say, "You and I must not train in this. It is not the Dharma. It is not the Vinaya. It is not the Buddha's teaching. It was not spoken by the Tathāgata." Rejecting the teachings them-

> selves, they also destroy others' faith. They corrupt their own and others' intentions. They delight in causing themselves and others to go to waste. With their desire to give up the Dharma, they induce others also to do so. If one so much as touches the shadow of such people who have accumulated the karma of destroying the Dharma . . .

The *Root Tantra of Mañjuśrī* states,

> Those on this earth who reject
> This, the most sublime teaching,
> The treasure of the Dharma taught by the conquerors,
> Will go to the Hell of Torment Unsurpassed,
> And there they'll cook for a great kalpa,
> As taught in detail many times.
> Once they have risen from there,
> Even if they are reborn in human form,
> They will be poor, and simple, afflicted by many ailments,
> Reborn in uncivilized lands.
> Despised by all the world,
> They will fall ill with leprosy.*
> Dumb, deaf, handicapped,
> Mentally retarded or blind,
> With ugly, ever fearful forms.
> On the earth, they will appear like hungry spirits,
> Badly dressed, with negative minds,
> And deformed fingernails and bodies,
> Devoured by parasites,
> Afflicted with boils and mange.
> Those who reject these sūtras
> Will have such destinies,
> And, wherever they take birth,
> They'll be reborn unintelligent and dull.

And in the *Perfection of Wisdom in Eight Thousand Lines*, we read,

***Leprosy* (Tib. *mdze*) in this context covers cancer and numerous other incurable diseases.

> Subhūti, those who accumulate the karma to be deprived of the Dharma will be reborn falling headlong into the lower realms and will suffer in the great Hell of Torment Unsurpassed. When it is their destiny for the universe to be dissolved in fire,* they will proceed from there to hells in other worlds. And when those worlds are in turn dissolved in fire, again they will be born in other hells, and so on, endlessly.

Similarly, the result of thinking ill of a bodhisattva spiritual friend who teaches the Dharma is described in the *Avalokinī Sūtra*[180] thus:

> People who act displeasingly
> To children of the buddhas
> Will abandon the states of gods and humankind
> For the experiences of the hells.
> People who cause harm
> To bodhisattvas
> Will suffer, eyeless or blind,
> Without anyone to help.
> Once dead, they will proceed to Torment Unsurpassed.
> There they'll blaze and be racked with fear.
> The bigger are their bodies,
> The greater the pain that they will feel.
> And in their series of lives
> They will have bodies a league in size,
> And round as a bag of waters,
> Completely eaten everywhere.
> And in those lives, upon their bodies
> There will grow five thousand heads,
> And in each head again
> A full five hundred tongues,
> On each of which a hundred ploughs
> Will plough their furrows on those very tongues.

*In other words, at the end of the kalpa, when the universe is destroyed by fire.

And there are other sūtras with similar accounts. It was with this in mind that the Buddha, in the *Heap of Jewels*, said,

> Kāshyapa, I or those like me can judge the teachings and individuals, but ordinary people should not judge individuals and the teachings because that would lead to a downfall.

The *Smaller Saṃvara Tantra* says,

> To sentient beings with different aspirations
> He teaches a variety of conducts.
> To disciples with different perceptions
> He teaches a variety of means.
> So when he teaches this profound Dharma,
> Even if it does not inspire you,
> You should not criticize it:
> Keep in mind the inconceivable ultimate reality.
> Those who are not proper vessels
> Do not understand the ultimate reality.
> Only the perfect buddhas and their children
> Know this with their great wisdom.

And in *Ornament of the Mahāyāna Sūtras*, we read,

> Negative states of mind are by nature harmful—
> It is wrong to have them even for illogical things,
> Let alone for teachings that one doubts.
> It's best, therefore, to be impartial, and thus free of fault.[181]

Impress these quotations on your mind, and make sure that you understand the importance of thus guarding yourself.

Besides this point, on which we have given a little supplementary explanation, there are other causes that lead to damaging our refuge vow, as is described in *Finding Rest in the Nature of the Mind*:

> Refuge is relinquished, in a sense,
> When the time for taking it is passed,

> But it is indeed abandoned through wrong view.
> Through the spoiling of the precepts
> You will fall to lower states.
> Therefore, rule yourself with care and mindfulness,
> Adopting and rejecting as you should.[182]

When one attains buddhahood and reaches "the essence of enlightenment," the duration for which one committed oneself in the refuge ritual is over.* Thus, in a nominal sense at least, enlightenment is a reason for giving up the refuge. The causes for abandoning the refuge in the true sense are giving rise to wrong views and forsaking the Three Jewels and being unable to keep the refuge precepts and giving back the vow. Breaking a few of the precepts—for instance, by paying homage to worldly gods, is known as "debasing the vow." The negative consequences of breaking the refuge precepts like this are boundless. One will be like a member of a corrupt dynasty and cease to be counted as a Buddhist. One will be like a merchant betrayed by his escort, and whatever one does, one will find oneself in danger. Like a fresco on a wall falling to ruin, all one's vows and precepts will be easily destroyed. Like poor folk at the bottom of the social ladder with no friends for support, one will suffer all kinds of harm and violence. One will be like a common lawbreaker: having broken one's promise, one will be reborn in the lower realms. So, reflecting on the faults of breaking the precepts, regret and confess your breaches, resolving not to repeat them in future, and take the precepts again. This will restore your refuge vow.

2. The benefits of keeping the precepts

The Master Vimalamitra says,

> Turning away from the ways of the tīrthikas,
> Not being born in the three, becoming a support,
> Absence of obstacles, few illnesses and longevity,
> Purification, and accumulation are the benefits.

In this way he lists eight major benefits: (1) One becomes a Buddhist, a

*When one takes refuge, one says "Until the essence (or heart) of enlightenment is reached, I go for refuge."

follower of the Buddha. (2) One will not be reborn in the lower realms. (3) One becomes a support for all vows. (4) One is free of obstacles. (5) One has few illnesses. (6) One has a long life. (7) One's negative deeds and obscurations are purified. (8) One will complete the two accumulations and swiftly attain buddhahood.

Simply taking refuge has the power to bar the entrance to the lower realms and to set one, in all one's lives, on the great path to the higher realms and liberation. This is stated in the *Tale with a Sow*:

> Those who have taken refuge in the Buddha
> Will not go to the lower realms.
> They will abandon their human bodies
> And be reborn with celestial forms.*

And regarding the fact that one will swiftly complete the two accumulations of merit and wisdom, the *Mahāparinirvāṇa Sūtra* declares,

> Those who go for refuge in the Three
> Will acquire the supreme accumulations of merit and wisdom,
> Develop the buddha qualities in this world,
> And thereby attain buddhahood.

One will acquire boundless good qualities and never be separate from the constant presence of the Three Jewels. We can read in the *Sūtra of the Questions of the Boy Ratnadatta*,

> Those who have gone for refuge in the Buddha increase all virtuous qualities. They have a sense of decency. They have a sense of shame. Those who have gone for refuge in the Dharma are careful. They have numerous sets of qualities. They always remember their past lives. They enjoy the fortune to receive the teachings. Those who have gone for refuge in the Saṅgha have workable minds. They possess numerous doors of concentration and powers of memory. They are always of noble family. Even in their

*The *Tale with a Sow* (*Sūkarikāvadāna-sūtra*) tells the story of a dying god's distress when he sees that he is going to take birth in the womb of a sow. Indra advises him to take refuge in the Three Jewels. This he does, and then dies. He is immediately reborn in the Tuṣhita heaven.

> dreams they never separate from the Buddha, the Dharma, and the Saṅgha.

They will be protected by virtuous gods, and their sources of good will grow ever greater, as the same text says:

> Moreover, the gods who delight in virtue will protect them. Their sources of good will increase.

All fear and danger will be dispelled and one will not be oppressed by the violence of demons and the lower realms. The *Supreme Victory Banner Sūtra* declares,

> Monks, wherever you are, in solitary places, cemeteries, empty wastes, and the like, take refuge in the Three Jewels and you will be free from fear, suffering, and hair-raising experiences.

And in the *Essence of the Sun Sūtra*, it is said,

> Beings who go for refuge in the Buddha
> Cannot be killed by ten million demons.
> Even if they have broken their vows and their minds are disturbed,
> They will surely go beyond birth.

To sum up, on a temporary level, taking refuge protects us from all adverse factors such as the defilements, danger, the paths of lower vehicles, and cyclic existence and the lower realms. It serves as the foundation of all good qualities. It enables us to obtain all our goals—both higher rebirth and ultimate excellence. Ultimately, by taking refuge in the Buddha, we will accomplish buddhahood. By taking refuge in the Dharma, we will turn the Wheel of Dharma. And by taking refuge in the Saṅgha, we will gather around us an ocean-like assembly of nonreturners. By this means, we will dispel all the ills of existence. These are just some of the boundless benefits we will have, as is stated in *Ornament of the Mahāyāna Sūtras*:

> Constantly, against the whole host of defilements,
> Against all kinds of negative actions,
> And even aging and death,

The enlightened state gives complete protection.
Because it protects from every kind of trouble,
From the lower realms, from improper paths,
From the view of the transitory composite, and from lesser vehicles,
It is the supreme refuge.[183]

And in the *Mahāparinirvāṇa Sūtra*, we read,

Those who go for refuge in the Three
Will swiftly attain buddhahood.

The *Heap of Jewels* declares,

Someone who goes for refuge in the Three
Will fully complete the accumulations,
Accomplish buddhahood,
And gain the qualities of the Dharma and Saṅgha.

And in the stainless sūtras, we find,

If the merit of taking refuge were to possess form, it would fill the whole of space and still there would be more.

B. Particular precepts: The precepts of the outer, inner, and secret refuge

The whole of the following section, describing the precepts of the outer, inner, and secret ways of taking refuge, is taken from the *Direct Instructions of the Teacher*.

1. The precepts of the outer refuge

These comprise (1) three particular precepts and (2) five common precepts, making eight in all.

a. The three particular precepts

These are the following: (1) after taking refuge in the Buddha, not to pay homage to other gods; (2) after taking refuge in the Dharma, to avoid harming sentient beings; and (3) after taking refuge in the Saṅgha, not to keep the company of those with non-Buddhist views.

i. Not to pay homage to other gods

If one pays homage to other gods—that is, worldly gods such as Pashupati, Viṣhṇu, and Maheshvara, one damages the refuge vow. When one has gone for refuge in them, the refuge vow is lost.

ii. To avoid harming sentient beings

The worst is to kill a sentient being. By doing so, the refuge vow is lost. Such acts as beating them out of anger, exploiting them, piercing their noses, penning them up, plucking their hair, and so forth damage the refuge vow.

iii. Not to keep the company of those with non-Buddhist views

Keeping the company of people who hold eternalistic or nihilistic views and who conduct themselves accordingly damages the vow. Agreeing with such views and modes of conduct results in the refuge vow being lost.

b. The five common precepts

i. To constantly venerate the Three Jewels, offering them the first part of one's food and drink

This involves setting out whatever offerings one can obtain before the supports of the Three Jewels and praying to them to come and receive the offerings. The actual offerings are of four kinds.

(1) The offering of homage

With your body straight and your hands folded, perform prostrations, bearing in mind the excellent qualities of the buddhas and bodhisattvas, and consider that you touch their feet, which are marked with a wheel.

(2) The offering of material things

Offer flowers and so forth, those that are owned and those that have no owner. Make offerings created by concentration. Offer even your own body.

(3) The offering of praises

These should be performed with melodious chants.

(4) The offering of practice

This is to meditate on bodhichitta, inseparable from emptiness and compassion, and to make prayers of aspiration that, through the resulting virtue, one will attain perfect buddhahood for the sake of all beings.

It is not that the Three Jewels need a single one of the bowls we fill with water or a single particle of the smoke we offer. Rather, these offerings are the causal factors that make it possible for us to be touched by the light rays from the buddhas.*

Offering the first part of everything you eat or drink involves dividing the first portion of your food into three tidbits and repeating OṀ ĀḤ HŪṀ over them, considering that thereby they become an ocean of nectar. Then consider that your yidam deity is present, surrounded by the infinite Three Jewels, and make the offering to them, thinking, "Please accept this offering of nectar." If you are unable to make the offering in that way, offer it to the Three Jewels, asking them to accept it. At the very least, if you have nothing to offer, offer a bowl of water every day. Failure to make such offerings damages one's refuge vow. The Three Jewels have no need of food, but the food torma is a way for one to accumulate merit imperceptibly.

ii. Not to abandon the Three Jewels even for the sake of one's body and life, for riches, or for reward

Not abandoning the Three Jewels for the sake of one's body means that you must never abandon them even if someone is about to take a knife to you, saying that they will gouge out your eyes, hamstring you, or cut off your ears, your nose, or any other member.

*That is, the buddhas' compassion.

Not abandoning them even for the sake of one's life means that you must never give up the refuge even if someone threatens you with death and is about to kill you.

Not abandoning them for the sake of riches or reward means that you must never abandon the refuge even if someone tells you that they will give you the whole world filled with precious things if you give up the refuge.

iii. Not to seek any other means of protection, whatever happens to one—sickness, joy, or sorrow

When things like illness and other misfortunes befall you, prepare a maṇḍala and the five offerings,* and offer them to the Three Jewels. Then take refuge and pray: "Teacher, Great Vajradhara . . . and all you buddhas and bodhisattvas, think of me. May my ailments and all my misfortunes, whether caused by humans, nonhumans, elemental spirits, or hindrance makers, be no more. May everything be peaceful, auspicious, and fortunate." It is also acceptable to use such means as accumulating merit through scripture readings, recitations, and torma offerings, as these involve taking refuge. If, however, these methods do not help, you must not give rise to wrong views, thinking, "The Three Jewels have no blessings; the Dharma is not true." Consider that you will recover from your illness once your bad karma has exhausted itself. Rather than seeking all kinds of other means such as soothsayers and magical rites, rely only on the refuge.

iv. Wherever one goes, to keep in mind the buddhas and bodhisattvas, making offerings and taking refuge

If you are going eastward tomorrow, for example, you should today prepare a maṇḍala and offerings and take refuge in the buddhas and bodhisattvas in that direction and pray: "Teacher, Great Vajradhara . . . and all you buddhas and bodhisattvas, think of me. From here until I get to my destination, may I not have any obstacles from human and nonhuman forces and may everything be auspicious." If you cannot do it today, do so when you are leaving. If you forget to take refuge within the first seven or ten paces of going out the door, you will diminish your refuge practice—meaning that you will not

*The five offerings are flowers, incense, lamps, scented water, and food.

benefit from their protection on this occasion. But you will not lose the vow. Once you again put your trust in the refuge, it will never fail you.

v. To train again and again, remembering the qualities of the refuge

Once you have taken refuge in the Three Jewels, you must put all your hopes in the Three Jewels, rely totally on the Three Jewels, go for protection to the Three Jewels only, direct your prayers to the Three Jewels only, and request blessings from the Three Jewels only. Consider that the representations of the Three Jewels that we use nowadays—whether in the form of cast or sculpted images, drawings or paintings, stūpas, or books and bound volumes of the scriptures—are the body of truth. Make prostrations, offerings, and prayers to them. As a result, it may even happen that you suddenly realize the essence of the body of truth. Even if that does not happen, by venerating the Three Jewels with prostrations, offerings, and so forth and establishing a karmic connection with them, in the future you will become a disciple of the Buddha. Think that all your good qualities and any happiness that you experience are the blessings of the teacher and the Three Jewels. By doing so, you will absorb their blessings. Reflect on the fact that your defects and any suffering that you experience are your own bad karma. In that way, all your bad karma will be exhausted. But if, rather than putting your trust in the Three Jewels, you hold wrong views, saying, "The Three Jewels do not have any blessings," you will never be freed from the depths of the hells.

There are eight benefits in taking refuge in this way. First, you are ranked as a Buddhist. Once you have gone for refuge in the Three Jewels, you are called a Buddhist. Unless you have given rise to the refuge, even if people say that you are a noble being, or a great meditator, or a real buddha, you cannot be ranked as a Buddhist.

Second, you are a suitable support for all the vows, beginning with the vows of individual liberation. If you break the refuge vow, all the vows that depend on it will also be broken. To restore them, it is sufficient to restore the refuge vow. For this, it is enough to think of the Three Jewels and, in their presence, take the vow.

Third, all your past negative deeds will be brought to an end. The vow of taking refuge in the Three Jewels, which precedes all the vows from the twenty-four hour *upavāsa* vow up to the secret Mantrayāna vows, attenuates and exhausts all our negative deeds. In this regard, it is said that the extraordinary refuge brings an end to obscurations forever, while the common refuge attenuates karmic obscurations.* Again, if genuine refuge takes birth in your mind stream, your karmic obscurations will be exhausted forever, while even the mere words of the refuge prayer will attenuate them. If you take refuge all the time, whether you are walking, moving around, lying down, or sitting, it will bring them to an end forever, while even taking refuge from time to time will attenuate them.

Fourth, your stream of being will possess a vast store of merit. Taking refuge results in mundane merit—a long life, good health, glory and splendor, immense wealth, and so forth. And the supramundane, unsurpassable enlightenment also comes from taking refuge.

Fifth, you will not be affected by any human or nonhuman factors creating obstacles for this life. Simply by genuinely giving rise to the refuge in your mind, you cannot be harmed either by people making obstacles to your present life or by nonhumans such as nāgas and *gyalpo*[184] spirits.

Sixth, you will fulfill all your wishes. When you genuinely give rise to the refuge in your stream of being, it is impossible for all your wishes not to be fulfilled. When you put your trust in the refuge, it is as if you had prayed to a wish-fulfilling jewel: everything you wish for happens.

Seventh, you will not fall into the lower realms, unfortunate rebirths, or erroneous ways. The lower realms refer to the hell, hungry spirit, and animal realms. Unfortunate rebirths refer to being reborn in places such as the borderlands, where the Dharma is absent. Falling into erroneous ways refers to those of the non-Buddhists with false views. Anyone who wishes not to fall into those states has only to take refuge.

Eighth, there is the benefit that you will swiftly attain manifest, perfect buddhahood. What need is there to mention any other benefits? It is taught in the Secret Mantrayāna of the Great Vehicle that one can attain buddhahood in a single lifetime and a single body. There is no faster way of attaining buddhahood. So get rid of the misconception that taking refuge from time to time will be sufficient and take refuge again and again, constantly, both day and night. If you do so, it is certain that you will swiftly attain manifest, perfect enlightenment.

If you are diligent in taking refuge, you will not need many other practices. You will have no fear of slipping off the path to enlightenment. If you are afraid that you have fallen into wrong paths, pray that you will meet

*For the extraordinary and common forms of taking refuge, see p. 246.

with the true path, and you will definitely find it. Even those who have little inclination for meditation on emptiness, meditation on the maṇḍala of the deity, and other profound teachings will, by taking refuge, purify their obscurations and accumulate merit, and thus come to realize those teachings.

As for the way in which one is protected by taking refuge like this, you might wonder whether the buddhas draw sentient beings directly out of cyclic existence, leading them by the hand. But that is not possible. If they could do so, there would not be a single being left that the buddhas, who are so compassionate and skilled in means, had not drawn out of cyclic existence. What, then, does protect us? It is the Dharma. Once you have given birth to the refuge in your being, you do not need any other teaching. It is impossible that the Three Jewels' compassion will not protect you.

2. The precepts of the inner refuge

As was the case for the previous precepts, the precepts of the inner refuge comprise (1) three particular precepts and (2) five common precepts, making eight in all.

a. The three particular precepts

1. Once one has taken refuge in the teacher, one should not, even in a dream, think badly or disparagingly of the teacher.
2. Having taken refuge in the yidam deity, one should not interrupt one's daily meditation on, and recitation of, the yidam.
3. Once one has taken refuge in the ḍākinī, one should not fail in the regular observance of offerings such as the *gaṇachakra* and confession and fulfillment.

b. The five common precepts

1. The first part of anything one eats or drinks should be blessed as nectar and offered to the teacher, visualized on the crown of one's head; to the yidam deity, visualized in one's heart center; and to the ḍākinīs, visualized in one's navel center.
2. Wherever one goes, one should do so praying to the teacher, yidam deity, and ḍākinī and visualizing the teacher on the crown of one's head, oneself

as the yidam deity, and the ḍākinīs and Dharma protectors around one as friends and helpers.

3. Even to save one's body and life, one should never abandon the Three Roots, and one should train in considering the teacher as dear as one's heart, the yidam deity as dear as one's eyes, and the ḍākinī as dear as one's body.

4. Whatever happens to one, whether one is sick, happy, or sad, one should train in praying to the teacher, making offerings to the yidam deity, and offering the torma and gaṇachakra feast to the ḍākinīs, without seeking any other means such as soothsayers and magical rites.

5. Remembering the qualities of the teacher, yidam deity, and ḍākinī, one should take refuge again and again. By taking refuge in the teacher, one will receive his or her blessings. By taking refuge in the yidam deity, one will attain the body of the Great Seal. And by taking refuge in the ḍākinī, obstacles will be dispelled.

As for the benefits of this inner refuge, by taking refuge in the teacher, you will be protected from the ordinary thoughts that fetter you, obstacles due to ignorance and bewilderment will be dispelled, the accumulation of profound insight and awareness will be completed, and spontaneous realization will be accomplished. By taking refuge in the yidam deity, you will be protected from ordinary deluded perceptions, anger and the sufferings of the vajra hell will be dispelled, the accumulation of self-arisen virtue will be gathered, and you will gain the accomplishment of the Great Seal. By taking refuge in the ḍākinī, you will be protected from obstacles due to elemental spirits, the sorts of poverty and deprivation that hungry ghosts suffer will be dispelled, the accumulation of liberation from clinging and freedom from attachment will be completed, and you will gain the accomplishment of the body of perfect enjoyment, great bliss.

3. The precepts of the secret refuge

The precepts of the secret refuge are divided into two groups, as before.

a. The three particular precepts

1. To train in having realization of the view. This is to train in the confidence that all sentient beings have the same basic nature as the buddhas* and that

*Tib. *rgyu*, lit. "cause, causal basis," refers to the buddha nature (Skt. *tathāgatagarbha*) that pervades all sentient beings.

there is, therefore, no buddhahood to be achieved elsewhere; and, by realizing that there is no distinction between appearances and the mind, to train in the confidence that appearance and emptiness are inseparable.

2. To train in having experience in meditation. This is to train in not settling the consciousness outside and not withdrawing it in but leaving it in the natural flow, at ease, without fixation.

3. To train in having the same taste in one's conduct. This is to train in not being distracted for a single instant in everything one does—walking, moving around, lying down, or sitting—even though there is nothing to meditate on.

b. The seven common precepts

1. Not to abandon the teacher even if one has realized one's own mind to be buddha.
2. Not to discontinue practicing compounded virtue even if one has realized appearances to be one's own mind.
3. To avoid the minutest negative deeds even if one is no longer afraid of the hells.
4. Not to criticize any teachings even if one no longer hopes to attain buddhahood.
5. Not to be proud or arrogant, even if one has oneself achieved an extraordinary degree of concentration.
6. Not to discontinue compassion for sentient beings even if one has understood that there is no distinction between self and others.
7. To constantly meditate in solitary places even if one has realized that there is no distinction between cyclic existence and nirvāṇa.

The different benefits of taking refuge like this are as follows: By taking refuge in the view, you are protected from eternalism and nihilism, obstacles due to wrong views and clinging will be dispelled, you will gather the accumulation of the radiant ultimate reality, and there will be no obstruction to accomplishing the three buddha bodies. By taking refuge in the meditation, you will also be protected by the view in your meditation, obstacles due to habitual clinging to emptiness will be dispelled, you will gather the accumulation of the nondual union, and you will gain the accomplishment of primordial liberation based on conviction. By taking refuge in the conduct, you will be protected from wrongdoing and nihilistic views, obstacles due to pretense and senseless behavior will be dispelled, you will naturally gather the accumulations, free of attachment, and you will gain the accomplishment that whatever you do will be virtuous.

This way of taking refuge on outer, inner, and secret levels is a pith instruction that includes in a single root the outer and inner teachings, high and low views, and the vehicles of characteristics and mantras. If you take refuge like this, the teachings will truly act as the Dharma, the Dharma will become the path, and the path will mature as the result. Lady of Kharchen,[185] know that it is thus.

This name "The Three Jewels"
Is hard to find in a billion kalpas,
So now, when you have the fortune gained through former accumulation,
Take them as your refuge and never separate from them, O fortunate ones!

This completes the instruction on going for refuge.

10. Arousing the Mind Set on Enlightenment, the Root of the Great Vehicle's Path That Distinguishes It from Lower Paths

The chapter on arousing the mind set on enlightenment has three sections: (1) the preparation, training the mind in the four boundless attitudes; (2) the main practice, showing how to arouse the mind set on enlightenment; and (3) the conclusion, how to keep the precepts, together with the benefits.

I. The preparation, training the mind in the four boundless attitudes

Finding Rest in the Nature of the Mind outlines these as follows:

> Those who thus have taken refuge
> Spread upon the ground of *love*
> The flowers of their *compassion*,
> Which in the cooling shade of *joy*
> Are moistened with pure waters of *impartiality*.
> They train their minds that through them they may be
> Of benefit to wandering beings.[186]

And in the *Middle Sūtra of the Perfection of Wisdom*, we read,

> Subhūti, for that, a bodhisattva mahāsattva must train in great love, great compassion, great joy, and great impartiality.

These four boundless attitudes, then, are defined as follows: Love is the wish that sentient beings may be happy. Compassion is the wish that they may be free of suffering. Joy is the wish that they may remain happy and free of suffering. Impartiality consists of letting go of attachment to those who are close to one and of aversion to those who are distant.

There are two categories of paths that employ these four attitudes: mundane and supramundane, as explained in the *Sublime Essence*:

> Shāriputra, love, compassion, joy, and impartiality that are not cultivated and followed up with the proper attitude are the four pure states, which are associated with the production of existence. Love, compassion, joy, and impartiality that are cultivated and followed up with the proper attitude are the four boundless attitudes, for they produce the path to nirvāṇa.

Regarding the four pure states,* their object is limited to one or two sentient beings. The form they take in the mind arises as love, compassion, joy, and impartiality that are not imbued with an intention to attain liberation. They act as causes of existence, or saṃsāra. This is exemplified in the case of a woman and her child who were drowned trying to cross the Ganges River: they died with such love for each other that they were reborn in the world of Brahmā. *The Way of the Bodhisattva* explains,

> A clear intent can fructify
> And bring us birth in such as Brahmā's realm.[187]

As for the four boundless attitudes, when their objects are all beings, the form they take in the mind arises as the four boundless attitudes with concepts. And when their object is suchness, the true nature of all phenomena, the form they take in the mind arises as the four boundless attitudes without concepts, as is mentioned in the *Treatises on the Stages*:

> In relation to beings and the true nature, the four boundless attitudes arise with concepts and without concepts.

*The four pure states (Tib. *tshangs pa'i gnas pa*, Skt. *brahmavihāra*) are attitudes in which Brahmā is said to constantly dwell. Furthermore, these attitudes, when cultivated without bodhichitta, result in rebirth in the celestial realms of the first *dhyāna*, such as The Pure.

Jamgön Mipham (1846–1912)

There are thus three categories of boundless attitudes: those whose object is sentient beings, those whose object is phenomena, and those that have no object. These three are related to different kinds of individuals, respectively: ordinary beings who have not realized no-self; noble listeners and solitary realizers who have realized "one-and-a-half" kinds of no-self—that is, just the individual no-self, or part of the no-self of phenomena; and noble bodhisattvas who have fully realized both kinds of no-self. These categories of the four boundless attitudes are mentioned in the *Bodhisattva Stage* as follows:

> Taking sentient beings as the object is shared with non-Buddhists. Taking phenomena as the object is shared with all listeners and solitary realizers. Having no object is not shared with any of them.

Nonconceptual love, compassion, joy, and impartiality are thus central to the path of the Great Vehicle. It is in such terms that the commentary of Padmasambhava's *Great Treatise on the Graded Path* states,

> Feeling affection for whomever is the object and thinking, "I must make them happy," is mundane love. Understanding that the objects, sentient beings, are one's parents and meditating with the thought "I must make them all happy" is Dharmic love. Continuously cultivating the concentration of love, which is to know that all such beings are one's parents and to give rise to the thought to benefit them, is what we call "boundless," or "great," love.
>
> There are three aspects to this. Love that takes sentient beings as its object is to understand that all sentient beings are one's parents and to give rise to the thought "I must make them happy." Love that takes phenomena as its object is to think, "Ultimately, they do not exist in any way, but, on the relative level, they exist as mere dreams or illusions, and in that respect may these mother beings be happy." Nonconceptual love results from the knowledge, at the very moment when one is meditating in this way, that the nature of everything, oneself and others, is emptiness, free of elaboration like space: it is the complete freedom from the concepts of the three spheres, the essential nature without thoughts

> or concepts, where continuous love radiates unobstructedly with the vivid realization of emptiness, the lack of innate existence.

Since Padmasambhava said this also applies to compassion, this passage can be used to describe the other two boundless attitudes as well. Here, these three aspects (taking sentient beings as the object and so on) are presented only from the point of view of the Great Vehicle. They refer respectively to bodhisattvas beginning the path, those who have some understanding and experience of distinguishing the two truths, and those who have realization of the natural condition of things. This should not be confused, therefore, with the above presentation in which the three categories are related to non-Buddhists and so on.*

The benefits of training in this way are as follows: As a result of training in love, on the temporary level, one will be appreciated by everyone, and ultimately one will transform anger into the realization of mirrorlike gnosis and attain the body of perfect enjoyment. This is mentioned in the *Lotus Pinnacle*:

> With love, anger is transmuted
> Into mirrorlike gnosis and the body of perfect enjoyment.

As a result of training in compassion, on the temporary level, one will never be in danger, and ultimately one will purify attachment into all-discerning gnosis and attain the body of truth. We read in the same text,

> With compassion, attachment is transmuted
> Into all-discerning gnosis and the body of truth.

As a result of training in joy, on the temporary level, one will be free of jealousy. Ultimately one will gain all-accomplishing gnosis, which is the nature of the wealth of buddha activities, and from transmuting jealousy, one will achieve the body of manifestation. The same text says,

> With joy, jealousy is transmuted
> Into all-accomplishing gnosis and the manifestation body,
> With all the sublime spontaneous deeds.

*That is, the way these three aspects are presented above in the *Bodhisattva Stage*.

As a result of training in impartiality, on the temporary level, one will have a fully functional mind. Ultimately, by transmuting pride and bewilderment, one will accomplish the gnosis of equality and the gnosis of the expanse of reality, and one will realize the adamantine (that is, unchanging) body of the essential nature and the body of manifest enlightenment, as is stated in the *Lotus Pinnacle*:

> With impartiality and great impartiality,
> Pride and bewilderment are transmuted
> Into the gnosis of equality and the gnosis of the expanse of reality
> And the adamantine body of enlightenment.

Furthermore, the four boundless attitudes lead to the temporary benefit and happiness of gaining a celestial or human body in the world of desire. They yield boundless benefits such as achieving the concentration of the world of form and all the qualities of pure rebirths.* In the *Sūtra of the Lion's Roar of Śrīmālādevī*, it is said,

> The tathāgatas alone can contemplate
> A person's training in the four boundless attitudes:
> In all respects, the benefits are boundless,
> Far exceeding the planets' paths in space.

With the above notions firmly established, we now come to the actual way of training in the four boundless attitudes. This should be done in stages, beginning with that which is easiest to develop. First, we shall consider the training in impartiality. This has two aspects: the object of meditation and the form impartiality takes. The object of meditation should be thoroughly examined and understood as follows.

At present, our mind is attached to those of our "in-group"—our parents, relatives, and so on—and it feels aversion to our enemies and those in our "out-group." This is not logical. In previous lives, our present enemies were our relatives, and our present relatives were our enemies. Nothing, therefore, is certain. Even now, our enemies cannot hurt us all the time, and if we make peace with them, they might even help us, like our relatives. Our relatives, too, say unkind things to us, quarrel with us, and misuse our

*Pure rebirths—that is, rebirth in the higher realms.

belongings; and when something untoward happens to those we love, it causes us much mental anguish. So they are, in fact, not unlike enemies. In the future, too, our relatives will become our enemies, and our enemies will become our relatives, and so on: it is all quite unpredictable. For this reason, we should give up mentally labeling people as close or distant, with thoughts of attachment to those of our in-group and aversion to those of the out-group. Instead, we should examine how relatives and enemies are, by nature, the same. We should view all sentient beings in this way. This is how we should consider the object.

As for the form impartiality takes in our minds, we should begin by training in an impartial attitude toward a single being, then extending this to two beings, then three, then a whole town, our country, the whole continent, the thousandfold universe, and all the beings filling the limits of space. At the end, we should train in the great impartiality free of concepts.

Once we have got used to this, we should train in love. This again has two aspects. The object of our love is all sentient beings. Just as we want all those of our in-group who are not happy to be happy, we should train in love for all beings, with complete impartiality, thinking, "May all those who are not happy meet with happiness." As for the form love takes in our minds, we should train by wishing that those close to our hearts—for example, our own parents—meet with happiness, then that others may do so, and finally that all beings may be happy. Afterward, we should settle evenly in the state where there is nothing at all to conceptualize.

Next, having got used to that, we should train in compassion. With regard to the object of our compassion, we should consider a being in the lower realms or a person with leprosy, for example, unbearably tormented by intense suffering. And for the form compassion takes in our minds, we should think, "May they be rid of this suffering." Meditating so intensely on compassion that tears well up in our eyes, we should extend the meditation from one being to all beings. We should conclude by settling in equanimity for a while in the state free from all concepts.

After that, we should train in joy, taking as the object of meditation all kinds of beings who are happy, and starting with someone in the higher realms, whatever the extent of their happiness and well-being. The form our meditation should take is to think, "May this happiness never desert them. May they, on the contrary, possess well-being and happiness, a long life, a large retinue, wealth, freedom from danger, great intelligence, and so on until they attain buddhahood." Apply this meditation to one being and then extend it to all beings. In particular, apply this again and again to your enemies who harm you and those who make you feel jealous. Finally, settle evenly in the state of emptiness.

Next, to develop proficiency in these, train in the four boundless attitudes in a fixed order—love, compassion, joy, and impartiality; then in the opposite order, from impartiality to love; then alternating them—love and joy, compassion and impartiality. Train in developing these from one instant to the next.

Practice all these without forgetting the three supreme methods concerning the preparation, main practice, and conclusion.

II. The main practice, showing how to arouse the mind set on enlightenment

There are two parts: (1) a presentation of the principles, and (2) the main teaching on the instructions for the practice. The first of these is divided into two: (1) an explanation of how these are generally presented, and (2) a specific explanation taken directly from the oral teachings of Orgyen, knower of the three times.

A. A presentation of the principles

1. An explanation of how these are generally presented

In *Finding Rest in the Nature of the Mind*, we read,

> When you are well practiced
> In the four unbounded attitudes,
> Meditate upon the twofold bodhichitta, root of all the Dharma.[188]

And in the *Bodhisattva's Scriptural Collection*,

> Those who wish speedily to attain unsurpassable, true, and perfect enlightenment should train in the extraordinary attitude that is the mind set on enlightenment.

For this, there are two sections: (1) the reasons one needs to train in this, and (2) the main explanation of how to arouse the mind set on enlightenment.

a. The reasons one needs to train in bodhichitta

Unless we attain the result of unsurpassable enlightenment in this present life, wherever we are reborn, whether in the higher or lower realms of cyclic existence, our condition will be characterized by faults and defects, like a mass of vomit and excrement. For we will not have transcended either its cause, our deeds and defilements, or their results, the three kinds of suffering. It is said in a sūtra:

> I see that the world of desire is full of defects, that likewise the world of form is full of defects, that the formless world is full of defects, and that nirvāṇa alone is without defect.

You might wonder, "Well, in that case, is it sufficient just to attain liberation from cyclic existence as an arhat, in nirvāṇa, which is the result of the listeners' and solitary realizers' paths?" No, it is not sufficient. It is true that, compared to us beginners, who are ordinary beings, the noble listeners and solitary realizers are to be marveled at and have immense qualities, for they have realized their result, nirvāṇa, which is the cessation of suffering and its origin. But compared to the bodhisattvas in the Great Vehicle, there is an enormous difference in qualities, as much as the difference between the volume of water in the ocean and that in a puddle formed by a hoofprint. Even as far as their own fulfillment is concerned, the listener and solitary realizer arhats have not achieved complete elimination: they have eliminated the defilements and their seeds, but they have not entirely eliminated the cognitive obscurations. Neither is their realization complete, for although they have certainly realized the individual no-self and have a limited realization of interdependence on the temporary level, they have not realized the phenomenal no-self and interdependence on the ultimate level. There is also a difference in their qualities. Apart from a few qualities here and there, they do not have all the qualities complete—neither the qualities of buddhahood, such as the ten strengths, four fearlessnesses, and eighteen distinctive qualities, nor the noble bodhisattvas' qualities of the path.

As far as others' fulfillment is concerned, the arhats' means and wisdom are limited in extent, so they have little ability to benefit sentient beings. And after all their sources of good and their enlightened qualities have come to cease in the expanse without residual aggregates, they again have to engage in the Great Vehicle for a long period of time. Chandrakīrti explains this in his *Seventy Stanzas on Refuge*:

> The tree of the Great Vehicle
> Is burnt without a trace by their own path,
> Leaving them like paupers
> Among the bodhisattvas.
> Their minds afraid—they're frightened by existence—
> They gain two kinds of enlightenment,
> And when they die, they're happy,
> Thinking they've attained nirvāṇa.
> Theirs, however, is not nirvāṇa:
> It's true they will no longer take
> A rebirth in the triple world;
> Instead they'll dwell in uncontaminated space,
> Unconscious and without defilements.
> In order that they leave that state,
> The buddhas, later, will arouse them:
> Gathering the accumulations for enlightenment,
> They'll thus become the guides of all the world.

And Noble Nāgārjuna says,

> Even followers of the two vehicles
> Emerge into the Great Vehicle.
> For those weary of the path of existence,
> There is rest, but it is not the ultimate state.
> Until the buddhas have aroused those listeners,
> They remain in a wisdom body,
> Senseless and intoxicated by concentration.
> Once roused, they take all kinds of forms,
> Delighting in the benefit of beings,
> And having gathered merit and wisdom,
> They will attain enlightenment as buddhas.

For a period that depends on how much merit they accumulated on the path of training, arhats remain in the expanse of cessation, in a state of unconsciousness brought about by concentration. Then, roused by the rays of light of the buddhas' compassion, they regain their senses and subsequently enter the Great Vehicle. When they do so, because of their having formerly followed their lower paths, they are hindered by the negative habitual tendency of keeping their own welfare in mind. As a result, their progress on the path is extremely slow, as is stated in the *Tantra of Vairocana's Enlightenment*:

> With the paths of the listeners and solitary realizers, one is eighty thousand great kalpas away from the result, unsurpassable enlightenment.

There are other disadvantages as well, as we can read in the *Letter to a Disciple*:

> Beings drowning in the ocean of saṃsāra,
> As if fallen into its immensity, take birth and die,
> So, seeing them, we fail to recognize our very kin.
> To leave them there and make our own escape—
> Nothing could bring greater shame!
> Because of love they nourished us,
> Their helpless newborn babes,
> With milk that trickled from their breasts;
> They bore so many hardships, bore them all with love.
> Now who could stoop so low as to desert them here?

In their beginningless series of lives, all beings have been our parents, showing us nothing but the greatest kindness. To seek one's own peace and happiness alone without doing anything for their benefit would be to carry a load of ingratitude and disregard for their kindness, to behave like the lowest, most despicable, shameless kind of person. In particular, the principal causal factor that runs counter to the path of the Great Vehicle is to completely give up the bodhichitta vow, which is a fault even more serious than the radical defeats.* The *Verses That Summarize the Perfection of Wisdom* states,

*Tib. *phas pham pa*. These are the most basic monastic vows, the breaking of which results in the ordination being completely annulled.

> Even if one has practiced the path of the ten virtues for a billion kalpas,
> When one wishes to attain arhathood as a solitary realizer,
> One's discipline is damaged, one's discipline is breached.
> Such a spiritual intent is graver than a radical defeat.

For this reason, Lord Maitreya says in *Ornament of the Mahāyāna Sūtras*,

> Just as those who wish themselves good physically avoid
> Poison, weapons, thunderbolts, and enemies,
> Bodhisattvas direct their three kinds of activities
> Away from the two lower vehicles.[189]

What, then, should we be trying to achieve? Our goal should be unsurpassable, perfect enlightenment. This is quite different from the above kinds of enlightenment in terms of the following unique features:

- its unique elimination, for the two obscurations, together with the habitual tendencies have been completely eliminated
- its unique realization, for there is direct and full knowledge of everything that is to be known, both in its nature and in its multiplicity
- its unique, altruistic activities, which happen effortlessly, spontaneously, and continuously until cyclic existence is emptied, as a result of which, even in the expanse without residual aggregates, a mass of merit arises uninterruptedly, as vast as the expanse of reality

In short, such enlightenment represents the complete and ultimate fulfillment of one's own and others' goals, and so it is this that we should achieve. The causal factor for doing so is the precious bodhichitta itself, as we read in the *Introduction to the Middle Way*:

> The Shravakas and those halfway to buddhahood are born from the Mighty Sage,
> And Buddhas take their birth from Bodhisattva heroes.
> Compassion, nonduality, the wish for buddhahood for others sake
> Are causes of the children of the Conqueror.[190]

And in the *Verses That Summarize the Perfection of Wisdom*, we find,

Just as from the first drop to the last,
Little by little, a pot will gradually fill,
So, too, the first thought, the cause of supreme enlightenment,
Will gradually result in buddhahood, complete with virtuous qualities.

The other specific benefits will be explained later.

Some small-minded persons might get discouraged, thinking, "Perfect enlightenment does indeed have enormous qualities, but it is difficult to attain, and to do so one has to train in the great waves of bodhisattva activities. How would I ever be able to do that?" We should not think like this, for as we find in the *Sūtra of the Questions of Subāhu*:

> Subāhu, bodhisattvas train as follows, thinking, "If even lions, tigers, dogs, jackals, vultures, cranes, crows, owls, worms, bees, flies, and bluebottles will attain buddhahood, then why should I, a human being, curtail my efforts—even to save my life—in trying to attain enlightenment?" Subāhu, you should also train as follows: "If a hundred or a thousand human beings realize and attain buddhahood, why should I, too, not realize and attain it?"

And in this regard, the *Basket's Display* gives the following illustration:

> Then the bodhisattva Avalokiteshvara appeared from the island of Siṃhala and at that time manifested in the form of a bee in the great city of Vārāṇasī, in a cesspit inhabited by many hundreds of thousands of kinds of insects. The bee buzzed the words "I submit obeisance to the Buddha." The insects remembered his words "I submit obeisance to the Buddha" and, having destroyed with adamantine gnosis the twenty peaks of the view of the transitory composite,* they became bodhisattvas, bearing the name Perfumed Breath and were reborn in the Sukhāvatī buddha-field.

*The twenty peaks comprise four aspects of the view of the transitory composite (see glossary, s.v. "transitory composite [view of]") for each of the five aggregates—namely, the four beliefs that (1) the self is the same as form (or one of the other four aggregates), (2) the self owns form, (3) the self dwells in form, and (4) form dwells in the self.

It is for this reason that *The Way of the Bodhisattva* states,

> "Oh, but how could I become enlightened?"
> Don't excuse yourself with such despondency!
> The Buddha, who declares the truth,
> Has truly spoken and proclaimed
> That if they bring forth strength of perseverance,
> Even bees and flies
> And gnats and grubs will gain
> Supreme enlightenment so hard to find.
> And if, by birth and lineage of human kind,
> I'm able to distinguish good from ill
> And do not leave aside the Bodhisattva deeds,
> Why should I not attain the state of buddhahood?[191]

And,

> Merit is the true cause of the body's ease,
> While happiness of mind is had through understanding.
> What can sadden those who have compassion,
> Who remain within saṃsāra for the sake of beings?
> For through their power of bodhichitta,
> Former sins are totally consumed,
> And merit, ocean-vast, is gathered in,
> It's therefore said that they excel the Shrāvakas.
> Mounted on the horse of bodhichitta,
> Which puts to flight all mournful weariness,
> What lucid person could be in despair
> Proceeding in this way from joy to joy?[192]

And in *Ornament of the Mahāyāna Sūtras*, we find,

> Sentient beings born as humans,
> In infinite numbers, in every instant,
> Attain perfect enlightenment,
> So do not give in to losing heart.[193]

Noble Nāgārjuna sums this all up as follows:

For the sake of immeasurable beings,
They wish for immeasurable enlightened qualities
And practice immeasurable virtue.
Even though enlightenment itself is immeasurable,
How, with the accumulations
Garnered with those four immeasurables,*
Could they not attain it without undue delay?
With the accumulation called "infinite merit"
And that called "infinite gnosis"
They swiftly dispel
All physical and mental pain.
Hunger, thirst, and other physical sufferings
In the lower realms arise from evil deeds.
Because of their merit in not doing evil,
Bodhisattvas do not have such suffering in other births.
Attachment, fear, desire, and other mental sufferings
Arise through ignorance.
Because of the gnosis that knows these are without foundation,
They are rapidly eliminated.
If they are thus not greatly hurt
By physical and mental pain,
Why should guiding beings
In the furthest reaches of the world make them lose heart?
Short-lived pains are difficult to bear,
Not to mention those that last a long time.
For those who have no suffering and are happy,
What will harm them, even in infinite periods of time?
They have no physical suffering,
How could they have mental suffering?
Yet they have compassion, because of which
They remain for ages in this world.†

*The four immeasurables are immeasurable time (mentioned in the first line of verse 219 of *Jewel Garland*, "Remaining for immeasurable periods of time," which has been omitted in this quotation), immeasurable beings, immeasurable enlightened qualities, and immeasurable virtue.

†A commentary on Nāgārjuna's *Jewel Garland* explains that although bodhisattvas do not suffer physically or mentally, they do have a sort of pain—the compassion they feel when they see others suffering—and this is by no means an unwanted "pain."

So do not feel discouraged,
Thinking, "Buddhahood will take so long."
To end your faults and gain good qualities,
Make a constant effort to accumulate merit.[194]

Accordingly, since bodhisattvas have abandoned the causal factors—that is, karmic deeds and defilements—the suffering that would result from these does not occur. On the contrary, with every moment that passes, they gather an immeasurable accumulation of merit, as a result of which they proceed to ever greater happiness. Who could get disheartened at that? That being the case, we should develop enormous enthusiasm for this wondrous, marvelous way.

b. The main explanation of how to arouse the mind set on enlightenment

Having learned of the advantages of training in bodhichitta and the disadvantages of not doing so, we come now to the main explanation of how to arouse the mind set on enlightenment, which is the root of the Great Vehicle's path. This is divided into two parts: (i) the nature of the potential, the basis of being fortunate, and (ii) a presentation of arousing bodhichitta, which is the basis for applying the precepts.

i. The nature of the potential, the basis of good fortune

The term *potential* generally refers to a constituent, seed, or cause. In this case, it refers to the cause, or seed, of liberation and omniscience. There are a great many different views and opinions regarding this, which are related to the various philosophical tenet systems, but here we shall present it in terms of the extraordinary view of the Great Vehicle, as mentioned in the *Sublime Continuum*:

Like the treasure and the fruit tree,
The potential should be understood to have two aspects:
Intrinsic presence without beginning,
And unsurpassed full adoption.[195]

The potential is thus held to be of two kinds: the naturally existing potential and the evolving potential. The naturally existing potential is further clarified as referring to the uncompounded true nature, for which there is nothing to be removed and nothing to be added:*

> Likewise, within their mind there is a precious treasure
> Undefiled, the true nature with nothing to add or remove;
> But because they do not realize it, these living beings
> Continually experience all the many sufferings of poverty.[196]

This point is generally associated with the sūtras of the final turning of the Wheel of Dharma and the textual tradition of Maitreya, who commented on them, and his followers. Here in Tibet, although there have appeared a variety of different schools of thought based on the Mādhyamika and Chittamātrin systems, the followers of our own tradition, that of the Ancient Translations, should adhere to the position of Orgyen, knower of the three times, the Omniscient Dharma King Longchenpa, and other vidyādharas of the past. Thus, we find in the Great Omniscient One's *Great Chariot of the Definitive Teachings*,

> Thus it is asserted in the final teachings that there is a constituent that is naturally pure and possessed of qualities from the beginning,† but that, at the time of practicing on the path, qualities appear to arise. And according to the mantra teachings, the natural maṇḍala is present in all beings. There is no difference between these two explanations: their ground is the same, their path is the same (being the two accumulations based on means and wisdom), and their result is the same (being the bodies and gnoses). Thus, Padmasambhava and other great masters of the past explained them from outer and inner points of view.

Rigdzin Jigme Lingpa, too, establishes this in his commentary on the *Treasury of Precious Qualities*, while his lineage master, the great Shāntapurīpa,[197] also declares:

*There are no defects to be removed and no qualities to be added.

†The use of the term "beginning" in expressions like "from the very beginning" (*ye nas*) or "pure from the beginning" (*ye dag*) should not be understood as referring to a first moment of origin, or creation, in the distant past but rather to the fact that the pure nature has always been intrinsically present.

To have no doubts that all apprehended phenomena are
completely devoid of existence,
And that the apprehending consciousness, too, is an illusion,
And to establish nondual gnosis as the ground to be purified—
These are the stages of the path of the final turning of the Wheel
of Dharma.
They were elucidated by Lord Maitreya and Nāgārjuna
In the *Four Treatises of Maitreya* and the *Collection of Praises*,
Whose commentaries in the writings of Asaṅga and his brother*
Bathed with sunlight the snowy peaks of Tibet.
Although these marvelous scriptural works
By the Conqueror Maitreya, Asaṅga, and Vasubandhu
Were commented on numerous times
Separately according to the Mādhyamika and Chittamātrin
traditions,
There is no doubt that they reflect the tradition of the Middle
Way.

The Dharma lords, father and son, of the Minling tradition† and other great authentically learned and accomplished masters were all of the same mind with regard to this. Furthermore, Lord Buddha himself directly introduced the ultimate, definitive teachings in terms of the potential, or constituent, using such analogies as a jewel that must be cleansed. Nobody, therefore, can dispute this.

In the general tradition of the Middle Way, it is held that the true nature of all sentient beings is the naturally radiant expanse of reality. When this nature is enclosed in the shell of the defilements, it is called the "essence of the sugatas." This is the naturally existing potential. By means of different positive conditions such as hearing and reflecting on the teachings of the Great Vehicle and arousing bodhichitta, the naturally existing potential is nurtured, and this is held to be the evolving potential.

However, with regard to the extraordinary tradition of the Ancient Translations, the Omniscient Dharma King says,

*Asaṅga's brother (and principal disciple) was Vasubandhu.

†Gyurme Dorje Terdak Lingpa (1646–1714) and his spiritual son (and younger brother) Lochen Dharmashrī (1654–1717).

> Buddha-potential is the basis
> Of the virtue that gives rise to liberation.
> Luminosity is the character of the mind.
> It is the stainless element:
> The *potential naturally present*,
> Whose appearing aspect is the twofold kāya.
> It has been described by nine comparisons.
> The nature of compassion, present from the first,
> Is *the potential that may be developed*,
> So the Sugata has said.
> Its root is primal wisdom, luminous, self-knowing,
> And it is virtue, being free of the three poisons.[198]

And in the commentary, we read,

> In this regard, mind, which is naturally pure and whose essential nature is uncontaminated, is the supreme gnosis of the buddhas, the radiant nature of the mind, present from the beginning. From its appearance aspect, there arise the spontaneously accomplished qualities of the buddha's form body, as shown by nine analogies. And in its emptiness aspect, there are the qualities of the body of truth, analogous to space. This is explained in all the sūtras and tantras. The inseparability of these two is the beginningless sphere of reality, which is virtue. Since it is unchanging, it is called the "naturally existing potential." And since, from cleansing it of contaminants, qualities develop and become manifest, it is called the "evolving potential." But at root, it is the radiant gnosis of awareness.

Taking this explanation literally, the Omniscient Jigme Lingpa says,

> It is not bound by objects that appear, for it is empty,
> Yet it has a core of natural luminosity.
> It is awareness that with qualities, the wisdoms and the kāyas,
> Is conjoined, like sun and sunlight, never to be parted.[199]

So although it is explained as two kinds of potential, their essence is the same; they are merely distinguished as isolates. In fact, the nature of mind free of elaboration—spontaneously arisen gnosis, the basic nature—does not exist in any way. Yet its radiance manifests unobstructedly as naked, clear, innate knowledge. It is this that is the seed of the wisdom of omniscience, or sugata essence. We read in the *Sūtra of the Play of Mañjuśrī*,

> Sisters, it is thus. Let us make an analogy of a fire burning in space: the fire cannot burn that space. Sisters, in the same way, although adventitious defilements may occur on something naturally radiant, those adventitious defilements can never defile that natural radiance.

And in the *Sublime Continuum*, the Lord Maitreya says,

> That very nature of mind, luminosity,
> Like space, is without change.
> Adventitious stains arising from incorrect notions
> Such as desire and so forth do not defile it.[200]

And in his *Praise of the Vajra Mind*, Nāgārjuna writes,[201]

> Just as water in the middle of the earth
> Remains uncontaminated,
> Gnosis in the midst of the defilements
> Remains, likewise, uncontaminated.

And in the *Tantra of Vairocana's Enlightenment*, we read,

> Ordinary beings obscured by ignorance
> Do not know things in this way:
> They look for buddhahood elsewhere.
> Not realizing that it is present here,
> Never will they find the buddha state
> In any other world or realm.
> Mind is the perfect buddha:
> Buddhahood has not been shown to be elsewhere.

In the *Rampant Elephant Tantra*, we find,

The nature of the mind is the great space of the expanse of reality;
Phenomena are perfectly pure—they are radiant light from the very beginning.
The expanse of union with the basic nature is beyond word and thought:
To that sameness, the mind of enlightenment, I constantly bow down.

And the *Guhyagarbha Tantra* has,

Nowhere in all the ten directions and the four times
Will you find the perfect buddha state.
The nature of mind is the perfect buddha:
Do not look for buddhahood elsewhere.

In the *Tantra of the Vajra Tent*, we read,

The expanse of reality is sublime peace.
It is called the "jewellike mind."
It fully grants the desired result.
The ultimate nature of the mind is natural purity.

And in a *dohā*,

Mind alone is the seed of everything;
From it existence and nirvāṇa manifest.
Like a wishing jewel, it grants the result that is desired:
To that same mind I submit obeisance.

How can we be sure that this sugata essence is present, pervading all beings like this? There are three means by which we can be certain of this: scriptural authority, reasoning, and evidence.

Scriptural Authority

The *Sūtra That Teaches the Tathāgata Essence* states,

> Whether or not the tathāgatas have appeared, sentient beings have always had the tathāgata essence.

And in the *Sūtra of the Ornament of the Buddhas*, we find,

> Among all the different kinds of beings, there is not a single being who is not completely imbued with the full wisdom of the tathāgatas.

The *Mahāparinirvāṇa Sūtra* has,

> In the past, when I spoke the *Sūtra of Transcendent Wisdom*, I explained that all phenomena are emptiness in order to free immature beings of their clinging to self. But in truth, only the tathāgata essence is the ultimate truth.

And,

> Let us make an analogy with butterfat, which is present throughout all milk. In the same way, the tathāgata essence, too, is present in all sentient beings, pervading them throughout.

In *Ornament of the Mahāyāna Sūtras*, we read,

> Suchness is present in all, and not different,
> Yet purified it is the Tathāgata.
> Thus it is that all beings
> Are imbued with its essence.[202]

And Nāgārjuna says,

> The pure state that is achieved
> By cleansing away saṃsāra's very causes
> Is nirvāṇa; it is the body of truth.

And,

> In spring we say that the water is warm,
> In winter we say that it is cold.

> When covered by the net of defilements,
> We speak of sentient beings;
> And when freed of defilements,
> We talk about buddhas.

In Jowo Atisha's *Lamp for the Path*, it says,

> From the point of view of the Great Vehicle's tenet system, there is no one who is not a suitable vessel for the Great Vehicle, for all sentient beings are of the same potential: they all have the tathāgata essence.

And this ultimate secret is taught in all the tantras. The chapter on gnosis in the *Kālacakra Tantra* says,

> Sentient beings are buddhas: there are no other, greater buddhas here in this world.

And the *Guhyasamāja Root Tantra* states,

> Fortunate children, however many beings there are who belong to the category of sentient beings, they all dwell in buddhahood, they are adamantine enlightenment.

In the *Tantra of the Vajra Tent*, we read,

> Apart from the precious mind,
> There are no beings and no buddhas.

And in the *Two Segments*,

> Sentient beings are the buddha state itself,
> Yet they are obscured by adventitious stains.
> Divested of those stains, they are true buddhas.

The *Ornament of the Indestructible Essence* has,

> In all the elements and things composed of them
> There is the Bhagavan, great bliss.
> Samantabhadra and Vajradhara
> Are ever present, permeating all.

In the *Tantra of Victory by Nonduality*, we read,

> The major and minor marks of the Sugata
> Are surely present on the bodies of all sentient beings.
> They appear without anything being added or taken away.
> Thus the secret meaning is taught.

There are an infinite number of such statements, which are summed up in the *Guhyagarbha Tantra*:

> The Buddha himself could never find
> Something other than that buddha nature.

And in the *Mirror of the Heart of Vajrasattva*:

> In all the sentient beings in the universe there dwells the tathāgata essence, like the oil pervasively present in a sesame seed.

Thus it is by means of these quotations from the scriptures that we can know of the presence of the sugata essence.

Reasoning

In the *Sublime Continuum*, it is said,

> Because the kāya of perfect buddhahood emanates,
> Because suchness is indivisible,
> And because they have that potential, all beings
> Have always had the essence of buddhahood.[203]

As we mentioned earlier, there is no contradiction between Lord Buddha's teachings in the middle and final turnings of the Wheel of Dharma—that is, between the emptiness aspect (the essential nature) and the appearance aspect (the natural expression—the bodies, gnoses, and so forth). The gnosis of the union of appearance and emptiness is the adamantine union sameness, the great, uncompounded, naturally arisen, ultimate truth, ultimately unclassifiable like the essence of space. It is this that we label with such terms as *expanse of reality*, *sugata essence*, or (in the Mantra Vehicle) *innate mind of luminosity*. When its ultimate purity becomes manifest, divested of everything that can obscure it, it is referred to as Buddha, the body of truth. There is nothing else to consider than that.

Now there are three reasons that prove that the buddha essence is present in the mind streams of sentient beings. First, from the mind streams of individuals who formerly had been ordinary and completely fettered, the qualities, as infinite as space, of the ultimate body of truth eventually became manifest. Second, if the potential were not present, those qualities could never have become manifest in that way, however much diligence those individuals had. And third, the qualities of the resultant body of truth are, in essence, unchanging, uncompounded, and eternal. These three reasons for the presence of the buddha essence in the mind streams of beings constitute the proof by means of *reasoning on the basis of dependency*.*

Furthermore, because suchness, the emptiness nature of all the phenomena of saṃsāra and nirvāṇa, is indivisible and of one single taste in the primordial, great luminosity, even the apparently existing beings that manifest because of adventitious delusion have never moved away, even slightly, from the ultimate true nature that is the actual condition of things. This is the proof that beings possess the buddha essence using *reasoning in terms of the nature of things*.

Finally, for all beings without distinction there exists the possibility of ridding themselves of the adventitious contaminants in their mind streams and the possibility of realizing the body of truth in which the qualities are primordially present. For this reason, they must have the potential for buddhahood. And if they have it, they must have the buddha essence. This is the proof by means of *reasoning on the basis of functioning*.

A detailed explanation of all this can be found in *Lion's Roar: A Great Summary of the Sugata Essence* and other works.[204]

*This proof corresponds to the first line of the above quotation from the *Sublime Continuum*. The two proofs that follow correspond to the second and third lines, respectively.

Evidence

The *Sublime Continuum* states,

> Without the constituent of buddhahood
> Disenchantment with suffering would not be felt,
> Nor would there be any wish for nirvāṇa,
> Interest in it, or aspiration toward it.
> That recognition of saṃsāra's suffering and faults
> And nirvāṇa's happiness and benefits
> Is the effect of having the potential. Why?
> Because those without it have no such recognition.[205]

The fact that beings who are disenchanted with the suffering of existence give rise to the thought of aspiring to the happiness of liberation is sure evidence that from the beginning it is possible for one's mind stream to be free of suffering and to attain nirvāṇa.

It is important to begin with this certainty regarding the way in which the potential, or constituent, of great enlightenment, the sugata essence, is present within us. Without such certainty, we will never give rise to the wish to accomplish buddhahood. Unless there were the conviction, for example, that there was gold under the earth, one would never think of wanting to mine it. As Nāgārjuna says,

> If the element is present,
> Work will bring the sight of finest gold.
> If the element is not there,
> Work will bring you trouble and nothing more.[206]

Some small-minded people might have doubts, thinking, "If this sugata essence is present in us, why is it not visible now?" It is because it is obscured by the deeds, defilements, and tendencies to which we have been habituated from time without beginning. This is indicated by the analogy in the *Sublime Continuum* of the gold statue covered with mud:

> Although without beginning, they have an end:
> To those who have that naturally pure, eternal element,

It is invisible, covered by a shell since beginningless time,
Like the golden statue still concealed.[207]

And the *Praise of the Expanse of Reality in the Middle Way* gives the analogy of the jewel hidden in ore:

The precious beryl
Always shines with light,
Yet when contained in rock,
Its light cannot be seen.
Likewise, when obscured by the defilements,
The expanse of reality, though utterly free of stain,
In saṃsāra does not show its light,
But in nirvāṇa it glows radiant again.[208]

To sum up, the Omniscient Prajñārashmi[209] says,

The sugata essence, the nature of the constituent,
Is present as the body of gnosis, the primordial protector,
Yet it is completely insubstantial:
Even the lords of the ten levels cannot see it.
It is perceived only by the buddhas of the three times.

Does all this mean, then, that the wisdom of the ten strengths is present in the mind streams of beings such as dogs and pigs? The qualities of the wisdom of the ten strengths are present in the sugata essence in their mind streams. Since they are the qualities of their own true nature, they are inseparable, like fire and heat. If the constituent is present, the qualities are present too, but they are not visible. They are like a sword's ability to cut: when the sword is sheathed, that ability to cut is no longer evident. Or like the features that appear reflected in a mirror: they may be there, but when the mirror is put away in a box, they can no longer be seen. Because the qualities of the constituent present in the mind stream of ordinary individuals are obscured, they are invisible. Even though the true nature of their own minds, which is the emptiness supreme in all aspects, is present, if they have not been introduced to it and become used to it, it will not be evident.

Merely having an understanding of the basic, actual condition of things is not much help. We need to apply ourselves diligently to getting rid of our obscurations, and the best way to do that is to arouse the bodhichitta, as is stated in the *Sūtra of the Questions of Maitreya*:

> Maitreya, if bodhisattvas possess a single teaching, they completely abandon all the lower realms and they do not fall into the hands of evil companions. Instead, they swiftly attain perfect, manifest buddhahood in unsurpassable, true, and perfect enlightenment. What is that one teaching? It is this: the superior intention, bodhichitta. Maitreya, if you possess that one teaching, you will completely abandon all the lower realms and will not fall into the hands of evil companions. Instead, you will swiftly attain unsurpassable, true, and perfect buddhahood in perfect, manifest enlightenment.

Unless one gives rise to bodhichitta, there is no other way to attain buddhahood. In a commentary on bodhichitta, we read,

> Unless the bodhichitta is aroused,
> Buddhahood will never be attained;
> No other means is there in cyclic existence
> For accomplishing one's own and others' goals.

Whether bodhichitta is aroused through habituation to virtuous deeds, or through hearing the scriptures of the Great Vehicle, or through being instructed by a spiritual friend, it takes birth in someone who has the signs of the potential having been awakened. So what are the signs of the evolving potential having been awakened? *Ornament of the Mahāyāna Sūtras* lists them as follows:

> Compassion prior to joining the path,
> Interest, resilience,
> And practicing perfect virtue—
> These are explained as being sure signs of the potential.[210]

As for the signs of the naturally existing potential having been awakened, we can find them in the *Introduction to the Middle Way*:

Certain simple, ordinary people,
When they hear of emptiness, will feel
A joy that leaps and surges in their hearts.
Their eyes will fill with tears, the hairs upon their skin stand up.
They have the seed of wisdom, perfect buddhahood.[211]

If someone who has these signs of the potential having been awakened arouses the precious mind set on supreme enlightenment exactly in accordance with the complete ritual of either of the two traditions* and then properly trains in the precepts, he or she will, without undue delay, attain the level of the omniscient king of Dharma and become a refuge, a protector and helping friend, for the whole infinity of beings. As the Omniscient Dharma Lord has said,

All beings without exception have the sugata essence:
Inside the shell of adventitious contaminants that covers it,
There dwells from the beginning a radiant lamp, the Dharma constituent.
The spontaneously accomplished qualities of the bodies and gnoses
Are within oneself, spontaneously present.
Devote yourself to the essence of emptiness and compassion,
And that constituent will gain the name "enlightenment,"
Bringing benefit and happiness to the whole host of beings.

And Noble Nāgārjuna says,

Just as a lamp enclosed within a pot
Cannot be seen by anyone,
Likewise, inside the pot of the defilements,
The expanse of reality is never seen.
If holes are pierced in the pot's walls,
Whichever sides the holes are made,
On those same sides

*The two traditions in this case are Nāgārjuna's tradition of the profound view and Asaṅga's tradition of the extensive practice.

The light will naturally appear.
And when the vajra concentration
Breaks the pot, destroying it,
It is then the light will shine
Unto the furthest reaches of the sky.*

To sum up, Orgyen, knower of the three times, says,

From the beginning, pure awareness
Dwells as the primordial body of truth:
Like a precious jewel located
Under a poor man's house,
If it is not recognized, one is deluded in cyclic existence.
When it is introduced and recognized,
One realizes the gnosis of the expanse of reality:
One is renowned as "Buddha."

And the Omniscient Dharma Shrī writes,

The unchanging, primordial wisdom that pervades the whole of existence and peace is the nature, or fundamental way of being, of the buddhas. It is inconceivable, completely beyond the understanding of intellectuals, in terms of the following points:

- The constituent: Although this buddha essence or sugata essence is uncontaminated since the very beginning, until it has been freed of the two obscurations, we cannot attain buddhahood. It is the naturally existing potential or contaminated suchness.
- Enlightenment: even when it is associated with contaminants, those contaminants are adventitious appearances that do not actually exist, so they have never sullied its own essential nature; it is naturally pure.
- The qualities: although all the qualities of buddhahood are spontaneously present in the ground from the very beginning,

*Nāgārjuna, *Praise of the Expanse of Reality*, 5–7. These three verses refer, respectively, to lack of realization of the buddha nature (in ordinary beings), partial realization (by bodhisattvas on the levels), and full realization (by a buddha).

unless they are activated by the practice of virtue, their power cannot be released.

- Activity: The buddha activity is present as the all-pervading protector and elixir for all beings without distinction, dispelling suffering and giving rise to happiness on both temporary and ultimate levels. It is accomplished spontaneously, without any concept of an actor or of performing the activities.

The *Sublime Continuum* expresses this as follows:

The buddha constituent, buddha enlightenment,
Buddha properties, and buddha activity,
Even for pure sentient beings, cannot be conceived;
They are the domain of the guides.[212]

If we consider the detailed accounts in the sūtras of the definitive teachings and reflect on their meaning without error, we will be freed of the fetters of doubt and gain the eye of perfect intelligence. Indeed, the Omniscient One in the Age of Strife, Patrul Rinpoche, has written extensively on this in *Benefits of Seeing the Mahāyāna Sūtras*, of which here is an extract:

Utterly pure, the uncontaminated expanse of reality,
The Capable One's body of truth, is present in the nature of infinite beings,
Like a manifested buddha dwelling in the heart of a lotus.
The knowledge that it is there comes from reading the sūtras.
"Suchness, the nature of the ground, path, and result,
The unchanging truth, like precious gold,
Is not sullied by the faults of defilements and concepts."
This perfect knowledge comes from reading the sūtras.
Great compassion, the potential of all the buddhas,
Is like a treasure or a fruit tree,
Increasing more and more the qualities that are realized.
Awakening that potential comes from reading the sūtras.
When the nature of the constituent is freed of contaminating obscurations,
Enlightenment as a sugata is the ultimate result;
Even though it has never been obscured, it becomes purified of stains.

That inconceivable fact is known by those who have read the sūtras.
The wisdom of realization is not something new that is acquired:
It shines like the sun that has been freed of clouds.
It is the great truth, the eternal nature of the three bodies.
Seeing it as it is comes from reading the sūtras.
All the qualities of freedom and maturation
Are boundless, inconceivable, and perfectly pure,
Inseparable when realized.
Seeing that nature as it is comes from reading the sūtras.
When true gnosis, which hitherto was bound
By the fetters of conception, is cut free,
The strengths and other qualities of knowledge are deployed unobstructedly.
Those who have read the sūtras attain the level of a conqueror,
Able to display to beings a form body with the major and minor marks.
The buddhas' effortless activities for beings' sakes
Are like a wish-fulfilling jewel—eternal, all-pervading, and spontaneous,
Unobstructedly deployed according to the fortune of those to be benefited.
Absence of confusion on this point comes from reading the sūtras.

ii. A presentation of arousing bodhichitta, which is the basis for applying the precepts

This is divided into two: (1) an explanation of the kind of birth that is a support for arousing bodhichitta, and (2) an explanation of the nature of the bodhichitta that is supported.

(1) The kind of birth that is a support for arousing bodhichitta

According to the Mind-Only tradition, bodhichitta in action has to be aroused on the basis of any one of the seven vows of individual liberation. Thus, the physical support for arousing bodhichitta must be a man or woman in the three continents,* as we find in the *Lamp for the Path*:

*The three continents here refers to three of the four continents in the traditional Buddhist cosmology, including our world, Jambudvīpa. Beings in the northern continent of Uttarakuru are the exception: they are not suitable supports for taking vows because they are lazy and distracted, with no interest in practicing the Dharma.

Those who constantly hold other vows—
The seven vows of individual liberation—
Have the fortune to take the bodhisattva vow,
But this is not the case for anyone else.

The Middle Way tradition does not have such stringent requirements. The sūtras indicate that many kinds of beings, including gods, nāgas, demigods, gandharvas, and garuḍas, can give rise to the mind set on supreme enlightenment, so it is accepted that this does not depend on the physical support.

As for our own tradition, the Great Omniscient One describes this as follows:

> It should be understood that even though there are these two traditions, they are not contradictory. Even if, at the time of arousing bodhichitta, one has not nominally taken a vow of individual liberation, one necessarily has the capacity to promise not to take life and so on, which comes to the same thing. So, in that respect, it is clear that any support will do, for one is definitely turning the mind away from doing harm. If one does not have the ability to keep any of the vows of individual liberation, then bodhichitta can never arise in one, for the precepts of bodhichitta itself will always risk being contravened.

Whichever the case, in both these traditions, it is one's intention that constitutes the most important support. There are numerous presentations of this, but they all include three points: faith in the Buddha, compassion for sentient beings, and confidence gained from hearing of the benefits of bodhichitta, along with a desire to take the vow. This is mentioned in the *Sūtra of the Precious Lamp*:

When one gains faith in the buddhas and the buddhas' teachings,
When one has faith in the ways of the buddhas' children,
When one has faith in unsurpassable enlightenment,
It is then that the spiritual intent of the wise can take birth.

Besides this, compassion is the principal and indispensable causal factor for attaining enlightenment. If one has compassion, that alone is sufficient, as is stated in the *Sūtra That Perfectly Summarizes the Dharma*:

> Avalokiteshvara replied, "Lord, those who wish to attain buddhahood will not have to train in many practices. They have to train in a single practice. What is it? It is great compassion. Lord, it is like this. Wherever the universal monarch's precious wheel goes, there all his troops go too. Lord, in the same way, wherever a bodhisattva's compassion is present, there all the Buddha's qualities are present too.

Accordingly, the most important thing is an attitude that comprises great compassion.

(2) The main explanation of the nature of the bodhichitta that is supported

The main explanation is divided into four parts: (1) essence, (2) etymological definition, (3) categories, and (4) how to take the vow of bodhichitta.

(a) Essence

In his *Ascertaining the Three Vows*, Paṇḍita Pema Wangyal writes,

> In essence, it is the intention to avoid negative deeds with the three doors
> In someone whose entire being is moistened with love and compassion
> And who wishes to attain enlightenment for the sake of others.

Bodhichitta thus has two points or aspects: a purpose and a goal. The purpose is to focus on others' benefit with compassion. The goal is to focus on perfect enlightenment with wisdom. Both of these—the wish to benefit others and the wish to attain perfect enlightenment—must be present; neither of them on its own constitutes arousing bodhichitta. If one does not want to attain ultimate perfect enlightenment, whatever other benefit and happiness, temporary or ultimate, one may wish to bring to other sentient beings, it will be nothing more than simple love and compassion. And the wish, on its own, to attain the level of perfect buddhahood for one's own benefit is taught even in the listeners' scriptural tradition.

In short, if these two aspects—the thoughts "For the sake of sentient beings" and "I will attain the level of perfect enlightenment"—are not both present, one will not have genuine bodhichitta. It is important, therefore, to properly recognize the difference between love, compassion, and bodhichitta. This is affirmed in the *Ornament of Clear Realization*:

> The arousing of bodhichitta is the wish,
> For others' benefit, to attain perfect enlightenment.[213]

There are three kinds of bodhichitta, which depend on the degree of one's courage. The wish to first bring all sentient beings to buddhahood and, only after that, to attain buddhahood oneself is the incomparable way of arousing bodhichitta. This is called "the shepherd's way." The wish that oneself and all others attain buddhahood at the same time is the way of arousing bodhichitta with sacred wisdom, which is the boatman's way. And the wish to first attain buddhahood for oneself and then liberate others is the way of arousing bodhichitta with the great wish, which is the king's way. With these different degrees of courage, it is said that buddhahood can be attained after three, seven, and thirty-seven measureless kalpas, respectively.

(b) Etymological definition

Derived from the Sanskrit word *bodhichitta*, the Tibetan *byang chub kyi sems* (lit. "mind of enlightenment") is so termed because it is a mind (*sems*) focused on ultimate, perfect buddhahood, the great nondwelling nirvāṇa in which all the obscurations to be eliminated have been purified (*byang*) and everything to be realized has been fully mastered (*chub*). This is accompanied by the fervent wish that oneself and others may attain that level.

(c) Categories

Ascertaining the Three Vows speaks of the categories as follows:

> As for the categories, the two traditions of Nāgārjuna and Asaṅga are well known,
> Each having categories from one to six, and again two each.
> The first is emptiness, whose essence is compassion;
> Then there are two categories—the training in the two accumulations, and relative and ultimate;

And three—the trainings of discipline, concentration, and
wisdom;
Four—bodhichitta practiced through aspiration on the paths of
accumulation and joining,
The bodhichitta of the utterly pure attitude on the seven impure
levels,
Fully ripened bodhichitta on the three pure levels,
And the pure bodhichitta of the buddha level,
Great compassion free of all obscurations;
Five—related to the five paths; and six, the six transcendent
perfections.
There are twenty-two aspects analogous to earth, gold, moon, fire,
and so on,
Corresponding to the stages up to the tenth level.

In each of the two traditions there are two ways of categorizing bodhichitta: one consisting of groups of from one to six elements and another related to the different stages. Each tradition also has two categories related to bodhichitta itself, those of aspiration and action.

Of the categories in groups from one to six, the first is what is known as the bodhichitta of emptiness, whose essence is compassion. This refers to the development of the enlightened mind as the wisdom that is the realization of emptiness guided by compassion for those who have not realized it. The Protector Maitreya speaks of this as follows:

With their wisdom, they have severed in its entirety all holding to
a self;
But those with love abstain from peace because they hold to
beings.
Thus, using understanding and love—the means of
enlightenment—
The noble ones neither circle in saṃsāra nor pass into nirvāṇa.[214]

And Nāgārjuna says,

Emptiness whose essence is compassion
Is for those who are accomplishing enlightenment.

This bodhichitta refers to emptiness and compassion—two entities having a single nature. But if we so much as isolate and distinguish them—that is, if we separate these two—we are turning away from perfect enlightenment. This is stated in the *Verses That Summarize the Perfection of Wisdom*:

> A separate wisdom, without means, veers toward the listeners' state.

And in the *Chapter on Mañjuśrī's Magical Display*, we find,

> Discerning emptiness and forsaking beings is the work of demons. Failing to investigate things with wisdom and holding on to great compassion is the work of demons.

Saraha, too, says,

> Those who engage in emptiness without compassion
> Have not found the supreme path.
> If they meditate only on compassion,
> They will remain here in saṃsāra and not attain liberation.
> Those who are able to combine both
> Do not remain in saṃsāra or dwell in nirvāṇa.

Indeed, all the sūtras and treatises speak of bodhichitta as the union of emptiness and compassion. Some scriptural traditions also speak of great compassion and nonconceptual compassion, and in the commentary of Padmasambhava's *Great Treatise on the Graded Path*, too, we read:

> Nonconceptual compassion results from the understanding, at the very moment one is meditating in this way, that the nature of everything, oneself and others, is space-like emptiness. It is the complete freedom from the concepts of the three spheres, the essential nature without thoughts or concepts, where continuous compassion radiates unobstructedly with the vivid realization of emptiness, the lack of innate existence.

Second, bodhichitta can be divided into two categories, either in terms of the two accumulations (the accumulation of merit with concepts and the accumulation of gnosis without concepts), or as the plain, relative bodhichitta engendered conventionally and the subtle, ultimate bodhichitta that arises through the strength of meditation on the true nature.

Third, there are three categories of bodhichitta distinguished in terms of the three trainings. These are discipline, which brings about purity; concentration, which brings about stability; and wisdom, which brings about freedom. Alternatively, there are three categories related to the three categories of discipline—refraining from negative deeds, gathering positive deeds, and benefiting others.

Fourth, there are the following four categories: (1) On the paths of accumulation and joining, there is *bodhichitta practiced through aspiration*, referring to faith and aspiration for the ultimate truth, emptiness. (2) On the seven impure levels, there is the *bodhichitta of the pure superior intention*, referring to the superior intention that comes from directly seeing the truth of ultimate reality and to the purification of the conceptual contaminants that are eliminated on the path of seeing. (3) On the three pure levels, there is *fully ripened bodhichitta*, referring to the fact that the obscurations of the defilements have been completely eliminated and that one has gained the strength of nonconceptual gnosis. (4) On the buddha level, there is *bodhichitta of great compassion free of obscurations*, referring to the fact that every one of the two kinds of obscurations has been eliminated.

Fifth, there are five kinds of bodhichitta related to the five paths: (1) the beginner's bodhichitta on the path of accumulation, (2) fully trained bodhichitta on the path of joining, (3) bodhichitta related to perceiving the true nature on the path of seeing, (4) bodhichitta related to perfect liberation on the path of meditation, and (5) inconceivable bodhichitta on the path of no more training.

Sixth, there are six kinds of bodhichitta distinguished in terms of the six transcendent perfections—namely, generosity, discipline, patience, diligence, concentration, and wisdom.

The second way of categorizing bodhichitta is based on the different stages, as presented in the *Ornament of Clear Realization*:

> Earth and gold and moon and fire,
> Treasure, mine of jewels, and sea,
> Diamond, mountain, healing draught,
> Virtuous teacher, wishing gem,
> Sun, melodious song, and king,

Treasure house and broad highway,
Perfect steed, a reservoir,
Strain of music, river, cloud:
Thus it is of twenty-two kinds.[215]

These similes are associated with the corresponding categories of bodhichitta as follows:

Bodhichitta associated with a yearning for enlightenment is like the earth: it is the ground for buddhahood and its causes—namely, all the virtuous practices related to the two accumulations.

Bodhichitta endowed with that constant intention is like gold, for the excellent intention to achieve benefit and happiness for others by means of the six transcendent perfections never changes until enlightenment.

Bodhichitta endowed with the superior intention that causes that same intention to grow ever greater is like the waxing moon, for all virtuous practices, such as the thirty-seven elements leading to enlightenment, increase more and more.

Bodhichitta endowed with a combination of sustained calm and profound insight based directly on nonconceptual wisdom is like fire: it rapidly consumes the fuel of obscurations.

Bodhichitta endowed with transcendent generosity is like a great treasure: with the Dharma and material riches, it brings satisfaction to all beings without ever running out.

Bodhichitta endowed with transcendent discipline is like a jewel mine: it is the source of priceless qualities such as the strengths and fearlessnesses.

Bodhichitta endowed with transcendent patience is like the sea: even though all kinds of unwanted things such as fire and weapons may be encountered, the mind is never troubled.

Bodhichitta endowed with transcendent diligence is like a diamond: because of one's firm confidence in unsurpassable enlightenment, the four demons have no chance of destroying it.

Bodhichitta endowed with transcendent concentration is like the king of mountains: distracting concepts cannot stir the mind from concentration.

Bodhichitta endowed with transcendent wisdom, the realization of the two kinds of no-self, is like a wonderful medicine. It completely cures the illness of the obscurations that derive from defilements such as attachment and the cognitive obscurations such as conceptual grasping at reality.

Bodhichitta endowed with transcendent means is like a spiritual teacher:

because of one's mastery of compassion and skillful means, one never abandons sentient beings' welfare, whether in times of prosperity or decline.

Bodhichitta endowed with transcendent aspiration is like a wish-fulfilling jewel: it makes whatever result one has prayed for come true.

Bodhichitta endowed with transcendent strength is like the sun: it has the power to ripen the crop of virtue in beings' minds.

Bodhichitta endowed with transcendent gnosis is like the melodious song of a gandharva: it teaches the Dharma that beings yearn for in accord with their different natures.

Bodhichitta endowed with the six kinds of preternatural knowledge is like a great king: it has the immense power to bring about others' welfare.

Bodhichitta endowed with the two accumulations is like a treasure house: it is the source of inconceivable merit and wisdom.

Bodhichitta endowed with the thirty-seven elements leading to enlightenment is like a great highway: it is the path that all the buddhas of the three times and their children have trodden, are treading, and will tread.

Bodhichitta endowed with both means and wisdom is like an excellent steed: it travels easily to the land of the nondwelling nirvāṇa without falling into either of the two extremes of existence and peace.

Bodhichitta endowed with both the power of memory that retains whatever one has heard without forgetting it and the confident eloquence to teach it to others without impediment is like a reservoir: it never gets low or runs dry.

Bodhichitta endowed with the feast of the teachings on the four summaries (impermanence, suffering, no-self, and peace) is like a strain of music, sweetly resounding.

Bodhichitta associated with the sole path to tread is like a flowing river: it engages effortlessly in others' benefit, with wisdom and compassion.

Bodhichitta concurrent with the body of truth is like a cloud: present in the Tuṣhita realm, it ripens the crop of beings with the great rain of Dharma from the great cloud of the display of the twelve deeds.

The stages referred to here are as follows: The three categories of bodhichitta with yearning and so on correspond to the three stages on the path of accumulation—lesser, middle, and greater. The combination of skillful means and profound insight corresponds to the path of joining. The ten transcendent perfections from generosity to gnosis correspond to the ten levels on the paths of seeing and meditation. The five categories from preternatural knowledge to memory and confident eloquence apply to all three pure levels of the extraordinary path. The three categories related to the feast of the teachings, the sole path, and the body of truth correspond to the so-called buddha level (the Mahāyāna equivalent of the level of candidacy for arhatship), which comprises the preparation, main practice, and conclusion of the tenth level.

One might well wonder whether or not there is such a thing as bodhichitta on the buddha level. While it is true that the bodhichitta one had acquired through the conventional process of the ritual is no longer present because the time limit of one's commitment has expired,* nevertheless, on the ultimate level, bodhichitta is present. For the naturally acquired bodhichitta has been attained, growing ever greater without diminishing; and it is through the bodhichitta of unobscured great compassion that others are effortlessly benefited.

All the above can be condensed into the two categories of aspiration and action, as is stated in *Ascertaining the Three Vows*:

> All these can be subsumed in two aspects: aspiration and action.
> These comprise the intention and its application—
> As it were, the wish to go and the going itself.

The difference between these two is explained in *The Way of the Bodhisattva*:

> Bodhichitta, the awakened mind,
> Is known in brief to have two aspects:
> First, aspiring, *bodhichitta in intention*;
> Then *active bodhichitta*, practical engagement.
> As corresponding to the wish to go
> And then to setting out,
> The wise should understand respectively
> The difference that divides these two.[216]

To pledge, "For the sake of all other sentient beings, infinite in number, whatever it takes, I will attain the precious level of perfect buddhahood," is arousing bodhichitta in aspiration, which is like the wish to make a journey. And, having pledged to train properly in the six transcendent perfections

*The commitment made during the ritual of the bodhisattva vow is "until enlightenment is reached."

and other stages of the path in order to achieve that, to engage in its practical application is arousing bodhichitta in action, which is like actually going.

This has to be put into practice by means of seven causally related branches, as follows:

- first training over a long period of time in an impartial attitude with regard to all sentient beings, free of attachment to those close to us and aversion for those who are distant, and subsequently recognizing that, again and again in our past lives, they have all been our mothers
- remembering their kindness on those occasions in helping us and protecting us from harm
- giving rise to the wish to repay their kindness and making a promise to bring about their benefit and happiness
- wishing that they all meet with happiness and its causes (that is, love)
- wishing that they be free of suffering and its causes (that is, compassion)
- thinking, "I alone must bring them happiness and free them from suffering" (that is, the altruistic attitude)
- on the basis of these causal factors, giving rise to their result, the real bodhichitta, whose nature is aspiration and action

This is reiterated in the following verse:

> Recognizing our mothers, remembering their kindness, repaying their kindness,
> Love, compassion, and the altruistic attitude are the cause;
> Bodhichitta is the result.

(d) How to take the vow of bodhichitta

Ascertaining the Three Vows states,

> The way to first obtain the vow, for those who have not already done so,
> Is to receive it from a spiritual friend who observes the vow.
> Disciples who have faith and are suitable vessels for the Great Vehicle

Offer the seven branches, after which they take the vows of aspiration and action together
And meditate on rejoicing for themselves and others.
These stages constitute the tradition of Nāgārjuna. Asaṅga's way
Is to take the vow of bodhichitta in aspiration without necessarily taking a vow of individual liberation,
But to take the vow in full, it must be preceded by one of the seven vows.
Then inquiries are made concerning obstacles, the precepts are taken, and so on.
Thus the vows of aspiration and action are taken in separate rituals.
Both traditions agree that it is permissible to use buddha supports.*
The point at which one has received the vow is at the last of the three repetitions.

The Middle Way tradition begins with preparation, as follows. With the special instructions, one corrects one's attitude. To the special object, one offers the maṇḍala and makes prayers. To the special support, the Three Jewels, one goes for refuge. And as the special means, one accumulates merit with the seven branches.† Next, for the main part of the vow ritual, after first training the mind in cherishing others more than oneself, one makes the request and then repeats the verses of the vow three times. In this way, one takes the vows of bodhichitta in aspiration and in action together, and one acknowledges that one has received them. For the conclusion, one practices rejoicing for oneself and others, followed by giving thanks and proclaiming the precepts.

In the Mind-Only tradition, the two aspects, aspiration and action, are taken separately. The details can be found in the individual rituals, but we will not expand on them here.

For these rituals, even if neither a teacher nor a support is available, if we

*Tib. *rgyal ba'i rten*. If one cannot take the vow from a teacher, it is permissible to do so in front of an image (a "support") of the Buddha, or failing that, by visualizing the buddhas and bodhisattvas in front of one.

†Seven branches: see glossary, s.v. "seven branches," and the detailed description below p. 547–54.

have the ability to take the vow on our own, we should take it as mentioned in Jowo Atisha's *Lamp for the Path*, visualizing the buddhas and bodhisattvas in the sky in front of us and receiving the vow from them. This accords with the *Sūtra of the Array of Qualities of Mañjuśrī's Buddha-Field*, which states:

> All phenomena arise from conditions,
> They depend on the intention.

2. A specific explanation taken from the *Direct Instructions of the Teacher*, the oral teachings of Orgyen, knower of the three times

Once they have entered the Great Vehicle, it is extremely important for bodhisattvas to train in benefiting others, for unless they do so they will regress to the lower vehicles. To explain this in detail, there are countless teachings in the sūtras of the Great Vehicle and in the tantras. Nevertheless, the training can be condensed, in accord with those teachings, into three topics: (1) training on the outer level, (2) training on the inner level, and (3) training on the secret level.

a. Training on the outer level

The training on the outer level is divided into twelve sections: essence, etymological definition, categories, the marks of the practitioner, the object from which the vow is taken, the ritual for taking the vow, the benefits of the training, the reasons for training like this, the disadvantages of not training, the precepts that have to be kept, the defining points at which one receives and gives up the vow, and the methods for repairing breaches.

i. Essence

The essence of the training is the wish and commitment to attain unsurpassable enlightenment in order that all sentient beings be released from cyclic existence.

ii. Etymological definition

This is an intention to benefit others that one has not previously engendered.

iii. Categories

There are numerous different categories taught in the sūtras, but they can be condensed into bodhichitta in aspiration and bodhichitta in action. Bodhichitta in aspiration is the mental aspiration to accomplish the welfare of sentient beings. This alone is not sufficient: it is important to actually engage in benefiting all sentient beings.

iv. The marks of the practitioner

Unlike a listener or solitary realizer, the sort of person who arouses bodhichitta needs to be someone who is interested in the teachings of the Great Vehicle. It is someone who is broad-minded, has no doubts whatsoever, has come under the protection of a master and the Three Jewels, has mentally renounced wrong and base ways, and is naturally calm and gentle.

v. The object from whom the vow is taken

The bodhichitta vow needs to be taken from a teacher who has aroused the spiritual intent of the Great Vehicle. He or she should be someone who possesses the power of love and compassion, who does not, even for an instant, do anything for his own benefit, and who keeps the precepts without deteriorating them.

vi. The ritual for taking the vow

The ritual will not be mentioned here: it is clearly described in the text of the ritual.

vii. The benefits of the training

The benefits are far superior to those of the listeners and solitary realizers. We enter the assembly of the Great Vehicle. Defilements, evil deeds, and obscurations are eradicated. All the virtuous deeds we perform become meaningful. We complete the vast accumulation of merit in our mind streams. The buddhas, bodhisattvas, and great protectors of the Dharma constantly think of us. All beings treat us with affection as if we were their only child and are happy to see us. We never separate from the teachings of the Great Vehicle. In short, we accomplish the immense qualities of the buddhas according to our wishes and swiftly attain manifest perfect buddhahood. Because of these and other inconceivable benefits, we should apply ourselves assiduously to this very bodhichitta.

viii. The reasons for training like this

We might think that attaining liberation for oneself alone is quite sufficient and wonder why it is necessary to free all sentient beings from cyclic existence. It is because all beings have been our parents, and their kindness to us is inconceivable. In order to repay that kindness, we need to train in doing so. In what way were they so kind? It was in dependence on them that our body and life energy were produced. From when we were small, they nourished us with plenty of food and drink. They experienced all kinds of sufferings and difficulties for us. They cherished us more than themselves: we were more important to them than their own hearts. Then they passed on to us a share of their wealth, educated us, and introduced us to the sacred Dharma. In these and other respects, their kindness is inconceivable, so we have to free them from cyclic existence. Moreover, we are related to them in that all sentient beings have the same causal factor, the essence of enlightenment, so we must free them from cyclic existence. If we wish for peace and happiness for ourselves alone, we will never attain perfect buddhahood.

ix. The disadvantages of not training

The disadvantages of not training are that it will make us regress to the states of the listeners and solitary realizers and it will act as a hindrance to attaining great enlightenment. Everything we do will be pointless. We will be constantly harmed by nonhumans. Everyone will be displeased with us and be hostile toward us. We will never accomplish anything we want. These are some of the innumerable disadvantages. Woe betide those who hope to follow the Great Vehicle without having bodhichitta.

x. The precepts that have to be kept

The precept that has to be kept for bodhichitta in aspiration is that one should train again and again in bodhichitta, with the attitude of never forsaking sentient beings. If, with the prior intention to reject another sentient being, one does things like getting angry with and beating that being, and a day passes without one's applying an antidote, one's bodhichitta in aspiration will be lost. The antidote to this is to help others by always being calm and controlled and to adopt the four white actions and avoid the four black actions.*

The precept that has to be kept for bodhichitta in action is to avoid the ten negative actions, to practice the ten positive actions that are their antidotes, and to train in the ten transcendent perfections, which are the activities to be engaged in.

xi. The defining points at which one receives and gives up the vow

The moment one receives the vow is when, after gathering a great accumulation of merit, one has purified one's mind stream, given rise to the thought that one must unerringly work for sentient beings' welfare, and recited the full ritual. It is at the last of the three recitations that one receives the vow.

The moment one gives up the vow is when one gives rise to wrong view. This leads to one's abandoning the Three Jewels and transgressing the precepts, so that one loses the vow. It is important, therefore, to make an effort to keep the vow with the guard of mindfulness and vigilance.

xii. The methods for repairing breaches

If one breaks the vow at the root, one should retake the vow as before, while if one deteriorates a branch precept, one must confess it in the presence of the master and the Three Jewels.

b) Training on the inner level

Arousing bodhichitta on the inner level is again divided into twelve sections, as above.

i. Essence

The essence of the inner bodhichitta is the ultimate reality, the true meaning free of elaboration. And it is the spiritual intent to benefit those who have not realized that.

*See below, p. 333.

ii. Etymological definition

Because that kind of bodhichitta does not depend on outer activities of the body and speech but is aroused solely with the mind, it is referred to as "inner."

iii. Categories

There are two categories: aspiration and action. Bodhichitta in aspiration is the wish that beings who do not have such realization may gain it. It is not enough to mouth this wish and leave it at that: it is important to make every possible effort to enable all sentient beings to obtain that realization.

iv. The marks of the practitioner

In addition to having the above-mentioned qualities, a person who engages in the training must be someone with little conceptual elaboration.

v. The object from whom the vow is taken

The vow has to be taken from a teacher who has trained in the three kinds of wisdom, who has realized the meaning of the two kinds of no-self, and who is free of the eight ordinary preoccupations.

vi. The ritual for taking the vow

The ritual consists of completely purifying the concepts of the three spheres, mentally renouncing all worldly activities, and requesting the authentic instructions.

vii. The benefits of the training

These are superior to those of wrong paths and lower vehicles: having eliminated the concepts of an ego and of subject and object, one necessarily realizes the meaning of no-self.

viii. The reason for training in this sort of bodhichitta

The reason is that one needs to set all sentient beings on the true path and in the meaning of the two kinds of no-self.

ix. The disadvantages of not training

The disadvantages of not training are that one will mistake the meaning of no-self and, because of apprehending individuals and phenomena as real, one will create existence.

x. The precepts that have to be kept

The precepts involve training in the meaning of no-self. This has two aspects. The precepts of bodhichitta in aspiration consist of, first, never interrupting the constant aspiration "May all sentient beings realize the meaning of no-self"; second, training in rejoicing three times day and night at others who meditate on no-self; and third, constantly training in never straying from the view of no-self.

Second, the precepts of bodhichitta in action consist of outer and inner precepts. The first of these, the outer precepts, are four in number:

(1) as long as one has not realized the meaning of no-self, not to separate from the spiritual friend who teaches it

(2) to abandon partiality—with regard to places, communities, enemies, and friends

(3) to listen, reflect, and meditate on the teachings that teach no-self and emptiness

(4) not to identify oneself with a name, bloodline, or body

The inner precepts are also four. They involve training in the following:

(1) not considering conventional designations to be ultimate, for all the names and conventional designations applied to external phenomena are nothing other than the nature of mind

(2) recognizing that everything in the universe and the beings it contains are like a dream, in that they appear but have no intrinsic existence

(3) three times a day and three times a night, looking for the nature of mind—awareness, the agent that apprehends those things in all their variety, even though they do not exist in any way

(4) not straying from the truth that is free from extremes, nameless, and cannot be found, however much one may look for it

xi. The defining points at which one receives and gives up the vow

The moment one receives the vow is when one receives the pith instructions from one's teacher. The moment one gives up the vow is when one fails to realize that things have no intrinsic existence and, because of one's ordinary, dualistic ways of apprehending things, one follows chains of thoughts. That is when one should apply the antidote.

xii. The methods for repairing breaches

The way to repair breaches is to train in not being distracted from the above-mentioned points. By training like this, the knot of dualistic apprehension will automatically be untied.

c. Training on the secret level

Guru Padmasambhava taught the secret bodhichitta in eleven points, but since these are connected to the extraordinary practice of the main path, they will not be explained at this stage.

B. The main teaching on the instructions for the practice

Having clearly understood the general presentation above, we come now to the main teaching on the instructions for the practice, which is divided into (1) a general exposition of how to arouse bodhichitta and (2) the actual instructions on the specific points to be considered.

1. A general exposition of how to arouse bodhichitta

In *Finding Rest in the Nature of the Mind*, we read,

> In a clean and pleasant place adorned with offerings,
> Prepare by setting up an image of the Buddha
> Together with the other necessary articles.
> And then imagine, in the space in front of you,

The buddhas and the bodhisattvas
Like great banks of cloud that fill the sky.[217]

As the preparation, beautifully arrange whatever offerings you have in front of a support of the Three Jewels. In the sky above, visualize the teacher, the Three Jewels, yidam deities, ḍākinīs, and Dharma protectors densely gathered like banks of cloud. Then, in their presence, accumulate merit with the seven branches: perform prostrations, with yourself and all sentient beings using body, speech, and mind together; make offerings; confess negative deeds; rejoice in virtue; pray to the objects of refuge to turn the Wheel of Dharma; request them to remain without passing into nirvāṇa; and dedicate the accumulated merit to enlightenment.

After that, as the same text says,

Take refuge three times in the Triple Gem
Of Buddha, Dharma, and Supreme Assembly,
And then proclaim:
"O Protectors, you and all your offspring, think of me!
Just as all the buddhas of the past, together with their heirs,
Have brought forth the awakened mind,
And in the precepts of the bodhisattvas lived and trained,
Likewise, for the benefit of beings,
I will bring to birth the awakened mind,
And in those precepts I will live and train myself.
I will carry over those who have not fully crossed,
And liberate all those who are not free,
I will bring relief to those not yet relieved:
All beings will I place in buddhahood."

Thrice by day and thrice by night,
Strive thus to cultivate the twofold bodhichitta.
Engender with the first enunciation
Bodhichitta in intention,
Then with the second, active bodhichitta.
And with the third one make the two both pure and firm.[218]

Accordingly, for the main part of the ritual, begin by praying to the buddhas and bodhisattvas to think of you, and take refuge three times, saying,

"Until the essence of enlightenment is reached," and so on.[219] Then recite three times the verses of the vow as they appear in *The Way of the Bodhisattva*: "Just as all the Buddhas of the past . . ." and so on.[220] With the first recitation, you take the vow of bodhichitta in aspiration, with the second, that of bodhichitta in action, and with the third, the vows of arousing bodhichitta in aspiration and action together, making both stable. After that proclaim,

> "From this day forward, I will be
> The ground of sustenance for every being.
> I assume the name of Bodhisattva,
> Heir and offspring of the Conqueror.
> And in saṃsāra fearlessly,
> I will secure the good of wandering beings.
> Constantly, with diligence, I will bring them only benefit
> And thus make meaningful this human life of mine."[221]

As is indicated by these lines, meditate on rejoicing for oneself and others with "Today my life has given fruit,"[222] and make prayers of aspiration. Train in the practices of the bodhisattvas, without ever relinquishing mindfulness, vigilance, and carefulness.

Where the passage cited earlier speaks of sentient beings "who have not crossed," it refers to hell beings, hungry spirits, and animals, who have not crossed over the ocean of suffering in the lower realms. "I will carry over" means: "I will enable them to attain the celestial and human states by setting them on the path to the higher realms and releasing them from the sufferings of the lower realms." Similarly, "those who are not free" refers to gods, humans, and other beings in the higher realms, who have not been released from the iron-like fetters of the defilements. They are to be set on the path to certain excellence and freed from the fetters of the defilements, enabling them to attain liberation. "Those who are not yet relieved" are the listeners and solitary realizers, who have not found relief in the Great Vehicle. They are to be induced to arouse bodhichitta and given relief in the Great Vehicle's view and conduct, setting them on the ten bodhisattva levels. Beings who have not completely gone beyond suffering are bodhisattvas, for they have not attained the nondwelling nirvāṇa: one vows to set them in buddhahood, the level of total nirvāṇa.

2. The actual instructions on the specific points to be considered

In the sky in front of you, visualize the fields of accumulation as you did the objects of refuge. In their presence, reflect as follows:

"From whichever of the ten directions one examines it, there is no end to the universe, and the whole of it, every last bit, is filled with sentient beings. All those beings have been my father and mother countless numbers of times, and on those occasions, they took good care of me and showed me nothing but kindness, just like my present parents. What they want, all of them, is to be happy, but what they have achieved are the causes for suffering: in their actions they achieve quite the opposite of what they really want, as if they were mad. How pitiful! What can be done for all these beings, my parents, who, without wanting to, experience all kinds of sufferings? What good is saying, 'How pitiful,' and leaving it at that? I must draw them out of the sufferings of cyclic existence by quickly setting them on the level of supreme liberation—unsurpassable, true, perfect buddhahood. Right now, I do not have the ability to do that, so I must, in this very life, attain buddhahood, with the power to liberate all beings." So thinking, arouse bodhichitta in aspiration. And arouse bodhichitta in action by making the following promise and being diligent in actually putting it into practice: "In order to attain buddhahood, I will train on the profound path of the generation and perfection phases in a main practice like that of Glorious Vajrasattva."

In this way, taking the fields of accumulation as your witness, recite the lines of bodhichitta as a pledge, for example:

> HOḤ. From now until saṃsāra is emptied,
> I shall arouse the mind intent on supreme enlightenment,
> Mastering the activities of all the buddhas,
> And setting all beings without limit in the ground of nirvāṇa.[223]

And accumulate the numbers—a hundred, thousand, ten thousand, or a hundred thousand. As you do so, avoid slipping into irrelevant talk and letting your gaze be distracted, and rather than just repeating the words, keep your mind focused one-pointedly. By this means, train continuously: develop faith in the teacher and the Three Jewels, thinking, "The objects of refuge, the fields of accumulation, surely know exactly what I am thinking and doing." Cultivate compassion, the wish to free all sentient beings from suffering. And, in order to free them, give rise again and again to the superior intention, never relinquishing your intense determination to attain perfect buddhahood.

At the end, the fields of accumulation joyfully melt into light and dissolve into you and all other sentient beings. Consider that the love, compassion, bodhichitta, and unmistaken view of realization of the actual condition of reality that are present in the minds of the objects of refuge take birth in the minds of yourself and all other beings. Then rest for a short while in equipoise in the nonconceptual state.

After that, train in the bodhichitta practices of equalizing and exchanging oneself and others, as follows:

Considering others as equal to oneself involves meditating with intense, sincere longing, thinking, "All sentient beings and I are the same: we are equal in that we all want to be happy, we do not want to suffer, and we are always pleased if we are happy and well. Yet because beings fail to recognize that the causes of happiness and suffering are positive and negative actions, and because they are confused as to the behavior they should adopt or avoid, they constantly experience the three kinds of suffering. How sad this is! How I wish that beings who are unhappy could find happiness, that those who are worn down by suffering could be free of suffering, that those who are comfortable and happy could never lose that joy and happiness, and that those who are attached to their kin and hate their enemies could remain impartial and free of attachment and hatred. How I wish that they could all engage in the path to liberation and constantly practice virtue and that I and all sentient beings could swiftly attain perfect buddhahood!"

After that, exchanging oneself and others is practiced as follows: Begin by considering in front of you a single being for whom you feel compassion. Then, mentally, completely relinquish all your happiness and excellence, your body, possessions, and sources of good, casting them off like pieces of clothing, and give them to that being, making him or her happy. Take back all the suffering and evil that that being may have, laying it on yourself so that it becomes your own suffering. Feel joyful that the other being is now free of suffering, eagerly undertaking the exchange as if you were swapping clothes. When you are training like this, as you breathe out, give your happiness to the being; as you breathe in, take on the being's suffering. Expand this practice of sending and taking from a single being to all sentient beings. Finally, give rise to an extraordinary thought of love, like the love a mother with only one child has for that child. Think, "Whether I remain in cyclic existence, whether I am sick, whether I die, whatever misfortunes befall me, I can put up with them, but how can I bear the fact that all these sentient beings, my mothers, are wandering in cyclic existence and suffering?" And thinking, "I have a responsibility to take care of all beings," look with the altruistic attitude of bodhichitta on all beings filling the ends of space, beginning with those beings whom you can see and hear—whether they are your enemies, close to you, or neither. It is important to train in this in whatever way you can.

At the end of the session, seal the practice by dedicating the merit in a manner completely free of concepts regarding the three spheres. And between sessions, make an effort to preserve the experience of the session and to constantly help sentient beings. In particular, arouse bodhichitta as mentioned in the section on perfectly pure conduct in the *Sūtra of the Ornament of the Buddhas*. It is said in this text that when bodhisattvas enter a building, they arouse bodhichitta with the thought "May all beings reach the city of liberation." Similarly, when they lie down, they think, "May they attain the body of truth of the buddhas." When dreaming, "May they realize that all phenomena are like a dream." On waking up, "May they awake from the slumber of ignorance." When rising, "May they attain the form body of the buddhas." When getting dressed, "May they be clothed in a sense of shame and a sense of decency." When putting on a belt, "May they be linked to the root of virtue." When seated, "May they attain the diamond throne." When leaning their backs against something, "May they be supported by the bodhi tree." When lighting a fire, "May they burn up the fuel of the defilements." When the fire is well alight, "May the fire of wisdom blaze." When they have finished cooking, "May beings obtain the nectar of wisdom." When they are eating, "May beings acquire the food of concentration." When they go outside, "May beings be liberated from the city of cyclic existence." When going down steps, "May I enter cyclic existence for the benefit of beings." When opening a door, "May I open the gates of the city of liberation." When closing a door, "May I close the door to the lower realms." When setting out on the road, "May beings set out on the noble path." When going uphill, "May all sentient beings be set in the happiness of the higher realms." When going downhill, "May they cut the stream of the three lower realms." When meeting a sentient being, "May this being meet the Buddha." As they place their foot on the ground, "May I go forward for the welfare of all sentient beings." When lifting their foot off the ground, "May I draw them out of cyclic existence." When they see someone wearing ornaments, "May they acquire the major and minor marks." When they see someone without ornaments, "May they possess the qualities of training." When they see a full container, "May beings be full of qualities." When they see an empty vessel, "May they be devoid of defects." When they see beings who are joyful, "May they delight in the Dharma." When they see beings who are joyless, "May they not delight in compounded things." When they see beings who are happy, "May they attain the bliss of buddhahood." When they see those who are suffering, "May they put all sufferings at peace." When they see those who are ill, "May they be freed from their illness." When they see someone being grateful, "May all beings repay the kindness of all the buddhas and bodhisattvas." When they see someone being ungrateful, "May they show their discontent toward wrong views." On seeing a dispute, "May they be able to subjugate all adversaries."* When seeing someone making praises, "May beings praise all the buddhas and bodhisattvas." When seeing someone talking about the Dharma, "May they acquire the confident eloquence of the buddhas." When seeing a sacred image, "May there be nothing to prevent beings from seeing all the buddhas." When seeing a stūpa, "May all beings become objects of veneration." When they see someone doing business, "May they obtain the seven noble riches." When they see someone performing prostrations, "May they gain the crown protuberance, which is invisible to ordinary beings and even to the gods."

Furthermore, we should train in the eight thoughts of a great being. These are to think the following:

(1) "When will I be able to dispel the sufferings of all sentient beings?"

(2) Similarly, "When will I be able to bring great riches to beings stricken by poverty?"

(3) "When will I be able to benefit sentient beings with this body of flesh and blood?"

(4) "When will I be able to help sentient beings, even though it may mean staying for ages in the hells?"

(5) "When will I be able to fulfill sentient beings' hopes with great wealth, mundane and supramundane?"

(6) "When will I attain buddhahood and be able to eliminate all the sufferings of sentient beings?"

(7) "In all my series of lives, may I never have a life that does not help beings, may I never enjoy alone the taste of the ultimate truth, may I never

*"Adversaries" in this case refers to defilements such as hatred and attachment.

say words that do not please everyone, may I never have a livelihood, body, intelligence, riches, or power that do not benefit others, and may I never delight in harming others."

(8) "May the results of beings' negative actions ripen on me and the results of my virtuous actions ripen on them, so that all beings are happy."

Moreover, although there are countless millions of prayers of aspiration that the noble bodhisattvas have made, they can be condensed into ten great prayers of aspiration, so we should make similar aspirations and train our minds in these aspirations:

(1) The aspiration to venerate all the buddhas with all kinds of offerings

(2) The aspiration to hold and preserve all the sacred teachings

(3) The aspiration to manifest unimpeded forms in the presence of all those who perform the marvelous deeds of the buddhas of the ten directions and to fulfill their extraordinary deeds

(4) The aspiration to constantly practice all the activities of the bodhisattvas

(5) The aspiration to bring all sentient beings to full maturation oneself

(6) The aspiration to create infinite worlds—buddha-fields in which beings can become enlightened

(7) The aspiration to train solely in infinite purity, creating, for example, manifested buddha-fields of infinite, inconceivable scope, filled with supreme bodhisattvas

(8) The aspiration to be one with all bodhisattvas in thought and deed

(9) The aspiration to accomplish on an infinite scale only the conduct and practice that is most beneficial

(10) The aspiration to attain manifest, perfect enlightenment by displaying infinite deeds in all the furthest reaches of space

All these have to be made on an infinite scale, wishing and praying, and training the mind. This is the indispensable root of the whole practice of the Great Vehicle, as we read in the *Prayer of Good Action*:

> As far as space itself does reach,
> That far, too, the sum of beings extends.
> As far as their deeds and defilements go,
> That far, too, will all my prayers extend.

Even if one develops confidence in this way of making aspirations just once, it will serve as the entrance for boundless merit, for the same text continues:

Though someone might adorn with precious gems
The boundless realms of the ten directions,
Offering them to the buddhas,
Or offer the supreme happiness of gods and men
For aeons as numerous as the atoms in the universe,
The merit of those who,
Hearing this, the king of dedications,
Yearn for supreme enlightenment
And give rise to faith just once,
Is infinitely more sublime.

This refers to the unsurpassable, highest concentration by which bodhisattvas skilled in means fully gather merit.

III. The conclusion: How to keep the precepts, together with the benefits

Generally speaking, the bodhisattvas' precepts consist of devoting oneself entirely to helping others, along with everything that serves as the basis for benefiting them. In practice, however, in our present situation as ordinary beings beginning the path, it is hard for us to really benefit sentient beings on a vast scale, and we do not have the capacity to undertake the bodhisattvas' difficult deeds. Nevertheless, the most important thing is to assimilate the bodhisattvas' motivation, the thought of only helping others. Subsequently, as far as our deeds are concerned, we should be diligent in the means for freeing our own minds of their fetters by refraining from negative deeds and increasing our virtuous activities. By doing so, we will incidentally be benefiting others. Once we have attained the levels of the noble bodhisattvas, when we have the capacity to fulfill others' goals, we will not neglect to do so even for an instant, and our thoughts and deeds will only be beneficial for others. In that way, we will also fulfill our own goal, incidentally completing our own elimination and realization. Finally, on the level of buddhahood, both our own and others' goals will be achieved effortlessly and spontaneously. We therefore have to be skilled in giving, protecting, purifying, and increasing our body, possessions, and accumulation of virtue, according to our ability.[224]

This training can be divided into four sections: (1) identifying the precepts that have to be kept, (2) how to keep them without deterioration, (3) indicating the fault in deteriorations and how to restore the vow, and (4) a teaching on the benefit of training in that way.

A. Identifying the precepts that have to be kept

There are two sections: (1) a detailed classification of the precepts, and (2) a summary. The first of these is divided into (1) the precepts of bodhichitta in aspiration and (2) the precepts of bodhichitta in action.

1. Detailed classification of the precepts

a. The precepts of bodhichitta in aspiration

The bodhisattva Chandraprabhākumāra[225] taught the precepts of bodhichitta in aspiration as follows:

> Do not abandon sentient beings,
> Remember the benefits of bodhichitta,
> Gather the two accumulations,
> Train again and again in bodhichitta,
> And adopt and avoid the eight white and black actions—
> These five summarize the precepts of bodhichitta in aspiration.

(1) The first of these, never abandoning sentient beings, is the principal means or causal factor for not losing the precious bodhichitta, as is mentioned in the *Sūtra of the Questions of the Nāga King Anavatapta*:

> If bodhisattvas possess one teaching, they hold all the teachings of the Buddha, supreme in all aspects. Were you to ask, what is that teaching, it is the intention to never abandon sentient beings.

(2) Remembering the benefits of bodhichitta is the means for preventing bodhichitta from deteriorating. So we should constantly recite and reflect on these as described in detail in sūtras such as the *Sūtra of the Arborescent Array* and summarized in the *Prayer of Maitreya*:

> Turning us from all the lower realms,
> It shows us the road to higher birth,

And leads us where there's no old age and death:
To this bodhichitta, in homage, I bow.

(3) Constantly gathering the accumulations of merit and wisdom is the means for developing the strength of bodhichitta, as is mentioned in *Advice on Accumulation*:

"Today, what should I do
To gather merit and wisdom?
What should I do to succor beings?"
Thus do bodhisattvas constantly reflect.

(4) Training again and again in bodhichitta is the way to make bodhichitta grow more and more. It involves training the mind in the four boundless attitudes (love and the others), meditating on the bodhichitta of equalizing and exchanging oneself and others, and taking the vow of bodhichitta by oneself, six times day and night. The Omniscient Dharma Lord has written,

"All the sufferings of beings I will take upon myself;
My happiness I give to them to bring them joy,
Until they gain enlightenment, may they never lose such bliss."
With such thoughts train yourself, and turn by turn,
Give them all your happiness, their sorrows take upon yourself.
These are the precepts of bodhichitta in intention.
Likewise train in the four boundless attitudes.
Eradicate whatever acts against them;
Place a guard upon your mind.[226]

And the Bodhisattva Shāntideva says,

If I do not interchange
My happiness for others' pain,
Enlightenment will never be attained,
And even in saṃsāra, joy will fly from me.[227]

This is explained in detail in the text I have written on the mind training.[228]

As to how to take the vow of arousing bodhichitta six times a day, this can be done using the general ritual, or in condensed form, simply by saying the four-line prayer "In the Buddha, the Dharma, and the Supreme Assembly . . ."[229] The words are to be found in the ritual for arousing bodhichitta by Jowo Atisha[230] and also in the *Direct Instructions of the Teacher*.

(5) Adopting and avoiding the eight white and black actions are the means that prevents one, throughout one's series of lives, from forgetting this same bodhichitta. For this, the four black actions, which are to be avoided, are mentioned in the chapter of the *Discourse for Kāśyapa* in the *Heap of Jewels*:

> Kāshyapa, if one possesses four actions, one will forget the bodhichitta. What are these four? To deceive the teacher and those worthy of veneration. To create regret in another person who has no reason for regret. To maliciously speak of faults in a bodhisattva who has aroused bodhichitta. And to behave slyly and deceitfully with regard to sentient beings.

It is said in the *Direct Instructions of the Teacher* that if any of these four should occur, and the antidote is not applied within twenty-four hours, one will lose the vow of bodhichitta in aspiration.

The opposites of these four are the four white actions, which should be used and practiced as their respective antidotes, as is mentioned in the above-named sūtra:

> Kāshyapa, if one has four actions, one will never forget the bodhichitta. What are these four? To not knowingly tell a lie. To consider bodhisattvas as one's teachers. To maintain an altruistic attitude without deceiving sentient beings. And to properly introduce all sentient beings to the Great Vehicle.

In addition we should give rise to four thoughts as the means for making bodhichitta more stable. These are described in the *Sūtra of the King of Concentrations*:

> Young man, if one has four thoughts, one's bodhichitta will become more stable. What are these four? To consider an authentic spiritual friend as a buddha. To consider his teaching as the path. To consider those who practice it as companions on the path. And to consider all sentient beings as one's only child.

This is why the Omniscient Dharma Lord says,

> Four black actions are, in brief, to be rejected;
> Four white actions should be carefully adopted.[231]

b. The precepts of bodhichitta in action

The Omniscient Teacher explains these as follows:

> The precepts, then, of active bodhichitta
> Are the practice of the six transcendent virtues.
> Strive therein, removing all opposing forces.[232]

Peerless Gampopa says,

> Generosity, discipline, patience,
> Diligence, concentration, and wisdom:
> These six include
> The precepts of bodhichitta in action.[233]

And in the *Sūtra of the Questions of Subāhu*, we read,

> In order for bodhisattva mahāsattvas to quickly attain manifest, perfect enlightenment, they must constantly work to complete these six transcendent perfections. What are these six? They are transcendent generosity, transcendent discipline, transcendent patience, transcendent diligence, transcendent concentration, and sixth, transcendent wisdom.

These will be dealt with under two headings: (1) a general presentation, and (2) a detailed explanation of their different branches.

i. General presentation

Here is Lord Gampopa's presentation:

> Under these six heads—number, order,
> Characteristics, etymological definitions,

Subdivisions, and groupings—
The six transcendent perfections are subsumed.[234]

The number of the six transcendent perfections

The number of the six transcendent perfections is established in terms of two aspects: attaining the higher realms and attaining ultimate excellence. Three of the transcendent perfections lead to the higher realms: generosity is practiced for wealth, discipline for bodily perfection, and patience for a perfect entourage.* The other three lead to ultimate excellence: diligence is practiced in order to make good qualities increase, concentration to achieve sustained calm, and wisdom to achieve profound insight. There are, thus, six transcendent perfections in all. This follows the explanation in *Ornament of the Mahāyāna Sūtras*:

Abundant wealth, a perfect body,
And perfect entourage within the higher realms, . . .[235]

Alternatively, the transcendent perfections can be counted as six from the point of view of all the practices of the bodhisattvas being included in the three trainings. Generosity, discipline, and patience comprise the training in discipline, in terms of their being, respectively, its cause, essence, and special feature, or result. Concentration corresponds to the training in meditative concentration, and wisdom to the superior training in wisdom. These are direct correspondences, while diligence is an accessory to all of them. In the same text, it is written,

These six transcendent perfections
The Buddha has clearly explained in terms of the three
trainings:
Three perfections in the first, two in the last two,
And one included in all three.[236]

*Wealth; a fine, healthy body; and a large, harmonious entourage are not, of course, ends that bodhisattvas seek in themselves but rather advantages that enable them to benefit others on a greater scale.

The order of the six transcendent perfections

As a result of generosity, one loses one's concern for one's body and possessions, and thus takes up discipline. Having the four principles of a renunciate* leads to patience. If one is patient, one is able to undertake things with diligence. Diligent practice gives rise to concentration. And when one settles the mind evenly in concentration, one comes to a heightened knowledge of things as they truly are. The six transcendent perfections are thus classified in order of cause and result.

Another explanation of their order is given in the *Discourse on Discipline*:

> As different as are the ocean
> And a cow's hoofprint in size,
> So is the difference
> Between generosity and discipline.

They are thus classified in order of superiority, the first transcendent perfections being inferior to the subsequent ones, which are superior. The text continues:

> Even butchers and those of evil nature
> Can give with generosity,
> But they are quite unable
> To observe any form of discipline.

In other words, they are classified in terms of the first transcendent perfections being gross and easy to practice, while the subsequent ones are subtler and more difficult to practice. For these reasons, *Ornament of the Mahāyāna Sūtras* speaks of their order as follows:

> Because the next one arises in dependence on the preceding one,
> And each is superior to the former one,
> And because each is more subtle than the former one,
> They are taught one after the other.[237]

*The four principles of a renunciate (Tib. *dge sbyong*, Skt. śramaṇa) are not to return abuse with abuse, not to get angry even if someone is angry with you, not to strike anyone even if you have been struck yourself, and, even if your faults are exposed, not to find fault in return.

The characteristics of the six transcendent perfections

The six transcendent perfections have four distinguishing features. Generosity and the other perfections weaken their opposites—stinginess and so forth. They are accompanied and supported by gnosis, which is free of the concepts of the three spheres. Their function is, by their respective means, to fulfill all other beings' wishes. And by those means, they bring to full maturation the minds of those to be trained, depending on their fortune. This is stated in the same text as follows:

> Generosity counters its opposite,
> Is endowed with nonconceptual gnosis,
> Fulfills all wishes,
> And ripens beings in three ways.[238]

Ornament of the Mahāyāna Sūtras also contains analogous verses that apply to discipline and the others.[239]

Etymological definitions of the six transcendent perfections

The term common to them all is *transcendent perfection* because they are of the highest perfection compared to all the virtuous activities of mundane beings and of listeners and solitary realizers and because they transcend both existence and peace.

As for their specific names, generosity is so called because it gets rid of poverty, discipline because it enables one to obtain coolness,* patience because it bears anger, diligence because it connects one to virtue or what is supreme, concentration because it keeps the mind inwardly focused, and wisdom because it knows the ultimate, actual condition of things. The same text says,

> One perfection banishes poverty,
> One obtains coolth, one puts an end to anger,
> One connects one to what is supreme, one keeps the mind
> focused,
> And one knows the ultimate—thus are they explained.[240]

*In other words, discipline protects one from the heat of the defilements.

Subdivisions of the six transcendent perfections

Generosity and the other five transcendent perfections are each subdivided into six aspects. The generosity aspect of each transcendent perfection (the generosity of generosity and so on) is to introduce others to the six transcendent perfections. Similarly, the discipline aspect of each of them is to practice each without being tainted by its respective opposite—that is, stinginess, lax discipline, anger, distraction, and aberrant understanding. The patience aspect of each involves putting up with hardships in practicing each one. The diligence aspect involves practicing each with joy and enthusiasm. The concentration aspect involves using such diligence to focus the mind and practicing each transcendent perfection without distraction. The wisdom aspect involves training in each of the six transcendent perfections without any concepts related to the three spheres. This makes thirty-six subdivisions in all, as explained in *Ornament of Clear Realization*:

> By grouping these practices
> Variously into six—generosity and so on,
> The armor-like practice
> Is explained in six sets of six.[241]

To the above subdivisions, Orgyen, knower of the three times, adds four transcendent perfections—namely, means, strength, aspiration, and gnosis, as he mentions in the *Direct Instructions of the Teacher*:

> Overcoming stinginess and poverty by giving without any hope of a reward constitutes the transcendent perfection of strength. Doing so while free of the attitudes of ordinary beings and the lower vehicles constitutes transcendent means. Giving things away while thinking, "May my own and all sentient beings' poverty cease," is transcendent aspiration. Giving things away in a state completely purified of the concepts of the three spheres is gnosis.
>
> Similarly, overcoming negative activities with discipline free of any wish for samsaric results constitutes strength. Keeping one's vows without any thoughts related to the eight ordinary preoccupations constitutes means. Without any desire for celestial or human rebirth for oneself alone, wishing, "May all beings con-

tinuously practice discipline," constitutes aspiration. Absence of concepts related to the three spheres constitutes gnosis.

Overcoming anger by accepting everything impartially constitutes strength. Doing so without mundane motives, such as by craft and deceit, constitutes means. Without any desire for a beautiful form in the celestial or human realms for oneself alone, wishing that all sentient beings, too, may be relieved of ugliness constitutes aspiration. Practicing all this with the support of nonconceptuality with regard to the three spheres constitutes gnosis.

Overcoming laziness by diligence in calling to mind good qualities constitutes strength. Being diligent in the Dharma, rather than in mundane activities with all sorts of expectations and so on, constitutes means. Wishing that beings may cease being lazy and may strive on the true path constitutes aspiration. Being diligent with the support of nonconceptuality with regard to the three spheres constitutes gnosis.

Overcoming distraction through concentration, in which the form and formless states are abandoned, constitutes strength. Practicing concentration in order to achieve the abundant and perfect qualities of unsurpassable enlightenment without wishing for celestial or human states constitutes means. Wishing that all beings cease to be distracted constitutes aspiration. All this with absence of concepts related to the three spheres constitutes gnosis.

Destroying conceptual attributes with the wisdom that embodies emptiness and compassion constitutes strength. Never parting from that state throughout the three times constitutes means. Wishing that oneself and all others may realize the true meaning constitutes aspiration. And recognizing that one's mind is by nature this wisdom, this knowledge present since the beginning, is the transcendent perfection of gnosis.

Groupings of the six transcendent perfections

The six transcendent perfections are included within the accumulations of merit and wisdom. Generosity and discipline belong to the accumulation of merit, wisdom belongs to the accumulation of wisdom, and the other three perfections are accessories of both. Moreover, when they are all imbued with complete freedom from the concepts of the three spheres, they correspond to the accumulation of wisdom. This is stated in *Ornament of the Mahāyāna Sūtras*:

> Generosity and discipline are the accumulation of merit;
> Wisdom is that of wisdom;
> The other three belong to both;
> Five, in part, are wisdom too.[242]

How the transcendent perfections are practiced

In addition to the above heads,[243] here is how the transcendent perfections should be practiced. Give generously without any expectation regarding a reward or the ripened effect of your deed. Keep your vows without hopefully aspiring to rebirth in happy states. Train in being patient with all sentient beings, without feelings of hostility. Undertake things with diligence, with a natural enthusiasm for gathering all kinds of virtuous qualities for yourself and others. Settle in equipoise in concentration that transcends the absorptions of the worlds of form and formlessness. And practice wisdom inseparable from compassionate skillful means. As *Ornament of the Mahāyāna Sūtras* says,

> Generosity without expectation,
> Discipline with no desire for higher rebirth,
> Patience with all in every respect,
> Diligence in gathering all good qualities,
> Likewise, concentration that is not intended for the formless world,
> And wisdom possessed of skillful means—
> Those who are steadfast in these six perfections
> Are applying them authentically.[244]

All these transcendent perfections need to be untainted by the stains of the seven forms of attachment, which are incompatible with them, and to be practiced with six or twelve supreme contributory factors.

The seven forms of attachment are attachment to (1) the respective factors that are incompatible with the transcendent perfections—stinginess, lax discipline, and so forth; (2) procrastination; (3) being satisfied with practicing just a little; (4) expectation of reward in this life; (5) expectation of karmic retribution in subsequent lives; (6) the latent seeds of incompatible factors; and (7) the distractions of attentiveness to lower paths and of concepts related to the three spheres. We have to ensure that the transcendent perfections are not tainted by these stains, as is mentioned in the previous work:

> In their generosity, bodhisattvas are
> Unattached, unattached, unattached,
> Quite without attachment,
> Unattached, unattached, and unattached.
> In their discipline, bodhisattvas are . . .

and so on: these lines apply to all the transcendent perfections.[245]

The six supreme contributory factors are as follows:

1. The supreme support, which is to have bodhichitta
2. The supreme "substance" or basis, which is to engage in the transcendent perfections wholly, not just partially
3. The supreme purpose, which is to apply them to the welfare of all sentient beings
4. The supreme means, which is to permeate them with wisdom, free from the concepts of the three spheres
5. The supreme dedication, which is to transform them with the aspiration for unsurpassable enlightenment
6. The supreme purity, which is to use them as the direct antidote for the two obscurations

The twelve supreme factors are listed in *Distinguishing the Middle from Extremes*:

> Their immensity, duration,
> Purpose, inexhaustibility,
> Continuity, facility,
> Mastery, embrace,
> Commencement, attainment, causal compatibility
> And accomplishment are held to be supreme.[246]

Supreme immensity refers to bodhisattvas' wish to attain the great enlightenment, which is superior to any mundane perfections. *Supreme duration* refers to the fact that bodhisattvas train for three measureless kalpas and so on. *Supreme purpose* refers to the fact that they practice in order to benefit all sentient beings. *Supreme inexhaustibility* refers to the fact that since the transcendent perfections are dedicated entirely to the great enlightenment, they are never spent. *Supreme continuity* refers to the fact that because of the bodhisattva's appreciation of the sameness of oneself and others, the six transcendent perfections of all beings are completed. *Supreme facility* refers to the fact that simply rejoicing in others' acts of generosity and so forth enables one to complete the transcendent perfections. *Supreme mastery* refers to bodhisattvas' mastery in completing generosity and the other transcendent perfections through their having attained the Sky Treasury concentration and other powers. *Supreme embrace* refers to the fact that the transcendent perfections are embraced by nonconceptual gnosis. *Supreme commencement* refers to their great acceptance on the level of earnest aspiration, *supreme attainment* to the first bodhisattva level, *supreme causal compatibility* to the second to ninth levels, and *supreme accomplishment* to the accomplishment of the final bodhisattva level and the level of buddhahood on the tenth level and the tathāgata levels, respectively. Practices that have these twelve factors are thus distinguished from those of the lower vehicles and so on and are the authentic transcendent perfections of the Great Vehicle's path. In the *Compendium of the Great Vehicle with Appended Commentary*, we read,

> For those who are like rhinoceroses,
> The words *six perfections* do not even exist.
> The state of bhagavan alone
> Dwells on the crown of the six transcendent perfections.

The transcendent perfections should also possess four special qualities: they are (1) vast, in that their objective is perfect enlightenment for others' sake; (2) disinterested, for they are devoid of their respective incompatible factors such as hope of any reward or ripened effect; (3) immensely beneficial, in that they set all sentient beings in higher rebirth and the ultimate excellence of the three kinds of enlightenment; and (4) inexhaustible, for they are each imbued with the skillful means of emptiness and compassion united and with the dedication, so that they grow greater and greater. This is mentioned in *Ornament of the Mahāyāna Sūtras*:

Vast, disinterested,
Immensely beneficial, and inexhaustible—
Such are the four qualities that should be known
Of all the perfections such as generosity.[247]

By putting the six transcendent perfections into practice, on the temporary level we will experience the effect similar to the cause. As a result of generosity, our wealth will increase and we will never lack for anything. Because of discipline, we will be immune to harm from others, and we will obtain happy states free of lack of opportunity. Through being patient, we will have a handsome physique and our minds will be untroubled by any kind of harm. As a result of diligence, we will take delight in virtue and become increasingly resplendent with good qualities. Because of concentration, we will be at peace from distraction by concepts and achieve joy through meditative absorption. And as a result of wisdom, our minds will be freed from their fetters and we will make people happy with our excellent explanations. The same text states,

They relieve the destitute, avoid all forms of harm,
Bear injury, are not discouraged by their task,
Make others happy, and give clear explanations.
Thus they fulfill the aims of others, and this is their
own aim.[248]

And in the *Jewel Garland*, we find,

Generosity results in wealth, discipline in happiness,
Patience in a handsome body, diligence in splendor,
Concentration leads to peace, and wisdom to liberation,
Compassion accomplishes every goal.[249]

Ultimately, we will obtain the results of the two accumulations—namely, the two buddha bodies. This is explained in the same text:

Stated briefly, the form body
Arises from the accumulation of merit.
Stated briefly, the body of truth,
O King, is born from the accumulation of wisdom.[250]

ii. Detailed explanation of their different branches

There are six sections: (1) generosity, (2) discipline, (3) patience, (4) diligence, (5) concentration, and (6) wisdom.

(1) Generosity

Definition

Transcendent generosity is that which is based on the virtuous attitude of freely giving and has the four distinguishing features.*

Etymological gloss

The Tibetan word for *generosity* is derived from the Sanskrit word *dāna*, "to give," with the meaning "that which banishes others' poverty."

Categories

According to *Ornament of the Mahāyāna Sūtras*, there are three categories of generosity:

> It is endowed with freedom from stinginess,
> And comprises the gifts of Dharma, of material gifts, and of
> freedom from fear:
> Knowing that such is generosity,
> The wise accomplish it perfectly.[251]

(a) Material gifts

Material gifts serve to make others' physical condition secure. In essence, they involve giving one's own possessions—first of all, giving a little, and then gradually training in this so that in the end one gives away everything. Material gifts can be divided into three, as is stated in the *Sūtra of the Questions of Lokadhara*:

*For the four distinguishing features of the six transcendent perfections, see under the heading "The characteristics of the six transcendent perfections," p. 337.

> In this regard, material gifts complete the accumulation of merit, and the gift of Dharma completes the accumulation of wisdom; the two together serve to attain omniscience. What, then, is material giving? It comprises ordinary generosity, great generosity, and utmost generosity. Ordinary generosity refers to giving others food, clothes, conveyances, and elephants. Great generosity refers to giving one's sons, daughters, and spouse. Utmost generosity refers to giving those things that are hard to give, such as one's head, eyes, hands, and legs.

(b) The gift of protection from fear

The gift of protection from fear makes others' lives secure, as is detailed in the *Bodhisattva Stage*:

> The gift of protection from fear should be understood as protecting from danger caused by lions, tigers, marine predators, tyrants, robbers, water, and so forth.

(c) The gift of Dharma

The gift of Dharma makes others' minds secure. It is divided into three. The above scripture continues:

> What is the gift of Dharma? Giving pens, ink, and books is the small gift of Dharma. Teaching the Dharma of the Listeners' Vehicle, Solitary Realizers' Vehicle, and Unsurpassable Vehicle in accordance with beings' capacities is the great gift of Dharma. Inducing beings to seize unsurpassable enlightenment and giving them the inconceivable sky-like teachings is the exceedingly great gift of Dharma.

The first two of these forms of generosity mainly concern making others happy in this life, while the gift of Dharma mainly concerns achieving their happiness in future lives. A further explanation is that lay bodhisattvas mainly practice material giving and those who have taken monastic ordination mainly give the gift of Dharma. Actually giving away one's kingdom, children, spouse, head, legs, and so forth is taught as being the domain of bodhisattvas who have acquired the acceptance that phenomena are unborn.* On the mental level, though, it is important to train the mind in giving away everything from the beginner's stage onward, and to train in this way until gradually one becomes capable of giving away everything in reality.

The gift of Dharma can only be made by those who possess the eye of Dharma—noble beings or learned beings who possess the true pith instructions—and it is otherwise not the domain of ordinary beings. Nevertheless, we should recite the profound sūtras and incantations and mantras with the aspiration that doing so will free the mind streams of all sentient beings. We should also pray again and again to fulfill the hopes of all beings with the nectar of the teachings in the future.

Whichever of these three one is practicing, what makes it pure is wisdom and skillful means—emptiness and great compassion. Whatever their magnitude, virtuous deeds that are imbued with these two, the extraordinary means and wisdom, will not become causal factors leading to samsaric existence or to the one-sided nirvanic peace of the lower vehicles. They will, rather, lead to the great unsurpassable enlightenment. They are, therefore, completely pure, as is stated in the *Compendium of Precepts*:

> Activities that contain
> The essence of emptiness and compassion
> Lead to pure merit.

As for the means that prevents acts of generosity from being exhausted and makes them increase more and more, it is said in the *Bodhisattva's Scriptural Collection*:

> Shāriputra, wise bodhisattvas can multiply even the smallest acts of generosity. Through the strength of their gnosis, they make them greater; through the strength of wisdom they make them vaster; through the strength of dedication, they make them infinite.

In this regard, the strength of gnosis refers to the realization that the three spheres are completely pure: the giver is like an illusion, the thing given is like an illusion, and the object to whom the gift is made is also like an illu-

*That is, bodhisattvas on the eighth bodhisattva level.

sion. As for the strength of wisdom, whatever kind of gift one is making, if in the first place, one gives in order to set all sentient beings in the level of buddhahood, in the middle, one is free of attachment to the gift itself, and at the end, one has no expectations as to the ripened effect of one's generosity, this makes the merit of the act of giving expand or multiply. The *Verses That Summarize the Perfection of Wisdom* states,

> Having made a gift, they cease to dwell upon substantiality and have no expectation of ever experiencing the ripened effect. By giving in that way, the wise give away everything: the smallest acts of giving are multiplied immeasurably.

Through the strength of dedication, as a result of dedicating those acts of generosity to unsurpassable enlightenment for the sake of all sentient beings, the effects of those deeds increase beyond measure and will never be spent, as we find in the *Sūtra of the Teaching of Akṣayamati*:

> Venerable Shāriputra, here is an analogy. Just as a single drop of water that has fallen into the great ocean never dries up until the end of the kalpa, in the same way, a source of good that has been dedicated to enlightenment will never ever be spent until one dwells in the heart of enlightenment.

These two factors—purity and increase—do not apply only to acts of generosity. It is important to understand that they should accompany every source of good on the path of the Great Vehicle: so they apply equally to discipline and the other transcendent perfections.

The faults or negative consequences of not practicing generosity like this are, in most cases, rebirth as a hungry spirit. Even if one is reborn as a human, one will be wretched and poverty-stricken, as we read in the *Verses That Summarize the Perfection of Wisdom*:

> Those who are miserly will be reborn in the realms of the hungry spirits. Even if they are reborn as humans, at that time they will be destitute.

If one practices generosity properly, on the temporary level, one will have quite the opposite results, as the same sūtra states:

> Bodhisattvas' generosity bars them from birth as hungry spirits. It puts an end to poverty and likewise to all the defilements. As they experience the result, they will gain vast and limitless wealth.

The ultimate result of generosity is the attainment of enlightenment, as the *Bodhisattva's Scriptural Collection* states:

> For those who give generously, enlightenment is not difficult to find.

In this context, if you wish to read a few stories about generosity, you will find relevant accounts in my own collection of stories taken from other sources.

(2) Discipline

Definition

Transcendent discipline is that which is based on the virtuous attitude of abstention and has the four distinguishing features.

Etymological gloss

The Tibetan word for "discipline" is derived from the Sanskrit word *śīla*, for it is "that which enables one to obtain coolness" instead of being overwhelmed by the torments of the sense objects.

Categories

According to the *Heap of Jewels*,

> Kāshyapa, a bodhisattva's discipline is of three kinds: the discipline of restraint, the discipline of gathering virtue, and the discipline of accomplishing sentient beings' welfare. With the discipline of restraint, one guards the mind from nonvirtue. With the discipline of gathering virtue, one creates sources of good. With the discipline of accomplishing sentient beings' welfare, one devotes oneself to helping others.

And the Omniscient Dharma Lord says,

> Avoiding evil, doing good,
> And working for the benefit of beings:
> These three disciplines are kept by bodhisattvas at all times.[252]

(a) The discipline of refraining from negative actions

The discipline of restraint refers to avoiding everything in general related to nonvirtue. If we consider this from the point of view of the vows of individual liberation, there are two kinds of discipline: temporary and long-term. Temporary discipline refers to vows such as the eight-branch twenty-four-hour vow. Long-term discipline refers to the seven forms of individual-liberation ordination—that is, male and female lay ordinees who have first taken the threefold refuge, male and female intermediate ordinees, women novices in training for full ordination, and fully ordained monks and nuns.

These vows may be taken with a variety of motivations. In some cases, the motivation is to be protected from fear in this life. People who are afraid of being punished by the authorities, having to pay taxes, and so on take vows in order to be protected from such difficulties.* Others are motivated by the wish to better their lot. They take vows with a view to attaining celestial or human states in the next life and, in this life, to leading a comfortable existence with adequate food and clothing. Neither of these two attitudes can result in liberation. On the other hand, if one has realized that the whole of the three worlds of cyclic existence is, by nature, suffering and one then takes vows out of a desire to attain liberation from cyclic existence for oneself alone, one is following the discipline of certain deliverance. That is the genuine discipline of individual liberation of the lower vehicles. If it is then imbued with the motivation of bodhichitta, of taking the vows for the benefit of other sentient beings, it becomes the individual-liberation discipline of the Great Vehicle. When one first takes vows, even if one takes them in order to be protected from fear or with a wish to better one's lot, if one subsequently develops an attitude of renunciation, one's discipline will become that of certain deliverance. And if one then gives birth to the bodhichitta,

*Becoming a monk or nun used to confer a certain immunity from some of the difficulties facing normal citizens.

the spiritual intent of the Great Vehicle, that discipline will become the individual-liberation discipline of the Great Vehicle.

In this context, if we consider discipline from the point of view of the root downfalls of the bodhisattva vow, there are two traditions: the Middle Way tradition, and the Mind-Only tradition.

(i) The Middle Way tradition

The Middle Way tradition is Nāgārjuna's tradition based on the *Sūtra of Ākāśagarbha* and the *Sūtra of Skill in Means* and taught by Shāntideva in his *Compendium of Precepts*. In essence, there are twenty root downfalls, listed in *Ascertaining the Three Vows* as follows:

> To appropriate the property of the Three Jewels; to reject the Dharma;
> To punish monks, whether they have kept their vows or not, or force them to give up their precepts and so on;
> To commit the five crimes with immediate retribution; and to hold wrong views—these are the five downfalls for a king.
> With destroying a house, village, town, city, or province,
> There are the five established for a minister.
> To frighten the untrained by speaking of emptiness so that they aspire to the listeners' path;
> To turn people away from perfect enlightenment so that they develop the attitudes of the lower vehicles;
> To make them abandon individual liberation and train in the Great Vehicle;
> To turn them away from the Listeners' Vehicle saying that it does not counter attachment and the like,
> Thereby making their efforts fruitless;
> Out of jealousy, to praise oneself and criticize others;
> For the sake of riches and esteem, to promote oneself;
> To have a monk punished or accept the bribe he offers;
> And to give the property of a mendicant to a reciter of the scriptures,
> Inducing the former to abandon sustained calm—these are the eight established for ordinary people.

Though presented in terms of individual likelihood, they all apply to everyone.
Called eighteen, they are really fourteen.
These, along with abandoning bodhichitta in aspiration and in action, are the root downfalls.

The Five Downfalls That Kings Who Are Bodhisattvas Might Risk Committing

The first is to steal the property of the Three Jewels. This is to knowingly steal, or induce someone else to steal, the property of the Buddha (the materials for a stūpa or image), the property of the Dharma (books and the implements of a teacher), the property of the Saṅgha (anything in general belonging to the Saṅgha), and anything that has been dedicated to the Three Jewels, down to the oil for filling a lamp or a measure of grain.

The second is to give up the sacred Dharma. This means rejecting it oneself or inducing someone else to do so, saying, "The Dharma that the Buddha taught, whether the Great Vehicle or lesser vehicles, is not the way to attain liberation."

The third is to inflict punishment upon an ordained person. This is to punish anyone who bears the signs of having taken ordination, whether or not he or she has kept their vows, to imprison them, force them to give up their vows, or to kill them.

The fourth is to commit any of the five crimes with immediate retribution—namely, killing one's father, killing one's mother, killing an arhat, creating a schism in the Saṅgha, or malevolently causing a buddha to bleed.

The fifth is wrong view—that is, wholeheartedly engaging in negative actions while denying the karmic law of cause and effect and the existence of past and future lives.

The Five Downfalls That Ministers Might Risk Committing

These comprise the first four of the above faults, from stealing the property of the Three Jewels to crimes with immediate retribution, to which is added laying waste to different forms of habitation. This refers to destroying any of the following habitations: a dwelling housing up to a single family, a village inhabited by all four castes,* a town in which all eighteen trades are represented,† a city in which large numbers of merchants live, or a country—for example, a province like Champā.‡

The Eight Downfalls That Are Established as Might Occur for Ordinary People

The first is, without checking whether they are suitable vessels, to give people who have not trained their minds in the Great Vehicle the profound teachings on emptiness. If one does so, they may take fright at those teachings and give up bodhichitta and aspire to the listeners' path.

The second is to induce someone who has engaged in the Great Vehicle, the path to perfect enlightenment, to give rise to the spiritual intent of the lower vehicles by telling them, "You will not be able to go through all the hardships over many measureless kalpas. Instead, you should engage in this path of the listeners and solitary realizers. Then you can be certain of deliverance from cyclic existence without any difficulty."

The third is, unless there is a specific reason for doing so, to induce someone who has the listeners' potential and is training in the path of individual liberation, or wishes to do so, to give up the path of individual liberation and train in the Great Vehicle by telling them, "What use is keeping the vows of individual liberation purely? If instead you arouse the bodhichitta, any breaches of the vow of individual liberation that you commit will be annulled by the force of bodhichitta."

The fourth is to believe, or cause someone else to believe, that, however much one trains in the Listeners' Vehicle, it will not counter defilements such as attachment and that one should, therefore, turn away from it.

The fifth is, out of jealousy, to express faults in another bodhisattva who is revered and to proclaim that one has qualities when one has none.

The sixth is, for the sake of gain and respect, to deceive others with lies about one's having sublime qualities that one does not have, telling them,

*The four castes of traditional Indian society were those of the warriors, priests, merchants, and commoners.

†The eighteen trades are those of merchant, potter, garland maker, wine seller, cattle seller, barber, oilseed presser, smith, carpenter, fortune teller, weaver, leather worker, fisher, dyer, basket maker, butcher, hunter, and cart maker.

‡Champā was one of the six great cities of ancient India.

for example, that one has realized the meaning of profound emptiness when one has not.

The seventh is to slander another monk so that someone in power, such as a king, punishes the monk; and should the monk steal the property of the Three Jewels and offer it to one as a bribe, to accept it or give it to the person in power.

The eighth is to impose inappropriate rules that disturb renunciate meditators and thereby interrupt their practice of concentration and so on; and to use a variety of means, such as stealing the belongings they have acquired and so forth and giving them to monks who are reading and reciting the scriptures, to interrupt their practice and induce them to abandon their concentration.

All these downfalls lead to rebirth as beings in the great hell, as is stated in the *Compendium of Precepts*:

> These are the root downfalls:
> They are the causes of beings in the great hell.

This presentation of the root downfalls of kings, ministers, and ordinary people is made in terms of the downfalls that those individuals are more likely to commit, but that does not mean they cannot become downfalls for the others. Every bodhisattva has to guard against all these downfalls.

Although the sūtras nominally distinguish eighteen kinds of downfalls, in fact they comprise fourteen because the first four of the ministers' downfalls are no different from the first four of the king's downfalls.

To these eighteen are added two more: abandoning bodhichitta in aspiration, as is stated in the *Sūtra of Skill in Means: The Great Secret of All the Buddhas*:

> Fortunate child, for a bodhisattva to abide with the listeners' and solitary realizers' attitude is a serious root downfall of the bodhisattva vow;

and giving up bodhichitta in action and failing to practice virtue, as is mentioned in the *Heap of Jewels*, making twenty in all.

(ii) The Mind-Only tradition

The essence of what the Noble Asaṅga compiled from various sūtras of the Great Vehicle and taught in the *Bodhisattva Stage* is presented by the Marvelous Master, the great Chandragomin,* in his *Twenty Verses on the Vows of a Bodhisattva*:

> Because they arise from intense defilements,
> There are four faults that destroy the vow.
> They are considered to be comparable to radical defeats.
> Out of attachment to riches and esteem,
> To praise oneself and criticize others;
> Out of stinginess, not to give the Dharma or riches
> To those who suffer and are without protector;
> Without listening, though the other apologizes,
> To strike another person out of anger;
> And to reject the Great Vehicle and teach a semblance of the sacred Dharma.

There are four root downfalls that are comparable to the listeners' radical defeats, for they are caused by intense defilements like attachment and destroy the bodhisattva vow:

- out of attachment, through excessive clinging to gain in the form of offerings and to esteem in the form of things like being offered a throne, to praise oneself and criticize others who have good qualities
- on account of stinginess, to fail to give material things to those who are suffering and helpless, and not to give teachings to those who are suitable vessels
- out of hatred, to fail to change one's mind and to harbor a grudge, even though the other person has reasonably apologized and asked to be pardoned, and not satisfied with angrily showering abuse upon the other person, to harm them by hitting and beating them

*Chandragomin was one of the Two Marvelous Masters (Tib. *rmad byung gi slob dpon gnyis*), the other being Shāntideva.

- out of lack of discernment, to disparage the teachings of the Great Vehicle and reject them, and to teach, or cause others to teach, a sham path, a semblance of the Dharma that one has invented oneself

In terms of the attitudes that motivate them, these are presented as four root downfalls, but as the above list shows, in terms of their application, they each constitute two downfalls. Jowo Atisha maintains that they should therefore be categorized as eight downfalls.

Furthermore, both traditions teach a number of minor, secondary faults: eighty minor faults as mentioned in the *Compendium of Precepts*, forty-six minor faults taught in the *Twenty Verses on the Vows of a Bodhisattva*, and so on.[253]

To sum up, the avoidance of all physical, verbal, and mental actions that are harmful to others, along with their basis, constitutes the discipline of refraining from negative actions.

(b) The discipline of gathering virtue

This involves training in the six transcendent perfections for others' sake, in the manner described above, and directly or indirectly accomplishing the benefit of others, along with its basis. In short, it means training in accomplishing an ocean-like accumulation of virtue in connection with the two accumulations and avoiding everything that goes counter to that. Moreover, it is said in the *Bodhisattva Stage*,

> Relying on, and abiding by, the bodhisattvas' discipline, they are diligent in listening, reflecting, meditating, and delighting in solitude. They venerate and serve their teachers, attend and nurse the sick, give generously, and proclaim good qualities. They rejoice at others' merit and put up with contempt. They dedicate merit to enlightenment and make prayers of aspiration. They make offerings to the Three Jewels and apply themselves with diligence. They conduct themselves carefully, are mindful of the precepts, and guard themselves with vigilance. They control their senses and are moderate in their eating. They are diligent in not sleeping during the first and last parts of the night. They

> follow sublime beings and spiritual friends. Having examined their own mistakes, they acknowledge them and give them up. Accomplishing such virtues, they preserve them and make them grow. This is what is known as the "discipline of gathering virtue."

(c) The discipline of benefiting sentient beings

The *Bodhisattva Stage* lists twelve different ways of benefiting beings, as follows:

> They assist beings in useful activities. They dispel the suffering of beings who are suffering. They give proper instruction to those who are ignorant of the right way. They are grateful and appreciative of actions done, and they help beings in return. They protect beings from different kinds of danger. They dispel the distress of those who suffer. They give provisions to those who lack provisions. With the teachings, they properly gather around them a following of disciples. They act in accord with beings' wishes. They inspire beings with their genuine qualities. They subjugate beings appropriately. And, by means of their miraculous powers, they cause beings to be afraid of nonvirtue and yearn for virtue.

In particular, we find in *Ascertaining the Three Vows*,

> The discipline of benefiting beings comprises the four ways of attracting disciples.
> Having first attracted disciples with generous gifts,
> They catch their attention with pleasant conversation.
> They act in their interests, leading them through the nine graded vehicles,
> And in order to guide them, they themselves practice the meaning.

Accordingly, the four ways of attracting disciples are as follows:

First, in order to bring together a group of many disciples to be trained, one first makes them content by giving them material gifts, as is stated by the sublime scholar Ashvaghoṣha in his *Heaped Lotuses*:

> Gracefully summon with the beckoning hand of generosity, . . .

Second, having attracted a following, one gradually captures their attention with pleasant conversation. In other words, by teaching them the sacred Dharma, one induces the disciples to feel eager and enthusiastic about pursuing its practice, as we read in the same text:

> And receive with pleasant conversation, . . .

Third, one induces the disciples to follow the practice of the Dharma in accord with their individual mental capacities, in the same way that, when feeding children, one gradually introduces them to food that is coarser and less soft. The same text reads,

> Give good advice according to need . . .

Fourth, in order to connect those beings to the sacred Dharma and to virtue, one trains oneself in those accordingly, as the same text says:

> And reassure by acting according to the teaching.

Furthermore, to prevent themselves from degenerating and to make others gain faith, on the physical level, bodhisattvas should avoid impure activities: pointlessly running and jumping and the like. Verbally, they should avoid a lot of pointless talk, digging out others' faults, and so on. And mentally, they should avoid such things as delighting in riches, esteem, sleep, and lethargy. They should be physically peaceful and controlled in their pure activities and in the four daily activities. In what they say, they should use gentle words and speak fittingly. And mentally, they should be free of deceit and maintain superior mental states like faith. In *The Way of the Bodhisattva*, we read,

> Be the master of yourself
> And have an ever-smiling countenance.
> Rid yourself of scowling, wrathful frowns,
> And be a true and honest friend to all.[254]

And in the *Moon Lamp Sūtra*, we find,

> Even if you see a person doing wrong,
> Never proclaim aloud that person's faults.
> Whatever deeds you do in that respect,
> Will give the corresponding fruit.*

And in the previous scripture,

> Speak coherently, appropriately,
> Clear in meaning, pleasantly.
> Rid yourself of craving and aversion;
> Speak gently with moderation.[255]

In the *Sūtra That Inspires a Superior Intention*, we read,

> Maitreya, bodhisattvas should understand that riches and honors give rise to attachment. They should know that riches and honors give rise to aversion. They should know that riches and honors give rise to bewilderment. They should know that riches and honors give rise to deceit. They should understand that riches and honors have never been sanctioned by any of the buddhas. They should understand that riches and honors plunder sources of good. They should understand that riches and honors are like prostitutes who cheat others.

Shāntideva sums this up as follows:

> And all that you have seen, or have been told,
> To be a cause of scandal—that you should avoid.[256]

For all these three kinds of discipline, we should, as mentioned earlier, rely on the extraordinary means and wisdom, and be skilled in the ways to make them perfectly pure and to increase them.

*While one may act responsibly to correct someone who has acted mistakenly, one should not take advantage of the situation to meanly criticize them. In Patrul Rinpoche, *Words of My Perfect Teacher*, 115, Patrul Rinpoche tells the story of a nun who called another nun a bitch, as a result of which she was herself reborn as a bitch five hundred times.

As for the faults in not observing discipline in this manner, *Introduction to the Middle Way* says,

> Enjoyment, in the lower realms, of fruits of generosity
> Occurs through fracturing the limbs of discipline.*

The benefits of observing discipline are as follows: On the temporary level, according to the *Verses That Summarize the Perfection of Wisdom*,

> Through their discipline, they will avoid the multitude of animal births
> And the eight states without opportunity: thus will they always gain freedom.

And in the *Bodhisattva's Scriptural Collection*, we find,

> Shāriputra, there are no glories and perfections, human or celestial, that bodhisattvas with perfectly pure discipline will not experience.

The result of discipline on the ultimate level is described in the *Bodhisattva Stage*:

> Having completed the bodhisattvas' transcendent perfection of discipline, one will attain perfect buddhahood in truly perfect, manifest enlightenment.

Accordingly, by means of these three kinds of discipline, we will accomplish the path of the three trainings and complete the two accumulations. Subsequently, at the moment of attaining buddhahood, we will, as a result of the discipline of refraining from negative actions, attain perfect elimination—the elimination of the two obscurations together with habitual tendencies. As a result of the discipline of gathering virtue, we will attain

*Chandrakīrti, *Introduction to the Middle Way*, chap. 2, v. 4. The result of practicing generosity is riches in future lives, but if one has failed to practice discipline, which would normally result in rebirth in the higher realms, one will be reborn in the lower realms as, for example, a wealthy nāga, and enjoy those riches there.

perfect realization—knowing things truly and knowing things to the full extent. And as a result of the discipline of benefiting sentient beings, we will acquire the perfect buddha activities in accord with the needs of beings to be trained, thus leading to the spontaneous accomplishment of the two goals.

(3) Patience

Definition

Transcendent patience is that which is based on a virtuous state of mind that is imperturbable and has the four distinguishing features.

Etymological gloss

The Tibetan word for "patience" is derived from the Sanskrit word *kṣānti*, for it is "that which bears suffering and the like."

Categories

In *Ascertaining the Three Vows*, we read of three kinds of patience:

> Patiently accept anger, the profound, and suffering.

(a) The patience of thinking nothing of the harm that has been done to us

Whatever harm others may inflict on us and those related to us, and in whatever way, we should think, "This is the result of my having harmed them in the past. They have harmed me like this now because their minds are confused and they cannot help it, as if they were driven mad by some demonic force. As a result, in future lives, they will have to experience the sufferings of the lower realms—how pitiful!" We should also think, "By relying on this method and training in patience, the karmic effect of many of my evil deeds will be exhausted and my accumulation of merit will grow. So my aggressors are actually being very kind, like spiritual friends." And, "In return for their kindness, I will share whatever virtuous deeds I have done with them." By these means, we should train in not letting our minds be disturbed by harm, in not retaliating, in not harboring resentment, and so on, as we read in *The Way of the Bodhisattva*:

> No evil is there similar to anger,
> No austerity to be compared with patience.
> Steep yourself, therefore, in patience,
> In various ways, insistently.

And,

> In just the same way in the past
> I it was who injured living beings.
> Therefore it is right that injury
> Should come to me, their torturer.

And,

> My enemies are helpers in my Bodhisattva work
> And therefore they should be a joy to me.
> Since I have grown in patience
> Thanks to them,
> To them its first fruits I should give,
> For of my patience they have been the cause.[257]

If we check carefully, the victim, the aggressor, and the harm are, all three, devoid of intrinsic existence. They are like things in a magical display, so who would get angry at them? The same text says,

> Knowing this, we will not be annoyed
> At things that are like magical appearances.

And,

> With things that in this way are empty
> What is there to gain and what to lose?
> What is there to give me joy and pain?
> May beings like myself discern and grasp
> That all things have the character of space![258]

(b) The patience of happily accepting suffering

Even though, in order to accomplish the Dharma, we may have to experience different hardships and momentary physical sufferings such as sickness, heat and cold, and hunger and thirst, on the temporary level, these are exhausting the results of our evil deeds, and ultimately they will lead to our attaining unsurpassable enlightenment. So we should accept them enthusiastically, like swans arriving at a lake of lotuses. As we read in *The Way of the Bodhisattva*,

> Is it not a happy chance if when, condemned to death,
> A man is freed, his hand cut off in ransom for his life?
> And is it not a happy chance if now, to escape hell,
> I suffer only the misfortunes of the human state?
> The hardships suffered on the path to Buddhahood
> Are limited in their extent
> And likened to the pain of an incision
> Made to cure the harms of inward ills.[259]

(c) The patience of certainty with regard to the teachings

This refers to fearless acceptance. It comprises great compassion and great wisdom. Because of great compassion, one is not afraid of fulfilling the vast goal of sentient beings' welfare until the end of the kalpa. And as a result of great wisdom, one is not afraid of the profound teachings on the actual condition of things—the teachings on emptiness, the ultimate nature that is the actual condition of all phenomena; the teachings on intrinsic natural luminosity; those on the self-arising uncompounded wisdom; those on the essence of the sugatas; the teachings on the inconceivable; and so on.

For these three kinds of patience, too, we should be skillful in the methods for making them pure and increasing them with extraordinary means and wisdom.

The faults in not having such patience are as Shāntideva has said:

> All the good works gathered in a thousand ages,
> Such as deeds of generosity,

And offerings to the Blissful Ones—
A single flash of anger shatters them.[260]

As for the results of training in patience, the same text describes the temporary results as follows:

For patience in saṃsāra brings such things
As beauty, health, and good renown.
Its fruit is great longevity,
The vast contentment of a universal king.[261]

And the sūtras mention five great benefits:

> Little enmity, little discord, much well-being and happiness, no regrets when one comes to die, and once the body has perished, rebirth in happy states in the higher realms.

Ultimately, one will attain manifest enlightenment, and as we read in the *Sūtra of the Meeting of the Father with the Son*:

From meditating constantly on love,
Thinking, "Anger is not the Buddha's path,"
Enlightenment will thus take birth.

(4) Diligence

Definition

Transcendent diligence is that which is based on the virtuous attitude of enthusiasm and has the four distinguishing features.

Etymological gloss

The Tibetan word for "diligence" is derived from the Sanskrit word *vīrya*, for it is "the undaunted fortitude that connects one to what is sublime."

Categories

In *Ascertaining the Three Vows*, we read of three kinds of diligence:

> Set about things with diligence that is armor-like, gathers virtue, and benefits others.

(a) Armor-like diligence

Armor-like diligence is related to one's attitude. From the moment one first starts practicing, to avoid being trampled on by demons, one should give rise to this courageous attitude, thinking from the bottom of one's heart, "Until I have set all sentient beings in perfect enlightenment, I will never give up making every effort to accomplish the great waves of bodhisattva activities." We find in the *Bodhisattva's Scriptural Collection*,

> Shāriputra, you must don the inconceivable armor: until the end of cyclic existence, do not relax your efforts to achieve enlightenment.

And in the *Sūtra of the Display of Armor*,

> In order to gather sentient beings,
> Bodhisattvas must put on armor.
> There is no limit to sentient beings,
> And therefore no limit to the armor they must wear.

And the *Sūtra of the Teaching of Akṣayamati*,

> Bodhisattvas do not seek enlightenment, counting the kalpas, "For this many kalpas, I will don the armor, and for that many kalpas, I will not don the armor." They have to wear inconceivable armor.

(b) Diligence in application

Diligence in application is related to one's application in putting things into practice. It is to have joy and enthusiasm in acquiring the qualities of elimination and realization that enable one to complete the five paths and the ten levels. The causal factor for obtaining these is to engage in amassing an ocean-like accumulation of virtue through such things as listening, reflecting, and meditating. Once one has engaged in that, one has to exert oneself with constant application and devoted application, by never becoming discouraged in the practice, never being satisfied with having acquired just a few temporary qualities, and never being put off by such things as others' ingratitude.

In this regard, constant application is described in the *Jewel Cloud Sūtra*:

> In undertaking all the bodhisattva activities with diligence, they pursue them whatever happens, without becoming wearied physically or disheartened mentally. This is what is known as the bodhisattvas' constant diligence.

Devoted application is to act joyfully, enthusiastically, and speedily. As it is said,

> The elephant, tormented by the noonday sun,
> Will dive into the waters of a lake,
> And likewise I must plunge into this work
> That I might bring it to completion.[262]

(c) Diligence in benefiting beings

Diligence in working for sentient beings' welfare is the causal factor for accomplishing one's own and others' goals. This involves, all the time, night and day, in thought or deed, putting one's efforts exclusively into the means for directly or indirectly accomplishing sentient beings' benefit and happiness.

> Directly, then, or indirectly,
> Do nothing that is not for others' sake.
> And solely for their welfare dedicate
> Your every action to the gaining of enlightenment.[263]

In the context of these different kinds of diligence, it is important to give up laziness, which is the counteragent of diligence. There are three kinds of laziness: the laziness of indifference, the laziness of defeatism, and the laziness of a liking for what is base or for evil activities.

The first of these refers to attachment to the pleasures of taking it easy—lying down, forgetting it all, falling asleep, and so on. The remedy for this is to be mindful of impermanence, as we read in a sūtra:

> Monks, your consciousness will dim, your life force will be severed, and even the Teacher's doctrine will definitely disappear. Why do you not practice with diligence and consistent effort?

And *The Way of the Bodhisattva* has,

> Gather merit as swiftly as you can.[264]

Second, the laziness of defeatism comes about when we get discouraged and are unable to apply ourselves, thinking, "Even if I try, how can a worthless person like me attain enlightenment?" To remedy this, we should encourage ourselves as has already been explained above.*

Third, the laziness of attachment to negative activities comes about through attachment and clinging to negative, worldly activities like subduing enemies, protecting relatives and friends, and engaging in business and agriculture. Since these lead directly to suffering, we should avoid them, as Atisha has advised:

> Look at all the activities of the worldly:
> All they do is pointless and leads to suffering.
> Whatever one thinks of, it is devoid of essence,
> So look at your own mind and train in that.

The methods for making diligence pure and increasing it are the same as for the previous transcendent perfections.

The faults or defects in not having diligence in anything and being overpowered by laziness are described in the *Sūtra of the Questions of Sāgaramati*:

> Those who are lazy have neither generosity, nor wisdom, nor any of the other transcendent perfections. Those who are lazy can

*For example, by reflecting on the fact that we possess the buddha nature.

> never benefit others. For those who are lazy, enlightenment is a very, very long way away.

The result of being properly diligent is that, on the temporary level, we will gain the highest happiness in existence, as is mentioned in *Ornament of the Mahāyāna Sūtras*:

> Through diligence, one obtains the enjoyments one desires in saṃsāra.[265]

The ultimate result is the attainment of enlightenment. The above sūtra has this to say:

> Those who have undertaken things with diligence have no difficulty attaining unsurpassable enlightenment. Why is this? Sāgaramati, where there is diligence, there is enlightenment.

And in the *Sūtra of the Questions of Pūrṇa*, we read,

> Those who always do things with diligence
> Have no difficulty reaching enlightenment.

(5) Concentration

Definition

Transcendent concentration is that which is based on the virtuous state of mind of one-pointedness with regard to an object and has the four distinguishing features.

Etymological gloss

The Tibetan word for "concentration" is derived from the Sanskrit word *dhyāna*, for when the mind moves, concentration "holds it without it being distracted elsewhere."

Categories

The *Sūtra on Entering Laṅka* lists three kinds of concentration:

> The concentration practiced by the childish, clearly discerning concentration, and the excellent concentration of the tathāgatas.

(a) The concentration practiced by the childish

The concentration practiced by the childish is the concentration that even those who have not entered the path to liberation possess in their mind streams. Its categories are the four states of concentration* free of the concepts of the world of desire and the four formless absorptions free of the concepts of the world of form. Of these, the absorptions of the four states of concentration comprise the sustained calm that serves as the foundation for profound insight. The four formless absorptions are meditational errors. In brief, the childish concentration does not transcend the four states of concentration, which, however stable they may be, are states in which the mind is merely settled with sustained calm alone, without being imbued with genuine profound insight. Neither does the childish concentration transcend the formless absorptions, which are mostly analytical ways of holding the mind, however well honed they may be. This is mentioned in the *Chapter on Gathering Concentration*[266] as follows:

> However stable it may be,
> Concentration that is clung to
> Is called "childish concentration."
> It will not lead to attaining nirvāṇa.

(b) Clearly discerning concentration

This is the concentration present in the minds of those who have entered the path and who are on the paths of accumulation and joining. Unlike the previous concentration, which is just sustained calm on its own, this concentration unites sustained calm and clear discernment of its object—that

*The four states of concentration, or four dhyānas (Tib. *bsam gtan bzhi*), are the states associated with the world of form.

is, discerning, profound insight. By meditating in this way, one progressively acquires the extraordinary qualities of the paths of accumulation and joining, as they have been taught; and by means of some minor preternatural powers, one is also able to benefit others in appropriate ways. *The Way of the Bodhisattva* declares,

> Penetrative insight joined with calm abiding
> Utterly eradicates afflicted states.
> Knowing this, first search for calm abiding,
> Found by people who are happy to be free from worldly ties.[267]

(c) The excellent concentration of the tathāgatas

The excellent concentration of the tathāgatas is the uncontaminated concentration in the minds of noble beings, starting from the path of seeing and the first bodhisattva level. It consists of absorption on the object of the tathāgatas' gnosis, as the Lord Maitreya says:

> From intellectual understanding that there is nothing other than
> the mind,
> They then realize that neither does the mind exist.
> Once the wise have seen that both do not exist,
> They abide in the expanse of reality devoid of those.[268]

To actually practice concentration, begin by reflecting on the nature of change and impermanence. Everything that is born ends up dying. Everything that is gathered ends up being separated. Everything that is accumulated ends up being consumed. All prosperity ends in decline. It is all deceptive and devoid of essence. The appearances of this life are like manifestations in a dream; their nature is impermanent and changing, and it is attachment to them that is so utterly ruinous for beings. So think, "Soon, I, too, will die. I am certain to die. There is no guarantee that I will not die tomorrow, or even tonight, and I will be helpless to prevent it, so what is the point of the activities of this present life, which is just an illusion? The only sure aid at the time of death will be my teacher's profound instructions. So I must meditate one-pointedly on them and make every effort to train in concentration." It is said in the sūtras,

Who knows if tomorrow death will come?
Train and practice now, this very day!
The Lord of Death and his great host
Are not by any means your friends.

Next, reflect on the negative consequences of desire. The things we desire have numerous drawbacks. We are occupied with accumulating, preserving, and increasing them. On account of them, we commit more and more negative actions, we get into disputes with everyone, and we are never satisfied with what we have. We become more and more arrogant and miserly. We are afraid of our possessions being used up, afraid of their being destroyed, and afraid of their being robbed. They get shared with everyone—thieves and the like. Even if we store them up, it is in the nature of things that when we die, they will be left behind and separated from us. However many possessions we acquire, they bring even more suffering. They are quite incompatible with the way to complete liberation—listening, reflecting, meditating, practicing discipline, and so on. The noble beings completely despise them, as we read in *Letter to a Son*:

The pain of gaining, keeping, and losing all!
See the endless hardships brought on us by property![269]

We should therefore train in being content with few desires, as is stated in *Letter to a Friend*:

Of all great wealth, contentment is supreme,
Said he who taught and guided gods and men.
So always be content; if you know this
Yet have no wealth, true riches you'll have found.[270]

After this, reflect on the disadvantages of having children and friends, as follows: "The company of gatherings of people, laypeople or monastics, friends, relatives, companions, enemies, and all those in between is overwhelming. They are evil in nature, unappreciative of what we do for them, and harm us in return for help. Always wanting things, unsatisfied, aggressive, and rude, they do only what they themselves want and naturally harm others. They consider only the short term, and they abandon and abuse us when their wealth dwindles. They have no fear of shame and no respect for the Buddha's teachings, sacred commitments, and so on, nor are they wary of retribution and the ripened effect of their actions. They have numerous projects and activities, are very difficult to please, quarrelsome, violent, and jealous. Thus they let their lives slip by, misled by exclusively non-Dharmic ways. Noble beings avoid and keep their distance from these immature beings, in whose mere company virtue diminishes and evil grows. For that reason, I, too, must not keep the company of anyone, for they will interrupt the accomplishment of the highest liberation. I will practice peaceful concentration alone." *The Way of the Bodhisattva* states,

> For if I act like childish beings,
> Sure it is that I shall fall to evil destinies.
> So why do I keep company with infants,
> Who lead me to a state so far from virtue?
> One moment friends,
> The next, they're bitter enemies.
> Even pleasant things arouse their discontent:
> Ordinary people—it is hard to please them!
> A beneficial word and they resent it,
> Turning me instead from what is good.
> And when I close my ears to what they say,
> Their anger makes them fall to lower states.
> Jealous of superiors, they vie with equals,
> Proud to those below, they strut when praised.
> Say something untoward, they seethe with rage.
> What good was ever had from childish folk?

And,

> For they will bring no benefit to me,
> And I in turn can bring them nothing good.
> Therefore flee the company of childish people.[271]

Now reflect on the negative consequences of being diverted by distracting occupations, as follows: With regard to experiences in the world in general and activities devoted to this life in particular, there never comes a time when they are completed and we are satisfied. We are constantly busy and distracted, for little purpose. However much effort we make, it is all in vain. There is no end to the enemies we need to put down. There is no end to the friends and relatives we have to protect. All the efforts we put into trade, agriculture, manufacturing, and intellectual endeavors are simply for food and clothing. Apart from that there is not so much as an atom's worth of meaningful activity that helps us progress on the path of the Dharma. Constantly, night and day, we pass the time in distracting bustle and diversion. What is the use of it all? Instead, I should abandon the preoccupations related to this life and practice concentration. For as the Great Orgyen has said,

> Unless you leave your native land, you will not overcome the demon of pride. If you do not give up household activities, you will not find the time to practice the Dharma. If you do not follow the Dharma when you have developed faith, you will never finish your tasks. Do not blame other people for your own lack of faith. If you do not throw your belongings to the wind, you will never make up your mind about worldly ways. If you do not distance yourself from your relatives, you will never cut the stream of attachment and aversion. If you do not practice the teachings now, you cannot be sure where you will be born later. Stop lying to yourself and decide what you really want—practice the Dharma! In due course, you will have to depart, leaving behind your relatives, spouse, and everything. So if you could abandon them now, it would be truly meaningful. Instead of continuing to engage in politics, which will certainly not help you, engage in virtue, which is what you really need. Instead of making plans for next year's projects, which may or may not be necessary, apply yourself to virtue, which definitely is necessary.

And,

> Idle chatter, jokes, and laughter
> Are obstacles to meditation, so avoid them.
> Relatives, companions, and disciples
> Are anchors for the eight worldly preoccupations, so abandon them.
> Possessions, diversions, and riches

Distract one from the Dharma, so renounce them.
Sleep, idling around, and laziness
Are practitioners' archenemies, so give them up.

Finally, reflect on the advantages of solitude, as follows: By practicing in quiet forests, all the buddhas and bodhisattvas in the past discovered ambrosia, so I, too, should make use of solitude. In isolated places, there is no bustle and distraction. There is nothing to do, no stress, no business, no agriculture, no children or companions. With birds and deer for company, I will be filled with happiness. The water, plants, and so on will be suitable for my ascetic's diet. My dwelling in a cave or at the foot of a mountain will accord with the teachings. With no friends or acquaintances, I will naturally be at peace from defilements such as attachment and aversion. With many conditions to inspire disenchantment and renunciation, virtuous activities will naturally increase. Awareness will naturally become clearer, so that wisdom will grow radiant and clear. Since there are so many such advantages in lonely places, from now on I must live in solitude. For as we read in the *Sūtra of the Questions of Pūrṇa*,

The wish to stay in mountains and forests
Is the source of good qualities and makes them grow.
Making use of lonely places
Banishes attachment to the five pleasures.
And so, because there are no diversions,
Those with virtue will not degenerate.
Because one does not walk to and fro,
Or ask questions, or speak words,
The buddhas give the highest praise
To empty solitudes and peaceful hermitages.
Bodhisattvas, for this reason,
Should forever dwell in lonely sites,
Remaining unattached to urban life.

In the *Sūtra of Individual Liberation*, it is said,

Happy are those who've studied much
And now grow old deep in the forest.

To live in lonely places like this is what noble beings aspire to, as did Shāntideva:

> In woodlands, haunt of stag and bird,
> Among the trees where no dissension jars,
> It's there I would keep pleasant company!
> When might I be off to make my dwelling there?
> When shall I depart to make my home
> In cave or empty shrine or under spreading tree,
> With, in my breast, a free, unfettered heart,
> Which never turns to cast a backward glance?
> When might I abide in such a place,
> A place unclaimed and ownerless,
> That's wide and unconfined, a place where I might stay
> At liberty, without attachment?[272]

Moreover, staying in solitary retreat is the very best way to serve the buddhas, and, as it is said in the *Moon Lamp Sūtra*:

> One might not venerate the buddhas, lords of beings,
> With food and drink, and likewise clothes,
> With flowers or incense or offerings in rows,
> But should one deeply wish for enlightenment
> And, revulsed by compounded evil states,
> Take seven steps to live in solitude for beings' sake,
> The merit gained thereby will be much more.

In particular, we will swiftly achieve concentration, as the same sūtra points out:

> Flee the delights of villages and towns
> And stay forever in lonely forest dwellings.
> Rhino-like, constantly practice nonduality:
> Shortly you will achieve the highest concentration.

Having distanced and isolated ourselves physically from crowds and distracting entertainments, we need to isolate ourselves mentally from such diversions, so we should ask ourselves, "Why have I come to this lonely place?" It is out of fear, to escape places full of distractions like towns and cities, that one seeks solitude. "Fear of what?" we might then ask. The answer is to be found in the *Sūtra of the Questions of the Householder Ugra*:

> Fearful of distracting crowds, fearful of riches and esteem, fearful of the company of evil folk, fearful of false teachers, fearful of attachment, aversion, and bewilderment, fearful of the demons of the aggregates, defilements, death, and "child of the gods," fearful of the hells and hungry spirit and animals realms—fearful of such things, I have come to a lonely hermitage.

Motivated by such fears, once we have arrived at our solitary retreat we must then check: "Now that I am living in this isolated place, what should I be doing with my body, speech, and mind?" And when we find ourselves passing the time in negative or indeterminate activities, we should berate ourselves: "Oh dear, if I am no different from the beasts of prey, hunters, bandits, birds, deer, monkeys, and other inhabitants of the forest, what was the point in my wanting to come to an isolated retreat? It was pointless." We should make an effort to apply the antidotes and stop those activities immediately.

Having thus achieved all the conditions for concentration, we come to the actual practice of concentration. How this is done is explained in *Finding Rest in the Nature of the Mind*:

> With crossed legs, take your seat in such a place,
> Remain with concentrated mind,
> Not stirring from the state of meditative equipoise.
> Thus you will accomplish various concentrations:
> The one that gives delight to childish beings,
> Then the concentration clearly discerning,
> And finally the sublime concentration of the Tathāgatas.[273]

Adopting the seven-point posture of Vairocana in a solitary place, go for refuge and arouse bodhichitta, and rest in a clear, undistracted state, without thinking of anything or grasping at anything. Without blocking off the objects of perception, develop the concentration that pacifies conceptual grasping. For this, settle the mind one-pointedly on any suitable meditation support, avoiding the faults of mental agitation and sinking. In this way, you will achieve sustained calm, in which the mind is not distracted. This is the concentration that delights childish beings.

When one has ascertained the meaning of no-self with discriminating wisdom and achieved profound insight free from all assertions, to settle evenly in that state and practice the path that unites sustained calm and profound insight is the clearly discerning concentration.

Through training in that over a long period of time, the dualistic perceptions of apprehending subject and apprehended object subside into the expanse of reality: one attains the path of seeing, the first bodhisattva level, and abides in the excellent concentration of the tathāgatas. From the first level up to the seventh, there is a difference between formal meditation and postmeditation because in formal meditation one rests in the nonconceptual state, while in postmeditation there is still some partial subject-object duality. On the other hand, from the eighth level onward, there is no real difference between meditation and postmeditation: the difference is purely nominal. On the buddha level, one is in constant meditation from which it is impossible ever to move.

After remaining in meditative equipoise like this, we should make the dedication.

There are three other categories of concentration. By training like this, conceptual perceptions subside and inwardly one acquires the joy and bliss that arise from concentration. This is the *concentration that procures a feeling of well-being in this life*. When one is accomplishing a mass of wholesome deeds such as the six transcendent perfections, one achieves innumerable kinds of mental one-pointedness or powers of perceptual domination and limitlessness and so on, along with the perfect freedoms and the power of memory and confident eloquence.[274] This is the *concentration that produces excellent qualities*. By concentrating one-pointedly on sentient beings' welfare or manifesting miraculous displays and transformations as desired from the mental state of the actual concentration, one acts for the benefit of beings. This is the *concentration that benefits sentient beings*.

Making concentration pure and making it grow is as explained above.

The faults or disadvantages of not having concentration and being mentally distracted are as indicated in *The Way of the Bodhisattva*:

> Recitations and austerities,
> Long though they may prove to be,

If practiced with distracted mind,
Are futile, so the Knower of Reality has said.
All those who fail to understand
The secret of the mind, the greatest of all things,
Although they wish for joy and sorrow's end,
Will wander to no purpose, uselessly.[275]

And in the *Kāśyapa Chapter*, we read,

Just as someone carried out to sea
Will slowly come to die of thirst,
One may seek teachings more and more
But fail to meditate attentively,
And, though on Dharma's ocean one remains,
One ends up going to the lower realms.

The benefits of properly training in concentration are that, on the temporary level, one will banish attachment to the pleasures of the senses and achieve numerous good qualities such as preternatural powers and meditative concentration. This is stated in the *Verses That Summarize the Perfection of Wisdom*:

By means of concentration, one will despise and abandon the pleasures of the senses,
And achieve knowledge, preternatural powers, and meditative concentration.

The ultimate result is the attainment of enlightenment, as is explained in the *Bodhisattva Stage*:

Having completed transcendent concentration, bodhisattvas have attained manifest perfect buddhahood in unsurpassable, true and perfect enlightenment; they are attaining it; and they will attain it.

(6) Wisdom

Definition

Transcendent wisdom is that which is based on the virtuous state of mind that perfectly discerns phenomena and has the four distinguishing features.

Etymological gloss

The Tibetan word for "wisdom" is derived from the Sanskrit word *prajñā*, for it is "that which realizes or fully comprehends ultimate reality," the object that is to be realized.

Categories

Nāgārjuna lists these as follows:

> What makes wisdom grow is listening
> And reflection; if one has these two
> And meditates on them, then wisdom will arise.

There are thus three kinds of wisdom, those that come from listening, reflecting, and meditating.

(a) The wisdom that comes from listening

What we have to listen to is mainly the "inner science,"* that is, the Buddha's excellent words along with the commentaries on their intended meaning. However, caring for beings by means of the inner science also requires that we train accessorily in the other four common sciences. To defeat opponents, we need to learn grammar and logic. To take care of beings, we need to learn the arts and medicine. All these sciences are indispensable for attaining the level of omniscience, as Lord Maitreya has said:

> Without being learned in the five sciences,
> Even the highest of noble beings will not attain omniscience.

*Tib. *nang rig pa*. One of the five sciences, which deals with spiritual development.

Therefore, in order to subjugate others, to care for them,
And to know all things themselves, they must be diligent in these.[276]

More particularly, to gain a complete understanding of the intended meanings of the Buddha's teachings, we need to properly determine the differences between the Buddhist and non-Buddhist philosophical tenet systems, the philosophical positions of the higher and lower Buddhist vehicles, the distinctions between the ultimate and expedient teachings and the implied and indirect teachings, the analysis of knowable phenomena in terms of the two truths, and so on. Therefore, we have to follow a learned teacher endowed with wisdom and study the great scriptural traditions of the sūtras and mantras in general, and in particular, in our own tradition, the works of such masters as the Omniscient Dharma King, Rongzom Chökyi Zangpo, the omniscient brothers of Mindrölling, Rigdzin Jigme Lingpa, the Dharma Lord Katokpa and his spiritual sons, and our own teachers, the three omniscient masters of the age of strife.[277] Their marvelous writings are free of fault, of perfect import, beautiful in expression, consistent with scriptural authority, and supported by reasoning. They unmistakenly establish the intended meaning of the pith instructions of the lineage of buddhas and vidyādharas. Thus, on the external level, they are firmly grounded in the philosophical tenets; on the internal level, they include all the crucial points of the practice; and on the secret level, they have not lost the flavor and potency of their blessings. These excellent texts are like precious wish-fulfilling jewels, which appear but rarely in the past, present, or future. By studying them repeatedly, we should give rise to the immaculate wisdom that comes from listening. It is said in a sūtra,

Just as a sighted person
Can see different forms,
Likewise, one who has listened
Will know virtuous and nonvirtuous ways.

In the *Bodhisattva's Scriptural Collection*, we read,

By listening, one will know all things,
By listening, one will turn away from evil deeds,
By listening, one will avoid what is meaningless,
By listening, one will attain nirvāṇa.

Other extensive passages in praise of listening to the teachings are to be found in all the sūtras and treatises. To sum up, it has been said that, let alone actually listening to the teachings, merely hearing the sound of the drum or gong bestows the fruit of enlightenment, as we find in the *Sūtra of the Gong*:

> The signal that the sacred teaching will begin—
> The beating of the drum or wooden gong—
> Will bring enlightenment to those who hear,
> So what need mention they who come to listen there?

(b) The wisdom that comes from reflecting

We should not be content with merely listening to the topics we are studying: we need to thoroughly investigate their meaning. For this, from the point of view of how objects of valid cognition appear to the minds of us ordinary beings, there are three kinds of such objects: manifestly evident, occult, and extremely occult. And there are three kinds of valid cognition that evaluate these objects—direct valid cognition, valid cognition by inference, and valid cognition by scriptural authority. Of these three, the one that we should mainly rely on is valid cognition based on scriptural authority—that of the buddhas' words. The *Sūtra of the Densely Ornamented Array* declares,

> Those who present the teachings
> Without the scriptures in which to have confidence,
> Will, because their presentations are conceptual,
> Throw themselves to waste, and others too.

With regard to these scriptures, depending on the stage at which the disciples are, there are different kinds of teachings—ultimate and expedient, implied and indirect, literal and not literal, and so forth. Therefore, we need to examine the scriptures critically and use reasoning to determine their meaning, in much the same way that when we use water to cleanse away contaminants, the water itself must first be purified with mantras:

> Like gold that has been flamed, cut, and rubbed,
> My words may be accepted after proper examination,
> But never simply out of respect.

The reasoning we use may be of two kinds, superficial and genuine. Of these, the latter comprises three kinds of valid cognition that serve (1) to investigate relative, conventional appearances, (2) to investigate the ultimate, actual condition of things, emptiness, and (3) on the ultimate level, to investigate the two truths without separating them. Provisionally, it is very important to distinguish which of these three objects of investigation we are dealing with, without mixing them up. And ultimately, as Lord Buddha has said,

> Rely on the meaning and not on the words,
> Rely on gnosis and not on intellectual knowledge,
> Rely on the ultimate teachings and not on the expedient
> teachings,
> Rely on the teachings and not on the individual.

Reliance here signifies "following." So, without contradicting the above, as we examine the ultimate meaning or establish it with the reasoning of the true nature of things, we should give rise in our mind streams to genuine, profound insight. This is the discriminating wisdom that realizes, with the nonconceptual gnosis that transcends the object of ordinary dualistic knowledge, the adamantine, uncompounded nature, like the heart of space, the inexpressible sameness and indivisibility of all phenomena. We read in the *Play in Full*,

> Profound, peaceful, stainless, lucid, and unconditioned—
> Such is the nectar-like truth I have realized.
> Were I to teach it, no one would understand,
> So I think I will silently remain in the forest.
> I have discovered the supremely sublime and astonishing absolute,
> The ineffable state, untainted by language,
> Suchness, the sky-like nature of phenomena,
> Completely free of discursive, conceptual movement.
> This meaning cannot be understood through words;
> Rather it is comprehended through reaching their limit.
> Yet when sentient beings, whom previous victorious ones took
> under their care,
> Hear about this truth, they will develop confidence in it.

Realizing this properly cannot be achieved by determining it simply with ordinary, superficial reasoning and the scriptural authority of the expedient teachings. We have to delve into the enlightened thinking of the profound sūtras and tantras of the ultimate teachings. In particular, having sought teachers who have realization of the true lineage, we should receive their oral instructions and acquire the secret treasury of their enlightened minds. This alone is the cherished jewel of all the practice lineage. We must grasp it as the pure essence of their hearts.

Moreover, we should reflect again and again on topics such as the difficulty of finding the freedoms and advantages, in the ways mentioned above, and blend our minds with the teachings.

(c) The wisdom that comes from meditating

The wisdom that comes from meditating is the profound nonconceptual wisdom related to profound insight that is to be cultivated in one's mind stream by meditating one-pointedly on the points that one has determined by listening and reflecting. How one meditates is described by the Omniscient Teacher in his *Essential Instructions for Finding Rest in the Nature of the Mind*:

> First, the view of the nature of appearances, with the eight similes of illusion.
>
> As in a dream, all the external objects perceived with the five senses are not there but appear through delusion.
>
> As in a magic show, things are made to appear by a temporary conjunction of causes, circumstances, and connections.
>
> As in a visual aberration, things appear to be there, yet there is nothing.
>
> As in a mirage, things appear but they are not real.
>
> As in an echo, things can be perceived but there is nothing there, either outside or inside.
>
> As in a city of gandharvas, there is neither a dwelling nor any inhabitants.
>
> As in a reflection, things appear but have no reality of their own.
>
> As in a city created by magic, there are all sorts of appearances, but they are not really there.

Meditate on these, considering that even at the moment things appear, they are false and devoid of substance, and are thus no more than empty forms.

This is extensively taught in such scriptures as the *Sūtra of the King of Concentrations*:

Just as at night the reflection of the moon
Appears upon a lake whose waters are crystal clear,
Yet the reflection is an empty counterfeit, quite essenceless,
Know that, likewise, are all phenomena.

Next, investigate the empty, ultimate reality. On the outer level, break down the gross objects that appear and the substance of your own body into minute particles. By doing so, you will reach the definite conclusion that there are no objects—they are empty. On the inner level, scrutinize your mind, the apprehending subject, in terms of indivisible instants. In this way, you will come to the definite conclusion that there is no apprehending subject—it is empty. In that state of realization that neither subject nor object exist, rest in meditative equipoise, in emptiness without fixation.[278]

This is stated in the *Perfection of Wisdom*:

Those who do not dwell on form, who do not dwell on feeling, who do not dwell on perception, who do not dwell on mental factors, who do not dwell on consciousness, but who dwell on their true nature are practicing the sublime, transcendent wisdom.

After properly determining this,

Settle in equipoise on the meaning of the middle way free from extremes. Begin by taking refuge and arousing bodhichitta. With the body motionless, the voice silent, and the mind free of conceptual thoughts, object-grasping concepts regarding the unceasing appearance of outer objects are brought to peace, subject-clinging elaborations regarding the emptiness-clarity of

> inner awareness are brought to peace, and in between, the ultimate reality dawns in the unsupported mind. Remain in equipoise for as long as it lasts in the state of awareness, empty and clear like the sky, the ever-present wisdom of the great inexpressibility, thatness, the middle way beyond concepts.[279]

The *Perfection of Wisdom* expresses this as follows:

> Recognizing that deluded beings are like deer caught in a trap,
> Those with wisdom fly like birds in the sky.
> When those with perfect conduct do not pursue forms,
> And do not pursue consciousness, perception, feeling, or mental factors,
> Their conduct is thus completely free of all attachment,
> And freed of attachment, they experience the wisdom of the sugatas.
> Clear-minded, wise bodhisattvas who practice like that
> Sever attachment and proceed without attachment to liberation.
> They are as bright as the sun uneclipsed by the planet Rāhu.
> And as, once started, a fire burns up all the grass and trees and woods,
> When bodhisattvas view with transcendent wisdom
> All phenomena as pure, completely pure,
> With no concepts even of an agent, no concepts of any phenomena,
> They are practicing the sublime practice of transcendent wisdom.

Maitreya says,

> In it there is nothing at all to remove,
> Or the slightest thing to add.
> The truth truly looked at,
> When truly seen, is liberation.[280]

And Nāgārjunagarbha,[281]

> Do not conceptualize anything, do not think of anything,
> Relax naturally, without fabrication.

The uncontrived, unborn state is a precious treasury;
It is the wisdom mind of all the buddhas of the three times.

Afterward, having arisen from that state, recognizing all phenomena to be like illusions, dedicate the merit, and train in the path that unites the two accumulations, giving teachings to others and so on. In the *Verses That Summarize the Perfection of Wisdom*, we read,

When bodhisattvas meditating on the sublime wisdom
Arise from that and speak the untainted Dharma
And dedicate it as the cause for enlightenment for beings' sake,
Their merit has no equal in the three worlds.

In this context, if one wishes, one should give explanations of such topics as the presentation of the ground middle way (the two truths), the path middle way (the two accumulations), and the resultant middle way (the two buddha bodies).

The methods for making wisdom pure and making it grow are as previously explained.

The fault in not being imbued with wisdom like this is that however much one exerts oneself in the five other transcendent perfections (generosity and the rest), they will not be genuine transcendent perfections. Without wisdom, they cannot join one directly to omniscience, as the same text points out:

A million billion beings blind from birth and without a guide,
Who do not know the road, can never find their way into a town.
Without wisdom, the five eyeless perfections
Will lack a guide and cannot reach enlightenment.
But when they're thoroughly imbued with wisdom,
They'll find their sight and gain their very name.*

The benefits or results of wisdom are that, on a temporary level, we will have every kind of mundane and supramundane excellence, as is mentioned in the previous text:

*In other words, only when generosity and the others are imbued with wisdom can they truly be called "transcendent."

As much happiness and well-being as have the buddhas,
Bodhisattvas, listeners, solitary realizers, gods, and all beings,
All of it comes from the supreme, transcendent wisdom.

Ultimately, we will attain the great enlightenment. The same text says,

Once one fully understands, with wisdom, the nature of phenomena,
One will go beyond the three worlds without exception.
As a leader of humanity, one will turn the precious wheel,
And in order to bring all suffering to an end, reveal the Dharma to beings.

2. Condensed precepts

A condensed presentation of the precepts for beginner bodhisattvas or those with dull faculties, who are unable to train extensively in the above precepts, is given in the *Sūtra of Advice to the King*:

> Great King, you who have so many duties, so many activities—you cannot train completely and all the time in the transcendent perfections from generosity to wisdom. Therefore, Great King, whether you are moving around, staying still, lying down, waking up, eating, or drinking, all the time, with constant mindfulness, keep in mind and cultivate three things: the wish to attain true, perfect enlightenment; faith; and the aspiration to pursue that. Rejoice at others' positive deeds. Having rejoiced, offer that rejoicing to the buddhas, bodhisattvas, listeners, and solitary realizers. Having made that offering, share it with all sentient beings. Then, every day, dedicate it to unsurpassable enlightenment, so that all sentient beings will perfect the Buddha's teachings. Great King, in that way you can rule your kingdom, you will not fail in your royal duties, and you will also complete the accumulations for enlightenment.

Accordingly, the foundation of the path of the Great Vehicle is never to separate from an earnest desire to attain perfect enlightenment for others' benefit, from faith in that, and from a complete aspiration to do so; to rejoice at others' good deeds and offer their sources of good to the buddhas; and to dedicate to sentient beings. In short, the root of arousing bodhichitta in aspiration is never to reject sentient beings, and to make every possible effort to avoid harming others and that which is the cause of harming others; and to help others and accomplish that which is the cause of helping others. All this should be reinforced with the three supreme methods.

The three supreme methods are (1) the preparation, arousing bodhichitta; (2) the main practice, free of concepts; and (3) the conclusion, dedication.

(1) Preparation. This is to reflect on one's motivation: "Sentient beings, who have been my own parents, all want to be happy, yet they are deprived of happiness. They do not want to suffer, yet they constantly indulge in the causes of suffering and experience much misery as a result. In order to free them from the realms of suffering and set them in the supreme and everlasting happiness of perfect liberation, I must do whatever it takes to attain the precious level of perfect buddhahood. And in order to do that, I will do this practice, performing virtue and avoiding evil."

In short, we should never cease to maintain three states of mind: faith and confidence in the law of cause and effect; the loving wish to bring benefit and happiness to sentient beings; and to that end, the earnest aspiration to attain perfect enlightenment. As long as we maintain these three, the smallest positive act—generously giving a single butter lamp, a drop of water, or just a mouthful of dough; keeping the precepts for just twenty-four hours; reciting a single *maṇi*;[*] or making a single prostration—will become a source of good on the path of the Great Vehicle. It will never be wasted until we reach the essence of enlightenment, and it will grow more and more. It will become one taste, inseparable from the emptiness of nonrejection, and will never come to an end even in the expanse without residual aggregates.[†] In such ways, it will have inconceivable benefit and purpose. This is mentioned in the *Perfection of Wisdom in Eight Thousand Lines*:

> Venerable Shāriputra, there are sources of good that, after resulting in rebirth among gods and humans, will lead to unsurpassable

[*] *Maṇi* is the name by which the mantra of Avalokiteshvara (OṂ MAṆI PADME HŪṂ) is known.

[†] When listeners and solitary realizers who have attained cessation die and pass into the expanse without residual aggregates, all their accumulated merit, too, comes to an end. The merit of a bodhisattva who has dedicated it to perfect buddhahood, on the other hand, continues to grow and does not come to an end when that bodhisattva attains buddhahood and passes into nirvāṇa.

> buddhahood. What are they? They are any of the ten virtuous deeds, the four concentrations, the four formless absorptions, and the six transcendent perfections that are performed with a single intent to attain unsurpassable enlightenment. In the meanwhile, they will never be spent or come to an end.

And in the *Sūtra of the Questions of Maitreya*, we read,

> Let us take an analogy. However many single drops of water fall into the ocean, they will never evaporate for kalpas on end. Maitreya, in the same way, a positive deed imbued with the mind set on enlightenment will never be consumed until one attains buddhahood in unsurpassable enlightenment. Maitreya, it is thus: just as any seeds sown in the right place will all develop and grow, a source of good imbued with bodhichitta will increase on a vast scale.

And in the *Basket's Display*,

> Mañjushrī, it is thus: if trees of any kind are nourished with the four elements, they will grow and spread. Mañjushrī, in the same way, if a source of good is backed by bodhichitta and dedicated to omniscience, it will grow and spread.

And in the *Sūtra of Advice to the King*,

> Great King, as the fully ripened effect of the positive deeds that you have done with your mind intent on unsurpassable, true, and perfect enlightenment, you have been born numerous times among the gods and you have been born numerous times among humans. And in all those lives as gods or humans, you have been in a position of power. Even now, the positive deeds that you have performed with your mind intent on unsurpassable, true, and perfect enlightenment will never be seen to diminish or increase.

In the *Sūtra of the Arborescent Array*, we find,

> Fortunate child, everything that those who have the spiritual intent to achieve supreme enlightenment undertake with their body, speech, or mind will be fruitful, always of the same taste.

(2) Main practice. When one is practicing in this manner, if one is bound by concepts of things existing truly, one's practice will go counter to the path of the Great Vehicle. We read in the *Perfection of Wisdom*,

> Subhūti, it is difficult enough for those with conceptual notions to achieve an approximation of acceptance, let alone unsurpassable, true, and perfect enlightenment.

And in the *Verses That Summarize the Perfection of Wisdom*,

> Like eating nourishing food with which some poison has been mixed,
> So too, the buddhas say, are virtuous actions mixed with conceptual thoughts.

So, if you know how to and are able, you should at all times reinforce the practice with the absence of concepts related to the three spheres. What are the three spheres? Yourself, the person who is doing the practice; the virtuous practice you are doing or the beings for whose sake you are doing it; and the method, or result, of the practice. You should know that all three appear but are devoid of intrinsic existence, like a dream or magical illusion, as is stated in the *Jewel Cloud Sūtra*:

> You should gather the accumulations of merit and wisdom without any concept of anyone for whom one is practicing virtue, without any concept of how it is to be done, and without any concept of anyone making the effort to do so. You should practice accordingly, with the thought that everything is like a magical illusion, like a mirage, like a visual aberration, like a magical creation.

And in the *Sūtra of the Questions of Upāli*, we read,

> When a magician creates a world with many hundreds of beings, even if he kills everyone he has created, it is not as if the illusion of them being killed truly exists. In the same way, all these beings are, by nature, an illusion, and there is no seeing any end to it all.

And,

> Although the spiritual intent to achieve enlightenment for beings' sake
> Has been taught as the very highest form of practice,
> It is not that enlightenment objectively exists,
> Or any wish whatsoever to attain it.

And,

> Though the praises of generosity are sung by all,
> It is not that this antidote to stinginess objectively exists.
> So, too, for the inconceivable qualities of the buddhas,
> There is nothing to observe, nothing to see.

In the *Sūtra of the King of Concentrations*,

> With mental notions and conceptual beliefs,
> One thinks that seeing the sugatas and making offerings to them gladdens the buddhas.
> But they are unborn, and there are no offerings that have been made:
> They are like the dreams people have inside their homes.

And in the *Sūtra of the Questions of Druma*,

> Upon a mirror's polished disk
> The image of one's face appears
> Without a face being truly there.
> Know, Druma, that all things are, likewise, so.

If you do not know how and are unable to practice like this, you should practice diligently with faith, respect, and enthusiasm. You should think that on the ultimate level, by nature, no phenomena truly exist, yet on the relative level, actions are infallibly followed by their results and that these are the immaculate words of the victorious ones, the perfect buddhas.

(3) Conclusion. In the *Middle Sūtra of the Perfection of Wisdom*, it is said,

> Subhūti, you should dedicate these positive deeds only to the level of buddhahood. Do not dedicate them to the levels of the listeners or solitary realizers, or to any other levels.

Accordingly, we should not dedicate all the positive deeds we have just performed merely to the temporary result of happiness as gods and humans, or to the inferior results of the listeners and solitary realizers. Rather, we should transform our aspiration, thinking, "Just as the buddhas and bodhisattvas of the three times and their disciples have dedicated, will dedicate, and are dedicating positive deeds for the benefit of others, so, too, will I fully dedicate them to the great, perfect enlightenment!" And using the buddhas' words—the *Prayer of Good Action*, for example—or those of extraordinary, sublime beings who have accomplished words of truth, we should say dedication prayers. Positive deeds that have been dedicated in this way will never be consumed but will grow more and more and turn into perfect enlightenment. This is illustrated in the *Sūtra of the Questions of Sāgaramati*:

> Sāgaramati, it is thus. Let us make an analogy. A drop of spit cast onto the dust will quickly evaporate. If it is spat into the great ocean, that drop of spit will not dry up until the great ocean dries up and disappears. Sāgaramati, in the same way, if you regret the positive deeds that you have performed, or feel that you could have given less, or dedicate them for a lower purpose, or dedicate them for wrong purposes,* they will be consumed. However, if you dedicate them to the great ocean of the wisdom of omniscience, they will not be consumed but will grow ever greater.

And in the *Sūtra of the Teaching of Akṣayamati*, we read,

> To dedicate for the purpose of enlightenment any virtuous thought that occurs is the inexhaustible achievement of a bodhi-

*"Lower purpose," for example, dedicating in order to become famous; "wrong purpose," for example, dedicating in order to harm someone.

> sattva. Why is that? Because it is dedicated to enlightenment: a source of good dedicated to enlightenment will never be consumed or come to an end until one is at the heart of enlightenment. Venerable Shāradvatīputra, it is like this. Let us use an analogy. A drop of water that has fallen into the great ocean will not be spent or destroyed until it is evaporated by the fire at the end of the kalpa. In the same way, a source of good that has been dedicated to enlightenment will never be spent or come to an end until one is at the heart of enlightenment.
>
> What is called "authentic practice" refers to authentic practitioners (that is, those who have authentically engaged in the path) authentically performing positive deeds and dedicating those positive deeds in order to protect all sentient beings, to bring sentient beings to full maturity, and to introduce all sentient beings to positive deeds. They dedicate those positive deeds in order to truly accomplish the wisdom of omniscience. They dedicate those positive deeds in order to sustain all sentient beings. They dedicate those positive deeds in order to take sentient beings beyond suffering and set them in the wisdom of omniscience. This is the inexhaustible achievement of a bodhisattva.

In short, the buddhas' and bodhisattvas' skill in means is inconceivable. Simply through their attitude and motivation, using such means as rejoicing, they include others' positive deeds in their ocean-like practices for enlightenment, not to mention the positive deeds they actually perform themselves. The *Sūtra of Skill in Means: The Great Secret of All the Buddhas* gives the following explanation:

> Fortunate child, for this, bodhisattva mahāsattvas are skilled in means, in that when they give even a mouthful of food to a being born in the animal realm, they give with the thought of its attaining omniscience, and they dedicate that positive deed so that all sentient beings perfect the Buddha's qualities. With two causal factors, they dedicate it fully to all sentient beings. What are these two? The thought of omniscience and skill in making a full dedication. It is this, fortunate child, that constitutes the skill in means of bodhisattva mahāsattvas.
>
> Fortunate child, furthermore, bodhisattva mahāsattvas are

> skilled in means in that they rejoice in the positive deeds that others have done, and after rejoicing, they also make a full dedication, sharing their deeds and giving them to sentient beings. Those positive deeds that have been dedicated to omniscience overpower givers and benefactors who have no thought of enlightenment, and they overpower those who receive the gifts. This, fortunate child, is the skill in means of a bodhisattva mahāsattva.
>
> Fortunate child, furthermore, bodhisattva mahāsattvas are skilled in means in that they mentally take and gather all the flowering trees, incense trees, flowers, flower garlands, incense, aromatic powders, and perfumes in the ten directions that are not owned or claimed by anyone and offer them to all the buddhas. They further give that positive deed to all sentient beings: they give it completely away and dedicate it to omniscience. All scents and fragrances carried by the wind of all the flowering trees, flowers, flower garlands, incense, incense powders, and perfumes in the ten directions that are owned or claimed, they offer with the bodhisattvas' skill in means to all the buddhas. They further fully dedicate all those positive deeds so that they and all sentient beings may perfect the state of omniscience. Because of that positive deed dedicated to omniscience, they will gain on an infinite scale the aggregates of discipline, concentration, wisdom, perfect freedom, and the vision of the gnosis of perfect freedom. Fortunate child, this is the skill in means of a bodhisattva mahāsattva.

Thus, if it is imbued with such skillful means, giving even the most basic thing such as a single handful of food to the most lowly of beings such as a blind person or beggar, or a dog or pig, comprises all six transcendent perfections. Giving with a generous attitude for another's benefit is generosity itself. At the same time, the fact that one is refraining from negative deeds physically, verbally, or mentally comprises discipline. Giving with one's mind undisturbed is patience. Giving joyfully is diligence. Doing so with one's mind undistracted is concentration. And understanding that the three spheres have no true existence is wisdom. We should be able to apply this inclusive method to everything we do.

Besides that, the *Twenty Verses on the Vows of a Bodhisattva* tells us,

Whether it is for others or for oneself,
Do what is beneficial, even if it is painful;
Do whatever brings benefit and happiness,
And avoid doing what is not beneficial, even if it is pleasant.

Even if they bring us difficulty in this life, we ourselves should perform both positive deeds that will benefit us and others in future lives and those that will bring us benefit and happiness in both this and future lives, and we should encourage others to perform them as well. We ourselves should avoid negative deeds that, even if they produce happiness in this life, will lead to suffering in future lives, along with those that will harm us both in this and future lives, and we should encourage others to avoid them also. There is nothing that is not included in these two precepts of what to adopt and what to avoid. If our deeds are motivated by great love and compassion and we can definitely see that they will be of great benefit to others, they cannot have negative consequences; we should undertake them enthusiastically, for as the same text points out:

Because they are compassionate and loving,
For those whose minds are virtuous, there is no fault.

Even if we cannot benefit others directly, as long as we do not let our altruistic intentions diminish, we will in fact be engaging in doing so, as we read in a commentary on bodhichitta:

Even if you do not have the power to work for others' sake,
Always have the wish to benefit.
Those who have that aspiration
Are, in truth, engaged in that.

So, as we are told in *The Way of the Bodhisattva*,

Directly, then, or indirectly,
Do nothing that is not for others' sake.
And solely for their welfare dedicate
Your every action to the gaining of enlightenment.[282]

B. How to keep the precepts without deterioration

How to keep the precepts without deterioration is divided into three sections: (1) avoiding the seven adverse conditions that cause one's own and others' practice to deteriorate, (2) training in favorable conditions—the factors that prevent the precepts from deteriorating and the conditions that reinforce them, and (3) training in constantly guarding them with mindfulness, vigilance, and carefulness.

1. Avoiding the seven adverse conditions that cause one's own and others' practice to deteriorate

This first section is divided into avoiding, for one's own sake, the three hindrances to wisdom and avoiding, for others' sake, the four faults in conduct.

First, there are the three hindrances to wisdom that have to be avoided:

- not being interested in listening
- being distracted when reflecting
- relaxing one's meditation

Second, there are the four faults in conduct that have to be avoided:

- great laziness in applying oneself
- making others lose faith through one's conduct
- lack of compassion in one's motivation
- performing activities in the wrong way

2. Training in favorable conditions—the factors that prevent the precepts from deteriorating and the conditions that reinforce them

Training in favorable conditions is divided into training in the three causal factors that prevent one from deteriorating the precepts and training in the nine conditions that reinforce them.

First, the three causal factors that prevent one from deteriorating the precepts comprise three groups:

1. Three things to remember, which prevent the precepts from deteriorating in this life:

- to repeatedly remind oneself of the benefits of arousing the bodhichitta
- to repeatedly remind oneself of the negative consequences of deteriorating it
- to repeatedly remind oneself of the difficulty of acquiring the bodhichitta

2. Three unmistaken means, which prevent the precepts from deteriorating in future lives:

    - to perform the seven branches in the three times*
    - to pray to the buddhas and bodhisattvas
    - to avoid demonic activities that go counter to the Dharma

3. Five things to be cherished, which prevent the precepts from deteriorating in both this life and future lives. These consist of training in the following:

    - considering sentient beings more important than ourselves, for it is their welfare that we must accomplish
    - considering the Dharma more important than riches, for it is what enables us to accomplish beings' welfare
    - considering bodhichitta dearer than our hearts, for it is bodhichitta that is the most essential thing
    - considering spiritual friends more important than our parents, for they constitute the dominant condition[283]
    - considering buddhahood more important than wealth, for buddhahood is what we must attain

Second, the nine conditions that reinforce the precepts comprise five things to remember and the four things to be done:

1. The five things to remember:

    - the changeable nature of compounded phenomena
    - the end of suffering

*The "three times" here refers to the morning, the middle of the day, and the evening. It could also refer to when one is happy, when one is unhappy or in pain, and when one is neither happy nor unhappy.

- the benefits of the Dharma
- the greatness of the Teacher
- the benefits of bodhichitta

2. The four things to be done:
   - to look with the eye of vigilance
   - to travel on the supreme steed of diligence
   - to goad oneself with the whip of renunciation
   - to keep in mind the city of liberation

3. Training in constantly guarding the precepts with mindfulness, vigilance, and carefulness

The Omniscient Dharma Lord has said,

> At all times, mindfully, with watchful introspection,
> And with attentive care remove your negativities
> And gather stores of merit ocean-vast.[284]

The causes of downfalls occurring are ignorance, carelessness, many defilements, and disrespect.

Ignorance

If we do not know what defines downfalls and so on, however much effort we put into the training, downfalls will occur. So, as the remedy for this, it is important to have received and learned the teachings on the precepts.

Carelessness

Even if we know what the downfalls are, we may not see their negative consequences, or even if we see them, we may not have mindfulness and vigilance, as a result of which downfalls will occur. The remedy for this is to train in mindfulness, vigilance, a sense of shame, a sense of decency, and carefulness. Mindfulness means not forgetting what we should be adopting and what we should be avoiding. Vigilance enables us to examine our three doors and to know whether we are engaging in good and turning away from evil. A sense of shame is what, in our own regard or from the point of view of the Dharma, makes us refrain from negative deeds. A sense of decency makes us refrain from negative deeds because we are afraid of others' low opinions or afraid of doing what is conventionally unacceptable. And carefulness means exercising the greatest circumspection, out of fear of the fully ripened effects of negative activities.

Many Defilements

Even if we try to be a bit careful in refraining from negative actions, the three poisons may be too strong in us and because of our defilements, downfalls will occur. The remedy for this is to examine our own minds and make an effort to employ the antidotes to whichever defilements are strongest. We should never remain unconcerned, thinking that even if something contravenes the precepts, it is only a small fault.

Disrespect

We might know what the downfalls are and so on, but if we are inclined to base ways and do not apply the precepts, downfalls will occur. The remedy for this is to respect the Teacher and the rules he laid down.

The above mental states also distinguish the gravity of any downfalls we commit. Those that occur through ignorance or carelessness are of minor significance, those that occur because of an abundance of defilements are of moderate significance, while those that occur out of disrespect are of major significance. Therefore, at the risk of our lives, we must be assiduous in applying the training to the different kinds of conduct to be adopted or avoided. It is said in the *Sūtra of the King of Concentrations*,

> At that time, the precepts that I explained
> For householders wearing layman's clothes
> Will no longer be held or kept
> Even by ordained monks.

At this time, when even monks do not keep the five basic precepts that were taught for lay ordinees, the result of being diligent in the precepts is even greater, as the same text explains:

For many a million kalpas, numerous as the Ganges' sands,
One might, with faithful mind, venerate a myriad billion buddhas
With food and drink, with parasols and banners and rows of lamps.
But when the sacred Dharma has been destroyed
And the teaching of the Sugata has ceased to be,
Greater still will be the merit of those
Who keep a single precept for just one night and day.

C. An explanation of the negative consequences of deteriorating the precepts and of how to restore the vow

This explanation is divided into two sections: (1) the negative consequences of deteriorating the precepts, and (2) how to restore the vow if they are deteriorated.

1. The negative consequences of deteriorating the precepts

Generally speaking, there are three causes for giving up the bodhichitta vow: giving up its foundation, bodhichitta in aspiration; the occurrence of a root downfall that runs counter to bodhichitta; and returning the vow, which leads one to abandon bodhichitta. The direct negative consequences of the deterioration, when any of these occur, are of two kinds: (1) the general negative consequences of downfalls, and (2) the particular negative consequences of root downfalls.

a. The general negative consequences of downfalls

There are three general negative consequences of downfalls.

By breaking one's promise, one will be an object of contempt. One has deceived the Buddha, our Teacher, so the buddhas are displeased. One has deceived the object, sentient beings, so they are not content. By deceiving oneself, one has undermined one's own welfare. One will therefore be a source of universal contempt, as we can read in the *Sūtra of the Questions of Sāgaramati*:

> Having aroused bodhichitta like that, if bodhisattvas do not act as they have said they will, they deceive the gods and all the world.

By failing to live up to one's name,* one will attract all kinds of unwanted things. Like a king who lets his kingdom go to ruin, in this life one will have all sorts of misfortunes, and at the moment of death, one will be tormented by anguish.

By committing a serious fault, in the next life one will fall into the lower realms and it will be hard to get free. The *Compendium of Precepts* states,

> If one fails to make effort
> As the perfect buddhas have taught,
> One will go to the lower realms.

b. The particular negative consequences of root downfalls

All the positive deeds made with the bodhichitta that one previously aroused will be reduced to dust. One will, by the very fact of having committed a root downfall, have deceived the Three Jewels and the gods. Because of that, one will be reborn in general in the lower realms and in particular as a being in the great hells, as the same text points out:

> These root downfalls
> Are the causes of beings in the great hells.

As for returning the vow, if one is unable to keep the vows of individual liberation, it is permissible to return them. However, if one returns the bodhisattva vow, this is an extremely serious fault, for one has given up the promise one made in the presence of the buddhas and bodhisattvas to accomplish beings' benefit and happiness. We read in *The Way of the Bodhisattva*,

> How can I expect a happy destiny
> If from my heart I summon
> Wandering beings to the highest bliss,
> But then deceive and fail them?

And,

*Lit. "losing one's name (the title of bodhisattva) and its significance (the responsibilities that go with it)."

Destroy a single being's joy
And you will work the ruin of yourself.
No need to speak of bringing low
The joy of beings infinite as space itself![285]

2. How to restore the vow if the precepts are deteriorated

Restoring the vow has two parts: (1) how to confess faults, and (2) if one has given up the vow, how to take it again.

a. How to confess faults

There are three ways that have been taught for confessing one's faults, depending on the individuals concerned. "Individuals of modest capacity, because of their belief that things are real, should remorsefully confess their faults in the presence of someone else and vow to refrain in the future. By this means, over time they progressively arise from their faults."[286] Therefore, in the presence of the object of confession (if one can find one, a bodhisattva in person, who is not tainted by downfalls, or otherwise a suitable support*), one should begin by requesting refuge, with an attitude of bodhichitta, and then apply the antidote of confession with the four strengths. In particular, one should confess, night and day, with the recitation of such scriptures as the *Sūtra in Three Sections*. This is stated in *The Way of the Bodhisattva*:

Reciting thrice by day and thrice by night,
The *Sūtra in Three Sections*,
Relying on the Buddhas and the Bodhisattvas,
Purify the rest of your transgressions.[287]

"Individuals of middling capacity rise from their downfalls by pleasing a deity of the knowledge mantras and secret mantras, such as the bodhisattva Ākāshagarbha, and receiving the deity's pardon." Thus, with great remorse and with the fear of falling into the lower realms, one should, if one is able, behold Noble Ākāshagarbha and confess directly to him. Otherwise, one should rise before dawn, and with ritual cleanliness make offerings in the eastern direction. After praying to the "deity of the dawn" and returning to

*"Support" here refers to a statue or image of the Buddha, a stūpa, and so on.

sleep, one should confess one's downfalls before him when he appears in one's dream, perform prostrations, recite incantations, and so on. By these means, one should do the confession until one actually beholds the Noble One or a sign appears that one's negative deeds have been purified. This is mentioned in the *Compendium of Precepts*:

> In your dream,
> Seated before the Noble Ākāshagarbha,
> Make the confession.

"Individuals of supreme capacity recognize that the very thing they are admitting as a downfall is devoid of intrinsic attributes, and with that realization of bodhichitta, they purify it without difficulty, as is explained in the *Sūtra of the Great Vehicle That Teaches All Phenomena as Being Without Origin*: 'Mañjushrī, bodhisattvas who know that there are no actions and no fully ripened effects attain the complete purification of their karmic obscurations.'"

b. How to take the vow again when it has been given up

One gives up the vow if one has given up bodhichitta in aspiration or a root downfall occurs with a high degree of entanglement,* which is equivalent to a radical defeat. In such a case, one should confess, vow to refrain in the future, and be assiduous in purification and accumulation. In the presence of a spiritual friend or a representation, one should take the vow again. Downfalls committed with a middling degree of entanglement, which are similar to defeats, can be purified by confessing and vowing to refrain in the future in the presence of at least three bodhisattvas. And root downfalls committed with a slight degree of entanglement and any kinds of minor infractions other than those (which, depending on their motivation, may or may not be with defilements and may or may not constitute downfalls) can be purified by confessing and vowing to refrain in the presence of at least one person. All this is stated in the *Twenty Verses on the Vows of a Bodhisattva*:

*"A high degree of entanglement" (Tib. *kun dkris chen po*) refers to committing a downfall continuously, without shame or embarrassment, being pleased with what one has done, and not regarding it as wrong. These four are less present in the middling and slight degrees of entanglement.

The vow must be taken again.
Middling taints should be confessed to three.
In front of one, confess the rest,
Depending on whether one's mind was defiled or not.

D. A teaching on the benefits of training in that way

If we were to categorize the benefits in detail, they would be limitless, but in brief they are of two kinds: (1) temporary, and (2) ultimate.

1. Temporary benefits

There are seven temporary benefits: a change of one's name and status, the elimination of very powerful evil deeds, the acquisition of vast merit, the acquisition of infinite good qualities, benefits indicated by analogies, the benefit of the training serving as an offering to all the buddhas, and benefits detailed in the scriptures.

1. One's name and status are changed, as described in *The Way of the Bodhisattva*:

> Should bodhichitta come to birth
> In those who suffer, chained in prisons of saṃsāra,
> In that instant they are called the children of the Blissful One,
> Revered by all the world, by gods and humankind.[288]

2. One eliminates intensely evil deeds, as stated in the *Sūtra of the Arborescent Array*:

> As it burns up all negative deeds, it is like the fire at the end of the kalpa. Because it consumes all nonvirtue, it is like the underworld.

3. One acquires vast merit, as is mentioned in the *Sūtra of the Questions of Vīradatta*:

> If the merit of bodhichitta
> Were to take material form,
> It would fill the whole of space
> And still there would be more.

And in an instruction,

> One who meditates on bodhichitta
> Even for a single instant
> Gains such a quantity of merit—
> Even buddhas cannot measure it!

4. One will acquire infinite excellent qualities, as is stated in the *Sūtra of the Precious Lamp*:

> The self-arisen mind, basis of enlightenment,
> Aroused in the very beginning—
> The praises of its qualities are infinite:
> Even the peerless ones cannot express them.

And in the *Sūtra of the Questions of Sāgaramati*,

> Wishing for perfect enlightenment, holding the teachings,
> Practicing the teachings, and loving all that lives—
> The qualities of these four are infinite:
> Their full extent no buddha can describe.

5. The benefits indicated by analogies are threefold: The transformation from lowly to sublime is indicated by analogy with alchemy, as mentioned in *The Way of the Bodhisattva*:

> For like the supreme substance of the alchemists,
> It takes our impure flesh and makes of it
> The body of a Buddha, jewel beyond all price.
> Such is bodhichitta. Let us grasp it firmly![289]

The rarity and great worth of bodhichitta is indicated by analogy with a jewel. In the same text, we read,

> Since the boundless wisdom of the only guide of beings
> Perfectly examined and perceived its priceless worth,
> Those who wish to leave this state of wandering
> Should hold well to this precious bodhichitta.[290]

The inexhaustible, ever-increasing fruition of bodhichitta is indicated by analogy with a wish-fulfilling tree. The same text states,

> All other virtues, like the plantain tree,
> Produce their fruit, but then their force is spent.
> Alone the marvelous tree of bodhichitta
> Constantly bears fruit and grows unceasingly.[291]

6. The training is an offering to the buddhas, as is shown in the *Sūtra of the Questions of Sāgaramati*:

> These three are unsurpassable offerings to the tathāgatas: arousing the bodhichitta, holding the sacred teachings, and loving living beings.

And the *Sūtra of the Questions of Vīradatta* has,

> Greater by far than the merit
> Of someone who fills with the seven precious substances
> All the buddha-fields, numerous as the Ganges's sands,
> And offers them to the buddhas
> Is the merit of one who, with folded hands,
> Bows before the bodhichitta:
> That merit knows no bounds.

And in the *Sūtra of the King of Concentrations*, we read,

> All the boundless offerings
> In a million billion buddha-fields,
> Constantly offered every day to the sublime beings,
> Could never match a fraction of a loving mind.

7. There are the benefits detailed in the scriptures. In the *Sūtra of the Arborescent Array*, we read,

> Fortunate child, the mind set on enlightenment is like the seed of all the buddhas' teachings. It is like the soil, for it enables all the virtuous deeds of all beings to grow. It is like the earth, for

> it supports the whole world. . . . It is like a father, for it protects all bodhisattvas. . . . Likewise, it is like Vaishravaṇa, the god of wealth, for it removes all poverty. It is like the king of wish-fulfilling gems, for it accomplishes all goals perfectly. It is like the excellent vase, for it completely fulfills all wishes. It is like a lance, for it vanquishes the defilements that are our foes. It is like an armor, for it shields us against improper use of the mind. It is like a sword, for it decapitates the defilements. It is like an axe, for it fells the tree of the defilements. It is like a weapon, for it protects us from all danger. It is like a hook, for it draws up to the surface those drowning in the river of cyclic existence. It is like the maṇḍala of the wind, for it completely scatters the straw covering of obscurations. It is like a concentrate, for it includes the activities and prayers of aspiration of the bodhisattvas. It is like a shrine in the world for gods, humans, and demigods. Fortunate child, bodhichitta, thus, has these benefits and boundless other specific benefits.

In like manner, Lord Maitreya used about 230 similes in all to describe the benefits of arousing bodhichitta to the young Sudhana.

2. Ultimate benefit

The ultimate benefit is that it enables us to complete all the Buddha's teachings, as is stated in the *Bodhisattva's Scriptural Collection*:

> Shāriputra, if bodhisattva mahāsattvas possess one teaching, they will completely hold these teachings of the Buddha and infinite others. What is that one teaching? It is this: the perfect attitude that is the mind set on enlightenment. Shāriputra, if bodhisattva mahāsattvas possess this one teaching, they will completely hold these teachings of the Buddha and infinite others.

In the same way, it enables us to never separate from the buddhas and the light of the Dharma, and through their blessings to swiftly attain enlightenment. In the *Sūtra That Perfectly Summarizes the Dharma*, it is said,

> Lord, the perfect intention is the root of all the teachings. For

> those who do not have that intention, the Buddha's teachings are a long way away. Lord, to those who have the perfect intention, the victorious, virtuous, transcendent buddhas appear and teach them the Dharma, even though they may be in other worlds. Even if the buddhas are not present, the sound of the Dharma resounds from the sky, from walls, and from trees. To bodhisattvas with pure intention, there appear, from their own discernment, all the instructions and follow-up teachings. This is why bodhisattvas have the perfect intention. Lord, it is thus. Just as those who have feet can walk, likewise, those who have this intention will have the Buddha's teachings. Lord, it is thus. Those who have a head, the foremost of all the limbs, have life. Likewise, those who have the superior intention have enlightenment.

The *Sūtra of the Arborescent Array* sums up,

> In brief, the qualities and benefits of bodhichitta are as numerous as all the Buddha's teachings and the qualities of buddhahood. Why is that? Because all the maṇḍalas of bodhisattvas arise from this, and all the tathāgatas who have appeared in the past, those who will appear in the future, and those who are appearing at present, are born from this.

Accordingly, we should apply ourselves diligently, all the time, to the supreme, single path trodden by all the buddhas and bodhisattvas of the three times, the precious bodhichitta that dispels all the troubles of existence and peace and grants every kind of benefit and happiness that we could wish for.

The qualities of buddhahood are achieved by helping others,
All the evils of saṃsāra come from cherishing oneself;
So recognize the harm and good these two can bring
And cultivate the supreme bodhichitta, O fortunate ones!

This completes the instruction on arousing the mind set on enlightenment.

Dudjom Rinpoche (1904–1987)

11. The Meditation and Recitation of Vajrasattva, Which Purifies the Negative Deeds and Obscurations That Act as Unfavorable Conditions

This chapter has three parts: (1) a general exposition of the nature of the four strengths, (2) the main explanation of the specific meditation and recitation of Vajrasattva, and (3) a concluding description of the signs of proficiency in purifying negative deeds and obscurations and the benefits.

I. General exposition of the nature of the four strengths

What has caused us to circle perpetually in cyclic existence in our beginningless series of lives and has prevented us from attaining the level of freedom in enlightenment is our negative deeds and obscurations—hence the need to purify them. How this is done is described by the Bodhisattva Shāntideva as follows:

> The things to be purified, the six doors of evil deeds,
> Are purified by the agents of purification, the four remedial
> powers.
> And the method of purification depends on the purity
> Of the preparation, main practice, and conclusion.

Of these three—what has to be purified, what does the purifying, and the method of purification—the first is what has to be purified.

A. What has to be purified

What has to be purified refers to the six doors of negative deeds, which are as follows:

The door of motivation refers to the three defiling poisons. Any acts that are motivated by these poisons are by definition unvirtuous, and their effect is to give rise exclusively to suffering. The *Jewel Garland* states,

> Attachment, aversion, and bewilderment—
> Actions created by these are unvirtuous.
> From nonvirtue arise all kinds of suffering
> And, likewise, all the lower realms.[292]

And in *The Way of the Bodhisattva*, we read,

> How instead can I make sure
> To rid myself of evil, only cause of sorrow?
> This should be my one concern,
> My only thought both night and day.[293]

The door of entrance refers to the body, speech, and mind. The door of the object refers to the Three Jewels, one's parents, preceptors, instructors, and so on. The door of time covers from time without beginning until the present. The door of the nature refers to all naturally negative deeds such as the ten negative actions and all downfalls that violate edicts (for example—eating after midday if one is an ordained person). Downfalls can be summarized as any transgressions, on the outer level, of the vows of individual liberation, on the inner level, of the bodhisattva vows, and on the secret level, of the sacred commitments of the vidyādhara mantras. In the *Prayer of Good Action*, one recites,

> Whatever faults I have committed
> By body, speech, or by mind
> Because of craving, hatred and ignorance,
> I confess each one of them.

The door of implementation refers to acts that one has done oneself, has incited others to do, or has rejoiced in. *The Way of the Bodhisattva* reads as follows:

In this and all my other lives,
While turning in the round without beginning,
Blindly I have brought forth evil,
And incited others to commit the same.
Deceived and overmastered by my ignorance,
I have taken pleasure in such sin,
And seeing now the blame of it,
O great protectors, I confess it earnestly!
Whatever I have done against the Triple Gem,
Against my parents, teachers, and the rest,
Through force of my defilements,
In my body, speech, and mind,
All the evil I, a sinner, have committed,
All the wicked deeds that cling to me,
The frightful things that I contrived,
I openly declare to you, the teachers of the world.[294]

B. The agents of purification

The agents of purification are the four powers, which are listed in the *Sūtra of the Teaching on the Four Qualities*:

> Maitreya, if one possesses four qualities,[295] all the negative deeds one has gathered will be completely overwhelmed. What are these four? They are the application of regret, the application of the antidote, the power of restoration, and the power of the support. The first of these is great remorse if one has committed a negative deed. The second is, having committed negative deeds, extreme diligence in performing positive deeds. The third is to take one's vows correctly and receive the vow not to perform negative actions. The fourth is to take refuge in the Buddha, Dharma, and Saṅgha and never to give up bodhichitta.

These four will now be explained in order. For ease of explanation, we will begin with the power of the support.

1. The power of the support

The power of the support is twofold.

The object as support is the object to which one confesses one's negative deeds. This can be the spiritual friend who is one's teacher. Alternatively, one may use a sacred representation of the body, speech, or mind of the Tathāgata, surrounded by material offerings, and invite the buddhas and bodhisattvas, visualizing them in the sky in front and considering that they are actually present as witnesses. This is the manner described in *The Way of the Bodhisattva*:

> The Buddhas and the Bodhisattvas both
> Possess unclouded vision, seeing everything.

And,

> To perfect Buddhas and to Bodhisattvas,
> In all directions where they may reside,
> To them who are the sovereigns of great mercy,
> I press my palms together, praying thus.[296]

One's own mind as support refers to taking refuge and arousing bodhichitta. With the compassionate wish to free all sentient beings and a yearning to attain perfect enlightenment, one should go for refuge in the general manner. In particular, one should pray to the buddhas to protect one from fear—for example, with the *Prayer to the Lord of the Victorious Ones* taken from *The Way of the Bodhisattva*.* How taking refuge purifies evil deeds is described in the *Mahāparinirvāṇa Sūtra*:

> By going for refuge in the Three Jewels,
> One will obtain freedom from fear.

And how arousing bodhichitta purifies our negative deeds is described in *The Way of the Bodhisattva*:

*See appendix 2.

Just as by the fire that will destroy the world,
Great sins are surely and at once consumed by it.[297]

2. The power of regret

The power of regret involves reminding oneself of the negative acts and downfalls that one has committed in the past and, with intense remorse, mentioning each one of them by name and confessing them. How are we to regret them? There are three ways of giving rise to regret: (1) by examining how pointless our negative deeds have been, (2) by examining how fearful they are, and (3) by examining the urgent need to rid ourselves of them.

a. Examining how pointless negative deeds are

The negative acts that we have committed were done sometimes in order to get the better of our enemies, sometimes to protect our kin, sometimes in order to achieve honor and fame, sometimes for our physical well-being, and sometimes in order to gather property and wealth. Yet when we die and move on to the next world, none of these things—enemies, kinfolk, country, body, riches, and so forth—will accompany us. Instead, only the negative deeds and obscurations associated with our bad karma will go along with us and, wherever we are reborn, they will rear up as our executioners to attack us. It is said in the *Sūtra of the Questions of Vīradatta*,

My parents, siblings, children, wife,
And servants, wealth, and friends—
None of them will go to my next life once I am dead.
My actions, though, will follow after me.

And,

At that time, as my pain becomes extreme,
My wife and children will not help.
Alone I will experience suffering,
At that time they'll not share my fate.

And in *The Way of the Bodhisattva*, we find,

And we must pass away, forsaking all.
But I, devoid of understanding,
Have, for sake of friend and foe alike,
Provoked and brought about so many wrongs.
But all my foes will cease to be,
And all my friends will cease to be,
And I will also cease to be,
And likewise everything will cease to be.[298]

If it was on account of enemies and friends, our bodies, possessions, and so forth that we committed negative actions, we will not have the company of all these things for very long. When we have fallen into the lower realms, where we are so very wretched and the most in need, they will no longer be by our sides or of any use to us. We alone will have to experience the suffering that is the ripened effect of those negative deeds. Therefore, reflecting on how much trouble negative actions involve, and for so little point, give rise to intense regret.

b. Examining how fearful negative deeds are

We might think that although negative acts are pointless, they will not harm us, but this is not the case. The result of having performed negative deeds produces the most terrible fear as we approach death, when we are dying, and after we have died. As they are dying, people who have done negative actions go through the unbearable suffering of their lives being severed and other hallucinatory experiences, as we read in *The Way of the Bodhisattva*:

There I'll be, prostrate upon my bed,
And all around, my family and friends.
But I alone shall be the one to feel
The cutting of the thread of life.[299]

Then, at the moment of death, the brutal, vicious henchmen of the Lord of Death, with their black faces, bloodshot eyes, and terrifying roars, will catch us by the throat with their nooses. Wielding fiery cudgels, sabers, and other weapons, they will beat us and drive us outside, crying "Strike! Strike! Kill! Kill!" They will pursue us into the fearful abodes of the hells—the plain of weapons, the ground of blazing rocks, and so forth—where we will be helpless to prevent the most terrible sufferings from being inflicted upon us. This is affirmed in *Letter to a Disciple*:

> With the noose of time* tied around your throat,
> Yama's thugs will chase you with their clubs.

And in *The Way of the Bodhisattva*,

> The day they take him to the scaffold,
> Where they will tear off his limbs,
> A man is changed, transfigured by his fear:
> His mouth is dry, his eyes start from his brow.
> No need to say how stricken I shall be
> When overcome and sick with dreadful fear,
> I'm seized by forms so horrible to see,
> The frightful servants of the Lord of Death.

And,

> And when the heralds of the Deadly King have gripped me,
> What help to me will be my friends and kin?
> For then life's virtue is my one defense,
> And this, alas, is what I shrugged away.[300]

As for the terrors we will experience after death, as a result of our negative deeds, we will fall into the evil destinies of the great hells, where we will experience the unbearable sufferings of being boiled, burned, hewn, and torn to pieces. Of this, *Letter to a Friend* says,

> The very instant that they cease to breathe
> The wicked taste the boundless pains of hell.
> And he who hearing this is not afraid
> A thousandfold is truly diamond hard.
> If simply seeing pictures of the hells

*The "noose of time" is a Tibetan metaphor for the moment of death.

And hearing, thinking, reading of them scares,
Or making sculpted figures, need we say
How hard to bear the ripened fruit will be?[301]

So, deeply fearful of the results of your negative deeds, again and again give rise to regret for them.

c. Examining the urgent need to rid ourselves of our negative deeds

We might think that it is all right to confess our negative actions later. But this will not do, for there is the risk that we might die before purifying our negative actions. *The Way of the Bodhisattva* warns,

It may be that my death will come to me
Before my evil has been cleansed.
How then can I be freed from it?
I pray you, quickly grant me your protection![302]

Nor should we think that we will not die before we have been able to purify our negative deeds. We cannot depend on it, for without looking to see whether or not we have purified our negative deeds, the demon of death snatches away our lives as soon as it gets the chance. The same text has,

We cannot trust the wanton Lord of Death.
The task complete or still to do, he will not wait.
In health or sickness, therefore, none of us can trust
Our fleeting, momentary lives.[303]

Since there is the risk, therefore, that we might die without having purified our negative actions, we must make an effort to confess them urgently. In this regard, when we speak of confessing or "acknowledging and parting,"* if we hide the wrong actions we have committed and keep them secret, they will grow ever greater, whereas if we recognize them as defects and openly declare them to the assembly without hiding or keeping them secret, the strength of

*"Acknowledging and parting" is a literal translation of the two aspects of the Tibetan expression *mthol bshags*, which is usually rendered as "confession," but this is a loose translation as the term "confession" only covers the first aspect, acknowledging.

those negative actions will diminish and will never increase. To declare to the assembly, which is the principal object of confession, "I have committed such-and-such a fault" is to acknowledge it. And, to accept that one's deed is a fault, with one's mind tormented by intense regret, thinking, "It was very wrong of me to do this, what a fool I've been!" is to part from it. Feeling dismayed and humbled because of the faults we have committed and realizing that those who do not have such faults are truly wondrous and sublime on account of their good qualities, we should respectfully think of them on the crown of our head and, ashamed of the wrong deeds we have done, speak openly, saying from the depth of our hearts: "Care for me with your love, please purify these deeds!" This is the essence of what is meant by confession.

3. The power of the application of the antidote

This power refers to different kinds of virtuous practice as an antidote to negative actions. Among these, I have selected a few that are easy to implement and of great benefit, known as the "six means for applying antidotes."

a. Remembering the names of the buddhas and bodhisattvas

In the sūtras, there are extensive mentions of the names of numerous buddhas and bodhisattvas and of how bringing them to mind will purify karmic obscurations. For example, it is said that hearing the name of our Compassionate Teacher* purifies the negative actions committed over eighty thousand great kalpas. There are also texts such as the Omniscient Jampel Dorje's compilation *Garland of Jewels of a Hundred Thousand Names*.[304] We should recite these ourselves or arrange for others to recite them.

b. Crafting images and building stūpas

Crafting images and building stūpas also includes producing copies of the Buddhist scriptures. Purifying negative deeds by creating representations of the Buddha's body is mentioned in the *Chapter on Images of the Tathāgata*:

> Fashion images of the Tathāgata. Restore ones that are damaged. Repair those that are broken. If one fashions images of the

*That is, Buddha Shākyamuni.

> Tathāgata, one will not be born in any of the lower castes, among beings who commit negative actions, or as those who have wrong views. One will not be in any way handicapped. Even if one has committed the five crimes with immediate retribution, if one gains faith in the Tathāgata and creates an image of him, one will experience only a little of the experiences in the hells and one will be certain of deliverance through any of the three vehicles. Just as someone who touches something foul can get rid of the unpleasant smell by washing thoroughly and putting on perfume, so, too, will someone who has committed a crime with immediate retribution be rid of its negative consequences. And if those who indulge in the ten nonvirtuous actions gain faith in the Tathāgata and make an image of him, the negative consequences of their deeds will vanish like oil being burned in a bonfire and disappearing without even a trace of smoke.

The purification of negative deeds by building stūpas is mentioned in the *Incantation of Vimaloṣṇīṣa*, in which, after clearly explaining the ritual methods for building stūpas, the Buddha gave a detailed description of the benefits. Here are some of them:

> One will give rise to the same sources of good as if one made offerings to tathāgatas as numerous as a million billion times the number of grains of sand in the Ganges. One will gain an immense store of merit. One will completely purify the obscurations associated with the five crimes with immediate retribution. One will be liberated from birth as a hell being, from birth as an animal, and from the lower realms that are the world of the Lord of Death. One will have a long life. Like a snake shedding its skin, having abandoned one's body, one will similarly rid oneself of one's obscurations and go to the Blissful Realm.* Henceforth, one will never be affected by the taints of the womb.

And in other texts, such as the *Incantation of Sarvanīvaraṇaviṣkambhin*, there are numerous statements to the effect that, simply from seeing a stūpa

*Tib. *bDeba can*, Sukhāvatī, Amitābha's buddha-field of bliss.

and hearing the ringing of its bells, the five crimes with immediate retribution and so on will be purified and after death one will be born in Sukhāvatī, the buddha-field of bliss.

As to how obscurations are brought to an end by copying the Buddha's excellent words, preserving them, reading them, and so on, there are countless references—in the respective texts, for example. And in the *Prayer of Good Action*, we find,

> All the evil deeds they've done because of ignorance—
> Even the five crimes with immediate retribution—
> Will be quickly purified
> By those who recite this *Prayer of Good Action*.

And,

> Just to hold or teach or read
> This *Prayer of Good Action*
> Will yield a ripened fruit known only to the buddhas:
> Without a doubt, it is supreme enlightenment.

c. Venerating and circumambulating sacred supports

This refers to accumulating merit by submitting obeisance to representations of the Buddha's body, speech, and mind and to the Saṅgha, making offerings, offering maṇḍalas, and so on. Those who have entered the Mantra Vehicle perform the feast offering and confession and fulfillment. Best of all is serving the teacher. We read in the *Incantation: The Heap of Flowers*,

> Those who venerate the Tathāgata, Arhat, true and perfect Buddha with pleasing offerings for one year, one hundred years, or one thousand years and who, once the Tathāgata has passed into nirvāṇa, make offerings of flowers to his reliquaries, sprinkle the water filling their cupped hands on them, offer a drop of saffron-scented water, wipe off pollen and dirt, or make offerings of scented unguents, resins, incense, or lamps, or to make such offerings, take a few paces with a joyful attitude, saying, "I submit obeisance to Lord Buddha!"—those beings, Prancing Lion, will

> not, for a hundred kalpas, or a thousand kalpas, or even a hundred thousand kalpas, migrate to states in which they fall upside down into the lower realms.

And in the *Vajra Sun*, we read,

> For a transgression, confess with the feast offering,
> For a deterioration, replenish it with your own possessions,
> For a breach of limit, repair it with your child, spouse,
> Relatives, body, speech, mind, and possessions.
> When the commitments have been torn apart, repair them with your own life.*

And in the *Vajra Net*,

> Of all kinds of merit, the feast offering is the best.
> In this life, all one's wishes will be fulfilled
> And obstacles and interruptions removed.
> And in the next life, in a buddha-field of the vidyādharas,
> One will attain the level of Samantabhadra.

In the *Ocean of Gnosis Tantra*, we find,

> Pleasing one's teacher
> With an offering of sandalwood, camphor, or perfume
> Has far greater merit than making offerings
> For many thousands of kalpas
> In hundreds of thousands of buddha-fields.
> Infinitely greater than the merit
> Of decking countless thousands of statues
> Of the buddhas and bodhisattvas
> With the five kinds of precious substances
> Is that of adorning a single hair of the teacher's head or body
> With the five kinds of precious substances.

*These four cases refer to different degrees of broken Vajrayāna commitments, depending on how long they have been left unconfessed. See Jigme Lingpa and Longchen Yeshe Dorje, *Treasury*, bk. 2, 225.

> Offering a banquet seven times
> To six million two hundred thousand
> Monks who have kept their vows
> Cannot compare to a hundredth, a thousandth,
> A ten thousandth, or a hundred thousandth
> Of the merit of serving one's teacher
> Seven grains of cooked rice.

And the *Guhyagarbha Tantra* has,

> To offer the five enjoyments to the teacher,
> The lord of all the maṇḍalas,
> Is to make an offering to all maṇḍalas,
> Not to mention the minor maṇḍalas.
> All one's faults will be purified,
> And all good qualities acquired.

d. Reading or reciting the profound sūtras and tantras

Generally speaking, there is no difference between the various scriptures containing the Buddha's words. Nevertheless, when it is mainly in order to purify negative deeds and obscurations, we should read and recite profound sūtras and tantras such as the *Praise and Confession of the Bodhisattva Downfalls* and the *Sūtra of Great Liberation*: their particular benefits and other details are as indicated in the texts themselves.

e. Reciting incantations and mantras

For purifying evil deeds, the *Hundred Syllables of the Tathāgatas*, the *Incantation of Akṣobhya*, and so on are especially recommended. Moreover, we should read such works as the collection of incantations compiled by the Omniscient Jampel Dorje[305] and gain confidence in their particular benefits.

f. Meditating on emptiness

If you have been introduced to the natural state and are able to maintain that view, you should rest in that state. If not, you should examine the negative deed itself, the person who has committed it, the consciousness that holds the seed of the negative deed, and the suffering that is its result. In each case, ask yourself what is the cause from which it arises, what is its essential nature, where does it reside, where does it finally cease to be, and so on. After analyzing things in this way, at the end, settle in the nonconceptual state free of elaborations, for as we read in the *Sūtra of Great Liberation*:

> Those who regret and wish to purify themselves
> Should sit up straight and truly look,
> Watching truly the truth itself.
> Truly seeing, they are freed.
> Of ways to regret and purify, this is the best.

And in the *Sūtra of the Buddha's Treasury*,

> Even if one has killed one's father or mother or a solitary realizer,
> By meditating on emptiness, one will be liberated.

In short, the negative deeds that we have committed are brought to an end by using virtuous activities as their antidotes, as is explained in the Vinaya scriptures:

> Any negative actions one has done
> Are brought to cessation by virtue,
> Like the sun and moon emerging from the clouds
> And shining on the world.

We might wonder whether when we perform virtuous activities as the antidotes for negative deeds, we have to perform as many positive deeds as the negative deeds we have committed. But this is not necessary, for it is said in the *Mahāparinirvāṇa Sūtra*:

> Even a single virtuous action annuls numerous negative deeds.

And,

> Just as a small diamond can destroy a huge mountain, a tiny spark can destroy a forest, and a little poison can kill a living being, so too, a small virtuous deed can overcome great evil.

4. The power of restoration

Anyone who has any knowledge of the effects of a poison will make a point of never drinking it. In the same way, out of fear of the fully ripened effects of our actions, we should make the promise "In the future, even if it costs me my life, I will never do these negative actions again," and refrain from wrongdoing, as is expressed in *The Way of the Bodhisattva*:

> I pray you, guides and guardians of the world,
> To take me as I am, a sinful man.
> And all these actions, evil as they are,
> I promise I will never do again.[306]

C. The method of purification

This comprises the preparation, main practice, and conclusion. Of these, the preparation consists of visualizing countless buddhas and bodhisattvas and taking refuge in them. For the main practice, recalling all your negative actions and regretting them, imagine all your own and others' negative deeds as a black mass on your tongue, and confess them. Think that as a result of your confession, light rays issue forth from the buddhas and bodhisattvas, especially from their foreheads, immediately purifying you. The conclusion consists of considering that, as a result of the emanation of numerous rays of light, all your negative actions are purified and your body becomes like a mass of crystal. The words for confessing negative deeds are to be found in such texts as the *Confession of the Bodhisattva Downfalls*, the *Prayer of Good Action*, and *The Way of the Bodhisattva*, or you may recite prayers like "Teacher, great vajra holder, . . ."* At the end, settle in the state free of the concepts of a support for one's confession, negative actions to be confessed, or a person confessing them. In this way, you should practice with the preparation, main practice, and conclusion complete.

II. The main explanation, comprising the instructions for the practice in the specific meditation and recitation of Vajrasattva

The obstacles that hinder our accomplishing perfect enlightenment for the

*See appendix 3.

benefit of others are our negative deeds and obscurations, so they need to be purified. And the best way to purify them is the meditation and recitation of Vajrasattva. So, saying to yourself, "I am going to engage in this profound practice," rest at ease physically and mentally, then think of yourself in your ordinary form. On the crown of your head visualize an eight-petaled white lotus, with its cluster of anthers. It is facing upward and its root is planted in your crown opening. On top of it is a full-moon disk.

When all this is clear, consider that on top of it is a radiant, clear-white syllable HŪṀ, from which five-colored rays* of light shine forth brightly, making offerings that please the body, speech, and mind of the buddhas and bodhisattvas in the ten directions and touching all beings, purifying their negative deeds and obscurations. As the light rays are gathered back, the HŪṀ transforms into your kind root teacher in the form of the virtuous, transcendent conqueror Glorious Vajrasattva. His body is white in color, shining majestically like a snow-capped mountain in the light of the rising sun. He has a radiant face, attractive and smiling, and is beautified with the thirty-two major marks and eighty minor marks of excellence. He has one face and two hands. With his right hand holding a five-pronged vajra at the level of his heart and the left on his hip holding a bell, he embraces his wisdom consort. He is seated cross-legged in the bodhisattva posture. He is in union with his consort Vajragarvā, who is also white and embraces him with her hands round his neck holding a curved knife and a skull cup.

Furthermore, both of them display the nine modes of expression of the peaceful deities: (1) As a sign that they have both transmuted pride, rather than renouncing it, their hands and legs are as supple as gold leaf. (2) As a sign that they have not rejected aversion but have transmuted it, their fingers are as pliant as a serpent's tail. (3) As a sign that they have not rejected attachment but have transmuted it, they—means and wisdom—are entwined with each other like the green leaves of sprouting barley. (4) As a sign that they have not rejected bewilderment but have transmuted it, their waists are as straight and flexible as pine trees. (5) As a sign that they have not rejected jealousy but have transmuted it, they are in the full bloom of youth, like eight-year-old children. (6) As an indication that they have no ignorance in their minds, they are as radiant as the moon. (7) As an indication that their qualities are spontaneously accomplished, they are as dazzling as the sun. (8) As a sign that they have all the major and minor

*The five colors are blue, white, yellow, red, and green.

Vajrasattva

marks perfect and complete, they give out a sense of grandeur like Mount Meru. And (9) as a sign that they outshine all, they have the majestic presence of a hundred thousand lions parading.

They are beautifully adorned with the five silken garments (the upper garment of gold-embroidered white silk, the skirt of multicolored silk, the tasseled headdress of five-colored silks, the two-colored silk sash,* and the long dancing shawl) and the eight jeweled ornaments (multijeweled crown, earrings, necklet, short necklace, bracelets, anklets, girdle, and long necklace).[307] Endlessly emanating infinite rays of light, they are present as the essence of bliss and emptiness inseparable.

In Vajrasattva's heart, upon a lotus and moon, is a white five-pronged vajra in an upright position. Within its hub, visualize a white syllable HŪṂ surrounded by the white chain of the hundred-syllable mantra turning to the right. All this, considering Vajrasattva as the embodiment of all sources of refuge, constitutes the power of the support.

> Visualizing myself as ordinary, upon my crown is a lotus and moon,
> Upon which a white syllable HŪṂ radiates light and reabsorbs it, transforming into Vajrasattva,
> Shining brilliant white, holding a vajra and bell and adorned with the ornaments of the body of enjoyment,
> Embraced by his consort, who is like him, and majestic with all the major and minor marks.
> He is seated in the bodhisattva's posture. In his heart center, upon a lotus and moon,
> Is a brilliant white five-pronged vajra, and in its center the syllable HŪṂ
> Surrounded by the garland of Vajrasattva's mantra,
> Turning clockwise and resounding on its own.
> From the mantra garland and his body a stream of nectar flows down,
> Purifying all the stains of negative actions, obscurations, and transgressions.[308]

Now, call to mind, above all, the negative deeds that you can actually

*The sash is blue on the outside and red inside.

remember doing in the past, that you urged others to do, or that you rejoiced at when others did them—nonvirtuous actions in general, and specifically acts that have transgressed the limits of the three vows, especially those deeds that have violated the body, speech, and mind of your teacher, the vajra master. With an intense attitude of shame and remorse, think from the very depth of your heart: "Teacher, Vajrasattva, in you I put my trust! Whatever the negative deeds that I and all sentient beings have committed in the past out of ignorance, disrespect, and our manifold defilements, I will keep nothing secret, I will not hide them: all of them I acknowledge and confess. Please cleanse and purify the whole multitude of stains from my negative actions and downfalls." This sort of attitude is the power of regret.

Then, think, "From now on, whatever the consequence, even if it costs me my life, I will not commit such negative deeds even in my dreams, let alone in reality. May I never act like that again!" Thinking like this constitutes the power of refraining from committing negative deeds again.

Practicing the meditation and recitation of Glorious Vajrasattva as the remedy for one's previous deeds constitutes the power of the application of the antidote.

Keeping in mind the key points of these four powers, recite the hundred-syllable mantra a hundred, a thousand, ten thousand, or a hundred thousand times, purely and clearly, without being interrupted by such things as ordinary talk, until you see signs that you have purified your negative deeds and obscurations. As you are doing the recitation, consider that a white stream of ambrosial bodhichitta floods down, first from the seed syllable in Vajrasattva's heart, then from the tips of his big toes, from the secret space of the point of union of Vajrasattva and his consort, and finally from all the parts of his body. Swirling down the lotus stem, it enters you through your crown opening. Every illness in the form of blood, pus, and foul matter; all kinds of negative forces in the form of scorpions, snakes, and other small creatures; and every one of your negative deeds and obscurations in the form of black liquid, like liquid charcoal or liquid smoke, emerge from all your sense doors and the pores of your body. In short, everything is rinsed out, like silt being washed away by a mountain torrent, resulting in your body becoming like a pure heap of crystal.

Again, pray as before. Consider that, as a result of your prayer, the ambrosial stream of bodhichitta fills you completely, from the crown of your head to your toenails, so that the obscurations and habitual tendencies of your body, speech, and mind are purified and you obtain the empowerments and accomplishments of the deity's body, speech, mind, qualities, and activities. In particular, you are blessed as a suitable vessel for being able to give rise effortlessly to all the qualities of the path of the main practice.

Finally, to conclude the session, pray as follows:

> Protector, ignorantly and stupidly
> I have transgressed and damaged the sacred commitments.
> O my teacher and protector, grant me refuge!
> Principal deity, holder of the vajra,
> You who embody great compassion,
> In you, sovereign of all beings, I take refuge.
> I confess all deteriorations of the root and branch commitments and of the commitments related to your body, speech, and mind.
> Purge and purify all my negative actions, obscurations, faults, downfalls, and stains, I pray.[309]

Consider that as a result of your prayer, the Teacher Vajrasattva smiles with pleasure and gives his consent, saying, "Fortunate child, all your negative actions and obscurations are purified!" At this, visualize the Teacher Vajrasattva above your head melting into light from his crown jewel downward and from his lotus throne upward. His heart becomes a sphere of five-colored light, which enters you through your crown opening and dissolves into the center of your heart. Look directly at the nature of the negative deeds and obscurations that have to be purified and what it is that purifies them, and finally rest in equipoise as long as you can in the state of great bliss beyond description, completely purified of the concepts of the three spheres. Then conclude with the dedication.

III. Concluding description of the signs of proficiency in purifying negative deeds and obscurations and the benefits of doing so

By confessing one's negative deeds in this way, concentrating on the four powers, signs of purification will occur in one's dreams, as listed in the *Incantation of the Goddess Cundā*:

> If in one's dreams one vomits rotten food, drinks yoghurt and milk, sees the sun and moon, travels through space, sees a blazing

> fire, is capable of taming wild buffalos and negative forces, sees an assembly of monks and nuns, climbs on top of a tree with milky sap, on an elephant, bull, mountain, lion throne, or palace, hears the Dharma, and so forth, one is free of negative acts.

Other dreams may occur that one is bathing, wearing white clothes, has a vision of the teacher and yidam deity, hears their teachings, and so on. And in reality as well, all kinds of qualities of the path may take birth in one's mind stream—a feeling of contentment, clear awareness, an increase in one's virtuous activities, the effortless arising of wisdom and compassion, and so on.

As for the proofs or benefits of purifying negative deeds and obscurations by relying on the four powers, these can be found in stories from the past. The brahmin's son Atapa, known as Aṅgulimāla,* had the evil karma of having killed 999 people. Yet by using the power of regret and confessing his negative deeds, he purified them and, in the very same life, became an arhat. Similarly, although the youth Shaṅkara had the evil karma of having killed his mother, he purified his negative deed by means of the power of application of the antidote and was reborn as a god, whence he attained the result of a noble stream enterer. Nanda had the evil karma of excessive attachment to his wife, but he purified his negative karma by means of the power of restraint† and subsequently attained the level of arhat. Then there was the prince Darshaka,‡ who had the evil karma of having killed his father, but with the power of the support he purified that negative deed and became a bodhisattva. These are all referred to in *Letter to a Friend*:

> Those who formerly were careless
> But then took heed are beautiful and fair,
> As is the moon emerging from the clouds,
> Like Nanda, Aṅgulimāla, Darshaka, Shaṅkara.[310]

*The name Aṅgulimāla (Tib. Sor mo phreng ba can) means "Garland of Fingers" and refers to his making a garland from the fingers of each of his victims in the mistaken belief that if he killed a thousand people he would go to the celestial realms.

†Tib. *sdom pa'i stobs*, another name for the power of restoration.

‡Darshaka is another name for Ajātashatru, who killed his father King Bimbisāra, one of the Buddha's principal patrons.

Furthermore, we read in the *Sovereign Lord of Sūtras: The Sublime Golden Light*,

> Those who for one thousand kalpas
> Have committed the most terrible evil deeds,
> By making full confession once
> Will purify them all.

And in the *Sūtra of Maitreya's Great Lion's Roar*,

> Whatever negative actions I have done unknowingly,
> I confess them.
> The wise, by confessing their faults,
> Live no longer with their deeds.

The *Sūtra on the Classification of Acts* states,

> If I reproach myself for the terrible deeds I've done,
> They will lose their strength.
> By confessing them and vowing to refrain,
> They will be completely eradicated.

In particular, the benefits of practicing the meditation and recitation of Vajrasattva are as mentioned in the *Tantra Common to All the Secret Teachings*:[311]

> Visualizing Vajrasattva,
> The single embodiment of all the buddhas,
> Daily, in the six periods,
> Recite twenty-one times
> The hundred syllables according to the ritual.
> By doing so, downfalls and the like will be blessed
> And will never grow greater.
> If you recite it one hundred thousand times—
> So the greatest accomplished beings have clearly explained—
> You will become the very embodiment of total purity.

And in the *Tantra of the Flower Array*,

By the power of meditating on Vajrasattva
And of the self-arisen hundred syllables,
The two obscurations will be purified.

In the *Tantra of the Three Verses on the Wisdom Mind*, we read,

Those who meditate on Vajrasattva
And recite the mantra perfectly
Will purify all their negative actions
And become the same as Vajrasattva.

Blanketed by the overwhelming darkness of the two obscurations,
We fail and languish in the forest of existence.
Lighting the way with the jeweled torch of the four powers,
Proceed to the isle of perfect liberation, O fortunate ones!

This completes the instruction on the meditation and recitation of Vajrasattva.

Dilgo Khyentse Rinpoche (1910–1991)

12. The Maṇḍala Offering, the Method for Completing the Two Accumulations

The maṇḍala offering is presented in three sections: (1) a general explanation of the principles, (2) a specific teaching on how to make the offering, and (3) a supplementary explanation of a few of the benefits of venerating the Three Jewels.

I. General explanation of the principles

Those who wish to better themselves cannot realize the result, omniscience, the greatest of goals, without relying on its causes, the two accumulations. And in particular, the heart of the main practice, the wisdom that is the realization of no-self, or the inexpressible innate gnosis that is profound emptiness, depends on the accessory conditions that are the two accumulations. We find this in the *Perfection of Wisdom*:

> Until one has completed the two sacred accumulations,
> One will never realize sacred emptiness.

And in the *Sūtra of the Play of the River That Leads to Peace*,

> Innate absolute wisdom can come
> Only as the mark of having accumulated merit and purified obscurations
> And through the blessings of a realized teacher.
> Know that it is foolish to seek any other means.

Now, although there are many ways to gather the two accumulations, the one that is easiest to practice, and the most beneficial, is the offering of the maṇḍala. As is stated in a tantra:

> If one offers to all the buddhas in the buddha-fields
> The universe of three billion worlds without exception
> Adorned with all things pleasing to the senses,
> One will perfect the gnosis of the buddhas.

It would be inappropriate to begin without first having some knowledge of a few essential points that need to be understood regarding the maṇḍala offering, so we will explain these under five headings: (1) the disadvantages of not offering the maṇḍala, (2) the reasons it is necessary to offer it, (3) when to offer it, (4) how to offer it, and (5) the benefits of offering the maṇḍala.

A. The disadvantages of not offering the maṇḍala

Unless one relies on the accumulation of merit, one will never complete its result, the accumulation of wisdom. And without completing the latter, one will not achieve any temporary and ultimate results that one may wish for, as is stated in a scripture:

> Should someone wish to accomplish the unsurpassable Great Vehicle
> But fail to offer the maṇḍala respectfully to the teacher and deity,
> He will not at once accomplish that same desired goal,
> And ultimately his progress to pure lands will be delayed.

And,

> Without relying on the path of the two accumulations,
> One will not accomplish anything.

B. The reasons it is necessary to offer the maṇḍala

The reasons it is necessary to make the maṇḍala offering amount to the opposite of the above disadvantages—namely, that on the temporary level one will accomplish everything one wishes, and ultimately it will bear fruit as enlightenment. We read in the *Essential Ornament*, by the master Mañjushrīkīrti,

> If one is diligent in the activities
> Of offering the maṇḍala, circumambulating stūpas,
> Performing fire offerings, consecrations,
> And torma rituals for the elemental spirits, greater and lesser,
> One's life span and merit will increase.
> These are the very causes of enlightenment,
> So exert yourself in these activities.

C. When to offer the maṇḍala

In general, you should offer the maṇḍala at all times, and in particular, at times when you think of the deity and the teacher, as the Great Orgyen has said:

> For people who want to attain freedom and omniscience quickly, the utmost diligence in offering the maṇḍala is extremely important, at all times and in all situations.

And,

> When you think of the deity and teacher,
> Or in the midst of an ocean-like gathering or when the Dharma is taught,
> Offer the maṇḍala, the essence of all Dharma practice.

D. How to offer the maṇḍala

There are three ways to offer the maṇḍala: (1) outwardly, (2) inwardly, and (3) secretly.

1. Offering the maṇḍala in an outward way

There are two sections: (1) the accomplishment maṇḍala, and (2) the offering maṇḍala. The first of these is divided into three: (1) the materials for the maṇḍala, (2) the materials for the piles, and (3) the arrangement and visualization.

a. The accomplishment maṇḍala

i. The materials for the maṇḍala

It has been taught that the best materials for the maṇḍala are gold and silver. Second best are common materials such conch shell and bell metal. Least good are clay, stone, and wood. We should use whatever we have and can afford.

As for the size, if the maṇḍala is of gold, it should be four fingers across, if it is of silver, a hand span, and if of other ordinary materials such as bell metal, no less than a cubit.

ii. The materials for the piles

The materials for the piles should correspond to whatever we can afford and is available. The best materials are jewels, second best are different kinds of medicinal fruits. Least best are various kinds of grains, and if they are not available, even stones, pebbles, and so on are acceptable. Whichever of these we offer, it is important to avoid factors such as showing off, being stingy, or choosing the easiest option, as these are faults that will spoil the offering.

iii. The arrangement and visualization

Wipe the maṇḍala free of dust with your hand and sprinkle it with scented water containing the purifying ingredients from a cow.* Set out as many piles as there are principal deities in the maṇḍala, or alternatively, following the general fashion, five piles—one in the center and four in the four directions. Place the accomplishment maṇḍala high on the altar in front of you. If you have them, also arrange any suitable offerings around it.

*Tib. *ba byung*. According to Kriya tantra, five ingredients collected under specific circumstances are especially pure: the milk, butter, cheese, urine, and dung of a red cow, born at an auspicious moment, and which has just calved for the first time. These have to be obtained during a lunar eclipse by a fully ordained monk who has been ordained fifteen years, kept his vows perfectly, and now renews his vows before milking the cow.

Visualize the piles as the deities of the maṇḍala according to your textual tradition, or just visualize them in the general way—that is, in the same way as the object of refuge described above. For detailed practice, there is a traditional way of performing the ritual for inviting the wisdom deity and dissolving it into the accomplishment maṇḍala, but this is not mentioned in most of the instruction texts, so for unelaborate practice it is not necessary.

In the case of someone with meager resources who cannot afford more than one maṇḍala or someone who cannot find one when there is an urgent need to make the maṇḍala offering, the point of the practice will still be achieved if they imagine the field of accumulation in the sky in front of them, for it depends mainly on their intention. We know this from the *Middle Sūtra of the Perfection of Wisdom*:

> For those who keep the Tathāgata in mind and say, "I pay homage to the Buddha!" the Tathāgata is present in front of them.

And in the *Sūtra of the Array of Qualities of Mañjuśrī's Buddha-Field*,

> All phenomena arise from conditions,
> They depend on the intention.
> Whatever prayers a person makes,
> He will accordingly obtain the fruit.
> For all who think of the Buddha,
> He dwells there in front of them:
> He continually blesses them
> And frees them from all evil.

In the *Sūtra of the King of Concentrations*, it is written,

> Whether they are walking, sitting, standing, or sleeping,
> For people who think of the moonlike Buddha,
> The Teacher is always there before them.
> They will attain the vast nirvāṇa.

And also,

> It is the buddhas' and their children's vow
> To come for anyone who thinks of them.

Alternatively, it is said in Padmasambhava's *Great Treatise on the Graded Path* that if you only have one maṇḍala, you should first arrange on it the piles as for the accomplishment maṇḍala. In them, visualize the field of accumulation, to which you should make offerings and prayers. After that, transfer the visualization of the field of accumulation into the sky above and gather up the piles. Wipe the maṇḍala clean, and use it again as the offering maṇḍala.

b. The offering maṇḍala

The materials and other details for the maṇḍala and piles are the same as those explained above.

In this context, when you are offering the maṇḍala one hundred thousand times or so, if you can afford to, renew the piles with fresh materials, and do not offer the old piles again. The old grains may be heaped up in front of a representation of the Three Jewels or given as charity to the poor, but you should never enjoy the use of them yourself. If you cannot afford to do that, add fresh materials for the piles to the old ones. In that way, make the offerings, counting the numbers. Whatever the case, it is important that the materials should be pure and clean and unspoiled by stinginess and so on.

As for when you are distributing the offerings on the maṇḍala, the practice is to hold the maṇḍala plate up in your left hand and set out the piles with your right hand. If it becomes too heavy—for example, as a result of accumulating large numbers of the offering—and you can no longer hold up the maṇḍala in your hand, place the maṇḍala on the table in front of you and replenish the piles there. There are numerous different instructions concerning the numbers of piles, the particularities of the Ancient and New Traditions, the maṇḍalas of the three buddha bodies, and so on. You should therefore practice according to your specific tradition. Here, because it is so well known, we shall explain the thirty-seven-element maṇḍala that is said to have been composed by the Protector of Beings, Chögyal Phakpa.[312]

First, wipe clean the maṇḍala plate with your hand while reciting the hundred syllables and the "Cloud of Offerings" incantation. This does not only imply that there are some impurities on the maṇḍala plate that need to be cleaned: it is in order to purify the contaminants in your own mind stream.

The maṇḍala of the universe

Next, take a few grains of barley* in your left hand and hold the maṇḍala plate on top of them. With the right hand, in order to symbolize soaking your mind stream with love and compassion, thoroughly sprinkle the maṇḍala base with scented water containing the purifying ingredients from a cow. As you do so, recite OṀ VAJRA BHŪMI and so on, and visualize it as the mighty golden ground, level, broad, and vast. Then, take a heap of flowers between your right thumb and ring finger, and as you say the mantra OṀ VAJRA REKHE and the other words, dispose the flowers in a circle, anticlockwise, on the maṇḍala base, and finally in the center, imagining that the mighty golden ground is encircled all around by the ring of mountains made of iron. If you have a ready-made ring of iron mountains† to place on the maṇḍala, you should do so at this point.

Next, as you recite "The king of mountains, Mount Meru," place a single large pile in the center, and visualize in the center of the mighty golden ground the king of mountains, Mount Meru, its four sides made of the four kinds of precious substances—the east side made of crystal, the south of beryl, the west of ruby, and the north of gold. It has four terraces, stepped one on top of the other, respectively, from the bottom up: Adamantine Turquoise, Piled High, Shining Crystal Light, and Tiered Wheels. Outside those, Mount Meru is surrounded by the seven square-shaped ranges of golden mountains, in order Yugaṃdhara, Īṣhādhara, Khadiraka, Sudarshana, Ashvakarṇa, Vinataka, and Nimiṃdhara. In between them are the seven seas of enjoyment, and outside them, the outermost ocean.

Next, set out the four continents, the eastern continent of Pūrvavideha and so on. Whether you do so with the "east" pointing toward you or pointing toward the object to which you are making the offering, the procedure is the same. In either case, distribute the piles clockwise in turn, starting with the east. The eastern continent, Pūrvavideha, is made of crystal, white in color and semicircular in shape, with its diameter facing Mount Meru and its circumference pointing toward the iron mountains. In the south is Jambudvīpa, which is made of beryl, blue in color and trapezoidal in shape, with the widest side facing Mount Meru and the smallest part pointing toward the perimeter. In the west is Godānīya, which is made of ruby, red in color

*Or other grains, medicinal fruits, or precious stones, depending on the materials being used for the offering.

†That is, the first of the three maṇḍala rings, if you have them.

and circular in shape. In the north is Uttarakuru, which is made of precious gold, yellow in color and square in shape.

After that, when you set out the piles for the subcontinents, Deha, Videha, and the others, for each continent arrange two subcontinents, one on the clockwise side and the other on the anticlockwise side of each continent in turn. In other words, place Deha on the clockwise side of the eastern continent, and Videha on its anticlockwise side. Similarly, place Chāmara and Aparachāmara on the clockwise and anticlockwise sides of the southern continent, Sāthā and Uttaramantriṇa on the clockwise and anticlockwise sides of the western continent, and Kuru and Kaurava on the clockwise and anticlockwise sides of the northern continent. These are all of the same substance, shape, color, and disposition as their respective main continents, but half their size.

With regard to the proportions of the mountains, continents, and so forth, there is no contradiction in adopting those generally given in the Abhidharma and Kālacakra scriptures. However, in our tradition we should mainly adopt the description given by the Great Omniscient One in the *Precious Treasury That Fulfills All Wishes*, though we will not mention this in detail here. In the context of the maṇḍala offering, I have given a summary above, but if you wish to know the details, you should look in that text.

Continue to set out the piles in order, matching them with the elements in the prayer. Next, in the eastern continent, are mountains of jewels made from all kinds of precious substances and of incalculable size. In the southern continent are wish-fulfilling trees, having the nature of the seven kinds of precious substances, their branches bending under the weight of their foliage, flowers, and fruit, and endowed with the capacity to grant every wish. In the western continent are golden-red bountiful cows, of beautiful form, a delight to the eyes, which have the quality of granting whatever one desires. In the northern continent are abundant crops that grow naturally without being cultivated or planted and are full of nourishment.

In front of the jewel mountains is a thousand-spoked wheel made of gold from the Jambu River and shining like the sun. In front of the wish-fulfilling trees is an eight-sided beryl stone, whose light rays dispel all the darkness around, up to a distance of a hundred leagues. It has the power to cool when it is hot and to warm when it is cold, and it sends down a rain of everything one could wish for. In front of the bountiful cows is the precious queen, who is free of all the defects of womankind and full of all excellent qualities; her mere touch has the power to give rise to the gnosis of bliss-emptiness. In front of the uncultivated crops is the precious minister, who is handsome, powerful, and skillful, full of abundant and perfect qualities, and enjoys an inexhaustible wealth of possessions.

To the southeast, between Deha and Aparachāmara, is the precious elephant, which is ash white and has six tusks. Its red, lofty crown is covered with a lattice of jewels, and it is as strong as a thousand ordinary elephants. To the southwest, between Chāmara and Uttaramantriṇa, is the marvelous and precious horse, beautifully colored like the blue feathers on a peacock's neck. It is a fine animal, free of physical illness and weaknesses, and can gallop round our world of Jambudvīpa three times in a day. To the northwest, between Sāthā and the subcontinent of Kaurava is the precious general, who is courageous, skillful, and well versed in the arts of war. He is thus adept at advancing and withdrawing the four regiments of his army. He is fitted out in a coat of armor of dazzling brilliance. To the northeast, between Aparachāmara and Kuru, is the great treasure vase, which is full of everything one could need or want and decorated with jewels.

In front of the precious wheel, in the east, is the lady of charm, who is white, graceful, and lovely to behold. She holds a mirror and displays an inconceivable range of charming manners. To the south, in front of the precious jewel, is the lady of garlands: she is blue and holds a garland of precious stones. In front of the precious queen in the west is the red lady of song, who holds a *vīṇā** and is singing melodiously. In front of the precious minister in the north is the green lady of dance, performing a dance with different choreographic gestures.

To the southeast, in front of the precious elephant, is the lady of flowers, who is white and holds a flower. In front of the precious horse in the southwest is the lady of incense, who is yellow and holds an incense burner. In front of the precious general in the northwest is the lady of lamps, who is red and holds a light. In front of the great treasure vase in the northeast is the lady of perfume: she is green and holds a conch filled with scented water.

In the sky above the lady of charm is the maṇḍala of the sun, made of fire crystal and blazing with light. In the sky above and in front of the lady of song is the maṇḍala of the moon, made of water crystal, clear and radiant. In the sky in front of the lady of dance is the precious parasol, which is white with a handle of gold. And in the sky in front of the lady of garlands is the

*The vīṇā is an Indian instrument similar to the lute.

banner of universal victory, which is straight and supple and embellished with filigree ornaments.

These last two are replaced in some traditions, such as the those of the *Wheel of Time* and *Spontaneous Freeing of the Mind*, by Rāhu and Ketu—the dark blue Rāhu in the east and yellow Ketu in the west.* Both of them shine brightly, emitting rays of light, and are circular in shape.

Whichever tradition you adopt, in the middle of all of these and in the intervening spaces, everything is completely filled with all the abundant and perfect riches of the celestial and human worlds, utterly pure and pleasing. All these elements radiate a wealth of offerings in keeping with their respective qualities, teeming like dust particles densely gathered in rays of sunlight. And inside each of those tiny particles of dust are amassed as many maṇḍalas again, as we have just described, all manifested by means of concentration, limitlessly, beyond what the ordinary mind can measure. Offering all this is well known as the way of making offerings described in the life story of the bodhisattva Samantabhadra. In some traditions, one imagines that from the heart of one bodhisattva Samantabhadra issue forth countless billions of myriad rays of light, and on the tip of each light ray is an emanation of Samantabhadra, each offering the maṇḍala; and from the navel of each of those emanations, similar light rays emanate, creating an offering that fills the whole of space. This is held to be Samantabhadra's way of making the maṇḍala offering.

Thus, we read in the *Guru's Graded Path of the Practice of Dharma*,

> The foundation is the mighty golden ground,
> Encircled outside by the mountains of precious iron,
> In the middle of which is the supreme, lofty king of mountains
> Made of five kinds of precious substance and spontaneously
> formed,
> Perfectly shaped, beautiful and lovely to behold,
> Surrounded by the seven golden mountain ranges and the seven
> seas of enjoyment.
> In the east is Pūrvavideha, in the south Jambudvīpa,
> The west is adorned with Godānīya,
> The north by the great continent of Uttarakuru,

*Tib. sGra can dus me, Skt. Rāhu and Ketu, two figures in Indian mythology representing the ascending and descending lunar nodes that give rise to eclipses.

With their eight subcontinents—
Deha and Videha, Chāmara and Aparachāmara,
Sāthā and Uttaramantriṇa, and Kuru and Kaurava.
The sun and moon, Rāhu and Ketu,
And all the wealth and pleasures of gods and humans, perfect and complete—
This I offer to the Teacher, the Three Jewels, and all the retinue.

2. Offering the maṇḍala in an inward way

There are two sections: (1) visualizing the object of offering, the accomplishment maṇḍala, and (2) presenting the offering maṇḍala.

a. Visualizing the object of offering, the accomplishment maṇḍala

The true nature of all the phenomena that comprise one's own body—the aggregates, constituents, and senses-and-fields—exists from the very beginning as the complete three seats, the wheel of the maṇḍala of the deity. This is the accomplishment maṇḍala, as described in the *Secret Essence of the Magical Display*:

The vajra aggregates
Are known as the five perfect buddhas.
All the many senses-and-fields
Are the maṇḍala of bodhisattvas.
Earth and water are Locanā and Māmakī,
Fire and wind are Pāṇḍaravāsinī and Samayatārā,
Space is Dhātvīshvarī.
The three worlds are a buddha-field from the beginning.
Everything without exception, the whole of phenomena,
Is nothing other than the enlightened state.
Phenomena that are other than buddha
Cannot be found, even by the buddhas themselves.

This being so from the very beginning, one only has to visualize it with the certainty of knowing that it is so. Apart from that, there is no need whatsoever for generating the deity, dissolving it, and so on.

b. Presenting the offering maṇḍala

When a correspondence is made between the inner phenomena of the aggregates, constituents, and senses-and-fields that make up one's own body and the outer container, the universe embellished with the four continents and so on, we offer the maṇḍala considering that our skin is the mighty golden ground. Our blood is the scented sprinkling water. The vertebral column is the ring of iron mountains. The head is the central Mount Meru. The right arm is the eastern continent, Pūrvavideha. The left arm is the southern continent, Jambudvīpa. The right leg is the western continent, Godānīya. The left leg is the northern continent, Uttarakuru. Our two eyes are the sun and moon. The fingers and toes are the subcontinents. The ribs are the seven golden mountain ranges. The intestines are the seven seas of enjoyment. The lungs are the wish-fulfilling trees. The heart is the great treasure vase. The kidneys are the bountiful cows. The liver is the uncultivated crop. The brain is the ambrosia of the gods. The hair and eyebrows are the forest of sandalwood trees. The hairs on one's body are hills covered with saffron crocuses. The five sense organs are the goddesses of the sense pleasures. The bodhichitta is the mass of human and celestial riches.

In the *Graded Path of the Practice of Dharma*, we read,

> In the pure, measureless palace of my own body, with its channels and elements,
> Adorned with the luster of the five sense organs,
> The constituents and senses-and-fields are perfectly pure.
> These I offer to the teacher and Three Jewels in the enjoyment-body buddha-field.

3. Offering the maṇḍala in a secret way

Again, there are two sections.

a. The accomplishment maṇḍala

In the nature of mind—the expanse of the one and only essence free from elaboration since the very beginning—all the phenomena of saṃsāra and nirvāṇa are complete in being spontaneously present from the beginning, without having to be sought. This is the accomplishment maṇḍala, as indicated in the *Tantra of the All-Creating King*:

> Oh! The center, the essence of the unmistaken meaning,
> Completely embodies its surroundings—saṃsāra and nirvāṇa, great bliss.*
> This is the essential maṇḍala, the root of all.
> Understand that it includes all maṇḍalas without exception.

b. The offering maṇḍala

The correlation between the secret maṇḍala offering and the relative maṇḍala is as follows: The ground, the nature of mind that is the actual condition of things free from elaboration, the primordial ground of all, pervading everything, is the mighty golden ground. The inseparability of that state from the moisture of compassion and bodhichitta is the scented sprinkling water. The essential nature's abiding without bias or limitation is the outer rim of iron mountains. The five kinds of gnosis—mirrorlike gnosis and so on—are Mount Meru, the king of mountains, in the center and the four great continents. The eight consciousnesses, clear and unobstructed, are the eight subcontinents. The play of the five pleasures of the senses boundlessly arising as the objects of the six consciousnesses comprises the offerings, complete and perfect, of existence and peace. All these are liberated as they arise in the expanse of primordial purity, awareness-emptiness, arising in the state free of fixation. The wisdom that realizes this is the sun. Manifesting from that is skillful means, great compassion for sentient beings who do not have such realization. The effortless arising of that compassion is the moon.

In short, everything that comprises phenomenal existence, saṃsāra and nirvāṇa, is complete as the self-manifestation of the empty nature of mind. If we realize this, we are offering the absolute maṇḍala, which transcends all concepts of offering, a recipient of the offering, and a person making the offering. The *Graded Path of the Practice of Dharma* expresses it thus:

*These two lines refer to the two elements of the Tibetan word *dkyil 'khor*, which translates the Sanskrit word *maṇḍala*; *dkyil* means "center," while *'khor* refers to all that surrounds that center.

In the pure, measureless palace of the nature of mind realized as
the body of truth,
Resting in the nonconceptual state of emptiness-clarity, free of
grasping,
Is innate gnosis, pure from the very beginning.
This I offer to the teacher and Three Jewels in the truth-body
buddha-field.

E. The benefits of offering the maṇḍala

In the *Compendium of the Teacher's Wisdom*, a treasure discovered by Sangye Lingpa, we find,

> The result and benefits of having offered the maṇḍala are as follows: On the temporary level, we will have great wealth—abundant riches and freedom from the sufferings of poverty and deprivation. Unshakable faith in the sublime teacher and extraordinary confidence in the teachings of the Great Vehicle will be born in us. We will delight all beings and be respected by everyone.
>
> The mass of merit from respectfully offering the maṇḍala once, on a special day, in the presence of the teacher and sacred representations of the Three Jewels and so forth, will exceed that of the extensive deeds of making outer and inner offerings and prayers to all the sugatas and their assemblies for countless kalpas. All our wishes will be accomplished. All the host of evil deeds, obscurations, and transgressions that we have amassed over kalpas and kalpas will be cleansed and purified. From offering the maṇḍala once, all the prayers and aspirations we have made with faithful minds will be accomplished without effort. For this reason, the sublime beings of future generations should be diligent in performing the maṇḍala offering.

And,

> Of all the forms of merit that condense all virtuous practice, the merit of offering the maṇḍala is by far the greatest. Extraordinary concentration and realization will be born in us. Ultimately,

> in our future lives, we will enjoy everything we could wish for, acquire glory and wealth, and travel to the buddha-fields. All the sugatas will keep us in mind and so on. No one can measure such a mass of merit.

In the *Maṇḍala Sūtra*, too, we read,

> Generosity in adding cow's dung and urine,*
> Discipline in cleaning,
> Patience in removing insects,
> Diligence in the endeavor one applies,
> Concentration as one thinks of these,
> Wisdom in very clear visualization—
> These are the six transcendent perfections
> That make the Capable One's maṇḍala the perfect deed.
> For those who do this practice physically,
> A golden complexion will be theirs;
> From every kind of sickness they'll be free.
> Far superior to gods and humans,
> They'll have the splendor of the moon,
> An abundance of precious stones and gold.
> And in the very best of households they'll be born,
> In royal or Buddhist families.

The master Ashvaghoṣha also taught in a similar way. And in the *Secret Tantra of Vajrakīlaya*, it is written,

> To prepare the maṇḍala to gather virtue is diligence,
> To clear it of insects and other creatures is the highest patience.
> To wipe it clean is the discipline of enlightenment,
> To suffuse the offering with medicinal substances and scented water is generosity.
> To crown it with flowers is wisdom.
> To consider the offerings as deities is concentration.
> Inviting the deities, requesting them to be seated, obeisance, offering, and circumambulating are to be known as skillful means.

*That is, the purifying ingredients from a cow. See footnote on p. 436 above.

Purifying the two obscurations and completing the two
accumulations is strength.
The result one obtains from it is gnosis.
Knowing that it is for beings' sake is aspiration.
Thus the maṇḍala truly completes the transcendent perfections.
Be diligent, therefore, in actually practicing the maṇḍala.

To sum up, by offering the maṇḍala, the six or ten transcendent perfections are completed, so that one achieves all the corresponding benefits. For this reason, as it is said in the scriptures,

The virtue of offering the maṇḍala,
Which gives rise to vast qualities—
Even the noble beings dare not tell.

Thus, the *Fifty Verses on the Teacher* states,

With the utmost devotion, three times a day,
Offer maṇḍalas of flowers, join your hands,
Honor the masters who teach you,
And make obeisance with your crown at their feet.

And in the *Approach to the Ultimate*, we read,

In the three breaks between sessions, observing extreme purity,
Wash your mouth, hands, and feet,
Then take some perfect flowers and before the teacher
Perform the perfectly round maṇḍala of the victorious ones.

You should make a constant effort to practice accordingly.

II. Specific teaching on how to make the offering

If you have an accomplishment maṇḍala actually set up in front, use it as the support for your visualization. Otherwise, visualize the maṇḍala of the field of accumulation in the sky in front of you as you did the object of refuge. Now, for the offering maṇḍala, take a maṇḍala made of precious substances, or whatever you can afford, or if you do not have one, an earthen base. Wipe it clean, and sprinkle it with scented water containing the purifying ingredients from a cow. Then, physically, distribute the piles of flowers. Verbally, with one voice together with all sentient beings, recite the lines of the maṇḍala ritual according to your own textual tradition, for example:

> The golden ground, Mount Meru and its perimeter,
> The rings of golden mountains, the seas of enjoyment, the four continents and the eight subcontinents,
> All the riches of gods and men completely filling the universe
> I offer, visualized as a pure buddha-field.[313]

Mentally, make the offering, visualizing inconceivable thousands of millions of universes comprising Mount Meru resting on the mighty golden ground, with the seas, the four continents, the subcontinents, the sun and moon, and so forth as described above, piled high and completely filled with all the magnificent and abundant riches and possessions of the gods and humankind.

In addition, you should visualize and offer on a vast scale the pure manifested buddha-fields, beautifully embellished with boundless riches, completely filled with hosts of buddhas and bodhisattvas. They contain manifested gods and goddesses offering immense clouds of offerings, and a boundless wealth of the teachings of the Great Vehicle. All these are manifested through the immeasurable power of the noble beings' completion of the two accumulations and the strength of their powers of memory, concentrations, aspirations, and gnosis. Offer everything there is, reaching the furthest limits of space, dwelling as the expanse of reality and as the realm of sentient beings, and arising in the ever-revolving wheel of eternity. Offer also the bodies, possessions, and sources of good accumulated by yourself and others throughout the three times. All these offerings should be mentally combined into one and continually manifested as an inconceivable offering like that displayed by the bodhisattva Samantabhadra.

At the same time, pray one-pointedly for your wishes to be fulfilled. Pray that the extraordinary qualities of experience and realization may swiftly arise in your own and others' minds—qualities such as faith, determination to be free, love, compassion, bodhichitta, the correct view, and the wisdom of realization of the actual condition of things. Pray that you may attain the highest realization and have uninterrupted experiences. Pray that everything you perceive appears as an auspicious link and that whatever you do will benefit others.

With this, perform the offering for as long as you can—a hundred, thousand, ten thousand, a hundred thousand times, and so on. At the end, the field of accumulation and the maṇḍala of offerings take the form of the letter HŪṀ and dissolve into you. Then rest for a little while in the state of great bliss, devoid of concepts related to the three spheres. After that, conclude the practice with suitable prayers of dedication and aspiration, such as:

> By this positive action may all beings
> Complete the accumulation of merit and wisdom
> And attain the two supreme kāyas,
> Which arise from merit and wisdom.

In between sessions, instead of being careless all the time, be diligent in increasing your accumulations of merit and wisdom by such means as prostrating to the representations of the Three Jewels, making offerings to them, and circumambulating them.

III. A supplementary explanation, related to the above, of a few of the benefits of venerating the Three Jewels

There are three sections: (1) the essence, (2) the etymological definition, and (3) the different aspects of veneration.

A. Essence

The essence of veneration is to make physical, verbal, and mental offerings to those worthy of esteem and to please them by means of material gifts.*

B. Etymological definition

The Sanskrit term *pūjā*, meaning "veneration," refers to something that is

*Throughout this section we have translated the Tibetan term *mchod pa*, usually rendered as "offering," in its broader sense of "veneration," which covers such "offerings" as prostrations, music, songs, praises, and so on. Another translation in this context could be "worship."

prepared beforehand, is offered repeatedly to please the object of veneration, and is actually presented in the form of respectful offerings that serve the recipient.

C. Different aspects of veneration

A general explanation is given in *Ornament of the Mahāyāna Sūtras*:

> In order to complete the two accumulations,
> Those whose minds are full of faith
> Offer to the buddhas robes and so forth,
> In both real and imagined ways.
> The offering of one who has made the prayer
> That the coming of the Buddha be beneficial,
> Offered without conceptualizing the three spheres,
> Is a complete offering to the Buddha.[314]

A complete act of veneration is thus taught as being one made with six aspects: (1) What leads one to engage in an act of veneration is faith associated with clarity of mind. (2) The way the act is dedicated takes the form of the aspiration that oneself and others complete the two accumulations. (3) The object of one's veneration may be a support that is actually present before one or one that is visualized. (4) The materials that are offered are pleasing articles such as garments and ornaments. (5) The causal factors behind the act of veneration are the aspiration prayers made in one's previous lives that the coming of the Buddha will be beneficial. And (6) the act of veneration is performed with gnosis: it is imbued with wisdom free from the concepts of the three spheres—namely, an act of veneration, a venerator, and an object of veneration.

Furthermore, it is said that the act of veneration should have the following six features: It should be devoid of complacency,* vast, joyous, beneficial, untainted, and made with a virtuous attitude. The *Commentary on Difficult Points in "The Way of the Bodhisattva"* speaks of six supreme features: The supreme support is the attitude, the wish to attain enlightenment. The supreme purpose is the welfare of all sentient beings. The supreme materials

*One should never be satisfied with acts of veneration and feel that one has done enough.

are those that are pleasing. The supreme skill in means is the perfect purity of the three spheres. The supreme purity is freedom from counteractive contaminants. And the supreme dedication is the transformation of one's aspiration into great enlightenment.

In the *Bodhisattva Stage*, we read of ten forms of veneration: veneration of the Buddha's body, veneration of shrines, veneration in person, indirect veneration by visualization, veneration performed by oneself, veneration that one has entrusted others to perform, veneration with riches and honor, veneration on a vast scale, veneration without defilements, and veneration through practice. The Dharma and the Saṅgha are to be venerated in similar manner, as appropriate.[315]

Thus, there are numerous different ways of classifying veneration, but here we will give an explanation in terms of the purity of four things: (1) the fields, (2) the intention, (3) the materials, and (4) the implementation.

1. Pure fields

The bodhisattva Shāntideva speaks of three fields in general:

> You will reap great virtues in the fields of excellence
> In the fields of benefits and sorrow.[316]

Fields of excellence are one's teachers and the Three Jewels. Fields of benefits are one's parents and fellow spiritual practitioners. Fields of sorrow are beings such as the sick, the destitute, and those without a protector.

The *Sūtra of Pure Aspiration*, on the other hand, mentions two fields—the object of offering, which is the field of the buddhas, and the object of giving, which is the field of sentient beings:

> Formerly did I tend the field of beings
> And the field of the mighty ones,
> From which I've harvested the perfect crop
> Of a buddha's boundless qualities.

There are numerous other ways of classifying the fields, but the most important ones are the Three Precious Jewels, as is explained in the *Sūtra of the King of Dharma*:

In the world with all its gods,
Apart from the Three Jewels,
There are none worthy of offerings,
So offer everything to them.

And in the *Garret Sūtra*,

There is no teacher like the Buddha,
No protection like the Dharma,
No fertile field like the Saṅgha.
Make offerings, therefore, to these three.

And in the *Heap of Jewels*,

Thus, in the world with all its gods, the Three Jewels are the ones worthy of homage, worthy of salutation with folded hands; they are the supreme fields of merit.

Even greater than all of them is one's teacher, as we read in the *Sūtra of the Ornament of the Light of Gnosis*:

Sons or daughters of good family with the greatest faith who serve a spiritual friend will acquire a boundless, immeasurable heap of merit, greater than that of venerating the buddhas for kalpas as numerous as the grains of sand in the Ganges River.

And in the *Tantra of Supreme Gnosis*,

Better than the heap of merit
From venerating the Buddha for a kalpa
Is that of anointing with a drop of oil
A single hair of one's teacher's body.

2. Pure intention

In the *Bodhisattva Stage*, we read,

> Bodhisattvas do not give for the sake of fame or in order to hear their praises sung. They do not give in order to compete with others. They do not give out of fear of becoming poor.* They do not give in worship of Indra, the universal monarch, or Īshvara. They do not give with a view to a future result. Everything they give is given and dedicated for the sake of unsurpassable, true, and perfect enlightenment.

And in the *Sūtra of the Questions of Subāhu*, there is an extensive explanation, beginning as follows:

> Subāhu, were you to ask how bodhisattva mahāsattvas complete transcendent generosity, Subāhu, bodhisattva mahāsattvas practice transcendent generosity in their search for the wealth of the teachings, and not for reasons contrary to the Dharma. They give equally and not partially. They do not harm other creatures or other sentient beings. They give gifts without creating fear. They do not give for the sake of different forms of fame and praise. It is not in order to avoid others' negative comments. It is not out of fear. It is not in the hope of being benefited in return. It is not in order to reach the higher realms. It is not with hypocrisy. It is not in order to be flattered. It is not out of contempt.

In brief, bodhisattvas do not give with defiled motivations such as rivalry with others, or with the intention of striving for prosperous circumstances in existence, such as happiness and fame in this life and any resultant samsaric happiness in future lives. Furthermore, they do not give with the inferior intention of striving just for the result of nirvāṇa. This does not mean that there is no ripened karmic effect in general of giving with such attitudes, but that doing so does not yield the most complete result.

A defiled motivation is like eating delicious food mixed with poison: it will never nourish the life force of liberation. On the other hand, even if we strive for the result of happiness in the celestial and human worlds or for the results of the listeners and solitary realizers, these respective results

*Bodhisattvas' practice of generosity is not motivated by fear of the karmic result of stinginess and failure to give, which is poverty in future lives.

will ripen once and then be consumed, like the plantain tree, which gives fruit once and then is spent. Furthermore, if they encounter other powerful conditions like anger, these positive results are interrupted and go to waste. So this is not what we should wish for.

What, then, should our intention be? As explained repeatedly above, our acts of veneration should be imbued with the thought of enlightenment, the excellent intention of striving for perfect enlightenment for others' benefit. If they are so imbued, all the faults that have just been mentioned will be prevented, and the results, instead of going to waste, will grow more and more, like the excellent wish-fulfilling tree, as has been explained in detail above. In the *Mass of Jewels Sūtra*, too, it is said that to toss a single flower in offering without parting from the thought of attaining omniscience* creates greater merit than that of all the beings in the three worlds each building a stūpa as big as Mount Meru and venerating it for as many kalpas as there are grains of sand in the Ganges. And in the *Sūtra on Maitreya's Setting Forth*, we read,

> Were all beings to become buddhas,
> Endowed with unlimited confidence and eloquence,
> And for all the previous kalpas of saṃsāra
> A single being were to venerate them,
> Far greater than this being's merit would be that
> Of a single wise person who has aroused
> The intention to attain supreme enlightenment
> And offers a single flower.
> Even if one set about explaining that merit
> For many myriads of kalpas,
> One would never finish
> Describing the merit that results.

The reasoning behind the benefits being so great is explained in the *Jewel Garland*:

> As boundless as are the realms of sentient beings,
> So too are the benefits.[317]

*That is, with bodhichitta.

And Shāntideva says,

If with kindly generosity
One merely has the wish to soothe
The aching heads of other beings,
Such merit knows no bounds.
No need to speak, then, of the wish
To drive away the endless pain
Of each and every living being,
Bringing them unbounded excellence.[318]

And,

If the simple thought to be of help to others
Exceeds in worth the worship of the Buddhas,
What need is there to speak of actual deeds
That bring about the weal and benefit of beings?[319]

3. Pure materials

Even if the fields and the intention are pure, if the materials are not pure, they will not be suitable as offerings to the Three Jewels. We read in a sūtra,

Do not offer goods that have been stolen or seized,
The property of the Three Jewels, or things that harm others.
The best are things one really values,
That give pleasure, or are beneficial.

And,

Offer things that are not contaminated by evil deeds
And that will help and please the Saṅgha and others.

Furthermore, it is said in the *Jewel Ornament of Liberation*, summarizing what is written in the *Bodhisattva Stage*, that bodhisattvas do not give to those who ask for poison, fire, weapons, and other things that the recipients might use to harm themselves or bring harm to others. They do not give to those who ask for nets, traps, or hunting equipment, or instructions on how to use them—in short, anything that will cause injury and suffering. They do not give their parents or leave their parents as a pledge. They do not give their spouses or children against their will to others who want them. They do not make small gifts if they are wealthy.

The *Sūtra of the Questions of the Ṛṣi Vyāsa* speaks of thirty-two instances of generosity that are impure because of their field, intention, application, or materials. They have been summarized by the learned beings of the past in the following verse:

> Gifts that lead to wrong view and lack of faith,
> Gifts that reward, or that lead to attachment,
> Gifts to kings or fire sacrifices or water offerings,*
> Gifts to those of whom one is afraid,
> Gifts of poison, weapons, and the meat of animals that have been killed,
> Gifts of alcohol made to the careless,
> Gifts made in order to gain influence over people,
> Gifts to musicians who will sing one's praises,
> Gifts to astrologers, gifts of others' riches to one's friends,
> Gifts of someone else's grain for wild animals to enjoy eating,
> Gifts to artisans, to doctors,† and gifts made contemptuously,
> Gifts that lead to doubt as to the karmic result, or to regret,
> Gifts made with the thought that they will help one in a future life,
> Gifts made so that one will experience the fully ripened effect oneself,
> Invocations and offerings made to help when one is old, sick, or dying,
> Gifts made in order to be celebrated elsewhere,
> Gifts to show that one really can be generous,
> Gifts to procure a woman, or because one does not have children,‡
> Gifts made with a view to gain in future lives,

*These three forms of giving are impure because they involve selfish, or self-furthering, motives.

†Giving to artisans and doctors refers to making gifts in the hope that they will freely provide their services later.

‡That is, giving one's wealth indiscriminately for lack of anyone to inherit it.

And those made to the rich while neglecting the poor—
These are the thirty-two forms of impure gift.

Moreover, there are numerous mentions in the scriptures regarding things such as the three Dharma robes that bodhisattvas who have taken monastic ordination must not give. The most important thing, however, is that whatever the quality or quantity of the things one offers, if their production has involved shameful deeds, inflicting harm on others—for example, things that have been stolen or robbed from others, or that have been produced by businesses in which animals are killed—then offering such things is not the way to please the buddhas. This has been mentioned in detail above and is reiterated in the following quotation from a sūtra:

To help sentient beings is to respect me: not to respect others is
not to respect me.
My activities and those of the respectful are never without
compassion:
Acting without compassion is the inferior way.
Through compassion, one understands what harms: without it,
one does not.
Those who are filled with compassion for sentient beings
Are venerating me; they hold my doctrine dear.
Those with discipline, learning, compassion, and intelligence
Will always thus make offerings to the Sugata.
It was in terms of helping beings that I accomplished this:
This buddha body was produced solely by benefiting beings.
How can those who, even in intent, do harm to sentient beings
Follow me? They have nothing to do with me.
Those who cultivate a joyful heart are venerating me,
So even helping beings a little is an offering to me.
Offerings that are violent in nature and bring about harm to others
Are not true offerings, however perfectly performed.
You might, with joy in mind, make gifts
Of your spouse, your children, power and wealth and kingdom,
Your flesh, blood, fat, your body and your eyes;
But if in doing so you injure anyone, it is me you harm.
To bring the greatest benefit to sentient beings is the greatest
offering to me.

To gravely harm sentient beings is the worst injury to me.
Beings' happiness is mine, their suffering is mine,
So when someone harms a sentient being, what do you think it does to me?
It was in dependence on beings that I pleased the buddhas and gathered virtue;
Thanks to beings, too, I achieved the transcendent perfections, the fulfillment of their welfare.
With beings' benefit in mind, I cultivated diligence and subdued the demons,
And in that way, all I did for beings' sake brought me to buddhahood.
If, throughout my lives, I had had no wish to bring joy to living beings,
Whom could I have relied on for the birth of loving-kindness and compassion?
On whom, what field or ground, could my quest for liberation, my joys and suchlike have depended?
For their sake, over long periods of time, I trained my mind in compassion.
To those very living beings I gave many gifts, of elephants and the like,
And from beings who were suitable vessels I accepted gifts.
For beings who suffered all sorts of woes, I grew in compassion.
Other than caring for beings, I had no other goal.
If it were not for living beings overwhelmed by the many miseries in cyclic existence,
For whom would I have taken birth and made my own their never-ending pains?
If it were not to bring joy to sentient beings, for whom would I have achieved this state,
That of a great being adorning saṃsāra—a sugata?
As long as my doctrine shines on beings in this world,
You should remain to bring the highest benefit to others and to equalize yourselves and others.
Apart from the unstinting application of my teachings to benefit sentient beings,
There is no point in tiring yourself nurturing this body with food.

The Venerable Dhārmika Subhūtighoṣha sums this up as follows:

To benefit oneself and others
And avoid harming others
Is merit, the opposite is sin,
So the Buddha has said.

Accordingly, it is very important that anything we offer should be unadulterated by negative actions and prepared cleanly and purely, without any taint of things like stinginess. *Ornament of the Mahāyāna Sūtras* states,

The tender generosity of bodhisattvas
Is free of shameful deeds, is based on purity,
Leads to happiness, and is protective,
Unquestioning, and without stain.[320]

4. Pure implementation

Even if the materials are pure, if they are offered impurely, the offering will be flawed. This is why it is said in the *Sūtra of the Sublime Being*:

> The Lord spoke, "Monks, these five constitute the gifts of a sublime being. What are the five? They are gifts made by a sublime being with faith. Gifts made respectfully. Gifts made with that person's own hand. Gifts made in a timely fashion. And gifts made without inflicting harm on others."

And it goes on to describe these in detail, together with their benefits. In the *Teaching on the Benefits of Generosity*, we read,

> In order to eliminate stinginess, give with faith. Give in a timely fashion. Make gifts that are completely pure in the three respects approved by the Tathāgata.* In order to eliminate all the faults related to disturbances of the mind, give respectfully. In order make the best use of your body, which is without essence,† give with your own hands.

*The recipient, the gift itself, and the intention should be perfectly pure.
†Lit. "in order to take the essence of the body, which is without essence," meaning "to make the best use of the body, even though it is empty by nature."

And,

> If you make gifts while in a state of love, you will be free of malice. Similarly, if you make gifts while in a state of compassion, you will never be harmed. If you give with joy, you will obtain the gift of no fear. If you give with equanimity, you will be rid of unhappiness. If you make different kinds of gifts, you will obtain all kinds of riches. If you give without any hope of reward, you will attain the fully ripened fruit of unsurpassable, true, and perfect enlightenment. Monks, the wise practice generosity in these thirty-seven ways.

The *Sūtra on the Perfection of Generosity* states,

> By giving with your own hands, you will be honored. By giving gifts respectfully, you will be revered by others, even by relatives and others with whom you are on familiar terms.* By making gifts in a timely fashion, riches will come to you at the proper time and they will multiply. By making fine gifts in an appropriate manner, you will be able to appreciate the nice things you have, such as your bed and clothes. By giving things that do not harm others, you will acquire lasting wealth. By giving things while accepting unhappy situations, you will be loved by those around you.

And it gives a lengthy explanation, beginning:

> In practicing generosity in that way, do not give with attachment. Do not give with hatred. Do not give when you are upset. Do not give with contempt. Do not give with blows. Do not give in order to exterminate. Do not give while despising people. Do not give while criticizing people. Do not give with arrogance and pride. Do not give to show off. Do not give just what is left. Do not give things that are rotten or spoiled.
>
> Instead, you should give whatever gifts you make respectfully. Give as if to a superior. Give as if making an offering. Give with expressions of courtesy. Give in plenty. Give what is of good

*Those with whom you are familiar might not normally treat you with great reverence.

> quality. Give with the greatest joy, give gladly. Give purely and on a vast scale. Give with your own hands. Give politely and respectfully. Give with a pure, virtuous intention. Give without stinginess. Give without holding back. Give unhesitatingly. Give without fear. Give magnanimously.

In this regard, it is stated in the sūtras that the Three Jewels are particularly important objects,* for they are the supreme refuge, receiving the homage of the gods and all beings. The Three Jewels are the object of veneration and the field of merit for the gods and all beings, worthy of their respect and possessed of a boundless mass of qualities. So even a slightly negative action directed toward the Three Jewels, involving lack of faith, disrespect, and other such factors, gives rise to boundless karmic consequences. For this reason, in venerating the Three Jewels, you should not be tainted by faults such as disrespect, carelessness, lack of cleanliness, limiting the offering, scornfulness, laziness, and miserliness. Instead, with faith in the Three Jewels, and keeping in mind the particular benefits, you should maintain a clear state of mind, with boundless joy and enthusiasm, in which your senses are restrained from careless behavior. The flowers and so forth that you have to offer should be of good quality, clean, and beautifully arranged. You should make the offering with pure intention and respectful implementation, and set it out perfectly and bountifully in a way that has the power to inspire and delight you and anyone else who sees it, as is described in the *Prayer of Good Action*:

> All arranged as perfectly as possible,
> I offer to all the conquerors.

And in *The Way of the Bodhisattva*,

> To the Buddhas, those thus gone,
> And to the sacred Dharma, spotless and supremely rare,
> And to the Buddha's offspring, oceans of good qualities,
> That I might gain this precious attitude, I make a perfect offering.[321]

*The Tibetan word *gnyan*, here translated as "important," is often used for powerful spirits, whom one never risks upsetting, and for haunted places where it is best to tread softly. The implication here is that the Three Jewels are never to be taken lightly.

The actual forms that this sort of perfectly pure veneration take can be categorized in many ways, but here they will be indicated under two headings: (1) common, limited forms of veneration, and (2) the unsurpassable form of veneration.

a. Common, limited forms of veneration

Generally speaking, all forms of veneration to those supreme fields, the Three Jewels, are unsurpassable. However, in this context, they are distinguished in terms of material veneration and veneration through one's accomplishment. Material forms of veneration will be discussed in the order in which they are indicated in the *Prayer of Good Action* and other texts.

With regard to forms of veneration that are made in reality, let us begin with the benefits of paying homage to representations of the Three Jewels. It is said in the Vinaya texts,

> Monks, the fully ripened effect of your prostrating with faith to stūpas containing the hair and nails of a tathāgata is that as long as you do not give rise to anger toward your fellow monks, you will experience the happiness of a universal monarch as many times as the number of atoms beneath you down to the mighty golden ground, and you will be born among gods and humans.

And in the *Garret Sūtra*,

> Ānanda, those beings who fold their hands and prostrate, saying, "I submit obeisance to the Bhagavan, the Tathāgata, Arhat, true and perfect Buddha," I will care for, and they will pass beyond suffering.

And the *Avalokinī Sūtra* gives lengthy explanations, for example:

> Greater than the merit of honoring a hundred thousand myriad buddhas
> For immeasurable millions of kalpas

Will be the merit of prostrating to a stūpa*
In the future terrible ages of this kalpa.

In the *Sūtra on the Classification of Acts*, it is said that by prostrating to representations of the Three Jewels, folding one's hands before them, sweeping the place clean, and offering canopies, bells, pennants, flowers, garlands, lamps, perfumed substances and incense, musical instruments and cymbals, one will, in each case, obtain ten great benefits, and by clothing them, one will obtain twelve benefits. These and other benefits can be referred to elsewhere in my writings. In the *Vajra Net Tantra*, we find,

If the merit of one who,
With reverence in body, speech, and mind,
Prostrates to the body of the Buddha
Were to take form, the world could not contain it.

The benefits of singing praises are mentioned in a sūtra, where it is said that in the past our Teacher sang a single verse in praise of the Tathāgata Tiṣhya, as a result of which he gathered nine kalpas' worth of merit. And in the *Sūtra of the Fortunate Kalpa*, it is said,

When the Sugata King Knower of Time
Was a poet, he sang a verse in praise
Of the Sugata Sublime Grass
And aroused bodhichitta for the first time.

In the *Four Stanzas*, we read,

One who praises the Tathāgata
With these four stanzas

*The Tibetan term *mchod rten* is usually translated as "stūpa," but its literal meaning (a support or object for veneration) can include any representations of a buddha's body, speech, and mind in the form of statues and images, books, and stūpas and reliquaries, respectively. Throughout this section, therefore, we have used a variety of words to translate this term, depending on the context, but, as is mentioned below, in many cases it would be appropriate to bear the full range of meanings in mind.

> Will not, for ten billion kalpas,
> Go to the lower realms.

And the *Verses for Prasenajit*,

> To those who praise the Buddha's reliquary,
> Sweet melodies of flutes and songs
> And other pleasing sounds will come,
> And perfect knowledge, too, they'll gain.

And in a tantra also we find,

> These are the vast and perfect qualities
> Of all the buddhas.
> By voicing them just once
> One will accomplish all the buddhas.

The benefits of making offerings of flowers to representations of the Three Jewels are mentioned in the *Sūtra of the Questions of the Girl Sumati*:

> Lady, if bodhisattvas possess four teachings, they will be reborn miraculously in a jeweled lotus in the presence of the victorious, virtuous, and transcendent buddhas. What are these four? They are these. To fill one's hands with incense powders, or utpala flowers, or lotuses, or water lilies, or white lotuses, and offer them to a representation of the Tathāgata or to a reliquary of the Tathāgata. To avoid giving rise to harmful intentions toward others. To place a lotus under a representation of the Tathāgata. And to have vast faith and conviction in the Buddha's enlightenment. Lady, if you have these four teachings, you will be reborn miraculously in a jeweled lotus in the presence of the victorious, virtuous, and transcendent buddhas.

And the *Avalokinī Sūtra* states,

> Those who, with a joyful mind, take some flowers and, arousing faith,
> Scatter them in a rain upon the Protector of the World

Will possess the fortune of the human realm.
Enthroned as kings, they will venerate the conquerors.

In the *Verses on Circumambulating Reliquaries*, we find,

Were a wise person, with joyful mind, to heap some flowers
Before a stūpa of the Buddha,
Even a hundred thousand containers full of Jambu River gold
Could never match or equal that.

Similarly, about offering garlands of flowers, jewels, and so forth, it is said in the *Avalokinī Sūtra*,

Those who make a garland of flowers
And offer it to a stūpa
Will never lack for anything.
When they die, they will migrate
From the human state to the Thirty-Three,
And there acquire a measureless palace
Made of all kinds of precious gems.

And in the *Verses for Prasenajit*,

Those who offer an abundant rain of flower garlands
To the statues of the buddhas in this life
Will be adorned with all kinds of lovely things
In the human and celestial worlds.

And,

Wise persons who, with faithful minds,
Drape garlands on the Sugata's reliquary
Will have such merit that they'll be crowned
With golden garlands decorated with many gems.
Those who hang ornaments and garlands on the stūpas of the Teacher
Will proceed through their lives with bodies bedecked
With the finest necklaces, garlands of ornaments, jewels,
Bracelets, and armlets.

In the *Verses on Circumambulating Reliquaries*,

> Were a wise person, with joyful mind,
> To drape a flower garland on a stūpa of the Buddha,
> Twenty million measures of Jambu River gold
> Could never match or equal that.

About offering music, with the sounds of different kinds of musical instruments, whether blown, clashed, or struck, it is said in the *Avalokinī Sūtra*,

> One who makes an offering of musical sounds to the Best of Men
> Will come as a king, powerful and free of suffering,
> With a voice that delights the human world,
> A voice that is complete and pure in sound.

And,

> By offering the sounds of musical instruments to the Conqueror's reliquary,
> One will have the perfect confidence and eloquence that comes from profound knowledge and correct elocution.
> One's voice will have all five qualities,* the words one says will please,
> And one's fame will spread throughout the world.

And,

> From offering bells to the Conqueror's reliquary,
> One's words will have authority and great renown.
> With the pleasing melody of Brahmā's voice, one will remember one's births.

With regard to offering perfumed substances such as fragrant oils and incense, the *Avalokinī Sūtra* says,

*The five vocal qualities are a deep voice and one that is pleasant, attractive, clear, and worth listening to.

If one has offered incense and scented water to the Conqueror's reliquary,
When the Bhagavan's teachings are destroyed,
One will no longer be reborn in Jambudvīpa
And will become a lord, at that time, in the higher realms.

And the *Verses for Prasenajit* state,

Those who anoint a stūpa of the Sugata
With oils mixed with the finest scents
Will be venerated with incense, and their bodies,
Anointed with sandalwood, will shine like the light of the sun.

On the benefits of making offerings of parasols, canopies, banners, victory banners, tassels, and so forth, the *Avalokinī Sūtra* states,

If one has given rise to the aspiration to become a buddha in the world
And offered a banner for a stūpa of the Bhagavan,
One will be worthy of veneration by many beings,
Enjoy supreme enlightenment, and experience sublime peace.

And,

By offering a victory banner to a supreme being,
Free of the dust of defilements,
One will, without undue delay, acquire much wealth,
One will possess the abundant treasure of infinite wisdom,
And never have a cowardly or ignoble mind.

And the sūtra gives the following extensive account, which begins:

When the Buddha, the sublime Best of Men, is walking,
And someone who has faith in that incomparable guide
Offers the Conqueror a parasol of jasmine flowers
To stop the sun's rays falling on the Teacher's body,
Because of his devotion with this beautiful deed,
He will be born a hundred thousand times as mighty Indra,
He will be the lord of brahmās in all worlds.

It continues through to:

> Those who offer parasols to the Bhagavan's stūpa
> Will never abandon their intent to attain enlightenment.
> Abiding in love, they will never have base intentions,
> Their understanding will never decline.

And in the *Verses for Prasenajit*, we read,

> If some with faithful minds
> Should offer a canopy for a stūpa or statue,
> They will have dominion over the earth,
> Beyond the ends of the ocean—
> They will be the only ruling king.
> By joyfully hanging vast, manifold canopies
> Over the stūpas of the sugatas,
> They will be like Indra is for gods and men—
> Like canopies over the human and celestial worlds.
> People who attach manifold beautiful banners
> To reliquaries containing the sacred relics,
> Which are sources of uncontaminated merit,
> Will become powerful, objects of veneration in the three worlds.
> Those who attach cloth ornaments to the reliquaries of the sugatas
> Will obtain the power and glory of humans, the power and glory of gods.
> Having experienced the greatest happiness,
> They will obtain the extraordinary crown of perfect liberation.

About offering butter lamps and other bright lights, it is said in the *Avalokinī Sūtra*,

> Those who offer a single lamp to the Buddha's reliquary
> Will, from then on and up to the peak of existence,
> Have splendor like a buddha-field filled with Jambu gold—
> A splendor that can never come to an end.
> Those who have offered a lamp to the Sugata's reliquary
> Will never have an ugly body.
> They will acquire a handsome form, strong and steady,

And travel everywhere in the world.
One might be able to count, measure, and describe
The grains of mustard heaped to fill
Ten thousand billion buddha-fields,
But not the merit of a single lamp offered to the Sugata.

And,

It is possible to finish filling with precious jewels and beryl stones
This entire realm, our world of Endurance,
But there is no possible end
To the glory of offering a single lamp to the Buddha's reliquary.

In the *Verses for Prasenajit*, we read,

By offering lamps to the peerless reliquary of the Buddha,
One will gain the unobscured divine eye,
An eye like the petal of a fully bloomed blue utpala,
Clear and lovely, and beautifully almond shaped.
Those who present a row of lamps before a stūpa
Will have lovely eyes, fully opened treasures,
Oval eyes, in color azure blue,
Catching the looks of men and women.
Those with fortune, who in the evening sit with folded hands
Before the Mighty One and offer wicks for lamps,
Will harvest the result in other lives:
Their bodies will shine with light like real jewels.
And when the lamps they've offered to the Conqueror go out,
If they, with happy minds, rejoice at this,
Requesting that they may reach the essential goal,
The five eyes, too, will surely be obtained.*

There are further extensive explanations in the *Sūtra on Offering Lamps* and other texts.

*Instead of being sad that the lamps have gone out, this is seen as a request to attain enlightenment and pass into nirvāṇa. By keeping this in mind as one makes the offering, one will gain the five kinds of eye, corresponding to progressively heightened powers of clairvoyance: the flesh eye, divine eye, wisdom eye, dharma eye, and buddha eye.

On making an incense offering by burning sweet-smelling substances, whether prepared or in their natural form, the *Avalokinī Sūtra* declares,

> As I relate the benefits for one who takes a little incense,
> No bigger than a mustard grain,
> And burns it before the stūpas of the Bhagavan—
> Listen with a clear mind, free of dust and contaminants.*
> Possessed of merit, that person will travel everywhere,
> And free of illness, will have a careful, stable mind.
> He will practice the way and subdue misery,
> Rejoicing and delighting many beings.
> He will become a king and venerate the supreme conquerors.
> He will become universal monarch, powerful and wise,
> A gold-hued buddha bedecked with all the marks,
> Spreading the perfume of the teachings throughout the world.

And in the *Verses for Prasenajit*, we read,

> By offering the Buddha's reliquary sweet fragrances,
> Offering incense made of aloe wood
> And preparations of many copious incense substances,
> One's whole body will bear a fragrant scent.

About offering different kinds of clothes such as silken garments, it is said in the *Avalokinī Sūtra*,

> Those who make an offering, with joyful, delighted mind,
> Of fabric to the Bhagavan's reliquaries
> Will always acquire the loveliest clothes,
> Ten billion, ten trillion, or infinite in number.

And,

> Those who make an offering of fabrics
> To the Bhagavan's reliquary and to the peerless guides
> Will here obtain an incomparable body,

*"Dust" here refers to doubts and "contaminants" to defilements such as the five poisons.

Marked with the flowers of the thirty-two marks.
If they wrap cloths round the Bhagavan's reliquaries,
For infinite kalpas on end, from the palms of their hands
Will come forth lovely strings of pearls
Of various kinds, magnificent chains,
And beautiful golden threads.

And,

It is possible to reach the end of the glory
Of filling the whole thousandfold universe
With the seven supremely precious substances,
But not that of a single offering of cloth to the Conqueror's
reliquary.

And in the *Verses for Prasenajit*, we read,

By offering clothes to the reliquary of the Conqueror,
One will be clothed with the raiment of merit, love, and modesty;
One will be joyful, possessed of all good qualities, free of
miserliness;
One's color, too, will be soft, of golden hue.

Sprinkling saffron water and so on and offering different kinds of sweet-smelling waters for drinking, ablutions, and so on result in the following benefits according to the *Verses for Prasenajit*:

Those who, in spring, settle the dust
Around a stūpa by sprinkling pure water
Will be fanned delightedly by women
With golden-handled fans.

And,

People who sprinkle the Munindra's stūpa
With scented water, pure and clear,
Will have no sorrows: their bodies free of smell,
They'll know no torment, and have soft complexions.

And in the *Verses on Circumambulating Reliquaries*,

> Were a wise person, with joyful mind,
> To sprinkle scented water on a stūpa of the Buddha,
> Even a hundred thousand heaps of Jambu River gold
> Could never match or equal that.

Moreover, with regard to sweeping the dust at a temple or stūpa, we read in the Vinaya texts,

> Those who sweep away the dust obtain five benefits: they will accumulate sources of good, so that their own minds become clear, others are inspired, the gods rejoice, and they become beautiful. And when their bodies disintegrate, they will be reborn in happy states, in the worlds of the gods.

And in the *Avalokinī Sūtra*,

> Those who, seeking merit, wield a broom
> And thus respectfully venerate the Bhagavan's stūpa,
> Will not have a body that is despised or unclean.
> Their every pore will emit the fragrance of sandalwood.
> Those who sweep before the Bhagavan's Nirvāṇa Stūpa
> Will, for a million myriad kalpas, obtain
> A sublime body, with perfect limbs,
> Beauty, and the armor of all the marks.

And,

> If, with the power of faith aroused, one sweeps away
> The dried-out flowers and dirt before a stūpa of the Bhagavan,
> One will be rid of the base desires that lead to suffering
> And please the Guide possessed of the ten strengths.
> Those who sweep away the wilted flowers from before a stūpa
> Will be physically beautiful and pure.
> They will be worthy of the veneration and gaze of many beings,
> And kings will never think of harming them.

And in the *Verses for Prasenajit*, we read,

> By removing the old flowers from the stūpa of the Conqueror,
> One will be free of attachment, never become angry,
> Be rid of confusion, and have no attachment to wrong views.
> One will make people delighted and happy.

Wiping away the cobwebs and so on from a representation of the Three Jewels results in the following benefits, according to the *Avalokinī Sūtra*:

> Whoever removes the cobwebs from the stūpa
> Of that field of merit, the incomparable Light of the World,
> Will become careful and tear away the web of Māra.
> He will always abandon the ground of the lower realms
> And constantly revere the buddhas, free of dust.
> He will always become a powerful universal monarch.
> Having been reborn in the human world, he will possess merit
> And become the object of veneration of all the kings.
> Among the gods, by Indra will he be revered.

And in the *Verses for Prasenajit*, we read,

> From having cleaned the stūpa of the Mighty One,
> One will be exceedingly lovely and beautiful to see,
> With a fine complexion, the color of a lotus,
> And free of all the flaws of existence.

On repairing leaks in the roof of a temple and so on, the *Avalokinī Sūtra* gives a lengthy explanation, beginning:

> Listen with a clear mind, free of defiling stains,
> To my explanation of the benefits
> For someone ordinary who, aspiring to gain buddhahood,
> Clears a stūpa overgrown with grass:
> One will in future lives see the sublime conquerors,
> Those supreme, powerful and noble beings,
> And offer them the most sublime offerings.

One will always acquire sublime faith.
Having seen the buddhas, the leaders with the ten strengths,
One will venerate those incomparable guides,
Who with gladdened hearts will prophesy:
"You will be a buddha adorned with all the marks."

About repairing ruined or cracked stūpas, or building an assembly hall, a shrine room, and so on, it is said in the *Verses for Prasenajit*,

Those who build a dwelling for a teacher of the world,
Of grass or wood or brick,
Or engage others to do so,
Will be as shelters, as it were, for beings.
Those who build a shrine hall for the Buddha
Will, while circling still as beings in saṃsāra,
Obtain a house that shines with light,
Like the residence of Indra, mightiest of gods,
And be possessed of happiness at all times.
Within the higher realms, in places that result from their good ways,
They will find happiness for many kalpas long
And live forever joyfully, free of suffering,
And in the end they will attain the state of peace.
Those who, at the main door of the Buddha's stūpa,
Build an arch, in beauty like a rainbow's curve,
Will in other lives obtain a house
With ornamented entrances.
Those who faithfully construct a moat and gate
In order to protect the bodily relics of the Teacher
Will in other lives be immune to enemies
Depriving them of their glory and possessions.
Those who, not at others' request
But of their own free will,
Repair the cracks in ancient stūpas
Will have fine physiques,
And with the highest qualities they will be adorned.

In the *Sūtra on Grasping the Roots of Virtue*, it is said that by venerating a stūpa of the Tathāgata, repairing it and cleaning it, one will realize four pure and sublime aspirations—those concerning the body, the leisure to practice, the full taking of vows, and beholding the Tathāgata. And the *Sūtra of Ambrosial Speech* states,

> It is thus. Uninterruptedly making the gift of Dharma, and likewise, making the gift of protecting all beings from danger, meditating on the four boundless attitudes, restoring old stūpas, and inspiring all sentient beings with the wish to achieve buddhahood—Maitreya, if bodhisattvas possess these five virtues, they will not be obstructed by any kinds of demons, they will not be overpowered by any of the demons' retinues; they will, because of their love for all sentient beings, have long lives, protecting others, and they will swiftly attain buddhahood in unsurpassable, true and perfect, manifest enlightenment.

Offering plaster, paint, and so forth for a temple, stūpa, and so on has the following benefits, according to the *Verses for Prasenajit*:

> Those who apply plaster or cow dung
> Upon a reliquary of the Sugata
> Will be reborn as gods and humans,
> Beautiful in body and complexion,
> Pure, unblemished, and leading happy lives.

And,

> Those who decorate the Buddha's stūpas,
> Images, or temples with different colored paints
> Will gain, one after another,
> All the qualities of the Sugata.

And,

> Those who paint the stūpa of the Mighty One with whitewash
> Will, in the worlds of gods and humans, have long lives,
> Be free of physical and mental illness and pain,
> And always be happy and have abundant wealth.

About offering jewel insets and so on for stūpas and statues and so forth, the same text says,

> Those who offer to the world's protectors
> Pleasing jewels that blaze with light
> Will obtain the seven precious substances
> And the branches of enlightenment, like stainless jewels.

And,

> Those who offer to the Omniscient Ones
> Lovely mirrors, spotless as the moon when full,
> Will, in all successive lives,
> Be worthy to behold by gods and men.

And in the *Avalokinī Sūtra*,

> One who, with joyful mind, develops the force of respect
> And offers chains of jewels to the Bhagavan's stūpa
> Will become a king, adorned with the major marks,
> The highest and the mightiest—a universal monarch.

About making an offering of food, with different things to eat and drink, to the Saṅgha at such times as religious festivals, it is said in the *Verses for Prasenajit*,

> Those who make an offering of delicious food
> To a Saṅgha of ordained persons or hermits in retreat
> Will, when dwelling in solitude in saṃsāra,
> Obtain colorful, tasty things to eat.
> Those who make an offering of plenteous drink
> To a Saṅgha of ordained persons or hermits in retreat
> Will, when dwelling in solitude in saṃsāra,
> Obtain colorful, tasty things to drink.

And in the *Sūtra on the Perfection of Generosity*, we read,

> When they make a gift of food,
> The wise are thereby giving

Long life, a beautiful appearance, strength,
Happiness, and, fifth, confidence and eloquence.
Those who make a gift of food will themselves be joyful,
Long-lived, healthy and happy, and strong.
These steadfast, cheerful people
Will have unobstructed confidence and eloquence.
Wealth and glory will be theirs.
People who are gentle and intelligent,
Possessed of merit, peaceable and wise,
Are so from having given food.

And,

By making gifts of drink, the wise
Will never fall and be reborn as hungry ghosts,
Burning everywhere and blazing furiously;
For them the torments of thirst will not occur.

On offering clothes the same text states,

Those who offer clothes will have the greatest glory.
Always of good family and beautiful physique,
They will be people who are full of decency,
People who are famed and fortunate.

On offering a place to stay and sleep, it is stated in the same text,

Those who give a place, a celestial palace,
Will, wherever they are born,
Become the owner and lord
Of the household, place, and surrounding land.

And,

People who make an offering of bedding and pillows
Will be born learned in the treatises,
They will acquire sustained calm and give magnanimously,
From a lotus they will emerge, endowed with majesty and youth.

And,

Made of the seven various precious substances,
And two yojanas in height,
With a perimeter of one yojana,
Resplendent like Mount Meru,
And fully ornamented with the measureless palace,
Surrounded by hundreds of magical, jeweled trees,
Covered with lattices of chimes and tinkling bells,
And brightly embellished with precious jewels—
One who gives chairs, seats, and tables
To those whose conduct is perfectly pure
Will, while circling in states of saṃsāra,
Obtain seats of a similar kind.

About offering everyday necessities such as medicines,

Because of gifts of elixirs and medicines,
They will be free of disease, like the full moon,
And live happily, comfortably, with little to harm them.
Such people will have long lives.

And,

By fully giving life's necessities,
Wherever they take birth again
They will have all the qualities complete,
Branches of the most sublime.

Circumambulating a representation of the Three Jewels has the following benefits, as stated in the *Avalokinī Sūtra*:

Those who, in order to benefit all living beings,
Arouse the mind intent on enlightenment
And perform circumambulations
Around the stūpas of the world's protectors
Will, in all their series of lives,
As they practice the activities of the bodhisattvas,

Have mindfulness, intelligence,
And fortune, and be free from fear.

And in the *Verses for Prasenajit*,

Those who with faith circumambulate
The stūpa or a statue of the Mighty One
Will, in their next lives, receive obeisance from their greatest enemies;
They will be excellent vessels and possess good qualities.

And, in particular, in the *Verses on Circumambulating Reliquaries*, we find an extensive explanation, beginning:

Those who circumambulate a stūpa
Will be worshipped by gods, nāgas,
Yakṣhas, gandharvas, demigods,
Garuḍas, kinnaras, and mahoragas.
They will obtain the freedoms, so hard to find,
And from completing even a single series
Of circumambulations round a stūpa,
They will abandon the eight states with lack of opportunity.
They will have mindfulness, intelligence,
A beautiful complexion, and wisdom.
They will always be venerated.
As gods and, likewise, humans,
They will have long lives too,
And gain great fame as well.

And,

They will acquire the four close mindfulnesses,
The four boundless attitudes,
And the four bases of miraculous powers.
They will, as results, obtain the four noble truths,
The powers and strengths,
And the elements leading to enlightenment.
Possessed of the six preternatural powers, and free of taints,

They will eliminate all defilements
And become arhats with great miraculous abilities.
Eliminating attachment and aversion,
And abandoning all followers,
They will attain enlightenment as solitary realizers.
They will attain the level of tathāgata in all worlds,
Adorned with the marks
And with bodies of golden hue.
Bodily one circumambulates,
Verbally one circumambulates,
Mentally one circumambulates,
Making prayers of aspiration one circumambulates.
By making circumambulations in this way,
The difficult journey is easily accomplished.
The benefits of circumambulating
The stūpas of the world's protectors
Are impossible to properly describe
With just a few, limited words.

In the above contexts, *stūpa* is explained as referring to representations of the Three Jewels in general.

The *Sūtra Teaching on the Magical Display of Miracles* gives the following summary:

Those who have stūpas, paintings, and statues made,
And venerate and pay homage to them,
Who thus call to mind the buddhas' names
And live for the sake of enlightenment,
Will all attain liberation.

And the *Sūtra of the White Lotus of the Sacred Dharma* states,

Those who to the relics of the Sugata make a little offering,
And strike and make the cymbals sound just once,
Or offer just a single flower to them,
And, even if with their minds disturbed,
Venerate a fresco of the Sugata drawn upon a wall
Will one day come to see ten million buddhas.

Those who fold their hands before a stūpa,
Completely, or raise just a single hand,
Or momentarily bow their heads,
And likewise bow their bodies once,
And those who, even with distracted minds, prostrate
To places where the relics rest,
Voicing the one word *Buddha* a few times,
Will all attain this supreme enlightenment.

And the *Jewel Cloud Sūtra* has the following:

> Fortunate child, the Tathāgata is the embodiment of the Dharma. By venerating the Dharma, fortunate children will be venerating all the tathāgatas.

In short, as the *Sūtra of the Ten Wheels of Kṣitigarbha* states,

All the happiness and well-being in the three worlds
Arises from venerating the Three Jewels.
Therefore, those who wish for happiness and well-being
Should be diligent in venerating the Three Jewels.

And the *Avalokinī Sūtra*,

Listen, then, to these great benefits,
And by offering the Protector
Flower garlands, victory banners,
The finest raiment, sounds of music,
And canopies, unguents, and scents,
Attain to buddhahood!

These are words of instruction given by the compassionate Buddha himself.

Now, one might wonder whether there is any difference between making offerings to the Buddha present in person and, as nowadays, to his representations. In fact, there is not the slightest difference, as is stated in a sūtra:

> Great Sage, I teach that the fully ripened effect for someone who makes offerings to the Bhagavan who has passed into nirvāṇa

> and for someone who makes offerings to the Bhagavan who is present now is equal; it is the same. Should you ask why, it is for the following reason: while the Tathāgata's form body is distinct from the body of truth, the body of truth is not distinct from the form body. Because the mental state is the same in those who make offerings to the Buddha who is present and in those who make offerings to the Buddha who has passed into nirvāṇa, there is not the slightest difference in merit between the two.

And,

> Making offerings to me, now,
> And making offerings to images in the future,
> Both have the same merit and the same ripened effect.
> There is not the slightest difference between these two.

And,

> Those who faithfully offer their respect
> To the conquerors who have passed into nirvāṇa
> And to the ones who are present now
> Have the same virtuous attitude,
> So they acquire the same heap of merit.

Furthermore, the *Detailed Explanations of Discipline* mentions seven kinds of merit derived from material gifts:

> Gifts of gardens, temples, and bedding,
> Continuous provisions, occasional meals,
> Gifts made to the sick and to their nurses,
> And gifts of humanitarian aid
> Are seven kinds of merit derived from material gifts.[322]

And in particular, *Distinguishing the Middle from Extremes* speaks of ten Dharma activities:

> Copying the scriptures, making offerings, charity,
> Listening, reading, memorizing,

Teaching, reciting, reflecting, and meditating—
These ten activities yield boundless stores of merit.

It is important to perform these activities, mainly in the postmeditation period.

b. The unsurpassable form of veneration

The unsurpassable form of veneration is referred to in a sūtra as follows:

> Brahmin, these three are the unsurpassable forms of veneration and service to the Tathāgata. They are the unsurpassable forms of veneration that give rise to boundless merit. What are these three? Arousing the mind set on unsurpassable, true, and perfect enlightenment. Holding the teachings of the tathāgatas. And accomplishing the teachings one has heard accordingly.

Of these, the benefits of bodhichitta have already been explained. As for the benefits of holding the sacred teachings, generally speaking the merit of hearing, expounding, practicing, and accomplishing the teachings of the Great Vehicle is inconceivable. We read in the *Sūtra of the Questions of Sāgaramati*,

Greater than the merit of offering the sugatas
This great thousandfold universe filled with gold
Is that of hearing and gaining faith
In the treasury of the teachings.
Greater than the merit of offering the tathāgatas
Ten thousand world systems filled with precious things
Is that of applying oneself to studying these sūtras—
Such merit the former cannot ever yield.
Greater than the merit of making gifts
Of ten thousand world systems filled with precious things
Is that of reading aloud and teaching this sūtra—
No previous merit matches a part of that.
Greater than the merit of offering
A million myriad realms filled with precious things
To the buddhas, masters and protectors of the world,

Is introducing beings to this way.
And compared to offering to the conquerors
Worlds in the ten directions as many as the Ganges's sands,
All filled with jewels,
To properly abide by whatever has been taught
Yields merit for which there is no equal.

In particular, the benefits of holding the sacred teachings at times such as ours, when the teachings are close to disappearing, are even more inconceivable. The *Avalokinī Sūtra* declares,

Those who hold the Victor's sacred Dharma
When the teachings are in decline
Have power and strength, and are endowed with diligence.
Wandering everywhere among common men,
They serve one hundred thousand buddhas.
Those who hold the Victor's sacred Dharma
When the teachings are in decline
Have utterly resplendent forms and are possessed of wisdom.
The world of humans honors them;
By kings, the wise, and learned are they praised.

And,

Greater than venerating a thousand buddhas,
Or a hundred thousand, or ten million,
For kalpas numerous as the Ganges's grains of sand,
Is the merit of one who holds, by day and night,
The sacred teachings of the world's Protector.
When the doctrine is in decline.
One who, as the doctrine disappears, holds the teachings
In which the wisdom of the Buddha dwells,
And that of all the buddhas of the past,
Is venerating me.
Those who, as the sacred Dharma disappears,
Preserve the Teacher's doctrine
Will never, in ten thousand million kalpas,
Weaken and degenerate.
They will experience physical well-being

And never be struck by illness.
Never will they be robbed of happiness.
Because they have preserved the Teacher's doctrine,
They will have patience in abundance,
Be gentle, clear-minded, and adaptable,
And be loving toward sentient beings.

And,

Those who in the future hold this sūtra
Are my children, constantly in tune with me.
Ten million buddhas might sing their eulogies,
But never would they finish praising them.

And in the *Sūtra of the Questions of Sāgaramati*, we find,

Those who hold the Tathāgata's sacred teachings
Are showing their gratitude to the Tathāgata.
They hold and trust the treasury of the conquerors
And venerate the buddhas in the ten directions.
The heap of merit of offering the tathāgatas
The many worlds that fall within the buddhas' gaze,
All filled with precious things, can never surpass that
Of holding the teachings when they are coming to an end.

And,

Were they to tell for kalpas without break
The qualities and benefits of these,
They would never reach the end of telling
These benefits of holding the sacred teachings.

And the *Sūtra of the Questions of Gaganagañja* states,

Just as, even if described for ten thousand million kalpas,
There is no end to the buddhas' wisdom,
Neither is it possible to assess
The merit of holding the Tathāgata's sacred teachings.

The benefits of properly practicing the meaning of the teachings one has heard are referred to in the *Sūtra of the King of Concentrations* in a passage beginning:

> Young man, there are ten benefits for great bodhisattvas who are diligent in correctly settling the mind inward. Their minds are free of turbidity. They act carefully. They remember the Buddha's qualities. They have faith in the practice. Their wisdom is free of fluctuation. They repay the Buddha's kindness. They do not give up the Dharma. They observe complete restraint. They acquire true discipline. And they realize the four kinds of perfect knowledge. Young man, these ten are the benefits for bodhisattva mahāsattvas who are diligent in correctly settling the mind inward.

And it ends as follows:

> When those bodhisattvas die and transmigrate,
> They will go to the Blissful Realm.
> Hearing the excellent teachings from Amitāyus,
> They will obtain the acceptance that phenomena are unborn.

In particular, the benefits are even greater than those of deeds such as generosity, as is mentioned in a sūtra:

> Mañjushrī, compared to a bodhisattva who, for a thousand god years, gives whatever is necessary to the Three Jewels, another bodhisattva who, for a duration as little as a finger snap, investigates things, thinking, "All compounded phenomena are impermanent; all compounded phenomena are suffering; all compounded phenomena are empty; all compounded phenomena are devoid of self," gives rise to an immeasurable amount of merit.

And in the *Sūtra of Maitreya's Great Lion's Roar*, it is said that greater than an offering to the Tathāgata of this third-order universe of one thousand million worlds, all filled with offerings, offered three times by day and three times by night for one hundred thousand years, is the merit of someone striving for enlightenment who abides by the aggregate of discipline and who receives the transmissions from a preceptor, recites them, and keeps in mind the meaning of as little as four lines, and who, shunning distractions and diversions, takes seven steps toward a lonely hermitage. Moreover, it is said that if one were to compare the offering of all kinds of gifts that King Rim-Holder made for eighty-four thousand years to the Tathāgata Manifold Flowers and the meditation on the teaching that all phenomena are unborn that someone dwelling in a lonely hermitage performs for a duration as little as a finger snap, one would never get near counting how many more times the latter offering exceeds the former—a thousand, ten million, a hundred million, and beyond.

The benefits of practicing are even greater than listening and so on, as we read in a sūtra that teaches thatness:[323]

> Shāriputra, many times greater than the merit of someone who listens to the teachings for one kalpa is the merit of one who trains in the concentration of thatness for the duration of a mere finger snap. Therefore, Shāriputra, put all your efforts into teaching others this concentration of thatness.

And in the *Sūtra of the Great Crown Protuberance*,

> Greater than the merit of listening and reflecting for many kalpas is that of meditating for one day on the meaning of ultimate reality. Should you ask why, it is because it takes one far beyond the path of birth and death.

This is also the antidote for the accumulation of obscurations that counter enlightenment, as we read in passages such as these, from the *Heap of Jewels*:

> Taking the analogy of holding up a lamp in a dark room, in the same way, Kāshyapa, even deeds and defilements that have been accumulated over one hundred thousand years will be annulled by once properly using the mind to analyze phenomena.

And,

> Kāshyapa, by once properly using the mind to analyze phenomena, deeds and defilements accumulated in a hundred thousand kalpas are purified.

Similarly, attachment to the sense pleasures is counteracted and preternatural knowledge and concentration arises, as is mentioned in the *Verses That Summarize the Perfection of Wisdom*:

> With concentration, one looks down upon the pleasures of the senses and abandons them. One manifestly accomplishes understanding, preternatural knowledge, and concentration.

As for how it removes doubts, the *Sūtra of the Ten Wheels of Kṣitigarbha* states,

> Training in concentration will clear away all doubts,
> But nothing else can do so.
> Therefore, meditation on concentration is the best:
> The wise should exert themselves in this.

It also enables us to develop great compassion and see the true meaning, as a result of which we realize the result, nirvāṇa. This is explained in the *Sūtra That Perfectly Summarizes the Dharma*,

> By settling the mind in equipoise, one will see the true nature as it is. By seeing the true nature as it is, bodhisattvas manifest great compassion for sentient beings.

As for the particular quality of being able to bring disciples to full maturation, the *Sūtra of the Perfection of Wisdom* states,

> A bodhisattva mahāsattva practices the transcendent perfection of wisdom, abides in the three meditative concentrations,* and brings sentient beings to maturation.

*Tib. *ting nge 'dzin gsum*: the illusory concentration, the great compassion concentration, and the indestructible concentration.

And in *Ornament of the Mahāyāna Sūtras*, we read,

> Through that very concentration, they bring all beings to the three levels of enlightenment.*

Moreover, settling evenly on the meaning of thatness, the actual condition of things, includes and completes all the paths of the sūtras and tantras. This can be known from scriptural authorities such as the Dharma Lord Gampopa's *Jewel Ornament of Liberation*.[324] In short, as we read in the *Sūtra of the Questions of Sāgaramati*,

> The mind intent on perfect enlightenment, holding the teachings,
> Accomplishing the teachings, and having compassion for living beings—
> The merit of these four elements is limitless:
> Of their limits, the sugatas do not speak.

Here, the separate mention of "compassion for living beings" shows that actions such as ransoming lives, which are motivated by bodhichitta, are also unsurpassable forms of veneration and that they, in fact, obtain the same benefits as described above.

If we have not stocked the treasury of the jewellike two accumulations,
We will never gain the extraordinary riches of the two buddha bodies.
So abandon all careless activities,
And be diligent in being one-pointed, O fortunate ones!

This completes the instruction on the maṇḍala practice for gathering the accumulations.

*Maitreya/Asaṅga, *Ornament of the Mahāyāna Sūtras*, chap. 17, v. 40 (3rd line) (English translation from Maitreya and Jamgön Mipham, *Feast*, p. 83). The three levels of enlightenment are the enlightenment of the listeners, that of the solitary realizers, and the perfect buddhahood attained by the bodhisattvas.

Kangyur Rinpoche (1897–1975)

13. The Instruction on the Guru Yoga, Which Enables the Extraordinary Blessings to Enter One's Being

There are three sections: (1) a general explanation of how to follow the spiritual friend, who is the source of good qualities; (2) the main explanation of how specifically to train in the profound practice; and (3) a concluding exposition of the benefits of following the teacher and practicing in that way. The first of these is divided into three: (1) the reasons one needs to follow a teacher, (2) the marks of a teacher who should be followed, and (3) how to follow such a teacher.

I. A general explanation of how to follow the spiritual friend, who is the source of good qualities

A. The reasons one needs to follow a teacher

If we follow a genuine spiritual friend, all that teacher's qualities and good aspects will rub off on us in the same way that ordinary wood placed next to sandalwood takes on its sweet fragrance. This is explained in the Vinaya texts:

> Those who rely on sublime beings,
> Like a creeper on a sal tree,*
> Will be held by an abundance of good qualities.

*The sal tree is an Indian tree esteemed for its wood, leaves, and resin, the latter being used medicinally and for incense.

For this reason, we need to follow a spiritual friend and virtuous companions, for all our own virtue and good qualities will thereby grow and flourish. The *Sūtra of the Questions of Maitreya* states,

> Know that all the aggregates of perfect liberation and of the vision of the gnosis of perfect liberation attained by the listeners, solitary realizers, and unsurpassed buddhas come from following a spiritual friend. Maitreya, know too that all the benefit and happiness that sentient beings may have comes from their own virtuous deeds and that the source of those is a spiritual friend.

And,

> O fortunate child, serve a spiritual friend. By doing so, you will fully understand how merit and nonmerit are gathered and will thereby completely eliminate all wandering in cyclic existence.

If, on the other hand, we do the opposite and follow a false teacher and unvirtuous companions, their faults will naturally rub off on us—as if we were surrounded by filth, like kusha grass tainted by rotten fish. In the Vinaya texts, we read,

> If, for all the world to see,
> Some rotten fish is wrapped in kusha grass,
> The kusha grass, before too long,
> Will start to smell just like the fish.
> And so it is, the same occurs
> For those who follow unholy men.

For this reason, it is important for us to avoid friends in evil* and unvirtuous companions, for we need to reduce and abandon everything that has to do with nonvirtue so as to annihilate it. The *Sūtra of the Arborescent Array* declares,

> Fortunate child, those who truly wish for sources of good must follow a spiritual friend. They must never rely on unvirtuous

*Tib. *mi dge ba'i bshes gnyen*, the opposite of a spiritual friend or friend in virtue (*dge ba'i bshes gnyen*) companions. Should you ask why, it is because the latter obstruct everything that is virtuous.

Moreover, no one other than a teacher can give us advice on accomplishing the lasting happiness of enlightenment, so we need to follow him or her. In the *Compendium of the Buddhas' Wisdom*, it is said,

For those who wander in the darkness here,
The ones who show the path of light toward great bliss
Are those very teachers, the greatest refuges.
No one else than them is capable of showing it.

Another reason for following a teacher is that there is no one else who can teach us the notions of adopting things we ought to do and avoiding things we ought not to do. It is said in the *Magical Manifestation Tantra in One Hundred Chapters*,[325]

They show us every single one
Of the great treasures of their precious qualities
And, eradicating each and all of our defilements,
Help us to attain the unsurpassed result.
Much worthier of our homage and respect
Than kings with power to rule the land,
They should be loved by us and cherished
More than our parents, so kind and dear,
Who physically engendered us.

The attainment of enlightenment depends on the two accumulations, and there is no better object for creating merit than the teacher, so this is yet another reason for following a teacher. In the *Tantra of Complete Union*, we find,

The supreme master of all the buddhas,
Whose name is "Mind of All Gnoses,"
Bestows all the accomplishments without exception.
Therefore, the wise should constantly venerate him;
For greater than the merit of making offerings
To the buddhas and bodhisattvas in the ten directions

> Is that of venerating a single pore of the teacher's body.
> Only the buddhas and bodhisattvas can comprehend
> The benefit of making offerings to the master.

The teacher is the unsurpassable refuge and protector, able to guard us from every kind of danger and suffering, so for that reason too, we should follow a teacher. The *King of Tantras: The Magical Display* states,

> The supreme being who gives sure protection
> From the fears of cyclic existence and leads us beyond all pain
> Is the teacher, and no one else.

Again, we should follow a teacher because there is no one else who can make all the wealth of good qualities grow in our mind streams. As the *Story of Śrīsambhava* tells us,

> All the excellent qualities of the bodhisattvas come from their having a spiritual friend.

And because there are no better instructors than spiritual teachers, it is them we should follow. In the *Guhyasamāja Tantra*, we read,

> The teacher is the same as all the buddhas,
> The teacher is greater than all the buddhas.
> I bow my head to the glorious teacher,
> Who is a treasure of sublime qualities.

Moreover, in the *Sūtra of the Arborescent Array*, it is said,

> You must never tire of seeking spiritual friends. Even when you have found them, serve them by never neglecting to follow in their footsteps. Develop the notion of never tiring of all your responsibilities, like the earth. Develop the notion of obeying all they tell you, like a servant.

Accordingly, constantly seek sublime teachers and follow them.

B. The marks of a teacher who should be followed

On a general level, you should learn the characteristics of a spiritual friend according to the Omniscient Teacher's detailed explanation in the *Precious Treasury That Fulfills All Wishes* of the points taught in the sūtras, tantras, and treatises. Here, however, we shall refer to the most important points taught in the *Essential Instructions for Finding Rest in the Nature of the Mind*. These are divided into two: (1) common characteristics, and (2) extraordinary characteristics.

1. Common characteristics

Like merchants who rely on a skillful pilot to guide them to an island of jewels, we have to rely on the spiritual friend who is our teacher to enable us to reach the island of liberation and attain buddhahood. We need, therefore, to follow someone whose physical, verbal, and mental activities are without fault and who is adorned with all the right qualities: someone who is learned, very loving, with boundless knowledge and compassion, who sets all those connected with him or her on the path to liberation, and who can put up with fatigue and difficulties. It is said in *Ornament of the Mahāyāna Sūtras*,

> Take as a teacher someone disciplined, peaceful, totally at peace,
> Possessed of superior qualities, diligence, and knowledge of the texts;
> Who has full realization, is skilled in explanation,
> Full of love, and indefatigable.[326]

2. Extraordinary characteristics

Just as wealth, servants, power, and prosperity in this life depend on their being granted by a good king such as a universal monarch, our attainment of the unsurpassable result and qualities in a single life depends on a guru, a supreme vajra holder who is learned and accomplished. We need, therefore, to follow someone who possesses all the blessings of the lineal transmission of sublime teachers and who has received all the empowerments and kept the sacred commitments perfectly. It is someone who is well versed in the essential points of the tantras and pith instructions, who has acquired the power of the profound approach and accomplishment, who has genuine realization of the view, concentration, and confidence, and whose numerous, perfect activities are of benefit to others. The *Indestructible Net of Magical Manifestations* describes such teachers as follows:

> They have studied many teachings, have great wisdom,
> And have definite realization of the wisdom transmitted in the teachings.
> Never pursuing material gain,
> They are hardly discouraged by difficult practices,
> Have all the pith instructions, and transcend the path.*
> They know their disciples' potentials and can recognize the signs of progress.
> Endowed with bodhichitta, they have great compassion.
> They hold the lineage and know how to accomplish the teachings that have come down to them.
> They possess the treasure of the teachings; in them the river of blessings is complete.
> Having liberated their own mind streams, they are diligent in benefiting others.
> These are the signs that they are teachers of the Secret Mantra Vehicle.

Again and again, we should think, "May I meet with sublime teachers like these whom I have not met until now. May I never separate from those whom I have met. And may I always please my teachers and be guided by their compassion."

C. How to follow such a teacher

There are two parts: (1) the attitude one should have in following one's teachers, and (2) the conduct one should adopt in following one's teachers.

1. The attitude one should have in following one's teachers

This is divided into three: (1) calling to mind the teachers' qualities, (2) calling to mind the teachers' kindness, and (3) regarding the teacher as a buddha.

*Lit. "they are free from the path"—that is, they are not caught by attachment to the path.

a. Calling to mind the teachers' qualities

In the *Sūtra of the Arborescent Array*, there is the following passage:

> O fortunate child, spiritual friends are like great ships delivering us from the ocean of cyclic existence. They are like guides for those who have set out on the path to liberation. They are like the king of wish-fulfilling jewels, for they clear away the woes of existence. They are like the waters that extinguish the fire of deeds and defilements. They are like bountiful clouds, pouring down the great rain of the teachings.

And it continues with numerous other similes, which the Great Omniscient One summarizes in his *Essential Instructions for Finding Rest in the Nature of the Mind* thus:

> In this world, the coming of a buddha is as rare as the appearance of the udumbara flower. And just as rare is the appearance of sublime spiritual friends, who are the emanations of the Buddha's compassion. Authentic spiritual friends such as our present sublime teacher and glorious protector have boundless qualities. They are like ferrymen helping us to cross the ocean of existence. They are like skilled guides leading us along the road to liberation. They are like a wish-fulfilling jewel dispelling the troubles of existence and peace. They are like streams of nectar extinguishing the fires of the defilements. They are like bountiful rain clouds, pouring down the great rain of the teachings. They are like the sound of the celestial drum, delighting all beings. They are like the king of doctors, curing all the ailments caused by the three poisons. They are like the light of the sun and moon, dispelling the gloom of ignorance. They are like a great wishing tree, providing everything we could hope for. They are like the orb of the sun, shining with the thousand light rays of their activities. Marvel, therefore, at all the qualities they have.

And further,

> Thus, the realization of sublime spiritual friends is as vast as the

sky, their concentration shines with light like the sun and moon, their knowledge is as fathomless as the ocean, their compassion as powerful as a river. Their minds are as steadfast as Mount Meru. They are as pure as a flawless lotus. They think of beings as impartially as parents think of their children. Their qualities appear spontaneously, like treasure from a treasure trove. They are sublime leaders, like worldly conquerors. It is impossible to gauge each of their qualities. How wondrous they are! May I always delight them and be held with their compassion.

Thus, simply through our seeing these glorious protectors, our sublime teachers, through our hearing them, thinking of them, or touching them, they plant the seed of liberation and wrest us out of cyclic existence. In this respect, they are the same as all the buddhas, and the activities they perform are the same. Since they guide us on the path to liberation, we are supremely fortunate. They come as the Fourth Jewel, as the essence of the *heruka* in the maṇḍala, bestowing complete empowerment and performing the activities of all the buddhas. For their disciples, their kindness is much greater than that of the buddhas. Such are their qualities.

In the *Sūtra of the Ornament of the Buddhas*, it is said,

> Were one to relate in detail, for kalpas on end, the qualities and praises of the spiritual friend, one could never finish doing so. Therefore, constantly rely on a spiritual friend.

And in the *Root Tantra of Saṃvara*, we read,

> By seeing, touching,
> Hearing, and remembering,
> One will be freed from all evils.
> Of that there is no doubt at all.

The *Tantra of the Union of All the Buddhas* states,

> The Buddha, Dharma, Saṅgha,
> And Teacher are the four.

And the *Sūtra of Untainted Space* has the following:

> Ānanda, the Tathāgata does not appear to all sentient beings, but spiritual friends will appear and teach the Dharma, planting the seed of liberation. For this reason, you should consider spiritual friends as superior to the tathāgatas.

Therefore, reflect and practice, thinking, "How glad I am that nowadays someone like me can meet and follow a spiritual teacher. In all my lives may I follow and serve the glorious protectors, my gracious teachers, who, in this life, set me on the profound path of maturation and liberation. May they bless me with their compassion."

b. Calling to mind the teachers' kindness

In the *Sūtra of the Arborescent Array*, we read,

> Spiritual friends show us everything that we should do and everything we should not do. They eradicate worldly ways. They counteract all evil and careless ways. They purify all obscurations. They draw us out of the city of cyclic existence. They sever the noose of the demons. They dispel the darkness of ignorance. They cut the fetters of wrong views. They remove the pains of misery. They clear away the gloom of lack of understanding. They save us from the river of existence. They draw us out of the swamp of desire. They show us the path of the bodhisattvas. They introduce us to our yidam.* They set us to practicing assiduously. They show us the way to freedom. They foster in us great compassion. They help us to develop the eye of wisdom. They help us to develop our bodhichitta. They show us the activities of the bodhisattvas. They give us the instructions on the transcendent perfections. They set us on the ten levels. They enable us to abide by all the Buddha's teachings.

And in the same text, we find,

*Yidam here refers not only to the sādhana practice of the yidam deity but also to any practice that suits one's particular needs and constitutes one's main practice.

> All the activities of the bodhisattvas depend on spiritual friends. All avenues of aspiration arise through them. It is they who produce all sources of good. It is they who accomplish all the accumulations of merit and wisdom. All the gateways of the Dharma are illuminated by them. The whole of the perfectly pure path originates from them. They are the root of all pure, altruistic attitudes. All the teachings on arousing bodhichitta come from them. It is the light of their memory and confident eloquence that reveals everything. It is they who hold the whole treasury, providing access to perfect purity. All the visions of gnosis are produced by them. All extraordinary aspirations lie in their hands.

And again,

> Like the eldest child of a universal monarch, spiritual friends are born in the family of the buddhas. Like mothers, they give rise to all the right qualities. Like fathers, they bring about vast benefit. Like nursemaids,[327] they protect us from doing wrong. Like schoolmasters, they teach us what we have to learn. Like guides, they lead us along the path of the transcendent perfections. Like doctors, they cure the disease of the defilements. Like heroes, they protect us from danger. Like ferrymen, they help us to cross the river of cyclic existence. On spiritual friends all the practices of the bodhisattvas depend.

And in the *Sūtra of the Ornament of the Buddhas*,

> Sudhana, spiritual friends protect us from all evil destinies. They enable us to realize the sameness of all phenomena. They show us how to distinguish the paths to happiness and unhappiness. They instruct us in wholly virtuous activities. They point out the way to the city of omniscience. They take us to the state of omniscience. They plunge us into the ocean of the expanse of reality. They show us the ocean of knowable phenomena of the past, present, and future. They reveal to us the maṇḍala of the assembly of noble beings. Spiritual friends make all our virtuous activities grow.

And,*

"Our spiritual friends teach us the Dharma,
They show us the qualities of the whole path,
Teaching the way of the bodhisattvas."
With this single-minded thought, he has come here.
"They have given birth to virtue, so they are like our mothers.
Like wet nurses, they have fed us the milk of good qualities.
It is they who train us in the elements of enlightenment.
These spiritual friends repel all harm.
Like doctors, they put an end to aging and death.
Like the mighty Indra, they rain down nectar.
Like a full moon, they make virtuous ways grow.
Like a newly risen sun, they show the way to peace.
Like mountains are they with regard to enemies and friends,
And like an ocean, their minds are never ruffled.
Like a ferryman, they protect us completely."
With such thoughts in mind, has Sudhana come here.
"They have given rise to the bodhisattvas' mind.
They produce the enlightenment of the buddhas and their
children.
They, our spiritual friends, are praised by the buddhas."
With such virtuous thoughts, he has come here.
"Protecting the world, they are like brave heroes,
They are our guides, our protectors and refuge.
They are for us the eye of bliss and strength."
Thinking thus, he venerates spiritual friends.

Accordingly, we should be sincerely mindful of their kindness. It is our spiritual friends who protect us from the sufferings of cyclic existence and the lower realms. It is they who show us the right road to the higher realms and liberation, who grant us abundant and perfect wealth, in both the short and long terms. It is they who, through numerous skillful means, turn us away from the slightest wrongdoing and connect our mind streams to good

*The following passage from the *Sūtra of the Ornament of the Buddhas* is part of the declaration Maitreya makes on the arrival of Sudhana, explaining why Sudhana has come to request guidance from him.

qualities, one by one. In particular, according to the tradition of the Diamond Vehicle of the secret mantras, spiritual friends possess the threefold kindness of bestowing empowerment, explaining the tantras, and teaching the pith instructions; in this respect they are superior to the buddhas. So we should rely on them like our very heart or like the eyes in our forehead. We read in the *Song of Pith Instructions of the Inexhaustible Treasury*,

> Those who show us that all the various phenomena
> Are one and the same are the sublime teachers,
> Supremely holy beings, who are like the swan's bill:*
> Place them on the crown of your head, with great devotion in your mind.
> Those who point out the all-inclusive nature of the mind are the teachers;
> The ground for pointing it out lies in the very heart of the disciple.†
> Through realizing that, in an instant, all our suffering is destroyed;
> They are thus true heroes, full of kindness.
> So, knowing this, in order to repay their kindness,
> Always consider them as kings of physicians.

And further on,

> Skillfully they transmute all the defilements,
> And through the essential pith instructions
> Give certain deliverance from the pain of concepts
> That are impossible to transmute.
> Through the power of the holy ones, one will gain certainty.
> Therefore, the wise should always follow those
> Who possess the blessings of the lineage
> And teach in timely fashion, skillfully.

*Like the swan's bill, which reputedly filters milk from water, a sublime teacher extracts the essence of the teaching, showing us what to relinquish and what to develop. Another explanation is that the bill is the swan's most vital and indispensable part, by means of which it eats and drinks, calls, breathes, preens itself, and so on. We should realize that the teacher is similarly indispensable.

†It is because the disciples have the tathāgatagarbha, or buddha nature, that the teacher can introduce them to the nature of the mind.

And in *Finding Rest in the Nature of the Mind*,

> Enlightened masters, the fourth Jewel,
> Are herukas in the maṇḍala, powerful and glorious.
> They labor in this age of dregs
> For beings difficult to teach,
> For whom they thus surpass all buddhas.
> Vajra masters are the root of all accomplishment.
> Attend such masters purely and with honesty
> In thought and word and deed,
> Revering them above your head.[328]

Furthermore, in the *Sūtra on the Samādhi in Which the Buddhas of the Present All Stand Before One*, we read,

> Spiritual friends are difficult to find, so you should enthusiastically serve preceptors and instructors. You should develop the thought and certainty that anyone from whom you hear the Dharma or from whom you request to write a scripture is the Buddha and that he or she is your spiritual friend. And in order that they give you the teachings and bring you to maturation in perfect enlightenment, cultivate especially great joy and respect in their regard.

And the *Sūtra of the Ten Qualities* states,

> When you respectfully make a request to those who hold the teachings, cultivate the notion that they are illuminating lamps. Think of them as the Buddha. Consider them as spiritual friends. Consider them as the ones who will save us from the ocean of existence. Consider them as the ones who seek us out, we who are wandering in cyclic existence. Consider them as the ones who rouse us from the slumber of bewilderment. Consider them as the ones who draw us out of the mire of cyclic existence. Consider them as the ones who indicate the right path to show those who have embarked on the wrong one. Consider them as the ones who release us from our shackles in the prison of existence. Consider them as doctors healing those who are afflicted by chronic

> illness. Consider them as rain clouds quenching the blazing fires of the defilements.

And in the well-known story of Noble Sadāprarudita, we read,*

> Gratefully acknowledge those from whom you receive the *Perfection of Wisdom* by considering them as buddhas. And cultivate the thought that those who teach the Dharma are your teachers, thinking, "By hearing the Dharma from them, I will swiftly attain irreversible enlightenment; by serving the buddhas, I will be reborn in their buddha-fields; I will completely abandon states without opportunity; and I will obtain all the perfect freedoms."

Moreover, the Omniscient Teacher says,

> Ask yourself, "If non-Buddhists can exert themselves so intensely in such pointless ascetic practices as the ordeal with five fires,† why should I not do something meaningful like revering and serving teachers who will lead me to ever-increasing happiness?" Similarly, think, "If ordinary people serve and venerate rulers and the like in order to gain their protection, why do I not venerate teachers who can protect me from all the sufferings of cyclic existence? If people who are afraid of short-term danger rely on brave men, why do I not rely on teachers who will liberate me forever from cyclic existence and the lower realms? If people make offerings to their kings of precious things, music, parasols, and so on, why do I not revere and serve my teachers, who can bestow on me a greater dominion, of lasting worth? If craftsmen and the like venerate masters who teach worldly skills, why do I not revere and serve my teachers, who show sentient beings how to attain buddhahood? If people make offerings to doctors who restore imbalances in their constitution, why do I not revere and serve my teachers, who can rid me of the chronic illness caused

*For the story of the bodhisattva Sadāprarudita, see Patrul Rinpoche, *Words of My Perfect Teacher*, 153–57.

†The ascetic practice of supposedly purifying oneself by enduring the heat of four fires in the four cardinal directions and of the sun overhead.

by the five poisons? If people respectfully make offerings to an escort who protects them from everyday hazards, why do I not revere and serve my teachers, who protect me from my enemies, the four demons? If people are prepared to give away their lives for the sake of things of little benefit, like food and clothes and money, why do I not revere and serve my teachers who bestow on me all the wealth I could need or want? People happily make offerings to friends who will accompany them but for a short while, so why do I not revere and serve my teachers, my sublime, eternal friends who introduce me to the profound and sacred Dharma? Ordinary folk esteem those who lovingly prepare them for projects in this life, so why do I not revere and serve my teachers, who prepare my lasting welfare?"

With such thoughts, revere and serve your teachers, considering the numerous difficulties, examples, and different aspects with regard to following them.* As a result of serving your teachers, because the result is as great as its cause, you will be praised and venerated by others, you will have a longer life, better health, and greater wealth, and you will fulfill all your wishes. You will die happily and be protected from fear in the intermediate state. In your next life, you will take miraculous birth on a lotus in a pure realm in which the Buddha is truly present and attain enlightenment. These are among the qualities you will obtain.

c. Regarding the teacher as a buddha

Generally speaking, even if, as far as the teachers are concerned, they are present like the real Buddha, our share of their blessings and accomplishment will be proportionate only to our own devotion. If we have the devotion of seeing the teacher as the Buddha in person, the blessings that we receive will be those of the Buddha in person. If we see our teacher as a bodhisattva or as a special spiritual friend, the blessings we receive will be respectively equivalent. And if we consider that our teacher is an ordinary person, we will not get any blessings at all.

Once, Geshe Drom Tönpa asked Jowo Atisha why it was that although

*"Difficulties" here refers to how difficult it is to find teachers and to have the fortune to be able to follow them.

there were plenty of people practicing meditation in Tibet, there were none who had acquired extraordinary qualities. Atisha replied, "All the qualities, great and small, that arise with the Great Vehicle arise in dependence on the teacher. But you Tibetans only think of the teachers as ordinary persons, so how can you develop any qualities?" On another occasion, a disciple called out loudly to Jowo, "Atisha, give me some advice!" "Ha!" replied Atisha, "No need to shout. I can hear you perfectly well! I'll give you a pith instruction—Faith! Faith! Faith!" This shows just how important it is to have faith.

For this reason, people who wish to realize the buddhas' wisdom easily, through the power of devotion to the teacher, must see their teacher as the Buddha in person. This is stated in the *Tantra of the Empowerment of Vajrapāṇi*:

> Lord of Secrets, if you were to ask how disciples should view their masters, they should see them as the Lord Buddha. Their minds will thus constantly give rise to virtue. They will become buddhas, bringing benefit to the whole world.

This is not a case of contriving to imagine that someone who is not really a buddha is a buddha. Rather, the teachers themselves are, from the very beginning, the Buddha in person. The reason for this is that all the buddhas of the three times constantly reside in the expanse of sameness that is the body of truth, without anything being removed or added in the expanse of their realization. From that state, their essential nature, the buddhas' untainted gnosis, manifests in all kinds of ways. This happens when the interdependently arising causes and conditions come together, as a result, on the one hand, of the aspirations those buddhas made for beings' welfare in the past, when they were on the path of training and so on, and on the other hand, of an increase in their potential disciples' virtue. Like the different reflections that appear through the coinciding of vessels of water and the moon in the sky, the maṇḍala of the body of perfect enjoyment and the array of the body of manifestation (supreme manifestations, manifestations through birth, and manifestations in art) are displayed in accordance with each being's fortune, uninterruptedly until cyclic existence is emptied. It is said, in the *Sūtra of the Ornament of the Light of Gnosis*,

> The Tathāgata is the natural reflection
> Of untainted virtue,

And in it there is neither thusness nor gone-to-thusness.
It appears everywhere, reflected in all the world.

And in the *Sublime Continuum*,

Just as in the clean ground of beryl
The reflected body of the lord of gods appears,
Likewise, in the clean ground of beings' minds,
Arises the reflection of the Munindra's form.[329]

Again, in *The Way of the Bodhisattva*, we read,

As the wishing jewel and tree of miracles,
Fulfill and satisfy all hopes and wishes,
Likewise, through their prayers for those who might be trained,
The physical appearance of the Conquerors occurs.[330]

And in the *Guhyagarbha Tantra*,

Without moving from the expanse of suchness,
They display the form body of true liberation
And diverse forms as are appropriate
To benefit the totality of beings.

In bygone times, when the Buddha was training beings, he appeared in person and people could actually see him. Subsequently, he benefited beings by appearing as arhats and paṇḍitas. At those times, these manifestations of him compiled his original teachings and composed the treatises. Nowadays, he benefits beings by manifesting as spiritual friends, who uphold the doctrine and teach the path to liberation. This is explained in the *Sūtra of the Supreme Concentration*,

Fortunate child, in future lives, in future times, I will manifest as spiritual friends and teach this concentration. Therefore, the spiritual friends are your teachers, so until you reach the heart of enlightenment, follow them, serve and honor them.

The *Tantra of the Vajra Tent* states,

However Vajrasattva is,
He takes the form of masters:
Seeing beings who need his care,
He dwells in ordinary form.

And in the *Secret Essence of the Magical Display*, we find,

The symbolic seal of all the tathāgatas
Is this Secret Essence.
Whoever realizes it and speaks of it
Is me, empowered by me.

Orgyen, knower of the three times, says too,

In every valley, a treasure finder;
There, in every place I practiced, a treasure place.
In every district, a famous siddha.
In every village, a respected master.
In every family, a venerated monk,
And, likewise, a mantra adept subduing spirits.
In the future, as the doctrine disappears, they will multiply:
All of them will be my manifestations.
Cultivate pure vision, O you Tibetans of times to come.

As shown above in scriptures such as the *Vajra Mirror* and the *Tantra of the Union of All the Buddhas*, the teacher is equal to the buddhas and is the essential embodiment of the Three Jewels, or the Fourth Jewel. Again, the Great Master says,

The teacher is Buddha, the teacher is Dharma,
Likewise, the teacher is Saṅgha;
The unsurpassable embodiment of all
Is the teacher, the great glorious heruka.

And in the *Infinite Secret*, we read,

The mighty lord of the maṇḍala, the heruka,
Is the sublime teacher, the source of great accomplishments.

And that is not all. For while, in terms of some of their aspects—their naturally pure character, their work for sentient beings' welfare, and their extensive activities—our teachers can be thought of as being the equals of the buddhas, in terms of their kindness to us, they are more important than the buddhas. This is shown in the *Guhyasamāja Tantra*:

> Because their characters and activities
> Are the same in nature,
> The teachers are equal to all the buddhas.
> Because they show the path to beings,
> They are superior to the buddhas.

And in the *Compendium of the Buddhas' Wisdom*,

> To the wise who have benefited them
> All the conquerors who have gone to bliss,
> Who dwell in the buddha-fields in the ten directions
> And in all the three times,
> Have come and given praise, paying homage with devotion.

And,

> Compared to the buddhas of a thousand kalpas
> You should hold the teacher in greater awe.
> Why? Because the buddhas throughout the kalpas
> All appear in dependence on a teacher.

In particular, when they are giving empowerments and teaching the profound instructions, and when they are present as the masters of gatherings of practitioners, on such occasions the Heruka, Vajrayoginī, and so on, joyfully, through love and compassion, enter the vajra masters' bodies and benefit infinite beings who see, hear, think of, or touch them. This is mentioned in the *Root Tantra of Saṃvara*:

> At all times, there is no doubt,
> The Great Glorious One manifests in them.
> Dwelling in their hearts is Varāhī,
> Together with myself,

The ḍākas, yoginīs, and messengers.
Those beings who visualize them properly
Will come to see the merit.

Keeping fully mindful of the meaning of these and other quotations, and maintaining heartfelt devotion, we should see the teacher as the truth-body buddha in person. This is the most important key point in this chapter.

2. The conduct one should adopt in following one's teachers

The conduct one should adopt is divided into two parts: (1) avoiding inappropriate behavior, and (2) adopting appropriate behavior.

a. Avoiding inappropriate behavior

In the *Compendium of the Buddhas' Wisdom*, we read,

Without following a master,
Buddhahood can never happen:
I have never seen it truly happen,
And if it has, it contradicts the sacred teachings.

And the *Tantra of the Wheel of Bliss* states,

Thus, the root of all the Dharma
Is explained as being the teacher, the vajra holder.
It is impossible to gain accomplishments
That do not come from the teacher.
It is impossible for so-called buddhahood to occur
That does not occur through the teacher.
It is by an authentic teacher
That one is led upward out of existence.

The dominant condition—that is, the principal means or causal factor—for accomplishing unsurpassable buddhahood is following a sublime teacher, a spiritual friend. Such accomplishment depends solely on this. For this reason, when we follow our teacher, demons and evil beings put all their efforts into trying to hinder us. They create differences between master and disciple. They make us discouraged by the scarcity of favorable conditions and the abundance of difficulties that get in our way. They induce negative states of mind, such as wrong views with regard to the teacher and the Dharma. At such times, therefore, we should recognize that these are demons creating obstacles for liberation. Ridding ourselves of such obstacles, we should follow the teacher with renewed devotion, as is explained in the *Verses That Summarize the Perfection of Wisdom*:

> The Dharma is as rare as a jewel, but there are always many difficulties.

And in the *Middle Sūtra of the Perfection of Wisdom*,

> Just as one must diligently and enthusiastically take care of a precious jewel against the depredations of numerous demons, when you truly seek the precious, transcendent wisdom, demons and evil beings will do their best to hinder you. They will turn your mind away by making all sorts of mischief, trying by all means to make sure you do not hear the teachings and to separate you from the spiritual friend. At that time, bodhisattva mahāsattvas should think, "Demons and evildoers are obstructing my virtuous practice. Without a doubt, I must do whatever I can not to fall under their influence." Thinking thus, they should don the great armor of diligence.

For this reason, the Omniscient Teacher writes in *Finding Rest in the Nature of the Mind*,

> Disciples such as these are ever mindful
> Of their teachers' qualities.
> They never think that they have defects,
> And if perchance they see them,
> They will take them for good qualities.
> Sincerely they tell themselves, "The master has no defects—
> This is just my own perception."
> They thus confess their error and,
> Resolving to refrain from it,
> They implement the antidotes.

All the teacher does not like should be avoided.
Strive instead to please him by all means
And never disobey what he commands.
Regarding as himself all those around him whom he cherishes,
Never take his entourage as your disciples.
Request instead both teachings and empowerments.
In the presence of the teacher,
Hold in check your body, speech, and mind.
Don't stretch out your legs or sit in vajra posture.
Do not turn your back or have a somber look,
And do not crease your face with frowns.
Don't speak out of turn, and do not lie or slander others.
Don't discuss another person's faults
Or speak unpleasantly and harshly.
Avoid all careless and unseemly talk.
Do not covet what the teacher owns,
And wish no harm or malice
To himself or to his entourage.
In the various deeds and conduct of the teacher
See no error, no hypocrisy.
Do not think his deeds are wrong
Or even slightly untoward:
All such false, mistaken views should be rejected.
When the teacher has a wrathful look,
Reflect that it is surely your own fault.
Make confession and restrain yourself.
Meditate upon the teacher; seeing him above your head,
Make fervent prayers to him.
By pleasing him you swiftly gain accomplishment.[331]

We should never, therefore, imagine faults in our teachers; we should be mindful only of their qualities. If it should happen that we have a slight lack of faith and see faults, they appear in this way because of our own wrong perception, just as when someone with an eye disorder perceives a conch to be yellow. Thinking, "I am sure that they do not have faults like that," train in pure perception, and make confession, resolving to refrain in the future. Even if such thoughts occur in our dreams, we should confess them as soon as we wake up. The *Tantra of the Display of the Wheel of Perfection* says,

> Should you, in your dreams,
> See faults in the teacher,
> Confess as soon as you awake.
> If you fail to confess,
> It will grow and lead to Torment Unsurpassed.

All the time, check yourself with regard to the things that could displease your teachers (that is, the ones you know about; if you do not know, ask others) and avoid them. Train exclusively in the ways to please them. Do not disobey even the smallest things they say. You should respect the teachers' attendants and other persons whom they hold dear as much as you do the teachers themselves. The reason for this is that by failing to respect them, you will also displease your teachers.

Moreover, you should not attract your teachers' disciples into your own following in order to increase your own importance. Nor should you independently engage in Dharma activities such as giving empowerments and teachings or performing consecrations in the vicinity of your teachers unless you have first consulted them and received their permission to do so. This is mentioned in the above work:

> If you act as they have said,
> Even if there seems to be a mistake,
> It will turn out to make good sense—
> It goes without saying you will accomplish your goal.
> Treat those close to them, whom they hold dear, just as you would
> your teachers.
> Do not take their followers as your disciples,
> And request permission for giving teachings and empowerments,
> Performing consecrations, fire ceremonies, and the like.

Besides this, in your teachers' presence you should avoid disrespectful physical behavior: drawing attention to yourself, sitting with your legs stretched out or leaning against anything, spitting, blowing your nose, vomiting in places such as the teachers' rooms, stepping on their shadows or in their footsteps, measuring their bodies, stepping over their clothes or seats, using their personal belongings without their permission, and so on. This is stated in the *Three Stages*,

> Regarding physical activities in the teacher's presence,
> Sit cross-legged, and do not lean on anything;
> Do not frown or scowl.
> In short, act bodily with care.

And in the *Compendium of the Buddhas' Wisdom*,

> Show your teachers the highest respect:
> Even if they are not sublime beings,
> Revere them as you would the most sublime.
> If ever you show contempt or scorn,
> In hell you'll roast, turned upside down.

And in the *Tantra of the Sublime Yoginī*,

> One who steps upon the teacher's pillow
> Will end up climbing the shālmali hill.
> A person who assesses the teacher's height
> Will be transpierced by three hundred darts.

In the *Tantra of the Secret Ḍākinī*, we find,

> Do not come behind the teacher,
> Or step in their footsteps.
> Do not go before the teacher.
> Turning your back, which to others would appear
> disgraceful,
> Would constitute the crime of contempt.
> Do not stay on the teacher's right,
> But, as ordinary people would approve,
> Walk behind them, on the left.

And in the *Method for Accomplishing Uṣṇīṣacakravartin*,

Teachers reveal to us the meaning of the truth.
By stepping on the shadow of their head and similar,
We abandon the true path and fall down into hell.

Careless behavior with your speech should be avoided: teasing and laughing, irrelevant gossip, unkind ridiculing, telling lies, harsh words, divisive speech, criticizing others, and so on. Speaking in this way just once in the teacher's presence is a far more serious negative action than doing so a hundred thousand times at other times. Even if what you say is true, it will result in very negative consequences for you, the person who has said these things. Why? Because the teacher will be shamed and upset. And to upset the teacher even for an instant gives rise to enormous negative consequences.

Avoid speaking careless, irrelevant words
Within the teachers' presence.
If you get angry with an ordinary person,
You will fall into the ephemeral hells.
Someone who displeases their teacher
Will roast for ten billion kalpas
In the pitch-black Hell of Torment Unsurpassed.[332]

For this reason, the *Sūtra to Vyūharāja on the Qualities of All Dharmas* states,

There are four demons: disrespecting the teacher, not keeping the Dharma in mind, speaking arrogantly, and thinking only of this life.

In the *Tantra of the Secret Ḍākinī*, we read,

Those who secretly gossip much
About their teacher, who, by nature, is a buddha,
Will be crushed in the Crushing Hell and choke.

And,

For those who say he is stupid behind his back,
It is impossible to meet with the path to enlightenment.

And in the *Sublime Ornament*,

> Those who fill their mouths with abusive words
> Will fall into hell for a thousand kalpas.
> Those who criticize the profound words
> Of the sacred vajra master
> Will fall into the Hell of Torment Unsurpassed.

In the *Tantra of the Equalizing Secret*, we read,

> One who arrogantly claims
> That he has greater qualities
> Than the sublime teacher
> Will, for many thousands of kalpas,
> Go upside down into the hells.

And in the *Display of the Secret*,

> Those who find fault in their teachers
> Will roast in the vajra hell.
> Do not criticize the teacher, even in jest.
> Refrain completely from wrongdoing with your speech.

As for lack of restraint in your mental conduct, you should not, even for a second, have such thoughts as coveting your teachers' belongings, or bearing ill will toward those close to them or their disciples. You should never regard them with lack of faith and wrong views, thinking that there are shortcomings in their physical, verbal, and mental activities. In the *Root Tantra of the Accomplishment of Gnosis*, we read,

> Avoid critical or covetous thoughts with regard to
> The teachers' belongings, followers, and relatives.
> Their multifarious deeds are a great magical show,
> A great means for benefiting sentient beings.
> Cast away wrong views, seeing faults
> In the infinite ocean of their intentions and deeds.

In the *Sūtra on the Samādhi in Which the Buddhas of the Present All Stand Before One*, we find,

If you have malicious, angry, or hateful thoughts toward those who teach,
Or fail to regard the teacher as a buddha,
You will never gain their qualities;
It will be impossible for you to receive teachings that you have not yet received,
And impossible for the teachings that you have received not to go to waste.
Because of your lack of respect, the teachings will disappear.

And in the *Tantra of Secret Union*,

By rivalling one's teachers
And rejecting the buddha-deity, one's yidam,
Accomplishing the conquerors' enlightened state becomes
As impossible as going all the way round the ocean mounted on a lame ass.
Those who covet the teacher's property
Will remain hungry spirits for two kalpas.

The *Tantra That Drives Back Armies* states,

Those who angrily and resentfully upset
Their teachers and their circle
Will cook in Torment Unsurpassed
For kalpas as many as the atoms in the universe.

And,

In us they have aroused the forces that lead to enlightenment and happiness,
So we should never criticize the vajra teachers.
Do not think, "They have the five poisons—
Attachment, aversion, and the rest."
Those who have such thoughts
Are burned on the ground of Torment Unsurpassed.

And the *Ocean of Scriptures*,

From thinking oneself equal to the vajra wish-fulfilling king
And hankering after his food and drink and wealth,
One will be roasted in the Hell of Ten Extremes.
Never knowingly let pride affect your attitude
When thinking of the king, the one who tells the supreme secret.
That fault will make you tumble into states of constant strife.

Again, in the *Sūtra That Includes the Many*, it is said,

By thinking, "My teacher is dependent on my kindness,"
You will be reborn in Torment Unsurpassed.
For those who imagine defects in the master,
Gathering virtue is pointless, they have rejected the deity:
Malevolent gods, nāgas, and the like
Will swiftly kill them and they will fall into the hells.

The *Tantra of Taking the Essence* states,

If ever you intend to harm the father
Who has introduced you to the supreme mantras,
You will surely fall into the coldest hells.

For these reasons, never imagine faults in your teacher. Even if someone contrives to create conflicts between you and your teacher and the teacher appears to be angry with you, confess even if you are blameless, and think of it as a means for exhausting your negative actions. In this way, follow your teachers, reflecting on their qualities. If you fail to do so and displease your teachers, the negative consequences are inconceivable, as is explained in the *Tantra of the Empowerment of Vajrapāṇi*:

"Lord, what is the fully ripened effect for those who show contempt for the master?" The Bhagavan replied, "Vajrapāṇi, do not speak of such things. It will frighten the gods and others in this world. Nevertheless, Lord of Secrets, I will tell you a little of it. Courageous One, listen attentively. I have explained the terrible results of acts such as the crimes with immediate retribution, which are the hells. It is those places that I would describe, and they last for infinite kalpas. Therefore, never, in any circumstances, show contempt for the master."

And in the *Word of Mañjuśrī*,

> Any being who in the future
> Shows contempt for a diamond holder
> Will have shown contempt for me:
> Therefore, I have avoided contempt at all times.

The *Tantra of Kīlaya* states,

> It's through your masters that accomplishment is gained.
> If you should show contempt for them,
> The pains of hell are what you will obtain.
> And even when you have escaped from those,
> Then for a billion kalpas multiplied by ten
> The mention of "Sacred Dharma" will never once be heard.

And the *Tantra of the Net of Magical Display*,

> The crime of criticizing teachers
> And upsetting them is such
> That one will suffer misery
> For as long as it would take to sprinkle
> All the water from the ocean with a single hair.

In the *Tantra of the Vajra Ḍāka*, we read,

> Those who criticize the master
> Will suffer in this very life.
> Laid low by plagues, by venoms,
> Toxic minerals, and ḍākinīs,
> And slain by evil forces and savage fiends,
> They'll be dispatched to rebirth in the hells.

And in the *Fifty Verses on the Teacher*,

Stupid fools who criticize the master
Will die from epidemics, leprosy, and other illnesses,
From evil forces, plagues, or poisons.
Killed by monarchs, fire, or venomous snakes,
Drowned, or killed by witches, thieves,
Negative forces, or demonic fiends,
They'll be reborn as denizens of hell.
Don't do anything to disturb your masters' minds.
If, through foolishness, you do,
You'll surely cook and roast in hell.
In Torment Unsurpassed and all the rest,
Those terrifying hells that have been taught,
It has been well explained that there will stay
All those who've criticized their masters.[333]

Since the Mantrayāna vajra masters are the supports for all the root vows, criticizing them is very serious. And besides them, we should consider, and keep as our teachers, even those who teach us how to read. Failure to do so is an extremely serious fault, as is mentioned in a tantra:

If you don't consider as your teachers
Those from whom you've heard a single verse,
It's as a dog you'll be reborn a hundred times,
And as an outcaste you'll take birth.

"Outcastes" in this context are said to be low-caste, flesh-eating beings who live in charnel grounds, but some texts explain them as referring to sentient beings who eat their own flesh.

For these reasons, we should diligently practice the advice given in the *Great Chariot of the Definitive Teachings*:

> In general, whomever you disagree with, half of the quarrel definitely depends on you. If you were not there, the quarrel could not occur, as would be the case for two people on different continents* getting angry. For a quarrel to occur, there would have to be the conditions of their seeing each other, hearing each other,

*Lit. two people on Jambudvīpa and Uttarakuru.

and so on, making contact like a drum and stick. It is not right, therefore, for you to quarrel because doing so serves as the objective condition for the other person's negative deed and because, by stirring up your own anger and hatred on a lasting basis, it creates the seed for rebirth in the hells. You should therefore imagine the person with whom you have quarreled above your head and confess. By doing so, in a few days your resentment and obscuration will definitely be purified.

It is particularly wrong to have a dispute with one's teachers, so you should visualize your teacher on the crown of your head, submit obeisance, and make offerings. With your hands folded and tears of intense regret welling up in your eyes, pray as follows:

O Precious Teacher,
I have no one other than you in whom to place my hopes.
Look on me with your compassionate gaze.
Overcome by ignorance and delusion,
I have committed negative deeds with my body, speech, and mind.
With great regret, I confess all these.
I have transgressed the three kinds of vows,
And my mind is tainted with the stains of evil deeds:
With your compassion, in this very instant,
Cleanse them all away.
Through ignorance and stupidity,
I have unknowingly committed evil acts,
So, as before, I will wander in cyclic existence.
Now, compassionate teacher, in this very instant,
Clear away all my obscurations.
When you see childish, ignorant beings
Acting mistakenly like this,
If you do not all the more turn your compassionate gaze on them,
How do you think they will ever change?
Like a mother who corrects
Her children's misdoings and protects them,
You first aroused bodhichitta
For us beings in the six realms

And vowed to help us:
Why do you now not think of me?
If you do not look on us deluded beings
And hold us with compassion,
How do you think your activities
Will benefit those who need training?
Even though there have been countless buddhas in the past,
They abandoned us and proceeded to liberation.
Now, when the conquerors in the ten directions
Have exhorted you and, for our sake,
You are manifesting as our teacher,
Do you dare to reject us?
Like a bodyguard deserting one when things get dangerous,
Today, are you abandoning us?
Even the precious wishing gem
Grants us all that we desire when we pray to it:
You are so loving and skilled in means,
Why, then, are you not looking on me?
Even flesh-eating spirits give up their former angry ways
As soon as offerings are made to them
And the words of truth are pronounced.
So why are you, the compassionate father of beings,
Not watching over me, as with fervent devotion, veneration,
And anguished mind I confess my wrongdoing?
Unless I purify all my negative deeds
I will take other rebirths,
And I cannot but be roasted in the fires of hell.
If you will not consider now my plight,
How can you be the embodiment of compassion?
Alas! I pray, please purify
My evil actions, each and every one!
This very instant, think of me compassionately.
Grant me empowerment and bless me.
Bestow on me the supreme and common accomplishments.
Dispel my hindrances from obstacle makers and those who lead us astray.
Fulfill all my wishes in this life,
Remove the pains of dying at the moment of death,

Save me from all the fears of the intermediate state,
And lead me to the "Unexcelled."

Recite this prayer day and night, seven times in each of the four sessions. By doing so, you will purify all degenerations and breaches and swiftly obtain the supreme and common accomplishments. There is no more profound way than this for restoring degenerations and breaches.

b. Adopting appropriate behavior

In the *Sūtra of the Arborescent Array*, it is said,

> Your mind should bear all kinds of responsibilities untiringly, like the earth that bears different loads. Like a vajra, your mind should not be swayed by conflicts. Like a city wall, it should be impenetrable by suffering. Like a servant, it should do whatever it is asked. Like a sweeper, it should have completely abandoned pride and self-esteem. Like an elephant, it should carry the heaviest loads. Like a dog, it should not get angry with its owner. Like a ship, it should never tire of coming and going. Like a mother, it should not be discouraged by defilements. Like the all-knowing horse, it should be completely tame and gentle. Like a mountain, it should be unmoved by circumstances. Like an outcaste, it should be without any sense of self-importance. Like a bull with a broken horn, it should be without arrogance. Like a well-brought-up child, it should look up to the spiritual friend. It is with such attitudes that you should serve your spiritual friend.

In this way, you should revere your teachers without ever going against what they say. How to do this is described in *Finding Rest in the Nature of the Mind* as follows:

When you see the teacher, rise and bow to him.
When he wishes to be seated, bring to him a seat
With all the needed comforts,
And with folded hands and pleasant speech extol him.
When he leaves, stand up

And like a servant tend on him.
Be at all times mindful, careful, vigilant,
Respectful, humble, full of awe.
In the teacher's presence be restrained—
Just like a newly wedded bride—
In body, speech, and mind.
Be without distraction, agitation, or vain ostentation.
Respect him in a manner free from partiality,
Without a wish for fame or personal advantage,
Free from all hypocrisy and all deceit,
Without duplicity and biased exclusivity.
Offer to the teacher wealth, if you possess it.
Serve him with respect and reverence
In your body, speech, and mind.
And please him with your practice,
Abandoning this life's concerns.
When others denigrate your teacher,
You should stop them.
If you are unable, think only of his excellence.
Block your ears and with compassion help the slanderers.
But do not stay with them nor chat with them on easy terms.
To act like this brings benefit in all your future lives.
You will encounter holy beings and hear the supreme Dharma.
Grounds and paths of realization,
The power of dhāraṇī and of concentration—
All this wealth of excellence will be completely yours,
And to beings you will bring a feast of happiness
and peace.[334]

Therefore, with devotion free of all pretension, prostrate to your teachers when you see them,* prepare a seat for them to sit on, and offer them whatever they need. Folding your hands, praise their qualities aloud. When they arrive or leave, get up and greet or escort them. In these and other ways, you should do everything to please them. In the *Sūtra on the Samādhi in Which the Buddhas of the Present All Stand Before One*, it is said,

*This can also refer to prostrating to a place where they are living or have lived.

> When bodhisattvas come into the presence of a teacher of the Dharma, they should consider the latter to be our Teacher, the Buddha: they should attend him and do everything to serve him. If, just to hear the teachings, they should follow their teachers for as long as they live, it goes without saying that they should do so in order to receive transmissions, request advice, and meditate. At all times, they should put aside their own personal interests and act in accordance with their teachers' wishes.

And in the Vinaya texts, we read,

> As soon as you see the preceptor, rise from your seat.

It is said in the *Hundred Parables on Action* that if one fails to rise from one's seat, for five hundred lifetimes one will be reborn as someone who is crippled. If one rises and serves the teacher, one will obtain the major and minor marks of a buddha. This is affirmed in the *Commentary on the "Ornament of Clear Realization"*:

> Those who welcome their teachers, escort them, and so forth will possess the marks of a wheel on their hands and feet.

The *Tantra of the Supreme Samaya* shows that, even in this present life,

> Whoever serves and venerates
> The teacher as best they can
> With body, speech, and mind,
> For them, there's no impediment to being blessed
> With a host of powers and abilities.

Moreover, whether you are in your teacher's presence or somewhere else (at home, for example), you should always maintain mindfulness. Keep vigilant, refraining from every kind of wrong conduct with your body, speech, and mind. Maintain carefulness, using your mind to watch your mind and controlling it so that it does not slip under the influence of defilement. By remaining peaceable and controlled, like a newly wed bride, or a newly ordained monk, your wishes will be fulfilled. As we read in *The Way of the Bodhisattva*,

This rampant elephant, my mind,
Once tied to that great post, reflection on the Teachings,
Must now be watched with all my strength
That it might never slip away.
Those who strive to master concentration
Should never for an instant be distracted.
They should always watch their minds, inquiring,
"Where is now my mind engaged?"

And,

All you who would protect your minds,
Maintain your mindfulness and introspection;
Guard them both, at cost of life and limb,
I join my hands, beseeching you.[335]

For those who are respectful and diligent in accompanying their teachers, in receiving instructions from their preceptors, in keeping fearful of the sufferings of the lower realms and cyclic existence, and in following the practice themselves, mindfulness, vigilance, carefulness, and numerous virtuous deeds come about naturally. The same text states,

Through fear, and by the counsels of their abbots,
And staying ever in their teacher's company—
In those endowed with fortune and devotion
Mindfulness is cultivated easily.[336]

Thus, at all times and in all situations, you should perform positive actions and serve your teachers in this manner,* without any self-interest, desire for gain or fame, deceit, hypocrisy, or partiality. Whether you are doing so visibly or discreetly, you will complete the accumulations and purify your obscurations.

In particular, you should follow your teachers, glorious protectors, by pleasing them in three ways.

*"In this manner," that is, while examining your mind and using mindfulness, vigilance, and carefulness.

The least effective way to please one's teachers

The least effective way to please one's teachers is with material offerings. This is not merely a case of unstintingly offering them any things you have and of delighting them. It also involves making an offering of relating their good qualities to others.

As soon as you intend to offer anything that will please your teachers, you should immediately offer it without holding back. And if there is a choice between two things to offer, you should offer the best one to the teacher. By offering one's sublime teachers things that repay their kindness and teachings, you will gain numerous different qualities. Yet even venerating them for a whole kalpa for each letter of the teachings you receive could never fully pay for those teachings, let alone repay the kindness of the teachers themselves. In the *Sūtra of the Questions of the Householder Ugra*, we read,

> Bodhisattvas who earnestly seek to receive a teaching and to recite it might venerate the master from whom they obtain or receive a single verse on the six transcendent perfections, the bodhisattva paths, and so forth by seeking, serving, and making all kinds of offerings to that master for as many kalpas as the letters in the teaching, but their respect for the master would still not be sufficient, let alone their respect for the teachings.

The benefits of making such offerings are boundless, as will be explained in detail below. Thus, in all the world with its gods, there are no greater sources of qualities than the sublime teachers and no greater kindness is there than theirs. So we should never seek any advantage or keep accounts in making an offering of just a few ordinary material riches, for it could never repay our teachers' kindness and it is impossible to put a price on the qualities of the Dharma. Ordinary people show their gratitude for the teachers' kindness in their presence, and then, behind their backs repeatedly tell others, "I made this offering," while at other times they regret having made the offering. You should never act in this way. It is said in the sūtras that relating how many good deeds you have done destroys their effect, as does regretting them.

Moreover, our teachers are the ones who dispel all our troubles in cyclic existence and enable us to gain the riches of buddhahood, teaching us the precious, unsurpassable Dharma and introducing us to the fact that the nature of the mind is buddha. To fail to repay their kindness and expect them to return our kindness in making them a small material gift is utterly inappropriate. Put another way, when we make an offering in order to increase our own merit, in accepting it, it is our teachers who are being immensely kind. They have never insisted on our making an offering, so why should they be grateful to us?

Therefore, you should reflect on their kindness and be indefatigable and diligent in serving your teachers, offering them the best of whatever you have, in order to accomplish happiness and well-being in this life and the next and to gather the provisions for the path. We read in the *Sūtra of the Arborescent Array*,

> Fortunate child, to repay your spiritual friends' kindness, you should make every effort to venerate them. Should you ask why, it is because they hold all virtuous qualities in their hands.

And in the *Stainless Wisdom*,

> Those who honor and attend to
> The teacher, the treasury holder,
> Must never proclaim it or relate it.
> Those who do so
> Will have no result and will be ruined.

The middling ways to please one's teachers

The middling ways to please them are to serve them with one's body and speech.

Serving one's teachers with one's body

On the outer level, we should prostrate to our teachers, circumambulate them, and make offerings such as incense and lamps. On the inner level, we should please them with the feast offering of blessed food and drink. And on the secret level, we should please them with our realization, concentration, wisdom, and so on. Whether when they are alive, after they have passed away, or on the anniversaries of their passing, we should make offerings to them night and day and repay their kindness by respectfully making gifts to beings and so on. We should protect our teachers from obstacles due to fire, water, precipices, beasts of prey, or enemies. We should act as emissaries for the teachers' activities in different countries, attend to their everyday requirements as needed, prepare seats for them to sit on, sweep the path, put our own cloth or silks on the path, and so on. Welcoming them and accompanying them with incense, we should sprinkle perfumed water and sweep the area around their residence. We should offer maṇḍalas, welcome them and see them off by providing a means of transport such as a horse or palanquin, and make offerings. When we see our teachers, we should perform prostrations and request their blessings, rising and folding our hands, and so on.

Requesting blessings refers to the present-day custom of receiving blessings from the teacher's hand. This is the meaning intended in the sūtras and tantras of taking the teacher's feet on the crown of one's head. Its purpose is as follows: Because the teachers are inseparable from the lords of the maṇḍala, the three seats are complete in their bodies and the infinite Three Roots are present, pervading the whole of their bodies to the tips of their hairs, like sesame seeds in a pod. So the merest contact with their hands, feet, or any other part of their body instantly purifies all the negative actions and obscurations that one has accumulated in the past and enables one to attain the level of the heruka without delay. How this is so is explained in a tantra:

> Those who have realized the glorious heruka, great wisdom,
> With all the marks of perfect purity,
> Are the source of bliss for the practitioner.
> Master and heruka being not two, they are inseparable:
> Contact with that inseparable union
> Purifies one, destroying all negative actions.
> Even their touch and voices
> Will free one from all evil.
> Freed of every kind of evil,
> One's body completely purified,
> One will become the best of humans,* devoid of fault.
> One will attain the level of a tathāgata,
> With every negative action purified.
> Purified of all negativity,

*Tib. *mi mchog*, the "best of humans" is an epithet of a buddha.

> One will be reborn in the family of the tathāgatas
> And become a Dharma-holding king.

According to the Lord, the Great Treasure Discoverer and Dharma King,* the implication of this quotation is that the most important factor is the faith and devotion of the person receiving the blessing.

Besides all this, we should point our pillow in the direction where our teacher is staying. Whatever we eat or drink, we should remember our teachers and offer the first part to them. Whatever we are doing, we should think that it is what our teacher has told us to do and, with vigilance, make every effort to succeed in our task.

In short, we should at all times keep our teachers as the objects of our yearning and respect, as is mentioned in the *Sūtra of the Arborescent Array*:

> Again, the merchant's son Sudhana, aspiring and diligently undertaking to achieve great enlightenment, attended and praised the spiritual friend, Noble Mañjushrī. Mañjushrī declared, "Accompanying and serving teachers is the basis for accomplishing great enlightenment. You should never tire of following and accompanying them."

Serving one's teachers with one's speech

Serving one's teachers with one's speech also involves a respectful mental motivation. On this basis, we should praise our teachers, go for refuge in them, and hold the teachers and all those connected with them in respect. Explicitly or discreetly, repeat the most essential of the sublime teachers' words, memorize the words and meaning of their teachings and, without forgetting them, proclaim them to others.

If it should happen that what they say is slightly unclear, you should reflect, thinking, "I am not managing to understand the true import of this: the fact that these words appear to be contradictory is a defect in my own understanding." You should consider that even if your teachers' words, whether related to the teachings or to ordinary subjects, appear to be mistaken, it is you who have failed to understand them. And if others ask you,

*Tib. rJe gter chen chos kyi rgyal po, refers here to the treasure discoverer Gyurme Dorje, Terdak Lingpa (1646–1714), the founder of Mindrölling Monastery in Tibet.

you should reply that you have not understood the intended meaning. Not for an instant should you say or think, "What the teacher has said cannot be right," for that is even more negative than criticizing a buddha's words. Thus, you should do whatever your teachers tell you. Even if what you have to do appears to be wrong,* you should first be guided by what they have said. Once you have started, the benefits of carrying out their wishes and the disadvantages of not doing so will become clear and you will surely understand what they had in mind. So, thinking, "Whatever they tell me is bound to be good for me," reflect on their qualities, rejoicing and praising them. To people who do not know them, or if they do, only slightly, and when you are traveling elsewhere, speak of your teachers' definite qualities. And in the four sessions, or all the time, think of your teachers and pray to them with the sweetest of melodies.

Furthermore, you should use your voice to praise them, to speak pleasantly and gently, without ever defying them, to talk honestly, and to relate their qualities to others too. Whatever they ask you to do, respectfully and politely reply that you will do it. When you yawn or sneeze, cover your mouth. Whatever you are doing, seek your teacher's approval. When you begin any virtuous activities, first think of your teachers, praise them, and pray to them. The *Jewel Cloud Sūtra* says,

> When serving them, sit on a seat; give praise; offer your esteem.

Serving one's teachers with one's mind

With the utmost faith, think of your teachers' qualities, and cultivate faith and devotion, thinking how difficult it is to encounter a teacher. Regarding your teachers as the Fourth Jewel, consider that they are equal to, or even superior to, the buddhas, so that when you hear their names, see their faces, meet them as a result of your aspirations, seek and find them, and hear their teachings, and even when they simply touch you on the head, you feel immense joy, thinking, "How wonderful it is that someone like me has actually met a spiritual friend like this," and realizing how rare it is to have the chance of meeting them. Think of how you can serve them in all kinds of ways, reflecting on how rare it is for such sublime beings to appear

*Even if the teacher asks you to do something that would normally be considered a fault, as when the Indian siddha Tilopa told his disciple Naropa to go and steal something.

in this world, how difficult it is to meet them, and how one cannot know when they will leave. Respectfully attend all those beings, too, whom the teachers have accepted as disciples, developing devotion and pure perception in such ways as saluting them and serving them. By these means, you will accomplish everything that is excellent in this life and in your future lives. The *Jewel Cloud Sūtra* states,

> Wherever those who teach the Dharma reside, think of those places as sacred places. Think of those who proclaim the teachings as masters, as spiritual friends, as guides. And when you see them, be happy and rejoice.

And the *Sūtra of the Arborescent Array*,

> By never separating from the thought of the spiritual friend, all one's goals will be fulfilled.

And the *Compendium of the Buddhas' Wisdom*,

> To an authentic teacher,
> The conquerors of the three times and ten directions,
> The bodhisattvas, gods, human beings,
> And likewise the vidyādharas of the nāgas,
> Yakṣhas, and rākṣhasas with wrong views
> All assemble and bow down,
> Tossing flowers and singing praises.
> Know that, just as mothers beget their children,
> The bodhisattvas and vidyādharas
> Are born from sublime beings.

The best way to please one's teachers

The best way to please one's teachers is to offer the practice one has done in accordance with their instructions. Of all kinds of offering, this is the very highest. Indeed, this is the reason that the teachers who have successively appeared since the time of the Buddha teach the Dharma and appear in the world. So everything we hear them say we should accomplish, clearly distinguishing between what to avoid and what to adopt. Hearing the teachings depends on there being a teacher, a sublime being, so you should practice by first impartially seeking out numerous sublime beings and following and receiving teachings from them. Then, you should practice by reflecting on the teachings you have heard, so that you gain an unmistaken knowledge of them. And without being content with mere knowledge, you should practice by making an experience of the meaning. That sort of practice should not be a mere facade: you should practice by blending the teachings with your whole being. For this, you must unite skillful means and wisdom, practicing diligently without leaving things at the level of aspiration. Practicing in this way is an offering that pleases all the teachers, buddhas, and bodhisattvas; it is the way of sublime beings. The *Ornament of Clear Realization* speaks of

> the way that delights the buddhas.[337]

And the *Middle Sūtra of the Perfection of Wisdom* states,

> All the buddhas have commended, praised, and revered diligence in practicing the spiritual friend's instructions.

In the *Compendium of the Buddhas' Wisdom*, we read,

> The sublime sugatas of the past
> Served a sublime guide
> And, abandoning all, departed to remote hermitages.
> There they practiced, and many attained liberation.
> So if we train as they did,
> We will inherit the perfect freedom of the conquerors.
> Therefore, to sublime beings whose kindness is so great,
> Make an offering of unflagging faith,
> Of flexibility, without being rigid and stubborn,
> Material offerings, without stinginess,
> Reverence without doubts,
> Honest words, free of deceit,
> A mind free of self-interest,
> Intelligence without confusion,

And a stainless altruistic attitude.
These eight you should offer to those sublime beings in their
entirety.

In short, all the piṭakas and tantras speak of the sublime teachers as being manifestations of the Buddha. By practicing in accordance with their life stories, we will be following the example of the Buddha. For this reason, we should regard the qualities of the teachers' body, speech, and mind as being the same as those of the buddhas. Thinking, "I, too, must do exactly the same," we should train in following the teachers' deeds and spend our time listening, reflecting, and meditating. By doing so, we will swiftly obtain the supreme and common accomplishments. The *Ocean of Gnosis Tantra* declares,

The teacher is Buddha, the teacher is Dharma,
Likewise, the teacher is Saṅgha:
The jewel of the teacher is our object of contemplation.
Do not abandon the teacher, respect the teacher,
And with the specific devotion and attitude
See the teacher as no different from Vajradhara.
The accomplishments that arise from doing so
Are what the practitioners enjoy.
By this means, they attain the glorious state of perfect
buddhahood.
The fulfillment of all the accomplishments
Arises from pleasing the teacher.

And in the *Tantra of the Net of Magical Display*, it is said,

Should you ask how one should view the master,
The teachers are the equal of all the buddhas.
They are ever Vajradhara.
They are the crown jewel of the tathāgatas.
They are an ocean of wisdom,
Granting us a precious wish-fulfilling jewel.
Remember the qualities of your masters,
Never think of their faults.

Those who remember the teachers' qualities gain the
 accomplishments,
While those who think of their faults lose all accomplishment.

Furthermore, the *Guhyasamāja Tantra* states,

Low-caste people, menial workers,[338] and the like,
And those whose minds are set on taking life,
Will gain accomplishment in this supreme vehicle,
The Unsurpassable Great Vehicle.
Even beings who perform great evil,
Like committing crimes with immediate retribution,
Will attain accomplishment in this supreme vehicle,
The great ocean of the Diamond Vehicle.
Those who make heartfelt criticism of the master
Will never, even if they practice, gain full accomplishment.

Its commentary, the *Shining Lamp*, explains that if one is close friends with people who genuinely criticize one's teachers, even if one has not criticized the master directly, it is no different from doing so. Therefore, if people speak badly of your teacher and you can prevent them from doing so, whether by peaceful or forceful means, stop them. Otherwise, reflect on the teacher's qualities, block your ears with your fingers, and do not associate or mix freely with those people. To do so would be an extremely serious fault, as is mentioned in the *Source of Nectar Tantra*:

If people criticize the vajra master,
Stop them by peaceful or forceful means.
If you do not have the ability,
Mindfully cover up your ears.
Do not associate or talk with them.
If you mix with such people,
You will be boiled in the lower realms.

All the methods for examining the spiritual friend mentioned in the sūtras and tantras apply to the time when one has not yet made a connection with the teacher. But once one has made a connection with one's teachers, whatever happens, one must follow them with devotion, seeing everything they do as excellent. The *Compendium of the Buddhas' Wisdom* states,

> Once you have taken them as sublime beings,
> Whether or not you are certain that they are perfect,
> How could you disobey and reject their word?
> If you break the link with them,
> You will be thoroughly boiled in the vajra hell.

Even from a general point of view, the buddhas, bodhisattvas, and great accomplished vidyādharas display inconceivable skillful means, concentration, wisdom, and confident eloquence, adapted to the different ways in which they can train beings. This is not something that ordinary, limited minds can imagine, so even if they appear to be at fault, one can never be sure that this is so. The *Sūtra of the Ornament of the Buddhas* speaks of this at length, beginning,

> With multifarious ways and means,
> They roam the world and work for beings' good.
> Like a lotus in water, unattached to worldly things,
> To create joy and faith, they take on different forms.
> As kings of poets, they compose poetry.
> As dancers, drummers, athletes, and musicians,
> Beautifully adorned, with ornaments and garlands they dance,
> And as magicians, display everywhere many forms.
> They appear as villagers, village chiefs, governors,
> And likewise guides, merchants, and householders.
> Kings, ministers, secretaries, envoys,
> Physicians, experts in worldly treatises and rituals,
> They are as wish-fulfilling trees in the wilderness.

And in the *Perfection of Wisdom in One Hundred Thousand Lines*, we read,

> Some bodhisattva mahāsattvas, in order to bring sentient beings to full maturity through their skill in means, appear to enjoy the pleasures of the five senses: they manifest from within the retinue of consorts and attain buddhahood in unsurpassable, true, and perfect enlightenment.

In his *Graded Path of the Magical Manifestation Tantra*, the master Buddhaguhya writes,

> Sometimes peaceful, sometimes wrathful,
> To the lustful, they appear lustful,
> To the hateful, they appear wrathful,
> To the arrogant, they appear hard,
> And to the stupid, they appear stupid.
> Sailing as on the ocean, against the wind or with it,
> They skillfully adapt their conduct
> And activities in carrying us across.

For this reason, Rigdzin Jigme Lingpa states in *Treasury of Precious Qualities*,

> Never look askance at what the teacher does,
> For most of the great siddhas of the Noble Land
> Were menials or outcasts, evildoers,
> And, even by the worst of standards, dissolute.
> If those who have not mastered their own minds
> Ascribe faults to their teacher, then their sin is measureless.
> Although he knew by heart the twelve parts of the scripture,
> Bhikshu Sunakshatra, overmastered by the power of sin,
> Perceived as false the actions of the Buddha.
> Reflecting well thereon, reform yourself.[339]

Accordingly, we should reflect only on our teachers' qualities, without ever ascribing faults to them. We should consider that they are the Buddha in person, as is explained in the *Jewel Cloud Sūtra*:

> "If I follow a teacher, my virtuous activities will increase and my negative deeds will diminish." With this in mind, whether or not your preceptors are learned, whether or not they are knowledgeable, whether or not they are disciplined, consider them as the Buddha.

This is why some of the accomplished masters of the Kagyu tradition in the past used to say,

> These precious, authentic teachers—
> All that they do is excellent;
> Whatever they do is a virtue.
> Even if they act as murderers or butchers,
> Be content, all is well;
> It is certain that they are holding beings with compassion.
> Even if they appear to have loose sexual morals,
> Good qualities are increasing, good qualities arise:
> It is a sign that they are uniting skillful means and wisdom.
> In fooling others with their lies,
> They are using a variety of gestures and means
> To guide all beings on the path to freedom.
> Even though they act as thieves, robbers, or gangsters,
> They are transforming others' property to accumulate merit
> And reducing people's poverty.
> In truth, when teachers like these
> Deliver a reprimand, it is a wrathful mantra:
> It is sure to dispel bad circumstances and obstacles.
> When they give a beating, it is a blessing:
> It gives rise to all accomplishments.
> You who have devotion, be glad!

That is the sort of faith and devotion that we need to cultivate. If we have this sort of approach, it is impossible for us not to be freed from cyclic existence. As Rigdzin Jigme Lingpa said,

> The marks of teachers and disciples and the extremely secret essential points of the practice are widely taught in the profound sūtras and tantras. However, as I can testify from my own experience, they all boil down to the following crucial point. Think, on the one hand, of a master, someone whose mind has been definitively freed from cyclic existence by a realized noble teacher and who possesses great compassion. And take, on the other hand, a person full of devotion, who has abandoned his or her own interests and does whatever the teacher says—someone like Nāgabodhi, clad in the great armor of faith, or like Palgyi Yeshe, whose mind is so stable that it is unaffected by circumstances and

who serves the teacher with no regard for body or life. Now, if such a disciple prays from the depths of their heart to that master and mingles their mind with the master's wisdom mind, it is impossible for them not to attain liberation. Why? Because what brings about blessings and accomplishments does not lie in strenuous practice but in pure devotion. It does not lie in the pith instructions but in faith. Thus, when Nāgabodhi snatched up a piece of snot that the noble master Nāgārjuna had discarded and put it in his mouth, at that very moment he attained the first bodhisattva level and realized the truth. And when Palgyi Yeshe killed two jailers and extricated his master Nyak Jñanakumāra from prison, he immediately gained accomplishment.

When I saw the writings of the Second Buddha, Longchenpa, I realized that up until then I had never, anywhere, come across such a profound and vast path, and I felt an inconceivable devotion to him. He actually appeared to me in his wisdom body and guided me. Again, immense devotion dawned in me, to the point that I was willing to give my life, and my mind was abruptly freed of all taints. Up until now, I have guided more than a hundred disciples. The ones who persevere in meditation do not advance beyond the worldly concentrations;* the intelligent ones might at first see the meaning of the lack of inherent existence, but on account of their fleeting devotion, they are cut off from profound realization. The way realization of the natural state arises appears to depend solely on the scale of their devotion.

The reason for this is to be found in the *Compendium of the Buddhas' Wisdom*:

> Even if one does not know or understand all the teachings,
> By fully honoring and serving a sublime teacher,
> One will cross the ocean of cyclic existence.
> It is as when a seed is planted in a fertile field:
> It is bound to grow and flourish.

*"Worldly concentrations" refers to states of concentration that result in rebirth in the world of form but do not enable one to be freed from cyclic existence.

II. The main explanation of how specifically to train in the profound practice

The way to train is widely mentioned in the secret tantras, among them, the *Tantra of the Precious Gathering of All*:

> Greater than meditation for a hundred thousand kalpas
> On a hundred thousand deities
> Is the brief thought of one's teacher:
> The merit of this is infinite.

And the *Great Array of the Sublime*,

> One who meditates on his kind teacher
> Above the crown of his head,
> On the palm of his hand,
> Or in the center of his heart
> Will also grasp the qualities of a thousand buddhas.

And the *Tantra of the Three Verses*,

> On someone who venerates the vajra master,
> Meditating on him or her above the crown of the head,
> The conquerors will bestow their blessings.

The unique source of all blessings and accomplishments, the root of the path of the Diamond Vehicle of the Secret Mantras, is the profound path that is the Lama Sādhana, the method for accomplishing the teacher. The reason for this is that when one first enters the Mantra Vehicle, the means of entry is the empowerment. And during the empowerment, the one who bestows empowerment, the lord of the maṇḍala, is the vajra master, while the empowering deities of the maṇḍala of the three seats complete are manifestations of the master's concentration. There are numerous accounts of disciples who were unaware of this and considered the yidam to be the chief of the maṇḍala rather than the teacher, thus barring their chances of attaining accomplishment. Later, too, when one is practicing the path of the main practice and training in the generation, recitation, and perfection phases, there is not even a minute part of these that is anything other than an aspect of the root teacher's body, speech, and mind. In particular, the ultimate perfection phase is the practice of uniting with the ultimate reality, nonconceptual gnosis. Since this is the very essence of a realized teacher's mind, it is from mingling one's own mind with the teacher's mind that the qualities of realization take birth in one's being.

Furthermore, when as a result of one's deity practice, one has visions of one's teachers and receives teachings from them, in this life, future lives, or in the intermediate state, these are also nothing other than mere appearances that are brought about by the teachers' compassion and one's own faith and devotion. They do not, even a tiny bit, happen just like that. There are some who are ignorant of this and who think that once the teacher has given them the empowerments, pith instructions, introductions, and so on, which are merely skillful means, they will then receive the main blessings and accomplishments from the yidam, ḍākinī, and others, as if these were superior to the teacher. The great vajra holders of the Ancient and New Traditions have repeatedly said that to think like this is the greatest obstacle to attaining accomplishment. And in the *Hevajra Tantra*, too, it is stated,

> That which is innate and inexpressible
> Cannot be found by any other means.
> Know that it is from the teacher's timely introduction
> And the merit one has gained oneself.

And in his *Five Stages*, Nāgārjuna writes,

> One who tumbles from a lofty peak
> May think, "I must not fall," but fall he will.
> One to whom a teacher has kindly given the beneficial
> transmission
> May not wish for freedom, but he will still be freed.

Glorious Saraha says,

> The teacher's words that have entered your heart
> Are like a treasure resting on the palm of your hand.

In Indrabhūti's *Accomplishment of Gnosis*, we read,

Without our grasping the oars,
The boat will never cross to the other side.
Even if we have all the qualities complete,
Without a teacher, there is no end to saṃsāra.

And in the *Profound Path*,

Even though the sun is burning hot,
Without a lens, the fire will not ignite.
So too, without the presence of a teacher,
The buddhas' blessings cannot possibly occur.

The *Tantra of the Supreme Samaya* states,

For faithful ones who seek accomplishment,
It comes from serving their teacher devotedly.
Defilements, subsidiary defilements,
And faults will all be thus consumed.

And in a song by the great Chetsun,[340]

When yearning for the teacher occurs,
Experiences and blessings will surely dawn.

As for how one should practice, generally speaking, there are numerous different methods. In Rigdzin Jigme Lingpa's tradition, the outer practice, at the beginning of the path when one takes refuge, consists of visualizing the teacher as the field of accumulation and so on. The inner practice, in order to purify one's stream of being, consists of meditating on the teacher as the embodiment of all the buddhas on the crown of one's head. The secret practice, in order for blessings to enter all at once, consists of visualizing the teacher in the center of one's heart and so on. And in the most secret practice, one visualizes one's own body as the teacher or when one is practicing the generation phase, one similarly arises as the teacher in the form of the yidam deity.

There is also the ultimate practice, where one realizes that the teacher and one's mind are inseparable and one rests in the state of thatness beyond anything to be practiced and anyone who is practicing.

Here, in the context of the Guru Yoga, there are also a number of different ways of visualizing the root and lineage teachers—one above the other, as a large gathering, in the manner of the jewel that includes all, and so on. These are explained according to the individual instruction manuals.

In the present case, we shall follow the approach taken in the *Primary Instructions on the Practice of Vajrasattva*,* which consists of five sections: (1) visualizing the support, (2) offering the seven branches, (3) praying, (4) receiving the empowerments, and (5) mingling one's mind with the teacher's and settling in meditative equipoise.

A. Visualizing the support

The *Primary Instructions* states,

> Visualize the object of your prayer in the sky in front, as you did previously for the object of refuge.

If you have been going straight through the preliminary practices and have not dissolved the object of refuge visualized earlier, simply continue the same visualization. Otherwise, meditate again as was explained above in the refuge section, clearly visualizing the object of refuge. All the refuges appear as an illusion-like display, which is the appearance aspect of the bliss-emptiness that is your root teacher's mind, in which there are no fluctuations in compassion and no differences in the level of realization. Visualize them awakened in all their splendor, blessing you and all other sentient beings with their gaze. You should understand that your root teacher's body is the Saṅgha, his† speech is the sacred Dharma, his mind is the Buddha: he embodies all the Three Jewels. He is the embodiment of the Three Roots: his body is the lama, his mind is the yidam deity, his qualities and activities are the ḍākinīs and Dharma protectors. And he is the essence of the four buddha-bodies inseparable: his body is the body of manifestation, his speech is the body of perfect enjoyment, his mind is the body of truth, and

*As in previous sections, Shechen Gyaltsap refers to the Minling Dorsem, whose instruction manual, the *Primary Instructions*, he mentions here.

†The teacher in this case is visualized as Vajrasattva, hence the use of the masculine pronoun in this context, which obviously does not preclude the same principles applying to a woman teacher.

their inseparability in him is the body of the essential nature. This is stated in the secret tantras,

> In the body of the vajra master
> The bodies of the sugata-conquerors are complete.
> The teacher is the Buddha, the teacher is the Dharma,
> Likewise, the teacher is the Saṅgha.
> The teacher is the Great Glorious Heruka,
> The king of all is the teacher.

And in *Immaculate Light*, the great commentary on the *Wheel of Time Tantra*, we read,

> The vajra master who teaches the *Tantra of the Wheel of Time* should be regarded by those who strive for liberation as the Lord Mañjushrī, as the Primordial Buddha in the Wheel of Time.

And in the *Guhyagarbha Tantra*,

> If one makes offerings of the five enjoyments to the Lord, . . .

and so on, indicating by the term *Lord*[341] the teacher, who is the sovereign of the maṇḍala. The sovereign of the maṇḍala is likewise denoted by the term *heruka*, which is used in the old texts of the Ancient Translations when speaking of the teacher. In some texts, the term *guru* is also used. The All-Powerful Lord Virūpa[342] says,

> Make no distinction between
> The teacher and Vajrasattva.
> The teacher is Buddha, Dharma,
> And likewise Saṅgha.
> Those who wish for the highest level of accomplishment
> Should please their teacher in every way.
> In this time of strife, Vajradhara, embodiment of all the buddhas,
> Appears for our sake, in tune with everyone.
> Knowing this, rely upon him truly, in every circumstance,
> And you will attain great bliss, the accomplishment
> Of all the buddhas, present, past, and yet to come.

The precious master Drikung Kyobpa[343] says,

> Unless the sun of devotion shines
> On the snowy range of the teacher's four bodies,
> The stream of his blessings will never flow.
> So earnestly arouse devotion in your mind!

And Lord Buddha, too, said,

> Shāriputra, it is through faith that the ultimate is to be realized.

B. Offering the seven branches

1. Obeisance

The *Sūtra of Great Liberation* speaks of obeisance as follows:

> With both hands joined above my head
> Like an opening lotus bud,
> And countless bodies amassed in clouds,
> I prostrate to the buddhas of the ten directions.

The Omniscient Teacher gives a corresponding explanation:

> Then like a lotus bud appearing in a lovely pool
> And opening with the rising of the sun,
> Make a gesture with your two hands joined above your head.
> With melodious praises, with countless emanated forms,
> Bow down to them devotedly.[344]

Accordingly, consider yourself and all other sentient beings emanating as many bodies as there are atoms in the universe in the presence of the extraordinary fields of accumulation, recalling their supreme qualities and singing their praises. Join your two hands to resemble the newly opening flower of a white lotus. As you touch your hands to your forehead, your physical obscurations are purified. Touching them to your throat purifies the obscurations of your speech. And touching them to your heart purifies your mental obscurations. Then, perform what we call "touching the ground with the five points of your body." This means, submit obeisance by touching the ground with your forehead, the two palms of your hands, and your two knees, making five points of contact. The benefits and purposes of doing so are that you purify the five poisons or defilements in your stream of being; you obtain the fivefold empowerments and blessings of the body, speech, mind, qualities, and activities of the fields of accumulation; and ultimately you will gain the unfathomable crown protuberance on a buddha's head.

If you have been accumulating the numbers (one hundred thousand, for example) for the other sections of the preliminary practice, you must be sure to accumulate the number of prostrations too. Nowadays, it appears to be the custom in some practice traditions to perform prostrations during the refuge practice in conjunction with the recitation of the refuge prayer. There is certainly nothing wrong in doing so, but the explicit teaching of most textual traditions is that the prostrations should be counted at this stage, so it is best to do so here.

The benefits of submitting obeisance have already been described above.* They are also described in *Finding Rest in the Nature of the Mind*:

> As many as may be the drops of water in the sea,
> Or atoms in earth and in the king of mountains,
> Merits such as this cannot be found in all the triple world.
> Thanks to such prostration,
> For as many times as there are atoms in the earth,
> Down to the strong foundation of the universe,
> You will become a Cakravartin king,
> And finally you will attain
> The state of supreme peace.[345]

2. Making offerings

The same text instructs us as follows:

> Presented in reality and imagined in your mind,
> Make offerings in vast and unsurpassed array.[346]

In other words, arrange whatever material offerings you may have, and men-

*See above, p. 464.

tally emanate and offer every possible kind of untainted offering to delight the senses, as Noble Samantabhadra's clouds of offerings—all the offerings of the celestial and human worlds, filling the heavens and the earth, including the following:

- incense, flowers, lamps, and the like
- boundless manifested creations such as palaces and landscapes
- the seven attributes of royalty (the wheel, jewel, queen, minister, supreme horse, elephant, and general)
- the eight auspicious symbols (the parasol, golden fish, vase, lotus, white conch shell, eternal knot, victory banner, and wheel)
- the eight auspicious objects (white mustard seed, *durva* grass, bezoar, vermilion powder, curd, *vilva* fruit, mirror, and right-spiraling conch shell)
- the seven semiprecious articles (shoes, cushion, carriage, bedclothes, throne, sword, and snakeskin)
- all the most beautiful displays in this and other worlds of all kinds of emanated gods and goddesses, with cloud-like offerings of song, dance, and music
- the inner samaya substances of the secret mantras, the feast liquor, meat,* and other varieties of offerings to be eaten, drunk, licked, and tasted.

Through the power of his concentration, the bodhisattva Samantabhadra emanated from his heart thousands of billions of multicolored rays of light as numerous as the dust particles in countless buddha-fields. On the tip of each of those rays of light, he projected a bodhisattva Samantabhadra identical to himself. From the heart of each one of them were emanating light rays in the same manner, and on the tip of each again another Samantabhadra, and so on in an infinite progression until the number of emanations was utterly inconceivable. Each of these manifestations of Samantabhadra was venerating the buddhas and bodhisattvas of the ten directions with an inconceivable variety of boundless offerings, in what are known as "Samantabhadra's clouds of offerings." It is in this same way that you should make offerings, mentally creating as many emanations as possible.

*Tib. *ru rdir*. This does not refer to meat that has been killed for ordinary consumption, but the meat of a naturally dead animal offered as a samaya substance.

The benefits of this sort of offering are mentioned in the *Sūtra of the White Lotus of the Sacred Dharma* as follows:

> Those who to the relics of the Sugata, however few,
> Strike and make the cymbals sound just once,
> Or offer just a single flower to them,
> And, even if with their minds disturbed,
> Venerate a fresco of the Sugata on a wall
> Will one day come to see ten million buddhas.

And so on. They have been described in detail above.

3. Confessing negative actions

In the presence of the extraordinary fields of accumulation, fold your hands, and remorsefully and regretfully confess all the negative deeds, whether you remember them or not, that you have gathered with your body, speech, and mind throughout your beginningless series of lives until now:

- acts of disrespect with regard to your parents, preceptors, instructors, fellow practitioners, sublime beings, and others
- the ten nonvirtuous deeds
- the five crimes with immediate retribution
- the five crimes that are almost as grave
- misuse of the Three Jewels' property
- acting stingily and preventing others from being charitable, and so on
- in particular, your transgressions of the root and branch sacred commitments with regard to the body, speech, and mind of your vajra-holder teachers, brought about by your considering them to be ordinary persons
- your faults through mixing with those who have broken the sacred commitments and your damaging the sacred commitments yourself, and so on

In short, confess all the shameful deeds (both naturally shameful and shameful because they violate edicts) that act as obstacles to your attaining the supreme and common accomplishments. Imagine that all these are gathered into a black heap on top of your tongue, and confess them. At the very instant you do so, consider that from the body, speech, and mind of the fields of accumulation, who are your support, white light streams forth and touches you, so that you are cleansed and purified. Using the antidote of vowing to refrain from such misdeeds in the future, recite the words of the confession.

The benefits are as mentioned in detail above and are also described in the *Hundred Thousand* as follows:

> For those who, the instant they remember,
> Recall their evil deeds and remorsefully confess,
> All those deeds will be consumed.
> Bodhisattva, vow in the future to refrain!

4. Rejoicing

From the depth of your heart, genuinely rejoice in the virtuous activities performed for others' benefit by the buddhas of the ten directions and the four times—their turning the Wheel of Dharma and so on. Rejoice in the bodhisattvas' virtue, the great waves of activities performed for enlightenment. Rejoice in the aggregates of wisdom and liberation of the noble listeners and solitary realizers. Rejoice in the virtue consistent with ordinary merit produced by all sentient beings. And rejoice in all the deeds that you have performed in the past, are performing at present, and are certain to perform in the future.

The benefits of doing so are described in the *Verses That Summarize the Perfection of Wisdom*:

> Rejoice with bodhichitta and a pure intent.
> One may assess the weight of a billion Mount Merus
> But not the merit of rejoicing.
> Just as a single precious beryl outshines
> A whole great pile of jeweled trinkets,
> A single thought of rejoicing with bodhichitta
> Outshines the whole vast heap of all beings' charity and other deeds.

5. Exhorting the teachers to turn the Wheel of Dharma

Among the buddhas, bodhisattvas, teachers, and great spiritual friends who have come to perform vast activities for others' benefit, there are those who wish to give others an opportunity to request the teachings, or who are tired of the ungrateful and discouraging attitudes of their disciples; they remain silent without teaching the Dharma. Imagine that in their presence you request them to turn the Wheel of Dharma, just as did Brahmā and Indra in the past, emanating many billions of bodies and manifesting in their presence, making offerings of right-spiraling white conch shells, thousand-spoked golden wheels, and so forth. As a result of your request, they are all delighted and accept, turning the Wheel of Dharma in the ever-revolving wheel of eternity in accordance with the aspirations of beings to be trained.

There are infinite benefits that result from this. For example, obscurations from having rejected the Dharma will be purified, and from one life to the next, throughout one's series of lives, one will never cease to hold the sacred Dharma in one's being. In the *Sūtra of the Questions of Ratnacūḍa*, we read,

> He who makes a prayer
> To a buddha in meditation
> Is like the king of jewels:
> Other kinds of merit are but mere trinkets.

6. Praying to the teachers not to pass into nirvāṇa

In this and other worlds, there are teachers, buddhas, and bodhisattvas who have completed their work benefiting sentient beings and who now intend to leave their manifestation bodies and pass into nirvāṇa. In their presence, entreat them as did Upāsaka Chunda in the past, mentally producing numerous emanations of yourself. Consider that, as a result of your prayer, they remain, benefiting beings on a vast scale until cyclic existence is emptied.

Among the infinite benefits that result from making such a prayer are both the purification of a short life span, untimely death, and the negative consequences of endangering others' lives and the attainment of infinite life. In the *Sūtra of the Questions of Brahmaviśeṣacintin*, we find,

> Listen, King of the Brahmā realm,
> The merit of praying to the Bhagavan

Is particularly exalted.
The Buddha will not pass into nirvāṇa.

7. Dedication

Taking as representative these sources of good that you have now created (from obeisance through to praying to the teachers not to pass into nirvāṇa), you should dedicate all the merit that you and all other sentient beings have accumulated, are accumulating, and will accumulate to your own fulfillment and that of all other sentient beings. Seal it with nonconceptual wisdom and dedicate it to the level of perfect buddhahood in the same way as did Venerable Mañjushrī and Noble Samantabhadra.

The particular benefits are referred to in the *Sūtra of the Questions of Sāgaramati* as follows:

> Just as a drop of spit falling into the ocean
> Will never dry up until the ocean has dried,
> So too, a good deed fully dedicated to enlightenment
> Will never be consumed until enlightenment is attained.

This has been explained in detail above.*

Having ascertained all this, combine these visualizations with reciting as much as you can the following:

> To the Glorious Teacher, Vajrasattva,
> The Three Jewels, the buddhas and bodhisattvas,
> Bowing fully, I submit obeisance
> And offer infinite outer and inner offerings.
> Turning away from negative actions,
> I rejoice in all merit.
> I respectfully pray,
> May you constantly turn the Wheel of Dharma
> And remain as long as beings exist.
> Through the merit of this, may beings as countless as the sky is vast
> Attain the state of unsurpassable buddhahood.[347]

*See the quotation and explanation on p. 391.

The general benefits of performing these seven branches are mentioned in the *Śrīgupta Sūtra*:

> For those who, thinking of the buddhas of the ten directions,
> Fold their hands together
> And submit obeisance, make offerings,
> Rejoice in all merit,
> Purify their negative actions,
> Exhort, and pray,
> A heap of merit constantly arises
> Filling the whole of space.

C. Praying

Your teacher is the embodiment of all the buddhas. Repeatedly clear away your doubts as to this and gain the absolute conviction that he or she is the one, all-sufficing sovereign. Recalling your teacher's qualities and kindness and relying totally* on him or her, you should unburden all your hopes and expectations, and with intense yearning recite the prayer to the lineage teachers:

> To the all-pervading lord, the Primordial Protector Samantabhadra,
> Glorious Vajrasattva, union of bliss and emptiness,
> And to his representative, the teacher Garab Dorje,
> I pray, may my mind stream be blessed.
>
> To Shrī Siṃha, who perfected the union nature,
> The holder of the secret treasure, Dorje Hūṁ Dze,
> And to Vimalamitra, who realized the essential meaning of the profound path
> I pray, may my mind stream be blessed.
>
> To Pema Jungne, actual embodiment of all the buddhas of the three times,
> Yeshe Tsogyal, sovereign of the celestial pure lands,

*Lit. trusting that "whatever I do, you know."

And to the Lord Vairocana, who elucidated the excellent path of
the definitive meaning,
I pray, may my mind stream be blessed.

To Terdak Lingpa, who bestowed the sublime gift of maturation
and liberation,
Rinchen Namgyal, the incarnation of Vimalamitra,
And to Mingyur Peldrön, who was as Tsogyal appearing in
reality,
I pray, may my mind stream be blessed.

To Uḍḍiyāna, knower of all things,
Rigdzin Gyurme Trinle Namgyal,
And the primordial protector Trinle Chödrön
I pray, may my mind stream be blessed.

To my root teacher, whose kindness is incomparable,
The yidam deity, illusory display of great bliss,
And to the ḍākinīs and Dharma protectors whose activities are
unobstructed
I pray, may my mind stream be blessed.

Through the merit obtained by this prayer, may I and all beings,
countless as the sky is vast,
Train in bodhichitta, may all that arises appear as the deity,
May we perfect the view of *trekchö*
And reach the end of the profound path of *thögal* where there is
no change.[348]

On the subject of the attitude that we should have while we are praying, the Omniscient Tāranātha has said, "Whatever his or her actual appearance, it is not a case of regarding one's root teacher as an ordinary person or as a noble being on the path of training or as an ordinary spiritual friend. One must meditate on him or her as the Buddha in person. Although, in truth, it does not make any difference whether there is one buddha or many, there is a difference insofar as the way we apply devotion is concerned. It is not as if one's root teacher embodies one or two buddhas. He or she is the essence and embodiment of all the buddhas of the ten directions and the three times and therefore also embodies all the Dharma and all the Saṅgha. So your teacher is in actual fact the embodiment of all the precious ones. The teacher *is* the Three Jewels; the Three Jewels themselves are the teacher.

"Yet, from our point of view, the teacher is much kinder than the Three Jewels. The buddhas in the ten directions are universally bounteous, but they have not appeared to us, nor have their teachings reached us. Were the Buddha, the yidam deity, the bodhisattvas, ḍākinīs, or Dharma protectors to appear to us in person, there is nothing they could do for us or teach us more than does our glorious teacher. At this time, when we do not have the fortune to actually meet them, we should feel immensely grateful that everything they could do for us is being done by our teacher. To combine faith in the teacher's infinite qualities, having realized that he or she is the embodiment of all the buddhas, with recognition of the teacher's immense kindness is the best way to understand what devotion really is.

"Although we may have understood this well theoretically, our devotion may develop only from time to time and at other times we will cease to think of our teacher. And even when we do think of him or her, if it is not with such longing that our hairs stand on end, our devotion will be simply intellectual. This is not the sort of devotion that can make experiences and realization happen right away. When we feel the sort of intense yearning that has the power to stop all ordinary perceptions and that is able to transform our awareness, the blessings immediately enter us, defilements are suddenly stopped, and gnosis instantly manifests.

"By thinking of the teacher in this way again and again, we will constantly progress in meditation, and through habituation we will eliminate all our faults and develop all good qualities. But if we do not see our teacher as the Buddha in person, any devotion we have will be a mundane conceptual thought, tainted by feelings of partiality, affiliation, and attraction, and so it will not have the power to free us. As long as we consider the teacher to be an ordinary spiritual friend and an ordinary accomplished being, our faith will be no more than a mundane concept. Stupid people say, 'My teacher is the Buddha,' but they call anyone who is a good person or who helps them with food or money a buddha. They do not have the faintest idea what the term *Buddha* really means. That sort of devotion is not of the slightest help in freeing the mind.

"We, therefore, need to know what are the Buddha's qualities, and then we need to have the devotion that these are complete in our teacher. Thus, knowing that the teacher is the Buddha involves thinking of the Buddha, the supreme, supramundane being. This is the essence of all practice on the path. It is, in general, the way for all the buddhas' blessings to enter; and in particular, it is the way for the immediate blessings of the yidam deities, received from our teacher, to enter us swiftly. If we fail to remember our teacher's kindness, on a general level we are being ungrateful and utterly lacking in shame and decency, which is the root of all sorts of faults and misfortunes. All our merit, prosperity, happiness, and excellence will decline as if swept away. In particular, by not thinking of their kindness in enabling us to receive the teachings, we will cease to value the Dharma and lose faith, as a result of which all our efforts will be fruitless. Even more particularly, we will be stained by the first root downfall.* On the other hand, remembering the teacher's kindness is the foundation of all virtue and excellence and automatically gives birth to great respect. Thus, if you have the devotion that includes these four special qualities—recognizing that the teacher is the Buddha, remembering their kindness, intense yearning, and thinking of them again and again without forgetting them—you will have 'reached the full measure of devotion,' as this is known. Thus it is that when disciples who have kept the commitments meditate and pray with this sort of devotion to an authentic vajra master, without any other means they will achieve all the accomplishments that they have wished for, both supreme and common." You should understand that this is one of the most crucial points of all the pith instructions.

A great meditator once asked Jamgön Sakya Paṇḍita the Great[349] whether one received the supreme accomplishment from the teacher or from the yidam deity. "It does not come from these two separately" was the reply. "It comes from the realization that the teacher, the yidam deity, the buddhas of the three times, one's own mind, and the whole of saṃsāra and nirvāṇa are inseparable."

To sum up, train and familiarize your mind again and again in remembering the teacher's qualities and kindness and in seeing him or her as the Buddha, as described above. In this way, maintain constant devotion, with the conviction that your teacher is the truth-body Buddha.

If you have been accumulating numbers (one hundred thousand, for example) in the other sections of the preliminary practice, you should complete a hundred thousand of this prayer too. If you find it difficult to

*The first root downfall is to show disrespect to the vajra master. See Jigme Lingpa and Longchen Yeshe Dorje, *Treasury*, bk. 2, 183.

manage that with such a long prayer, I myself heard the Vajradhara Khyentse Wangpo say that you can begin by doing as many repetitions of the lineage prayer as you can and then, visualizing the teacher in the manner of the jewel that includes everything, you can recite the Seven-Line Prayer,* which is the king of all prayers to the Guru, counting the numbers with that prayer. You might think that there is a contradiction here between visualizing and praying to the teacher as Vajrasattva† and directing your prayer to the Precious Orgyen. But this is not the case. All the buddhas are of one essence in the expanse of gnosis, so however they may appear to beings to be trained, they do not in the slightest way exist as different streams of being. Vajrasattva, therefore, is the Great Orgyen, and the Great Orgyen is Vajrasattva himself. Moreover, because of the different beings to be trained, the infinite deities of the Three Roots appear in all their different peaceful and wrathful manifestations, but they are all the appearance aspect of the root teacher's mind—bliss and emptiness—the display of a single gnosis. Therefore, if we complete the practice of the preliminaries and the main practice (the approach, accomplishment, and so on) on a single deity such as our own root yidam, Vajrasattva, we in fact accomplish all the others. We can understand this from the *Auspicious Awareness Cuckoo Tantra*:

> The body of truth is of one taste, its activity in benefiting beings is the same:
> It appears differently to the minds of the faithful.
> Because all its manifestations are one in the expanse of gnosis,
> Meditation on one sugata leads to the state of all the buddhas.

D. Receiving the empowerments

After praying like that again and again, consider that rays of light emanating from the root teacher's body touch all the surrounding retinue—the lineage teachers, the Three Jewels, and so on. They melt into light and one by one dissolve into the root teacher's body. As the essence embodying all sources of refuge, the root teacher blazes with majesty even more brilliantly than

*See appendix 4.

†It should be remembered that the liturgy Shechen Gyaltsap refers to here is the Minling Dorsem, in which the Guru Yoga practice involves visualizing the teacher as Vajrasattva.

before. His incomparable body is marked on his head with a white OṀ, on the throat with a red ĀḤ, and at the heart with a blue HŪṀ. These embody the vajra body, speech, mind, and wisdom of all the buddhas. Again, with boundless devotion, pray fervently as follows:

> Lord of the four kāyas, Vajra Holder,
> Think upon us beings with your compassion:
> Fill our being with the sublime wisdom
> Of the vase, secret, wisdom, and absolute empowerments.
>
> From the syllable OṀ in the teacher's crown center, rays of white light emanate;
> They dissolve into my own crown center, and I receive the vase empowerment,
> The defilements of my body are purified,
> I am empowered to practice the path of the generation phase,
> And I gain the fortune to attain the manifestation body as the result.
> From the syllable ĀḤ in the throat center, red rays of light emanate;
> They dissolve into my own throat center, and I receive the secret empowerment,
> The defilements of my speech are purified,
> I am empowered to practice the path of the channels and energies,
> And I gain the fortune to attain the enjoyment body as the result.
> From the syllable HŪṀ in the heart center, blue rays of light emanate;
> They dissolve into my own heart, and I receive the empowerment of wisdom,
> The defilements of my mind are purified,
> I am empowered to practice the path of the essence,
> And I gain the fortune to attain the body of truth as the result.
> Again, from the three centers emanate white, red, and blue rays of light;
> They dissolve into my own three centers, and I receive the fourth empowerment,

> The defilements obscuring wisdom are purified,
> I am empowered to practice the path of the Great Perfection,
> And I gain the fortune to attain the body of the essential nature as the result.[350]

As a result of your prayer, consider that, from the syllable OṀ in the teacher's crown center, infinite rays of white light stream forth, as from a rising moon, and dissolve into your forehead, between the eyebrows. You thus receive the vase empowerment. The factors to be purified—namely, the negative deeds (taking life, and so on) that you have accumulated with your body and the obscurations of the body and subtle channels—are purified. You are empowered to practice the purifying factor—namely, the generation phase or yoga of form, the path of appearance and emptiness. And you gain the fortune to attain the result of the purification—the vajra body, the body of manifestation.

Again, from the syllable ĀḤ in the teacher's throat, infinite rays of red light stream forth, like chains of lamps, and dissolve into your throat. By this means, you receive the secret empowerment. The factors to be purified—namely, the negative deeds (telling lies, and so on) that you have accumulated with your speech and the obscurations of the speech and subtle energies—are purified. You are empowered to practice the purifying factor—namely, the mystic heat practice, the path of clarity and emptiness. And you gain the fortune to accomplish the result of the purification—the vajra speech, the body of perfect enjoyment.

Again, from the syllable HŪṀ in the teacher's heart center, infinite rays of blue light stream forth, like molten lapis lazuli in color, and dissolve into your heart center. You thus receive the empowerment of wisdom and gnosis. The factors to be purified—namely, the negative deeds (covetousness, and so on) that you have accumulated with your mind and obscurations of the mind and subtle essence—are purified. You are empowered to practice the purifying factor—namely, the path of yoga with a consort. And you gain the fortune to accomplish the result of the purification—the vajra mind, the body of truth.

Again, from the three centers of the teacher's body, infinite rays of white, red, and blue light stream forth all together and dissolve into your three centers, like falling rain. In this way, you receive the fourth empowerment, the precious word empowerment. The factors to be purified—namely, your three doors together and the cognitive obscurations—are purified. You are empowered to practice the purifying factor—namely, the path of the Great Perfection, combining trekchö related to primordial purity and thögal related to spontaneous presence. And you gain the fortune to attain the result of the purification—the vajra gnosis, the body of the essential nature. With that, rest in equipoise.

If you wish to practice in a more detailed way, you may also consider that from the centers in the teacher's body different symbols stream forth and dissolve into you. These are deity forms, symbolic of his body; chains of letters, syllables, and mantras, symbolic of his speech; and hand attributes, symbolic of his mind. This is the way taught in the *Profound Meaning of Ati*. However, the main teaching in the *Primary Instructions* is as has been described above.

Generally speaking, we should not practice any of the paths of the Diamond Vehicle of Secret Mantras without the support of the maturing empowerment. The *Guhyagarbha Tantra* states,

> Unless one serves the master
> And unless one obtains the empowerments,
> All one's efforts in receiving the teachings and so on
> Will be fruitless and destructive.

And in another tantra, we read,

> Without empowerment, there is no accomplishment.
> Even if put through a press, sand will never yield oil.

The essence of empowerment is that it introduces into one's stream of being the gnosis that needs to be attained and brings it to maturation. The Tibetan word for empowerment translates the Sanskrit word *abhiṣeka*, literally meaning "dissipating" or "pouring." Thus, empowerment involves cleansing the contaminants in one's mind stream and introducing into it the extraordinary gnosis.

As for the different categories of empowerment, the *ground empowerment* takes place when a qualified master first admits a disciple who is a suitable vessel into the maṇḍala of the king of the supreme secret and bestows empowerment. Subsequently one takes the *path empowerment*, using practices such as the Guru Yoga to receive the four empowerments by oneself, by means of profound concentration and so on, without depending on some other person or condition. Finally, at the time of the result, there is the *result empowerment*, when one receives the empowerment of great light rays, or empowerment of the indivisibility of profundity and clarity, and attains manifest buddhahood. In this sense, the whole of the path of the Diamond Vehicle is included within the maturing empowerment. Thus, not only is empowerment important here in the preliminary practice, but prior to doing any practice, such as meditating on the generation and perfection phases of the main practice, it is indispensable to rely on the Guru Yoga to take the four empowerments and mingle one's mind with the teacher's mind. In the *Tantra of the Vastness of Space*, it is said,

> To meditate on the teacher is to meditate on the body of truth.
> Meditating on a hundred million deities
> Could never match a fraction of the merit of that.
> Therefore, for those who practice the virtuous way,
> Whatever they are doing, be it listening, teaching,
> Meditating, memorizing, or making offerings or tormas,
> They should precede it with this.
> The teacher is the glorious embodiment of the buddhas of the three times.

The benefits of taking empowerment in this way are that, on the temporary level, one will give rise to effortless devotion to the teacher and have a clear mind for practicing concentration and so on. Ultimately, it will enable one to realize the great bliss, self-arisen gnosis. In the empowerment text of the *Great Compassionate One, Embodiment of All the Sugatas*, written by Guru Rinpoche, it is said,

> The first sign that one has been blessed
> By the qualities of empowerment thus bestowed
> Is that effortless devotion is born in one's mind.
> The second sign that one has been blessed
> Is that whatever one concentrates on is stable and clear.
> The third sign that one has been blessed
> Is that realization of self-arisen gnosis dawns.

E. Mingling one's mind with the teacher's and settling in meditative equipoise

After receiving the four empowerments like this, pray again mentally, with yearning devotion. As a result of your prayer, the teacher descends delightedly onto the crown of your head, melts into light, and dissolves into you. Rest in equipoise, in the state of the teacher and your own mind being inseparable.

How to rest in equipoise is described by Orgyen, knower of the three times, in his instructions to Ngok Sherab Gyalpo:

> Listen, old man. Look at this enlightened state of mind, self-awareness. It has no form, no color. It has no orientation or particularity. It has no center or circumference. In the beginning, there is nowhere from which it arises: it is empty. In between, there is no place it stays: it is empty. In the end, there is nowhere it goes: it is empty. This emptiness does not exist in any way. It is radiant and lucid. To see and recognize it is to know your own nature. It is to understand the true nature of phenomena. It is to see the nature of mind in your thoughts. It is to establish with certainty the way things actually are. It is to resolve all doubt concerning anything to be known.
>
> That awareness-bodhichitta does not in any way exist substantially. Self-arisen, it dwells within: it is not something to be sought elsewhere, and therefore the ultimate reality is easy to realize. In the ultimate reality, subject and object do not exist as entities. It is beyond the extremes of eternal existence and nihilistic nonexistence. There is no enlightenment to awaken to: enlightenment is your own awareness, clear and awake. There is no hell to go to: awareness is naturally pure. There is no Dharma to be practiced: the ultimate reality is naturally radiant. The great view of one's own nature is present within you, so decide that it is not to be sought elsewhere.
>
> When you have understood the view in this way and wish to put it into practice, wherever you are, your body is a mountain hermitage. Whatever external appearances arise, their appearance is your own perception, their emptiness is empty by itself.

Self-arising, self-subsiding, let them be, free from conceptual extremes.

In this way, external appearances arise as helpers, so that appearances are purified in their own state. Appearances are taken as the path, and by practicing in this way, whatever external appearances arise, there is bliss in practicing. On the inner level, whatever thoughts arise, whatever movements occur in your mind, they are without essential nature, they are empty. Thought movements are purified in their own state, and the nature of the mind appears clearly, so that thought movements are taken as the path and there is bliss in practicing. On the secret level, whatever defilements arise, if you look at the defilements, they arise and dissolve by themselves, without leaving any trace. Defilements are purified in their own state. Defilements are taken as the path, so that there is bliss in practicing.

When you practice in this way, the meditation is no longer a question of training in sessions. Everything arises as a support, and there is no fluctuation between clarity and obscurity in your experience, no interruption in your realization of the ultimate reality, no limitation in your conduct. Whatever your state, it never separates from the realization of the ultimate reality.

Once you have this sort of realization, however old your physical body is, the bodhichitta does not grow old—it makes no difference whether you are young or old. The realization of the ultimate reality is without partiality, so that when you recognize that that gnosis of the ultimate reality is present within you, it makes no difference whether your faculties are sharp or dull. Since the ultimate reality is without partiality, when you understand that it is present within you, it makes no difference whether you are learned or not. Even if your illusory body, made up of physical matter and consciousness, disintegrates, there is no interruption in the flow of awareness, gnosis, the body of truth. When you attain unwavering stability, it makes no difference whether you live long or not.

Old man, practice this authentic truth. Integrate the practice with your mind stream. Do not confuse the words and their meaning. Never part from the companionship of diligence. Imbue everything with mindfulness. Do not indulge in idle talk

> and gossip. Do not adulterate your mind with ordinary thoughts. Do not worry about your children. Do not crave food and drink. Beware of dying as an ordinary person. Life is too short for wasting time, so develop diligence. Old man, practice this instruction as you are dying.

Because Guru Rinpoche gave these instructions while pointing his staff at the old man's heart, they are known as "Instructions to the old man given with pointed staff." By means of these, Ngok Sherab Gyalpo was liberated and attained accomplishment. They have come down to us through the uninterrupted stream of both the oral transmission and treasure lineages. They constitute the root of all mind teachings, and as they are the adamantine words of Guru Rinpoche, their blessings are particularly powerful.

If you have the time, it is also good to go first through the general procedure of looking for the mind.* Whichever the case, at the end of your meditating in equipoise like this, perceive the whole of phenomenal existence as the manifestation of the teacher and conclude with appropriate prayers of dedication and aspiration, such as the following:

> By the merit of this practice
> May I swiftly accomplish the glorious protector, my teacher,
> And, not leaving out a single being,
> May I place them on that same level.

As part of this practice of Guru Yoga, when you are walking around, you should visualize the teacher in the sky above your right shoulder: this will serve as a way to circumambulate them. When you are seated, visualize them in the sky above your head, as the focus of your prayers. When you are eating or drinking, visualize them in the middle of your throat, so that the first part of everything you eat and drink is an offering to them. When you go to sleep, visualize them in the center of your heart: this is the essence of the practice of perceiving everything as luminosity. In short, at all times and on all occasions, constantly think of your teacher.

Whatever unwanted things happen to you, such as your falling ill or being affected by obstacles from negative forces, instead of thinking of how to get rid of them, be glad and think that with them, your teacher is

*The practice of examining the mind to see where it arises, where it stays, and where it goes.

compassionately providing you with a way to exhaust the consequences of your past negative deeds. When you feel happy and at ease and are able to do more virtuous activities, recognize that these are also signs of your teacher's compassion, and do not be proud or excited about them. During meditation, your concentration may be affected by your becoming discouraged, tired, dull, or agitated. When this happens, make an effort to mingle your awareness inseparably with the teacher's mind and preserve the innate radiance of the view of the natural state, combining this with reciting prayers and so on.

Tsele Natsok Rangdröl sums up the practice as follows:

> To think of the teacher with yearning faith and devotion
> Is the relative Guru Yoga, with effort.
> The mingling of the teacher's mind with one's own
> Is the ultimate, effortless Guru Yoga.
> To settle in uncontrived, relaxed awareness
> Is the Guru Yoga of the all-pervading body of truth.
> Lack of clinging to whatever appearances arise to the six consciousnesses
> Is the Guru Yoga of radiant clarity, the body of perfect enjoyment.
> Recognition of concepts, thoughts, and memories as one's own nature
> Is the Guru Yoga of the multifarious body of manifestation.
> All buddhas are one in the essential nature of the teacher:
> When one recognizes this, the blessings enter naturally.
> The hosts of deities without exception are expressions of the teacher:
> When one recognizes this, endless accomplishments occur.
> The ḍākinīs and Dharma protectors are the manifestations of the teacher:
> When one understands this, one accomplishes the four activities.
> The whole of phenomenal existence is the maṇḍala of the teacher:
> When one trains in pure perception, his compassion is everywhere.
> All the outer elements are manifestations of the teacher:
> They benefit beings with whatever they need.
> All beings contained in the world are manifestations of the teacher:

There are none that are not pervaded by the sugata essence, the body of truth.
All happiness, comforts, and enjoyments are the manifestations of the teacher,
Granting all the accomplishments one wishes for.
All ailments and difficulties, too, are the manifestations of the teacher:
The experience of suffering exhausts evil deeds and obscurations.
All-pervading, all-creating, source of all, universally good—
For this reason, to take the teacher as the path is a profound and crucial point.

And,

When we fail to realize that the teacher is inseparable from our own mind,
On the relative level, there is meeting and separating from the teacher in the form body.
The crucial point is to recognize one's own awareness as the truth-body teacher.
When we fail to realize that everything, good and bad, is the teacher,
There is no way that impartial, pure perception can arise.
If we do not train in pure perception, phenomenal existence will rise up as our enemy.
The crucial point is, rather, to recognize everything as manifestations benefiting according to need.
When we fail to recognize enemies, spirits, and difficulties as the teacher,
With every obstacle we avoid, another will appear:
This is the retribution for not having given up our ego-clinging.
The crucial point is to recognize everything that happens as the teacher's compassion.
If we do not remember the teacher as we are dying,
All the many things we have learned will be no more than a dream.
When our consciousness is wandering alone in the intermediate state,
We will have no other source of hope and refuge.

> So do not leave this profound and crucial point of taking the teacher as the path
> In words and letters but put it into practice.
> It is more profound than the eighty-four thousand teachings.
> Whether it is profound or not depends on whether it is put into practice:
> If you do not practice it, however profound it is, it will barely help.
> So, rely wholeheartedly* on this instruction.

This is how you should practice. Make every effort to do so.

III. A concluding exposition of the benefits of following the teacher and practicing in that way

Generally speaking, the benefits of following a spiritual friend are boundless. A few of them can be understood from the explanations above. In addition, we shall here quote the *Sūtra of the Arborescent Array*:

> Bodhisattvas who are guided by spiritual friends never fall into the lower realms. They never turn away from the Great Vehicle. They do not regress to the levels of the listeners and solitary realizers. They are barely affected by karmic deeds and defilements. They transcend the levels of ordinary beings. They do not transgress the precepts. Because they are guarded by spiritual friends, they cannot be led astray by evil companions. As they are protected by spiritual friends, they do not fall back from the very nature of a bodhisattva. They are unstained by worldly concerns, and so are truly noble. As they serve their spiritual friends, they practice all the bodhisattva deeds without error. Having been brought into being by spiritual friends, they never give up anything that they have undertaken. Guided by spiritual friends, they are never overwhelmed by demons.

And,

> The practice of the bodhisattvas depends on spiritual friends. The perfection of all excellent qualities is brought about by spir-

*Tib. *blo snying brang gsum*, literally "with your lungs, heart, and chest."

itual friends. All the qualities of buddhahood are obtained by attending spiritual friends.

In the *Bodhisattva's Scriptural Collection*, we read,

> In short, the attainment and perfection of all the practices of the bodhisattva, and likewise the attainment and perfection of the transcendent perfections, the levels, acceptance, concentration, preternatural knowledge, powers of memory, confident eloquence, dedications, aspirations, and all the qualities of buddhahood depend on the teacher. The teacher is their root, the teacher is their origin, the teacher is their birthplace and source. They are engendered by the teacher, they grow because of the teacher, they depend on the teacher. The teacher is their cause.

And in the *Tantra of the Wheel of Bliss*,

> Therefore, the root of the whole Dharma
> Is explained as being the teacher, the vajra holder.
> It is impossible to gain accomplishment
> That does not come from one's teachers.
> It is impossible for a so-called buddha to arise
> That has not arisen from a teacher.
> The one who steers one upward in existence
> Is the qualified teacher.

The *Compendium of the Buddhas' Wisdom* states,

> Without one's following a master,
> Buddhahood can never happen:
> I have never seen it truly happen,
> And if it has, it contradicts the sacred teachings.

Furthermore, Rigdzin Jigme Lingpa has said,

> In general, it is said in the sūtras that meritorious and nonmeritorious actions performed with regard to the highest objects—masters, preceptors, and instructors, and likewise those who

> teach the Dharma, bodhisattvas in their final existence, noble listeners and solitary realizers, one's parents, sick people, and so on—are so powerful that the effect can ripen even in this same lifetime without the passage of other lives in between. In particular, nowadays the times are degenerate and our concepts are very gross. This was not the case in past kalpas, in the age of enhancement, when beings' thoughts were very subtle and the effects of their positive and negative deeds ripened slowly in other lives. Now, they are much stronger, ripening in this very life. Happily, this is also true for the benefits of following and venerating a teacher. Look at those who, in ordinary life, are ignorant and uneducated (cowherds, for example), those who are poor and destitute, and those who are subject to everyone's contempt. Even they, by simply following a spiritual friend and engaging in the path of Dharma, easily gain ordinary people's esteem and respect and manage to find enough to eat and drink.

The *Bodhisattva's Scriptural Collection* describes the benefits in detail, beginning:

> Moreover, like medicinal plants growing on the slopes of a snow mountain, all one's sources of good will increase. Like a great lake containing water, one will become a container for all good qualities. Like the ocean that is the source of precious stones, one will become the source of all good qualities. Like gold that has been fully refined by the heat of the fire, one will fully train in bodhichitta. Like Mount Meru, towering above the ocean, one will rise above the whole world.

Accordingly, even in this life, for all to see, one will become enriched with qualities. And one will gladden the sublime beings—buddhas, bodhisattvas, and spiritual friends—and be cared for by them. As a result, one will achieve everything one desires, on both temporary and ultimate levels. This is affirmed in the *Sūtra of the Arborescent Array*:

> Fortunate child, bodhisattvas who follow the instructions of a spiritual friend will gladden the virtuous, transcendent conquerors. Bodhisattvas who abide by the instructions of their spiritual

> friend without violating them will come close to omniscience. Bodhisattvas who have no doubts about their spiritual friend's words will emulate the spiritual friends. Bodhisattvas who constantly keep in mind their spiritual friend will realize all their goals.

Furthermore, by following a sublime being in this way, even if one has the karma to experience the lower realms in one's future lives, minor troubles that affect one mentally or physically now, or even such troubles experienced in dreams, will bring that karma to exhaustion. And the benefit of having venerated one's teacher for one morning outshines the benefit of creating sources of good with respect to ten million buddhas. This is mentioned in the *Sūtra of the Ten Wheels of Kṣitigarbha*:

> When one is cared for by a teacher, mental and physical afflictions in this life such as infectious diseases and shortage of food will purify deeds that would lead to wandering in the lower realms for countless tens of millions of kalpas; even rebukes or dreams will purify them. All the sources of good made with respect to countless tens of millions of buddhas and produced by being charitable, making offerings, or keeping the precepts are eclipsed by a single morning serving a teacher. One who has venerated the teacher possesses inconceivable qualities.

All in all, one will be enriched with all the qualities of higher rebirth in this life and those of certain excellence in future lives.

As for the specific benefits, the benefits of offering material possessions to one's teacher are mentioned in the *Ocean of Gnosis Tantra*:

> Those who please the teacher
> With their own possessions and property
> Will find shelter from the three worlds of saṃsāra
> In the buddha-field of a manifestation body
> And reach the level of nirvāṇa.

And in the *Compendium of the Buddhas' Wisdom*, we read,

> Therefore, venerating a thousand buddhas
> For a thousand kalpas

Cannot match even a thousandth part
Of anointing with a single drop of sandal oil
A pore of the teacher's body.

And in the *Ocean-Like Source of Nectar Tantra*,

Offering the whole billionfold universe
Decorated with all kinds of precious things
To all the buddhas filling space
Cannot match even a hundredth part of the merit
Of anointing with a single drop of oil
A single one of the teacher's pores.

The *Guhyasamāja Tantra* states,

Far greater than the merit
Of making offerings to all the buddhas of the three times
Is that of anointing a single pore of the teacher's body
With a single drop of oil.

And the *Tantra of the Vajra Flame*,

The merit of making countless offerings in veneration
Of countless hundreds of thousands of buddhas and their retinues
In buddha-fields numerous beyond words
Cannot match a fraction of that of presenting offerings of gold
and suchlike
To the teacher, the teacher's entourage,
And following and attendants.

Moreover, there is greater merit in making an offering once when one's teacher is giving an empowerment or profound instructions than in making a thousand billion offerings at other times. In *Details of Empowerment*, it is said,

Compared to countless thousands of billions
Of offerings made to one's own teacher
At times when he is not bestowing empowerment,

Making a single one during an empowerment
Has boundless, infinite merit.

The reason for this is that on such occasions the totality of the hosts of root and lineage teachers, yidams, ḍākas and ḍākinīs, buddhas and bodhisattvas are indivisibly present in the body, speech, and mind of the vajra master, so these are times when blessing the disciples' mind streams, accepting their offerings, and so on multiply their accumulation of merit. This is affirmed in the *Word of Mañjuśrī*:

At times made meaningful by this,
I am present in the teacher's body,
Accepting offerings from others who are practicing.
Pleased by these, I purify
The karmic obscurations in their mind streams.

And the *Tantra of Complete Union* states,

The supreme master of all the buddhas,
Whose name is "Mind of All Gnoses,"
Bestows all kinds of accomplishments.
Therefore, the wise should constantly venerate him.

Furthermore, in the *Bodhisattva's Scriptural Collection*, is it said,

In order to make the best use of one's body, which is without essence, one should serve a teacher by offering, at the very least—if one has nothing at all to give—a pot full of water. By doing so, boundless sources of good will result and multiply.

And in the *Sūtra of the Ten Wheels of Kṣitigarbha*,

One who venerates the teacher
Will possess inconceivable qualities.

There are innumerable other scriptural sayings to this effect. And in his *Commentary on the "Precious Treasury That Fulfills All Wishes,"* the Omniscient Teacher writes,

> In short, [one will gain] both visible and invisible qualities*—the completion of the accumulation of merit and wisdom, the removal of all obstacles due to unfavorable circumstances, great glory and wealth, and the swift attainment of buddhahood. I myself benefited from making pure offerings, free of the concepts of the three spheres, to my sublime teacher Kumārarāja. As a result of these, my life span, which was running out, was lengthened, and I was able to gather more resources.† So if such definite benefits can occur in this very life, need one mention the benefits one will experience in other lives?

Moreover, there is extraordinary merit in always offering the first part of one's food and clothes, performing the feast and torma offerings, and making the maṇḍala offering and other offerings, both with materials such as precious substances, grains, and medicinal plants, if you have them, and in your imagination, if you do not. This is stated in the *Tantra of the Garland of Flames*:

> For wise practitioners
> Who sacrifice their own food and clothes,
> Offering them to the teacher,
> One can never finish telling
> The merit of once offering their teacher
> Their food or else their clothes:
> It is a hundred times greater
> Than giving a feast a thousand times
> To infinite numbers of monks
> In all the lands around.

And in the *Tantra of Vajra Vetālī*, we read,

> Those who always offer the teacher Vajradhara
> The first part of their food and drink

*Qualities that are apparent in this life and those that will be seen in future lives.

†Longchenpa had hitherto been extremely poor, but afterward his needs were always provided for.

Will in this life have more to eat and drink
And will attain the state of a universal monarch.

The *Tantra of the Vajra Staff of Vajrapāṇi* declares,

If one continually performs the complete ritual
Of the feast and torma offerings in the teacher's presence,
One will be wealthy, complete the accumulations,
Dispel all one's own and others' obstacles,
And, when one dies, be reborn in Vajrapāṇi's retinue.

The *Great Array* has the following:

One's horses, elephants, jewels,
Kingdom, children, spouse,
Precious gold, silver, copper, iron,
Food and drink, feasts and raiment,
Essential medicines, grains, flowers,
And all enjoyments, religious and material—
To please the teacher, offer these.
By doing so, you will attain right now, without delay,
All accomplishments without exception.
If you do not have such things,
Gather offerings created by your mind.
If you offer them as many times as you have years,
The merit thus will be the same as shown before.

In the *Five Stages of Guhyasamāja*, it is said,

Give up all other offerings
And set about making offerings to the teacher.
By pleasing him or her, you will attain
The highest gnosis of omniscience.
By making offerings to Vajrasattva,
The master who brings about the unsurpassable,
There is no merit that is not achieved,
No ascetic practice that has not been done.

Again, there are the benefits that result from attending and serving one's teachers with one's body and speech. In the *Tantra of the Supreme Samaya*, it is said,

> Those who venerate and serve their teacher as best they can
> With all their physical, verbal, and mental strength
> Will have no obstacle to being blessed
> With a host of powers and abilities.

Regarding the particular benefits of serving the teacher physically, the *Ocean of Gnosis Tantra* states,

> There is greater benefit for a fortunate being
> Proficient in doing what the teacher asks
> Than for one who makes obeisance
> To all the buddhas of the three times
> For six hundred billion kalpas.
> If one acts as instructed by the teacher,
> One will accomplish all one's wishes
> And gain infinite merit.

In the *Source of Nectar Tantra*, we read,

> The merit of saving the lives of a hundred thousand beings
> Could never match a fraction of that gained
> If one were to kill a person who, with evil mind,
> Undertakes to harm one's teacher.
> The same is true if one completes
> The tasks the teacher has given one.

The benefits of serving the teacher with one's speech are given in the *Tantra of the Display of the Wheel of Perfection*:

> For those of highest intelligence
> Who please their teacher with their speech,
> The merit is inconceivable, one hundred thousand times as great
> As that from many hundreds of kalpas spent reading aloud
> The teachings that the buddhas gave.

As for the benefits of serving the teacher with one's mind, the same text states:

> Of all good qualities, faith is the best.
> Offering a billion offerings
> To buddhas filling the billionfold universe
> Cannot match a fraction of pleasing the teacher through one's faith.

Then there are the benefits of pleasing one's teachers by practicing their instructions. These are referred to in the *Tantra of the Display of the Wheel of Perfection*:

> Greater than the merit of training in
> The generation phase for three kalpas
> Is the merit of a single instant
> Spent pleasing one's teacher through one's practice.

In *Ornament of the Mahāyāna Sūtras*, we find,

> They should rely fully on a spiritual master in order to possess the qualities
> For enjoying their share of the Dharma and not material gain.[351]

And in the *Series of Lives*,

> Those who make an offering in return for the benefit they have received
> Are those who put into practice the words of the instructions.

The *Middle Sūtra of the Perfection of Wisdom* has the following:

> Those who are diligent in accomplishing the instructions of a spiritual friend are praised, eulogized, and honored by all the buddhas.

In particular, everything we do on the physical and verbal level in attending to and serving our teacher, and, on the mental level, in practicing and accomplishing the Guru Yoga constitutes the ultimate accumulation of supreme merit. Mingling our mind with the teacher's mind and resting in equipoise in the ultimate reality constitute the accumulation of wisdom. Thus, the Guru Yoga is the ultimate result, or essential nature, of the two accumulations. It is, therefore, a universal path that is even swifter and more profound than practices such as training in the ocean-like methods of the generation phase. This is stated in the *Tantra of the Display of the Wheel of Perfection*:

> Better than meditating for ten million kalpas
> On the deity's form
> Is the thought, it has been taught, of one's teacher,
> The mightiest of all protectors.

And the *Supreme Wish-Fulfilling Tantra* declares,

> To take in the palm of one's hand
> A thousand buddha maṇḍalas,
> And take them round the billionfold universe,
> And absorb them a thousand times into one's heart
> Cannot match in power a hundredth or a thousandth
> Of the act of visualizing the teacher, one's inspirational deity,
> On the crown of one's head.
> With constant mindfulness, therefore,
> Think of the glorious teacher
> Ornamenting the wheel of your crown.

And in the *Tantra of the Great Samantabhadra Dwelling in Oneself*, we read,

> Those who visualize in their heart,
> In the palm of their hand, or on the crown of their head
> Their kind teacher, arisen from Ati,
> The Great Perfection—
> Such people will also hold
> The qualities of a thousand buddhas.

And the *Great Array of the Sublime* declares,

> Meditating on a hundred thousand deities
> Cannot match one hundred-thousandth
> Of the merit of correctly visualizing the teacher's form.
> A hundred billion recitations in the approach and accomplishment
> Cannot match in power one hundred-thousandth
> Of the merit of uttering three times a prayer to one's teacher.
> Abandoning all diversions and practicing
> Even for a kalpa the perfection phase
> Cannot match one twenty-thousandth
> Of the merit of the teacher appearing within one's mind.
> By visualizing, praising, and thinking of one's teacher,
> One is certain to accomplish the fruit of buddhahood instantaneously.

And the *Secret Lamp*,

> Better than a million recitations in the approach and accomplishment
> Is a single word of prayer to the teacher.
> Do not meditate on deities: meditate on the teacher.
> Meditation on the teacher has greater merit
> Than meditation on ten billion deities.

The *Tantra of the Array of Commitments* states,

> Through six months of unmoving devotion
> One will attain the level of Vajradhara.

And the *Manifestation of Gnosis*,

> The stages of the levels and paths
> Are accomplished in months and years through devotion to the teacher.
> If one does not separate from the thought of the teacher,
> One will remain inseparable from the buddhas.

These quotations are just a few examples from the infinite number of scriptural sources on this subject.

To sum up, we should keep in mind the following passage from *Treasury of Precious Qualities*:

> Engaging truly in the actions of enlightenment,
> Holy beings make supreme accumulation
> Of both merit and of wisdom.
> To serve and help them in their work,
> To carry messages and sweep the floor—
> Even tasks like these bear fruit
> And of accumulation are the supreme path.[352]

And in its commentary,

> In this way, all virtuous activities in which the preparation, main practice, and conclusion are complete serve as causes for liberation. Actions that are otherwise do not. It is difficult for our own activities to be entirely imbued with skillful means and wisdom. For this reason, we should join in the positive activities and accumulation of merit of a sublime teacher who is engaged in practicing the six transcendent perfections. We can do this by contributing materially with our own possessions, or by joining in with physical and verbal activities and with the activities of listening, reflecting, and meditating, or at least by being diligent in carrying messages, acting as a servant, and cleaning the place. Our own accumulation of merit will thus be in tune with the sublime teacher's completion of the two accumulations. This is what makes the mantra path so swift.
>
> From the point of view of that path, following a teacher and being diligent in serving him or her and in accumulating merit and purifying obscurations have been taught as being equivalent to the path of accumulation. Through that sublime being's blessings, one is introduced to nonconceptual gnosis (equivalent to the path of joining), and one sees the ultimate reality directly (the path of seeing). One then has to train in what one has seen (the path of meditation), and, by perfecting the training, one proceeds to the path of no more learning. This is also mentioned in a tantra:

Completely serving the teacher
And remaining in that sublime being's presence
Are what is called the path of accumulation.
Applying the sublime teacher's
Explanations and instructions
Is what I have taught as the path of joining.
Seeing the definitive truth in this life
Is what I have explained as the path of seeing.
Resting without separating
Meditation outside formal meditation
And nonmeditation inside formal sessions
Is what I have taught as the path of meditation.
Reaching perfection without dwelling
Is what I have explained as the path of consummation.

Unless the teacher's blessings have entered one's mind,
It will never be possible to realize the profound natural state.
The essence of the sūtras and tantras is just this,
So constantly practice on the teacher, O fortunate ones!

This completes the instruction on the Guru Yoga.

Concluding Remarks

Let me say a few words about my reason for compiling these few supporting instructions on the common preliminary practices based on the teachings of the sublime beings who appeared in the past.

In the tradition of the Diamond Vehicle, we generally speak of the maturing empowerment, liberating instructions, and supportive transmissions and commentaries. Of these, the initial entrance is the maturing empowerment, of which there are many different kinds, according to the different classes of tantra. However, the empowerments of the unsurpassable Mantra Vehicle are all included in the four empowerments—the vase empowerment, secret empowerment, wisdom empowerment, and absolute empowerment. The very life of these empowerments depends on the sacred commitments, so it is very important to keep the root and branch commitments without damaging them. Someone who does not have the empowerment and the sacred commitments does not even have the fortune to hear the profound secret teachings. For this reason, giving these teachings to such a person is very destructive for both master and disciple. The empowerment and commitments are thus of primary and fundamental importance.

The liberating instructions require a realized teacher who holds the true lineage, possesses the highest degree of experience in meditation, and is well versed in the essential points for removing obstacles and enhancing the practice. They also require disciples who are suitable vessels, who have faith and diligence, and who consider the practice to be the most important thing. To such disciples, the teacher gives the pith instructions that bring together the essential points in the form of direct, experiential instructions. Through these, disciples with the best faculties attain liberation at the same moment that the instructions are completed, those with middling faculties begin to have experiences and realization, while those with the most modest faculties embark on the path to liberation as they develop the power of positive qualities such as the determination to be free and weariness of cyclic existence, faith and devotion, love and compassion, and diligence in the practice.

With regard to the supportive transmissions, as a general rule, the person reading the text should have all the qualities of a sublime being, but the most important thing is that there should have been no interruption in the lineage or spoilage by faults such as breaches of the sacred commitments. The people listening should have faith, interest, and devotion. The text that is being read should be read out clearly and distinctly so as to be sure that the listeners can hear it, thus sowing in their minds habitual tendencies from what they have heard. For the transmission, then, the most important things are that the reader reads correctly and clearly and that the listeners have faith and keen interest.

As for the commentaries, the teacher should possess the three kinds of wisdom* and, in particular, should have freed his or her mind stream through having heard the teachings. The disciples receiving the teaching should be intelligent and diligent. The meaning of the words of the text being taught should be elicited from scriptural quotations and logical arguments, and the words should be expanded upon with detailed explanations. In this way, the wisdom that comes from reflection is aroused in the minds of the listeners and their doubts and misconceptions are dispelled. The most important thing in this case is the employment of the different kinds of reasoning related to the three kinds of valid cognition (direct, inferential, and based on scriptural authority) and analysis of the two truths. In particular, for explaining the profound, definitive teachings, without contradicting the four reliances,† the essential points of the Diamond Vehicle's six exegetical perspectives and four expository methods[353] should be explained on the basis of the presentations in the pith instructions of the lineage of vidyādharas. For such teachings, the dry methods of reasoning in conventional dialectics will lead nowhere.

Within this scheme of things, the transmissions mainly create positive habitual tendencies through listening. The explanations give rise to the wisdom that comes through reflection, and they resolve contradictions in the

*The three kinds of wisdom are those that come from listening or study, reflection, and meditation.

†For the four reliances, see the quotation on p. 381 above, "Rely on the meaning, and not on the words . . ."

words. The profound instructions give rise to the wisdom that comes from meditating, and they connect one to the lineage of the essential meaning. In this, the most important thing is to clear away obstacles, bring about progress, and introduce the disciple to the nature of mind on the basis of experience. There is no need for irrelevant explanations and a lot of words. This is why, in their practice manuals, the learned and accomplished beings of the past taught by condensing the profound essential points that they had grasped in their practice into visualization and practice texts. The mere fact that the transmission of the instructions has continued without being interrupted means that the adamantine words of the vidyādharas of the past have much more powerful blessings than other teachings, so communicating them by reading them precisely is truly useful and beneficial. There was even a tradition by which the practice of the sublime beings was transmitted in this way.

Nowadays, however, the age of accomplishment is largely over, and we are approaching the age of transmission when the teachings are merely symbolic. Consequently, people have little disenchantment and renunciation, they are disinclined to practice, and their minds cling to dry, conventional words. One cannot deny the possibility that there might be a few sublime beings around, but otherwise the continuous lineage of experience and profound instructions has mostly been interrupted. We have reached a stage where it seems no one can distinguish between the different kinds of instructions, transmissions, and explanations, and it would appear that there is no point in the teachers giving the profound instructions directly, or any point in disciples listening. This is why I compiled these teachings, as it seemed essential to communicate at least a few of the basic principles.

The most important thing, however, is not just that the teacher and the persons receiving the teaching should devote themselves to busily collecting words but rather that we should be diligent in applying them to our own mind streams and putting them into practice. This is stated in the *Sūtra of the Arborescent Array*,[354]

> One who hears the true Buddha's teaching
> Yet fails to accomplish it
> Is like a person swept away
> Along a river, helplessly,
> To finally die of thirst.
> So it is for those who fail to practice Dharma.

One might give many people
Things to eat and drink
But die, oneself, of hunger.
So it is for those who fail to practice Dharma.
One might be a skilled physician
With all the medicines one could need
Yet die of some abdominal disease.
So it is for those who fail to practice Dharma.
One might have counted all the many jewels
Inside a treasury of precious things
But not obtain a single one oneself.
So it is for those who fail to practice Dharma.
One might be born a courtier in a royal palace,
Possessed of every happiness,
And yet have nothing to eat or drink.
So it is for those who fail to practice Dharma.
A blindman in the middle of a marketplace
Might ask an artist to draw or paint the scene
But nothing will he see himself.
So it is for those who fail to practice Dharma.
A ferryman upon a great, wide lake
Might carry many passengers across
And yet himself be drowned in it.
So it is for those who fail to practice Dharma.
A person at a crossroads
Might speak of every wondrous thing
But fail to hear it all himself.
So it is for those who fail to practice Dharma.

And,

A swimmer whom the river sweeps away
Might have in mind the swimmer's art,
Yet until he actually swims, he will not save himself.
The same is true for those who know the Dharma but fail to meditate.
A farmer, skilled in cultivating land,

Might leave his fields to teach his friends good husbandry
But, when it comes to harvest time, will reap nothing for himself.
The same is true for those who know the Dharma but fail to meditate.

The *Sūtra of the King of Concentrations* states,

I have explained the excellent Dharma,
But unless you practice properly what you've heard,
You'll be like a patient holding up a bag of medicine
But unable to cure their own illness.

One may have heard a lot of teachings and be very learned, but there are numerous defects in being content with just talking about the Dharma, as we read in the *Sūtra That Inspires a Superior Intention*:

One's learning makes one proud and lacking in respect,
Attached to interpretations and debate,
Forgetful and devoid of vigilance.
These are the faults of being fond of talk.*
Concentration drifts off, far away,
One's mind and body are no longer fit,
One is full of arrogance and tied in knots.
These are the faults of being fond of talk.
Upon the Dharma the childish scarcely reflect,
Their minds become inflexible and wild
And far removed from calm and deep insight.
These are the faults of being fond of talk.
Always disrespectful to their teachers,
They like to chat of superficial things,
Nothing they say is heartfelt, their intelligence wanes.
These are the faults of being fond of talk.
Such people are not respected by the gods,
And then they cease to care about respect;

*Tib. *smra la dga' ba*, having a purely intellectual approach to the teachings without really putting them into practice.

Knowledge and discernment fade away.
These are the faults of being fond of talk.

And,

"Nothing have I accomplished, what can I now do?"
Thus will they lament as death draws near.
Finding nothing deep down, they'll suffer terribly.
These are the faults of being fond of talk.
Dithering and wavering, like windblown grass,
They're certain to be prone to doubt,
And never will they find stability of mind.
These are the faults of being fond of talk.
Like someone in a public spectacle
Acting out the exploits of the brave,
They themselves lack true zeal and grit.
These are the faults of being fond of talk.
Fickle and inconstant,
They put off ever starting anything,
For them the noble Dharma's far away.
These are the faults of being fond of talk.
Weak-minded, fond of honors and respect,
They are ignorant and whimsical,
With minds like monkeys, jumping up and down.
These are the faults of being fond of talk.
Their intelligence is poor,
And so these stupid beings depend on others;
They're overpowered by defilements.
These are the faults of being fond of talk.
Deluded by their sight and also by what they hear,
Deluded by their sense of smell, and likewise by that of taste,
They are deluded physically and mentally as well.
These are the faults of being fond of talk.
With minds attached to the consciousness of the ear,
They're satisfied with words but have no real insight;
They understand things wrongly and proceed on evil paths.
These are the faults of being fond of talk.

And the same sūtra continues with the following advice:

> For ages long they have been fond of talk,
> So they'll not have the essence to enjoy.
> They will obtain unlimited delight in words,
> But best would be reflection on a single word.
> There is no essence in the bark of sugarcane:
> The taste to be enjoyed is right inside.
> So those who eat the bark will never find
> The sugar they desire or its sweet taste.
> As with the bark, so with the words:
> The taste lies in reflecting on their sense.
> So give up all your fondness for mere words:
> Act constantly with care, and on the sense reflect.

It is for this reason that we read in a sūtra that teaches thatness,[355]

> Shāriputra, many times greater than the merit of someone who listens to the teachings for one kalpa is the merit of one who trains in the concentration of thatness for the duration of a mere finger snap. Therefore, Shāriputra, put all your efforts into teaching others this concentration on thatness.

And in the *Extensive Sūtra of the Great Realization*, it is said,

> One short session of concentration
> Is more beneficial than protecting the lives
> Of human beings filling the three worlds.

And in the *Sūtra of the Great Crown Protuberance*,

> Greater than the merit of listening and reflecting for many kalpas is that of meditating for one day on the meaning of ultimate reality. Should you ask why, it is because it takes one far beyond the path of birth and death.

And so on, as has been explained in detail above. Moreover, the *Heap of Jewels* states,

The buddhas of the past, protectors of the world,
Wherever they have reached nirvāṇa,
Have all relied on solitude and in perfect solitude
Found unsurpassed enlightenment.
Those who swiftly go to dwell in solitude
Dispel the craving of the desire realm
And, once they have discerned its faults,
Will turn their minds away from it.
Those who quickly give up household life
And stay alone in hermits' caves
Are wise, and with their perfect view
Train on the path the buddhas trod.
Those who strive to reach enlightenment
Rely on empty places, uninhabited,
And take delight in living all alone;
They have no liking for the household life.
They share the same activities
As did the buddhas in the past.
For those who set out on this path,
It is not hard to gain enlightenment.

And in the *Moon Lamp Sūtra*, we read,

Those who follow their desires,
Who are attached to wife and kids
And lead ignoble household lives,
Will never gain enlightenment, sublime and unsurpassed.
Those who give up their desires, regarding them like burning dung,*
Who give up all attachment to their wives and kids,
And fearful of the household life, renounce their homes—
For them it is not hard to gain supreme enlightenment.
Hitherto, no buddhas have appeared
Who gained enlightenment, sacred and sublime,
While still continuing to lead a household life;

*Dried cow dung, used as fuel in India, may not look very hot when it is lit, but if one touches it, one will be thoroughly burned.

No buddhas ever will come thus, and none are present now.
Their kingly states renounced like spit upon the dust,
They went to distant places where they dwelled in solitude.
Thus did they dispel defilements and destroy the demon hordes,
Attaining spotless enlightenment and uncompounded
buddhahood.
For those who truly wish enlightenment,
Who, disillusioned by the evils of compounded things,
Take seven steps for beings' sake toward a hermitage—
The merit of that act is especially sublime.
Those for whom there is no pleasure or unhappiness
Lead human lives of constant, utter joy.
Those who find delight in mountain solitudes
Will taste the utter joy of true renunciates.
Those with nothing they can call their own,
Who do not seize or grasp at anything at all,
And in this world dwell like rhinoceroses,
Can travel like the wind through space.
Those whose minds have no attachment to the world
Have, in the human world, the greatest bliss.
They're unattached to joy or misery,
Their minds have constant freedom, like the wind.
Having eliminated the two extremes—
The suffering of leaving those close to them
And unhappiness at difficult situations—
Such people who delight in the Dharma are happy.

And,

Rid of all the many kinds of faults,
Those who practice never have much to do.
For yogins who are diligent, there are no disputes.
The benefit for those who dwell in solitude
Is a mind forever disenchanted with compounded things
And no desire at all for worldly life;
The taints of the defilements will not increase.
The benefit of a life in forest groves
Is total absence of disputes,

> With constant peace and joy in solitude
> And full restraint of body, speech, and mind.
> The many virtues of this life in solitude
> Are consistent with becoming free;
> Peace and perfect liberation are soon realized.
> Forest dwellers who adhere to perfect liberation
> Will find all these qualities in their hermitage.

And,

> Give up your attachment for home and city life
> And constantly rely on forest solitudes.
> Like rhinos, always act without duality.
> Before too long, the highest concentration will be yours.

It is important to be fully mindful of, and properly implement, the meaning of these and the other extensive praises made in the precious sūtras of the benefits of having few desires, being content with what one has, and relying on solitude. Even if we ourselves are unable to strive in this sort of concentration, there is still inconceivable merit in not interrupting those who go into solitary retreat and practice meditation, and furthermore, of rejoicing at their doing so. The *Sūtra of the Fortunate Kalpa* has the following account:

> In the distant past, there appeared the Tathāgata Boundless Diligence, who had an entourage of one billion followers, to whom he taught meditative concentration. While he was teaching concentration, a king called Flower of Merit appeared, and having heard the Tathāgata, spoke to his thousand queens and thousand children, "We cannot understand the meaning of this concentration of limitless appearance.[356] And if we cannot understand it, we will be unable to realize it. Nevertheless, we should rejoice in the Tathāgata's excellent words." They rejoiced in this concentration that the Bhagavan had excellently spoken and explained. As a result of their doing so, the very instant that they rejoiced, they annulled eighty thousand kalpas' worth of rebirths in cyclic existence and turned away from cyclic existence, obtaining the power of memory called "possessed of a house."[357] Because of that

> virtuous deed, they pleased three hundred thousand buddhas, they always attained this concentration, and they never fell into wrong ways or states without opportunity. And through that causal factor alone, they became true and perfect buddhas.

The *Knowledge of the Ultimate* sums all this up as follows:

> Those who fail to drink the cool and soothing nectar
> Of their master's pith instructions until they are replete
> End up dying of thirst in the plain of misery,
> Anguishing over the meaning of a myriad treatises.

And Lord Atisha said,

> Life is short, there is so much to learn,
> There is no knowing how long we have to live.
> So like a swan extracting milk from water,
> Eagerly take the teachings you most desire.
> Look at those who practice worldly ways:
> All they do is meaningless and leads to pain.
> Whatever we think of, it has no essence,
> So train in watching your own mind.

Accordingly, those who wish the best for themselves should take to heart the oral advice of the sublime beings who hold the lineage and apply it as best they can to their own mind streams. This is the only thing that is truly important, so, folding my hands, I beseech you to do as they have said.

Concluding Poem

In earlier times, people felt true renunciation and disenchantment,
Disciples and the teachings came together, and people enjoyed one-pointed practice.
A single deep instruction matured and liberated fortunate beings.
At that time, a lot of explanation was superfluous and unnecessary.
These days, people mostly like to be entertained,
They fail to experience the essential meanings and only run after the words.
The continuous stream of instruction based on one's experience has been stopped,
And all is filled with the din of hollow talk.
Because of this, for those who wish for explanation, this compilation will be useful.
In this age of decadence, the land is filled
With frauds like me who hold the rank of lama
Yet have not trained themselves in the writings of the wise
And are not perfumed with the scent of experience in the practice.
When left to themselves, they carelessly distract themselves with frivolous diversions,
For important occasions, they tire themselves out by reading lots of books.
Like madmen, they speak irrelevantly, saying the first thing that comes into their heads,
And though their utterances might satisfy the foolish, to the wise they are an embarrassment.
They repeat what others say, like music echoed off a cliff,

And though it sounds quite good, it lacks the pith—the blessings of the lineage.
This is why these teachings of the greatest accomplished vidyādharas,
Collected here like drops of dew, are truly meaningful.
I myself am not a sublime being, or even a learned scholar;
I am utterly devoid of the perfume of good conduct, let alone accomplishment.
I have, however, encountered teachers who truly are the perfect buddhas
And I experienced just a few of their instructions.
Although I could not honor and attend them with my body and my speech,
My devotion to them is impossible to erase,
Engraved upon my heart as if on stone, so just because of this
I believe I have made use of my precious human life.
However, when I see the way that fickle people seem to be,
Their ever-moving thoughts shaking like the tips of kusha grass
With the cold wind of things and situations,
There is not a moment that I am relieved of sadness.
When I give explanations according to the Dharma, not a single person knows how to listen;
If I say something contrary to the Dharma, they listen, but the ripened effect will be so serious.
Who, then, can I benefit, whatever I do?
Alas, alack! Precious Teacher, only you know.
We do not do a single thing that is worthwhile;
We burden ourselves with a hundred projects that we never get done.
Even though we train in helping others, it ends up creating conflict.
When I see my following of disciples like this, I feel so sad.
If one's own mind is not tamed, how can one help others?
If one's own mind is tamed, whatever one does will be right.
Now, in what is left of my life, as brief as when the sun breaks through the clouds,
May I give up distractions and meditate one-pointedly.
Think of all our failures—our former plans that we failed to achieve;
Think of all the many things we did—and what was the result?
Now that I am independent, like a beggar,
I pray that I may humbly end up dying like a dog.

My only father, treasure of compassion beyond all concepts,
From the invisible expanse, think of me with love:
Bestow on me the blessing that I might have the freedom
To practice the sacred Dharma and accomplish all I wish.
I pray that when the perceptions of this life fade away
I may not die in anguish as life's thread is cut
But be welcomed by the pure perception of radiant light
And be reborn close to my teacher, the all-pervading lord.
Together with the hosts of vidyādharas gathered there,
Through the profound practice of the secret mantras,
May I without difficulty continue on the path
And realize the level of my teacher, the glorious protector.
Until I attain that state, in my successive lives,
May I never find myself in run-down monasteries, under false teachers;
May I not indulge in evil deeds, or be reborn as a king, minister, or their servant or messenger;
Or be reborn falling into the lower realms.
May I never be reborn as an intellectual who refutes the teachings through sophistry,
As one who pays lip service to emptiness and shows contempt for the law of cause and effect,
Or as one who deceives others, pretending that he is accomplished when he is not,
For I would thus bring ruin on others and myself.
May I never be reborn in virtueless positions—
As a monastery official, disciplinarian, and the like—
That the sublime beings condemn and avoid,
And may I never be separated from the sacred Dharma.
May I truly gain a precious human form
Enriched with the four wheels as positive conditions,*
And may I always serve my teachers, glorious protectors,
And hold the long tradition of the essential, definitive teachings.
Even in my dreams may I not have evil thoughts,
May bodhichitta never slip my mind.

*The four wheels are the four conditions conducive to spiritual practice: staying in a suitable place, following a spiritual teacher, the strong aspiration to accomplish enlightenment, and a great stock of merit accumulated from previous lives.

Completely and without mistake, may I practice
The path that delights the buddhas—the union of the two accumulations.
Especially, may I find a fully qualified teacher
To ripen my being with the four empowerments;
Keeping the sacred commitments purely,
May I perfectly complete the practice of the two phases,
And in that life traverse the ocean of existence.
One day, when I have fulfilled my own goal
And gained the power to effortlessly accomplish others' goals,
Without ever feeling discouraged even for an instant,
May I bring happiness and peace to all beings without exception.
By means of infinite manifestations, in pure lands filling all space,
May I venerate the buddhas, hold all the sacred teachings, and bring beings to maturity.
Having completed the ocean-like deeds of Samantabhadra,
May I accomplish all the activities of the teacher, glorious protector.
Oh please, if you have any faith in me,
Think carefully and do not deceive yourselves:
Anyone can get the food and clothes they need to live this present life,
But rare are those who have the Dharma that helps in future lives.
This precious human life is greater than a wishing gem,
A unique occasion, enriched with goodness gathered in the past.
If one is diligent, enlightenment is close at hand,
But if one fails to use it, returning with empty hands, one is, alas, a fool.
Youth, like a flower garland, quickly fades,
Wealth and glory, like dewdrops on the grass tips, are volatile and fleeting.
One's vital force and length of life are like the dance of lightning—what is there to trust?
From this day onward, I beseech you, marshal the forces of diligence.
The actions we perform will follow us like our shadows,
Happiness and suffering will be their unsought white and black results.
No one in the triple world is mightier than one's deeds.
So, essentialize the practice, adopt what's right, avoid what's wrong.
Unless we have an elixir for lasting youth and immortality,
We must wander in existence like someone chronically ill,
Whichever realm we're in, what chance is there of happiness?

The torments of the triple forms of suffering never cease.
Those with power to protect us from all these are the teacher and the Three Jewels,
And it is impossible for these refuges to ever let us down.
If we can rely on them for refuge with faith and confidence,
We will turn back the powerful stream of existence, not to speak of ordinary sufferings.
Some foolish beings go to ghosts and spirits for protection,
They do not trust the Three Jewels as sources of refuge.
Ruinous for themselves and other beings, this leads to rebirth in the hell and preta realms.
My heart grieves to think of them, and tears spring from my eyes.
Drawn along by the four boundless attitudes, as in the slipstream of a chariot,
One aspires and acts with bodhichitta, a radiantly white elixir,
An antidote to poison, removing the torments of existence and peace.
This is the sole root of the path of the Great Vehicle.
Wanting happiness for just oneself involves all kinds of wrongful deeds;
From helping others, the fruit of buddhahood matures.
So recognize what it is that you stand to gain or lose,
And please forever train on the path of the six perfections.
Recitation and meditation fan, with the wind of the four powers,
The destructive fire at the end of time that instantly consumes
The firewood of obscurations gathered over many aeons.
Those who are diligent in this are fair as the unclouded moon.
As when one sows good seed upon a fertile field,
And fills the granary with grain,
Those who make connection with the Three Jewels and Three Roots,
Venerating them with the riches of the three buddha bodies,
Will fill the storehouse of the two accumulations, winning, thus, the fruit.
Nowhere has a buddha appeared
Who has not purified the two obscurations
And completed the two accumulations.
Such a possibility would be untrue
And contradicts the sūtras, tantras, and oral teachings.
Hence the importance of being diligent in both accumulation and purification.

The root teacher, from whom you have received so much kindness,
Is shown in all the sūtras and tantras to be the Buddha in person,
Superior even to the buddhas in kindness.
Those who serve and please the teacher in the three ways are fortunate indeed.
If the blessings of realization through the true lineage are not transferred,
It is impossible to realize the actual state of being with one's beclouded mind.
For those with faith, it unfolds openly from within.
The Guru Yoga, therefore, is the best of paths.
Those who are skilled in means make obeisance and offerings,
Confess their evil deeds, rejoice, exhort, and so on,
Thus producing in an instant many kalpas' worth of accumulation.
Space would be too small to hold their merit, could one give it form.
In all you do, when praying or receiving empowerment,
Devotion to your teachers, seeing them as buddhas, is most important.
If you lack devotion, nothing you do will be of any help.
If you have devotion, everything you do will be all right.
Relatively, we meet and part from the teacher in the form body,
Yet fortunate disciples should not feel sad at this,
For ultimately there is no meeting or parting from the teacher in the body of truth:
If you realize your own mind to be the teacher, that is all there is to it.
So, fortunate beings, like-minded friends,
Keep the Guru Yoga as the essence of the path.
Mingle your mind with the teacher's mind and preserve the experience of that realization:
There are no crucial points for practice that are not included in this.
The practice of the generation phase, recitation, perfection phase, and so on
Amounts to this, the teacher's mind, the result of all the crucial points, and nothing else.
Therefore, you who have the good fortune of constant diligence,
Sublime friends, never separate from this.
By the merit of this explanation, may beings filling space
Always be guided by a sublime teacher,

And through making all the right connections on the path of the supreme vehicle,
May they perfect completion, maturation, and purification and attain buddhahood.
May the Buddha's doctrine spread, may those who hold the teachings have long lives,
May study and practice increase, and may happiness spread throughout the land.
As it was in the perfect age,* may the world and its inhabitants everywhere
Be filled with riches, glory, and auspiciousness.

*The perfect age, or age of complete endowment, is the first of the four ages, when beings had infinitely long lives, bodies of light, and miraculous abilities, and were nourished by a nectar-like elixir.

Colophon

Some time ago, Drodül Pawo Dorje,* who is the foremost of accomplished vidyādharas, said to me, "It would be good if you could produce a text explaining a bit about the preliminary practices." And although I had made some notes about them, up to and including the four practices for turning the mind, simply to refresh my own memory, for a number of reasons I did not see any relevant need for it and I put aside working on the project. Subsequently, the sublime precious emanation Pema Drimé Lekpai Lodrö,† whose nature is as immutable as refined gold, and my younger brother, Thubten Gelek Gyamtso, both urged me to continue, backing up their request by offering paper and ink and other writing materials. Merely so as not to refuse them, I, the old monk Gyurmé Pema Namgyal (or Jamyang Lodrö Gyamtso Drayang, as I am called by my bodhisattva name), who has had the fortune to have the perfect buddha Lodrö Thayé as my root teacher, wrote this in my fifty-first year, the year of the iron bird (1921), on auspicious days in the fourth month, in the isolated hut Tashi Chimé Drubpai Gatsel, above the beautiful retreat center Dechen Pema Öling in a forest of bodhi trees at Senge Namdzong in Dokham. May virtue ensue!

Printing Colophon

Straying from the heart of the sugatas, primordial radiant light,
Beings are tainted by adventitious dualistic delusions.
That they may be liberated in the level of primordial buddhahood, free
from the beginning,

*Drodül Pawo Dorje (1842–1924), also known as Adzom Drukpa, a disciple of Jamyang Khyentse Wangpo.

†Shechen Kongtrül Rinpoche, Jamgön Kongtrül Khyentse Özer (1904–1953/54). He was a reincarnation of Jamgön Kongtrül the Great.

Care for them, all-pervading teacher, Vajrasattva!
The buddhas' teachings are inconceivable:
Temporarily, they guide beings according to their temperaments and capacities,
And ultimately, they train and bring them to the profound definitive meaning.
These are one and the same vehicle, not two.
It is with that in mind that this introduction for beginners,
The basic teachings on the common preliminaries,
Was compiled from the teachings of the lineage of former vidyādharas
And arranged with the intention of benefiting himself and others.
At the time of the new moon in the month of miracles,
When the Buddha appeared in many forms,
Adren Dratshab Jampa Gelek,
Mingyur Dronma, and her son Gyurga,
Who see with the rich qualities of faith and generosity,
Made offerings with pure thought and deed, and thanks to these,
This book was printed in the great monastery of Tennyi Dargye Ling
In the male wood mouse year of the fifteenth sixty-year cycle (1924).
May all the virtuous deeds accumulated, beginning with this one,
Uncontaminated by the impurities of concepts regarding the three spheres,
And dedicated in the same way as did Mañjushrī and Samantabhadra,
Become blended as a single taste in the ocean of great enlightenment.
May all troubles in this life for the sponsors and their entourage be removed,
May longevity, merit, glory, wealth, the lineage, and religion grow greater.
May all beings never turn away from the path of the supreme vehicle,
And may the two goals and all their wishes be fulfilled.
May the obscurations of all beings filling space be swiftly purified,
Especially those of Jamyang Rabten, in whose name the offerings were made;
Abandoning states devoid of freedom, and in a body complete with the freedoms and advantages,
May they be enriched with the four wheels as favorable conditions.
In that state, may their propensity for the essential supreme vehicle be awakened,

And may they train properly and without error on the path of the sūtras
and mantras.
Perfecting completion, maturation, and purification without difficulty,
May they swiftly accomplish the all-pervading lord Vajrasattva.
Furthermore, may all those beings who hold the nonsectarian teachings
Live long, their lotus feet remaining firm for oceans of kalpas.
May they constantly turn the wheel of the profound and extensive
teachings,
And may the precious doctrine spread to the limits of space.
May the Saṅgha always live in harmony and accomplish all they wish,
May the land be filled with the light of happiness and the ten virtuous
deeds,
May the words for disasters—*plague*, *famine*, and *war*—never be heard,
And may all be satiated anew with the feast of the golden age.
May this miraculous, well-executed, marvelous publication
Endure forever without deteriorating until the end of existence.
May its activity in benefiting others be as vast as space,
And may it connect many beings to supreme perfect liberation.
May all be auspicious,
That the wisdom, qualities, and virtue
Of the buddhas and their heirs,
And the power of their spiritual intent,
Aspirations, knowledge, love, and ability
All appear to us, unobscured, at this very time.

These few words of aspiration were written as a printing colophon by Jamyang Lodrö Gyamtso* in accordance with the wishes of a virtuous practitioner.

*Jamyang Lodrö Gyamtso is another name of Jamyang Khyentse Chökyi Lodrö, who was one of Shechen Gyaltsap Rinpoche's disciples.

Appendix 1: Structural Outline of *A Chariot to Freedom*

Preamble

Part One: The Virtuous Beginning, Comprising an Explanation of How the Teachings Should Be Presented and Received

- Chapter 1: Attitude
  - I. The attitude related to the vast intention of bodhichitta
  - II. The attitude related to the vast skill in means of the Secret Mantra Vehicle
- Chapter 2: Conduct
  - I. Conduct to be avoided
    - A. Conduct to be avoided by the disciples listening to the teachings
      - The three defects of the pot
      - The six stains
      - The thirty-six faults
    - B. Conduct to be avoided by the master giving the teachings
    - C. Conduct to be avoided by both the teacher and the disciples
  - II. Conduct to be adopted
    - A. Conduct to be adopted by the disciples listening to the teachings
      - 1. Thirty-six qualities that one should possess
      - 2. The four correct notions that one should cultivate
      - 3. The six transcendent perfections that one should have
      - 4. Additional instructions on conduct
    - B. Conduct to be adopted by the master giving the teachings
    - C. Conduct to be adopted by both the teacher and the disciples

Chapter 3: A Supplementary, Inspirational Section Describing the Benefits of Teaching the Dharma and Listening to It
- I. The benefits obtained by the master giving the teaching
- II. The benefits obtained by the disciples listening to the teaching

Part Two: The Virtuous Middle, Comprising an Explanation on Training One's Being through the Four Common Practices for Turning the Mind

Section One: Preliminaries to beginning a session

Chapter 4: Preliminaries to Beginning a Session

Section Two: The specific, individual practices

Chapter 5: Reflecting on the Difficulty of Finding the Freedoms and Advantages
- I. Identifying the freedoms and advantages
  - A. Identifying the essence, freedom
    - 1. The eight states without opportunity that depend on one's own stream of being
    - 2. The eight intrusive circumstances that leave no freedom to practice the Dharma
    - 3. The eight incompatible propensities that leave no freedom to practice the Dharma
  - B. Identifying the particular qualities, the advantages
    - 1. The five individual advantages
    - 2. The five circumstantial advantages
- II. The difficulty of finding the freedoms and advantages
  - A. The very nature of the precious human body that makes it so difficult to find
  - B. The causes and conditions that make a precious human body so difficult to find
  - C. Analogies of how difficult it is to find a precious human body
  - D. Reflecting on numerical comparisons of how difficult it is to find a precious human body
- III. The importance of finding the freedoms and advantages
- IV. The benefits of meditating on the freedoms and advantages and the signs of having done so

Chapter 6: Reflecting on Death and Impermanence
- I. A general teaching on the impermanent nature of the vessel and contents

II. A detailed classification using twelve instructions
   A. Reflecting on the aggregates that form the support
   B. Reflecting on the lords of beings
   C. Reflecting on the formation and destruction of the universe and beings
   D. Reflecting on sublime beings
   E. Reflecting on how uncertain it is when we will die
   F. Reflecting on the nature of compounded phenomena
   G. Reflecting on the power of the causes of death
   H. Reflecting on how one will depart alone
   I. Reflecting on beings in time
   J. Reflecting on how there is nothing that one can rely upon
   K. Reflecting on the unpredictability of events
   L. Reflecting with intense longing
III. Essentializing the practice with nine reflections on death
   A. Three reasons why death is inevitable
      1. There is no one in the past whose life has been spared, who has been born and has stayed without dying, so we, too, are sure to die
      2. There is no adding to one's life span, it is constantly decreasing, so again, one is certain to die
      3. One's body and mind are compounded, so again, one is certain to die
   B. Three reasons why there is no certainty when one will die
      1. One's span of life has not been fixed in time, so there is no certainty when one will die
      2. The causes of death are numerous, so again, there is no certainty when one will die
      3. The body is frail and essenceless, so again, there is no knowing when it will perish
   C. Three reasons why nothing can help one when one is dying
      1. The wealth that one has accumulated cannot help one
      2. Those to whom one is related cannot help one
      3. The body with which one was born cannot help one
IV. The benefits of meditating on impermanence and signs of having done so
   A. Benefits
   B. The signs of having trained

Chapter 7: Reflecting on Actions: Cause and Result

- I. Identifying the nature of deeds
  - A. Nonvirtuous deeds to be avoided
    - 1. Definition
    - 2. Etymological definition
    - 3. Categories
      - a. Naturally shameful deeds
        - The five crimes with immediate retribution
        - The five crimes that are almost as grave
        - The ten nonvirtuous deeds
        - The sixteen serious faults
          - The four serious faults entailing reversal
          - The four serious faults entailing impairment
          - The four serious faults entailing contempt
          - The four serious faults entailing scorn
        - The eight perverse acts
      - b. Shameful deeds that violate edicts
      - c. Mundane shameful deeds
  - B. Virtuous deeds to be adopted
    - 1. Definition
    - 2. Etymological definition
    - 3. Categories
      - a. Virtuous deeds conducive to merit
      - b. Virtuous deeds conducive to liberation
      - c. Unsurpassable virtuous deeds
  - C. Indeterminate deeds
    - 1. Definition
    - 2. Etymological definition
    - 3. Categories
- II. A specific explanation of the ten actions
  - A. The ten nonvirtuous deeds to be avoided
    - 1. A synopsis according to the Great Omniscient One's *Finding Rest in the Nature of the Mind*
      - a. The three nonvirtuous deeds of the body
      - b. The four nonvirtuous deeds of speech
      - c. The three nonvirtuous deeds of the mind
    - 2. A presentation of the actual words of Orgyen, knower of the three times

- a. The three nonvirtuous deeds of the body
  - i. Taking life
  - ii. Taking what is not given
  - iii. Sexual misconduct
- b. The four nonvirtuous deeds of speech
  - i. Telling lies
  - ii. Divisive speech
  - iii. Worthless chatter
  - iv. Harsh speech
- c. The three nonvirtuous deeds of the mind
  - i. Covetousness
  - ii. Malice
  - iii. Wrong views

B. The ten virtuous deeds to be adopted

1. A synopsis according to the Great Omniscient One's *Finding Rest in the Nature of the Mind*
2. A presentation in the adamantine words of Guru Rinpoche
   - a. Definition
   - b. Etymological definition
   - c. Categories
   - d. Results

III. Additional teachings on distinctions and categories

A. Distinctions

1. The distinction between virtue and nonvirtue in terms of their object
2. Distinction in terms of the subject
3. Distinction in terms of acting as the direct antidote to, and direct cause of, existence
4. Distinction in terms of obscuration and nonobscuration of the way things are and of compatibility and incompatibility with the way things appear
5. Distinction in terms of the presence or absence of samsaric, conceptual elaboration
6. Distinction in terms of the fully ripened effect
7. Distinction in terms of the degree of skillful means and wisdom

B. Categories of deeds

1. A general exposition of the different kinds of deeds

2. Deeds that differ according to their intention and application
3. Differences from the point of view of the way in which the effects are experienced
4. Differences from the point of view of the way in which the effects are produced
5. Differences from the point of view of the classification of deeds as propelling and completing

IV. Reflecting on how everything is determined by deeds
V. The signs of having trained

Chapter 8: Reflecting on the Sufferings of Cyclic Existence

I. Reflecting generally on the sufferings of cyclic existence
II. Reflecting specifically on the sufferings in each of the six realms

A. The sufferings in the hells

1. The eight hot hells
   a. The Reviving Hell
   b. The Black-Line Hell
   c. The Crushing Hell
   d. The Screaming Hell
   e. The Great Screaming Hell
   f. The Hell of Heat
   g. The Hell of Intense Heat
   h. The Hell of Torment Unsurpassed
   The lesser hells
   The neighboring hells
2. The eight cold hells
   a. The Hell of Blisters
   b. The Hell of Bursting Blisters
   c. The Hell of Lamentation
   d. The Hell of Groans
   e. The Hell of Chattering Teeth
   f. The Hell of Utpala-Like Cracks
   g. The Hell of Lotus-Like Cracks
   h. The Hell of Great Lotus-Like Cracks

B. Reflecting on the sufferings of the hungry spirits

1. Hungry spirits that live in the underworld
   a. Hungry spirits whose perception of the outer world is obscured

- b. Hungry spirits whose perception of their inner world is obscured
- c. Hungry spirits whose perceptions are specifically obscured
- d. Hungry spirits whose perceptions are generally obscured

2. Hungry spirits that move through space

C. Reflecting on the sufferings of the animals

1. Animals that live in the depths
2. Animals that live scattered in different places

D. Reflecting on the sufferings of human beings

1. The four root sufferings
   - a. The suffering of birth
   - b. The suffering of aging
   - c. The suffering of illness
   - d. The suffering of death
2. The four branch sufferings
   - a. Encountering those we do not like
   - b. Being separated from those we like
   - c. Being deprived of what we want
   - d. The natural suffering of being tainted

E. Reflecting on the sufferings of the demigods

F. Reflecting on the sufferings of celestial beings

III. An instruction on the importance of accomplishing the means to become free from suffering

IV. The benefits and signs of having trained in this way

Part Three: The Virtuous Ending, Comprising an Explanation of the Main Preliminaries for the Path of the Diamond Vehicle

Chapter 9: Taking Refuge, Which Distinguishes This Path from Wrong Paths

I. A teaching on the nature of faith, the principal causal factor in taking refuge

II. An explanation of the actual practice, the way to take refuge

A. A general presentation of distinctions

1. The refuge of the causal vehicle of characteristics
2. The refuge of the system of the resultant Diamond Vehicle

B. A condensed presentation from the oral teachings of Orgyen, knower of the three times

1. The outer refuge
2. The inner refuge
3. The secret refuge

C. The main explanation of the instructions for taking refuge

III. A concluding explanation of the different precepts and benefits of taking refuge

A. General precepts

1. The actual precepts

a. Precepts of the causal refuge

i. Three precepts regarding things one must avoid

ii. Three precepts regarding things one should do

iii. Three ancillary precepts

b. Precepts of the resultant refuge

2. The benefits of keeping the precepts

B. Particular precepts: the precepts of the outer, inner, and secret refuge

1. The precepts of the outer refuge

a. The three particular precepts

i. Not to pay homage to other gods

ii. To avoid harming sentient beings

iii. Not to keep the company of those with non-Buddhist views

b. The five common precepts

i. To constantly venerate the Three Jewels, offering them the first part of one's food and drink

(1) The offering of homage

(2) The offering of material things

(3) The offering of praises

(4) The offering of practice

ii. Not to abandon the Three Jewels even for the sake of one's body and life, for riches, or for reward

iii. Not to seek any other means of protection, whatever happens to one—sickness, joy, or sorrow

iv. Wherever one goes, to keep in mind the buddhas and bodhisattvas, making offerings and taking refuge

v. To train again and again, remembering the qualities of the refuge

2. The precepts of the inner refuge

a. The three particular precepts
b. The five common precepts
3. The precepts of the secret refuge
a. The three particular precepts
b. The seven common precepts

Chapter 10: Arousing the Mind Set on Enlightenment, the Root of the Great Vehicle's Path That Distinguishes It from Lower Paths

I. The preparation, training the mind in the four boundless attitudes
II. The main practice, showing how to arouse the mind set on enlightenment
A. A presentation of the principles
1. An explanation of how these are generally presented
a. The reasons one needs to train in bodhichitta
b. The main explanation of how to arouse the mind set on enlightenment
i. The nature of the potential, the basis of good fortune
ii. A presentation of arousing bodhichitta, which is the basis for applying the precepts
(1) The kind of birth that is a support for arousing bodhichitta
(2) The main explanation of the nature of the bodhichitta that is supported
(a) Essence
(b) Etymological definition
(c) Categories
(d) How to take the vow of bodhichitta
2. A specific explanation taken from the *Direct Instructions of the Teacher*, the oral teachings of Orgyen, knower of the three times
a. Training on the outer level
i. Essence
ii. Etymological definition
iii. Categories
iv. The marks of the practitioner
v. The object from whom the vow is taken
vi. The ritual for taking the vow
vii. The benefits of the training
viii. The reasons for training like this

ix. The disadvantages of not training
x. The precepts that have to be kept
xi. The defining points at which one receives and gives up the vow
xii. The methods for repairing breaches
b. Training on the inner level
i. Essence
ii. Etymological definition
iii. Categories
iv. The marks of the practitioner
v. The object from whom the vow is taken
vi. The ritual for taking the vow
vii. The benefits of the training
viii. The reason for training in this sort of bodhichitta
ix. The disadvantages of not training
x. The precepts that have to be kept
xi. The defining points at which one receives and gives up the vow
xii. The methods for repairing breaches
c. Training on the secret level
B. The main teaching on the instructions for the practice
1. A general exposition of how to arouse bodhichitta
2. The actual instructions on the specific points to be considered
III. The conclusion: How to keep the precepts, together with the benefits
A. Identifying the precepts that have to be kept
1. Detailed classification of the precepts
a. The precepts of bodhichitta in aspiration
i. Never abandoning sentient beings
ii. Remembering the benefits of bodhichitta
iii. Constantly gathering the accumulations
iv. Training again and again in bodhichitta
v. Adopting and avoiding the eight white and black actions
b. Precepts of bodhichitta in action
i. General presentation
The number of the six transcendent perfections
The order of the six transcendent perfections
The characteristics of the six transcendent perfections

Etymological definitions of the six transcendent perfections
Subdivisions of the six transcendent perfections
Groupings of the six transcendent perfections
How the transcendent perfections are practiced
ii. Detailed explanation of their different branches
(1) Generosity
(a) Material gifts
(b) The gift of protection from fear
(c) The gift of Dharma
(2) Discipline
(a) The discipline of refraining from negative actions
(i) The Middle Way tradition
(ii) The Mind-Only tradition
(b) The discipline of gathering virtue
(c) The discipline of benefiting sentient beings
(3) Patience
(a) The patience of thinking nothing of the harm that has been done to us
(b) The patience of happily accepting suffering
(c) The patience of certainty with regard to the teachings
(4) Diligence
(a) Armor-like diligence
(b) Diligence in application
(c) Diligence in benefiting beings
(5) Concentration
(a) The concentration practiced by the childish
(b) Clearly discerning concentration
(c) The excellent concentration of the tathāgatas
(6) Wisdom
(a) The wisdom that comes from listening
(b) The wisdom that comes from reflecting
(c) The wisdom that comes from meditating
2. Condensed precepts
B. How to keep the precepts without deterioration
1. Avoiding the seven adverse conditions that cause one's own and others' practice to deteriorate

2. Training in favorable conditions—the factors that prevent the precepts from deteriorating and conditions that reinforce them
3. Training in constantly guarding the precepts with mindfulness, vigilance, and carefulness

C. An explanation of the negative consequences of deteriorating the precepts and of how to restore the vow
1. The negative consequences of deteriorating the precepts
   a. The general negative consequences of downfalls
   b. The particular negative consequences of root downfalls
2. How to restore the vow if the precepts are deteriorated
   a. How to confess faults
   b. How to take the vow again when it has been given up

D. A teaching on the benefits of training in that way
1. Temporary benefits
2. Ultimate benefit

Chapter 11: The Meditation and Recitation of Vajrasattva, Which Purifies the Negative Deeds and Obscurations That Act as Unfavorable Conditions

I. General exposition of the nature of the four strengths

A. What has to be purified

B. The agents of purification
1. The power of the support
2. The power of regret
   a. Examining how pointless negative deeds are
   b. Examining how fearful negative deeds are
   c. Examining the urgent need to rid ourselves of our negative deeds
3. The power of the application of the antidote
   a. Remembering the names of the buddhas and bodhisattvas
   b. Crafting images and building stūpas
   c. Venerating and circumambulating sacred supports
   d. Reading or reciting the profound sūtras and tantras
   e. Reciting incantations and mantras
   f. Meditating on emptiness
4. The power of restoration

C. The method of purification

II. The main explanation, comprising the instructions for the practice in the specific meditation and recitation of Vajrasattva
III. Concluding description of the signs of proficiency in purifying negative deeds and obscurations and the benefits of doing so

Chapter 12: The Maṇḍala Offering, the Method for Completing the Two Accumulations

- I. General explanation of the principles
  - A. The disadvantages of not offering the maṇḍala
  - B. The reasons it is necessary to offer the maṇḍala
  - C. When to offer the maṇḍala
  - D. How to offer the maṇḍala
    - 1. Offering the maṇḍala in an outward way
      - a. The accomplishment maṇḍala
        - i. The materials for the maṇḍala
        - ii. The materials for the piles
        - iii. The arrangement and visualization
      - b. The offering maṇḍala
    - 2. Offering the maṇḍala in an inward way
      - a. Visualizing the object of offering, the accomplishment maṇḍala
      - b. Presenting the offering maṇḍala
    - 3. Offering the maṇḍala in a secret way
      - a. The accomplishment maṇḍala
      - b. The offering maṇḍala
  - E. The benefits of offering the maṇḍala
- II. Specific teaching on how to make the offering
- III. A supplementary explanation, related to the above, of a few of the benefits of venerating the Three Jewels
  - A. Essence
  - B. Etymological definition
  - C. Different aspects of veneration
    - 1. Pure fields
    - 2. Pure intention
    - 3. Pure materials
    - 4. Pure implementation
      - a. Common, limited forms of veneration
      - b. The unsurpassable form of veneration

Chapter 13: The Instruction on the Guru Yoga, Which Enables the Extraordinary Blessings to Enter One's Being

- I. A general explanation of how to follow the spiritual friend, who is the source of good qualities
  - A. The reasons one needs to follow a teacher
  - B. The marks of a teacher who should be followed
    - 1. Common characteristics
    - 2. Extraordinary characteristics
  - C. How to follow such a teacher
    - 1. The attitude one should have in following one's teachers
      - a. Calling to mind the teachers' qualities
      - b. Calling to mind the teachers' kindness
      - c. Regarding the teacher as a buddha
    - 2. The conduct one should adopt in following one's teachers
      - a. Avoiding inappropriate behavior
      - b. Adopting appropriate behavior
        - The least effective way to please one's teachers
        - The middling ways to please one's teachers
          - Serving one's teachers with one's body
          - Serving one's teachers with one's speech
          - Serving one's teachers with one's mind
        - The best way to please one's teachers
- II. The main explanation of how specifically to train in the profound practice
  - A. Visualizing the support
  - B. Offering the seven branches
    - 1. Obeisance
    - 2. Making offerings
    - 3. Confessing negative actions
    - 4. Rejoicing
    - 5. Exhorting the teachers to turn the Wheel of Dharma
    - 6. Praying to the teachers not to pass into nirvāṇa
    - 7. Dedication
  - C. Praying
  - D. Receiving the empowerments
  - E. Mingling one's mind with the teacher's and settling in meditative equipoise

III. A concluding exposition of the benefits of following the teacher and practicing in that way

Concluding Remarks
Concluding Poem
Colophon

Appendix 2: Prayer to the Lord of the Victorious Ones (*gTso rgyal ma*)

Adapted from *The Way of the Bodhisattva* (*Byang chub sems dpa' spyod pa la 'jug pa*), chap. 2, verses 47–53 (English translation, p. 44).

From this day forward I take refuge
In the Buddhas, guardians of beings,
Who labor to protect all wanderers,
Those mighty ones who scatter every fear.

And in the Dharma they have realized in their hearts,
Which drives away the terrors of saṃsāra,
And in all the host of Bodhisattvas
Likewise I will perfectly take refuge.

Gripped by dread, beside myself with anguish,
To Samantabhadra I will give myself;
My body I myself will give
To Mañjughoṣha, gentle and melodious.

To him whose deeds of mercy never fail,
My lord Avalokita,
I cry out from depths of misery,
"Protect me now an evildoer!"

Now to the noble one, Ākāshagarbha,
And to Kṣhitigarbha, from my heart I call.

To all protectors, great, compassionate,
I cry to them in search of refuge.

To Vajrapāṇi I shall fly,
For at the sight of him
All vengeful things like Yama's host
Escape in terror to the four directions.

Formerly your words I have transgressed,
But having seen these terrors all around,
I come to you for refuge praying:
Swiftly drive away my fear!

Appendix 3: Confession Prayer

Taken from Dudjom Rinpoche Jigdrel Yeshe Dorje, *Collection of Liturgical Texts* (*Chos spyod kyi rim pa rnam par grol ba'i lam gyi shing rta*), pp. 25–26.

Teacher, great vajra holder, and all you buddhas and bodhisattvas dwelling in the ten directions, heed my prayer.

In all my beginningless lives in cyclic existence until now, overpowered by the defilements of attachment, aversion, and bewilderment, I, who am called . . . , have committed the ten negative actions with my body, speech, and mind.

I have committed the five crimes with immediate retribution and the five crimes that are almost as grave.

I have transgressed the vows of individual liberation, the precepts of the bodhisattvas, and the sacred commitments of the secret mantras.

I have disrespected my parents, disrespected my preceptors and instructors, and disrespected my fellow practitioners.

I have done violence to the Three Jewels, I have abandoned the sacred Dharma, I have slandered the noble Saṅgha, I have harmed sentient beings, and committed other deeds.

All these nonvirtuous deeds that I have committed, those done at my behest, and those done by others that I have rejoiced in—in short, the whole host of negative deeds and broken vows that I have committed, which will obstruct my gaining higher rebirth and liberation and will lead to my remaining in cyclic existence and being reborn in the lower realms—all these I confess in the presence of the teacher, great vajra holder, and of all the other buddhas and bodhisattvas dwelling in the ten directions.

None of them do I keep secret, none of them do I conceal. Henceforth, I will refrain from doing them.

If I acknowledge and part from them, I will abide in happiness. But if I fail to acknowledge and part from them, happiness will never come to me.

Appendix 4: The Seven-Line Prayer

HŪṀ
In Orgyen's land, upon its northwest rim,
On lotus, pistil-cup, and stem,
Wondrous, supreme mastery you found
And as the Lotus-Born you are renowned.
A ring of many ḍākinīs encircles you,
And in your footsteps, practicing, we follow you.
To grant your blessings, come we pray.
GURU PADMA SIDDHI HŪṀ

Glossary

Abhidharma (Skt., Tib. Chos mngon pa). One of the three baskets; the branch of the Buddha's teachings that deals mainly with psychology and logic.

accomplishment. (1) Tib. *dngos grub*, Skt. *siddhi*. The result (and goal) of spiritual practice. Common accomplishments include supernatural powers, which a bodhisattva may use to benefit beings. The principal goal, however, is the supreme accomplishment, which is enlightenment. (2) Tib. *sgrub pa*. In the context of the recitation of mantras, see **approach and accomplishment**.

Ānanda (Skt., Tib. Kun dga bo). "Ever Joyful." Buddha Shākyamuni's attendant and close disciple for twenty-five years. Renowned for his retentive memory and having heard almost every word the Buddha had spoken, he recited the sūtra section of the teachings at the First Buddhist Council.

Ancient Tradition (Tib. rNying ma pa). The followers of the first teachings of the Secret Mantra Vehicle propagated in Tibet by the great masters Vimalamitra and Padmasambhava in the eighth century.

Ancient Translations (Tib. sNga 'gyur). The first Buddhist teachings translated from Sanskrit and propagated in Tibet, those of the Ancient Tradition, as distinct from the teachings of the New Tradition that were translated and propagated from the tenth century onward.

approach and accomplishment (Tib. *bsnyen sgrub*). Two stages in practices involving the recitation of a mantra in a sādhana. In the first, practitioners approach the deity that they are visualizing by reciting the deity's mantra. In the second, they are familiar enough to identify themselves with the deity. See also **deity**.

arhat (Skt., Tib. *dgra bcom pa*). Lit., "one who has vanquished the enemy" (the enemy being defilements). A practitioner of the Basic Vehicle (that is, a listener or solitary realizer) who has attained the cessation of suffering—that is, nirvāṇa, but not the perfect buddhahood of the Great Vehicle.

Asaṅga (Skt., Tib. Thogs med). "Unimpeded." The great fourth-century Indian master and father of the vast activity tradition whose disciples established the Chittamātra, or Mind-Only school, of Mahāyāna Buddhism. His writings include the five great treatises that he received from Maitreya.

Ashvaghoṣha (Skt., Tib. rTa dbyangs). "He whose voice is a horse's neigh." An important Indian Buddhist writer of the first–second century.

Atisha (Skt., Tib. Jo bo A ti sha). 982–1054. The great Indian master and scholar Dīpaṃkara-shrī-jñāna, who spent the last ten years of his life in Tibet, propagating the teachings on refuge and bodhichitta and contributing to the translation of Buddhist texts. His disciples founded the Kadampa school, which emphasized the teachings on mind training.

Atiyoga (Skt., Tib. A ti yo ga). The highest vehicle in the Ancient Tradition's classification of nine vehicles. The vehicle of the Great Perfection.

Avalokiteshvara (Skt., Tib. sPyan ras gzigs dbang phyug). "The Lord Who Gazes Down [Compassionately on the World]." One of the Eight Great Close Sons, and the bodhisattva who incarnates all the buddhas' compassion, he is considered to be the principal bodhisattva protecting the people of Tibet, where he is known as Chenrezi.

awareness (Tib. *rig pa*, Skt. *vidyā*). In the teachings of the Great Perfection, the original state of the mind, fresh, vast, luminous, and beyond thought.

Basic Vehicle (Tib. Theg dman, Skt. Hīnayāna). Lit., "Lesser Vehicle" (in relation to the Mahāyāna, or Great Vehicle). The vehicle of the listeners and solitary realizers that leads to the state of arhat.

benefit and happiness (Tib. *phan bde*). The temporary benefit of happy states in cyclic existence and the ultimate happiness of nirvāṇa. This expression is therefore sometimes translated as *happiness and peace.*

bhagavan (Skt., Tib. *bcom ldan 'das*). An Indian term of veneration for someone of high spiritual attainment, used in Buddhism as an epithet of the Buddha. In its Tibetan translation, which might be conveyed in English as "transcendent, virtuous conqueror," it is defined as "he who has overcome (*bcom*) the four demons, who possesses (*ldan*) the six excellent qualities, and who does not dwell in either of the two extremes of saṃsāra and nirvāṇa but has gone beyond them (*'das*)."

bodhichitta (Skt., Tib. *byang chub kyi sems*). The mind set on enlightenment. On the relative level, it is the wish to attain buddhahood for the sake of all beings, as well as the practice of the path of love, compassion, the six transcendent perfections, and so forth necessary for achieving that goal; on the ultimate level, it is the direct insight into the ultimate nature.

bodhisattva (Skt., Tib. *byang chub sems dpa'*). A follower of the Great Vehicle whose aim is perfect enlightenment for all beings. One who has taken the vow of bodhichitta and practices the six transcendent perfections.

body of manifestation (Tib. *sprul sku*, Skt. *nirmāṇakāya*). The aspect of buddhahood that manifests out of compassion to help ordinary beings.

body of perfect enjoyment (Tib. *longs spyod rdzogs pa'i sku*, Skt. *saṃbhogakāya*). The spontaneously luminous aspect of buddhahood, only perceptible to highly realized beings.

body of the essential nature (Tib. *ngo bo nyid kyi sku*, Skt. *svabhāvikakāya*). The fourth body, which is the very essence, or aspect, of the inseparability of the body of truth, the body of perfect enjoyment, and the body of manifestation.

body of truth (Tib. *chos sku*, Skt. *dharmakāya*). Lit., "Dharma body." The emptiness aspect of buddhahood; also translated as *absolute dimension*.

Brahmā (Skt., Tib. Tshangs pa). Lit., "pure." The name given to a number of gods in the world of form.

brahmin (Skt., Tib. *bram ze*). A member of the priestly caste in Indian society.

buddha (Skt., Tib. *sangs rgyas*). One who has dispelled (Tib. *sangs*) the darkness of the two obscurations and developed (Tib. *rgyas*) the two kinds of omniscience (knowing the nature of phenomena and knowing the multiplicity of phenomena).

buddha body (Tib. *sku*, Skt. *kāya*). Any one of the forms, or aspects, of buddhahood. See also **three buddha bodies**.

buddha-field (Tib. *sangs rgyas kyi zhing khams*, also *dag pa'i zhing*). A pure land, or world, manifested by a buddha or great bodhisattva through the spontaneous qualities of his or her realization, in which beings can progress toward enlightenment without falling back into the lower realms of cyclic existence. Also, any place whatsoever when it is perceived as a pure manifestation of spontaneous wisdom.

buddha nature (Tib. *de gshegs snying po*, Skt. *tathāgatagarbha*). Also translated as *essence of buddhahood*. The potential of buddhahood present in every being.

Capable One (Tib. Thub pa, Skt. Muni). Often translated as *Mighty One*. An epithet of the Buddha Shākyamuni. He was called "capable" because when he was a bodhisattva and there were none who had the courage to tame the most unfortunate beings, those with extremely gross views, afflictive emotions, and actions, he, our kind Teacher, was the only one, of all the 1,002 buddhas of this Excellent Kalpa, who had the strength or capacity to vow to benefit them.

certain excellence (Tib. *nges legs*). A synonym for buddhahood, defined as "lasting happiness: the state of liberation and omniscience."

Chandragomin (Skt., Tib. Go mi dge bsnyen). "The Layman Moon." A seventh-century Indian master and proponent of the Chittamātra system, famous for his debate with the Mādhyamika master Chandrakīrti (author of *Introduction to the Middle Way*) and for his observance of the eight *upavasa* vows for lay practitioners.

Chārvākas (Skt., Tib. rGyang 'phen pa). Members of an ancient Indian philosophical school that denied the law of karma and the existence of past and future lives.

Chittamātrin (Skt., Tib. *Sems tsam pa*). Also called "Yogāchārin." A follower of the Mind-Only philosophical school of the Great Vehicle, based on the teachings of Asaṅga.

circumambulation (Tib. *skor ba*). An act of veneration that consists of walking clockwise, concentratedly and with awareness, around a sacred object—for example, a temple, stūpa, or sacred mountain, or the residence, and even the person, of a spiritual master.

commitments. See **sacred commitments.**

confidence and eloquence (Tib. *spobs pa*). Also translated as *confident eloquence.* A buddha's or bodhisattva's ability to expound the Dharma for limitless periods of time, without any fear of not knowing anything or of being contradicted.

conqueror (Tib. *rgyal ba*, Skt. *jina*). Also translated as *victorious one.* A general epithet for a buddha, one who has conquered the four demons.

crown opening (Tib. *tshang pa'i bu ga*). Lit., "aperture of Brahmā." In the anatomy of the subtle body, the point on the top of the head where the central channel (Tib. *rtsa dbu ma*) ends.

crown protuberance (Tib. *gtsug tor*, Skt. *uṣṇīṣa*). A prominence on the head of a buddha, one of the thirty-two major marks.

cyclic existence (Tib. *'khor ba*, Skt. *saṃsāra*). Lit., "wheel." The endless round of birth, death, and rebirth in which beings suffer as result of their actions and defilements. It should be noted that what Buddhists call "saṃsāra," and what they aim to transcend, includes all three worlds, while some non-Buddhists consider the two worlds of form and formlessness to be the ultimate attainment or spiritual goal.

ḍāka (Skt., Tib. *dpa' bo*). Lit., "hero." The male equivalent of a ḍākinī, a tantric bodhisattva.

ḍākinī (Skt., Tib. *mkha' 'gro ma*). Lit., "one who moves through space." The feminine principle associated with wisdom and with the enlightened activities of the teacher. This term has several levels of meaning. There are ordinary ḍākinīs, who are beings with a certain degree of spiritual power, and wisdom ḍākinīs, who are fully realized. The male equivalent is a ḍāka.

defilements (Tib. *nyon mongs pa*, Skt. *kleśa*). Also translated as *afflictive emotions* or *negative emotions.* Mental factors that influence thoughts and actions and produce suffering. See also **five poisons; three poisons.**

definitive teachings. See **ultimate teachings.**

degenerate age (Tib. *snyigs dus*, Skt. *kaliyuga*). A period in which beings have shorter life spans, their defilements increase, they themselves are particularly difficult to help, wars and famines proliferate, and wrong views are widespread.

deity (Tib. *lha*, Skt. *deva*). A buddha or wisdom deity, or sometimes a wealth deity or Dharma protector, as distinct from a nonenlightened god in the world of desire, the world of form, or the formless world.

demon (Tib. *bdud*, Skt. *māra*). In the context of Buddhist meditation and practice, any factor, on the physical or mental plane, that obstructs enlightenment. See also **four demons.**

determination to be free (Tib. *nges 'byung*). Also translated as *renunciation*. The deeply felt wish to achieve liberation from cyclic existence.

Dharma (Skt., Tib. Chos). The Buddha's doctrine; the teachings transmitted in the scriptures and the qualities of realization attained through their practice. Note that the Sanskrit word *dharma* has ten principal meanings, including "anything that can be known." Vasubandhu defines the Dharma, in its Buddhist sense, as the "protective dharma" (*chos skyobs*): "It corrects (*'chos*) every one of the enemies, the defilements, and it protects (*skyobs*) us from the lower realms: these two characteristics are absent from other spiritual traditions."

Dharma protectors (Tib. Chos skyong, Skt. Dharmapāla). Beings who fulfill the enlightened activities of the teacher by protecting the teaching from being diluted and its transmission from being disturbed or distorted. Protectors are sometimes emanations of buddhas or bodhisattvas, and sometimes spirits, gods or demons who have been subjugated by a great spiritual master and bound under oath.

dharmakāya (Skt.). See **body of truth.**

dhyāna (Skt., Tib. *bsam gtan*). A state of concentration.

Diamond Vehicle (Tib. rDo rje'i theg pa, Skt. Vajrayāna). Also called Secret Mantrayāna (Secret Mantra Vehicle). A branch of the Great Vehicle that uses the special techniques of the tantras, based on the realization of the diamond-like nature of the mind and taking the result as the path, to pursue enlightenment for the sake of all beings more rapidly.

Dīpaṃkara-shrī-jñāna (Skt.). Jowo Atisha's ordination name. See also **Atisha.**

disenchantment (Tib. *skyo shas*). The disillusionment, sadness, or weariness that comes with seeing the suffering inherent in cyclic existence.

dohā (Skt.). A song in which a siddha (notably Saraha or Virūpa) expresses his or her realization.

downfall (Tib. *ltung ba*). A fault due to the transgression of a rule (monastic or otherwise).

Drom Tönpa (Tib. 'Brom ston pa, also called 'Brom ston rgyal ba'i 'byung gnas). Atisha's principal Tibetan disciple, one of the first teachers of the Kadampa school and founder of Radreng (Rva sgreng) Monastery (often pronounced "Reting").

dualistic (Tib. *gnyis 'dzin*). Lit., "grasping at (or apprehending) two." Having the concept of "I" and "other" or of an apprehending subject and an apprehended object.

earnest aspiration (level of) (Tib. *mos spyod kyi sa*). A sort of prelevel before a bodhisattva reaches the first of the ten levels. It comprises the paths of accumulating and joining. Practitioners on these paths have not yet realized emptiness and cannot, therefore, practice the six transcendent perfections in a truly transcendental way. Their practice is more a question of willingness than of the genuine practice of a mature bodhisattva.

eight consciousnesses (Tib. *tshogs brgyad*). The consciousnesses of the five senses, the mind consciousness, emotional consciousness, and the consciousness of the ground of all.

eight ordinary preoccupations (Tib. *'jig rten chos brgyad*). The normal preoccupations of unrealized people without a clear spiritual perspective: gain and loss, pleasure and pain, praise and criticism, fame and infamy.

elimination and realization (Tib. *spangs rtogs*). The elimination of obscurations and the realization of wisdom.

empowerment (Tib. *dbang bskur*, Skt. *abhiṣeka*). Lit., "transfer of power." The authorization to hear, study, and practice the teachings of the Diamond Vehicle. This takes place in a more or less elaborate ceremony in which the diamond master introduces the disciple to the maṇḍala of a deity.

emptiness (Tib. *stong pa nyid*, Skt. *śūnyatā*). The absence of true existence (in the sense of any permanent, independent, and single entity) in all phenomena.

enlightenment (Tib. *byang chub*, Skt. *bodhi*). The purification (*byang*) of all obscurations and the realization (*chub*) of all qualities.

equipoise (Tib. *mnyam pa nyid*). Also translated as *sameness* or *evenness*. The meditative state and understanding that all things equally have the nature of emptiness.

eternalism (Tib. *rtag par lta ba*). The belief in an eternally existing entity, such as a soul. One of the extreme views refuted by the proponents of the Middle Way.

excellent words (Tib. *gsung rab*, Skt. *pravacana*). The words of the Buddha—that is, the teachings that he gave.

expanse of reality (Tib. *chos kyi dbyings*, Skt. *dharmadhātu*). Emptiness, which is the nature of the five aggregates.

expanse without residual aggregates (Tib. *phung po lhag med pa'i dbyings*). The state of nirvāṇa into which buddhas or arhats pass when they leave their earthly bodies.

expedient teachings (Tib. *drang don*). Teachings intended to lead unrealized beings toward the truth of the ultimate (or definitive) teachings.

five aggregates (Tib. *phung po lnga*, Skt. *pañcaskandha*). The five psychophysical components into which a person can be analyzed and that together produce the illusion of a self. They are form, feeling, perception, conditioning factors, and consciousness.

five bodies (Tib. *sku lnga*). The five buddha bodies: the three buddha bodies to which are added the unchanging adamantine body (Tib. *mi 'gyur rdo rje'i sku*, Skt. *vajrakāya*) and the body of perfect enlightenment (*mngon par byang chub pa'i sku*, Skt. *abhisambodhikāya*).

five degenerations (Tib. *snyigs ma lnga*). The degeneration of (1) life span, (2) defilements (that is, the five poisons increase), (3) beings (that is, it is difficult to help them), (4) times (that is, wars and famines proliferate), (5) views (that is, false beliefs spread).

five kinds of gnosis (Tib. *ye shes lnga*). Also translated as *five wisdoms*. Five aspects of the wisdom of buddhahood: the gnosis of the absolute space (Tib. *chos dbyings kyi ye shes*), mirrorlike gnosis (*me long gi ye shes*), the gnosis of equality (*mnyam nyid kyi ye shes*), discriminating gnosis (*so sor rtog pa'i ye shes*), and all-accomplishing gnosis (*bya ba grub pa'i ye shes*).

five paths (Tib. *lam lnga*). The paths of accumulation, joining, seeing, meditation, and no more learning.

five perpetuating aggregates (Tib. *nye bar len pa'i phung po lnga*). The five "tainted" aggregates produced by defilements and actions in a previous life and that will again produce further defilements and actions.

five poisons (Tib. *dug lnga*). The five defilements of bewilderment, attachment, aversion, pride, and jealousy.

five senses (Tib. *dbang po lnga*). Sight, hearing, taste, smell, and physical sensation.

form body (Tib. *gzugs sku*, Skt. *rūpakāya*). The body of perfect enjoyment and the body of manifestation considered together.

four activities (Tib. *phrin las bzhi*). Four types of activity performed by realized beings to help others and eliminate unfavorable circumstances: pacifying (*zhi ba*), increasing (*rgyas pa*), bringing under control (*dbang*), and forcefully subduing (*drag po*).

four bodies (Tib. *sku bzhi*). The three buddha bodies with the addition of the body of the essential nature.

four daily activities (Tib. *spyod lam bzhi*). Walking, moving around, sitting, and lying.

four demons (Tib. *bdud bzhi*). The demon of the aggregates, the demon of the defilements, the demon of the Lord of Death, and the demon of the sons of the gods (or demon of distraction). See also **demon**.

four empowerments (Tib. *dbang bzhi*). The vase, secret, wisdom, and absolute empowerments.

four noble truths (Tib. *'phags pa'i bden pa bzhi*, Skt. *caturāryasatya*). The truth of suffering, the truth of the origin of suffering, the truth of cessation, and the truth of the path. These constitute the foundation of Buddha Shākyamuni's doctrine, the first teaching that he gave (at Sarnath near Varanasi) after attaining enlightenment.

four times (Tib. *dus bzhi*). The past, present, future, and timeless time.

Gampopa (Tib. sGam po pa). Gampopa Sönam Rinchen (1079–1153), also known as Dagpo Rinpoche, the most famous disciple of Milarepa and the founder of the Kagyupa monastic order.

gaṇachakra (Skt., Tib. *tshogs*). A ritual feast in which offerings are made to the deities visualized in a sādhana. Because of the skillful means and wisdom employed in the gaṇachakra feast, it serves as a powerful method for purifying breaches of the sacred commitments and for accumulating merit.

gandharva (Skt., Tib. *dri za*). Lit., "one who feeds on smells." A kind of spirit that feeds on scents. Gandharvas are also classed as inhabitants of the lowest gods' realms, where they are renowned for their musical skills. The name is used as well for beings in the intermediate state: since they inhabit a mental body, they feed not on solid food but on odors.

garuḍa (Skt., Tib. *mkha' lding*). A mythological bird, master of the skies. Traditionally, it preys on the nāgas.

generation phase (Tib. *bskyed rim*, Skt. *utpattikrama*). The meditation associated with sādhana practice in which one purifies oneself of one's habitual attachments by meditating on forms, sounds, and thoughts as having the nature of deities, mantras, and wisdom. Contrast **perfection phase.**

gnosis (Tib. *ye shes*, Skt. *jñāna*). Also translated as *primordial wisdom* or *primal wisdom*. The knowing (*shes pa*) that has always been present since the beginning (*ye nas*); awareness, clarity-emptiness, naturally dwelling in all beings.

gods (Tib. *lha*, Skt. *deva*). Also translated as *celestial beings*. A class of beings who, as a result of accumulating positive actions in previous lives, experience immense happiness and comfort and are, therefore, considered by some non-Buddhists to have attained the ideal state to which they should aspire. According to the Buddhist teachings, however, they have not attained freedom from cyclic existence. Those in the world of form and the world of formlessness experience an extended form of the meditation that they practiced (without the aim of achieving liberation from cyclic existence) in their previous life. Gods like Indra, and others of the six classes of gods of the world of desire, possess, as a result of their merit, a certain power to affect the lives of other beings, and they are therefore worshipped, for example, by Hindus. The same Tibetan and Sanskrit term is also used to refer to enlightened beings, in which case it is more usually translated as *deity*.

Great Master (Tib. sLob dpon chen po). On its own, an epithet that usually refers to Padmasambhava, Guru Rinpoche.

Great Omniscient One (Tib. Kun mkhyen chen po). The name usually used to refer to Longchen Rabjam (Longchenpa).

Great Orgyen (Tib. O rgyan chen po). The great master from Uḍḍiyāna, another name by which Guru Padmasambhava is known.

Great Perfection (Tib. Dzogs pa chen po). Also called "Atiyoga." The highest of all the vehicles leading to enlightenment, by which it is possible to attain buddhahood in a single lifetime. *Perfection* means that within the mind all the qualities of the three buddha bodies are naturally present: its nature is emptiness, its natural expression is clarity, and its compassion is all-encompassing. It also means that the accumulations of merit and wisdom are perfect and complete. *Great* refers to the fact that this perfection is the natural condition of all things.

Great Vehicle (Tib. Theg pa chen po, Skt. Mahāyāna). The vehicle of the bodhisattvas, referred to as "great" because it leads to perfect buddhahood for the sake of all beings, and, according to Maitreya/Asaṅga's *Ornament of the Mahāyāna Sūtras*, chap. 20, vv. 59–60, because of the greatness of its object, accomplishment, gnosis, diligent application, skill in means, consummation, and activities.

ground consciousness (Tib. *kun gzhi* or *kun gzhi rnam par shes pa*, Skt. *ālaya*). The basis for the other consciousnesses and that in which the habitual tendencies are stored.

Guru Rinpoche (Tib. Gu ru rin po che). Lit., "Precious Teacher." The name by which Padmasambhava is most commonly known in Tibet.

habitual tendencies (Tib. *bag chags*). Habitual patterns of thought, speech, or action created by one's attitudes and deeds in past lives.

Heaven of the Thirty-Three (Tib. gSum cu rtsa gsum). The second of the six god realms in the world of desire. The abode of Indra and his thirty-two ministers.

higher realms (Tib. *mtho ris*). The god realms, the demigod realm, and the human realm.

incantation (Tib. *gzungs*, Skt. *dhāraṇī*). A mantra, often quite long, blessed by a buddha or bodhisattva, which has the power to help beings. Canonical works entitled "incantation" or "dhāraṇī" usually contain an account of the circumstances in which the incantation was taught, along with the benefits of reciting it.

individual liberation (Tib. *so sor thar pa*, Skt. *prātimokṣa*). The collective term for the different forms of Buddhist ordination and their respective vows, as laid down in the Vinaya.

Indra (Skt., Tib. brGya byin). "He who is honored with a hundred gifts." The ruler of the Heaven of the Thirty-Three.

intermediate ordinee (Tib. *dge tshul*, Skt. *śrāmaṇera*). A person with an ordination intermediate between lay followers who take the four basic vows and fully ordained monks and nuns. Although this level of ordination may serve as a novitiate until the ordinee is ready or old enough to take full ordination, it is incorrect to refer to intermediate ordinees as novices because some intermediate ordinees remain so all their lives without passing to higher ordination. This is the case with most nuns in Tibet, where the lineage for fully ordained nuns has been lost and full female ordination is possible only by taking the bhikṣhunī vows in another country whose lineage has continued unbroken.

intermediate state (Tib. *bar do*). Various stages of experience between death and the next rebirth. In a wider interpretation, it includes the various states of consciousness in life.

Jambu River gold (Tib. 'Dzambu'i chu gser). Gold from the Jambu River, the river flowing through Jambudvīpa. Gold of exceptional quality and purity.

Jambudvīpa (Skt., Tib. 'Dzam bu gling). "Land of the Jambu Tree." In the ancient Indian cosmology, it is the southern continent, the world in which we live.

Jigme Lingpa (Tib. 'Jigs med gling pa). 1729–1798. The discoverer of the Longchen Nyingtik teachings, which were revealed to him in a vision he had of Longchenpa. He is considered to be a combined emanation of Vimalamitra and King Trisong Detsen. Patrul Rinpoche is often considered to be the emanation of Jigme Lingpa's speech.

Jowo Atisha. See **Atisha.**

Kadampa (Tib. bKa' gdams pa). The first of the schools of the New Tradition, which followed the teachings of Atisha. It stressed compassion, study, and pure discipline. Its teachings were continued by all the other schools, in particular the Gelugpa, which is also known as the New Kadampa school.

kalpa (Skt., Tib. *bskal pa*). A unit of time (of inconceivable length) used in Buddhist cosmology to describe the cycles of formation and destruction of a universe and the ages of increase and decrease within them.

karma (Skt., Tib. *las*). The whole process of deeds (physical, verbal, and mental) leading to results in future lives. The force created by a positive or negative action is stored in an individual's stream of being and persists until it is experienced as pleasure or pain (usually in another life), after which the deed is said to be exhausted. The term *karma* (action) is sometimes used to signify the result produced by past deeds (Tib. *las kyi 'bras bu*), which some people wrongly equate with destiny or fate—that is, with something beyond one's control. However, the Buddha taught that everything one will experience in future lives depends on one's deeds and is, therefore, very definitely within one's control.

kinnara (Skt., Tib. *mi'am ci*). Lit., "is this human, or what?" A class of celestial beings, half human, half bird (or half horse according to some sources).

lama (Tib.). See **teacher.**

law of cause and effect (Tib. *las rgyu 'bras*). Lit., "action, cause, result." In the context of the Buddhist teachings, the process by which every action inevitably produces a corresponding effect, usually in a subsequent lifetime. See also **karma.**

Lesser Vehicle. See **Basic Vehicle.**

liberation (Tib. *thar pa*). Freedom from cyclic existence, either as an arhat or as a buddha.

lineage (Tib. *brgyud*). The process by which the Buddhist teachings have been transmitted from master to disciple in a continuous line from their original source until the present day. The transmission can be either from the teacher's mind to the disciple's mind (in the mind lineage of the conquerors), through symbolic gestures (in the symbol lineage of the knowledge holders), by the disciple's hearing the master's words (in the hearing lineage of ordinary beings), or by the teachings being transmitted to a disciple before being hidden as treasure to be rediscovered later by an incarnation of that disciple (in the treasure lineage). The fact that a teaching has been preserved and transmitted through an unbroken lineage is what makes the practice of that teaching a potent, living experience.

listener (Tib. *nyan thos*, Skt. *śrāvaka*). A follower of the Basic Vehicle, one whose goal is to attain liberation for himself or herself as an arhat.

Longchenpa (Tib. kLong chen rab 'byams pa). 1308–1363. Also known as the Omniscient Sovereign or King of Dharma. One of the most influential spiritual masters and scholars of the Nyingma school. He wrote more than 250 treatises covering almost all of Buddhist theory and practice up to the Great Perfection, including the Seven Treasures (mDzod bdun), the Four Parts of the Heart Essence (sNying tig ya bzhi), the Trilogy of Rest (Ngal gso skor gsum), the Trilogy of Natural Freedom (Rang grol skor gsum), the Trilogy of Dispelling Darkness (Mun sel skor gsum), and Miscellaneous Writings (gSung thor bu).

Lord of Secrets (Tib. gSang ba'i bdag po). An epithet of Vajrapāṇi.

lower realms (Tib. *ngan song*). The hell realm, the hungry spirit realm, and the animal realm.

Mādhyamikas (Skt., Tib. dBu ma pa). Those who follow Nāgārjuna and adhere to the Madhyamaka, the Middle Way that avoids the extremes of existence and nonexistence.

Mahāyāna (Skt., Tib. Theg pa chen po). See **Great Vehicle**.

mahoraga (Skt., Tib. *lto 'phye*). A class of serpent-like spirits with dominion over their surrounding lands.

main practice (Tib. *dngos gzhi*). In general, the main part of a practice, the actual practice as distinct from its preparation and conclusion. In the context of the Diamond Vehicle, the practice of sādhana, mantra recitation, yogic exercises, and so on associated with the generation and perfection phases, which can be followed only by practitioners who have completed the preliminary practices (*sngon 'gro*) described in this book.

Maitreya (Skt., Tib. Byams pa). "Love." One of the Eight Great Close Sons (the Buddha's eight closest bodhisattva disciples). As the future Buddha, he presently resides in the Tuṣhita heaven.

major and minor marks (Tib. *mtshan dpe*). The thirty-two major marks and eighty minor marks of excellence that characterize a buddha's physical form.

maṇḍala (Skt., Tib. *dkyil 'khor*). Lit., "center and circumference." The universe with the palace of the deity at the center, as visualized in the practice of the generation phase. Also, the visualized ideal universe in the form of an offering.

Mañjushrī (Skt., Tib. 'Jam dpal). "Gentle and Glorious." The bodhisattva who embodies the buddhas' knowledge and wisdom.

mantra (Skt., Tib. *sngags*). A manifestation of supreme enlightenment in the form of sound: a series of syllables that, in the sādhanas of the Secret Mantra Vehicle, protect the mind of the practitioner from ordinary perceptions and invoke the wisdom deities. The Sanskrit word is explained as meaning "that which liberates the mind."

Māra (Skt., Tib. bDud). Demon, the tempter in general, that which makes obstacles to spiritual practice and enlightenment. See also **demon**; **four demons**.

merit (Tib. *bsod nams*, Skt. *puṇya*). The first of the two accumulations. *Merit* is also sometimes used loosely to translate the Tibetan terms *dge ba* (virtue, positive action) and *dge rtsa* (sources of good for the future).

Middle Way (Tib. dBuma'i lam, Skt. Madhyamaka). The series of teachings on emptiness first expounded by Nāgārjuna and considered to form the basis of the Secret Mantrayāna. *Middle* in this context means that it is beyond the extreme points of view of nihilism and eternalism.

mind stream. See **stream of being.**

mundane (Tib. *'jig rten gyi*). The opposite of supramundane, anything that does not transcend saṃsāra. Translations of this term as *ordinary* or *worldly* can be misleading since non-Buddhist meditators who have mastered the four dhyānas (but without being liberated from saṃsāra) and who have immense powers of concentration, magical powers, and so forth cannot really be called "ordinary," nor are they necessarily worldly in the sense of being materialistically minded and interested only in the present world.

nāga (Skt., Tib. *klu*). A serpent-like being (classed in the animal realm) living in the water or under the earth and endowed with magical powers and wealth. The most powerful ones have several heads. In Indian mythology, they are preyed on by the garuḍas.

Nāgārjuna (Skt., Tib. kLu sgrub). "He whose accomplishment is related to the nāgas." The great first–second-century Indian master and father of the profound view tradition who rediscovered the Buddha's teachings on Transcendent Wisdom (Prajñapāramitā) in the realm of the nāgas and composed numerous treatises that became the basic texts for the proponents of the Madhyamika, or Middle Way, philosophical system.

nihilism (Tib. *chad par lta ba*). The view that denies the existence of past and future lives, the principle of cause and effect, and so on. One of the extreme views refuted by the proponents of the Middle Way.

nine vehicles (Tib. *theg pa dgu*). The three vehicles of the Sūtrayāna (those of the listeners, solitary realizers, and bodhisattvas) and the six vehicles of the Vajrayāna (Kriyātantra, Caryātantra, Yogatantra, Mahāyoga, Anuyoga, and Atiyoga).

nirvāṇa (Skt., Tib. *mya ngan las 'das pa*). Lit., "beyond suffering" or "the transcendence of misery." While this can be loosely understood as the goal of Buddhist practice, the opposite of saṃsāra, or cyclic existence, it is important to realize that the term is understood differently by the different vehicles: the nirvāṇa of the Basic Vehicle, the peace of cessation that an arhat attains, is very different from a buddha's "nondwelling" nirvāṇa, the state of perfect enlightenment that transcends both saṃsāra and nirvāṇa. Moreover, *nirvāṇa* in a Buddhist sense should never be understood as simply being a state of eternal happiness, as is the case for some non-Buddhist spiritual paths.

noble (Tib. *'phags pa*, Skt. *ārya*). An epithet applied, in the Great Vehicle, to someone who has attained the path of seeing, a bodhisattva on one of the ten bodhisattva levels; in the vehicles of the listeners and solitary realizers, it is used to refer to stream enterers, once-returners, nonreturners, and arhats.

nondwelling nirvāṇa (Tib. *mi gnas pa'i myang 'das*). The state of perfect enlightenment that transcends both saṃsāra and nirvāṇa.

no-self (Tib. *bdag med*, Skt. *anātman, nairātmya*). Also translated as *egolessness*. The absence of independent, or intrinsic, existence, either of oneself (Tib. *gang zag gi bdag med*) or of external phenomena (Tib. *chos kyi bdag med*).

obscurations (Tib. *sgrib pa*, Skt. *āvaraṇa*). Factors that veil one's buddha nature, maintaining one in cyclic existence and preventing one from attaining enlightenment. See also **two obscurations.**

Omniscient Dharma Lord (Tib. Kun mkhyen chos rjes). A title used to refer to Longchenpa.

Omniscient Teacher (Tib. Kun mkhyen bla ma). A title used to refer to Longchenpa.

Orgyen, knower of the three times (Tib. O rgyan dus gsum mkhyen pa). A title used to refer to Guru Padmasambhava, the Guru from Uḍḍiyāna (or Orgyen, as it is known in Tibetan).

Orgyen, the Second Buddha (Tib. O rgyan sangs rgyas gnyis pa). Guru Padmasambhava.

Padampa Sangye (Tib. Pha dam pa sangs rgyas). Eleventh/twelfth century. An Indian siddha who established the teachings of the Shijepa (Tib. Zhi byed pa) school. The teacher of Machik Labdrön, to whom he transmitted the Chöd teachings. He traveled to Tibet several times.

Padmasambhava (Skt., Tib. Padma 'byung gnas). The Lotus-Born Teacher from Uḍḍiyāna, often known as Guru Rinpoche. During the reign of King Trisong Detsen in the eighth century, this great master subjugated the evil forces hostile to the propagation of Buddhism in Tibet, spread the Buddhist teaching of the Diamond Vehicle in that country, and hid innumerable spiritual treasures for the benefit of future generations. He is venerated as the Second Buddha, whose coming was predicted by the first one, Buddha Shākyamuni, to give the special teachings of the Diamond Vehicle.

paṇḍita (Skt.). A scholar, someone learned in the five traditional sciences (crafts, medicine, philology, logic, and philosophy). The term is used to refer primarily to Indian scholars.

path of accumulation (Tib. *tshogs lam*). The first of the five paths, according to the Bodhisattva Vehicle. On this path, one accumulates the causes that will make it possible to proceed toward enlightenment.

path of joining (Tib. *sbyor lam*). The second of the five paths. Also known as the path of preparation, it connects the path of accumulation to the path of seeing, preparing the practitioner for seeing the two kinds of no-self on the path of seeing.

path of meditation (Tib. *sgom lam*). The fourth of the five paths, during which a bodhisattva traverses the remaining nine of the ten levels.

path of no more learning (Tib. *mi slob pa'i lam*). The last of the five paths, the culmination of the path to perfect enlightenment—buddhahood.

path of seeing (Tib. *mthong lam*). The third of the five paths, the stage at which a bodhisattva in meditation gains a genuine experience of emptiness and attains the first of the ten levels.

perfection phase (Tib. *rdzogs rim*, Skt. *saṃpannakrama*). (1) "With characteristics" (Tib. *mtshan bcas*): meditation on the channels and energies of the body visualized as a diamond body; (2) "without characteristics" (Tib. *mtshan med*): the meditation phase during which the forms visualized in the generation phase are dissolved and one remains in the experience of emptiness.

piṭaka (Skt., Tib. *sde snod*). Lit., "basket." A collection of scriptures, originally in the form of palm leaf folios stored in baskets. The Buddha's teachings are generally divided into three piṭakas: Vinaya, Sūtra, and Abhidharma.

pith instructions (Tib. *man ngag*, Skt. *upadeśa*). Instructions that explain the most profound points of the teachings in a condensed and direct way for the purposes of practice.

plantain tree (Tib. *chu shing*). Lit., "water tree." A banana tree. Because its "trunk" is actually a pseudostem made up of tightly packed tubular leaves, with no real heart or core, it is used as an analogy for phenomena being "devoid of essence." Furthermore, the pseudostem dies back after the fruit has been produced, and in this respect, it is used as an analogy for the ripening and exhaustion of karmic deeds.

preceptor (Tib. *mkhan po*). In the Nyingma tradition, the master from whom one takes monastic vows. A *khenpo* may also be a qualified tutor responsible for the study program in a monastery.

preta (Skt., Tib. *yi dvags*). A hungry spirit. A class of beings whose attachment and miserliness in previous lives result in constant hunger and the frustration of their desires.

profound insight (Tib. *lhag mthong*, Skt. *vipaśyanā*). The perception, through wisdom, of the true nature of things.

protectors. See **Dharma protectors.**

pure land. See **buddha-field.**

pure perception (Tib. *dag snang*). The perception of the world and its contents as a pure buddha-field, as the display of the buddha bodies and wisdoms. Pure perception, particularly in relation to the teacher and fellow practitioners, is fundamental to the practice of the Diamond Vehicle.

radical defeat (Tib. *pham pa*). The breaking of a basic vow or precept that results in ordination being completely annulled. This term is also used as the name given to such vows.

rākṣhasa (Skt., Tib. *srin po*). A kind of malignant spirit or ogre that feeds on human flesh.

relative truth (Tib. *kun rdzob bden pa*). Lit., "all-concealing truth." The apparent truth perceived and taken as real by the deluded mind, which conceals the true nature of things. Contrast **ultimate truth.**

renunciate (Tib. *dge sbyong*, Skt. *śramaṇa*). Lit., "one who trains in virtue." A general term for someone who has renounced worldly life and taken monastic ordination.

renunciation (Tib. *nges 'byung*). The deep wish to attain freedom from cyclic existence, above all by renouncing defilements such as attachment, without necessarily withdrawing from the world. See also the alternative translation **determination to be free.**

riṣhi (Tib. *drang srong*, Skt. *ṛṣi*). A sage, hermit, or saint; particularly the famous sages of Indian mythology, who had enormous longevity and magical powers.

root downfall (Tib. *rtsa ltung*). The breaking of a vow the observance of which is fundamental to successfully accomplishing the path. It has been defined as follows: if the vow is kept, it is the root that gives rise to all the excellent qualities of the path and result; if it is not kept, it becomes the cause of lower realms and the root of suffering, and as a result one falls further and further down in subsequent lives.

root teacher (Tib. *rtsa ba'i bla ma*). (1) The principal, or first, spiritual teacher from whom one has received empowerments, commentaries, and pith instructions. (2) The teacher who has introduced one to the nature of the mind.

sacred commitments (Tib. *dam tshig*, Skt. *samaya*). Lit., "promise." Sacred links between the teacher and disciple, and also between disciples, in the Diamond Vehicle. The Sanskrit word *samaya* can mean agreement, engagement, convention, precept, boundary, and so forth. Although there are many detailed obligations, the most essential samaya is to consider the teacher's body, speech, and mind as pure.

sādhana (Skt., Tib. *sgrub thabs*). The method for accomplishing the level of a particular deity—for example, the lama, yidam, or ḍākinī.

Sahā realm (Skt., Tib. Mi mjed 'jig rten). The realm of no fear, so called because beings are not afraid of the three poisons. The Sahā realm is our universe, which is the buddha-field of Buddha Shākyamuni.

Samantabhadra (Skt., Tib. Kun tu bzang po). "Universal Good." (1) The original Buddha (Ādibuddha), he who has never fallen into delusion, the absolute-body buddha, the source of the lineage of the tantra transmissions of the Nyingma school. He is represented as a naked figure, deep blue like the sky, in union with Samantabhadrī, as a symbol of awareness-emptiness, the pure, absolute nature ever present and unobstructed. (2) The bodhisattva Samantabhadra, one of the eight principal bodhisattva disciples of Buddha Shākyamuni, renowned for the way in which, through the power of his concentration, he miraculously multiplied the offerings he made.

samaya (Skt.). See **sacred commitments.**

samaya ingredient, or substance (Tib. *dam tshig gi rdzas*). An object or ingredient that is necessary for or enhances the practices of the Vajrayāna.

saṃsāra (Skt.). See **cyclic existence.**

Saṅgha (Skt., Tib. dGe 'dun). The community of Buddhist practitioners. The use of this term varies: it may include only noble beings (that is, those who have attained the path of seeing), the monastic community, or the disciples of a particular teacher.

Saraha (Skt., Tib. Sa ra ha). An Indian mahāsiddha (great accomplished being), author of three cycles of dohā (songs of realization).

Secret Mantra Vehicle (Tib. gSang ngags kyi theg pa). A branch of the Great Vehicle that uses the special techniques of the tantras to pursue the path of enlightenment for all beings more rapidly. Because these practices are based on the realization of the diamond-like nature of the mind, this vehicle is also known as the Diamond Vehicle.

Secret Mantrayāna. See **Secret Mantra Vehicle.**

self (Tib. *bdag*, Skt. *ātman*). In Buddhist philosophy, denotes the mistaken notion of a permanent, single, and independent entity, whether applied to a personal sense of "I" or a divine creator.

sense of decency (Tib. *khrel yod*). Also translated as *modesty* or *consideration of others*. To be ashamed because of what others might think if one commits negative actions. This is one of the seven noble riches.

sense of shame (Tib. *ngo tsha shes*). Also translated as *conscientiousness* or *honesty*. To be ashamed because of what one thinks of oneself if one commits negative actions. This is one of the seven noble riches.

senses-and-fields (Tib. *skye mched*, Skt. *āyatana*). Also called "sense bases," "sources of perception," and so on. The twelve āyatanas comprise the six sense organs and the six sense objects. Together, they give rise to the six sense consciousnesses.

seven branches (Tib. *yan lag bdun*). A form of prayer comprising seven parts: prostration, offering, confession, rejoicing, requesting the teachers to turn the Wheel of Dharma, requesting them not to pass into nirvāṇa, and dedication of merit.

seven noble riches (Tib. *'phags pa'i nor bdun*). Faith, discipline, generosity, learning, a sense of decency, a sense of shame, and wisdom.

seven precious attributes (Tib. *rin po che sna bdun*, Skt. *saptaratna*). Also called "seven attributes of royalty" (Tib. *rgyal srid sna bdun*). The seven special possessions of a universal monarch: the precious golden wheel, precious wish-fulfilling jewel, precious queen, precious minister, precious elephant, precious horse, and precious general.

seven-point posture of Vairocana (Tib. *rnam snang chos bdun*). The seven points of the ideal meditation posture: legs crossed in the diamond (vajra) posture, back straight, hands in the gesture of meditation, eyes gazing along the nose, chin slightly tucked in, shoulders well apart "like a vulture's wings," and the tip of the tongue touching the palate.

Shākyamuni (Skt., Tib. Sha kya thub pa). "Capable One of the Shākyas." The seventh of the thousand buddhas in this Fortunate Kalpa. The buddha of our time, who lived around the fifth century B.C.E.

shameful deeds (Tib. *kha na ma tho ba*). Lit., "that which cannot be mentioned" or "that which cannot be praised." This term covers every kind of action that results in suffering and not only the most serious kinds of wrongdoing. Shameful actions are divided into those that are naturally negative and those that are negative in that they involve breaches of vows.

Shāntideva (Skt., Tib. Zhi ba lha). "Peaceful God." The great seventh-century Indian poet and mahāsiddha (great accomplished being), author of the famous poem on the practice of bodhichitta *The Way of the Bodhisattva* (*Bodhicaryāvatāra*).

Shāriputra (Skt.). One of the foremost listener (shrāvaka) disciples of Buddha Shākyamuni.

siddha (Skt., Tib. *grub thob*). Lit., "one who has attained the accomplishments." Someone who has attained the result of the practice of the Secret Mantra Vehicle.

six consciousnesses (Tib. *rnam shes tshogs drug*). Lit., "six gatherings of consciousness." The gathering of a sense object, a sense organ, and a consciousness. The consciousnesses related to vision, hearing, smell, taste, touch, and mentation.

six elements of a person (Tib. *skyes bu khams drug*). Earth, water, fire, air, space, and consciousness.

six realms (Tib. *'gro drug*). Six modes of existence caused and dominated by a particular mental poison: the hells (anger or aversion), the hungry spirits realm (miserliness), animal realm (bewilderment or ignorance), human realm (desire), demigod realm (jealousy), and god realm (pride). These correspond to the deluded perceptions that are produced by beings' past actions and that are apprehended as real.

six transcendent perfections (Tib. *pha rol tu phyin pa drug*, Skt. *ṣaḍpāramitā*). Generosity, discipline, patience, diligence, concentration, and wisdom.

skillful means (Tib. *thabs*, Skt. *upāya*). Spontaneous, altruistic activity born from wisdom.

solitary realizer (Tib. *rang sangs rgyas*, Skt. *pratyekabuddha*). Followers of the Basic Vehicle who attain liberation (the cessation of suffering) on their own, without the help of a spiritual teacher. Although some solitary realizers with sharp intellects remain alone, "like rhinoceroses," others with dull minds need to stay in large groups, "like flocks of parrots." Their practice consists, in particular, of meditation on the twelve links of interdependent origination.

source of good (Tib. *dge rtsa*). A positive or virtuous act that serves as a cause propelling its perpetrator toward happy states.

spiritual friend (Tib. *dge ba'i gshes gnyen*, Skt. *kalyāṇamitra*). A spiritual guide or teacher.

stream of being (Tib. *rgyud*). Lit., "continuity" or "continuum." Also translated as *mind stream*, or simply *mind*. This term denotes that aspect of an individual that continues from one moment to the next and from one lifetime to the next, and that, therefore, includes the individual's stock of positive and negative deeds along with his or her positive and negative habitual tendencies.

stūpa (Skt., Tib. *mchod rten*). Lit., "support of offering." A symbolic representation of the Buddha's mind. It is the most typical Buddhist monument, which often has a wide, square base, a rounded midsection, and a tall, conical upper section, topped by a sun and moon. Stūpas frequently contain the relics of enlightened beings. They vary in size from tiny clay models to the vast stūpas at Borobodur in Indonesia and Bodha in Nepal.

Subhūti (Skt., Tib. Rab 'byor). "Greatly Endowed." One of the Buddha's foremost disciples, renowned for his understanding of emptiness.

sublime being (Tib. *skyes bu dam pa*, or simply *dam pa*). Also translated as *holy being*. A realized being who has the capacity to act for the benefit of others on a vast scale.

Sudhana (Skt., Tib. Nor bzang). "Excellent Treasure." The bodhisattva whose spiritual journey is recounted in the *Sūtra of the Arborescent Array* (*Gaṇḍavyūha*). He was named for the treasures that appeared when he was born.

sugata (Skt., Tib. *bde bar gshegs pa*). Lit., "one who has gone to bliss." An epithet of a buddha.

superior intention (Tib. *lhag bsam*). Also translated as *altruistic attitude*. The good heart and unselfish attitude that is an essential aspect of bodhichitta.

sustained calm (Tib. *zhi gnas*, Skt. *śamatha*). A calm, undistracted state of unwavering concentration, the basis of all concentrations.

sūtra (Skt., Tib. *mdo*). A scripture containing teachings given by the Buddha or by one of his disciples who was inspired by the Buddha.

tainted (Tib. *zag bcas*). A characteristic of actions or states in which the three concepts of subject, object, and action are present and that are, therefore, tainted by defilements, so that they cannot transcend cyclic existence.

tantra (Skt., Tib. *rgyud*). Any one of the texts on which the Diamond Vehicle teachings are based. They reveal the continuity between the original purity of the nature of mind and the result of the path, which is the realization of that nature.

tathāgata (Skt., Tib. *de bzhin gshegs pa*). Lit., "one who has gone to thusness." A buddha, one who has reached or realized thusness, the ultimate reality. Also, one who is "thus come," a buddha in the body of manifestation (*nirmaṇakāya*) who has appeared in the world to benefit beings.

teacher (Tib. *bla ma*, Skt. *guru*). One who gives spiritual guidance and instruction. The Tibetan term, which translates the Sanskrit, refers to the fact that no one is more important than one's spiritual teacher.

Teacher (Tib. sTon pa). An epithet for Buddha Shākyamuni, but also occasionally, in lowercase, used as a general term.

ten directions (Tib. *phyogs bcu*). The four cardinal points, the four intermediate points, and the zenith and nadir.

ten levels (Tib. *sa bcu*, Skt. *daśabhūmi*). The ten stages of realization by which a noble bodhisattva progresses toward enlightenment, beginning with the first level on the path of seeing. The nine other levels occur on the path of meditation. The eighth, ninth, and tenth levels are termed the "three pure levels," or "great levels."

ten transcendent perfections (Tib. *pha rol tu phyin pa bcu*, Skt. *daśapāramitā*). Transcendent generosity, discipline, patience, diligence, concentration, and wisdom, together with transcendent means, aspirational prayer, strength, and gnosis. Each of these ten is practiced predominantly on one of the ten bodhisattva levels—generosity on the first level, discipline on the second, and so forth. They are termed "transcendent" because their practice involves realization of the view of emptiness.

Terdak Lingpa (Tib. gTer bdag gling pa). Gyurme Dorje, Terdak Lingpa (1646–1714), founder of Mindrölling (sMin grol gling) Monastery in Tibet. Among the spiritual treasures that he discovered is the Vajrasattva sādhana cycle known as the Minling Dorsem (sMin gling rdor sems).

thirty-two marks (Tib. *mtshan nyid so gnyis*). The special physical features on a buddha's body, including the crown protuberance and the wheel markings on the palms and soles. These marks, which are the result of the immense merit accumulated by such beings, are also present, but to a lesser extent, on the bodies of universal monarchs.

three buddha bodies (Tib. *sku gsum*, Skt. *trikāya*). The three aspects of buddhahood: the body of truth, body of perfect enjoyment, and body of manifestation.

three doors (Tib. *sgo gsum*). The three ways through which a person acts—namely, through the body, speech, and mind.

Three Jewels (Tib. dKon mchog gsum, Skt. Triratna). Collectively, the object of refuge of all Buddhists: the Buddha, Dharma, and Saṅgha.

three poisons (Tib. *dug gsum*). The three defilements of bewilderment, attachment, and aversion. See also **five poisons**.

Three Roots (Tib. rTsa gsum). The teacher or lama, root or source of blessings; the yidam deity, source of accomplishments; and the ḍākinī (or protectors), source of activities.

three seats (Tib. *gdan gsum*). The aggregates and elements, āyatanas (the sense organs and their corresponding sense objects), and limbs of one's body, whose true nature, according to the pure perception of the Mantrayāna, is the maṇḍala of the male and female tathāgatas, the male and female bodhisattvas, and other deities.

three spheres (Tib. *'khor gsum*). Subject, object, and action, perceived as having real and independent existence.

three supreme methods (Tib. *dam pa gsum*). The supreme preparation—with bodhichitta; the supreme main part of the practice or deed—performed without distracting concepts; and the supreme conclusion—with the dedication of merit to the enlightenment of all beings.

three times (Tib. *dus gsum*). Past, present, and future.

three trainings (Tib. *bslabs pa gsum*, Skt. *triśikṣā*). The threefold training in discipline, concentration, and wisdom.

three vajras (Tib. *rdo rje gsum*). The unchanging, indestructible body, speech, and mind of an enlightened being.

three vehicles (Tib. *theg pa gsum*, Skt. *triyāna*). The vehicles of the listeners, solitary realizers, and bodhisattvas.

three vows (Tib. *sdom pa gsum*). The vows of individual liberation, the precepts of the bodhisattvas, and the sacred commitments of the Secret Mantrayāna.

three ways of pleasing one's teachers (Tib. *mnyes pa gsum*). Making material offerings; helping them through physical, verbal, or mental tasks; and practicing what they have taught.

three worlds (Tib. *khams gsum*). The world of desire, the world of form, and the world of formlessness. Alternatively (Tib. *'jig rten gsum, sa gsum, srid gsum*): the world of gods above the earth, that of humans on the earth, and that of the nāgas under the earth.

thusness (Tib. *de bzhin nyid*, Skt. *tathātā*). The ultimate nature of things, emptiness, the expanse of reality free from elaboration.

tīrthika (Skt., Tib. *mu stegs pa*). Denotes non-Buddhist proponents of nihilistic and eternalistic philosophical views. The Tibetan term refers to the fact that they are said to stay on the steps (*stegs*) leading down to the edge (*mu*) of the river—that is, the path flowing into the ocean of nirvāṇa.

torma (Tib. *gtor ma*). A ritual object, often modeled from flour and butter, which can be used to represent a deity, a maṇḍala, an offering, or occasionally a weapon to subdue negative forces.

transitory composite, view of (Tib. *'jig tshogs la lta ba*). The view whereby the five aggregates, which are transitory and composite, are regarded as a permanent, independent, and single "I" and "mine." This view is the basis of all other wrong views.

treatise (Tib. *bstan bcos*, Skt. *śāstra*). In the context of Buddhist literature, a work by an Indian or Tibetan master that comments on the Buddha's teachings or presents them in a condensed or more accessible form.

Trisong Detsen (Tib. Khri srong sde'u btsan). 790–844. The second of the three great religious kings of Tibet. It was thanks to his efforts that Guru Padmasambhava and other great masters came from India to establish Buddhism firmly in Tibet.

true nature. See **ultimate reality**.

Tuṣhita (Skt., Tib. dGa' ldan). Lit., "The Joyous." One of the realms of the gods in the world of desire, in which Buddha Shākyamuni took a final rebirth before appearing in this world. The future Buddha, Maitreya, is currently in the Tuṣhita heaven teaching the Great Vehicle.

twelve branches of excellent speech (Tib. *gsung rab yan lag bcu gnyis*). The twelve types of teaching given by the Buddha, which correspond to twelve kinds of texts: condensed (Tib. *mdo sde*, Skt. *sūtra*), melodious (Tib. *dbyangs bsnyan*, Skt. *geya*), prophetic (Tib. *lung bstan*, Skt. *vyākaraṇa*), verse (Tib. *tshigs bcad*, Skt. *gāthā*), spoken with a purpose (Tib. *ched brjod*, Skt. *udāna*), conversational—questions, talks, etc. (Tib. *gleng gzhi*, Skt. *nidāna*), concerning his past lives (Tib. *skyes rab*, Skt. *jātaka*), marvelous (Tib. *rmad byung*, Skt. *adbhutadharma*), establishing a truth (Tib. *gtan babs*, Skt. *upadeśa*), biographical or "expressing realization" (Tib. *rtogs brjod*, Skt. *avadāna*), historical (Tib. *de ltar byung*, Skt. *itivṛttaka*), and very detailed (Tib. *shin tu rgyas pa*, Skt. *vaipulya*).

twelve deeds of a Buddha (Tib. *mdzad pa bcu gnyis*). (1) Descending from the Tuṣhita heaven, (2) entering the womb of his mother, (3) being born, (4) enjoying youthful sports, (5) taking pleasure in his entourage of queens, (6) renouncing the world, (7) practicing asceticism, (8) proceeding to the vajra seat under the bodhi tree, (9) vanquishing Māra, (10) attaining perfect buddhahood, (11) turning the Wheel of Dharma, and (12) passing into nirvāṇa.

two accumulations (Tib. *tshogs gnyis*). The accumulation of merit (Tib. *bsod nams*) and the accumulation of wisdom (Tib. *ye shes*).

two buddha bodies (Tib. *sku gnyis*). The body of truth and the form body.

two fulfillments. See **two goals.**

two goals (Tib. *don gnyis*). One's own goal, benefit, or welfare (Tib. *rang don*) and that of others (Tib. *gzhan don*). It is often understood that the goal for oneself is achieved by the realization of emptiness, the body of truth (*dharmakāya*), and that the goal for others is achieved by compassion manifesting as the form body (*rūpakāya*).

two kinds of no-self (Tib. *bdag med gnyis*). The no-self of the individual (Tib. *gang zag gi bdag med*) and the no-self of phenomena (Tib. *chos kyi bdag med*). See also **no-self.**

two obscurations (Tib. *sgrib gnyis*). The obscurations of defilements and cognitive obscurations. See also **obscurations.**

two truths (Tib. *bden gnyis*). Relative truth and ultimate truth.

twofold purity (Tib. *dag pa gnyis*). Original purity (*rang bzhin ye dag*), which is the buddha nature present in all beings, and the purity from all adventitious stains (Tib. *blo bur 'phral dag*), which is the result of practicing the path. Only a buddha has this second purity.

udumbara (Skt.). The udumbara flower is said to blossom only once in a kalpa and is therefore used in Buddhist teachings as a symbol of exceptional rarity.

ultimate excellence (Tib. *nges legs*). The lasting happiness of liberation and omniscience—that is, buddhahood.

ultimate reality (Tib. *chos nyid*, Skt. *dharmata*). Also translated as *true nature*. The true nature of phenomena, which is emptiness.

ultimate teachings (Tib. *nges don*). Also translated as *definitive teachings*. Teachings that, unlike the expedient teachings, comprise the direct expression of truth from the point of view of realized beings.

ultimate truth (Tib. *don dam bden pa*). The ultimate nature of the mind and the true status of phenomena, which can be known only by gnosis, beyond all conceptual constructs and duality. Contrast **relative truth**.

universal monarch (Tib. *'khor los sgyur ba'i rgyal po*, Skt. *cakravartin*). An emperor who, with his golden, silver, copper, or iron wheel, has dominion over the beings of the four continents. Universal monarchs appear only in certain eras when the human life span is greater than eighty thousand years.

untainted (Tib. *zag med*). Uncontaminated by negative emotions, including concepts due to the defilement of ignorance.

utpala (Skt.). A kind of blue lotus flower.

Vaishravaṇa (Skt., Tib. rNam thos sras). One of the Four Great Kings (whose god realm is the first in the world of desire), guardian of the North and god of wealth.

vajra (Skt., Tib. *rdo rje*). Lit., "lord of stones." A diamond. The symbolic implement (representing skillful means) held by tantric deities and used in tantric rituals. Originally a stone thrown by Indra as a weapon (hence "Indra's thunderbolt"). In Buddhism it represents the unchanging, indestructible nature of reality, which has seven characteristics: it cannot be cut, is indestructible, true, hard, enduring, unimpeded, and invincible. This diamond-like nature gives its name to the Diamond Vehicle.

Vajradhara (Skt., Tib. rDorje 'chang). "Diamond Bearer." In the New Tradition, which follows the tantras translated and propagated in Tibet from the tenth century onward, he is the primordial Buddha, source of all the tantras. In the Ancient Tradition, which follows the teachings introduced to Tibet by the great master Padmasambhava in the eighth century, Vajradhara represents the principle of the teacher as enlightened holder of the teachings of the Diamond Vehicle.

Vajrapāṇi (Skt., Tib. Phyag na rdo rje). "Vajra in the Hand." One of the Eight Great Close Sons (the Buddha's eight closest bodhisattva disciples) and the manifestation of the Buddha's power. Also known as the Lord of Secrets (Tib. gSang ba'i bdag po).

Vajrasattva (Skt., Tib. rDo rje sems dpa'). "Diamond Being" or "Diamond Hero." In the Diamond Vehicle, the deity most widely practiced for purification.

Vajrayāna (Skt.). See **Diamond Vehicle**.

vehicle of characteristics (Tib. *mtshan nyid theg pa,* Skt. *lakṣaṇayāna*). Also called the "causal vehicle of characteristics." The vehicle that teaches the path as the cause for attaining enlightenment. It includes the vehicles of the listeners, solitary realizers, and bodhisattvas (that is, those bodhisattvas practicing the sūtra path and not that of the mantras). It is distinct from the resultant vehicle of the mantras, which takes the result (that is, enlightenment) as the path.

victorious one (Tib. *rgyal ba*, Skt. *jina*). Also translated as *conqueror*. A general epithet for a buddha, one who has won victory over the four demons.

vidyādhara (Skt., Tib. *rig 'dzin*). Lit., "knowledge holder." One who through profound means holds the deities, mantras, and the wisdom of great bliss.

Vimalamitra (Skt., Tib. Dri med bshes bnyen). "Stainless Friend." An Indian master who holds an important place in the lineages of the Great Perfection. He went to Tibet in the eighth century, where he taught extensively and composed and translated numerous Sanskrit texts. The quintessence of his teaching is known as the Vima Nyingtik.

Vinaya (Skt., Tib. *'Dul ba*). Lit., "taming." The section of the Buddha's teaching that deals with discipline, and in particular with the vows of monastic ordination.

virtue consistent with ordinary merit (Tib. *bsod nams cha mthun gyi dge ba'i las*). Positive actions that are not backed by bodhichitta and that, therefore, are not a direct cause leading to buddhahood. Such actions result in higher rebirth, but they contribute in only a limited way to liberation from cyclic existence.

Viṣhṇu (Skt., Tib. Khyab 'jug). An important Hindu god.

Wheel of Dharma (Tib. Chos kyi 'khor lo, Skt. Dharmacakra). The symbol of the Buddha's teaching. To turn the Wheel of the Dharma means to teach the Dharma. During his lifetime, the Buddha gave three major series of teachings, which are referred to as the first, second, and third turnings.

wish-fulfilling jewel (Tib. *yid bzhin nor bu*, Skt. *cintāmaṇi*). A fabulous jewel found in the realms of the gods or nāgas that fulfills all wishes.

world of desire (Tib. *'dod khams*, Skt. *kāmaloka* or *kāmadhātu*). The first of the three worlds, comprising the realms of the hell beings, hungry spirits, animals, humans, demigods, and the six classes of gods of the world of desire.

world of form (Tib. *gzugs khams*, Skt. *rūpadhātu*). The second of the three worlds, comprising the twelve realms of the four concentrations and the five pure abodes.

world of formlessness (Tib. *gzugs med khams*, Skt. *ārūpyadhātu*). The third of the three worlds, at the peak of existence. It comprises the spheres of infinite space, infinite consciousness, utter nothingness, and neither existence nor nonexistence.

wrong view (Tib. *log lta*, Skt. *mithyādṛṣṭi*). A false belief, particularly a view that will lead one to courses of action that bring more suffering. See also **eternalism; nihilism.**

yakṣha (Skt., Tib. *gnod sbyin*). A class of powerful spirits who, despite their Tibetan name of "harm doers," are as often beneficent as they are malignant.

Yama (Skt., Tib. gShin rje). The Lord of Death.

Yeshe Tsogyal (Tib. Ye shes mtsho rgyal). "Wisdom Sea of Victory." Padmasambhava's mystic consort and greatest disciple. She served him perfectly and helped him to propagate his teachings, in particular, by concealing spiritual treasures to be rediscovered later for the sake of future disciples.

yidam (Tib. *yi dam*, Skt. *devata*). A deity representing enlightenment, in a male or female, peaceful or wrathful, form and that corresponds to the practitioner's individual nature. The yidam is the source of accomplishments. Yidam practice involves performing the deity's sādhana and reciting its mantra.

yoga (Skt., Tib. *rnal 'byor*). Lit., "union (Tib. *'byor*) with the natural state (Tib. *rnal ma*)." A term for spiritual practice.

yogin (Skt., Tib. *rnal 'byor pa*). A person practicing a spiritual path.

yoginī (Skt., Tib. *rnal 'byor ma*). A female yogin.

Abbreviations

BDRC. Buddhist Digital Resource Center. https://www.tbrc.org/.

Dg. Derge edition of rNying ma'i rgyud 'bum (Collected Tantras of the Ancients). Website of the Tibetan and Himalayan Library. http://www.thlib.org/encyclopedias/literary/canons/ngb/catalog.php#cat=dg.

Ng. rNying ma'i rgyud 'bum (Collected Tantras of the Ancients). Website of the Tibetan and Himalayan Library. http://www.thlib.org/encyclopedias/literary/canons/ngb/.

NL. It has not been possible to locate a work with this title or containing the cited passage.

Pt. dPal brTsegs Edition of the Nyingma Gyübum. Website of the Tibetan and Himalayan Library.

Tb. Tsamdrak edition of rNying ma'i rgyud 'bum (Collected Tantras of the Ancients). Website of the Tibetan and Himalayan Library. http://www.thlib.org/encyclopedias/literary/canons/ngb/catalog.php#cat=tb.

Toh. Hakuju Ui et al. eds., *A Complete Catalogue of the Tibetan Buddhist Canons.* Sendai, Japan: Tohoku University, 1934. Tohoku University catalog of the Derge edition of the canon.

Notes

1. Gyurmé Pema Namgyal was the fourth in the reincarnation line that begins with Aja Lama Drupwang Pema Gyaltsen but the third of his reincarnations or regents, who bore the name Shechen Gyaltsap, Regent of Shechen. See Shechen Gyaltsap, *Practicing the Great Perfection*, 127n2.
2. Published in English translation as Zhechen Gyaltsab, *Path of Heroes*.
3. Included in Dilgo Khyentse Rinpoche, *Zurchungpa's Testament*, trans. Padmakara Translation Group (Boulder, CO: Snow Lion, 2020).
4. This quotation is attributed in other works to the *Tantra on Seizing the Essential Meaning* (*sNying po don len pa'i rgyud*). It has not been possible to identify either of these titles.
5. Longchenpa, *Precious Treasury*, chap. 10
6. Longchenpa, chap. 10.
7. *Ornament of Clear Realization*, chap. 1, v. 18.
8. Jigme Lingpa, *Treasury*, chap. 3, v. 14 (English translation, Jigme Lingpa and Longchen Yeshe Dorje, *Treasury*, bk. 1, p. 26).
9. Longchenpa, *Precious Treasury*, chap. 11.
10. Longchenpa, chap. 11.
11. Longchenpa, chap. 10.
12. Longchenpa, chap. 11.
13. Longchenpa, chap. 11.
14. Longchenpa, chap. 11.
15. Shechen Gyaltsap is quoting here from the instructions in Longchenpa's autocommentary on the *Precious Treasury That Fulfills All Wishes.*
16. Longchenpa, *Precious Treasury*, chap. 10.
17. Śāntideva, *Way of the Bodhisattva*, chap. 5. It comprises one line adapted from verse 89 and the first two lines of verse 90 (English translation, Shantideva, *Way*, p. 74).
18. Longchenpa, *Precious* Treasury, chap. 10.
19. Longchenpa, chap. 10.
20. Longchenpa, chap. 11.
21. The following introduction to the specific, individual practices has been brought forward from its original position in the Tibetan text immediately preceding chapter 5.

22. Longchenpa, *Precious Treasury*, chap. 13.
23. Longchenpa, chap. 13.
24. *Dal ba phun sum tshogs pa bcu gnyis bstan pa'i mdo*. We have been unable to identify a sūtra with this name or precise content.
25. Longchenpa, *Finding Rest in the Nature of the Mind*, chap. 1, v. 10 (English translation, p. 7).
26. Longchenpa, chap. 1, v. 10 (English translation, p. 7).
27. Longchenpa, chap. 1, v. 11 (English translation, p. 7).
28. Longchenpa, chap. 1, v. 12 (English translation, p. 8).
29. Longchenpa, *Precious Treasury*, chap. 13.
30. Śāntideva, *Way of the Bodhisattva*, chap. 4, vv. 17, 18 (English translation, Shantideva, *Way*, p. 55, last line slightly modified).
31. Chandrakīrti, *Introduction to the Middle Way*, chap. 2, v. 7 (English translation, Chandrakirti and Jamgön Mipham, *Introduction*, p. 63).
32. Nāgārjuna, *Letter to a Friend*, v. 61 (English translation from Nagarjuna and Longchen Yeshe Dorje, *Nagarjuna's "Letter,"* p. 51).
33. Śāntideva, *Way of the Bodhisattva*, chap. 1, v. 4 (English translation, Shantideva, *Way*, p. 31).
34. Nāgārjuna, *Letter to a Friend*, v. 59 (English translation from Nagarjuna and Longchen Yeshe Dorje, *Nagarjuna's "Letter,"* p. 51, second line modified).
35. Longchenpa, *Precious Treasury*, chap. 13.
36. Longchenpa, *Finding Rest in the Nature of the Mind*, chap. 1, v. 17 (English translation, p. 9).
37. Longchenpa, chap. 1, v. 19 (English translation, p. 9).
38. Longchenpa, chap. 1, v. 18 (English translation, p. 9).
39. Śāntideva, *Way of the Bodhisattva*, chap. 10, v. 47, line 3 (English translation, Shantideva, *Way*, p. 170).
40. Longchenpa, *Precious Treasury*, chap. 13.
41. We have taken the liberty of inserting a few words here to correct an apparent scribal omission in the copying of this passage from Longchenpa's autocommentary on the *Precious Treasury That Fulfills All Wishes*, which has resulted in reducing these two sentences to a single one. In translation it would otherwise read: "When you have an escort in a dangerous place, that is the time to make the most effort."
42. Śāntideva, *Way of the Bodhisattva*, chap. 7, v. 14 (English translation, Shantideva, *Way*, p. 99).
43. Longchenpa, *Precious Treasury*, chap. 13.
44. Padampa Sangye, *Hundred Verses of Advice*, v. 78 (English translation, Dilgo Khyentse and Padampa Sangye, *Hundred Verses*, p. 137).
45. Longchenpa, *Precious Treasury*, chap. 13.
46. Longchenpa, *Finding Rest in the Nature of the Mind*, chap. 2, v. 1 (English translation, p. 11).

47. Padampa Sangye, *Hundred Verses of Advice*, v. 5 (English translation, Dilgo Khyentse and Padampa Sangye, *Hundred Verses*, p. 12).
48. We have been unable to locate these lines in extant versions of *The Way of the Bodhisattva*.
49. Śāntideva, *Way of the Bodhisattva*, chap. 4, v. 16 (English translation, Shantideva, *Way*, p. 55).
50. Nāgārjuna, *Letter to a Friend*, v. 57 (English translation from Nagarjuna and Longchen Yeshe Dorje, *Nagarjuna's "Letter,"* p. 49).
51. Longchenpa, *Finding Rest in the Nature of the Mind*, chap. 2, v. 5 (English translation, p. 12).
52. Śāntideva, *Way of the Bodhisattva*, chap. 2, v. 39 (English translation, Shantideva, *Way*, p. 42).
53. Nāgārjuna, *Jewel Garland*, v. 278.
54. Longchenpa, *Finding Rest in the Nature of the Mind*, chap. 2, v. 8 (English translation, p. 13).
55. Longchenpa, chap. 2, v. 11 (English translation, p. 13).
56. Śāntideva, *Way of the Bodhisattva*, chap. 4, v. 16 (English translation, Shantideva, *Way*, p. 55).
57. Śāntideva, chap. 2, v. 58 (English translation, Shantideva, *Way*, p. 45).
58. Longchenpa, *Finding Rest in the Nature of the Mind*, chap. 2, v. 12 (English translation, p. 14).
59. Nāgārjuna, *Letter to a Friend*, v. 55 (English translation from Nagarjuna and Longchen Yeshe Dorje, *Nagarjuna's "Letter,"* p. 49).
60. Śāntideva, *Way of the Bodhisattva*, chap. 5, vv. 62–63 (English translation, Shantideva, *Way*, p. 70).
61. Śāntideva, chap. 2, v. 40 (English translation, Shantideva, *Way*, p. 43).
62. Nāgārjuna, *Letter to a Friend*, v. 56 (English translation from Nagarjuna and Longchen Yeshe Dorje, *Nagarjuna's "Letter,"* p. 49).
63. Lit. "take the Capable One's throne."
64. Śāntideva, *Way of the Bodhisattva*, chap. 2, v. 62 (English translation, Shantideva, *Way*, p. 46).
65. From Mipham Rinpoche's recitation text, *Illuminating the Path to Freedom*.
66. Longchenpa, *Precious Treasury*, chap. 14.
67. Geshe Cha-Yulwa (1075–1138) was a Kadampa master and one of Gampopa's teachers.
68. Sangye Tönpa (1207–1278) was a Kagyu master.
69. Geshe Chen-ngawa (1038–1103) was a Kadampa master and a disciple of Drom Tönpa.
70. The Kadampa master Drom Tön Gyalwa'i Jungne (1005–1064) was Atisha's principal disciple in Tibet.
71. Sangye Öntön (died 1210) was a twelfth-century Kadampa master.
72. Mokchokpa Rinchen Tsondrü (1110–1170) was a Kadampa master.
73. Nāgārjuna, *Jewel Garland*, v. 20.

74. Nāgārjuna, v. 20 (last two lines) and v. 21.
75. Śāntideva, *Way of the Bodhisattva*, chap. 7, v. 40 (English translation, Shantideva, *Way*, p. 103).
76. Śāntideva, chap. 7, v. 42 (English translation, Shantideva, *Way*, p. 103).
77. Longchenpa, *Finding Rest in the Nature of the Mind*, chap. 4, v. 1 (English translation, p. 35).
78. Longchenpa, chap. 4, v. 14 (English translation, p. 39).
79. Longchenpa, chap. 4, v. 15 (English translation, p. 39).
80. Longchenpa, chap. 4, v. 16 (English translation, p. 39).
81. Longchenpa, chap. 4, v. 17 (English translation, p. 40).
82. The Tibetan term used here is *mi tshangs par spyod pa*, meaning literally "impure conduct"— that is, the opposite of "pure conduct" or celibacy. However, below on p. 143, this section is headed *log par g.yem pa*, the term more usually employed for sexual misconduct.
83. Śāntideva, *Way of the Bodhisattva*, chap. 6, vv. 122–23 (English translation, Shantideva, *Way*, p. 94).
84. Śāntideva, chap. 7, v. 43 (English translation, Shantideva, *Way*, p. 103).
85. Nāgārjuna, *Letter to a Friend*, vv. 30–31 (English translation from Nagarjuna and Longchen Yeshe Dorje, *Nagarjuna's "Letter,"* p. 39, slightly modified).
86. Longchenpa, *Finding Rest in the Nature of the Mind*, chap. 4, v. 24 (English translation, p. 42).
87. Śāntideva, *Way of the Bodhisattva*, chap. 5, v. 11 (English translation, Shantideva, *Way*, p. 62).
88. Longchenpa, *Finding Rest in the Nature of the Mind*, chap. 4, v. 25 (English translation, p. 43).
89. Nāgārjuna, *Jewel Garland*, vv. 23, 24 (first two lines).
90. That is, Longchenpa, *Finding Rest in the Nature of the Mind*, chap. 4, v. 35 (English translation, p. 46).
91. Longchenpa, chap. 4, v. 36 (English translation, p. 46).
92. *dGe ba bcu bstan pa'i mdo*. Possibly the *Sūtra That Teaches the Ripening of Virtuous and Non-Virtuous Actions, dGe ba dang mi dge ba'i las kyi rnam par smin pa bstan pa'i mdo*, Toh. 355.
93. Longchenpa, *Finding Rest in the Nature of the Mind*, chap. 4, v. 37 (English translation, p. 46).
94. Śāntideva, *Way of the Bodhisattva*, chap. 9, v. 2 (last two lines) (English translation, Shantideva, *Way*, p. 137).
95. Nāgārjuna, *Jewel Garland*, v. 212.
96. Longchenpa, *Finding Rest in the Nature of the Mind*, chap. 4, v. 42 (English translation, p. 48).
97. Nāgārjuna, *Root Stanzas on the Middle Way*, chap. 24, v. 19.
98. Nāgārjuna, *Commentary on Bodhichitta*, v. 88.
99. Nāgārjuna, *Jewel Garland*, v. 57.
100. Nāgārjuna, v. 43.

101. Longchenpa, *Finding Rest in the Nature of the Mind*, chap. 4, vv. 43–44 (English translation, p. 48).
102. From Mipham Rinpoche's recitation text, *Illuminating the Path to Freedom*.
103. Longchenpa, *Finding Rest in the Nature of the Mind*, chap. 3, vv. 1–2 (English translation, p. 17).
104. Nāgārjuna, *Letter to a Friend*, v. 66 (English translation from Nagarjuna and Longchen Yeshe Dorje, *Nagarjuna's "Letter,"* p. 53).
105. Nāgārjuna, v. 68 (English translation from Nagarjuna and Longchen Yeshe Dorje, *Nagarjuna's "Letter,"* p. 53, slightly modified).
106. Nāgārjuna, v. 69 (English translation from Nagarjuna and Longchen Yeshe Dorje, *Nagarjuna's "Letter,"* p. 55).
107. To make sense of this passage, we have inserted this line, which is present in the source texts that we have consulted but has apparently been omitted in the Tibetan here.
108. Śāntideva, *Way of the Bodhisattva*, chap. 9, v. 156 (English translation, Shantideva, *Way*, p. 159).
109. Śāntideva, chap. 2, v. 61 and chap. 8, vv. 31–32 (English translation, Shantideva, *Way*, pp. 46 and 113).
110. We have inserted this second line (in Tibetan: *mi rnams kyis ni mi rtogs la*), which is present in the commentary but appears to have been omitted here.
111. Longchenpa, *Finding Rest in the Nature of the Mind*, chap. 3, v. 13 (English translation, p. 20).
112. Nāgārjuna, *Letter to a Friend*, vv. 86–87 (English translation from Nagarjuna and Longchen Yeshe Dorje, *Nagarjuna's "Letter,"* p. 61).
113. Longchenpa, *Finding Rest in the Nature of the Mind*, chap. 3, v. 14 (English translation, p. 20).
114. Nāgārjuna, *Letter to a Friend*, v. 78 (English translation from Nagarjuna and Longchen Yeshe Dorje, *Nagarjuna's "Letter,"* p. 57).
115. Longchenpa, *Finding Rest in the Nature of the Mind*, chap. 3, v. 15 (English translation, p. 21).
116. Nāgārjuna, *Letter to a Friend*, v. 78 (English translation from Nagarjuna and Longchen Yeshe Dorje, *Nagarjuna's "Letter,"* p. 57).
117. Longchenpa, *Finding Rest in the Nature of the Mind*, chap. 3, v. 16 (English translation, p. 21).
118. Longchenpa, chap. 3, v. 17 (English translation, p. 22).
119. Longchenpa, chap. 3, v. 17 (English translation, p. 22).
120. Longchenpa, chap. 3, v. 18 (English translation, p. 22).
121. Longchenpa, chap. 3, v. 18 (English translation, p. 22).
122. Longchenpa, chap. 3, v. 19 (English translation, p. 22).
123. Longchenpa, chap. 3, v. 19 (English translation, p. 22).
124. Longchenpa, chap. 3, v. 20 (English translation, p. 23).
125. Longchenpa, chap. 3, v. 20 (English translation, p. 23).
126. Longchenpa, chap. 3, v. 21 (English translation, p. 23).

127. Longchenpa, chap. 3, v. 21 (English translation, p. 23).
128. Longchenpa, chap. 3, v. 22 (English translation, p. 23).
129. Longchenpa, chap. 3, v. 23 (English translation, p. 23).
130. Longchenpa, chap. 3, v. 26 (English translation, p. 24).
131. Longchenpa, chap. 3, v. 27 (English translation, p. 24).
132. Longchenpa, chap. 3, v. 28 (English translation, p. 24).
133. Longchenpa, chap. 3, v. 29 (English translation, pp. 24–25).
134. Longchenpa, chap. 3, v. 30 (English translation, p. 25).
135. Śāntideva, *Way of the Bodhisattva*, chap. 5, v. 7 (last two lines) and v. 8 (first two lines) (English translation, Shantideva, *Way*, p. 62).
136. Longchenpa, *Finding Rest in the Nature of the Mind*, chap. 3, v. 32 (English translation, p. 25).
137. Nāgārjuna, *Letter to a Friend*, vv. 83–84 (English translation from Nagarjuna and Longchen Yeshe Dorje, *Nagarjuna's "Letter,"* pp. 59, 61).
138. Longchenpa, *Finding Rest in the Nature of the Mind*, chap. 3, v. 35 (English translation, p. 26).
139. Longchenpa, chap. 3, v. 36 (English translation, pp. 26–27).
140. Longchenpa, chap. 3, v. 36 (English translation, p. 27).
141. Longchenpa, chap. 3, v. 38 (English translation, p. 27).
142. Longchenpa, chap. 3, v. 38 (English translation, p. 27).
143. Longchenpa, chap. 3, v. 40 (English translation, p. 28).
144. Nāgārjuna, *Letter to a Friend*, v. 102 (English translation from Nagarjuna and Longchen Yeshe Dorje, *Nagarjuna's "Letter,"* p. 67).
145. Longchenpa, *Finding Rest in the Nature of the Mind*, chap. 3, v. 48 (English translation, p. 31).
146. As mentioned in the sections dealing with the duration of life in the first six hot hells above, the gods undergo the suffering of death for the equivalent of 350 human years in the realm of the Four Great Kings, and this duration increases in each god realm up to 11,200 human years in Mastery over Others' Creations.
147. We have taken the liberty to correct what appears to be a scribal error in the attribution of this quotation to *Letter to a Friend*: It does not occur in extant versions of that work. Other texts nevertheless attribute the same quotation to Nāgārjuna, although we have not been able to locate which of his works contains it.
148. Longchenpa, *Finding Rest in the Nature of the Mind*, chap. 3, v. 51 (English translation, p. 32).
149. Longchenpa, chap. 3, vv. 52–54 (English translation, p. 32–33).
150. From Mipham Rinpoche's recitation text, *Illuminating the Path to Freedom*.
151. Nāgārjuna, *Jewel Garland*, v. 5.
152. Longchenpa, *Precious Treasury*, chap. 15.
153. The word *gsungs* in the Tibetan text indicates that Shechen Gyaltsap has been quoting from a source text, in this case Longchenpa's autocommentary on his *Precious Treasury That Fulfills All Wishes*.

154. Impervious practitioners (Tib. *chos dred*) are ones who have received many teachings but have never taken them to heart and practiced them properly, so that they end up impervious to the Dharma, and instead of using situations to make their faith grow and to progress in the practice, they are carried away by their ordinary habits. They are like the leather bags used in Tibet to transport butter: no matter how much grease is added, the leather never loses its stiffness.
155. In the root text of the *Precious Treasury That Fulfills All Wishes*, whose auto-commentary Shechen Gyaltsap is quoting here, Longchenpa clearly refers to the three trainings (Tib. *bslab pa gsum*)—that is, the threefold training in discipline, concentration, and wisdom.
156. In Longchenpa, *Precious Treasury*, chap. 15.
157. Longchenpa, *Finding Rest in the Nature of the Mind*, chap. 6, v. 1 (English translation, p. 67).
158. Maitreya/Asaṅga, *Sublime Continuum*, chap. 1, v. 5.
159. Maitreya/Asaṅga, chap. 1, vv. 10, 11 (first two lines).
160. For further details, see Jigme Lingpa and Longchen Yeshe Dorje, *Treasury*, bk. 1, 454n84.
161. Maitreya/Asaṅga, *Sublime Continuum*, chap. 1, v. 14.
162. Maitreya/Asaṅga, chap. 1, v. 22.
163. Maitreya/Asaṅga, chap. 1, v. 19.
164. Longchenpa, *Precious Treasury*, chap. 19.
165. The eight dangers or fears (Tib. *'jigs pa chen po brgyad*) are those related to lions, elephants, fire, snakes, water, chains, robbers, and flesh eaters (harmful spirits and rākṣhasas). The sixteen dangers or fears (Tib. *'jigs pa chen po bcu drug*) are those related to (1) earth (earthquakes, landslides), (2) water (oceans, floods, drowning), (3) fire, (4) wind (cyclones), (5) lightning, (6) weapons, (7) imprisonment and the law, (8) robbers, (9) ghosts, (10) wild elephants, (11) lions, (12) poisonous snakes and food poisoning, (13) epidemics and disease, (14) untimely death, (15) poverty, (16) not accomplishing one's wishes. Other sources include in this list different illnesses, environmental disasters, and the influences of spirits and other nonhuman beings.
166. Although the Tibetan here reads *mthong zhing thos pas* ("seen or heard"), the source text reads *mthong zhing reg pas* ("seen or touched"). However, the analogy of seeing or hearing of this herb would go better with the following line in this verse.
167. Maitreya/Asaṅga, *Sublime Continuum*, chap. 1, v. 21.
168. Longchenpa, *Precious Treasury*, chap. 19.
169. Longchenpa, *Finding Rest in the Nature of the Mind*, chap. 6, v. 13.
170. Each tradition has its own specific instructions for visualizing the refuge tree and so on. If one is practicing the Longchen Nyingtik (Heart Essence of the Vast Expanse), for example, one should follow the instructions given in Patrul Rinpoche, *The Words of My Perfect Teacher*.

171. Nubchen Sangye Yeshe, one of the twenty-five principal disciples of Guru Padmasambhava.
172. The Eight Great Close Sons, the Buddha's closest bodhisattva disciples, are Mañjushrī, Avalokiteshvara, Vajrapāṇi, Maitreya, Samantabhadra, Ākāshagarbha, Kṣhitigarbha, and Sarvanivaraṇa-viṣhkambhin.
173. The Eight Supreme Listeners are Shāriputra, who of all the Buddha's listener disciples, was foremost in great wisdom; Maudgalyāyana, foremost in great miracles; Ānanda, foremost in having heard much; Kāshyapa, foremost in the good qualities of discipline; Kauṇḍinya, foremost in devotion to the precepts; Upāli, foremost in holding the Vinaya; Aniruddha, foremost in possessing the miracle eye; and Subhūti, foremost in questioning and answering.
174. The Sixteen Sthaviras, sometimes called the Sixteen Arhats, were close disciples of the Buddha, to whom he entrusted the preservation and propagation of his teachings after he passed into nirvāṇa. They included his own son, Rāhula.
175. Taken from the Minling Dorsem preliminary practices.
176. "Pursuer of virtue" is a literal translation of the Tibetan term *dge bsnyen* (*upāsaka* in Sanskrit), which refers to a lay ordinee. Although the term is often used to denote lay persons who keep the five basic precepts (not to kill, steal, indulge in sexual misconduct, lie, or consume intoxicants), it is also used for someone who has taken any one of these vows, or even one who has taken only the refuge vow, which is the basic vow without which it is impossible, in the Buddhist tradition, to take any other vows.
177. Longchenpa, *Finding Rest in the Nature of the Mind*, chap. 6, v. 16 (English translation, p. 71).
178. Longchenpa, chap. 6, v. 17 (English translation, p. 71).
179. The Sanskrit term *vaidalya* could refer to an early bodhisattva-piṭaka, or to *vaipulya*, one of the twelve branches of excellent speech, the section of the scriptures comprising very detailed texts. See glossary, s.v. "twelve branches of excellent speech."
180. The Tibetan title of this sūtra (*'Phags pa spyan ras gzigs kyi mdo*), which could be translated as "Sūtra of Avalokiteshvara," might mislead one into imagining that the sūtra features the bodhisattva Avalokiteshvara (or Chenrezi, as he is known in Tibetan). However, there is no mention of him at all in this sūtra. To avoid confusion, therefore, we have adopted the Derge Kangyur variant of the Sanskrit title, *Avalokinī Sūtra*.
181. Maitreya/Asaṅga, *Ornament of the Mahāyāna Sūtras*, chap. 2, v. 15 (English translation from Maitreya and Jamgön Mipham, *Feast*, p. 7).
182. Longchenpa, *Finding Rest in the Nature of the Mind*, chap. 6, v. 18 (English translation, p. 71).
183. Maitreya/Asaṅga, *Ornament of the Mahāyāna Sūtras*, chap. 10, vv. 7–8 (English translation from Maitreya and Jamgön Mipham, *Feast*, p. 30).
184. Tib. *rgyal po*. A kind of spirit.
185. Tib. mKhar chen bza', another name for Yeshe Tsogyal, who came from the

Kharchen family. Guru Padmasambhava is here ending his description of the refuge precepts addressed to Yeshe Tsogyal in the *Direct Instructions of the Teacher*.

186. Longchenpa, *Finding Rest in the Nature of the Mind*, chap. 7, v. 1 (English translation, p. 75).
187. Śāntideva, *Way of the Bodhisattva*, chap. 5, v. 15 (English translation, Shantideva, *Way*, p. 63).
188. Longchenpa, *Finding Rest in the Nature of the Mind*, chap. 8, v. 1 (English translation, p. 85).
189. Maitreya/Asaṅga, *Ornament of the Mahāyāna Sūtras*, chap. 16, v. 4 (English translation from Maitreya and Jamgön Mipham, *Feast*, p. 75).
190. Chandrakīrti, *Introduction to the Middle Way*, chap. 1, v. 1 (English translation, Chandrakirti and Jamgön Mipham, *Introduction*, p. 59).
191. Śāntideva, *Way of the Bodhisattva*, chap. 7, vv. 17–19 (English translation, Shantideva, *Way*, p. 99).
192. Śāntideva, chap. 7, vv. 28–30 (English translation, Shantideva, *Way*, p. 101).
193. Maitreya/Asaṅga, *Ornament of the Mahāyāna Sūtras*, chap. 11, v. 12 (English translation from Maitreya and Jamgön Mipham, *Feast*, p. 42).
194. Nāgārjuna, *Jewel Garland*, vv. 219 (second line)–227.
195. Maitreya/Asaṅga, *Sublime Continuum*, chap. 1, v. 152.
196. Maitreya/Asaṅga, chap. 1, v. 116.
197. Shāntapurīpa is another name for the great treasure finder Sherab Özer (1517–1584), one of whose treasures Jigme Lingpa practiced intensively in retreat.
198. Longchenpa, *Finding Rest in the Nature of the Mind*, chap. 4, v. 29 (English translation, p. 44).
199. *Treasury*, chap. 12, v. 5 (English translation, Jigme Lingpa and Longchen Yeshe Dorje, bk. 2, p. 51).
200. Maitreya/Asaṅga, *Sublime Continuum*, chap. 1, v. 63.
201. Some sources locate this quotation in Nāgārjuna's *Praise of the Expanse of Reality*.
202. Maitreya/Asaṅga, *Ornament of the Mahāyāna Sūtras*, chap. 10, v. 37 (English translation from Maitreya and Jamgön Mipham, *Feast*, p. 34).
203. Maitreya/Asaṅga, *Sublime Continuum*, chap. 1, v. 27.
204. Ju Mipham Gyamtso, *bDe gshegs snying po'i stong thun chen mo seng ge'i nga ro*.
205. Maitreya/Asaṅga, *Sublime Continuum*, chap. 1, vv. 40–41.
206. Nāgārjuna, *Praise of the Expanse of Reality*, v. 11.
207. This is a quotation from Asaṅga's commentary on the *Sublime Continuum* (*Theg pa chen po rgyud bla ma'i bstan bcos rnam par bshad pa*).
208. Nāgārjuna, *Praise of the Expanse of Reality*, vv. 9–10.
209. Prajñārashmi was the great treasure finder Sherab Özer (1517–1584).
210. Maitreya/Asaṅga, *Ornament of the Mahāyāna Sūtras*, chap. 4, v. 5 (English translation from Maitreya and Jamgön Mipham, *Feast*, p. 13).

211. Chandrakīrti, *Introduction to the Middle Way*, chap. 6, vv. 4 and 5 (one line) (English translation, Chandrakirti and Jamgön Mipham, *Introduction*, p. 68).
212. Maitreya/Asaṅga, *Sublime Continuum*, chap. 5, v. 1.
213. Maitreya/Asaṅga, *Ornament of Clear Realization*, chap. 1, v. 18.
214. Maitreya/Asaṅga, *Sublime Continuum*, chap. 1, v. 39.
215. Maitreya/Asaṅga, *Ornament of Clear Realization*, chap. 1, vv. 19–20.
216. Śāntideva, *Way of the Bodhisattva*, chap. 1, vv. 15–16 (English translation, Shantideva, *Way*, p. 33).
217. Longchenpa, *Finding Rest in the Nature of the Mind*, chap. 8, v. 15 (English translation, p. 88).
218. Longchenpa, chap. 8, vv. 32–33 (English translation, p. 92).
219. Śāntideva, *Way of the Bodhisattva*, chap. 2, v. 26 (English translation, Shantideva, *Way*, p. 41).
220. Śāntideva, chap. 3, vv. 23–24 (English translation, Shantideva, *Way*, p. 50).
221. Longchenpa, *Finding Rest in the Nature of the Mind*, chap. 8, v. 34 (English translation, pp. 92–93).
222. Śāntideva, *Way of the Bodhisattva*, chap. 3, vv. 26–28 (English translation, Shantideva, *Way*, pp. 50–51).
223. This is the four-line verse taken from the Minling Dorsem preliminary practice.
224. These four aspects of the bodhisattva vow are mentioned by Shāntideva in his *Śikṣāsamuccaya*:

    My body and my worldly wealth,
    My virtues present, past, and those to come,
    I will give them all to every being,
    And protect and purify and increase them.

    For a detailed explanation, see Jigme Lingpa and Longchen Yeshe Dorje, *Treasury*, bk. 1, pp. 317–18 and 475n205.
225. Chandraprabhākumāra was a doctor at the time of the Buddha. As predicted in the sūtras, he later manifested as the great Tibetan master Gampopa, who was also known by this name.
226. Longchenpa, *Finding Rest in the Nature of the Mind*, chap. 8, v. 36 (English translation, p. 93).
227. Śāntideva, *Way of the Bodhisattva*, chap. 8, v. 131 (English translation, Shantideva, *Way*, p. 128).
228. An English translation of Shechen Gyaltsap's commentary on the Seven-Point Mind Training has been published in Zhechen Gyaltsab, *Path of Heroes*. See also a similar commentary in Dilgo Khyentse, *Enlightened Courage*.
229. This well-known prayer is found at the beginning of many rituals and sādhanas:

    In the Buddha, the Dharma, and the Supreme Assembly
    We take refuge until we attain enlightenment.
    By the merit of practicing generosity and the like

May we attain buddhahood for the benefit of beings.

230. *Ritual for Arousing Bodhichitta.*
231. Longchenpa, *Finding Rest in the Nature of the Mind*, chap. 8, v. 38 (English translation, p. 94).
232. Longchenpa, chap. 8, v. 36 (English translation, p. 93).
233. Gampopa Sönam Rinchen, *Jewel Ornament of Liberation*, chap. 11.
234. Gampopa Sönam Rinchen, chap. 11.
235. Maitreya/Asaṅga, *Ornament of the Mahāyāna Sūtras*, chap. 17, v. 2 (English translation, modified, from Maitreya and Jamgön Mipham, *Feast*, p. 77).
236. Maitreya/Asaṅga, chap. 17, v. 7 (English translation from Maitreya and Jamgön Mipham, *Feast*, p. 78).
237. Maitreya/Asaṅga, chap. 17, v. 14 (English translation from Maitreya and Jamgön Mipham, *Feast*, p. 79).
238. Maitreya/Asaṅga, chap. 17, v. 8 (English translation from Maitreya and Jamgön Mipham, *Feast*, p. 78).
239. Maitreya/Asaṅga, chap. 17, vv. 9–13 (English translation from Maitreya and Jamgön Mipham, *Feast*, p. 78).
240. Maitreya/Asaṅga, chap. 17, v. 15 (English translation from Maitreya and Jamgön Mipham, *Feast*, p. 79).
241. Maitreya/Asaṅga, *Ornament of Clear Realization*, chap. 1, v. 43.
242. Maitreya/Asaṅga, *Ornament of the Mahāyāna Sūtras*, chap. 19, v. 40 (English translation from Maitreya and Jamgön Mipham, *Feast*, p. 104).
243. Tib. *gzhan yang*, literally, "furthermore." Having completed his explanation of the six heads listed by Gampopa at the beginning of this section, Shechen Gyaltsap adds a section on the practice of the transcendent perfections.
244. Maitreya/Asaṅga, *Ornament of the Mahāyāna Sūtras*, chap. 20, vv. 28–29 (English translation from Maitreya and Jamgön Mipham, *Feast*, p. 116).
245. Maitreya/Asaṅga, chap. 17, vv. 30–35 (English translation from Maitreya and Jamgön Mipham, *Feast*, p. 81). These six verses are identical except for the name of the respective transcendent perfection in their first lines.
246. Maitreya/Asaṅga, *Distinguishing the Middle from Extremes*, chap. 5, vv. 3–4.
247. Maitreya/Asaṅga, *Ornament of the Mahāyāna Sūtras*, chap. 17, v. 42 (English translation from Maitreya and Jamgön Mipham, *Feast*, p. 83).
248. Maitreya/Asaṅga, chap. 17, v. 4 (English translation from Maitreya and Jamgön Mipham, *Feast*, p. 77).
249. Nāgārjuna, *Jewel Garland*, v. 438.
250. Nāgārjuna, v. 212.
251. Maitreya/Asaṅga, *Ornament of the Mahāyāna Sūtras*, chap. 17, v. 18 (English translation from Maitreya and Jamgön Mipham, *Feast*, p. 79).
252. Longchenpa, *Finding Rest in the Nature of the Mind*, chap. 8, v. 44 (English translation, pp. 95–96).
253. See Jamgön Kongtrul, *Treasury of Knowledge: Book Five: Buddhist Ethics*,

trans. Kalu Rinpoché Translation Group (Ithaca, NY: Snow Lion Publications, 2003), 179–81 and 187–91.

254. Śāntideva, *Way of the Bodhisattva*, chap. 5, v. 71 (English translation, Shantideva, *Way*, p. 71).
255. Śāntideva, chap. 5, v. 79 (English translation, Shantideva, *Way*, p. 72).
256. Śāntideva, chap. 5, v. 93 (English translation, Shantideva, *Way*, p. 74).
257. Śāntideva, chap. 6, vv. 2, 42, 107 (last two lines), 108 (English translation, Shantideva, *Way*, pp. 77, 83, 92).
258. Śāntideva, chap. 6, v. 31 (last two lines); chap. 9, vv. 151 (first two lines), 152 (second line), 154 (first two lines) (English translation, Shantideva, *Way*, pp. 81, 158, 159).
259. Śāntideva, chap. 6, v. 72; chap. 7, v. 22 (English translation, Shantideva, *Way*, pp. 87, 100).
260. Śāntideva, chap. 6, v. 1 (English translation, Shantideva, *Way*, p. 77).
261. Śāntideva, chap. 6, v. 134 (English translation, Shantideva, *Way*, p. 96).
262. Śāntideva, chap. 7, v. 66 (English translation, Shantideva, *Way*, p. 106).
263. Śāntideva, chap. 5, v. 101 (English translation, Shantideva, *Way*, p. 75).
264. This line appears to be a contraction of the first two lines of Śāntideva, *Way of the Bodhisattva*, chap. 7, v. 7, which read (English translation, Shantideva, *Way*, p. 98):

    Death will swoop on you so swiftly.
    Gather merit till that moment comes!

265. Maitreya/Asaṅga, *Ornament of the Mahāyāna Sūtras*, chap. 17, v. 67 (first line) (English translation from Maitreya and Jamgön Mipham, *Feast*, p. 86).
266. It has not been possible to identify this source precisely.
267. Śāntideva, *Way of the Bodhisattva*, chap. 8, v. 4 (English translation, Shantideva, *Way*, p. 109).
268. Maitreya/Asaṅga, *Ornament of the Mahāyāna Sūtras*, chap. 7, v. 8 (English translation from Maitreya and Jamgön Mipham, *Feast*, p. 22).
269. A scribal error appears to have occurred in the attribution of this quotation to Nāgārjuna's *Letter to a Friend*: it does not appear in extant versions of that text. On the other hand, we have found it in Sajjana's *Letter to a Son*; it is also identical to two lines from Śāntideva's *Way of the Bodhisattva* (chap. 8, v. 79).
270. Nāgārjuna, *Letter to a Friend*, v. 34 (English translation from Nagarjuna and Longchen Yeshe Dorje, *Nagarjuna's "Letter,"* p. 41).
271. Śāntideva, *Way of the Bodhisattva*, chap. 8, vv. 9–12, 14 (last two lines), 15 (first line) (English translation, Shantideva, *Way*, pp. 110, 111).
272. Śāntideva, chap. 8, vv. 25–27 (English translation, Shantideva, *Way*, pp. 112–13).
273. Longchenpa, *Finding Rest in the Nature of the Mind*, chap. 8, v. 65 (English translation, p. 100).
274. For some of the different qualities listed here, see Jigme Lingpa and Longchen Yeshe Dorje, *Treasury*, appendix 9, 431–35.

275. Śāntideva, *Way of the Bodhisattva*, chap. 5, vv. 16–17 (English translation, Shantideva, *Way*, p. 63).
276. Maitreya/Asaṅga, *Ornament of the Mahāyāna Sūtras*, chap. 12, v. 60 (English translation from Maitreya and Jamgön Mipham, *Feast*, p. 53).
277. The lineage teachers Shechen Gyaltsap Rinpoche is referring to here are, respectively, the Omniscient Longchenpa (1308–1363), Rongzom Paṇḍita (1012–1088), the brothers Terdak Lingpa Gyurme Dorje (1646–1714) and Lochen Dharmashrī (1654–1717) of Mindrölling, Rigdzin Jigme Lingpa (1729–1798), Katokpa Dampa Deshek (1122–1192) and his successors, and Jamyang Khyentse Wangpo (1820–1892), Jamgön Kongtrul Lodrö Thaye (1813–1899), and Ju Mipham (1846–1912).
278. Shechen Gyaltsap is again quoting from Longchenpa, *Essential Instructions for Finding Rest in the Nature of the Mind.*
279. Longchenpa.
280. Maitreya/Asaṅga, *Sublime Continuum*, chap. 1, v. 157.
281. Although this quotation is attributed to kLu grub, the usual Tibetan name of Nāgārjuna, we have only been able to locate it in the *Ratnāsūkośa* (Toh. 3839) by Nāgārjunagarbha (Tib. kLu grub snying po).
282. Śāntideva, *Way of the Bodhisattva*, chap. 5, v. 101 (English translation, Shantideva, *Way*, p. 75).
283. See Jigme Lingpa and Longchen Yeshe Dorje, *Treasury*, bk. 1, p. 459n114 for an explanation of the significance of the dominant condition (Tib. *bdag po'i rkyen*).
284. Longchenpa, *Finding Rest in the Nature of the Mind*, chap. 8, v. 36 (English translation, p. 93).
285. Śāntideva, *Way of the Bodhisattva*, chap. 4, vv. 6, 10 (English translation, Shantideva, *Way*, p. 54).
286. This quotation and the two similar quotations below concerning individuals of middling and supreme capacity appear to be taken from Kṛishṇa Paṇḍita, *Ascertainment of Difficult Points.*
287. Śāntideva, *Way of the Bodhisattva*, chap. 5, v. 98 (English translation, Shantideva, *Way*, p. 75).
288. Śāntideva, chap. 1, v. 9 (English translation, Shantideva, *Way*, p. 32).
289. Śāntideva, chap. 1, v. 10 (English translation, Shantideva, *Way*, p. 32).
290. Śāntideva, chap. 1, v. 11 (English translation, Shantideva, *Way*, p. 32).
291. Śāntideva, chap. 1, v. 12 (English translation, Shantideva, *Way*, p. 33).
292. Nāgārjuna, *Jewel Garland*, chap. 1, vv. 20 (first two lines) and 21 (first two lines).
293. Śāntideva, *Way of the Bodhisattva*, chap. 2, v. 62 (English translation, Shantideva, *Way*, p. 46).
294. Śāntideva, chap. 2, vv. 28–31 (English translation, Shantideva, *Way*, p. 41).
295. Tib. *chos bzhi*, also translatable as "four things" or "four ways" (Skt. *dharmas*).
296. Śāntideva, *Way of the Bodhisattva*, chap. 5, v. 31; chap. 2, v. 27 (English translation, Shantideva, *Way*, pp. 65, 41).

297. Śāntideva, chap. 1, v. 14 (English translation, Shantideva, *Way*, p. 33).
298. Śāntideva, chap. 2, vv. 34–35 (English translation, Shantideva, *Way*, p. 42).
299. Śāntideva, chap. 2, v. 40 (English translation, Shantideva, *Way*, p. 43).
300. Śāntideva, chap. 2, vv. 43, 44, 41 (English translation, Shantideva, *Way*, p. 43).
301. Nāgārjuna, *Letter to a Friend*, vv. 83–84 (English translation from Nagarjuna and Longchen Yeshe Dorje, *Nagarjuna's "Letter,"* pp. 59, 61).
302. Śāntideva, *Way of the Bodhisattva*, chap. 2, v. 32 (English translation, Shantideva, *Way*, p. 41).
303. Śāntideva, chap. 2, v. 33 (English translation, Shantideva, *Way*, p. 42).
304. *mTshan'bum nor bu'i phreng ba las khol phyung gces btus*, a compilation by Mipham Rinpoche.
305. Mipham Rinpoche's *A Hundred Mantras That Cut the Stream of Karma and Obscurations* (*Las sgrib rgyun gcod gyi sngags brgya pa*).
306. Śāntideva, *Way of the Bodhisattva*, chap. 2, v. 65 (English translation, Shantideva, *Way*, p. 46).
307. A note in the corresponding passage in Dudjom Rinpoche's instructions on the preliminary practices points out that the short necklace reaches down to the breast, while the long one reaches down to the navel. See Dudjom Rinpoche, *A Torch Lighting the Way to Freedom*, trans. Padmakara Translation Group (Boston: Shambhala Publications, 2011).
308. For the sake of completeness, we have inserted this section of the recitation text for the Minling Dorsem preliminary practices.
309. Taken from the Minling Dorsem preliminary practices.
310. Nāgārjuna, *Letter to a Friend*, v. 14 (English translation from Nagarjuna and Longchen Yeshe Dorje, *Nagarjuna's "Letter,"* p. 33).
311. *gSang ba spyi rgyud*. This appears to be another name for Mañjuśrīkīrti's *Essential Ornament of the Rituals Common to All the Secret Teachings*.
312. Chögyal Phakpa (1235–1280) was a great scholar of the Sakya tradition.
313. This is the verse for the maṇḍala offering from the Minling Dorsem preliminary practices.
314. Maitreya/Asaṅga, *Ornament of the Mahāyāna Sūtras*, chap. 18, vv. 1–2 (English translation from Maitreya and Jamgön Mipham, *Feast*, p. 89).
315. For a detailed explanation of these ten forms of veneration, see Ārya Asaṅga, *The Bodhisattva Path to Unsurpassed Enlightenment*, trans. Artemus B. Engle (Boulder, CO: Snow Lion, 2016), chap. 16, pp. 387–96.
316. Śāntideva, *Way of the Bodhisattva*, chap. 5, v. 81 (last two lines) (English translation, Shantideva, *Way*, p. 72).
317. Nāgārjuna, *Jewel Garland*, v. 487 (last two lines).
318. Śāntideva, *Way of the Bodhisattva*, chap. 1, vv. 21–22 (English translation, Shantideva, *Way*, p. 34).
319. Śāntideva, chap. 1, v. 27 (English translation, Shantideva, *Way*, p. 35).
320. Maitreya/Asaṅga, *Ornament of the Mahāyāna Sūtras*, chap. 18, v. 59 (English translation from Maitreya and Jamgön Mipham, *Feast*, p. 97).

321. Śāntideva, *Way of the Bodhisattva*, chap. 2, v. 1 (English translation, Shantideva, *Way*, p. 37).
322. The seven forms of merit derived from material gifts (Tib. *dzas las 'byung ba'i bsod nams bdun*) are defined as follows: (1) the offering of temples to the monastic community; (2) the offering of gardens; (3) the offering of bedding and clothes; (4) the offering of nourishment on a continuous basis—that is, offering food and drink daily for months or years; (5) offering meals to monks who arrive unexpectedly; (6) offering supplies and provisions to the sick and nurses; (7) offering food and drink in times of disasters due to wind, rain, or famine.
323. *De kho na nyid bstan pa'i mdo*. Also referred to in other sources as *de kho na nyid nges par bstan pa'i mdo*. This quotation appears to be a résumé of a passage in the *Sūtra of the Meeting of the Father with the Son*.
324. The reference to Gampopa's work here in the text reads *Chos rje sgam po pas lam mchog rin chen thar pa'i rgyan*, which we have been unable to identify as a single work. Both Gampopa's *Lam mchog rin chen phreng ba* (*Jeweled Garland of the Sublime Path*) and his *Thar pa rin po che'i rgyan* (*Jewel Ornament of Liberation*) cover the whole path. However, Shechen Gyaltsap is most probably referring to the concluding section of the chapter on transcendent wisdom in the latter work.
325. Tib. *sGyu 'phrul brgya pa*. We have been unable to locate a tantra of this name. The source of this quotation is mentioned in the autocommentary of the *Precious Treasury That Fulfills All Wishes* as being *sGyu 'phrul rgyas pa* (*Extensive Magical Manifestation Tantra*), but we have failed to identify this work precisely. Could the title given here be a misprint for *sGyu 'phrul brgyad pa* (*Magical Manifestation Tantra in Eight Chapters*), G527 in the Collection of Old Tantras (*rNying ma rgyud 'bum*)?
326. Maitreya/Asaṅga, *Ornament of the Mahāyāna Sūtras*, chap. 18, v. 10 (English translation from Maitreya and Jamgön Mipham, *Feast*, p. 90).
327. Although the Tibetan here reads *ma lta bu*, "like mothers," we have followed the original source text, which reads *ma ma lta bu*, "like nursemaids."
328. Longchenpa, *Finding Rest in the Nature of the Mind*, chap. 5, v. 9 (English translation, p. 54).
329. Maitreya/Asaṅga, *Sublime Continuum*, chap. 4, v. 29.
330. Śāntideva, *Way of the Bodhisattva*, chap. 9, v. 35 (English translation, Shantideva, *Way*, p. 142).
331. Longchenpa, *Finding Rest in the Nature of the Mind*, chap. 5, vv. 16–21 (English translation, pp. 57–58).
332. Shechen Gyaltsap again quotes from the *Three Stages*.
333. Aśvaghoṣa, *Fifty Verses on the Teacher*, vv. 11–14.
334. Longchenpa, *Finding Rest in the Nature of the Mind*, chap. 5, vv. 22–26 (English translation, pp. 58–59).

335. Śāntideva, *Way of the Bodhisattva*, chap. 5, vv. 40, 41, 23 (English translation, Shantideva, *Way*, pp. 67, 64).
336. Śāntideva, chap. 5, v. 30 (English translation, Shantideva, *Way*, p. 65).
337. Maitreya/Asaṅga, *Ornament of Clear Realization*, chap. 4, v. 44 (last line).
338. Tib. *smyig ma mkhan*, people who do work that is despised. Another version of this quotation has *sme sha can*, referring to very low castes, which includes such people as butchers.
339. Jigme Lingpa, *Treasury*, chap, 5, vv. 39–40 (English translation from Jigme Lingpa and Longchen Yeshe Dorje, *Treasury*, bk 1, p. 46).
340. Chetsun Senge Wangchuk (lCe btsun seng ge dbang phyug), an eleventh–twelfth century Tibetan master in the lineage of the Great Perfection, whose teachings were rediscovered by Jamyang Khyentse Wangpo in the nineteenth century and written down as the *Heart Essence of Chetsun* (Tib. *lCe btsun snying tig*).
341. Tib. *dbang phyug*, lit. "almighty." The Tibetan also translates the name of Īshvara, the creator of the world according to some non-Buddhist Indian traditions.
342. Virūpa was one of the eighty-four mahāsiddhas of India and an important figure in the lineage of the Sakya tradition in Tibet.
343. Drikung Kyobpa (1143–1217), the founder of Drikung Monastery in Tibet and of the Drikung Kagyu school.
344. Longchenpa, *Finding Rest in the Nature of the Mind*, chap. 8, v. 16 (English translation, p. 88).
345. Longchenpa, chap. 8, v. 17 (English translation, p. 89).
346. Longchenpa, chap. 8, v. 18 (English translation, p. 89).
347. Taken from the Minling Dorsem preliminary practices.
348. The lineage prayer from the Minling Dorsem preliminary practices. The last two lines refer to the practices of the Great Perfection.
349. Sakya Paṇḍita Kunga Gyaltsen (1182–1251) was one of the foremost masters and scholars of the Sakya tradition in Tibetan Buddhism.
350. Taken from the Minling Dorsem preliminary practices.
351. Maitreya/Asaṅga, *Ornament of the Mahāyāna Sūtras*, chap. 18, v. 14ab (English translation from Maitreya and Jamgön Mipham, *Feast*, p. 91).
352. Jigme Lingpa, *Treasury*, chap. 5, v. 47 (English translation from Jigme Lingpa and Longchen Yeshe Dorje, *Treasury*, bk. 1, p. 47).
353. For the six exegetical perspectives and the four expository methods (or four ways of exposition), see Jigme Lingpa and Longchen Yeshe Dorje, *Treasury*, bk. 2, appendix 2, pp. 333–36.
354. The title *Sūtra of the Arborescent Array* is here being used to refer to the *Sūtra of the Ornament of the Buddhas*, of which it is the final section. This quotation is to be found in an earlier section in the *Avataṃsaka*.
355. *De kho na nyid bstan pa'i mdo*. Also called in other sources *de kho na nyid nges par bstan pa'i mdo*. This quotation appears to be a résumé of a passage in the *Sūtra of the Meeting of the Father with the Son*.

356. Tib. *ting nge 'dzin zad par snang ba.*
357. Tib. *khyim can zhes bya ba'i gzungs.* We have been unable to trace the original Sanskrit terms for this and the above-mentioned concentration: our translation of these terms should not be taken as definitive.

Bibliography

The bibliography comprises three main sections, each separately alphabetized: (1) works cited in *A Chariot to Freedom* (subdivided into canonical scriptures, canonical treatises, Tibetan works, preliminary practice texts, and works in English translation; (2) works mentioned but not quoted from in *A Chariot to Freedom* (subdivided into canonical scriptures and treatises, and Tibetan works; and (3) English-language sources

Works Cited in *A Chariot to Freedom*

Canonical Scriptures

Auspicious Awareness Cuckoo Tantra (*bKra shis rig pa khu byug gi rgyud*). Tb. 19.

Avalokinī Sūtra (*'Phags pa spyan ras gzigs kyi mdo, Avalokinī-sūtra*). Toh. 195.

Basket's Display (*Za ma tog bkod pa, Karaṇḍavyūha-sūtra*). Toh. 116.

Bodhisattva's Scriptural Collection (*Byang chub sems dpa'i sde snod, Bodhisattvapiṭaka-sūtra*). Toh. 56.

Chapter on Images of the Tathāgata (*De bzhin gshegs pa'i sku gzugs kyi le'u*). NL.

Chapter on Mañjuśrī's Magical Display (*'Jam dpal rnam par 'phrul pa'i mdo, Mañjuśrī-vikurvāṇaparivarta*). Toh. 97.

Chapters of Utterances on Specific Topics (*Ched du brjod pa'i tshoms, Udānavarga*). Toh. 326.

Close Mindfulness Sūtra (*Dam chos dran pa nyer ba'i bzhag pa'i mdo, Saddharmasmṛtyupasthāna*). Toh. 287.

Compendium of the Buddhas' Wisdom (*mDo dgongs pa 'dus pa, Samājasarvavidyāsūtra*). A tantra, one of the four root "sūtras" of Anuyoga. Toh. 829.

Complete Compendium of Vaidalya (*rNam par 'thag pa thams cad bsdus pa'i mdo, Sarvavaidalyasaṃgraha-sūtra*). Toh. 227.

Detailed Explanations of Discipline (*Lung rnam 'byed, Vinayavibhaṅga*). Toh. 3.

Details of Empowerment (*dBang rnam par phye ba*). NL.

Discourse on Impermanence (*Mi rtag pa'i gtam*). NL.

Display of the Secret (*gSang ba rol pa*). NL.

Essence of the Sun Sūtra (*Nyi ma'i snying po'i mdo, Sūryagarbha-sūtra*). Toh. 257.

Extensive Magical Manifestation Tantra (*sGyu 'phrul rgyas pa*). Another name for *The Secret Nucleus Definitive with respect to the Real*, also known as the *Eighty-Chapter Guhyagarbha Tantra* (*gSang ba'i snying po de kho na nyid nges pa*). Toh. 834.

Extensive Sūtra of the Great Realization (*rTogs pa chen po rgyas pa'i mdo*). Translated from the Chinese. Toh. 265.

Four Stanzas (*Tshigs su bcad pa bzhi pa, Caturgāthā*). Toh. 324.

Garret Sūtra (*Khang bu brtsegs pa'i mdo, Kūṭāgāra-sūtra*). Toh. 332.

Great Array. See *Great Array of the Sublime*.

Great Array of the Sublime (*A ti bkod pa chen po*). A tantra of the Great Perfection. Ng. 277.

Great Close Mindfulness Sūtra. See *Close Mindfulness Sūtra*.

Great Collection Sūtra of the Incantations of Ratnaketu (*'Dus pa rin po che'i tog, Mahāsannipātaratnaketu-dhāraṇī*). Toh. 138.

Guhyagarbha Tantra (*rGyud gsang ba snying po*). The *Tantra of the Secret Essence*. Toh. 832.

Guhyasamāja Root Tantra (*gSang 'dus rtsa rgyud*). Toh. 442.

Guhyasamāja Tantra (*gSang ba 'dus pa*). The *Tantra of the Union of Secrets*. Toh. 442.

Heap of Jewels (*dKon mchog brtsegs pa, Ratnakūṭa*). A collection of sūtras. Toh. 45–93.

Heruka Galpo (*He ru ka gal po*). One of the eighteen tantras of Mahāyoga. Ng. 646.

Hevajra Tantra (*He badzra*). Toh. 471.

Hundred Parables on Action (*Las brgya pa, Karmaśataka*). Toh. 340.

Hundred Thousand (*'Bum pa*). NL.

Incantation: The Heap of Flowers (*Me tog brtsegs pa'i gzungs, Puṣpakūṭa-dhāraṇī*). Toh. 516.

Incantation of the Goddess Cundā (*sKul byed kyi gzungs, Cundādevī-dhāraṇī*). Toh. 613.

Incantation of the Pure Immaculate Rays of Light (*'Od zer dri med kyi gzungs, Raśmivimalaviśuddhaprabhā-dhāraṇī*). Toh. 510.

Incantation of Vimaloṣṇīṣa (*gTsug tor dri med, Uṣṇīṣaprabhāsasarvatathāgatahṛdaya-samayavilokita-dhāraṇī*). Toh. 599.

Indestructible Net of Magical Manifestations (*sGyu 'phrul rdo rje*). Ng. 534.

Infinite Secret (*gSang ba rab 'byams*). NL.

Jewel Cloud Sūtra (*dKon mchog sprin, Ratnamegha-sūtra*). Toh. 231.

Kālacakra Tantra (*Dus 'khor*). Toh 362.

Kaśyāpa Chapter (*'Od srung gis zhus pa*). See *Sūtra of the Discourse for Kāśyapa*.

King of Tantras: The Magical Display (*sGyu 'phrul rgyal po*). See *Tantra of the Net of Magical Display*.

Knowledge of the Ultimate (*Don dam rig pa*). Possibly part of *Songs from the Treasury of Dohās* (*Do ha mdzod kyi glu, Dohākoṣagīti*). Toh. 2224.

Lotus Pinnacle (*Padma rtse mo*). NL.

Magical Manifestation Tantra in One Hundred Chapters (*sGyu 'phrul brgya pa*). Possibly a mistaken reference to the *Magical Manifestation Tantra in Eight Chapters* (*sGyu 'phrul brgyad pa*), Ng. 527.

Mahāparinirvāṇa Sūtra (*Mya ngan las 'das pa'i mdo, Mahāparinirvāṇa-sūtra*). Toh. 119.

Maṇḍala Sūtra (*Maṇḍala gyi mdo, Maṇḍalavidhi*). Toh. 376.

Manifestation of Gnosis (*Ye shes mngon phyung*). NL.

Mass of Jewels Sūtra (*Rin chen phung po'i mdo, Ratnarāśi-sūtra*). Toh. 88.

Method for Accomplishing Uṣṇīṣacakravartin (*gTsug tor 'khor los sgyur ba, Uṣṇīṣacakravartisādhana*). NL.

Middle Sūtra of the Perfection of Wisdom (*Yum bar ma*). Toh. 9.

Mirror of the Heart of Vajrasattva (*rDo rje sems dpa' snying gi me long*). Ng. 98.

Moon Lamp Sūtra (*Zla ba sgron ma'i mdo*). Apparently another name for the *Sūtra of the King of Concentrations.* Toh. 127.

Ocean of Gnosis Tantra (*Ye shes rgya mtsho'i rgyud*). NL.

Ocean of Scriptures (*gZhung rgya mtsho*). NL.

Ocean-Like Source of Nectar Tantra (*bDud rtsi rgya mtsho 'byung ba'i rgyud*). NL.

Ornament of the Indestructible Essence (*rDo rje snying po rgyan, Vajrahṛdayaalaṃkāratantra*). Toh. 451.

Perfection of Wisdom. A general reference to the Prajñāpāramitā sūtras indicated in the Tibetan as *Sher phyin, Sher mdo, Yum,* and so forth. Toh. 8–30.

Perfection of Wisdom in Eight Thousand Lines (*brGyad stong pa, Aṣṭasāhasrikāprajñāpāramitā*). Toh. 12.

Perfection of Wisdom in One Hundred Thousand Lines (*Sher phyin stong phrag brgya pa, Śatasāhasrikāprajñāpāramitā*). Toh. 8.

Play in Full (*rGya cher rol pa, Lalitavistara*). Toh. 95.

Praise and Confession of the Bodhisattva Downfalls. See *Sūtra in Three Sections.*

Prayer of Good Action (*bZang spyod smon lam, Bhadracaryā-praṇidhāna*). The final section of the *Sūtra of the Arborescent Array.* Toh. 44.

Profound Path (*Lam zab pa*). NL.

Rampant Elephant Tantra (*rGyud glang po rab 'bog*). A Mahāyoga scripture. Dg. 219.

Root Tantra of Mañjuśrī (*'Jam dpal rtsa rgyud, Mañjuśrīmūlakalpa*). Toh. 543.

Root Tantra of Saṃvara (*bDe mchog rtsa rgyud*). Toh. 368.

Root Tantra of the Accomplishment of Gnosis (*Ye shes grub pa'i rtsa rgyud*). NL.

Sayings on Impermanence (*Mi rtag pa'i tshoms*). NL.

Secret Essence of the Magical Display (*sGyu 'phrul gsang snying*). Another name for the *Guhyagarbha Tantra.* Toh. 832.

Secret Lamp (*gSang sgron*). NL.

Secret Tantra of Vajrakīlaya (*rDo rje phur pa'i gsang rgyud*). Pt. 343.

Smaller Saṃvara Tantra (*bDe mchog nyung ngu'i rgyud, Laghusaṃvara*). Toh. 368.

Source of Nectar Tantra (*bDud rtsi 'byung ba'i rgyud*). NL.

Sovereign Lord of Sūtras: The Sublime Golden Light (*gSer 'od dam pa'i mdo, Suvarṇaprabhāsottamasūtrendrarāja*). Toh. 557.

Śrīgupta Sūtra (*dPal sbas kyis zhus pa'i mdo, Śrīgupta-sūtra*). Toh. 217.

Stainless Wisdom (*Ye shes dri med*). NL.

Story of Śrīsambhava (*dPal 'byung ba'i rnam thar*). Part of the *Sūtra of the Arborescent Array*. Toh. 44.

Sublime Essence (*sNying po mchog*). NL.

Sublime Ornament (*rGyan dam pa*). NL.

Succession of Ṛṣi Teachers (*Phal po che'i drang srong bla ma'i rabs*). A section of the *Sūtra of the Ornament of the Buddhas*. Toh. 44.

Supplementary Tantra of Vairocana's Enlightenment (*rNam snang mngon byang gi rgyud phyi ma*). Toh. 494.

Supreme Victory Banner Sūtra (*mDo rgyal mtshan dam pa, Dhvajāgra-mahā-sūtra*). Toh. 293.

Supreme Wish-Fulfilling Tantra (*Yid bzhin mchog gi rgyud*). NL.

Sūtra in Three Sections (*'Phags pa phung po gsum, Triskandhaka-sūtra*). Also called the *Sūtra of the Three Heaps*. Toh. 284.

Sūtra of Advice to the King (*rGyal po la gdams pa'i mdo, Rājāvavādaka-sūtra*). Toh. 221.

Sūtra of Ambrosial Speech (*'Phags pa bdud rtsi brjod pa zhes bya ba'i theg pa chen po'i mdo, Āryāmṛtadāna-nāma-mahāyāna-sūtra*). Toh. 197.

Sūtra of Great Liberation (*Thar pa chen po'i mdo, Mokṣa-sūtra*). Translated from the Chinese. Toh. 264.

Sūtra of Individual Liberation (*So sor thar pa'i mdo, Prātimokṣa-sūtra*). Toh. 2.

Sūtra of Maitreya's Great Lion's Roar (*Byams pa seng ge sgra chen pos zhus pa'i mdo, Maitreyamahāsiṃhanāda-sūtra*). Part of the *Heap of Jewels*. Toh. 67.

Sūtra of Manifest Enlightenment (*mNgon par byang chub pa'i mdo*). Probably a reference to part of the *Play in Full*. Toh. 95.

Sūtra of Precious Space (*Nam mkha' rin po che'i mdo*). NL.

Sūtra of Pure Aspiration (*sMon lam rnam par dag pa'i mdo*). NL.

Sūtra of Skill in Means: The Great Secret of All the Buddhas (*gSang chen thabs la mkhas pa'i mdo, Sarvabuddhamahārahasyopāyakauśalyajñānottarabodhisattvaparipṛcchāparivarta-sūtra*). Also called the *Chapter of the Bodhisattva Jñānottara's Questions*. Toh. 82.

Sūtra of the Arborescent Array (*'Phags pa sdong po bkod pa'i mdo, Gaṇḍavyūha*). The final chapter of the *Avataṃsaka Sūtra*. Toh 44.

Sūtra of the Array of Qualities of Mañjuśrī's Buddha-Field (*'Jam dpal zhing gi yon tan bkod pa, Mañjuśrībuddhakṣetraguṇavyūha-sūtra*). Toh. 59.

Sūtra of the Buddha's Treasury (*Sangs rgyas mdzod kyi mdo*). Toh. 123.

Sūtra of the Densely Ornamented Array (*rGyan stug po bkod pa, Ghanavyūha-sūtra*). Toh. 110.

Sūtra of the Discourse for Kāśyapa (*'Od srungs kyi zhus pa, Kāśyapaparivarta-sūtra*). A chapter from the *Heap of Jewels*. Toh. 87.

Sūtra of the Display of Armor (*Go cha bkod pa'i mdo, Varmavyūhanirdeśa-sūtra*). Toh. 51.

Sūtra of the Fortunate Kalpa (*mDo sde bskal bzang*, *Bhadrakalpika-sūtra*). Toh. 94.
Sūtra of the Full Array of Qualities (*Yon tan yongs su bkod pa'i mdo*). NL.
Sūtra of the Gong (*Gaṇḍi'i mdo*, *Gaṇḍīsūtra*). Toh. 298.
Sūtra of the Great Crown Protuberance (*gTsug tor chen mo'i mdo*). Translated from part of the Chinese *Śūraṃgamasūtra*. Toh. 236.
Sūtra of the Great Vehicle That Teaches All Phenomena as Being Without Origin (*'Phags pa chos thams cad 'byung ba med par bstan pa zhes bya ba theg pa chen po'i mdo*, *Sarvadharmāpravṛttinirdeśa-sūtra*). Toh. 180.
Sūtra of the Inconceivable Secrets (*gSang ba bsam gyis mi khyab pa'i mdo*, *Tathāgatācintyaguhyanirdeśa-sūtra*). Part of the *Heap of Jewels*. Toh. 47.
Sūtra of the King of Concentrations (*Ting 'dzin rgyal po*, *Samādhirāja-sūtra*). Toh. 127.
Sūtra of the King of Dharma (*Chos kyi rgyal po'i mdo*, *Saddharmarāja-sūtra*). Toh. 243.
Sūtra of the Lion's Roar of Śrīmālādevī (*dPal phreng gi mdo*, *Śrīmālādevīsiṃhanāda-sūtra*). Part of the *Heap of Jewels*. Toh. 92.
Sūtra of the Magical Tree (*lJon shing gi mdo*). Included in mDo mang, a collection of short canonical texts and dharani, possibly translated from the Chinese canon. BDRC W1KG12536.
Sūtra of the Marks That Inspire the Development of Faith (*'Phags pa dad pa'i stobs bskyed pa la 'jug pa'i phyag rgya'i mdo*, *Śraddhābalādhānāvatāramudrā-sūtra*). Toh. 201.
Sūtra of the Meeting of the Father with the Son (*Yab sras mjal gyi mdo*, *Pitāputrasamāgama-sūtra*). Toh. 60.
Sūtra of the Ornament of the Buddhas (*Sangs rgyas phal po che*, *Buddhāvataṃsaka-sūtra*). Toh. 44.
Sūtra of the Ornament of the Light of Gnosis (*Ye shes snang ba rgyan gyi mdo*, *Sarvabuddhaviṣayāvatārajñānālokālaṃkāra-sūtra*). Toh. 100.
Sūtra of the Play of Mañjuśrī (*'Jam dpal rnam par rol ba*, *Mañjuśrīvikrīḍita-sūtra*). Toh. 96.
Sūtra of the Play of the River That Leads to Peace (*Zhi byed chu klung rol pa'i mdo*). NL.
Sūtra of the Precious Lamp (*dKon mchog ta la la'i mdo*, *Ratnolkādhāraṇīsūtra*). Toh. 145.
Sūtra of the Prophecy for the Magician Bhadra (*sGyu ma mkhan bzang pos zhus pa'i mdo*, *Bhadramāyākaravyākaraṇa-sūtra*). Toh. 65.
Sūtra of the Questions of Brahmaviśeṣacintin (*Tshangs par khyad par sems kyis zhus pa'i mdo*, *Brahmaviśeṣacintiparipṛcchā-sūtra*). Toh. 160.
Sūtra of the Questions of Candragarbha (*zLa ba'i snying po'i mdo*). Toh. 356.
Sūtra of the Questions of Druma (*lJon pas zhus pa'i mdo*)). Possibly part of the *Sūtra of the Meeting of the Father with the Son*, *Pitāputrasamāgama-sūtra*. Toh. 60.
Sūtra of the Questions of Gaganagañja (*Nam mkha' mdzod kyi mdo*, *Gaganagañjaparipṛcchā-sūtra*). Toh. 148.
Sūtra of the Questions of Lokadhara (*'Phags pa 'jig rten 'dzin gyi dris pas lung bstan pa'i mdo*, *Lokadharaparipṛcchā-sūtra*). Toh. 174.
Sūtra of the Questions of Maitreya (*'Phags pa byams pas zhus pa'i mdo*, *Ārya-maitreyaparipṛcchā-nāma-mahāyāna-sūtra*). Toh. 85.

Sūtra of the Questions of Nārāyaṇa (*Sred med kyi bus zhus pa'i mdo, Nārāyaṇaparipṛcchā-dhāraṇī*). Also called *The Incantation: The Questions of Nārāyaṇa*. Toh. 684.

Sūtra of the Questions of Pūrṇa (*Gang po zhus pa, Pūrṇaparipṛcchā-sūtra*). Toh. 61.

Sūtra of the Questions of Rāṣṭrapāla (*Yul 'khor skyong gi zhus pa'i mdo, Ārya-rāṣṭrapāla-paripṛcchā-nāma-mahāyāna-sūtra*). Part of the *Heap of Jewels*. Toh. 62.

Sūtra of the Questions of Ratnacūḍa (*gTsug na rin chen gyis zhus pa'i mdo, Ratnacūḍa-paripṛcchā-sūtra*). Part of the *Heap of Jewels*. Toh. 91.

Sūtra of the Questions of Sāgaramati (*bLo gros rgya mtshos zhus pa'i mdo, Sāgaramati-paripṛcchā-sūtra*). Toh. 152.

Sūtra of the Questions of Subāhu (*Lag bzang gis zhus pa'i mdo, Subāhu-paripṛcchā-sūtra*). Toh. 70.

Sūtra of the Questions of Suratā (*Des pas zhus pa'i mdo, Suratā-paripṛcchā-sūtra*). Toh. 71.

Sūtra of the Questions of the Boy Ratnadatta (*Khye'u rin chen byin byis zhus pa'i mdo*). Possibly another name for the *Sūtra Teaching the Conduct of a Bodhisattva* (*Byang chub sems dpa'i spyod pa bstan pa'i mdo, Bodhisattvacaryānirdeśa-sūtra*). Toh. 184.

Sūtra of the Questions of the Devaputra Susthitamati (*bLo gros rab gnas kyis zhus pa'i mdo, Susthitamatidevaputra-paripṛcchā-sūtra*). Toh. 80.

Sūtra of the Questions of the Girl Sumati (*bLo gros bzang mos zhus pa'i mdo, Sumatidārikā-paripṛcchā-sūtra*). Toh. 74.

Sūtra of the Questions of the Householder Ugra (*Khyim bdag drag shul can gyis zhus pa'i mdo, Ugra-paripṛcchā-sūtra*). Toh. 63.

Sūtra of the Questions of the Nāga King Anavatapta (*Ma dros pas zhus pa'i mdo, Anavataptanāgarāja-paripṛcchā-sūtra*). Toh. 156.

Sūtra of the Questions of the Ṛṣi Vyāsa (*Drang srong rgyas pas zhus pa'i mdo, Ṛṣivyāsa-paripṛcchā-sūtra*). Toh. 93.

Sūtra of the Questions of Upāli (*Nye bar 'khor gyis zhus pa'i mdo, Vinayaviniścayopāli-paripṛcchā-sūtra*). Toh. 68.

Sūtra of the Questions of Vīradatta (*dPas byin gyis zhus pa'i mdo, Vīradatta-paripṛcchā-sūtra*). Toh. 72.

Sūtra of the Sublime Being (*'Phags pa skyes bu dam pa'i mdo, Satpuruṣa-sūtra*). Toh. 327.

Sūtra of the Supreme Concentration (*Ting nge 'dzin mchog dam pa, Samādhi-agra-uttama*). Toh. 137.

Sūtra of the Teaching of Akṣayamati (*'Phags pa blo gros mi zad pa'i mdo, Akṣayamati-paripṛcchā-sūtra*). Toh. 175.

Sūtra of the Teaching on the Four Qualities (*Chos bzhi bstan pa'i mdo, Caturdharma-nirdeśasūtra*). Toh. 249.

Sūtra of the Ten Qualities (*Chos bcu pa'i mdo Daśadharmakasūtra*). Toh. 53.

Sūtra of the Ten Wheels of Kṣitigarbha (*Sa'i snying po 'khor lo bcu pa'i mdo, Daśacakrakṣitigarbha-sūtra*). Toh. 239.

Sūtra of the Treasury of Jewels (*Rin chen mdzod kyi mdo*). NL.

Sūtra of the White Lotus of the Sacred Dharma (*Dam chos pad ma dkar po, Saddharmapuṇḍarīka-sūtra*). Toh. 113.

Sūtra of the Wise and the Foolish (*mDzangs blun*). Toh. 341.

Sūtra of Untainted Space (*Nam mkha' dri ma med pa'i mdo*). NL.

Sūtra on Correct Moral Discipline (*Tshul khrims yongs su dag pa'i mdo, Śīlasaṃyukta-sūtra*). Toh. 303.

Sūtra on Entering Laṅka (*Lang kar gshegs pa, Laṅkāvatāra-sūtra*). Toh. 107.

Sūtra on Maitreya's Setting Forth (*'Phags pa byams pa 'jug pa'i mdo, Maitreyaprasthāna-sūtra*). Toh. 198.

Sūtra on the Classification of Acts (*mDo sde las rnam 'byed, Karmavibhaṅga*). Toh. 338.

Sūtra on the Concentration of the Magical Display That Ascertains What Is Peace (*Rab zhi rnam nges kyi mdo, Praśāntaviniścayaprātihāryasamādhi*). Toh. 129.

Sūtra on the Perfection of Generosity (*sByin pa'i phar phyin gyi mdo, Dānapāramitā-sūtra*). Toh. 182.

Sūtra on the Samādhi in Which the Buddhas of the Present All Stand Before One (*Da ltar gyi sangs rgyas mngon sum pa'i ting nge 'dzin, Pratyutpannabuddhasaṃmukha-avasthitasamādhi-sūtra*). Toh. 133.

Sūtra Teaching on the Magical Display of Miracles (*Cho 'phrul bstan pa'i mdo, Buddha-balādhānaprātihāryavikurvāṇanirdeśa-sūtra*). Toh. 186.

Sūtra That Includes the Many (*Du ma 'dus pa'i mdo*). NL.

Sūtra That Inspires a Superior Intention (*Lhag bsam bskul ba'i mdo, Adhyāśaya-saṃcodana-sūtra*). Toh. 69.

Sūtra That Perfectly Summarizes the Dharma (*Chos yang dag par bsdus pa'i mdo, Dharmasaṃgīti-sūtra*). Toh. 238.

Sūtra That Teaches the Tathāgata Essence (*De bzhin gshegs pa'i snying po bstan pa'i mdo, Tathāgatagarbha-sūtra*). Toh. 258.

Sūtra to Vyūharāja on the Qualities of All Dharmas (*Yon tan bkod pa'i mdo, Sarvadharmaguṇavyūharāja-sūtra*). Toh. 114.

Synopsis That Asserts the View of Mañjuśrī (*'Jam dpal gyi lta 'dod mdor bstan*). NL.

Tale with a Sow (*Phag mo'i rtogs brjod, Sūkarikāvadāna*). Toh. 345.

Tantra of Complete Union (*Kun tu kha sbyor gyi rgyud*). Toh. 1199.

Tantra of Kīlaya (*Phur pa'i rgyud*). NL.

Tantra of Secret Union (*sNyoms 'jug gsang ba'i rgyud*). NL.

Tantra of Supreme Gnosis (*Ye shes dam pa'i rgyud*). NL.

Tantra of Taking the Essence (*sNying po rnam par len pa'i rgyud*). NL.

Tantra of the All-Creating King (*Kun byed rgyal po'i rgyud*). Ng. 10.

Tantra of the Arising of Saṃvara (*sDom 'byung bde mchog 'byung ba'i rgyud, Saṃvarodaya-tantra*). Toh. 373.

Tantra of the Array of Commitments (*Dam tshig bkod pa'i rgyud, Samayavyūha*). Ng. 200 or 80.

Tantra of the Display of the Wheel of Perfection (*'Khor lo chub pa rol pa'i rgyud*). NL.

Tantra of the Empowerment of Vajrapāṇi (*Lag na rdo rje dbang bskur ba'i rgyud, Vajrapāṇyabhiṣeka-mahā-tantra*). Toh. 496.

Tantra of the Equalizing Secret (*gSang ba kun snyoms kyi rgyud*). NL.

Tantra of the Exhaustion of the Four Elements (*'Byung bzhi zad pa'i rgyud*). NL.

Tantra of the Flower Array (*Me tog bkod pa'i rgyud*). NL.

Tantra of the Garland of Flames (*Me lce phreng ba'i rgyud*). NL.

Tantra of the Great Samantabhadra Dwelling in Oneself (*Kun tu bzang po che ba rang la gnas pa'i rgyud*). Ng. 485.

Tantra of the Net of Magical Display (*sGyu 'phrul drva ba*). It has not been possible to identify this tantra with certainty.

Tantra of the Precious Gathering of All (*Kun 'dus rin po che'i rgyud*). NL.

Tantra of the Questions of Subāhu (*dPung bzang gi mdo Subāhu-paripṛcchā-tantra*). Toh. 805.

Tantra of the Secret Ḍākinī (*mKha' 'gro ma gsang ba'i rgyud, Ḍākinī-guhyajvāla-tantra*). Toh. 408.

Tantra of the Sublime Yoginī (*rNal 'byor ma dam pa'i rgyud*). NL.

Tantra of the Supreme Samaya (*Dam tshig mchog gi rgyud*). NL.

Tantra of the Three Verses on the Wisdom Mind (*dGongs pa tshigs gsum pa'i rgyud*). Ng. 341.

Tantra of the Three Verses. See *Tantra of the Three Verses on the Wisdom Mind*.

Tantra of the Union of All the Buddhas (*Sangs rgyas mnyam sbyor*). Ng. 538.

Tantra of the Vajra Ḍāka (*rDo rje mkha' 'gro'i rgyud, Vajraḍāka-tantra*). Toh. 370.

Tantra of the Vajra Flame (*rDo rje me lce'i rgyud*). NL.

Tantra of the Vajra Staff of Vajrapāṇi (*rDo rje be con gyi rgyud, Vajrapāṇi-nīlāmbara-vidhivajradaṇḍa-tantra*). Toh. 456.

Tantra of the Vajra Tent (*rDo rje gur Ḍākinī-vajrapañjara-tantra*). Toh. 419.

Tantra of the Vastness of Space (*Nam mkha' klong yangs kyi rgyud*). Pt. 20.

Tantra of the Wheel of Bliss (*'Khor lo bde ba'i rgyud*). NL.

Tantra of Vairocana's Enlightenment (*rNam snang mngon byang, Vairocanābhisaṃbodhi*). Toh. 494.

Tantra of Vajra Vetālī (*rDo rje ro lang gi rgyud*). NL.

Tantra of Victory by Nonduality (*gNyis med rnam rgyal*, which refers to *dPal de bzhin gshegs pa thams cad kyi gsang ba rnal 'byor chen po rnam par rgyal ba zhes bya ba mnyam pa nyid gnyis su med pa'i rgyud kyi rgyal po rdo rje dpal mchog chen po brtag pa dang po, Śrī-sarvatathāgata-guhyatantra-yoga-mahārāja-advayasamatā-vijaya-nāma-vajra-śrī-paramamahākalpa-ādi*). Toh. 453.

Tantra on Seizing the Essential Meaning (*sNying po'i don len pa'i rgyud*). NL.

Tantra That Drives Back Armies (*dPung rnam par bzlog pa'i rgyud*). NL.

Teaching on the Benefits of Generosity (*sByin pa'i phan yon bstan pa'i mdo, Dānānuśaṃsā*). Toh. 183.

Three Stages (*Rim gsum*). NL.

Torch of the Three Methods (*Tshul gsum pa'i sgron me*). Toh. 3707.

Two Segments (*brTag gnyis*). The condensed *Hevajra Tantra in Two Segments*. Toh. 417.

Vajra Garland (*rDo rje phreng ba*, *Vajramālā*). Toh. 445.
Vajra Mirror (*rDo rje me long*). Ng. 533.
Vajra Net (*rDo rje drva ba*). NL.
Vajra Net Tantra (*rDo rje dra ba'i rgyud*). NL.
Vajra Pinnacle Tantra (*rDo rje rtse mo*). Ng. 835.
Vajra Sun (*rDo rje nyi ma*). NL.
Verses for Prasenajit (*gSal rgyal gyis zhus pa*, *Prasenajidgāthā*). Toh. 322.
Verses on Circumambulating Reliquaries (*mChod rten skor ba'i tshigs bcad*, *Caitya-pradakṣiṇagāthā*). Toh. 321.
Verses That Summarize the Perfection of Wisdom (*sDud pa tshigs su bcad pa*, *Prajñā-pāramitāsaṃcayagāthā*). One of the Prajñāpāramitā sūtras. Toh. 13.
Vinaya scriptures. Toh. 1–7.
White Lotus of Compassion (*rNying rje pad ma dkar po'i mdo*, *Karuṇāpuṇḍarīka-sūtra*). Toh. 112.
Word of Mañjuśrī (*'Jam dpal zhal lung*). NL.

Canonical Treatises

Anon. *Prayer of Maitreya* (*Byams pa'i smon lam*, *Āryamaitreya-praṇidhāna*). Toh. 4378.
Āryaśūra. *Series of Lives* (*sKyes rabs*, *Jātakamālā*). Toh. 4150.
Asaṅga. *Bodhisattva Stage* (*Byang sa*, *Bodhisattvabhūmi*). One of the *Treatises on the Stages* by Asaṅga. Toh. 4037.
——. *Commentary on the "Sublime Continuum"* (*Theg pa chen po rgyud bla ma'i bstan bcos rnam par bshad pa*, *Mahāyānottaratantraśāstravyākhyā*). Toh. 4025.
——. *Treatises on the Stages* (*Sa sde*), which refers to Asaṅga's *Stages of Yogic Practice* (*rNal 'byor spyod pa'i sa*, *Yogācārabhūmi*) and its related treatises. Toh. 4035–42.
Asvabhāva. *Compendium of the Great Vehicle with Appended Commentary* (*Theg pa chen po bsdus pa'i bshad sbyar*, *Mahāyānasaṃgrahopanibandhana*). A commentary on Asaṅga's *Mahāyānasaṃgraha*. Toh. 4051.
Aśvaghoṣa. *Fifty Verses on the Teacher* (*bLa ma lnga bcu pa*, *Gurupañcāśikā*) Toh. 3721.
——. *Letter of Consolation* (*Mya ngan bsal ba*, *Śokavinodana*) Toh. 4177.
Atiśa Dīpaṃkaraśrījñāna. *Analysis of Actions* (*Las rnam 'byed*, *Karmavibhaṅga*). Toh. 3959.
——. *Lamp for the Path* (*Lam sgron*, *Bodhipathapradīpa*). Toh. 3947.
Bhāvaviveka. *Precious Lamp of the Middle Way* (*dBu ma rin po che'i sgron ma*, *Madhya-makaratnapradīpa*). Toh. 3854.
Buddhaguhya. *Graded Path of the Magical Manifestation Tantra* (*sGyu 'phrul lam rim*). NL.
Candragomin. *Letter to a Disciple* (*sLob spring*, *Śiṣyalekha*). Toh. 4183.
——. *Twenty Verses on the Vows of a Bodhisattva* (*sDom pa nyi shu pa*, *Bodhisattva-saṃvaraviṃśaka*). Toh. 4081.
Chandrakīrti. *Introduction to the Middle Way* (*dBu ma la 'jug pa*, *Madhyamakā-*

vatāra). Toh. 3861. Translated by the Padmakara Translation Group and published under the same title. Boulder, CO: Shambhala Publications, 2004.

——. *Seventy Stanzas on Refuge* (*sKyabs 'gro bdun cu pa, Triśaraṇa[gamana]saptati*). Toh. 3971.

Chapter on Gathering Concentration (*Ting nge 'dzin gyi tshogs le'u, Samādhisambhāra-parivarta*). Any one of five treatises with this title. It has not been possible to identify this treatise precisely.

Commentary on the First Part of the "Hundred Parables on Action" (*Las brgya pa'i stod 'grel*). NL.

Indrabhūti. *Accomplishment of Gnosis* (*Ye shes grub pa, Jñānasiddhi-nāma-sādhanopāyikā*). A commentary on tantra. Toh. 2219.

Jñānagarbha. *Distinguishing the Two Truths* (*bDen gnyis rnam par 'byed, Satyadvaya-vibhaṅga*). Toh. 3881.

Kaśmīri Buddhaśrījñāna. *Commentary on the "Ornament of Clear Realization"* (*mNgon rtogs rgyan gyi 'grel pa, Abhisamayālaṃkārabhagavatīprajñāpāramitopadeśaśāstravṛtti prajñāpradīpāvali*). Toh. 3800.

Kṛṣṇa Paṇḍita. *Ascertainment of Difficult Points in "The Way of the Bodhisattva"* (*Byang chub sems dpa'i spyod pa la 'jug pa'i rtogs par dka' ba'i gnas gtan la dbab pa zhes bya ba'i gzhung, Bodhisattvacaryāvatāraduravabodhananirṇaya-nāma-grantha*). Toh. 3875.

Kulika Puṇḍarīka. *Approach to the Ultimate* (*Don dam bsnyen pa, Śrīparamārtha-sevā*). Toh. 1348.

Lakṣmīṁkara. *Fourteen Root Downfalls* (*rTsa ltung bcu bzhi pa, Vajrayānacaturdaśa-mūlāpatti-vṛtti*). Toh. 2485.

Maitreya/Asaṅga. *Distinguishing the Middle from Extremes* (*dBus mtha' rnam 'byed, Madhyāntavibhāga*). Toh. 4021.

——. *Ornament of Clear Realization* (*mNgon rtogs rgyan, Abhisamayālaṃkāra*). Toh. 3786.

——. *Ornament of the Mahāyāna Sūtras* (*mDo sde rgyan, Mahāyānasūtrālaṃkāra*). Toh. 4020. Translated by the Padmakara Translation Group and published in *A Feast of the Nectar of the Supreme Vehicle*. Boulder, CO: Shambhala Publications, 2018.

——. *Sublime Continuum* (*rGyud bla ma, Mahāyānottaratantraśāstra-ratnagotra-vibhāga*). 4024.

Mañjuśrīkīrti, *Essential Ornament*. See Mañjuśrīkīrti, *Essential Ornament of the Rituals Common to All the Secret Teachings.*

——. *Essential Ornament of the Rituals Common to All the Secret Teachings* (*dPal gsang ba thams cad kyi spyi'i cho ga'i snying po rgyan, Śrīsarvaguhyavidhigarbhālaṃkāra*). Toh. 2490.

——. *Tantra Common to All the Secret Teachings* (*gSang ba spyi rgyud*). See Mañjuśrīkīrti, *Essential Ornament of the Rituals Common to All the Secret Teachings.*

Mātṛceṭa. *Advice on Abandoning the Four Errors* (*Phyin ci log bzhi spang ba'i gtam, Caturviparyaya[parihāra]kathā*). Toh. 4169.

Nāgārjuna. *Commentary on Bodhichitta* (*Byang chub sems 'grel, Bodhicittavivaraṇa*). Toh. 1800.

———. *Five Stages* (*of Guhyasamāja*) (*Rim lnga, Pañcakrama*). Toh. 1802.

———. *Jewel Garland* (*Rin chen phreng ba, Ratnāvali*). Nāgārjuna's advice to a king. Toh. 4158.

———. *Jewel Garland of the Middle Way* (*dBu ma rin chen phreng ba*). See Nāgārjuna, *Jewel Garland.*

———. *Letter to a Friend* (*bShes spring, Suhṛllekha*). Toh. 4182. Translated by the Padmakara Translation Group and published in *Nagarjuna's "Letter to a Friend."* Boston: Snow Lion, 2013.

———. *Praise of the Expanse of Reality in the Middle Way* (*dBu ma chos dbyings bstod pa, Dharmadhātu-stotra*). Toh. 1118.

———. *Praise of the Vajra Mind* (*Sems kyi rdo rje la bstod pa, Cittavajrastava*). Toh. 1121.

———. *Root Stanzas on the Middle Way* (*dBu ma rtsa ba'i tshig le'ur byas pa, Mūlamadhyamakakārikā*). Toh. 3824. Translated by the Padmakara Translation Group and published under the same title. Boulder, CO: Shambhala Publications, 2016.

Pundarika. *Great Commentary on the Wheel of Time Tantra: Immaculate Light* (*Dus 'khor 'grel chen dri med 'od, Vimalaprabhā-namā-mūlatantrānusāriṇīdvādaśasāhasrikālaghukālacakratantrarājaṭikā*). Toh. 1347.

Sajjana. *Letter to a Son* (*Bu la spring ba, Putralekha*). Toh. 4187.

Śāntideva. *Way of the Bodhisattva* (*sPyod 'jug, Bodhicaryāvatāra*). Toh. 3871. Translated by the Padmakara Translation Group and published under the same title. Boston: Shambhala Publications, 2006.

———. *Compendium of Precepts* (*bsLab pa kun las btus pa, Śikṣāsamuccaya*). Toh. 3940.

Saraha. *Song of Pith Instructions of the Inexhaustible Treasury* (*Mi zad pa'i gter mdzod man ngag gi glu, Dohākoṣopadeśagīti*). Toh. 2264.

Udbhaṭasiddhasvāmin. *Praise of the Most Noble* (*Khyad par du 'phags pa'i bstod pa, Viśeṣastava*). Toh. 1109.

Vasubandhu. *Treasury of Abhidharma* (*Chos mngon pa'i mdzod, Abhidharmakośa*). Toh. 4089.

———. *Advice on Accumulation* (*Tshogs kyi gtam, Sambhāraparikathā*). Toh. 4166.

———. *Discourse on Discipline* (*Tshul khrims kyi gtam, Śīlaparikathā*). Toh. 4164.

———. *Well-Explained Reasoning* (*rNam bshad rig pa, Vyākhyāyukti*). Toh. 4061.

Vimalamitra. *Six Points of Refuge* (*sKyabs 'gro yan lag drug, Ṣaḍaṅgaśaraṇa[gamana]*). Toh. 3972.

Tibetan Works

Aro Yeshe Jungne. *Practice of the Great Vehicle* (*Theg chen rnal 'byor*).

Chetsun. *Song by the Great Chetsun* (*lCe btsun che po'i mgur*).

Dharmaśrī. *Primary Instructions on the Practice of Vajrasattva* (*rDor sems rtsa khrid*). Dharmaśrī's commentary on the practice of Minling Dorsem.

Gampopa Sönam Rinchen. *Jewel Ornament of Liberation* (*Dam chos yid bzhin gyi nor bu thar pa rin po che'i rgyan zhes bya ba theg pa chen po'i lam rim gyi bshad pa*).

Gyurme Dorje Terdak Lingpa. *Great Compassionate One, Embodiment of All the Sugatas* (*Thugs rje chen po bde gshegs kun 'dus*). A treasure text by Padmasambhava rediscovered by Gyurme Dorje Terdak Lingpa.

Jigme Lingpa. *Treasury of Precious Qualities* (*Yon tan rin po che'i mdzod*). Translated with commentary by Longchen Yeshe Dorje, Kangyur Rinpoche by the Padmakara Translation Group and published under the same title. Boston: Shambhala Publications, 2010–2013.

Karma Lingpa. *Graded Path of the Practice of Dharma* (*Chos spyod lam rim*). Part of the treasure *Zab chos zhi khro dgongs pa rang grol* by Padmasambhava rediscovered by Karma Lingpa.

Longchenpa. *Commentary on the "Precious Treasury That Fulfills All Wishes."* See Longchenpa, *White Lotus*.

———. *Essential Instructions for Finding Rest in the Nature of the Mind* (*Sems nyid ngal so'i don khrid*). Longchenpa's instructions for putting *Finding Rest in the Nature of the Mind* into practice.

———. *Finding Rest in the Nature of the Mind: A Teaching of the Great Perfection*. (*rDzogs pa chen po sems nyid ngal gso*). Part of the Trilogy of Rest (*Ngal gso skor gsum*). Translated by the Padmakara Translation Group and published under the same title. Boulder, CO: Shambhala Publications, 2017.

———. *Great Chariot of the Definitive Teachings* (*Nges don shing rta chen mo*). Longchenpa's autocommentary on *Finding Rest in the Nature of the Mind*.

———. *Precious Treasury That Fulfills All Wishes* (*Yid bzhin rin po che'i mdzod*). One of the Seven Treasuries (*mDzod bdun*).

———. *Story of Losel Ribong* (*Blo gsal ri bong gi rtogs pa brjod pa*).

———. *White Lotus*. Longchenpa's autocommentary on the *Precious Treasury That Fulfills All Wishes*.

Ngari Panchen Pema Wangyal. *Ascertaining the Three Vows* (*sDom gsum rnam nges*).

Ngok Sherab Gyalpo. *Instructions to the Old Man Given with Pointed Staff* (*rGad po 'khar btsugs kyi gdams pa*). Instructions given to Ngok Sherab Gyalpo by Guru Padmasambhava.

Nyang Ral Nyima Özer. "Answers to the Questions of Yeshe Tsogyal." In Nyang Ral Nyima Özer, *Direct Instructions of the Teacher* from the *Treasure of Nyang*.

———. *Direct Instructions of the Teacher* from the *Treasure of Nyang* (*Nyang gter bla ma'i dmar khrid*). A treasure text by Padmasambhava rediscovered by Nyang Ral Nyima Özer.

———. *Jewel Garland*. The autocommentary of Padmasambhava's *Great Treatise on the Graded Path* (*Padma'i lam rim chen mo'i rang 'grel rin chen phreng ba*). Hidden as treasure and rediscovered by Nyang Ral Nyima Özer.

Padampa Sangye. *The Hundred Verses of Advice* (*Ding ri brgya rtsa ma*). Translated by the Padmakara Translation Group and published under the same title. Boston: Shambhala Publications, 2006.

Padmasambhava. *Great Treatise on the Graded Path* (*Padma'i lam rim chen mo*).

———. *Instructions to the King* (*rJe mga' bdag chen po la gdams pa*).

Patrul Rinpoche, Orgyen Jigme Chöwang. *Benefits of Seeing the Mahāyāna Sūtras* (*Theg chen mdo sde mthong ba'i phan yon tshig su bcad pa*).

Sangye Lingpa. *Compendium of the Teacher's Wisdom* (*bLa ma dgongs 'dus*). A treasure discovered by Sangye Lingpa.

Preliminary Practice Texts

Jamgön Mipham Rinpoche. *Illuminating the Path to Freedom: A Recitation Text for the Preliminary Practices* (*sNgon 'gro'i ngag 'don thar lam rab gsal*). In *gSung 'bum / Mi pham rgya mtsho*, vol. 32, pp. 287–94. Khreng tu'u: Gangs can rig gzhung dpe rnying myur skyobs lhan tshogs, 2007.

Jamyang Khyentse Wangpo. *The Recitation Text for the Preliminary Practices of the Accomplishment of the Heart of Vajrasattva* (*rDor sems thugs kyi sgrub pa'i sngon 'gro'i ngag 'don*). In *gSung 'bum / mKhyen brtse'i dbang po*, vol. 12, pp. 453–82. Gangtok: Gonpo Tseten, 1977–1980.

Works in English Translation

Chandrakirti and Jamgön Mipham. *Introduction to the Middle Way.* Translated by the Padmakara Translation Group. Boston: Shambhala Publications, 2004.

Dilgo Khyentse and Padampa Sangye. *The Hundred Verses of Advice.* Translated by the Padmakara Translation Group. Boston: Shambhala Publications, 2005.

Jigme Lingpa and Longchen Yeshe Dorje, Kangyur Rinpoche. *Treasury of Precious Qualities.* 2 bks. Translated by the Padmakara Translation Group. Boston: Shambhala Publications, 2010–2013.

Longchenpa. *Finding Rest in the Nature of the Mind.* Translated by the Padmakara Translation Group. Boulder, CO: Shambhala Publications, 2017.

Maitreya and Jamgön Mipham. *A Feast of the Nectar of the Supreme Vehicle.* Translated by the Padmakara Translation Group. Boulder, CO: Shambhala Publications, 2018.

Nagarjuna and Longchen Yeshe Dorje, Kangyur Rinpoche. *Nagarjuna's "Letter to a Friend."* Translated by the Padmakara Translation Group. Boston: Snow Lion, 2013.

Shantideva. *The Way of the Bodhisattva.* Translated by the Padmakara Translation Group. Rev. ed. Boston: Shambhala Publications, 2006.

Works Mentioned but Not Quoted from in *A Chariot to Freedom*

Canonical Scriptures and Treatises

Asaṅga. *Compendium of Topics from the Stages of Yogic Practice* (*rNal 'byor spyod pa'i sa las gzhi bsdu ba, Yogācārabhūmau vastusaṃgrahaṇī*). Toh. 4039.

Atiśa. "Ritual for Arousing Bodhichitta" (*Sems bskyed pa dang sdom pa'i cho ga'i rim pa, Cittotpādasaṃvaravidhikrama*). Toh. 3969.

Incantation and Practice of Uṣṇīṣavijayā (*gTsug tor rnam par rgyal ba'i mdo, Uṣṇīṣavijayādhāraṇī kalpasahitā*). Toh. 594.

Incantation of Sarvanīvaraṇaviṣkambhin (*sGrib sel gyi gzungs*). Toh. 891.

Incantation of the Casket of Secret Relics (*gSang ba ring bsrel za ma tog gi gzungs, Sarvatathāgatādhiṣṭhānahṛdayaguhyadhātukaraṇḍa-nāma-dhāraṇī-sūtra*). Toh. 507.

Jamgön Mipham Rinpoche. *A Hundred Mantras That Cut the Stream of Karma and Obscurations* (*Las sgrib rgyun gcod gyi sngags brgya pa*).

Kṛṣṇa Paṇḍita. *Commentary on Difficult Points in "The Way of the Bodhisattva"* (*Byang chub sems dpa'i spyod pa la 'jug pa'i rnam par bshad pa, Bodhisattvacaryāvatāravivṛttipañjikā*). Toh. 3873.

Lives of the Bodhisattva (*Byang chub sems dpa'i skyes rab*). The Jātaka Tales that recount the Buddha's former lives as a bodhisattva. Toh. 4157.

Maitreya/Asaṅga. Four Treatises of Maitreya (*Byams pa'i chos bzhi*). Four of the five treatises that Asaṅga received from Maitreya.

Nāgārjuna. *Collection of Praises* (*bsTod tshogs*).Toh. 1118 et seq.

Praise and Confession of the Bodhisattva Downfalls (*bsNgags pa byang chub ltung bshags*). Another name for the *Sūtra in Three Sections*. Toh. 284.

Śāntideva. "Prayer to the Lord of the Victorious Ones" (*gTso gyal ma*). A prayer taken from the second chapter of the *Way of the Bodhisattva*. Toh. 3871.

Sūtra of Ākāśagarbha (*Nam mkha'i snying po'i mdo, Ākāśagarbha-sūtra*). Toh. 260.

Sūtra of Dependent Arising (*rTen cing 'brel bar 'byung ba'i mdo, Pratītyasamutpāda-sūtra*). Toh. 212.

Sūtra on Grasping the Roots of Virtue (*dGe rtsa yongs 'dzin mdo, Kuśalamūlasamparigraha-sūtra*). Toh. 101.

Sūtra on Offering Lamps (*'Phags pa mar me 'bul ba'i mdo, Pradīpadānīya-sūtra*). Toh. 204.

Sūtra That Teaches the Conduct of a Bodhisattva (*Byang chub sems dpa'i spyod pa bstan pa'i mdo, Bodhisattvacaryānirdeśa-sūtra*). Toh. 184.

Wheel of Time (*Dus 'khor, Kālacakra*). Toh. 362.

Tibetan Works

Geshe Potawa. *Book of Analogies* (*Po ta ba'i dpe chos kyi khrid*). A list of analogies for different topics.

Gyurme Dorje Terdak Lingpa. *Profound Meaning of Ati* (*rDzogs pa chen po a ti zab don snying po'i chos skor*). A cycle by Padmasambhava revealed by Gyurme Dorje Terdak Lingpa.

Ju Mipham Gyatso. *Garland of Jewels of a Hundred Thousand Names* (*mTshan 'bum nor bu'i phreng ba las khol phyung gces btus*). A compilation by Ju Mipham Gyatso.

———. *Lion's Roar: A Great Summary of the Sugata Essence* (*bDe gshegs snying po'i stong thun chen mo seng ge'i nga ro*).

Karma Lingpa. *Spontaneous Freeing of the Mind* (*dGongs pa rang grol*) Refers to *Zab chos zhi khro dgongs pa rang grol*, a treasure text by Padmasambhava rediscovered by Karma Lingpa.

Shechen Gyaltsap. *Stairway on the Path to Perfect Liberation* (*Yang dag thar lam bgrod pa'i them skas*). A collection of tales from the sūtras compiled by Shechen Gyaltsap.

Shining Lamp (*[gSang ba 'dus pa'i] 'grel pa sgron gsal*). A commentary on the Guhyasamāja (author not certain).

English-Language Sources

Ārya Asaṅga. *The Bodhisattva Path to Unsurpassed Enlightenment*. Translated by Artemus B. Engle. Boulder, CO: Snow Lion, 2016.

Buswell, Robert E., Jr., and Donald S. Lopez Jr. *The Princeton Dictionary of Buddhism*. Princeton: Princeton University Press, 2014.

Choying Tobden Dorje. *The Complete Nyingma Tradition from Sutra to Tantra: Books 1 to 10: Foundations of the Buddhist Path*. Translated by Ngawang Zangpo. Boston: Snow Lion, 2014.

Dilgo Khyentse. *Enlightened Courage*. Translated by the Padmakara Translation Group. Ithaca, NY: Snow Lion Publications, 2006.

Dowman, Keith, trans. *The Legend of the Great Stūpa*. Berkeley, CA: Dharma Publishing, 1973.

Dudjom Rinpoche. *The Nyingma School of Tibetan Buddhism*. Translated by Gyurme Dorje and Matthew Kapstein. Boston: Wisdom Publications, 1991.

———. *A Torch Lighting the Way to Freedom*. Translated by the Padmakara Translation Group. Boston: Shambhala Publications, 2011.

Hopkins, Jeffrey. *Buddhist Advice on Living and Liberation: Nāgārjuna's "Precious Garland."* Ithaca, NY: Snow Lion Publications, 1998.

Jamgön Kongtrul. *The Treasury of Knowledge: Book Five: Buddhist Ethics*. Translated by Kalu Rinpoché Translation Group (Elio Guarisco and Ingrid McLeod). Ithaca, NY: Snow Lion Publications, 2003.

———. *The Treasury of Knowledge: Book One: Myriad Worlds*. Translated by the Kalu Rinpoché Translation Group. Ithaca, NY: Snow Lion Publications, 2003.

———. *The Treasury of Knowledge: Book Six, Parts One and Two: Indo-Tibetan Classical Learning and Buddhist Phenomenology*. Translated by Kalu Rinpoché Translation Group (Gyurme Dorje). Ithaca, NY: Snow Lion, 2012.

Khenpo Ngawang Pelzang. *A Guide to "The Words of My Perfect Teacher."* Translated by Dipamkara in collaboration with the Padmakara Translation Group. Boston: Shambhala Publications, 2004.

Patrul Rinpoche. *The Words of My Perfect Teacher*. Translated by the Padmakara Translation Group. Boston: Shambhala Publications, 1998.

Shabkar Tsogdruk Rangdrol. *Food of Bodhisattvas*. Translated by the Padmakara Translation Group. Boston: Shambhala Publications, 2004.

Shechen Gyaltsap Gyurmé Pema Namgyal. *Practicing the Great Perfection: Instructions on the Crucial Points*. Translated by the Padmakara Translation Group. Boulder, CO: Shambhala Publications, 2020.

Zhechen Gyaltsab. *Path of Heroes: Birth of Enlightenment*. Berkeley, CA: Dharma Publishing, 1995.

Index

The Padmakara Translation Group Translations into English

The Adornment of the Middle Way. Shantarakshita and Mipham Rinpoche. Boston: Shambhala Publications, 2010.

Counsels from My Heart. Dudjom Rinpoche. Boston: Shambhala Publications, 2003.

Enlightened Courage. Dilgo Khyentse Rinpoche. Ithaca, NY: Snow Lion Publications, 2006.

The Excellent Path of Enlightenment. Dilgo Khyentse. Ithaca, NY: Snow Lion Publications, 1996.

A Feast of the Nectar of the Supreme Vehicle. Maitreya and Jamgön Mipham. Boulder, CO: Shambhala Publications, 2018.

Finding Rest in Illusion. Longchenpa. Boulder, CO: Shambhala Publications, 2018.

Finding Rest in Meditation. Longchenpa. Boulder, CO: Shambhala Publications, 2018.

Finding Rest in the Nature of the Mind. Longchenpa. Boulder: Shambhala Publications, 2017.

A Flash of Lightning in the Dark of Night. The Dalai Lama. Boston: Shambhala Publications, 1993. Republished as *For the Benefit of All Beings.* Boston: Shambhala Publications, 2009.

Food of Bodhisattvas. Shabkar Tsogdruk Rangdrol. Boston: Shambhala Publications, 2004.

A Garland of Views: A Guide to View, Meditation, and Result in the Nine Vehicles. Padmasambhava and Mipham Rinpoche. Boston: Shambhala Publications, 2015.

A Guide to "The Words of My Perfect Teacher." Khenpo Ngawang Pelzang. Translated with Dipamkara. Boston: Shambhala Publications, 2004.

The Heart of Compassion. Dilgo Khyentse. Boston: Shambhala Publications, 2007.

The Heart Treasure of the Enlightened Ones. Dilgo Khyentse and Patrul Rinpoche. Boston: Shambhala Publications, 1992.

The Hundred Verses of Advice. Dilgo Khyentse and Padampa Sangye. Boston: Shambhala Publications, 2005.

Introduction to the Middle Way. Chandrakirti and Mipham Rinpoche. Boston: Shambhala Publications, 2004.

Journey to Enlightenment. Matthieu Ricard. New York: Aperture Foundation, 1996.

Lady of the Lotus-Born. Gyalwa Changchub and Namkhai Nyingpo. Boston: Shambhala Publications, 2002.

The Life of Shabkar: The Autobiography of a Tibetan Yogin. Ithaca, NY: Snow Lion Publications, 2001.

Lion of Speech: The Life of Mipham Rinpoche. Dilgo Khyentse. Boulder, CO: Shambhala Publications, 2020.

Nagarjuna's "Letter to a Friend." Nagarjuna and Longchen Yeshe Dorje, Kangyur Rinpoche. Boston: Snow Lion, 2013.

The Nectar of Manjushri's Speech. Kunzang Pelden. Boston: Shambhala Publications, 2010.

Practicing the Great Perfection: Instructions on the Crucial Points. Shechen Gyaltsap Gyurmé Pema Namgyal. Boulder, CO: Shambhala Publications, 2020.

The Root Stanzas on the Middle Way. Nagarjuna. Boulder, CO: Shambhala Publications, 2016.

A Torch Lighting the Way to Freedom. Dudjom Rinpoche, Jigdrel Yeshe Dorje. Boston: Shambhala Publications, 2011.

Treasury of Precious Qualities. Jigme Lingpa and Longchen Yeshe Dorje, Kangyur Rinpoche. 2 bks. Translated by the Padmakara Translation Group. Boston: Shambhala Publications, 2010–2013.

The Way of the Bodhisattva. Shantideva. Rev. ed. Boulder, CO: Shambhala Publications, 2008.

White Lotus. Jamgön Mipham. Boston: Shambhala Publications, 2007.

Wisdom: Two Buddhist Commentaries. Khenchen Kunzang Pelden and Minyak Kunzang Sonam. Dordogne: Editions Padmakara, 1999.

The Wisdom Chapter: Jamgön Mipham's Commentary on the Ninth Chapter of "The Way of the Bodhisattva." Jamgön Mipham. Boulder, CO: Shambhala Publications, 2017.

The Wish-Fulfilling Jewel. Dilgo Khyentse. Boston: Shambhala Publications, 1988.

The Words of My Perfect Teacher. Patrul Rinpoche. New Haven, CT: Yale University Press, 2010.

Zurchungpa's Testament. Zurchungpa and Dilgo Khyentse. Boulder, CO: Shambhala Publications, 2020.

Ekajati

Rahula

Dorje Lekpa

Shenpa Marnak

Tseringma

Durtrö Lhamo